ORACLE®

Oracle Press™

Java™ Programming

D0871050

About the Author

Poornachandra Sarang (popularly known as Dr. Sarang) has been a Java programmer since its inception way back in 1996. Over the last 15 years, Dr. Sarang has conducted many train-the-trainer programs, instructor authorization tests, and corporate training sessions based on Sun Microsystems' official curriculum. He has authored several books and journal articles on Java and various other similar topics. He has been a regular speaker at many international conferences, including the recent JavaOne 2011. He is also associated with the University of Mumbai and a few other universities of repute as a visiting/adjunct faculty and Ph.D. advisor in Computer Science. Dr. Sarang has been invited to deliver keynote addresses and technical talks at many international research and technology conferences. Besides Java coding, Dr. Sarang does some architecture work and is also well recognized in the Enterprise Architecture space.

Oracle Press™

Java™ Programming

Poornachandra Sarang

New York   Chicago   San Francisco
Lisbon   London   Madrid   Mexico City   Milan
New Delhi   San Juan   Seoul   Singapore   Sydney   Toronto

The **McGraw·Hill** Companies

Cataloging-in-Publication Data is on file with the Library of Congress

McGraw-Hill books are available at special quantity discounts to use as premiums and sales promotions, or for use in corporate training programs. To contact a representative, please e-mail us at bulksales@mcgraw-hill.com.

Java™ Programming

1 2 3 4 5 6 7 8 9 0   QFR QFR   1 0 9 8 7 6 5 4 3 2

ISBN   978-0-07-163360-4
MHID   0-07-163360-X

Sponsoring Editor	**Copy Editor**	**Composition**
Megg Morin	Bart Reed	Cenveo Publisher Services
Editorial Supervisor	**Proofreader**	**Illustration**
Jody McKenzie	Lisa McCoy	Cenveo Publisher Services
Project Managers	**Indexer**	**Art Director, Cover**
Harleen Chopra and	Rebecca Plunkett	Jeff Weeks
Sapna Rastogi	**Production Supervisor**	**Cover Designer**
Technical Editor	George Anderson	Pattie Lee
Danny Coward		

A deep reverence to my beloved late father-in-law

Contents at a Glance

Contents

Foreword

Java has been a part of my career and my life nearly since its beginning. I started using Java 1.0 in 1996, and joined the Java team at Sun later that year. It was a rocky beginning, but something quite special happened: Many brilliant people brought together countless ideas to create a platform that changed how people think about software. Many existing companies adopted Java as a core technology, and many new companies were formed either to add to the Java ecosystem or to leverage it in another arena.

Java isn't just a language. It is a platform that consists of many parts, including the Java language, the Java Virtual Machine (VM) core libraries, and many other components. These components make for a flexible, powerful, and versatile technology that reaches into the most diverse range of applications anywhere.

Java isn't just a platform. It is its own ecosystem. Built on top of the Java platform are IDEs, monitoring and management tools, libraries, application servers, test and debug tools, development tools, and, of course, applications of almost every variety.

Developer usage has grown in the years I've worked on Java. In the late 1990s, developers were counted in the tens and hundreds of thousands. Today, Oracle reports that over nine million developers use Java. Deployments, including Java ME on consumer devices, measure in the billions.

Java continues to improve. By some measures, Oracle JDK performance has nearly tripled since JDK 5. These improvements reflect changes throughout the platform.

The improvements don't stop with performance, but include a wide range of capabilities and features added in every release. The evolution of Java is carefully shepherded by talented technologists with a wide range of expertise who pay an enormous level of attention to maintaining compatibility and uniformity.

Even with this, the scope of a major Java release, combined with its occasional obscure characteristics, makes a book like *Java Programming* crucial for developers. Books like this one were a huge influence on the adoption of Java by millions of developers, including myself, and I am grateful that Poornachandra Sarang has the patience and skills needed, and has taken the time to effectively communicate the intricate details of the Java platform.

John Pampuch
Director, Java VM Technology, Oracle
December 15, 2011

xix

Acknowledgments

Since embracing Java in 1996, I have conducted several train-the-trainer programs and instruction authorization tests for Sun Microsystems (now Oracle). All these years, I always wanted to write a book on Java programming that provides accurate and authentic knowledge of the language to professionals who want to master Java. However, this goal always seemed to be a low priority until, finally, my dream took concrete shape when McGraw-Hill became interested in publishing this book. Naturally, my first thanks go to the acquisitions editors of McGraw-Hill. But thanks also go to the editorial and production teams who painstakingly helped me bring my idea for a book into a reality. I would like to specifically mention a few names from the teams with whom I had direct interactions. I wish to thank Joya Anthony, Jane Brownlow, and Megg Morin from the acquisitions department as well as Bart Reed, Harleen Chopra, and Sapna Rastogi from the editorial and production teams. Also, many thanks to Jody McKenzie, who helped in resolving several issues during production and creating this beautiful and technically accurate book.

My thanks also go to the members of the Oracle family. Without their help, this book would have never achieved the technical accuracy that it has today. I first wish to thank Pratik Parekh, a good long-time friend and the current Director of Production Management for Fusion Middleware at Oracle Corporation. Pratik helped in introducing and establishing contacts with the right people at Oracle. I wish to thank John Pampuch (Director, Java VM Technology at Oracle), who took immediate action on my request and provided me with the best person in the world to technically review the manuscript. That reviewer was none other than Danny Coward, Chief Architect of Client Software at Oracle. Danny's review and comments were so deep and insightful that I decided to rewrite the entire book. My special thanks go to Danny for agreeing to do a second round of technical reviews on the revised manuscript. On several occasions, he went out of his way to guide me and provide the accurate technical information that the book needed. I must admit that in spite of my many years of Java coding experience, I still had many misconceptions that were cleared up due to my constant interaction with Danny during the writing of this book. Danny was very particular in his reviews, even insisting on strictly following the naming conventions and observing the code formatting per JLS standards, thus taking care of some minor details such as required line spaces and the spacing between the characters. Without his critical reviews, I probably would have never achieved the level of technical accuracy that I desired for this book. Once again, many, many thanks to you, Danny. Whatever errors may have remained in the book are now solely mine.

My special thanks also go to my students, especially Ishita Patel, who read the manuscript with careful eyes, locating many errors and omissions. Ishita also helped in developing and testing all the code examples in this book. I also want to thank Rashmi Singh, who provided me with constructive feedback on several chapters. I must also mention Steven Suting, who helped in correcting all Java Language Syntax specifications in the book.

I am also indebted to Vijay Jadhav, who helped create the illustrations for this book as well as formatted, organized, and tracked the manuscript.

Finally, my sincere thanks go to John Pampuch, who readily agreed to provide the foreword to this book.

Introduction

You are holding a book that has been written by a veteran Java programmer and technically reviewed by none other than Sun Microsystems (now Oracle). This book provides in-depth coverage of Java language features, including the latest additions introduced in Java SE 7. So whether you are new to Java programming, a student studying for Java certification, or a professional programmer in other languages, you will find this book extremely useful in taking you into the Java domain.

How This Book Is Organized

The book consists of a total 24 chapters, with three initial chapters located on the Web (www.oraclepressbooks.com). The conventional Hello World program and basic Java syntax are covered in these three chapters. They have been placed on the Web because most of the readers of this book are likely to be professional programmers who want to jump directly into the more advanced topics of the language. After an initial introduction to Java and its path toward the latest version in Chapter 1, we jump directly to Java arrays in Chapter 2. Up to Chapter 9, you'll find an in-depth treatment of the Java language, focusing mainly on object orientation in Java and dealing with many intricacies such as the object-creation process; creating inheritance hierarchies; appropriate usage of final, static modifiers; effectively using public, protected, and private modifiers; defining nested, local, and anonymous classes; and, finally, how to effectively handle exceptions in your Java applications.

From here, we take a break from the Java language syntax and move into discussing Java libraries, covering I/O programming with several practical coding examples. Then we cover some more advanced syntax topics such as enums, autoboxing, annotations, and generics. The remainder of the book focuses on real-world application development, including GUI building, event and user gesture processing, understanding data structures, thread and network programming, and assorted important Java classes.

All the chapters of this book have been structured carefully to avoid forward references. Therefore, the book is meant to be read chapter by chapter. Those who know Java and want to get in-depth and accurate information on a particular topic can just read the relevant chapter of interest.

The Chapters

The book consists of 21 carefully organized chapters, with three additional chapters on Java syntax available at www.oraclepressbooks.com. Here's a rundown of the chapters in this book:

- Chapter 1 gives a brief history of Java, tells you why Java was created, what Java is, and what its prominent features are.

- Chapter 2 discusses how to declare and use both single- and multidimensional arrays.

- Chapter 3 begins your study of object-oriented language by discussing what a class is. This chapter covers the major features of an object-oriented language, such as encapsulation, inheritance, and polymorphism.

- Chapter 4 provides an in-depth treatment of the inheritance feature in regard to Java's object orientation. This chapter teaches you how to create single- and multilevel inheritance hierarchies.

- Chapter 5 explains the object-creation process and how superclass objects are constructed during object creation.

- Chapter 6 takes you further into the realm of object-oriented programming by discussing static fields, methods, and initializers.

- Chapter 7 provides a grand finale to Java's classes and covers nested, local, and anonymous classes.

- Chapter 8 talks about exception handling in Java. You may find this to be a nice change of pace after a heavy dose of the intricacies of the Java language in the previous two chapters.

- Chapters 9 and 10 cover I/O programming in Java, including the new java.nio package.

- Chapter 11 takes you further into Java language syntax and introduces enums, autoboxing, and annotations.

- Chapter 12 covers generics, giving you a deep technical understanding of its many features.

- Chapter 13 is a move toward practical application development in Java. It deals with GUI building and how events are processed in such GUI applications.

- Chapter 14 provides an in-depth treatment of the various layout managers used in creating sophisticated screen layouts.

- Chapter 15 shows you how to draw graphics and process user gestures.

- Chapter 16 is all about the Collections API—an important API for organizing your data.

- Chapter 17 is the first of three chapters on thread programming. It provides in-depth knowledge on how threading is implemented in JVMs and discusses the basic synchronization mechanism.

- Chapter 18 discusses blocking queues and synchronizers such as countdown latches, semaphores, and more.

- Chapter 19 covers callables, futures, executors, and the latest fork/join framework introduced in Java SE 7.

- Chapter 20 is on network programming, a very vital facet of Java applications.

- Chapter 21 provides the grand finale by discussing a few assorted classes and APIs that set a path for you to learn the rich repertoire of classes in Java.

NOTE
Syntax Reference 1, Syntax Reference 2, and Syntax Reference 3 discuss basic Java syntax and are available at www.oraclepressbooks .com. These three web chapters start with a discussion of the conventional Hello World program and walk you through basic constructs, operators, and control flow statements. The three web chapters are up to date with all the additions made to basic Java syntax up through Java SE 7. Many features that are easily missed are discussed in these chapters.

CHAPTER

1

Introduction to Java

ince its release in 1996, Java has been a popular language among developers worldwide. As of this writing, official sources (namely Oracle) claim that there are about 9 million active Java developers worldwide. Java has been widely accepted as the language of choice for developing almost every kind of application, ranging from small web-based Java applets to large distributed enterprise applications. You will also find Java being used in small-embedded devices as well as very large mission-critical applications. You will find Java being used in colleges by students doing their projects, in industries by developers for their commercial projects, in government for their scalable applications, in banks for their time-critical reliable applications, and in militaries for their robust mission-critical applications. You will find that Java is used in almost every corner of the world.

So what is it that has made Java so popular? Is Java merely a programming language like Pascal, C, or C++? Is it a tool for creating applications of various sizes and complexities? Is it a platform for running applications right from embedded to enterprise level? In this chapter, I will try to answer these questions and many more. You will learn what is so special about Java that has made it so popular. In particular you will learn the following:

- Why Java was created
- What Java is
- The features of Java
- Java's evolution

Why Java?

Java was publicly released in 1996. At that time, C++ substantially dominated the market and was widely used for creating many kinds of software applications. With C++ having such a stronghold in the market, almost nobody would have thought of bringing a new programming language into the world of computing—but Sun Microsystems did. When they came out with Java, they had specific reasons for developing a new language at that time. One of the primary goals for developing a new language was the need for an appropriate language in developing embedded device applications.

There were many issues with then existing languages. C++ has always been known as "resource hungry." C++ developers are required to manage memory themselves. A typical "Hello World" program written in C++ with, say, Microsoft's Visual Studio requires several megabytes of memory to run the code. Though C++ generates highly optimized code, the runtime requirements to run it are typically very high. This was also true for other development and runtime systems available in the market at that time, such as Borland C++ and Turbo Pascal—thus the strong need for a language that would generate small code and use a runtime environment that would not occupy a lot of memory space on the target device.

Programming for embedded devices also demands portability, and these devices typically use a wide variety of CPUs and different architectures. Each architecture made C++ applications behave differently and typically needed to be rewritten for new devices. The complexity of managing multiple build environments and codebases was the biggest challenge in supporting multidevice development. Java was an attempt to create a higher-level language that eliminated these problems— and it largely succeeded in its attempt. It eliminated the multidevice development problems with the introduction of a virtual machine (VM) and portable bytecode architecture. Sun Microsystems aptly came up with the marketing slogan "Write Once, Run Anywhere."

So What Is Java?

The previous section described why Java was created. It started out as a programming language that had a lot of similarities to C++ and Smalltalk, and it was designed to appeal to C++ developers. Java was created as a simpler, higher-level language that removes complexities such as memory management and security and relegates them to tasks managed by the VM.

NOTE
Today, Java is much more than a simple programming language.
It is a platform as well as a development and runtime environment.
By the end of this chapter, you will understand what Java is from the
perspective of today's computing environment.

The creators of Java wanted to establish an easy migration path for developers, most of whom were quite strong in C++ at that time. Although Java had lots of similarities to C++, such as being an object-oriented language, the creators eliminated the drawbacks and not commonly used features of C++ from their new language. This made Java not only small, but offered several side benefits, such as making it more robust, simple, and portable.

Before we cover Java's language features, let's look at its architecture and the concept of a "virtual machine."

Java Virtual Machine

A Java compiler translates the Java source program into what is known as *bytecode,* which is similar to the OBJ code generated by a C++ compiler or any other language compiler. The only difference is that most of these compilers generate the object code for a real CPU, whereas the bytecode generated by a Java compiler consists of the instructions for a "pseudo CPU." In other words, whereas C++ OBJ code consists of the instruction set for, say, an Intel 80x86 CPU or Motorola 68xxx CPU, or maybe even a SPARC workstation, Java bytecode represents an instruction set for a CPU that does not exist in reality. What Sun Microsystems did was to create a virtual CPU in memory, and they designed an instruction set for this virtual CPU, which itself is emulated in memory at runtime.

A Java virtual machine (JVM) emulates the aforementioned virtual CPU. The JVM provides the runtime environment for a Java executable (bytecode). It also provides a bytecode interpreter and a verifier that confirms the bytecode's validity before translating and running it on a real CPU. In addition, it has several more modules for security, memory and thread management, and other purposes. A JVM is essentially a machine (as its name suggests) that is capable of running a Java executable. The JVM and its essential components that are relevant to us at this time are shown in Figure 1-1.

The Java compiler stores the generated bytecode in a file with the extension .class. Your program will also use several .class files supplied by the Java Development Kit (JDK). The class loader in JVM loads these .class files in memory. Along with your .class files, JVM also loads other library files required by your application at the runtime. The JVM subjects the loaded classes to verification to ensure that they do not contain any undefined instructions for the pseudo CPU. The internal .class files need not go through such verifications. If the bytecode of your application program contains an invalid instruction, the JVM rejects its execution and unloads it from memory. After the code is verified, a built-in interpreter converts it to machine code. Now, the code is handed over to the execution unit to be run on the host.

Based on this understanding of Java's architecture, you will now be able to appreciate its features.

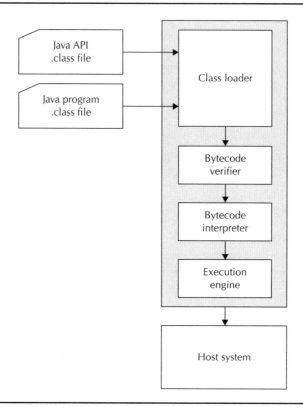

FIGURE 1-1. *Java Virtual Machine*

Features of Java

Java offers several benefits over other programming languages. It is small and simple, and it is object oriented. It may be treated as both a compiled and interpreted language. The executables generated by the Java compiler run on any platform that provides a JVM. The Java platform itself is robust and secure. Like many other languages, it supports multithreading, albeit in a much simpler form. And lastly, like a few other languages, it is dynamic in nature. We will now look at each of these features in more detail.

Small

As stated previously, the main motive behind creating Java was to develop a language for embedded systems programming. The executable code generated by Java is very small; typically, a Hello World application translates into just a few bytes. Compare this with similar code generated by a C++ compiler, which is easily a few kilobytes in size and additionally requires lot of memory for its runtime. The runtime environment required to run Java compiled code typically takes less than 1MB of memory space. Again, contrast this with the runtime required to run a C++ application, which involves not only hundreds of megabytes of code embedded in MFC (Microsoft Foundation Classes) or OWL (Borland's Object Windowing Library) but also requires a sophisticated operating system and hardware to deploy it. Although this was true for both stand-alone and GUI-based applications during the previous decade, Microsoft's current .NET platform provides an architecture similar to Java and its executables, and runtime environment requirements are comparable to those of Java's.

NOTE
*Both MFC and OWL were the popular libraries at the time
Java was introduced.*

Simple

Being object oriented, Java is simple to learn. It has often been said that people who never learned procedure-oriented languages such as C and Pascal will always leap-frog those who have when it comes to learning an object-oriented language. Those who have learned procedural-oriented languages typically find the migration to object-oriented languages difficult because it may require some undoing of what they have learned previously. Java is simple enough to be introduced as a first programming language in any computer science curriculums.

Object Oriented

The next important feature of Java is that it is object oriented. C++, which originated from C, allows global variable declarations, which means that the variables can be declared outside the scope of any object—to be more precise, outside of any class definition. This violates the rules of encapsulation—one of the important features of an object-oriented language (the features of object-oriented programming are covered in Chapter 3). Java does not allow global declarations. Similarly, in Java, there are no structures and unions like in C and C++ that break the rules of object orientation by making all their members public by default. The absence of these features in the Java language has made it a better object-oriented language.

In Java, the entire code consists of only fully encapsulated classes. You're probably wondering about the primitive data types. Are these, too, represented as objects in Java? To maintain efficiency, Java declares primitive data types as non-objects; however, it also provides wrapper classes for these primitive data types should you prefer to use objects holding the primitive data type items.

Compiled and Interpreted

Here lies the major difference between Java and languages such as C++, Pascal, and many others. These languages compile their source program into object code (an .obj file). The linker converts the generated object code into an executable (.exe file) by combining object code with the desired libraries. When you run the EXE, the loader in the operating system loads the executable code in memory, resolves the function references with the absolute memory addresses, and executes the code.

Compiling and running a Java program differs substantially from the preceding procedure. As explained earlier, a Java compiler translates the Java source program into what is known as *bytecode*, which is the set of instructions for a virtual CPU. No linker process is involved when you create an executable from a Java source program. In fact, the only executable that is created from a Java source program is the bytecode. So how does this bytecode run on a real CPU? When you run a Java executable (bytecode) on your machine, an interpreter converts each bytecode instruction into a real CPU instruction. This instruction then executes on the real CPU, so compiling and running a Java program involves both compilation and interpretation processes. Thus, Java is considered both compiled and interpreted.

As Java bytecode is interpreted into machine language instructions at runtime, Java code execution suffers in performance. To overcome this performance limitation, most JVMs implement a number of code optimization techniques, one of which is the use of a Just-in-Time (JIT) compiler that translates the bytecode into machine language code before the real CPU begins the program execution. Obviously, the JIT compiler cannot perform as many optimizations as an offline compiler such as the C++ compiler, because it has to translate the bytecode into machine language code in real time. If the JIT compiler were to attempt to do so, it would take a long time to start the program after the user fires it up from the command line. You have to consider the tradeoff between startup time and throughput. VMs employ a variety of optimization techniques these days. Most of them can be tuned to prefer startup over throughput, or how quickly they adapt the optimizations. There's a whole body of expertise on tuning VMs for performance, and for many apps, the Java version is as quick as (and sometimes quicker than) the C++ counterpart.

Platform Independent

A major benefit that is derived out of the introduction of a JVM is the resulting platform independence for a Java executable. As seen in the previous section, the JVM provides a runtime environment for Java executables. Also, you have seen that the JVM is a software program that runs on a target environment. Thus, as long as you have a JVM for a desired machine, your compiled Java code (bytecode) will run on that machine without requiring any changes in the binary or the source program. This way, a Java program becomes platform independent at the binary level. Any compiled Java application would run on any platform without any changes as long as the target platform provides a Java virtual machine. This turned out to be a great boon for application developers who could now easily create a portable application that would run on several operating systems without any code modifications. In the days before the introduction of Java, creating portable applications was a painstaking task for many developers. These developers lost important revenue if they were unable to port their popular applications onto other platforms—and those who were able still had to rewrite them for new devices. The platform independence of a Java application is illustrated in Figure 1-2.

As seen in Figure 1-2, a Java compiler compiles the given source program into machine-independent bytecode. Each of the three machines shown in the figure run a different operating system—that is, UNIX, Windows, and Mac OS. Each of these machines could be running on totally different hardware. For example, UNIX could be running on a Sparc workstation, Windows could be running on an Intel 80xx architecture, and Mac OS could be running on an architecture such as 68xxx or Intel 80xx. However, what is common among all three machines is the JVM. Note that the JVM, which is a software application itself, is not portable. Rather, every JVM is written for a particular target platform. The bytecode is portable across different JVMs and thus across different platforms that support the JVMs.

Robust and Secure

The introduction of the JVM in the architecture also helped developers in creating robust and secure Java applications. So what is meant by "robust and secure"? As described earlier, bytecode is interpreted by a JVM, and a JVM contains a bytecode verifier. The bytecode verifier not only verifies the validity of the bytecode, but also maintains the integrity of the memory space used by each application running on it. If the bytecode is invalid, JVM simply refuses to run the code. Similarly, if the bytecode tries to access a memory location that does not belong to the memory space of the current application, the JVM rejects the code.

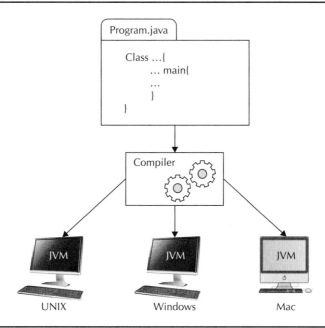

FIGURE 1-2. *Demonstrating Java Portability*

Now, in the first place, how can you have invalid bytecode or an invalid memory reference in a compiled Java application? The bytecode may be modified by a malicious hacker by opening the code in a binary editor, or it may simply get modified due to noise as it is transmitted over a network. Accordingly, even the memory references may get modified in the executable before it is referenced by the JVM at runtime. Fortunately, the JVM traps such intentional and nonintentional errors before the code is executed on a real CPU, resulting in a very robust application that won't crash your operating system.

Java code is highly secure in the sense that it cannot be used to spread a virus on a target machine. Java code that runs under the tight surveillance of the JVM does not have direct access to the operating system resources. Such access is made through the JVM, which ensures all the necessary security for the operating system.

Java has omitted one of the important features of C++, and that is pointer arithmetic. Java does not support the declaration of pointers and pointer arithmetic.

NOTE
Java supports object references that are essentially pointers. However, user-level pointer arithmetic is not supported.

The lack of pointers also makes Java programs more robust and secure. Pointers are notorious for allowing malicious access to locations outside the executing program's memory space. They can also be used for spreading viruses on the system. The elimination of pointers has helped developers in creating robust and secure applications in Java.

Java is both a statically and strongly typed language. The term *static* refers to compile time or the source code, whereas *dynamic* refers to the runtime or the bytecode. A programming language is said to use static typing when type checking is performed during compile time as opposed to runtime. In static typing, all expressions have their types determined at compile time, prior to when the program is executed. The word *strong* in the context of typing means that rules about the typesystem are enforced prior to the code being run. Thus, Java is considered to be both statically and strongly typed.

Another important consideration in making an application robust is the proper allocation and deallocation of memory and other system resources at runtime. In C++, memory allocation and deallocation are the responsibility of the programmer. A developer may sometimes forget to deallocate a memory resource after it has been used. The worst case is when he deallocates memory that is still in use by some other part of the application. This results in chaos and hard-to-track runtime errors. Java eliminates this issue totally by providing automatic garbage collection. The Java runtime assumes the responsibility of tracking the allocations and freeing memory resources when they are no longer referenced by any part of the application. This automatic garbage collection makes Java applications very robust.

Another reason behind why Java programs are so robust is the exception-handling mechanism. Whenever an error occurs in your running program, it will be handled by an exception handler in your code, provided you have one. As a developer, you are required to provide exception handlers at all appropriate places in your program. Java has an exception mechanism with two types of exceptions—checked and unchecked. The compiler makes the developer provide code to handle the checked exceptions, but not the runtime (unchecked) ones. This mandatory requirement for processing checked exceptions results in more robust applications with fewer application crashes.

Multithreaded

The fact that Java was a multithreaded language was one of the key features hyped when the language was introduced in 1996 (...as if other languages did not support multithreading). Although most other languages do support threading, what Java provided was simpler semantics for threading. Creating threads in C++ is as easy as creating threads in Java. The difference lies in the management of shared resources. To share a resource among multiple running threads, C++ uses several constructs, including critical sections and semaphores. These are low-level constructs provided by the operating system itself. Coding for these constructs is typically very complex. Java hides the use of all these constructs underneath a newly designed keyword called **synchronized**. You just declare a block of code or a class as **synchronized** and the Java runtime takes care of the thread concurrency in accessing the shared resources. This makes thread programming in Java very simple.

NOTE
*What was obscured from developers in early version of Java has been made available in its newer versions. The typical synchronization constructs such as semaphores, **CountDownLatch**, and many more are now accessible to programmers.*

Dynamic

Another important feature introduced in Java is its dynamic nature. As we have seen, a Java source program compiles into bytecode. This bytecode is stored in a file with the extension .class.

A running Java application can load a compile-time unknown .class file, understand the defined class, instantiate it, and use it for its own purpose. This process is called "introspection and reflection" in Java. A running Java program can introspect an unknown class, understand the attributes and operations defined in it, create an instance of the class, set the attributes of the created object, and invoke the member functions on the created object. It can also create an array of objects of this unknown type at runtime. This is the dynamic nature of Java.

NOTE
Smalltalk had this dynamic feature since the 1970s, Objective-C from the 1980s, and so do modern languages such as C#.

Java's Evolution

So far, we have discussed the features of Java referring to its first version, JDK 1.0. Over time, Java has expanded a lot and has had many new features added to its repertoire. You will learn several new features in this book. In this section, we discuss the way Java has evolved over the last decade and a half.

As mentioned earlier, although Java started as a programming language for embedded devices, it has evolved into a full-fledged platform. We will look at the major milestones in Java's evolution to its current state. Java is distributed in the form of a Java Development Kit (JDK). The several milestones in Java's evolution are identified by the version number assigned to this JDK. The following subsections list the major releases of the JDK and the features introduced therein.

JDK 1.0 (January 23, 1996): Codename Oak

This was the first version of Java, released officially in January 1996. Prior to that Java was known as "Oak" and was mainly used internally by Sun for the development of embedded software. Embedded devices demanded portability across a wide variety of hardware and a small footprint; Java carries both these capabilities. JDK 1.0 itself was really small, with about 212 classes and eight user packages, with one additional Sun package for debugging.

NOTE
A Java package provides a logical grouping of classes and interfaces.

Thus, this version of Java had very limited capabilities and was no match for the libraries provided in other languages at that time. The user interface provided in the java.awt (Abstract Windowing Toolkit) package was too primitive and did not even provide a printing facility. In spite of a small feature set, Java usage picked up early in the market and within one year of its introduction Java became extremely popular.

The success behind Java at that time was due to the increasing popularity of the Internet. Web pages back then did not possess dynamic capabilities; the web pages were only static. Java applets provided dynamic content generation and interactive capabilities for web pages. Every copy of the Netscape browser provided a Java runtime. Thus, developers were able to reach a massive user base very easily by writing Java applets. This resulted in the enormous popularity and quick acceptance of Java. JDK 1.0 also provided classes for network programming, and Java was hyped at that time as a network programming language.

NOTE
An applet is a small Internet-based program, written in Java, that can be downloaded by any computer.

JDK 1.1 (February 19, 1997)

The next major release for Java was in February of 1997. As you can see, this major release came just one year after its original release. One can imagine the popularity that Java must have gained in this short period of time. So what major additions were made to Java in this release? The number of classes in JDK 1.1 was 504 and the number of packages was 23. These figures speak to the number of additions made to the Java APIs. Thus, although the change in release number was minor, this was in fact a major change.

The major change in the Java language at this time was the new event-processing model. JDK 1.0 used the hierarchical event model used by Windows operating systems. JDK 1.1 and above use the delegation event model, which is more efficient compared to the older model. This helped improve Java's performance, which was highly desired because Java in those days lacked in performance due to its compiled and interpreted nature, as explained earlier. Programming for the delegation event model may employ the newly added anonymous and inner classes for improved efficiency.

JDK 1.1 had many minor releases over next two years, until its last release, which was JDK 1.1.8 in April 1999. Each release added new classes and interfaces to the library, and thus Java was growing every day. Some of the major milestones in these minor releases are detailed next.

Java Beans

The JavaBeans API was introduced during this period for component development in Java. *Java Beans* are reusable software components, written in Java, that can be manipulated visually in a builder tool. Thus, you could build sophisticated GUIs (graphical user interfaces) visually by using third-party components based on the JavaBeans API.

Remote Method Invocation

JDK 1.1 also introduced Remote Method Invocation (RMI), which allows a client to invoke a method on an application running on a remote server. RMI used a proprietary binary protocol called the Java Remote Method Protocol (JRMP). Later on, a newer protocol, called the Internet InterORB Protocol (IIOP), was widely accepted by the industry and became preferred over JRMP. IIOP was designed as part of the Common Object Request Broker Architecture (CORBA). To bridge the gap between the two protocols, Java also introduced RMI over IIOP.

The JAR File Format

A Java applet may consist of many source files. When such applet code is compiled, it generates a separate object code (.class) file for each public class or interface. When the applet code is downloaded to the client machine, all such .class files must be downloaded before the applet can begin its execution. The HTTP 1.0 protocol required the creation of a separate socket connection for each file download. Typically, each .class file is a few hundred bytes in size. The time required to make a connection and disconnection was much longer than the time required for each file download. To resolve this problem, JDK 1.1 introduced the JAR concept, whereby all applet .class files were archived in one single file using the PKZIP algorithm. The resultant JAR file was referenced in the **APPLET** tag of the HTML code. The client would now download one single JAR file using a single socket connection. This resulted in faster download and a much better application startup time on the client's end.

Digital Signatures

Another major change provided in JDK 1.1 was the introduction of digital signing. In JDK 1.0, a Java applet would run in a sandbox with several security restrictions and limited access to system resources; conversely, a stand-alone Java application runs outside the sandbox with full access to all the system resources. With digital signing, applets that were generally deployed on remote servers could now be trusted after their signatures were verified. The client would grant full privileges of a stand-alone application to such verified signed applets.

AWT Enhancements

The AWT, which contains the interfaces and classes for building the GUI, provided several enhancements in JDK 1.1. The most noticeable change was the new event model mentioned earlier. Besides this, several other additions were made to the AWT package. The GUI now supported data transfer using the clipboard so that you could cut/copy/paste the contents of your documents from even a native application to a Java application, and vice versa. You could set and use desktop colors in your Java applications. You could also define shortcut keys for menu items. It also became possible to create pop-up menus like the ones in applications running on Microsoft Windows.

Finally, AWT classes added printing support. Printing was not at all possible in JDK 1.0. AWT also added a **ScrollPane** container for displaying large documents in windows with scrollbars. Note that even such basic facilities were not available in JDK 1.0, and it received wide acceptance in the very short period of one year. Thus, Java had a promising future, as was proved by now.

Other Changes

Some of the other noticeable changes in JDK 1.1 included the introduction of object serialization classes, the Introspection and Reflection API, and the facility to define Inner classes. In addition, general performance improvements were made in several places.

J2SE 1.2 (December 8, 1998): Codename Playground

The next milestone for Java came in December 1998. This version had 1,520 classes and 59 packages. You can clearly see how fast Java grew in just three years. During this time, Sun also introduced a new terminology to describe Java technology—Java SE (Standard Edition). The name JDK is still used to describe an implementation of this technology.

The Introduction of Swing

The major feature introduced in Java 2 was Swing—the new Java-based GUI classes. This made the earlier AWT classes somewhat obsolete, except that Swing extended those classes. AWT components are considered heavyweight because they use many native operating system calls. The new Swing-based GUI classes are totally Java based and therefore are lightweight. These Java-based classes provided the advantage of on-demand installation in browsers that refused to add support to the new JDK versions; this was the case with Microsoft's Internet Explorer (readers may be aware of the famous legal suit between Microsoft and Sun Microsystems during this period). Swing classes also permitted the "pluggable look and feel" (PLAF) that allowed developers to change the look and feel of their applications to whatever they would like. Swing supported Windows, Motif, and Java native platforms.

NOTE
The Java platform at that time was commonly known as Java 2, even though the official name was J2SE 1.2.

The 2D API
The JDK now included classes for the 2D API to allow the user to create two-dimensional charts and graphs easily with the help of several predefined classes and interfaces. The 2D API is the basis for all the drawing in the Java SE platform, not just for charts and graphs.

Drag-and-Drop
J2SE 1.2 introduced the drag-and-drop facility for selecting contents in a Java application and then dragging and dropping them into a native application, and vice versa. Thus, you could now drag and drop the contents of a Microsoft Word document into a Java application, as well as the other way around. This is done without copying and pasting the contents to a clipboard.

Audio Enhancements
The JDK now provided classes for playing back MIDI files and a full range of .wav, .aiff, and .au files. It also provided much higher sound quality.

Java IDL
Java IDL is CORBA'S ORB (Object Request Broker) implemented on the Java platform. This facilitated integration of Java applications with existing CORBA clients and servers. Java provided both CORBA IDL (Interface Definition Language) to Java Interfaces mapping and Java to CORBA IDL reverse mapping. This made it possible to protect the investments in both existing Java Client and RMI-based Java applications.

Security Enhancements
Java security is now policy based. Digital signing was introduced in JDK 1.1. This allowed the identification of the applet source; however, it was not possible to assign different privileges, depending on the source of the applet. In other words, there was no differentiation between two different trusted applets or between a trusted applet and a stand-alone application. All would acquire the same privileges. J2SE 1.2 resolved this issue by creating policy-based security. One can now define a security policy based on the source of the applet. In this way, different applets would be subject to different policies defined by their user and thus acquire different sets of privileges. This also applies to stand-alone Java applications that were also subject to user-defined policies. The policy files are text based and easily configurable. Java also provided a policy tool to create and maintain policies. The policies enabled the fine-grain access control to system resources.

Other Enhancements
In addition to the aforementioned major changes, several enhancements were made to improve performance in general. The loaded classes now had better memory compression. The memory allocation and garbage collection had improved algorithms for faster allocations and deallocations. The Just-in-Time (JIT) compiler mentioned earlier was introduced in this version of Java. New classes such as **ArrayList** and **BufferedImage** and APIs such as Collections were added. DSA code signing was also added.

NOTE
At the time the Java 2 platform was introduced, Java ventured into another arena, known as server-side Java. A separate bundle of Java classes was introduced for this purpose and was called J2EE (Java 2 Enterprise Edition). This included classes for server-side component developments such as Servlets. J2EE has also gone through several major revisions and now includes classes for creating server-side components such as Enterprise Java Beans (EJBs), Java Server Pages (JSPs), Java Database Connectivity (JDBC), J2EE connectors, and more. By this time, Java was clearly split into two areas: the server-side Java (J2EE, now called Java EE) and the standard edition of Java (J2SE). Because this book focuses only on the standard edition of Java, we will not discuss J2EE further.

J2SE 1.3 (May 8, 2000): Codename Kestrel

The next major release of Java, known by this time as J2SE (Java 2 Standard Edition), came in May of 2000. It was codenamed Kestrel and was also called Java 2, Release 1.3. This version did not make lots of additions to its predecessor. The number of classes increased from 1,520 to 1,840, and the number of packages increased from 59 to 76. The notable changes included the bundling of the HotSpot JVM (first released in April 1999 for J2SE 1.2 JVM), JavaSound, Java Naming and Directory Interface (JNDI), and Java Platform Debugger Architecture (JPDA). JNDI provides Java-platform-based applications with a unified interface to multiple naming and directory services in the enterprise, including Lightweight Directory Access Protocol (LDAP), Domain Name System (DNS), Network Information Service (NIS), Common Object Request Broker Architecture (CORBA), and file systems. Like all Java APIs, JNDI is independent of the underlying platform. The service provider interface (SPI) allows directory service implementations to be plugged into the framework, which may make use of a server, a flat file, or a database.

The RMI API had several enhancements—strings longer than 64K could now be serialized, and **rmid** now required a security policy file, to name a couple. Two new methods were added in the **DataFlavor** class of the drag-and-drop API. Several additions were made to the Java 2D API, including support for Portable Network Graphics (PNG) format. Besides these, many changes were made to Swing, AWT, Security, and Object Serialization APIs. The **java.math** package was enhanced, and some classes were added, including the **Timer** class, the **StrictMath** class, the **print** class, and the **java.media.sound** class. This API introduced Hotspot and RMI over IIOP (discussed earlier). The RSA code signing was also added.

The next minor release was J2SE 1.3.1, codenamed Ladybird, which was released on May 17, 2001.

J2SE 1.4 (Feb 6, 2002): Codename Merlin

This was the first release of the Java platform developed under the Java Community Process (JCP) as Java Specification Request (JSR) 59. It consisted of 2,991 classes in 135 packages. Major changes included regular expressions modeled after Perl, exception chaining, an integrated XML parser, an XSLT processor (JAXP), and Java Web Start. To support regular expressions, a new package called **java.util.regex** was added that contained classes for matching character sequences against patterns specified by regular expressions. You will learn about exception chaining in Chapter 8. The JAXP

(Java API for XML processing) provides basic support for processing XML documents though a standardized set of Java Platform APIs. Java Web Start software provides a flexible and robust deployment solution for Java-technology-based applications.

NOTE

The JCP is the mechanism for developing standard technical specifications for Java technology. The JSR is the actual description of proposed and final specifications for the Java platform.

Besides these, several changes came in the AWT package to improve the robustness, behavior, and performance of GUI-based programs. Likewise, many new features were added to Swing, including a new spinner and formatted text field components as well as support for drag-and-drop. The **Popup** and **PopupFactory** classes were exposed to programmers, thus allowing them to create their own pop-ups. JDBC, which provides universal data access from the Java programming language, was enhanced to JDBC 3.0 API. The new features included the ability to set savepoints in a transaction, to keep result sets open after a transaction is committed, to reuse prepared statements, to get metadata about the parameters to a prepared statement, to retrieve keys that are automatically generated, and to have multiple result sets open at one time. It also included two new JDBC data types: BOOLEAN and DATALINK. The DATALINK data type makes it possible to manage data outside of a data source. The new I/O (NIO) APIs provided new features and improved performance. Besides these changes, additions were made to RMI, Math, Collections Framework, Accessibility, and the Java Native Interface (JNI).

The other minor releases that followed were J2SE 1.4.1 (September 16, 2002), codenamed Hopper, and J2SE 1.4.2 (June 26, 2003), codenamed Mantis.

J2SE 5.0 (Sept 30, 2004): Codename Tiger

Developed under JSR 176, Tiger added a number of significant language features, including the **for-each** loop, generics, autoboxing, and var-args. Because this book focuses on J2SE, we cover most of the additions made in this release. This release had 3,562 classes in 166 packages.

Generics allow a type or method to operate on objects of various types while providing compile-time type safety. This was added to all the classes in the Collections Framework. You learn about generics in Chapter 12. The enhanced **for** loop eliminates the drudgery and error-proneness of iterators and index variables when iterating over collections and arrays. (You can learn about this enhanced **for** loop in Syntax Reference 3, one of the three web chapters.) The autoboxing/unboxing feature eliminates the drudgery of manual conversion between primitive types and wrapper types. Chapter 11 fully covers this feature. The var-args allow you to specify a variable number of arguments on program invocation. This is covered in Chapter 9. Besides these, typesafe enums were introduced in this version, which are covered in Chapter 11. The newly added static import facility lets you avoid qualifying static members with class names without the shortcomings of the "Constant Interface anti-pattern." Additionally, changes and enhancements were made to Internationalization APIs. Internationalization is the process of designing an application so that it can be adapted to various languages and regions without engineering changes. Sometimes the term *internationalization* is abbreviated "i18n," because there are 18 letters between the first letter (i) and the last (n). Besides these, the following APIs were enhanced: JavaSound and Java 2D technologies, Image I/O, AWT, and Swing. The **java.lang** and **java.util** packages had several enhancements, including the new **Formatter** and **Scanner** classes, which you will be using in several programming examples in this book. There were lots of enhancements to Concurrency Utilities and the Collections Framework. We cover all major enhancements to Concurrency Utilities in Chapter 19 and those in the Collections Framework in Chapter 16. On the hardware front, AMD Opteron processors are now supported by the server VM on SUSE Linux and on Windows 2003.

Java SE 6 (Dec 11, 2006): Codename Mustang

This release facilitated the use of scripting languages (JavaScript using Mozilla's Rhino engine) with the JVM and provided Visual Basic language support. As of this version, Sun replaced the name "J2SE" with Java SE and dropped the ".0" from the version number. This release introduced several changes and additions to the Collections Framework. New interfaces, named **Deque**, **BlockingDeque**, **NavigableSet**, **NavigableMap**, and **ConcurrentNavigableMap**, were added. A few concrete implementation classes were added, and the existing classes were retrofitted to implement new interfaces. We discuss the Collections Framework in Chapter 16. Several enhancements were made in the **java.lang.instrument** package. The Instrumentation API provides services that allow Java programming language agents to instrument programs running on the JVM. We do not cover instrumentation in this book. The **java.io** package introduced a new class called **Console**, which will be covered in Chapter 9. This class contains methods to access a character-based console device; its **readPassword** method allows input of sensitive data such as passwords by disabling echoing of characters on the console. The **File** class now has several methods to retrieve disk usage information as well as setting and querying file permissions. We discuss this class in Chapter 9. The JAR and ZIP API was also enhanced. In addition, enhancements were made in Java Web Start and the Java Network Launching Protocol (JNLP), which provides a browser-independent architecture for deploying Java 2 technology-based applications to the client desktop.

Other major changes included support for pluggable annotations (JSR 269), lots of GUI improvements, including native UI enhancements to support the look and feel of Windows Vista, and improvements to the JPDA and JVM Tool Interface for better monitoring and troubleshooting.

Java SE 7 (July 7, 2011): Codename Dolphin

Java SE 7 is the major release to the Java SE platform, which came a long time after its previous release. It introduced many enhancements to the Java language. Integral types can now be expressed using the binary number system. Numerical literals can contain underscore characters for better readability. You can use strings in switch statements. A diamond operator is introduced in generics instance creation syntax. A new try-with-resources statement has been added. Multiple exception types may now be included in a single catch block. A new compiler option and two annotations are added to give you improved compiler warnings and errors when using nonreifiable formal parameters with var-args methods. Many of these features are covered in the relevant chapters in this book.

Java SE 7 introduced the NIO.2 API, which offers the ability to develop a custom file system provider for managing file system objects. The new additions to this API provide comprehensive support for file I/O and for accessing the file system. We cover this in Chapter 9. The JDBC 4.1 API enables you to use try-with-resources syntax to automatically close resources of type **Connection**, **Resultset**, and **Statement**. Additions have been made to **RowSet** that enable you to create all types of row sets supported by your JDBC driver. Java SE 7 adds support for Stream Control Transmission Protocol (SCTP) on Solaris and Sockets Direct Protocol (SDP), which is a wire protocol to support stream connections over InfiniBand fabric. This, at the time of this writing, was available for the

Solaris and Linux platforms. You can now develop and deploy Rich Internet Applications as applets or Java Web Start applications. Because this is an altogether different domain of applications that would require another book to describe, we do not cover these APIs in this book. The Java SE platform now supports the implementation of dynamically typed programming languages on the JVM; for this, a new instruction called **invokedynamic** was added to the JVM. Although the Introspection and Reflection API is covered thoroughly in Chapter 21, we do not cover the use of this instruction because it is not at all relevant to the context of this book. A lightweight fork/join framework is now added to the Concurrency API. This is covered fully in Chapter 19. On the client side, Java SE 7 adds a next-generation cross-platform look and feel for Swing—called Nimbus look-and-feel. This is used in several applications in this book. Besides these, there are several other enhancements that are not relevant to the context of this book. For example, the XML stack has been updated to support the most recent versions of XML processing, binding, and Web Services APIs. The MBeans API is enhanced to add more management functionality. In the Security and Cryptography API, a portable implementation of the standard Elliptic Curve Cryptographic (ECC) algorithms has been added. The Internationalization API is enhanced to support the 6.0 version of Unicode. The **Locale** class has been upgraded, and the handling of locales has been upgraded to separate formatting locales from user interface language locales. The reader is encouraged to visit the openjdk site (http://openjdk.java.net/projects/jdk7/features/) to look at the rest of the changes that came in the Java SE 7 platform.

Summary

Java, since its public introduction in 1996, has become extremely popular among developers worldwide—mostly because of its cross-platform nature. Today it has evolved into a full-fledged platform for creating, deploying, and running a wide variety of applications. To achieve portability, Java uses the concept of a virtual machine (VM). A Java source file compiles into bytecode consisting of an instruction set of a pseudo CPU. This CPU is emulated in memory by a running process, and the compiled bytecode runs on the emulator. This allows Java executables to run on any platform that has a JVM (Java Virtual Machine). Java's major features of note are that it is small, simple, object oriented, compiled and interpreted, platform independent, robust and secure, multithreaded, and dynamic. We discussed each of these features in depth in this chapter.

Java has undergone several revisions over the last 15 years. These revisions are marked by the versioning of the Java Development Kit. JDK 1.0 was introduced in 1996, and the next major release, JDK 1.1, came about just one year later. Over next several years, Java evolved into several distinct platforms: Java SE (Java Platform, Standard Edition), Java EE (Java Platform, Enterprise Edition), Java ME (Java Platform, Micro Edition), and Java Card technology. We discussed the important features and additions in all the major releases of the Java SE platform in this chapter.

With this brief introduction to the exciting Java platform, let's start learning it.

CHAPTER

2

Arrays

he previous chapter presented an overview of Java technology and its various stages of development. Now it's time to jump into coding. Most programming books start with a Hello World example, and I do not want to make an exception to this rule. However, there's not enough space in this book to cover basic syntax, so the publisher and I have decided to move that material to the Web (go to www. oraclepressbooks.com). There are a total of three Syntax Reference chapters that address language constructs, operators, and control flow statements. These chapters cover the latest additions and inclusions in Java 7, so I encourage you to read these online chapters. If you already have a good familiarity with other programming languages or know some Java, you may prefer to skim through the material merely to identify changes to Java 7.

Leaving the basic syntax to the three online chapters, we will now start with an important construct called *arrays*. Arrays facilitate the easy creation and access of several elements of the same data type. You learn how to create arrays and use them in your programs. You also learn to create arrays of single and multiple dimensions. In particular, you will learn the following:

- Declaring arrays
- Accessing/modifying array elements
- Runtime initialization of arrays
- Using array literals for initializations
- Multidimensional arrays
- Nonrectangular arrays
- Determining array length
- Copying arrays
- Understanding the class representation of an array

Arrays

You create arrays when you want to operate on a collection of variables of the same data type or pass them all around together. An array is essentially a collection of elements of the same data type. The elements are also called *components* of the array. Each element of the array is accessed using a unique index value, also called a *subscript*. For example, an array of integers contains several elements, each of type **int**, and an array of floating-point numbers contains several elements, each of type **float**. Because array elements are accessed using a single variable name coupled with a subscript, you do not need to create several unique variable names in your program code to store and access many variables having the same data type. A typical integer array is shown in Figure 2-1.

The array in Figure 2-1 stores five integer variables. Each variable will be accessed using the single name **numbers**, along with a unique index in the array. Each variable will hold an integer value that is independent of the values held by other elements. Each element can be accessed and modified individually. You will learn how to declare an array and access the array elements in the sections that follow.

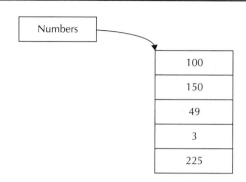

FIGURE 2-1.   *An array of five integer variables*

Declaring Arrays

The general syntax for declaring an array is as follows:

```
type arrayName [ ];
```

Java allows another syntax for array declaration, as follows:

```
type [ ] arrayName;
```

NOTE
*Though Java supports both types of declarations, convention discourages the first form. The square brackets indicate that the variable you want to declare is of the array type, and **type** indicates the type of element it is going to hold. It makes more sense to have the brackets appear with the type designation. Therefore, the latter is the preferred form of declaration and is used throughout this book.*

The square brackets in this syntax are also called the *indexing operator* because they specify the index of an element in an array. The **type** specifies the type of element that the array is going to store. The **arrayName** specifies the name by which the elements of the array are addressed in the program code. Note that like in many other languages, the declaration does not allow you to specify the size of the array.

To declare an array of integers, you would use the following declaration:

```
int[] numbers;
```

The name of the array in this declaration is **numbers**. Thus, each element of the array would be accessed using this name along with an appropriate index value.

To declare an array of **float**, you use the following declaration:

```
float[] floatNumbers;
```

The name of the array is **floatNumbers**, and each element of the array holds a floating-point number.

NOTE
These declarations simply create a variable of the array type. They do not create an actual array, and no memory space is yet allocated for storing the array elements.

Creating Arrays

Now that you know how to declare an array variable, the next task is to allocate space for the array elements. To allocate space, you use **new** keyword. For example, to create an array of 10 integers, you would use the following code:

```
int[] numbers;
numbers = new int[10];
```

The first statement declares a variable called **numbers** of the array type, with each element of type **int**. The second statement allocates contiguous memory for holding 10 integers and assigns the memory address of the first element to the variable **numbers**. An array initializer provides initial values for all its components. You may assign different values to these variables somewhere in your code, as explained in the next section.

To create an array of 20 floating-point numbers, you use the following code fragment:

```
float[] floatNumbers;
floatNumbers = new float[20];
```

The first statement declares a variable called **floatNumbers** of the array type. Each element of the array is of the floating-point type. The second statement allocates space for holding 20 floating-point-type elements and assigns the address of the first element to the array variable.

Accessing and Modifying Array Elements

Now that you know how to create an array, our next task is to access the array elements. You use an index to access the elements of an array. Each element of the array has a unique index value. An element of an array is accessed by using the array name followed by its index value written in square brackets. The general syntax of accessing an array element is as follows:

```
arrayName [ indexValue ] ;
```

For example, consider the following declaration of an array of integers:

```
int[] numbers = new int[5];
```

Note how the declaration and allocation are done in the same program statement.

In this declaration, there is a total of five elements in the **numbers** array. The array index starts with a value of zero. Thus, the first element of the array is accessed using the following syntax:

```
numbers[0]
```

This is illustrated in Figure 2-2.

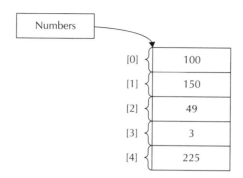

FIGURE 2-2.   *Accessing array elements using a subscript*

The subsequent elements will be accessed using syntax **numbers[1]**, **numbers[2]**, and so on. The last element is accessed using syntax **numbers[4]**. Note that using an index value of **5** will be illegal because **numbers[5]** will try to access the sixth element—which is out of bounds for the given array.

TIP
*Trying to access an element that is outside of the array's bounds results in the generation of an **ArrayIndexOutOfBounds** exception, which is explained in Chapter 8.*

TIP
*Whenever you come across a new class such as **ArrayIndexOutOfBounds**, it is strongly recommended that you open javadocs (http://docs.oracle.com/javase/7/docs/api/) and learn more about the class.*

The array elements are always stored in a block of contiguous memory. Figure 2-3 shows the memory allocation for an integer array consisting of five elements declared using the following statements:

```
int[] numbers;
numbers = new int[5];
```

Because an **int** takes 4 bytes of memory, you will notice in Figure 2-3 that each element of the array occupies 4 bytes. Therefore, the total allocation is 20 bytes of memory space. Usually, you will not have to worry about this memory allocation while accessing or modifying the elements of the array.

To modify the value of an array element, you use the following syntax:

```
arrayName [ index_value ] = data;
```

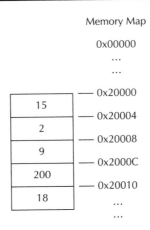

Memory Map

FIGURE 2-3. *Displaying the memory map of an integer array*

For example, in the **numbers** array declared previously, you can set the value of the element at index 3 to 100 using the following statement:

```
numbers[3] = 100;
```

Note that the index value of 3 refers to the fourth element of the array.

Initializing Arrays

At this point, you have learned how to declare an array, allocate the space for its elements, and access its elements. Now you will learn to initialize the entire array to a desired state before its elements are used.

CAUTION
Although Java provides a default initialization for array elements, with arrays of objects, the default initialization results in object references set to null. This may result in runtime exceptions in the code if the elements are not initialized to proper object references.

There are two techniques for initializing the array elements. The elements of the array may be initialized at runtime via value assignment, as shown earlier, or initialized via array literals.

Initializing at Runtime

An array element may be initialized at runtime using its index value, as discussed in the previous section. Consider the following declaration for an array of integers:

```
int[] numbers = new int[10];
```

Each element may now be initialized to a desired value by using a block of code such as the following:

```
numbers[0] = 10;
numbers[1] = 5;
numbers[2] = 145;
...
numbers[9] = 24;
```

If you decide to initialize all the elements of the array to the same value, you may use one of the loop constructs discussed in Syntax Reference 3. For example, the following **for** loop will initialize all the elements of the preceding array to zero:

```
for (int i = 0; i < 10; i++) {
    numbers[i] = 0;
}
```

Initializing Using Array Literals

Array literals provide a shorter and more readable syntax while initializing an array. For example, consider the following program statement:

```
int[] numbers = {15, 2, 9, 200, 18};
```

This statement declares an array of integers containing five elements. The compiler determines the size of the array based on the number of initializers specified in curly braces. When the JVM loads this code in memory, it will initialize those memory locations allocated to the array with the values specified in the curly braces.

This type of initialization is sometimes called *aggregate initialization* and is a much safer method of initializing an array. If you perform runtime initialization, as discussed earlier, the code is error-prone because you might accidentally specify a wrong value for the index while modifying an element. Using an array literal centralizes the entire code for initialization, and adding/removing elements is error-free. For example, to add one more element, you just need to write a new initializer in the list, and to remove an element, you simply delete one from the list. This cannot result in an array out-of-bounds error and is therefore safer to use.

It is also important to understand that the Java Virtual Machine architecture does not support any kind of efficient array initialization. As a matter of fact, array literals are created and initialized when the program is run, not when the program is compiled. For example, consider our earlier declaration of an array literal:

```
int[] numbers = {15, 2, 9, 200, 18};
```

This gets compiled into the equivalent of the following code:

```
int[] numbers = new int[5];
numbers[0] = 15;
numbers[1] = 2;
numbers[2] = 9;
numbers[3] = 200;
numbers[4] = 18;
```

Thus, array literals are just a shorthand for writing the runtime initialization code discussed earlier.

CAUTION
If you want to include a large amount of data in a Java program, do not use array literals, because the Java compiler will create lots of Java bytecode to initialize the array. The better way is to store the data in an external file, read its contents at runtime, and initialize the array elements using these values.

NOTE
Consider the following declaration:

```
long[] times = {System.nanoTime(), 0};
```

*The element at subscript **0** in the **times** array will hold the long value of the current time when the program is run, and not the time when the code is compiled.*

CAUTION
Like C++, Java does not allow you to specify the array size in square brackets. It determines the array size from the number of values specified in the RHS (right-hand side) of the expression. It is illegal to specify the array size. Thus, even if you specify the size equal to the exact number of values specified on the RHS, the program statement will not compile.

The memory representation of the preceding declaration is shown in Figure 2-4.

Let's now look at the use of arrays using a simple program. Listing 2-1 declares and uses an array of integers for storing the marks (scores) of students on a mathematics test. The program prompts the user to enter the mark obtained by each student. The input data is stored in an integer array. After accepting the scores of all students, the program computes the class average by accessing the scores stored in the array.

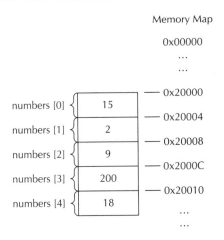

FIGURE 2-4.   *Displaying the memory map of an integer array*

Listing 2-1   *Program to Illustrate the Use of an Array*

```java
import java.io.*;

public class TestScoreAverage {

    public static void main(String[] args) {
        final int NUMBER_OF_STUDENTS = 5;
        int[] marks = new int[NUMBER_OF_STUDENTS];
        try {
            BufferedReader reader =
                    new BufferedReader(new InputStreamReader(System.in));
            for (int i = 0; i < NUMBER_OF_STUDENTS; i++) {
                System.out.print("Enter marks for student #" + (i + 1) + ": ");
                String str = reader.readLine();
                marks[i] = Integer.parseInt(str);
            }
        } catch (Exception e) {
            e.printStackTrace();
        }
        int total = 0;
        for (int i = 0; i < NUMBER_OF_STUDENTS; i++) {
            total += marks[i];
        }
        System.out.println("Average Marks " + (float) total / NUMBER_OF_STUDENTS);
    }
}
```

In the **main** method, we first create a constant for defining the number of students in the class:

```java
final int NUMBER_OF_STUDENTS = 5;
```

TIP

*Use the **final** keyword to create constants in your program. The variables declared with **final** can be initialized only once. After initialization, their values cannot be modified throughout the life of the program.*

It is always a good practice to create a constant in such situations; if the number of students in the class changes, we would need to modify only one statement and the rest of the program would remain unaffected (or at least would require minimal changes).

We then declare and create an array of integers called **marks** that has a size equal to **NUMBER_OF_STUDENTS**, as follows:

```java
int[] marks = new int[NUMBER_OF_STUDENTS];
```

We now read the mark for each student by prompting the user to enter it on the terminal. To read input from the terminal, we create a **BufferedReader** on the **System.in** object, as follows:

```java
BufferedReader reader = new BufferedReader(new InputStreamReader(System.in));
```

The use of the **BufferredReader** and **InputStreamReader** classes for accepting a string from the user was briefly explained in Syntax Reference 3.

The program now reads the marks by setting up a loop:

```
for (int i = 0; i < NUMBER_OF_STUDENTS; i++) {
```

For each student, we prompt the user using a **System.out.print** statement:

```
System.out.print("Enter marks for student #" + (i + 1) + ": ");
```

The user input is read by calling the **readLine** method of the **reader** object:

```
String str = reader.readLine();
```

The marks entered will be in the **String** format. We need to convert this string to an integer before assigning it to the array element. To convert a string into an integer, we use the **parseInt** method of the **Integer** class:

```
marks[i] = Integer.parseInt(str);
```

Because both **readLine** and **parseInt** methods can generate a runtime error, these are enclosed in a **try-catch** block. The exception handler prints a trace of the stack by calling the **printStackTrace** method on the **Exception** object:

```
e.printStackTrace();
```

After reading the marks from the user input and copying them into the array elements, we now set up a **for** loop for determining the total of all the marks:

```
int total = 0;
for (int i = 0; i < NUMBER_OF_STUDENTS; i++) {
    total += marks[i];
}
```

Finally, we print the average marks of the class on the user console using the following statement:

```
System.out.println("Average Marks " + (float) total / NUMBER_OF_STUDENTS);
```

Note that while computing the average, we convert the variable **total** to type **float**. If we do not do this, the compiler will perform an integer division on the two operands and the result will not be accurate.

This simple program illustrates the declaration of a single-dimensional array, initializing the array elements, and accessing the elements in the program code.

Now that you know a bit more about arrays, we can take a short break and return to our discussion on control flow for a moment. As you learned in Syntax Reference 3, Java provides yet another looping construct to iterate through the elements of an array: the **for-each** loop. This construct was introduced in J2SE 5.0, and we discuss it next.

The for-each Loop

The **for-each** construct allows you to iterate through an entire array without using the index values of the elements. The general form of the **for-each** loop is as follows:

```
for ( type  variableName : collection ) {
    loopBody
}
```

NOTE
*The **for-each** construct was introduced in J2SE 5.0. The official sources use several names for the construct. It is called the "Enhanced for" loop, "For-Each" loop, and "foreach" statement.*

The ***variableName*** specifies the type of variable and its name. The ***collection*** represents the name of the array. For each iteration of the **for** loop, the ***loopBody*** is executed once. The iterations continue until the last element of the array is processed. Using this construct, you will iterate through the **marks** array, declared in the previous section, as follows:

```
for (int m : marks) {
    System.out.println (m);
}
```

In each iteration of the **for** loop, the value of an element of the **marks** array is printed. After each iteration, the index in the array is automatically incremented to retrieve the next element. The **for** loop continues until the last element is retrieved. The **for-each** construct is very useful if you want to traverse all the elements of the array. Specifically, it allows you to iterate over collections and arrays without using iterators or index variables. (Collections are discussed in Chapter 16.) Although the **for** statement is quite powerful, it is not optimized for collection iteration.

TIP
*The **for-each** construct can be easily used to dump all the elements of an array on the user console. However, the same thing can be easily achieved by using the **toString** method of the **Arrays** class. The **Arrays** class is discussed later in this chapter.*

Though a powerful construct, **for-each** has certain restrictions. It can be used for accessing the array elements but not for modifying them. It is not usable for loops that must iterate over multiple collections in parallel—for example, to compare the elements of two arrays. It can be used only for a single element access and cannot be used to compare successive elements in an array. It is a forward-only iterator. If you want to access only a few elements of the array, you would need to use the traditional **for** loop.

Before we close this discussion on the **for-each** loop, you may like to know why the designers did not opt for introducing the new keyword **foreach** like in C# (Microsoft's .NET language). By not introducing the new **foreach** keyword, the designers ensured backward compatibility with any pre–J2SE 5.0 code that might use the keyword as an identifier. The general syntax for a **foreach** loop in other languages is as follows:

```
foreach (element in collection)
```

Using this syntax would also make the code incompatible with the previous versions because **in** is a keyword (for example, as in **System.in**).

Going back to our discussion on arrays, so far we have discussed single-dimensional arrays. Now we will discuss multidimensional arrays.

Multidimensional Arrays

Multidimensional arrays, as the name suggests, contain more than one dimension. You can create two-dimensional, three-dimensional, and *n*-dimensional arrays in Java (where *n* is any natural number). The number of dimensions may be any large number, subject to the restrictions imposed by the compiler. The JDK compiler puts this limit at 255, which is so large that developers need not worry about it.

Let's first discuss two-dimensional arrays.

Two-dimensional Arrays

A two-dimensional array can be visualized as a table consisting of rows and columns. Each cell of the table denotes an array element.

The general syntax for declaring a two-dimensional array is as follows:

```
type arrayName [ ] [ ] ;
```

or

```
type [ ] [ ]  arrayName ;
```

TIP
Although both syntaxes are valid, the preferred one is the second syntax, where the square brackets are placed immediately after the data type.

The ***type*** specifies the type of data that each array element will hold. The ***arrayName*** specifies the name for the array. The two square brackets indicate that the current array variable declaration refers to a two-dimensional array.

Suppose you have to write a program to store marks obtained by each student in a class in various subjects. Let's assume that each student takes five subjects and that 50 students are in the class. You will need to create a two-dimensional array to store this data. You would write the following block of code to create such an array:

```
final int NUMBER_OF_SUBJECTS = 5;
final int NUMBER_OF_STUDENTS = 50;
int[][] marks;
marks = new int[NUMBER_OF_SUBJECTS][NUMBER_OF_STUDENTS];
```

The first dimension of the array (that is, the row) specifies the subject ID, and the second dimension (that is, the column) specifies the student ID. You could easily interchange rows and columns in the preceding declaration by changing their order of declaration as shown in the following statement:

```
marks = new int[NUMBER_OF_STUDENTS][NUMBER_OF_SUBJECTS];
```

In this case, the first dimension specifies the student ID and the second dimension specifies the subject ID. The memory layout in tabular format for this second declaration is shown in Figure 2-5.

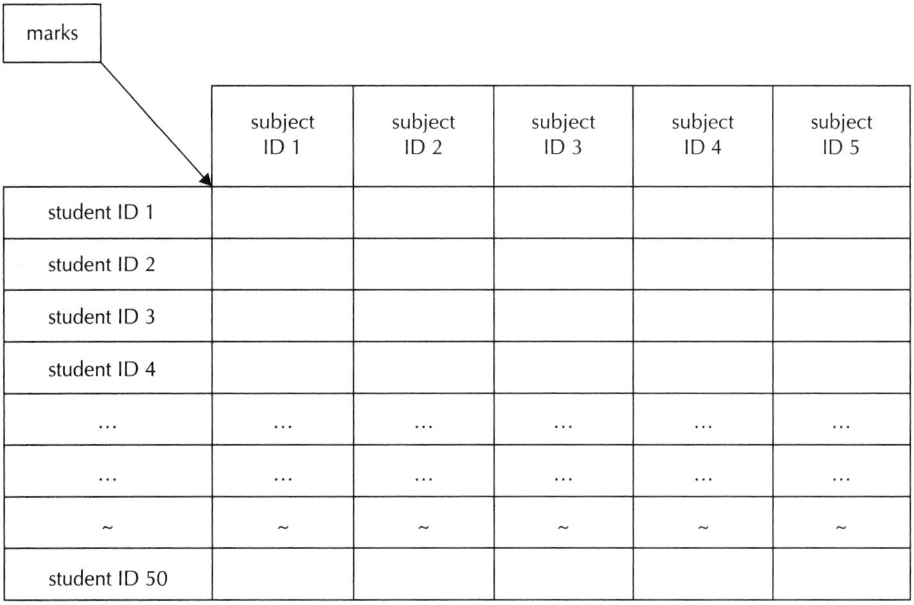

FIGURE 2-5. *Displaying the memory map of a two-dimensional array*

The tabular map displayed in Figure 2-5 shows both student and subject IDs starting with 1. (Generally, a student and a subject will not be assigned an ID equal to zero.) When you store the student marks in this array, you will need to adjust both indices by 1 to comply with Java's requirements of array indexing. For example, to assign the marks obtained by student with ID 6 in subject 4, you will use the following syntax:

```
marks[5][3] = 78;
```

Note that a row-index value of 5 indicates the sixth row in the table because the index always starts with zero. Similarly, a column-index value of 3 indicates the fourth column in the table.

As another example, the syntax **marks[0][0]** would denote the marks obtained by a student with ID 1 in the subject designated by subject ID 1. (Again, remember that the student IDs and subject numbers start with 1 in our notation.) Similarly, **marks[49][4]** would denote the marks obtained by the last student in the class (student ID 50) in the last subject (subject ID 5).

Initializing Two-dimensional Arrays

Just like you initialize a single-dimensional array by using runtime initialization or an array literal, you can initialize a two-dimensional array by using both techniques. Let's discuss both methods.

Initializing at Runtime

To initialize an element of a two-dimensional array, you use the syntax discussed earlier for accessing the element and then use an assignment statement to initialize it:

```
arrayName [ row ] [ col ] = data ;
```

For example, consider the following declaration for a two-dimensional array of integers:

```
int [] [] marks;
marks = new int [5] [50];
```

The individual elements of this array may be initialized using following program statements:

```
marks [0] [5] = 78;
marks [2] [10] = 56;
```

The first statement initializes the value of the array element addressed by the first row and the sixth column to 78. The second statement initializes the array element addressed by the third row and eleventh column to a value of 56.

You may use a nested **for** loop to initialize each element of a two-dimensional array to a specific value. Using the following nested **for** loop, you initialize each element of the array to a value of 0:

```
final int MAX_ROWS = 5, MAX_COLS = 50;
for (int row = 0; row < MAX_ROWS; row++) {
    for (int col = 0; col < MAX_COLS; col++) {
        marks [row] [col] = 0;
    }
}
```

Initializing Using Array Literals

You may define the values of individual array elements in curly braces on the right side of the assignment operator during the array declaration. The general syntax for initializing elements of a two-dimensional array using this method is shown here:

```
int [] [] subjectMarks = {
    {1, 98},
    {2, 58},
    {3, 78},
    {4, 89}
};
```

Note the use of nested curly braces to separate out the different rows of the data declarations. The Java compiler will generate the bytecode for the preceding declaration that is the equivalent of the following:

```
subjectMarks = new int [] [];
subjectMarks [0] [0] = 1;
subjectMarks [0] [1] = 98;
subjectMarks [1] [0] = 2;
...
```

As mentioned earlier, the array literals are just a shorthand for initializing an array element by element.

CAUTION

Unlike other languages such as C++, Java does not allow you to omit the inner curly braces that mark each row of a two-dimensional array. Therefore, the following declaration is invalid in Java:

```
int[][] subMarks = {1, 98, 2, 58, 3, 78, 4, 89};
```

This is because Java does not allow you to specify the dimensions of the array in the declaration statement.

We will now discuss the use of two-dimensional arrays with the help of a program. We will develop a program for storing and displaying the marks obtained by all the students in a class across all their subjects. As explained in the previous section, we will need to create a two-dimensional array for this purpose.

The program shown in Listing 2-2 demonstrates how to declare, initialize, and access a two-dimensional array.

Listing 2-2 *Program to Illustrate the Use of a Two-dimensional Array*

```
public class MultiDimArrayApp {

    public static void main(String[] args) {
        final int MAX_STUDENTS = 50, MAX_SUBJECTS = 3;
        int[][] marks = new int[MAX_STUDENTS][MAX_SUBJECTS];
        // Adding data to the array
        for (int id = 0; id < MAX_STUDENTS; id++) {
            for (int subject = 0; subject < MAX_SUBJECTS; subject++) {
                marks[id][subject] = (int) (Math.random() * 100);
            }
        }
        // Printing Array
        System.out.print("Student\t");
        for (int subject = 0; subject < MAX_SUBJECTS; subject++) {
            System.out.print("\t" + "Subject " + subject + "\t");
        }
        System.out.println();
        for (int id = 0; id < MAX_STUDENTS; id++) {
            System.out.print("Student " + (id + 1) + '\t');
            for (int subject = 0; subject < MAX_SUBJECTS; subject++) {
                System.out.print("\t" + marks[id][subject] + "\t");
            }
            System.out.println();
        }
    }
}
```

The program first creates two constants for defining the array sizes:

```
final int MAX_STUDENTS = 50, MAX_SUBJECTS = 3;
```

In practice, both constants may contain larger values than used here for simplicity. Next, we declare a two-dimensional array of integers using these constants:

```
int[][] marks = new int[MAX_STUDENTS][MAX_SUBJECTS];
```

Note that the first dimension is used for tracking students—each row will correspond to a unique student ID. The second dimension tracks subjects—each column will correspond to a unique subject number.

We will now add some data to the array. Rather than asking the program user to input the scores for each subject and each student, we will enter values in the array programmatically. We first set up a loop to iterate through all student IDs, as follows:

```
for (int id = 0; id < MAX_STUDENTS; id++) {
```

For each student ID, we will iterate through all subject IDs by setting up an inner **for** loop:

```
for (int subject = 0; subject < MAX_SUBJECTS; subject++) {
    marks[id][subject] = (int) (Math.random() * 100);
}
```

We initialize the individual array elements by assigning a random number in the range 0 to 99. The **random** method of the **Math** class generates a **double** value in the range 0 to 1.0 (excluding 1.0). This is multiplied by 100, the result is typecast to an **int**, and finally it is assigned to the element of the **marks** array.

Note that to access an [i, j]th element of the array, we use the syntax **marks[i][j]**. The nested **for** loops ensure that we visit each row and column of the array and initialize each individual element of the array. Once the entire array is filled with some values, we print the array values on the user console.

Once again, we set up the nested **for** loops to iterate through all the rows and columns. The individual array elements are accessed and printed on the console using following statement:

```
System.out.print("\t" + marks[id][subject] + "\t");
```

We print a tab character after each cell value to separate out the columns. The program prints tabs at the appropriate places to format the output. Partial output is shown here:

```
Student           Subject 0      Subject 1        Subject 2
Student 1            23             41               17
Student 2            72             44               46
Student 3            65             65               56
Student 4            12             11               76
Student 5            49             53               36
```

Looping Using the for-each Construct

You can easily use the **for-each** construct, discussed earlier, to loop through all the elements of a two-dimensional array. For example, to loop through the elements of the **marks** array declared in the previous example, use the following block of code:

```
int i = 0;
for (int[] student : marks) {
    System.out.print("Student " + i++ + '\t');
    for (int value : student) {
        System.out.print("\t" + value + "\t");
    }
    System.out.println();
}
```

The outer **for** loop iterates through each row of the array. The inner **for** loop visits each column of the array. The **value** variable holds the value of the array element. Thus, all the array elements are dumped on the console in a tabular format. Note that to print the student ID, we use another variable, **i**. This is because the outer **for** loop now refers to an integer array rather than an integer ID, as in the previous case.

N-dimensional Arrays

So far, we have discussed single- and two-dimensional arrays. The same concepts may be extended to represent and access *n*-dimensional arrays. For example, to declare a three-dimensional array, you will use following syntax:

```
type [] [] []   arrayName= new type [size] [size] [size] ;
```

An example follows:

```
int[] [] [] matrix = new int[5] [15] [10];
```

This declaration creates a three-dimensional array; the size of the first dimension is 5, the size of the second dimension is 15, and the size of the third dimension is 10. Each element of the array will store an integer value. The total number of elements for this array is 5 × 15 × 10 (that is, 750). The memory allocations for the entire array will be 750 multiplied by the size of **int** data type. Because the size of **int** data type is 4, the byte allocation will be 3000.

To access the [i, j, k]th element, you use the syntax **matrix[i][j][k]**. The array elements may be initialized by using either runtime initialization or array literals, as discussed earlier. The concepts may be extended further to create and access arrays having more than three dimensions.

Nonrectangular Arrays

So far you have seen the declaration and use of rectangular arrays. Java allows you to create nonrectangular arrays. A *nonrectangular array* is an array in which each row of the array may have a different number of columns. The memory layout for a nonrectangular array is illustrated in Figure 2-6.

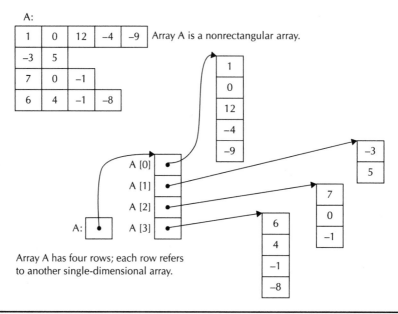

FIGURE 2-6. *Memory layout of a nonrectangular array*

As shown in Figure 2-6, Array A is a nonrectangular array having four rows. When allocated in memory, the variable **A** will refer to a contiguous memory allocation of four cells, where each cell holds a reference to another single-dimensional array. In our case, the first cell holds a reference to an array having five elements, the second row holds a reference to an array having two elements, the third row holds a reference to an array having three rows, and finally the fourth cell holds a reference to an array having four rows.

Runtime Initialization

Consider a two-dimensional array whose first dimension is, let's say, 5. Therefore, the array will contain five rows. You may now declare different column sizes for each row. For example, the first row may contain four columns; the second row may contain three columns, and so on. Such a declaration is shown here:

```
int[][] jaggedArray = new int[5][];
jaggedArray[0] = new int[4];
jaggedArray[1] = new int[3];
jaggedArray[2] = new int[5];
jaggedArray[3] = new int[2];
jaggedArray[4] = new int[4];
```

The **jaggedArray** is a two-dimensional array, as declared in the first statement. During the declaration, you initialize the first dimension of the array to 5, indicating that the array would contain five rows. Here, you do not specify the value for the second dimension.

On the next line, you initialize the first row of the **jaggedArray**. Each row consists of a certain number of cells of type **int**. The number of cells in each row is the column length of the array. You initialize this to 4. Thus, the first row (that is, the row with ID 0) would contain four columns. For the second row (row ID 1), you declare the column size 3. The second row therefore contains three columns. Likewise, for third row, you set a column size of 5; for the fourth row the column size is 2, and for the fifth row the column size is 4.

To access the elements of this array, you would use the syntax **jaggedArray[i][j]**, as in the case of the earlier examples. You will have to ensure that **i**, **j** values are within the range of the array declaration. For example, **jaggedArray[0][3]** is valid, whereas **jaggedArray[1][3]** is invalid because the second row contains only three columns.

This type of nonrectangular array is also called a "jagged" or "ragged" array. Sometimes, it is also called an "array of arrays." Note that like rectangular arrays (that is, arrays having the same number of columns in each row), each element of the nonrectangular array must be of the same data type.

Initialization Using Array Literals

The same way you initialize single-dimensional and other rectangular arrays using array literals, you can initialize a nonrectangular array. Consider the following declaration:

```
int[][] myArray = {
    {3, 4, 5},
    {1, 2}
};
```

Here, **myArray** is a two-dimensional array of integers. The first row of the array consists of three elements, whereas the second row consists of only two elements. Thus, this is a nonrectangular array. While accessing the elements of this array, you will have to take care to ensure that both indices lie within the bounds of the array for each row.

CAUTION
The material that follows requires knowledge of object-oriented programming and also contains some advanced concepts on classes. If you are a beginner in this field, skip the rest of this chapter and revisit it after studying classes in Chapter 3.

A Few Goodies

When you declare an array in Java, it is treated as an object of an internal class that defines useful attributes and methods. Using these, you will be able to determine the length of the array and make a copy of its contents, in addition to other useful operations. You will now learn how to perform these operations.

Determining the Array Length

The **length** field of the internal array class specifies the length of an array. The program in Listing 2-3 illustrates how to use this field.

Listing 2-3 *Determining the Length of an Array*

```java
public class ArrayLengthApp {

    public static void main(String[] args) {
        final int SIZE = 5;
        int[] integerArray = new int[SIZE];
        float[] floatArray = {5.0f, 3.0f, 2.0f, 1.5f};
        String[] weekDays = {"Sunday", "Monday", "Tuesday",
            "Wednesday", "Thursday", "Friday", "Saturday"};
        int[][] jaggedArray = {
            {5, 4},
            {10, 15, 12, 15, 18},
            {6, 9, 10},
            {12, 5, 8, 11}
        };
        System.out.println("integerArray length: " + integerArray.length);
        System.out.println("floatArray length: " + floatArray.length);
        System.out.println("Number of days in a week: " + weekDays.length);
        System.out.println("Length of jaggedArray: " + jaggedArray.length);
        int row = 0;
        for (int[] memberRow : jaggedArray) {
            System.out.println("\tArray length for row "
                    + ++row + ": " + memberRow.length);
        }
    }
}
```

In the **main** method, the program declares several arrays. **integerArray** is a single-dimensional array consisting of five elements with default initial values. **floatArray** is an array of floating-point numbers containing four initialized elements. **weekDays** is an array of **String** objects initialized to the values of the days of the week. **jaggedArray** is a nonrectangular initialized array. To determine the length of each of these arrays, we use the syntax *arrayName.length*. The program output is shown here:

```
integerArray length: 5
floatArray length: 4
Number of days in a week: 7
Length of jaggedArray: 4
Array length for row 1: 2
Array length for row 2: 5
Array length for row 3: 3
Array length for row 4: 4
```

Note the length of **integerArray**, where the elements are not explicitly initialized, is printed as 5; the length of **floatArray**, where the elements are initialized using literals, is printed as 4; and the length of array of **String**s called **weekDays**, which is also initialized using literals, is printed as 7. The interesting case here is determining the length of the **jaggedArray**. The expression **jaggedArray.length** returns the number of rows in this two-dimensional array. Each row is treated as an array; therefore, to determine the length of each row, we use the **for-each** loop discussed earlier to iterate through all the rows:

```
for (int[] memberRow : jaggedArray) {
```

Note how each element of the **jaggedArray** is considered an array of integers. The length of each row is obtained using the expression **memberRow.length**.

Cloning an Array

To make a copy of an array, you call the **clone** method on the array object. This is illustrated in Listing 2-4.

Listing 2-4   *Making an Array Clone*

```java
import java.util.Arrays;

public class ArrayCopyApp {

    public static void main(String[] args) {
        float[] floatArray = {5.0f, 3.0f, 2.0f, 1.5f};
        float[] floatArrayCopy = floatArray.clone();
        System.out.println(Arrays.toString(floatArray) + " - Original");
        System.out.println(Arrays.toString(floatArrayCopy) + " - Copy");
        System.out.println();
        System.out.println("Modifying the second element of the original array");
        floatArray[1] = 20;
        System.out.println(Arrays.toString(floatArray)
                + " - Original after modification");
        System.out.println(Arrays.toString(floatArrayCopy) + " - Copy");
        System.out.println();
        System.out.println("Modifying the third element of the copy array");
        floatArrayCopy[2] = 30;
        System.out.println(Arrays.toString(floatArray) + " - Original");
        System.out.println(Arrays.toString(floatArrayCopy)
                + " - Copy array after modification");
    }
}
```

In the **main** method, we declare an array of floating-point numbers called **floatArray** with its elements initialized to some value. To make a copy of this array, we use the following statement:

```
float[] floatArrayCopy = floatArray.clone();
```

The **clone** method copies all the elements of the **floatArray** into a new array called **floatArrayCopy**. To confirm that a new copy is made, we will try modifying an element of each of the two arrays, printing both each time. To print the contents of an array, we use the expression **Arrays.toString(floatArray)**, where **Arrays** is a Java-supplied class available since Java 2.

The **toString** method of this class takes an argument of the array type and converts its contents to a string. Another approach to print the elements of an array would be to use a traditional loop to iterate through all the array elements, printing each in the iteration cycle. The program first modifies the element at index 1 of the original array and then it modifies the element at index 2 of the copied array. Each time, both arrays are printed after modifications. The program output is shown here:

```
[5.0, 3.0, 2.0, 1.5] - Original
[5.0, 3.0, 2.0, 1.5] - Copy

Modifying the second element of the original array
[5.0, 20.0, 2.0, 1.5] - Original after modification
[5.0, 3.0, 2.0, 1.5] - Copy

Modifying the third element of the copy array
[5.0, 20.0, 2.0, 1.5] - Original
[5.0, 3.0, 30.0, 1.5] - Copy array after modification
```

I printed the legend after printing the array contents so that the elements of the two arrays appear one below the other for ease of comparison.

NOTE
*The **clone** method performs a shallow copy and not a deep copy. A shallow copy copies only the "surface" portion of an object. The actual object consists of this "surface," plus all the objects that the references are pointing to, plus all the objects those objects are pointing to, and so on. Copying this entire web of objects is called a deep copy.*

Finding Out the Class of an Array

As mentioned earlier, the material presented so far is considered advanced, requiring you to have a working knowledge of object-oriented programming. The material presented in this section is considered more advanced still. However, it is presented here for those advanced users who might be curious to know what the class of an array is. The program in Listing 2-5 answers this question.

Listing 2-5 *Finding Out the Class Representation of an Array*

```java
public class ArrayClassNameApp {

    public static void main(String[] args) {
        final int SIZE = 5;
        int[] integerArray = new int[SIZE];
        float[] floatArray = {5.0f, 3.0f, 2.0f, 1.5f};
        String[] weekDays = {"Sunday", "Monday", "Tuesday",
            "Wednesday", "Thursday", "Friday", "Saturday"};
        int[][] jaggedArray = {
            {5, 4},
            {10, 15, 12, 15, 18},
```

```
        {6, 9, 10},
        {12, 5, 8, 11}
    };
    Class cls = integerArray.getClass();
    System.out.println("The class name of integerArray: " + cls.getName());
    cls = floatArray.getClass();
    System.out.println("The class name of floatArray: " + cls.getName());
    cls = weekDays.getClass();
    System.out.println("The class name of weekDays: " + cls.getName());
    cls = jaggedArray.getClass();
    System.out.println("The class name of jaggedArray: " + cls.getName());
    System.out.println();
    cls = cls.getSuperclass();
    System.out.println("The super class of an array object: "
        + cls.getName());
    }
}
```

The **main** method declares four arrays of different data types, as in our earlier example from Listing 2-3. To obtain the class represented by an array object, we use the expression **arrayName .getClass()**. The **getClass** method is a method of the **Object** class that returns a class representation of the given object. Java defines a class called **Class** that provides (presents) this class representation (refer to Chapter 21 for more on **Class**). We obtain this class object in the following statement:

```
Class cls = integerArray.getClass();
```

Now, to print the name of the obtained class, we call the **getName** method of the **Class** class on the object **cls**. The following statement prints this name to the console:

```
System.out.println("The class name of integerArray: " + cls.getName());
```

Now, study the following program output:

```
The class name of integerArray: [I
The class name of floatArray: [F
The class name of weekDays: [Ljava.lang.String;
The class name of jaggedArray: [[I
The super class of an array object: java.lang.Object
```

The class name of the single-dimensional integer array is **[I**. The class name of the two-dimensional integer array is **[[I**. The name of the floating-point array class is **[F**, and finally the name of the local **String** type array class is **[Ljava.lang.String**. Although it is not explicitly stated anywhere in the Java language specifications, we can observe that the dimensions of the represented array object are indicated by the number of open square brackets and that the type of element is indicated by a trailing single character in the case of primitive types. In the case of a local class, the fully qualified name of the class is appended after the square bracket. For an array of the **Object** class, the name is **[Ljava.lang.Object**, and for an array of the **ArrayClassNameApp** class, the name is **[LArrayClassNameApp**.

Summary

In this chapter, we covered arrays in Java. When you want to perform common operations on a collection of items of the same data type, you use arrays. An array allows you to use a single variable name to access a large collection of variables. The elements of the array are accessed using the array name, followed by the array index enclosed in square brackets. Arrays may consist of a single or multiple dimensions. Java allows you to create both rectangular and nonrectangular arrays. After we covered the basic material on array creation and manipulation, some advanced concepts on arrays were presented. We talked about the internal representation of an array in Java and covered the techniques of determining the length of an array, making its copy, and getting its class representation.

The next chapter teaches you the most important feature of object-oriented programming—the class.

CHAPTER
3

Classes

he main motive behind using object-oriented programming is the code reuse. Java is an object-oriented programming language and therefore allows you to reuse your code. A typical Java application contains many objects. An *object* is an instance of a class. A program may contain many classes. In this chapter, you learn what a class is, what an instance of a class is, and how to use classes in your Java programs. We have looked at several Java programs in earlier chapters; however, all these programs used only one class. Therefore, object orientation was not really exploited in earlier chapters. This chapter introduces you to the concepts behind object-oriented programming and its features. We'll also talk more about classes. The chapter covers several features of a class and its use in Java programming.

In particular, you will learn the following:

- The template for class creation
- How to declare class attributes and methods
- How to define a class member's visibility
- How to define class constructors
- The layout of the source program
- The significance of the **package** statement
- How to import external classes

Object-Oriented Programming (OOP) Concepts

In nature, we see numerous objects—birds, animals, plants, and so on. Each object possesses certain characteristics that are unique to it. For example, a bird can fly, an animal has four legs, and a plant cannot move (unless you help it move to another location). The wings of a bird can be considered a characteristic that is unique to it. In object-oriented programming, we call this an *attribute* of an object. An object in nature, which is a real-world entity, exhibits unique behavior. For example, a bird can fly with the help of its wings. Flying may be described as an *operation* that an object performs. We call this as a *method* of an object. Our object-oriented programming derives several of its concepts from nature.

In object-oriented programming, we talk about objects—just as nature has various kinds of objects. Suppose we want to write a program for computing the monthly payroll for the employees in our company. We can immediately think of "employee" as one of the objects in such a system. Each employee object will have a unique ID, name, and gender, which are publicly declared characteristics of the employee object. The employee object will also contain some additional characteristics, such as basic salary, 401(k) plan account, leave travel allowance, and so on. Naturally, we would not want this data to be globally accessible to every other person in the company. This is sensitive data and should therefore be protected from the eyes of other employees. Also, when we define functionality such as computing the monthly salary of each employee, we consider that such functionality will be implemented in functions that operate on the data belonging to the particular employee under consideration.

Every employee object in our payroll system will hold data similar to every other employee object in the system, and every employee object will also exhibit functionality that is exactly identical to the functionality exhibited by every other employee object in the system. Naturally, we would want to create some template on which to base our employee object. In word processing, we create templates for various purposes, such as writing a resume, invoice, a memo, and so on. An applicant would create her resume to give to a prospective employer using a resume template. Every applicant could use the same template for writing the resume. In object-oriented programming, we create templates to define or to represent objects having common behavior. Such templates are called *classes* in object-oriented programming. A class is really the heart of object-oriented programming, the basis on which the entire system is built. By the end of this chapter, you will understand a class's various features.

First, however, let's look at the important features of object-oriented programming.

OOP Features

The three major features of object-oriented programming are encapsulation, inheritance, and polymorphism. We discuss each of these features in detail in this section.

Encapsulation

As described in the previous section, it is a good practice to provide a coupling between the data and the methods that operate on the data (*method* is another name for a function or a procedure, also called an *operation*). Such data should be hidden from the outside world; this means it should be inaccessible to code outside the current context (to be more precise, the current object). This process of information hiding and combining data and methods in a single logical unit is called *encapsulation*. We say that the data and the methods that operate on this data are encapsulated into a single unit called a *class.*

A class consists of data (more precisely called *attributes)* and methods. These are called the *members* of the class. The attributes of the class should be considered "private" to an instance of a class; only the class methods would have access to these attributes. When you define a class, you can set the visibility access to these attributes. They may be made visible to the code outside the current class definition. We talk more on this later in the chapter when we discuss classes in depth. Right now, just know that we encapsulate the data and the related methods in a logical unit called a class.

Inheritance

You know from earlier that a **class** contains attributes and the methods that operate on them. A class acts like a template. It is the basis on which different objects are created. Each object possesses data unique to it; however, all the objects of the same class type possess the same characteristics. For example, when we create an **Employee** class, each **Employee** object will contain the same data attributes, such as ID, name, base salary, 401(k) plan, leave travel allowance, and so on. The values assigned to these attributes will vary from employee to employee. Each **Employee** object exhibits the same functionality that is defined by the methods of the **Employee** class. At some later time, we may want to represent a manager in our software. For this, we would create a **Manager** class that inherits the characteristics of the **Employee** class; after all, a manager is also an employee.

In nature, we observe that children inherit some traits from their parents. We find various families of classes in nature, such as birds, animals, mammals, and so on. Each family consists of several objects. All objects in a given family share common characteristics (or in the context of object-oriented programming, a common functionality). The children in the family inherit these characteristics from their parents. A child may also exhibit characteristics (functionality) in addition to what it has inherited from its parents.

In software engineering, when we develop software, we search for the presence of a family of classes similar to what we observe in nature. For example, to represent different types of cars in a software application, we may design a parent class called **Vehicle**. The class **Vehicle** defines functionality that is common to all automobiles. We can further define classes based on this parent class (**Vehicle**), such as **Car**, **Truck**, and so on. Each such class adds some functionality to the functionality inherited from the **Vehicle** class. The added functionality is unique to the defining class. This means that a **Car** and a **Truck** will add some functionality to **Vehicle** that is different from the functionality of the other classes in the same family. For example, a **Car** may describe the passenger capacity as its characteristic, whereas a **Truck** may define the maximum load capacity as one of its added characteristics.

A **Car** may be further classified as a sports car, a passenger car, a sports utility vehicle (SUV), and so on. We can define classes for these classifications. An **SUV** class will inherit from the **Car** class, which in turn inherits from the **Vehicle** class. Thus, **SUV** exhibits the functionality of not only the **Car** class but also the **Vehicle** class. This class hierarchy is depicted in Figure 3-1.

The concept of inheritance helps preserve our investment in existing code by allowing us to extend the functionality of existing classes.

Polymorphism

In our classification of automobiles, we have different classes in our class hierarchy for the **Car** object. Each such **Car** object exhibits several common functionalities. For example, a "drive" method could be defined in each class that is applicable to all the **Car** objects. Because this is a common functionality, we should define this in our parent class. The child class will also define a "drive" method and may modify the inherited "drive" method. Both methods may use the same name (that is, **drive**). Driving a truck is different from driving a sports car or an SUV. However, we may say, "we drive the vehicle" with regard to both the vehicles. Thus, the name of the functionality remains the same, even though the implementation varies across objects. This feature is called *polymorphism* in object-oriented terminology. Polymorphism originates from the Greek word *polymorph,* meaning having different faces to the same object.

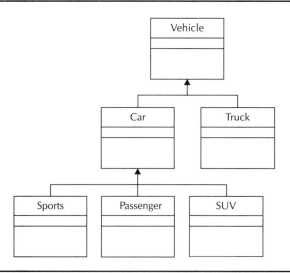

FIGURE 3-1. *Class hierarchy*

Polymorphism is an important feature of object-oriented languages and will be explained in depth in Chapter 4.

OOP Benefits

Now that we have examined the three main features of object-oriented programming, you can see how OOP helps us in creating well-structured programs where the code, once developed, is easily reusable. Programs can be easily extended with little effort, allowing us to reuse the existing code (which has been previously tested) and thereby reducing the maintenance cost for the software.

The Class

A class is a template that encapsulates data and the methods that operate on this data, as in the **Employee** or **Automobile** class described earlier. A class is a user-defined data type that embeds methods to operate on the enclosed data. You create objects based on this template, and you use the **new** keyword in Java to create an object (in which case, we say that the class is *instantiated*). You can create many objects from one single class. All these objects have the same type with a predefined set of data members. The values held in these data members vary from object to object. Although each object is similar to another object of the same type, each object has its own unique identity. For example, two cars of the same type and color will have two different vehicle identification numbers (VINs) as their unique identifiers.

Defining a Class

The general form for defining a class is as follows:

```
Modifiers_opt class ClassName{
    classbody_opt
}
```

NOTE
The notation used here is a pseudo notation. The Java Language Specification (JLS) defines the full grammar in JLS notation. Here is a partial definition of a class definition in JLS form:

```
ClassModifiers_opt class Identifier ClassBody
```

JLS is complex. For more information, you can download the Java Language Specification from http://java.sun.com/docs/books/jls/.

To define a class, you use the **class** keyword. The **ClassName** is a valid identifier that defines a unique name for a class. This name should be unique within the entire application. However, you may use the same name for classes belonging to two independent applications or Java packages.

NOTE
Every class has a fully qualified name that has the form
packagename.ClassName. *The* **ClassName** *may be repeated*
if the **packagename** *differs. This is explained in detail in Chapter 5,*
which describes Java packages.

The modifier in front of the **class** keyword defines the visibility of the class. Do not worry about this modifier right now. We discuss it in great detail later in this chapter as well as in subsequent chapters.

A typical class declaration looks like this:

```
class MyClass {

    // attributes
    // constructors
    // methods
}
```

NOTE
A class declaration may contain a declaration of another class, which
is then called a member class *of the outer declaring class.*

The class definition is enclosed in opening and closing braces. Within the body of the class definition, you define zero or more attributes, zero or more constructors, and zero or more methods. The attributes of a class are its data members. These are also called *fields*. The fields provide the state of the class and its objects. For example, for an **Employee** class, as described earlier, **ID** is its field. A class constructor is a special method of the class that we use while initializing new objects. A class may contain other methods that define the behavior of the class and its objects.

NOTE
The Java Language Specifications uses the term fields *in place*
of attributes. *Henceforth, the term* field *will be used to refer to*
a class attribute.

We'll now turn our attention to defining the fields, constructors, and methods of a class. We'll start with a very simple class that holds only the fields and no methods. Later on, we'll add more functionality to this base class template.

Declaring a Point Class

The following code snippet shows a declaration for the **Point** class.

```
class Point {

    int x;
    int y;
}
```

The class is defined using the keyword **class** followed by its name, **Point**. The modifier field is optional and is not applied in this definition. The modifier defines the class visibility, and the possible values for this modifier are discussed later. The body of the class is enclosed in braces. The body of this class consists only of fields.

NOTE
C++ requires a class definition to be terminated with a semicolon.
In Java, the use of a semicolon is not mandatory.

Our **Point** class declaration contains two fields, **x** and **y**, of type **int**. This simple **Point** class definition does not contain any methods. As mentioned earlier, methods define the functionality of a class. Our **Point** class currently does not exhibit any functionality.

As shown in this example, it is possible to create a class that does not contain any methods and has only fields. It is also possible to create a class that has an empty body—meaning no fields, no constructors, and no methods. However, creating such a class is usually meaningless, except for the name and/or whether it inherits from another one.

NOTE
*A top-level class such as **Vehicle** or **Employee** (discussed earlier) may*
have an empty body. The classes that inherit from these top-level
classes will have the fields and methods added to their definitions.

Using Classes

A class definition serves as a template from which you create objects for the use of your application code. For example, by using our class definition of **Point**, we can create several **Point** objects. Each **Point** object will be characterized by two distinct fields, **x** and **y**, which specify the x-coordinate and y-coordinate of the point, respectively. Each **Point** object will have its own copy of the data members **x** and **y**. These members are called *instance variables* of an object because they belong to a particular instance of the class. The process of creating an object from a class definition is called *class instantiation.* We say that a class has been instantiated when we create an object.

To create an object, we use the following declaration:

```
Point p = new Point();
```

We use the **new** keyword to instantiate a class. We specify the class name after the **new** keyword, followed by opening and closing parentheses. The opening and closing parentheses indicate a method call—a call to a class constructor. We discuss class constructors later in the chapter. Once a class is instantiated, memory will be allocated for the object of the class to hold its data. The reference to this memory allocation must be copied and saved somewhere so that the created object can be accessed at a later time in your program code. In the preceding statement, we copy this memory reference to the variable **p** declared on the left-hand side of the assignment operator. The type of variable **p** is **Point**, indicating that **p** holds a reference to a **Point**-type object.

When the preceding program statement is executed, an object of type **Point** is created at runtime. This **Point** object contains two fields: **x** and **y**. The object will be referred to by the variable **p** later in the program. The two fields, **x** and **y**, take a default integer value of 0. The default value assigned to a field depends on its type.

Accessing/Modifying Fields

Accessing the fields declared in the preceding example is simple. To access the x-coordinate of the point **p**, you use the syntax **p.x**, and to access the y-coordinate, you use the syntax **p.y**. The general form for accessing a field is **_objectReference.fieldName_**. With respect to our example, **_objectReference_** is **p** and **_fieldname_** is **y** or **x**.

The Class Example Program

We'll now write a Java program to declare a **Point** class, instantiate it, and use it in the application. Listing 3-1 gives the full program for declaring and using a **Point** class.

Listing 3-1   _The Class Example Program_

```
class Point {

    int x;
    int y;
}

class TestPoint {

    public static void main(String[] args) {
        System.out.println("Creating a Point object ... ");
        Point p = new Point();
        System.out.println("Initializing data members ...");
        p.x = 4;
        p.y = 5;
        System.out.println("Printing object");
        System.out.println("Point p (" + p.x + ", " + p.y + ")");
    }
}
```

The program output is shown here:

```
C:\360\ch03>java TestPoint
Creating a Point object ...
Initializing data members ...
Printing object
Point p (4, 5)
```

NOTE
To run the code, you need to specify **TestPoint** on the command line because the **main** method is defined in **TestPoint**.

The **Point** class definition in Listing 3-1 is the same as the one we discussed earlier. To test the **Point** class, you need to write another class. The preceding program defines this other class, called **TestPoint**. The **TestPoint** class declares a **main** method where the program execution begins. In the **main** method body, we create an instance of the **Point** class using the following program statement:

```
Point p = new Point();
```

We access the fields **x** and **y** of the created object using following statements:

```
p.x = 4;
p.y = 5;
```

These statements set the values of the two data members (that is, the fields). As stated earlier, these members are also called *instance variables* because they belong to a particular instance of the class; in this case, the instance is **p**. If we create another instance (say, **p2**), it will have its own copy of the **x** and **y** fields. Here, we use the syntax ***objectReference.fieldName*** to access a field. The two statements assign values to the two fields. We verify this assignment by printing the object contents in the next two lines of the program code:

```
System.out.println("Printing object");
System.out.println("Point p (" + p.x + ", " + p.y + ")");
```

Here, we use the same syntax, **p.x** and **p.y**, as in the earlier case for retrieving the instance variables.

Declaring Methods

Our **Point** class declared in the previous section contains only fields. Now, we will add a method to the **Point** class to help you understand the method declaration and calling syntax. The purpose of adding a method to the class definition is to provide some functionality to it. The functionality we are going to add to our **Point** class involves determining the distance of the point from the origin. Therefore, we will add a method called **getDistance** that returns the distance between the point and the origin.

The modified program is given in Listing 3-2.

Listing 3-2   *Program Illustrating How to Declare Methods in a Class*

```
import java.util.*;

class Point {

    int x;
    int y;

    double getDistance() {
        return (Math.sqrt(x * x + y * y));
    }
}

class TestPoint {

    public static void main(String[] args) {
        System.out.println("Creating a Point object ... ");
        Point p1 = new Point();
        System.out.println("Initializing object ...");
        p1.x = 3;
        p1.y = 4;
        double distance = p1.getDistance();
```

```
          StringBuilder sb = new StringBuilder();
          Formatter formatter = new Formatter(sb, Locale.US);
          formatter.format("Distance of Point p1(" + p1.x + "," + p1.y
                  + ") from origin is %.02f", distance);
          System.out.println(sb);
          System.out.println();
          sb.delete(0, sb.length());
          System.out.println("Creating another Point object ... ");
          Point p2 = new Point();
          System.out.println("Initializing object ...");
          p2.x = 8;
          p2.y = 9;
          distance = p2.getDistance();
          formatter.format("Distance of Point p2(" + p2.x + ","
                  + p2.y + ") from origin is %.02f", distance);
          System.out.println(sb);
      }
}
```

When we compile and run this program, we see the following output:

```
C:\360\ch03>java TestPoint
Creating a Point object ...
Initializing object ...
Distance of Point p1(3,4) from origin is 5.00

Creating another Point object ...
Initializing object ...
Distance of Point p2(8,9) from origin is 12.04
```

The **Point** class now has a method added to its definition. The method **getDistance** computes the point's distance from the origin and returns a **double** value to the caller:

```
double getDistance() {
    return (Math.sqrt(x * x + y * y));
}
```

The distance is computed using the **sqrt** method of the built-in **Math** class. You will learn to use many such built-in classes throughout this book.

In the **main** method of the **TestPoint** class, we first create an instance, **p1**, of the **Point** class and then initialize its data members using the syntax we used in our earlier example. Next, we call the **getDistance** method to determine the point's distance from the origin:

```
double distance = p1.getDistance();
```

To invoke a method, we use the syntax *objectReference.methodName*. In our case, *objectReference* is the reference to the **Point** object (that is, **p1**) and *methodName* is **getDistance**. To dump the object's contents along with the distance, we use the **StringBuilder** class (you used this in Syntax Reference 2):

```
StringBuilder sb = new StringBuilder();
Formatter formatter = new Formatter(sb, Locale.US);
```

```
formatter.format("Distance of Point p(" + p1.x + ","
        + p1.y + ") from origin is %.02f", distance);
System.out.println (sb);
```

NOTE
You could also use the printf method on **System.out**, *as described in an earlier chapter, instead of the* **Formatter** *class used here.*

After building the string, we print it to the console. To illustrate that we can create more than one **Point** object in our application using the same class definition, we have created another instance of the **Point** class called **p2**. The program initializes its fields to some values, computes its distance from the origin by calling the **getDistance** method, and dumps it along with the object's contents to the console. As you can see, the same functionality (**getDistance**) is exhibited by both objects of the **Point** class. Thus, the methods allow us to define a common functionality for all objects belonging to the same class type.

NOTE
The **delete** *method of the* **StringBuilder** *class clears the contents of its object, starting at an index specified by its first parameter and the number of characters specified by the second parameter.*

CAUTION
C++ allows you to define method bodies outside the class declaration. In Java, you must define the method body in the class declaration itself.

Memory Representation of Objects

The **Point** object contains two fields, **x** and **y**, of type **int**. The space for storing these fields is allocated within the object's memory space. An object occupies more space than the space occupied by its fields because it also holds some hidden information in its footprint to indicate its type. The memory representation of the **Point** object is shown in Figure 3-2.

You may create multiple **Point** objects by declaring several variables of the **Point** class type and assigning instances of the **Point** class type to each one of them. The following code fragment creates three **Point** objects:

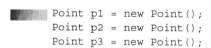

```
Point p1 = new Point();
Point p2 = new Point();
Point p3 = new Point();
```

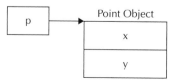

FIGURE 3-2. *Memory allocation of an object*

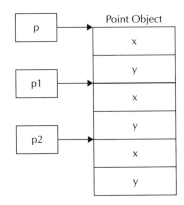

FIGURE 3-3. *Memory allocation for multiple objects*

For each variable declaration, an independent memory block is allocated, as shown in Figure 3-3.

Note that each **Point** variable declaration receives its own copy of instance variables **x** and **y**.

CAUTION
Although the memory layout in Figure 3-3 indicates the contiguous allocation for the three objects, this may not always be the case.

Information Hiding

In our everyday life, many of us oftentimes try to hide information from other people. In many situations, the information hiding is an essential part of our life. For example, when you go grocery shopping, do you allow the store clerk to withdraw money from your wallet? The wallet (which is an object in object-oriented terms) hides money (which is the information or attribute/field of an object) from outsiders. A wallet may provide a method called "pull out X dollars" that, when executed by an outside object, results in handing over X dollars to the caller without disclosing how much money is in it. This is called *information hiding* in object-oriented programming.

Let's now put these concepts to work via a practical example. The program shown in Listing 3-3 contains classes for the wallet and a person who pulls money out of a wallet object.

Listing 3-3 *Program to Illustrate the Concept of Information Hiding*

```java
class Wallet {

    private float money;

    public void setMoney(float money) {
        this.money = money;
    }
}
```

```
        public boolean pullOutMoney(float amount) {
            if (money >= amount) {
                money -= amount;
                return true;
            }
            return false;
        }
    }

class Person {

    public static void main(String[] args) {
        Wallet wallet = new Wallet();
        System.out.println("Putting $500 in the wallet\n");
        wallet.setMoney(500);
        System.out.println("Pulling out $100 ...");
        boolean isMoneyInWallet = wallet.pullOutMoney(100);
        if (isMoneyInWallet) {
            System.out.println("Got it!");
        } else {
            System.out.println("Nope, not enough money");
        }
        System.out.println("\nPulling out $300 ...");
        isMoneyInWallet = wallet.pullOutMoney(300);
        if (isMoneyInWallet) {
            System.out.println("Got it!");
        } else {
            System.out.println("Nope, not enough money");
        }
        System.out.println("\nPulling out $200 ...");
        isMoneyInWallet = wallet.pullOutMoney(200);
        if (isMoneyInWallet) {
            System.out.println("Got it!");
        } else {
            System.out.println("Nope, not enough money");
        }
    }
}
```

When we compile and run this program, we see the following output:

```
C:\360\ch03>java Person
Putting $500 in the wallet
Pulling out $100 ...
Got it!
Pulling out $300 ...
Got it!
Pulling out $200 ...
Nope, not enough money
```

The **Wallet** class declares one field called **money**, as you would expect it to do. Naturally, the type of this field is set to **float** so that we can keep our small change in the wallet:

```
class Wallet {

    private float money;
```

Notice the **private** keyword in front of this field declaration. This is the access modifier mentioned earlier. This access modifier controls the visibility of the declaration to which it is attached. In this case, it is attached to a field declaration. You can also apply access modifiers to class and method declarations. One such method we have used so far is the **main** method in our earlier programs. This **main** method has a **public** modifier attached to it. In Syntax Reference 1, when we used this method for the first time, we discussed that the **main** method is declared **public** so that it can be invoked by the JVM—or to be more precise, by an external object. It is mandatory for the **main** method to be declared **public**. The other methods we create in our class definition need not be **public**; for example, the **getDistance** method in our earlier example of the **Point** class is not **public**. (Note that when you do not specify the modifier, the visibility is package-private, which has a lesser scope than a public visibility.) We also apply the access modifiers to the class declarations. You will learn more about these two access modifiers—**private** and **public**—as you read the rest of this chapter.

Coming back to our definition of the **Wallet** class, the class defines a method called **setMoney**, as follows:

```
public void setMoney(float money) {
    this.money = money;
}
```

The method takes a **float** argument and does not return a value to the caller. The method is declared **public** and therefore can be invoked by the code in an external object, as you will soon see (obviously, you want to load the wallet with some money when you go shopping).

Inside the method's body, we copy the value of **money** received as the method parameter to the instance variable with the same name, **money**. Because the method parameter and the instance variable use the same name, we need to differentiate between them in our code. This is done with the help of the **this** keyword. The **this** keyword is a reference to the current object, and thus the syntax "**this.**" A dot following the object reference refers to some variable or a method within the object. The syntax **this.money** refers to the **money** field of the current object. We set this field to the value passed in the method parameter. This method helps in loading our wallet with some money. Incidentally, this method is called a *setter* or a *mutator* method because it sets the value of a field. Setter methods, by convention, start with the word **set**, followed by the name of the field on which they operate, with the first letter of the field capitalized. Similar to the setter methods, there are **getter** methods that start with the word **get** and return the value of a field to the caller. We will use getter methods in some of our upcoming programs.

Let's now look at the next method defined in our **Wallet** class. The **pullOutMoney** method takes a **float** value as a parameter and returns a **boolean** to the caller:

```
public boolean pullOutMoney(float amt) {
```

In this method's implementation, we check whether the requested amount is less than the current balance in the wallet; if so, we subtract the requested amount from the balance amount and return the amount to the caller:

```
if (money >= amount) {
    money -= amount;
    return true;
}
```

In case of insufficient funds, we return **false** to the caller.

Note that the **pullOutMoney** method declaration contains a **public** access modifier, indicating that this method is accessible to an external object.

Now we turn our attention to the **Person** class that uses this **Wallet**. In the **main** method of the **Person** class, we first create an object of the **Wallet** class:

```
Wallet wallet = new Wallet();
```

We load the wallet by calling the **setMoney** method:

```
wallet.setMoney(500);
```

This sets the **money** variable of the **wallet** object to 500. Because the method **setMoney** is declared **public**, it can be called from the code within the **Person** class. Had this been declared with a **private** modifier, the compiler would have complained with an "illegal access" error while compiling the **Person** class.

Now, let's try withdrawing some money from the wallet. We call the **public** method **pullOutMoney** on the **wallet** object. Because this method is declared **public** like the **setMoney** method, it can be invoked from the code in an external class:

```
boolean isMoneyInWallet = wallet.pullOutMoney(100);
```

Depending on the returned value, we print an appropriate message to the user's console. Note that the **pullOutMoney** method does not reveal what the current balance is (thus implementing information hiding). Next, we withdraw money for a second and third time. The second time we withdraw $300, and third time we withdraw $200. Note that none of these withdraw operations reveal the balance amount in the wallet. In fact, in the last withdrawal, when the operation fails, it still does not reveal how much can be withdrawn—an effective implementation of information hiding.

Now, what if we really want to know what the current balance in the wallet is? If so, we would provide a **public** getter method to read the field value. The getter method declaration is shown in the following code fragment:

```
public float getMoney() {
    return money;
}
```

NOTE
The getter methods are also called accessor methods because they are used for accessing attribute values.

The method **getMoney** uses the standard convention for a getter method—the **get** followed by the attribute's name, with its first letter capitalized. The method does not take any arguments and returns a **float** value to the caller. The implementation simply returns the current value of the **money** attribute. The method is declared **public** so that it can be invoked by an external object. To read the current balance in our code now, we use the syntax **wallet.getMoney()**.

TIP

According to the principles of object-oriented programming and good design practice, all fields in a class definition should be declared **private** *and you should provide the required getter/setter* **public** *methods to access them.*

Now the question is, why do we need to apply access modifiers to our declarations? So far, you have seen two access modifiers—**private** and **public**. The **private** modifier makes the corresponding field, method, or class declaration truly private to the code to which it belongs. In our example, the variable **money** is declared **private** and is therefore visible only to the code within the **Wallet** class. Therefore, using the earlier dot syntax (**wallet.money**) will result in a compilation error. The only way to access the **money** field is to use the **public** getter/setter methods that operate on this attribute. Making **money** private also helps in protecting it from any accidental modifications by an external code because one cannot use the *objectReference.fieldName* syntax to access it.

Encapsulation

In the previous section, you saw the importance of information hiding. Another big concept associated with object-oriented programming is encapsulation. Every class contains some data in its fields. We hide these fields by declaring them **private**. We define getter/setter methods to access them. When we assign a value to a field, do we validate the value before assigning it? By providing a setter method, we get an opportunity to provide such a validation. As an example, consider the definition of a **Date** class declared as follows:

```
class Date {

    public int day;
    public int month;
    public int year;
}
```

This class declares three public fields.

Although it is against the object-oriented programming best practices, these fields are declared **public** to illustrate the problems associated with public declarations.

If **d** is an object of the **Date** class, we could use the following statement to set its **month** value:

```
d.month = 13;
```

The code is syntactically correct and will execute without any errors. However, this is obviously a wrong assignment, which may be due to a simple typing error. To protect from such not-so-inevitable errors, be sure to make your fields **private**, define a setter method to assign values to them, and provide the validation in the setter methods before making an assignment. Thus, we could write the setter method for the **month** field as follows:

```
public void setMonth(int month) {
    if (month >= 1 && month <= 12) {
        this.month = month;
    } else {
        // print an error message to the user
    }
}
```

This implementation checks whether the value we are trying to assign is within the bounds of a calendar month. This ensures that an invalid value cannot be assigned to the **month** field. Similar validations can be performed in the setter methods for the **day** and **year** fields.

The process of putting the data and the methods that operate on this data together in the class definition is called *encapsulation.* As you saw, encapsulating getter/setter methods helps in creating robust objects. When we talk about encapsulation, we are not just referring to the getter/ setter methods. There could be other methods in the class that logically belong to it. For example, let's take a method called **printDate** that prints the values of the **date** attributes in some predefined date format. It makes perfect sense to declare and define the **printDate** method in the **Date** class itself. This is exactly what encapsulation is. You encapsulate the methods in a class definition that operate on the class's fields and make logical sense being in the class definition. The **Date** class, for example, could provide several methods, such as for the addition of dates, determining whether the current date is in a leap year, and so on. These should be defined in methods that belong to the **Date** class.

Here's something else to consider about using encapsulation: If you do not encapsulate the appropriate methods in a class definition, you will have to provide error-checking code in several places within your application. For example, if you do not provide the validations in the setter methods of the **Date** class, you will need to repeat the validation code in several places in your application, and if this validation ever changes, you will have the big task of ensuring that it occurs in every place you have set the field values.

NOTE
As a designer of an object-oriented system, it is your duty to identify and provide the encapsulation of appropriate data and methods in all your class definitions.

Declaring Constructors

A *constructor* is a special method that the runtime executes during the object-creation process. In an earlier section, you saw that the following statement calls the class constructor:

```
Point p = new Point();
```

When you instantiate a class using the declaration shown here, an object is created with some default values assigned to its fields. However, you may want to create an object with an initial state that is different from the default state set by the compiler. For example, you might want to create a **Point** object with its initial values **x** and **y** set to 4 and 5, respectively. This can be achieved with the help of a constructor. To create a constructor, you write a method as shown here:

```
public Point() {
    x = 4;
    y = 5;
}
```

This method has a name that is the same as the class name. This is one of the rules for defining a constructor. Also, note that the method does not declare any return type, not even **void**. This is the second rule for defining the constructor—a constructor does not have a return type. The rules for constructor declaration are summarized later in this section.

Now, let's look at the other features of the constructor. The constructor in this case does not take any arguments. In general, a constructor can accept zero or more arguments. If the constructor does not specify an argument, it is called a *no-argument constructor*. Sometimes, this is also referred to as a *default* or a *parameterless* constructor.

In the constructor body, we put two assignment statements that initialize the values of the **x** and **y** fields to the desired values. You may assign any values you choose. When the object is created, it will have those values.

Once you write a constructor like this in the class definition, any time you instantiate the class, your constructor is called. This is demonstrated in the program shown in Listing 3-4.

Listing 3-4   *A Program Illustrating a Class with a Constructor*

```
class Point {

    private int x;
    private int y;

    public Point() {
        x = 10;
        y = 10;
    }

    public int getX() {
        return x;
    }

    public int getY() {
        return y;
    }
}

class CustomConstructorApp {

    public static void main(String[] args) {
        System.out.println("Creating a Point object ... ");
        Point p = new Point();
        System.out.println("\nPrinting Point object");
```

```
        System.out.println("Point p (" + p.getX() + ", " + p.getY() + ")");
    }
}
```

The class **Point**, just like in our earlier examples, declares two fields, **x** and **y**, of type **int**. The class also declares a constructor, as follows:

```
public Point() {
    x = 10;
    y = 10;
}
```

The constructor initializes both fields to a common value of 10. This is a no-argument constructor. The class also declares two getter methods for accessing the values of the two fields. Note that we do not define any setter methods here because our program does not need to set the values of these fields to anything other than the default values set in the constructor.

In the **main** method of the **CustomConstructorApp** class, we instantiate the **Point** class, as follows:

```
Point p = new Point();
```

The execution of this statement results in calling the constructor we defined in the class definition. The constructor sets the values of both **x** and **y** fields to 10. We can verify this by dumping the object's contents via the following statement:

```
System.out.println("Point p (" + p.getX() + ", " + p.getY() + ")");
```

Note the use of getter methods for obtaining the **x** and **y** values. When we run the program, we get the following output:

```
Creating a Point object ...
Printing Point object
Point p (10, 10)
```

After the object is constructed, we may still call its setter methods (provided we defined them in the class definition) to change the value of data members to any other value. By providing a no-argument constructor, we ensure that any newly created object will have its data members set to the default values specified in the constructor.

Now, what if we want to set the data members to a different value each time we create an object? For this, we need to pass the values as parameters to the constructor. Therefore, we need to declare a constructor that takes parameters. Such a constructor is shown in the following code fragment:

```
public Point(int x, int y) {
    this.x = x;
    this.y = y;
}
```

We assign the values specified by the two parameters to the two instance variables using **this** as a reference to the current object. To call this constructor in our program code, we use the following statement:

```
Point p = new Point(4, 5);
```

When we call the constructor, we set the values for its arguments. The instance variables will now be initialized using these values. We can verify this by dumping the object's contents as illustrated in the previous example.

Sometimes, we may want to initialize only one of the instance variables while letting the other variable have some default value. In such a case, we declare another constructor for our **Point** class, as follows:

```
public Point(int x) {
    this.x = x;
    y = 10;
}
```

This constructor takes only one argument, the value of which is assigned to the **x** field. The other instance variable, **y**, is set to a value of 10. If we do not assign a value to the variable **y**, it will take a default value of 0, which is provided by the compiler. We can now call the constructor with the following statement:

```
Point p = new Point(5);
```

This creates the **Point** object **(5, 10)**, which can be verified by printing the object's contents.

NOTE
You cannot write two constructors that have the same number and type of arguments for the same class because the platform would not be able to differentiate between them. Doing so causes a compile-time error.

A class may declare more than one constructor in its definition. If this is the case, how do you know which constructor is called when the class is instantiated? The compiler decides which constructor to call depending on the number of parameters and their types. Look at the following code fragment:

```
Point p1 = new Point();
Point p2 = new Point(15);
Point p3 = new Point(5, 10);
```

The first statement calls the no-argument constructor and creates the object **p1(10, 10)**. The second statement creates the object **p2(15, 10)**, and the third statement creates the object **p3(5, 10)**. Thus, the compiler has decided which constructor to call depending on the number of parameters passed to it.

Default Constructor

In the previous section, you learned to write your own constructor. In all our previous examples, we hadn't written any constructors. So is there any constructor provided by default? Yes, there is. If you do not write a constructor, the Java compiler provides a constructor with no arguments. This is called the *default constructor,* and the implementation of the default constructor is null, which means it does not contain any code.

CAUTION

If you provide a constructor of your own—either a no-argument one or one with the arguments in the class definition—the compiler will not provide a default constructor.

NOTE

Like C++, Java does not provide destructors. Java relies on its garbage collector to clean up the resources held by unused objects.

For further details on constructors and how they are called, see Chapter 5.

Rules for Defining a Constructor

The rules for constructor creation can be summarized as follows:

- A constructor must have the same name as the class name.
- A constructor does not return anything, not even a **void** type.
- A constructor may take zero or more arguments.
- By default, the compiler provides a no-argument constructor.
- If you provide any constructor—either a no-argument constructor or a constructor with arguments—the compiler does not provide a default constructor.

Source File Layout

You have learned enough from the examples given thus far to get started writing Java programs. Now, let's discuss the complete structure of a Java source file. When you write a Java source program, it needs to follow a certain structure or template. This template is shown in Listing 3-5.

Listing 3-5 *Layout of a Java Source File*

```
/**

 * NewClass.java

 */

package javaapplication;

import classes;

public class NewClass {

    public NewClass() {
    }
}
```

The **import** statement makes the declarations of external classes available to the current Java source program at the time of compilation.

As stated earlier in the book, you may use any text editor for writing a Java source program. The entire program may consist of more than one source file. Each Java source file must have the same name as a **public** class that it declares. Each Java source file can contain only one **public** class declaration. The file extension must be **.java**. The filename is case-sensitive. Therefore, the preceding source code must be stored in a file named **NewClass.java**. The source file may contain more than one class declaration; however, not more than one such declaration can be public.

The source consists of three major sections—the **package**, **import**, and **class** definition—besides the comments, which you may embed anywhere in the source. A multiline comment is shown at the top of Listing 3-5, which shows the name of the file under which this code must be saved. We discussed the **class** declaration earlier, so let's turn our attention to the **package** and **import** sections.

The package Statement

The **package** statement allows you to group logically related classes into a single unit. In our earlier programs, we have used **import** statements such as the following:

```
import java.io.*;
import java.util.*;
```

Both **java.io** and **java.util** in these statements are packages. All I/O-related classes are grouped together and put under the package **java.io**. Similarly, all the utility classes are grouped together under the **java.util** package. The Java Development Kit defines many such packages, grouping the various classes in different logical units depending on their functionality. When you develop several classes in your application or when you create several applications, you may also want to arrange your classes into logical units. You do so by creating packages in your application. To create a package, you need to use a **package** statement. The basic syntax of the **package** statement is shown here:

```
package packagename;
```

A package name may consist of zero or more subpackage names, each separated by a dot. Here are a few valid package declarations:

```
package mypackage;
package mypackage.reports;
package mypackage.reports.accounts.salary;
```

The first statement declares a top-level package called **mypackage**. The second statement declares a subpackage called **reports** within **mypackage**. The third statement declares a package hierarchy where **mypackage** is the top-level package, with the **reports** package within it, the **accounts** package within **reports**, and finally the **salary** package within **accounts**.

When you declare a package, the declaration must follow certain rules:

- The package must be declared at the beginning of the source file before any other statement.

NOTE
A comment may precede the package statement because it is not treated as a program statement.

- Only one package declaration per source file is permitted.

- Package names must be hierarchical and separated by dots.

- If no package is declared, the compiler creates a default package and all classes that do not have a package declaration will be grouped under this default package.

As the first rule states, a package declaration must be a top-level statement in your source file. Writing a **package** declaration statement anywhere else in the source program results in a compile-time error.

As the second rule states, you cannot have more than one package declaration in a single source file. Note that a source file may contain multiple class declarations; however, it can contain only one **package** declaration. All classes defined in the source file will be grouped together in a package declared at the top of the source file.

As the third rule states, if you decide to use subpackages, the entire name must be hierarchical and the subnames must be separated by a dot. Imagine the hierarchical package name as a directory structure containing a main directory, followed by a subdirectory in each, until the end of the full package name. A class belonging to the package will be put under this last subdirectory following the entire directory structure. The directory layout for a source containing a **package** statement is described in the next section.

Finally, the last rule states that if the source file does not contain a **package** declaration, all classes defined in the source file will be grouped together in a default package. The directory for this default package is the current directory itself. Thus, all classes defined in this source file will be put in the current folder when compiled.

NOTE
The **package** *statement carries more meaning to it than just the logical grouping of classes. It controls the visibility of the classes, as well as the fields and methods defined in its source program. We discuss these visibility rules when we cover inheritance and visibility in Chapter 5.*

The import Statement

Immediately following the **package** declaration, you have **import** declarations. You use the **import** statement to tell the compiler where to find the external classes required by the source program under compilation. The full syntax of the **import** statement is as follows:

```
import packagename;
```

or

```
import packagename.* ;
```

Here are a few examples of the **import** statement:

```
import mypackage.MyClass;
import mypackage.reports.accounts.salary.EmployeeClass;
import java.io.BufferedWriter;
import java.awt.*;
```

The first statement imports the definition of the **MyClass** class that is defined in the **mypackage** package. The second statement imports the definition of **EmployeeClass** belonging to the **mypackage.reports.accounts.salary** package. The third statement imports the JDK-supplied **BuffferedWriter** class belonging to the **java.io** package. The fourth statement imports all the classes belonging to the **java.awt** package. Note that the asterisk (*) in the fourth statement indicates that all classes are included.

As the syntax suggests, you may import a single class or all the classes belonging to a package. To import a single class, you specify the name of the class, and to import all classes you specify *.

NOTE
*The **import** statement specifies the path for the compiler to find the specified class. It does not actually load the code, as is the case with an **#include** statement in C or C++. Therefore, the **import** statement with * does not affect the application's runtime performance.*

Directory Layout and Packages

You have learned how to create Java packages and how to import the classes defined in those packages. Now, let's look at the package hierarchies. As mentioned earlier, packages follow a hierarchical structure. When you compile your source program, the compiler generates a folder structure defined in your package and creates a .class file for your program in the innermost subfolder. To instruct the compiler to generate the folder hierarchy, you need to specify the **–d** option on the compiler command line. For example, let's say your source program called Employee.java contains the following **package** statement:

```
package mypackage.reports.accounts.salary;
```

When you compile this source program, use the following command line:

```
C:\360\ch03>javac -d . Employee.java
```

The **-d** option tells the compiler to create the folder hierarchy in the directory specified on the command line following the **-d** option. In this example, the starting directory is a dot (.), indicating that this is the current working directory. Therefore, when the compiler compiles the program, it creates a folder hierarchy, as shown in Figure 3-4, in the current working directory and creates a .class file in the **salary** subfolder, as shown.

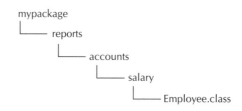

FIGURE 3-4. *Folder hierarchy for the compiled code*

If you do not specify the **-d** option during compilation, the compiler will generate the **Employee.class** file in the current folder. You will then need to create the folder structure yourself and copy the .class file in the **salary** folder. To run this .class file (assuming it contains a **main** method) from the command line, use the following command:

```
C:\360\ch03>java mypackage.reports.accounts.salary.Employee
```

Note that you need to mention the full folder structure while running the .class file. This is because the fully qualified name of Employee.class is *packagename.ClassName*. If you try running the **Employee** class without the package name, as shown next, you will get a "class not found" error at the runtime:

```
C:\360\ch03>java Employee            // generates runtime error
```

If you navigate to the **Salary** folder and try to run the **Employee** class from within the **salary** subfolder, as shown next, the runtime still generates an error:

```
C:\360\ch03\MyPackage\Reports\Accounts\Salary>java Employee       //error
```

CAUTION
*If you use a **package** statement in your Java source file to access the created .class file, you must use the fully qualified class name.*

TIP
*When you reference a class defined using a package, its fully qualified path must be available with respect to the current folder, assuming that the current folder is defined in your **CLASSPATH** environment variable. You may edit the **CLASSPATH** environment using the tools provided by your operating system. Alternatively, you may specify the **CLASSPATH** on the command line when you run the application.*

Summary

Java is object oriented. A Java program consists of classes. A class is a template for object creation. A running Java program contains several objects. You create an object by instantiating a class. A class may contain data members and methods that operate on this data. A class may be defined having a null implementation, in which case it does not have any data and method declarations. Each member of the class is declared with an access modifier that defines its visibility in the entire application. You used two types of modifiers in this chapter: **public** and **private**. It is recommended that all data members of the class be declared using the **private** modifier. A data member declared with a **private** modifier cannot be accessed by code external to the class definition using dot syntax. You need to define getter and setter methods, also called *accessor* and *mutator* methods, respectively, to access private variables from external code. This is known as *information hiding*. Defining setter methods for mutuating fields also helps in validating data input before it is assigned to the variables.

To instantiate a class, you use the **new** keyword. The instantiation results in calling a class constructor. A *constructor* is a special method defined in a class that is used for initializing the state of the created object. The compiler provides a default constructor with a null body. You may write your own constructors. A constructor can take arguments, which you can use to supply the initial values to the fields of the newly created object. A class may contain multiple constructors having different sets of arguments. A constructor declaration must obey a set of predefined rules. The compiler decides which constructor to call based on the number of parameters and their types.

A Java source program follows a predefined layout. It consists of **package**, **import**, and **class** definition sections. The **package** statement helps in grouping the logically related classes to control their visibility in the entire application. A package may create a hierarchical structure for logical organization of the classes. When a source program declares the **package** statement, the compiler generates a folder hierarchy defined in the **package** declaration. You must use the **-d** option on the compiler command prompt to enable the compiler to generate this hierarchy. You use the **import** statement to import the external classes in your source program. The **import** statement must specify the fully qualified name of the imported class.

In the next chapter, you will learn a very important principle of object-oriented programming—inheritance.

CHAPTER
4

Inheritance

ne of the major benefits of object-oriented programming is code reuse. Programmers develop lot of code over time. If this code can be reused, they can save time and effort in developing and testing a new project. In structured programming, if the code is arranged in appropriate independent functions, it can be reused in future applications. For object-oriented programming, the inheritance feature you'll learn about helps achieve code reuse. In the previous chapter, you learned to define classes. In this chapter, you learn how to write classes that extend the functionality of classes that already exist. You generally do so because you have already developed a few classes and you want to add some functionality to them without breaking the existing code or rewriting them entirely again. In some situations, you may even like to reuse the code developed by others and add more functionality. This is achieved with the inheritance feature of object-oriented programming, and that is what you are going to learn here.

In particular, you will learn the following:

- What inheritance is
- Implementing single-level inheritance in Java
- Creating multilevel inheritance hierarchy
- Accessing fields and methods of parent classes
- Overriding base class methods
- Understanding compile-time and runtime polymorphism
- Creating and traversing a heterogeneous collection of objects
- Learning typecasting rules for accessing a heterogeneous collection
- Preventing method overriding and subclassing
- Using the **super** keyword to access shadowed fields and methods

Why Inheritance?

Before you learn what inheritance is and how to implement it in your code, let me first give you a brief introduction to the importance of having inheritance. The major advantage of inheritance is code reuse. You will be able to use your tested code in your new applications, with desired additions, without really touching it. Even if the code has been distributed, you are able to add more functionality to your new applications without breaking the distributed code. For example, you may have been using OpenOffice for the last several years. Haven't you upgraded it several times during this period? When an application such as OpenOffice is upgraded, the developers do not rewrite the full code for every new version. They use the code of the existing version in terms of the classes they have defined and simply add more functionality to it without touching the source program of the existing code. This is what inheritance permits you to do. Besides this, by using inheritance, you will be able to model the real-world hierarchies. For example, to develop a payroll system, you could define classes such as Person, Employee, Staff, Manager, Director, and so on, that perfectly fit into an inheritance hierarchy. Because such classes have a lot of commonality, putting them in an inheritance hierarchy will make your code more maintainable in the future. The inheritance also allows you to create a set of pluggable items with the same "look and feel". As an example, consider the various GUI (graphical user interface) controls you use in dialog boxes of your daily applications. Most of these controls, such as text boxes, list boxes, buttons, labels, and so on, have lot of commonality in terms of their functions and their look and feel. The inheritance feature of object-oriented programming facilitates creating a set of such controls. As you read this chapter, you will learn these and several other benefits offered by inheritance. So let's start by discussing what inheritance is.

What Is Inheritance?

All of us have observed inheritance in nature. For example, a baby inherits the characteristics of her parents, a child plant inherits the characteristics of its parent plant, and so on. We attempt to bring this feature into our software by inheriting the characteristics of the existing classes and then extending their functionality. To identify the classes, which have some commonality and thus are probable candidates for creating inheritance hierarchies, object-oriented analysis techniques provide some rules. You will learn some of these as you read this section.

Let me illustrate inheritance with a concrete real-life example. Suppose we are asked to write some assets management software. Now, what are the classifications of assets a person may possess? A person might have a bank account, a few investments in securities, and a home in which to live. There may be many more types of assets, but we will restrict our discussion to the few mentioned here. We would like to represent these assets in our software, so let's start creating classes to represent them. The first thing that comes to mind is an **Asset** class, which is a common term for all the assets previously mentioned. We represent the **Asset** class as shown in Figure 4-1.

Note that this figure uses Unified Modeling Language (UML) notation to represent an **Asset** class. Each asset has a unique identifier represented by the **id** field in the class definition. Similarly, each asset has a certain type, such as bank account, security, real estate, and so on. We represent this type using the **type** field. The prefix in the definition of each field indicates its visibility within our program code. The hyphen (-) prefix indicates the private visibility, the plus sign (+) prefix indicates a public visibility, and so on. The variables declared with private visibility are accessible only to the methods defined in the class and are not visible to the code defined in other classes. The **Asset** class declares a method called **printDescription**. The method returns a **void** and its name is prefixed with a + sign, indicating that the method is publicly accessible.

NOTE
UML defines a widely accepted notation for creating artifacts of object-oriented design.

Next, we want to add classes to represent our real-world assets. Let's define a class to represent a bank account. As mentioned earlier, a bank account is a type of asset and would have an **id** and **type** associated with it. Each account is held with a particular bank; this information

Asset
–id : int –type : string
+printDescription() : void

FIGURE 4-1. *The Asset class*

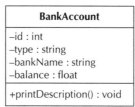

FIGURE 4-2. *BankAccount class*

will be captured in an attribute that represents the bank name. Let's call this field **bankName**. Each bank account will also contain a balance at any given time. We capture this by creating a field called **balance**. Thus, our **BankAccount** class will look like what is shown in Figure 4-2.

You can easily see that the **BankAccount** and **Asset** classes have certain characteristics in common. Because the **id** and **type** attributes (fields) are common to both classes, we will create a hierarchy such that the **BankAccount** class inherits these fields from the **Asset** class. This is represented in the UML notation shown in Figure 4-3.

We call this operation of extending the class functionality *subclassing*. We say that the **BankAccount** is a "subclass" of the **Asset** class. Alternatively, we say that **BankAccount** "extends" the **Asset** class. Another way of putting it is that **BankAccount** is "derived from" the **Asset** class. The class from which a subclass is created is called a *superclass*. Thus, **Asset** is a superclass of **BankAccount**. Alternatively, we say that **Asset** is a "base class" of **BankAccount**.

In Java, subclassing is achieved with the help of the **extends** keyword. UML notation has been used thus far to explain class inheritance. Now, you will see the class declarations for these classes (see Listing 4-1).

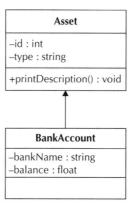

FIGURE 4-3. *Inheriting BankAccount from the Asset class*

Listing 4-1 *Program Snippet to Demonstrate Subclassing*

```java
class Asset {

    private int id;
    private String type;

    public int getId() {
        return id;
    }

    public void setId(int id) {
        this.id = id;
    }

    public String getType() {
        return type;
    }

    public void setType(String type) {
        this.type = type;
    }

    public void printDescription() {
        System.out.println("Asset ID: " + id);
        System.out.println("Asset type: " + type);
    }
}

class BankAccount extends Asset {

    private String bankName;
    private int accountNumber;
    private float balance;

    public int getAccountNumber() {
        return accountNumber;
    }

    public void setAccountNumber(int accountNumber) {
        this.accountNumber = accountNumber;
    }

    public float getBalance() {
        return balance;
    }

    public void setBalance(float balance) {
        this.balance = balance;
    }
```

```
public String getBankName() {
    return bankName;
}

public void setBankName(String bankName) {
    this.bankName = bankName;
}

public void printDescription() {
    super.printDescription();
    System.out.println("Name: " + bankName);
    System.out.printf("Account #: %d%n", accountNumber);
    System.out.printf("Current balance: $%.02f%n", balance);
}
}
```

Note that the **BankAccount** class definition does not contain any of the fields defined in the **Asset** class. These characteristics (fields and methods) are automatically made available to an object of **BankAccount** type. Note that the **id** and **type** fields of the **Asset** class are declared private. As stated earlier, private fields are not visible to the code outside the class definition. Therefore, to access these private fields, we create getter/setter methods for each field. These methods are declared public and can be called from the code outside the current class definition. To initialize these fields, we can use class constructors. How to do this is detailed in the next chapter, where we discuss the class constructors in depth.

NOTE
*With use of the **extends** keyword, the subclasses will be able to inherit all the properties of the superclass except for its private properties.*

TIP
The inheritance is captured by an "is a" relationship. After all, a BankAccount "is a" type of Asset. Examples are "BankAccount is an Asset," "Security is an Asset," "RealEstate is an Asset," and so on. While designing your classes, if you find the relationship between two classes can be represented by an "is a" relationship, then these classes are good candidates for creating an inheritance hierarchy.

Defining Single-level Inheritance

When a class inherits from a single class, as in the case of **BankAccount** inheriting from **Asset**, it is called *single-level inheritance* or simply *single inheritance*. In single inheritance, you create a class that inherits the properties of another single class. You may create multiple classes that inherit from a single class. This was stated earlier when I said that bank account, security, and real estate are types of assets. Thus, all these can be represented as classes inheriting from the **Asset** class, as shown in Figure 4-4.

Note that the newly defined classes **Security** and **RealEstate** both extend the **Asset** class and define the fields unique to each. Just like the **BankAccount** class, both the **Security** and **RealEstate** classes will have access to the base class fields and methods. You will learn more about this as you read the rest of the chapter.

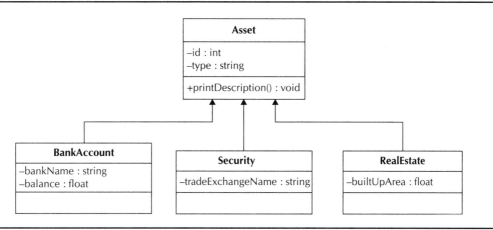

FIGURE 4-4. *Multiple classes inheriting the Asset class*

When a class inherits from a single class, known as the *parent* class, as in the case of the **BankAccount, Security**, and **RealEstate** classes inheriting from **Asset**, it is called single inheritance. If the class itself does not inherit from any other class, we call it a *top-level* class.

NOTE
*In Java, every class inherits from the **Object** class. Thus, **Object** is a top-level class.*

CAUTION
You may be wondering whether it is possible to inherit from multiple classes. C++ allows you to inherit from multiple classes. However, Java does not support multiple inheritance. This means a Java class cannot simultaneously inherit the characteristics of two or more Java classes. Java has interfaces, which provide a sort of multiple inheritance. Interfaces are discussed in Chapter 6.

Capturing Multilevel Inheritance

We will now extend our single-level class hierarchy to multiple levels. A **BankAccount** inherits from **Asset**. A bank account can be one of two types: savings or checking. Therefore, we can say the following:

- A bank account "is an" asset.
- A savings account "is a" type of bank account.
- A checking account "is a" type of bank account.

Thus, we could add two more classes, called **SavingsAccount** and **CheckingAccount**, to our class hierarchy to represent these additional real-life entities. This is shown in the UML diagram given in Figure 4-5.

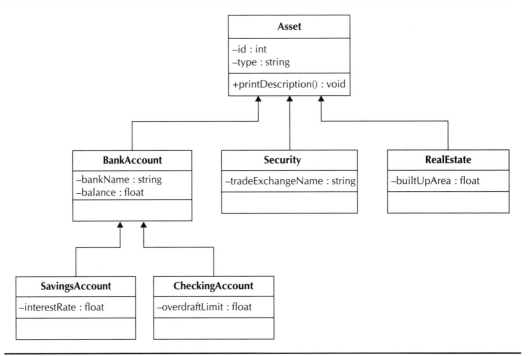

FIGURE 4-5. *Illustrating multilevel inheritance on bank assets*

The savings account draws monthly interest, but the bank does not pay any interest on the checking account. Thus, the **SavingsAccount** class defines a field called **interestRate**, whereas the **CheckingAccount** does not. Likewise, **CheckingAccount** has a unique field or attribute called **overdraftLimit**, which is missing in the **SavingsAccount** class. To get a better grasp of these inheritance hierarchies, we will now discuss a small program that illustrates the various concepts covered so far.

Writing a Multilevel Inheritance Program

The application discussed in this section is based on the asset management classes you have studied so far. We will now look at the concepts of multilevel inheritance with the help of program code. For this purpose, we will use the asset hierarchy discussed previously. The complete program that demonstrates multilevel inheritance is shown in Listing 4-2.

Listing 4-2 *Asset Management Application*

```
class Asset {

    // Same definition as in Listing 4-1
}
```

```
class BankAccount extends Asset {

    // Same definition as in Listing 4-1
}

class SavingsAccount extends BankAccount {

    private float interestRate;

    public void setInterestRate(float interestRate) {
        this.interestRate = interestRate;
    }

    public void printDescription() {
        System.out.println("A savings account");
        super.printDescription();
        System.out.printf("Interest rate (%%): %.02f%n", interestRate);
    }
}

class CheckingAccount extends BankAccount {

    private float overdraftLimit;

    public void setOverdraftLimit(float overdraftLimit) {
        this.overdraftLimit = overdraftLimit;
    }

    public void printDescription() {
        System.out.println("A checking account");
        super.printDescription();
        System.out.printf("Overdraft limit: $%.02f%n", overdraftLimit);
    }
}

public class AssetMgmt {

    private SavingsAccount tomSavingsAccount;
    private CheckingAccount iVisionBusinessAccount;

    public static void main(String[] args) {
        AssetMgmt manager = new AssetMgmt();
        manager.createAssets();
        manager.printAllAssets();
    }

    private void createAssets() {
        tomSavingsAccount = new SavingsAccount();
        tomSavingsAccount.setId(1001);
        tomSavingsAccount.setType("Bank Account");
```

```
        tomSavingsAccount.setBankName("Citi bank");
        tomSavingsAccount.setAccountNumber(526702);
        tomSavingsAccount.setBalance(15450.00f);
        tomSavingsAccount.setInterestRate(3.0f);

        iVisionBusinessAccount = new CheckingAccount();
        iVisionBusinessAccount.setId(1002);
        iVisionBusinessAccount.setType("Bank Account");
        iVisionBusinessAccount.setBankName("Bank of America");
        iVisionBusinessAccount.setAccountNumber(24689);
        iVisionBusinessAccount.setBalance(678256.00f);
        iVisionBusinessAccount.setOverdraftLimit(50000.00f);
    }

    private void printAllAssets() {
        String lineSeparator = "--------------------";
        System.out.println(lineSeparator);
        tomSavingsAccount.printDescription();
        System.out.println(lineSeparator);
        iVisionBusinessAccount.printDescription();
        System.out.println(lineSeparator);
    }
}
```

Here, we have first created an **Asset** class:

```
class Asset {

    private int id;
    private String type;
```

Note that the **Asset** class is not declared public because the Java compiler has a restriction of allowing only one public class declaration in a source file.

TIP
To create multiple public classes in your application, declare each class in a separate file, compile all the source files, and place the generated .class files in the CLASSPATH. The runtime will be able to locate these class files whenever called for in your application. If you are using NetBeans or some other IDE, create a project and add as many public classes as you want. Each public class will be put into a separate file under the project.

The **Asset** class declares two fields, which are private to the class definition. To access these variables, we provide the corresponding getter/setter methods.

NOTE
*Object-oriented design guidelines suggest that all class fields should
be declared* private *and one should provide getter/setter (also called
accessor/mutator) methods to access these private data members. Also,
note that the information that the **Asset** class holds is sensitive and
must be declared private by virtue of its nature. In the previous chapter,
when the **Point** class was introduced, we did not mark its fields private
because we had not talked about private/public modifiers yet.*

Besides the two fields, we declare a **printDescription** method in the class definition that prints
the values of these fields on the user console.

The **BankAccount** class inherits the **Asset** class:

```
class BankAccount extends Asset {

        private String bankName;
        private int accountNumber;
        private float balance;
```

The **BankAccount** class declares three fields; we once again provide the appropriate getter/
setter methods for each field and a **printDescription** method to print the values of these fields on
the console. Next, we declare a **SavingsAccount** class that inherits **BankAccount**:

```
class SavingsAccount extends BankAccount {

        private float interestRate;
```

The **SavingsAccount** class, as discussed earlier, has the unique characteristic of an interest
rate that does not apply to a checking account. Therefore, we declare a field to represent this
interest rate and a corresponding setter method to set its value. Note that a getter method was not
created for this field because we are not going to need it. The **printDescription** method, like in
the earlier cases, prints the value of the class field.

Likewise, we create a **CheckingAccount** class that derives from **BankAccount**:

```
class CheckingAccount extends BankAccount {

        private float overdraftLimit;
```

The checking account has the unique characteristic of an overdraft limit, which is represented
by the **overdraftLimit** field. Like in earlier cases, we provide the setter method for this field and a
printDescription method.

Our next task is to write a test application that uses these classes. We do so with the following
declaration:

```
public class AssetMgmt {
```

Note that this class is declared public, although in reality this is not necessary (you will understand why after you study Java packages and member visibility rules in Chapter 5). We define two variables that hold references to the **SavingsAccount** and **CheckingAccount** types, as follows:

```
private SavingsAccount tomSavingsAccount;
private CheckingAccount iVisionBusinessAccount;
```

tomSavingsAccount will be used for holding an instance of the **SavingsAccount** class. As the name suggests, this may be for representing the real-life savings account of a customer named Tom. Next, we declare another variable of the **CheckingAccount** type, which may represent a real-life business account of iVision, Inc.

We now write a **main** method where the program execution always begins:

```
public static void main(String[] args) {
    AssetMgmt manager = new AssetMgmt();
    manager.createAssets();
    manager.printAllAssets();
}
```

We first create an instance of the **AssetMgmt** class. Once an instance is created, we can invoke the instance methods on this object.

NOTE
A class declaration can contain both static and nonstatic methods.
The static methods can be invoked without creating an instance of
the class. The nonstatic methods can be invoked only on an object
*reference. The **static** keyword is discussed in Chapter 6.*

On the newly created manager object, we invoke the two methods **createAssets** and **printAllAssets**. As the names suggest, the first method creates a few assets and the second method lists those objects on the console.

```
private void createAssets() {
```

We declare the **createAssets** method to be private because we know for sure that this method need not be invoked by any code outside the class definition.

NOTE
It is generally considered a good practice not to expose the code to
the outside world unless you truly want to do so.

In the method definition, we first create an instance of **SavingsAccount** class:

```
tomSavingsAccount = new SavingsAccount();
```

We now invoke several set methods on the created object to set the values of various fields of the class:

```
tomSavingsAccount.setId(1001);
tomSavingsAccount.setType("Bank Account");
tomSavingsAccount.setBankName("Citi bank");
```

```
tomSavingsAccount.setAccountNumber(526702);
tomSavingsAccount.setBalance(15450.00f);
tomSavingsAccount.setInterestRate(3.0f);
```

Note that the **setId** and **setType** methods belong to the parent class **Asset**. These methods are public and therefore can be invoked by the **SavingsAccount** object we created.

NOTE

*Because **SavingsAccount** is a subclass of **Asset**, the **setId** and **setType** methods are automatically inherited in the subclass even if they were not declared public. You learn the member visibility rules when we discuss packages in Chapter 5.*

These methods set the two fields of the **Asset** object that is automatically created whenever you create a **SavingsAccount** object.

NOTE

Whenever you create an object of a subclass, its parent class object is automatically created. You learn the object-creation process in depth in the next chapter.

You set the values of three fields—bank name, account number, and balance—by calling the corresponding setter methods of the **BankAccount** class. Once again, note that the **BankAccount** object has been created for us automatically during the creation of the subclass object. Finally, we set the interest rate by calling the **setInterestRate** method of the **SavingsAccount** class itself.

Likewise, we create one more asset of the **CheckingAccount** type and set its fields by calling the appropriate setter methods of the various classes in the inheritance hierarchy.

Now we look at the **printAllAssets** method, which is also declared with a private modifier. The method prints the descriptions of the assets by calling the corresponding **printDescription** method on each object:

```
tomSavingsAccount.printDescription();
iVisionBusinessAccount.printDescription();
```

The two **printDescription** methods in the preceding statements need further explanation. If you look at the **printDescription** method of the **SavingsAccount** class, you'll see that it contains the following two statements:

```
super.printDescription();
System.out.printf("Interest rate (%%): %.02f%n", interestRate);
```

The second statement obviously prints the interest rate field to the console. The first statement uses the **super** keyword to access the super class object and invokes the **printDescription** method of this super object.

NOTE

*You can access any of the super class fields and methods from a subclass object by using the **super** keyword to reference the super class object's fields and methods.*

If you look up the **printDescription** method of the **BankAccount** class, which is a super class of **SavingsAccount**, you will find another call, **super.printDescription**. This call invokes the **printDescription** method of its super class, which is the **Asset** class. Thus, by using the **super** keyword, you are able to request each of the inherited objects to print their own descriptions. When you run the application, you will see the following output:

```
------------------
A savings account
Asset ID: 1001
Asset type: Bank Account
Name: Citi bank
Account #: 526702
Current balance: $15450.00
Interest rate (%): 3.00
------------------
A checking account
Asset ID: 1002
Asset type: Bank Account
Name: Bank of America
Account #: 24689
Current balance: $678256.00
Overdraft limit: $50000.00
------------------
```

Note how all the details of each account are printed to the console.

Polymorphism

In the code example described in the previous section, you might have noticed that we used the same name, **printDescription**, for defining a method in each of the three classes defined in the inheritance hierarchy. This is called polymorphism in the object-oriented paradigm. The word *polymorphism* comes from Greek and means "having many forms." In our case, the **printDescription** method declared in our classes—that is, **Asset**, **BankAccount**, and **SavingsAccount** (also **CheckingAccount**)—has different forms depending on the class to which it belongs.

Whenever we use the same method name across a class hierarchy, we say that the method is *overridden* in a subclass. This feature is called *method overriding*. Now, how does the compiler know which version of the method to call? The compiler decides this by looking at the object reference on which the method is invoked. Thus, when we invoke the **printDescription** method on an object of type **SavingsAccount**, the compiler first searches for this method within this class. If it's found, the compiler simply invokes this method. Otherwise, it looks for this method in its super class. If the super class provides the method definition, the compiler calls its implementation. Otherwise, it searches up the hierarchy until the method declaration is found. If any of the classes in the hierarchy, including the base class, do not define the method, the compiler finally gives a compile-time error. Thus, the compiler statically binds the method to an object that defines it. This is called *early binding*.

NOTE
Connecting a method call to a method body is called binding. *When binding is performed before the program is run (by the compiler and linker, if there is one), it's called* early binding. *When the binding is performed at the runtime, it is called* late binding.

In our code, we called the **printDescription** method on an object of type **SavingsAccount**. This results in calling the **printDescription** method defined within the **SavingsAccount** class and not the one defined in its super class. This feature is called *compile-time polymorphism.* The compiler resolves which implementation to call at the compile time, thus the name. We also have a feature called *runtime polymorphism,* whereby the Java runtime decides during program execution which implementation to call. You learn about runtime polymorphism in the next section.

Creating a Heterogeneous Collection of Objects

In the previous example, we created two assets and printed their descriptions by calling the overridden **printDescription** method on each. What if we have hundreds of such assets? Maintaining references to many such objects and calling **printDescription** on each one of them would be really tedious. You learned about arrays in a previous chapter—so why not create an array of assets? In our discussion of arrays, I said that an array consists of homogenous objects; so how can we put the references to different object types in a single array? Well, this is possible, as you'll see shortly. We call this a heterogeneous collection of objects. You learn how to create this type of array and how to traverse the elements of such an array in the program example that follows.

A Program That Demonstrates a Heterogeneous Collection

A few classes have been added to our earlier class diagram in Figure 4-5 to include more types of assets. The modified class diagram is shown in Figure 4-6.

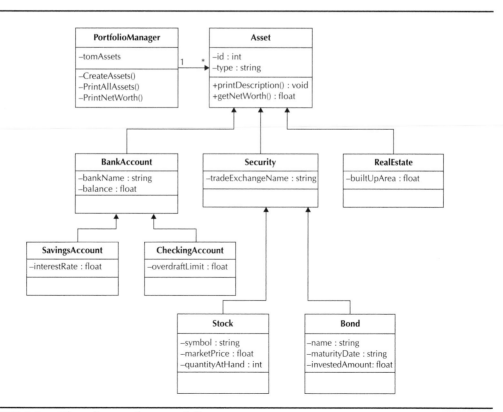

FIGURE 4-6.   *Class diagram for a portfolio management system*

The program in Listing 4-3 implements these classes. The **PortfolioManager** class defines the **main** method. It creates a heterogeneous collection of different asset types and demonstrates how to traverse its elements to print a description of each asset and how to compute the net worth of the entire portfolio.

Listing 4-3   *Portfolio Management System*

```java
class Asset {
    // Same definition as in Listing 4-1
    public float getNetWorth() {
        return 0;
    }
}

class BankAccount extends Asset {
    // Same definition as in Listing 4-2
    public float getNetWorth() {
        return balance;
    }
}

class SavingsAccount extends BankAccount {
    // Same definition as in Listing 4-2
}

class CheckingAccount extends BankAccount {
    // Same definition as in Listing 4-2
}

class Security extends Asset {

    private String tradeExchangeName;

    public String getTradeExchangeName() {
        return tradeExchangeName;
    }

    public void setTradeExchangeName(String tradeExchangeName) {
        this.tradeExchangeName = tradeExchangeName;
    }

    public void printDescription() {
        super.printDescription();
        System.out.println("Trade Exchange: " + tradeExchangeName);
    }
}

class Stock extends Security {
```

```java
    private String symbol;
    private float marketPrice;
    private int quantityAtHand;

    public void setMarketPrice(float marketPrice) {
        this.marketPrice = marketPrice;
    }

    public void setQuantityAtHand(int quantityAtHand) {
        this.quantityAtHand = quantityAtHand;
    }

    public void setSymbol(String symbol) {
        this.symbol = symbol;
    }

    public void printDescription() {
        System.out.println("Investment in securities");
        super.printDescription();
        System.out.println("Stock: " + symbol);
        System.out.printf("Today's market price: $%.02f%n", marketPrice);
        System.out.printf("Quantity at Hand: %d%n", quantityAtHand);
        System.out.printf("Net worth: $%.02f%n", marketPrice * quantityAtHand);
    }

    public float getNetWorth() {
        return marketPrice * quantityAtHand;
    }
}

class Bond extends Security {

    private String name, maturityDate;
    private float investedAmount;

    public void setName(String name) {
        this.name = name;
    }

    public void setInvestedAmount(float investedAmount) {
        this.investedAmount = investedAmount;
    }

    public void setMaturityDate(String maturityDate) {
        this.maturityDate = maturityDate;
    }

    public void printDescription() {
```

```java
        System.out.println("Investments in Bonds");
        super.printDescription();
        System.out.println("Bond name: " + name);
        System.out.printf("Invested Amount: $%.02f%n", investedAmount);
        System.out.println("Maturity Date: " + maturityDate);
    }

    public float getNetWorth() {
        return investedAmount;
    }
}

class RealEstate extends Asset {

    private String name;
    private float builtUpArea;
    private float currentMarketRate;

    public void setName(String name) {
        this.name = name;
    }

    public void setBuiltUpArea(float builtUpArea) {
        this.builtUpArea = builtUpArea;
    }

    public void setCurrentMarketRate(float currentMarketRate) {
        this.currentMarketRate = currentMarketRate;
    }

    public void printDescription() {
        System.out.println("Real Estate");
        super.printDescription();
        System.out.println("Name: " + name);
        System.out.printf("Built-up Area: sq.ft. %.02f%n", builtUpArea);
        System.out.printf("Current Market Rate(per sq.ft.): $%.02f%n",
                currentMarketRate);
        System.out.printf("Net worth: $%.02f%n",
                +builtUpArea * currentMarketRate);
    }

    public float getNetWorth() {
        return builtUpArea * currentMarketRate;
    }
}

public class PortfolioManager {
```

```
Asset[] tomAssets = new Asset[5];

public static void main(String[] args) {
    PortfolioManager manager = new PortfolioManager();
    manager.createAssets();
    manager.printAllAssets();
    manager.printNetWorth();
}

private void createAssets() {
    SavingsAccount tomSavingsAccount = new SavingsAccount();
    tomSavingsAccount.setId(1001);
    tomSavingsAccount.setType("Bank Account");
    tomSavingsAccount.setBankName("Citi bank");
    tomSavingsAccount.setAccountNumber(526702);
    tomSavingsAccount.setBalance(15450.00f);
    tomSavingsAccount.setInterestRate(3.0f);
    tomAssets[0] = tomSavingsAccount;

    CheckingAccount iVisionBusinessAccount = new CheckingAccount();
    iVisionBusinessAccount.setId(1002);
    iVisionBusinessAccount.setType("Bank Account");
    iVisionBusinessAccount.setBankName("Bank of America");
    iVisionBusinessAccount.setAccountNumber(24689);
    iVisionBusinessAccount.setBalance(678256.00f);
    iVisionBusinessAccount.setOverdraftLimit(50000.00f);
    tomAssets[1] = iVisionBusinessAccount;

    Stock ibmStocks = new Stock();
    ibmStocks.setId(5001);
    ibmStocks.setType("Security");
    ibmStocks.setTradeExchangeName("NYSE");
    ibmStocks.setSymbol("IBM");
    ibmStocks.setQuantityAtHand(100);
    ibmStocks.setMarketPrice(129.61f);
    tomAssets[2] = ibmStocks;

    Bond aaplBonds = new Bond();
    aaplBonds.setId(6000);
    aaplBonds.setType("Bonds");
    aaplBonds.setTradeExchangeName("NYSE");
    aaplBonds.setName("Apple Inc");
    aaplBonds.setInvestedAmount(25000.00f);
    aaplBonds.setMaturityDate("01/01/2015");
    tomAssets[3] = aaplBonds;

    RealEstate texasEstate = new RealEstate();
    texasEstate.setId(8000);
    texasEstate.setType("Real Estate");
    texasEstate.setName("House in Texas");
```

```
        texasEstate.setBuiltUpArea(2250);
        texasEstate.setCurrentMarketRate(950.00f);
        tomAssets[4] = texasEstate;
    }

    private void printAllAssets() {
        String lineSeparator = "-------------------";
        System.out.println("Entire Portfolio");
        for (Asset asset : tomAssets) {
            System.out.println(lineSeparator);
            asset.printDescription();
        }
        System.out.println(lineSeparator);
    }

    private void printNetWorth() {
        float total = 0;
        for (Asset asset : tomAssets) {
            total += asset.getNetWorth();
        }
        System.out.println("Net Worth of Tom's entire portfolio: $" + total);
    }
}
```

The program first defines the various classes for representing different asset types. We will not discuss these class definitions because they are identical to the asset classes used in the previous example. So let's jump to the main program—the **PortfolioManager** class. This class declares an array of the **Asset** type, as follows:

```
Asset[] tomAssets = new Asset[5];
```

We restrict the number of assets to five. You can create an array of a larger size if you want to store more assets, or better yet you can create an array that grows dynamically. You will learn how to create dynamic arrays in Chapter 16. In the **main** method, we create an instance of the **PortfolioManager** class and call its **createAssets** method:

```
PortfolioManager manager = new PortfolioManager();
manager.createAssets();
```

In the **createAssets** method, we first create an asset of the **SavingsAccount** type and set its various fields by calling its setter methods and all those of the superclasses:

```
SavingsAccount tomSavingsAccount = new SavingsAccount();
tomSavingsAccount.setId(1001);
...
```

After the **SavingsAccount** object is initialized, we copy its reference into the **tomAssets** array at index 0:

```
tomAssets[0] = tomSavingsAccount;
```

Note that this assignment is valid. The **tomSavingsAccount** represents an object of a class that is a subclass of **Asset**. You are allowed to copy the references of subclass objects into a collection of the superclass type. Likewise, we will create the various types of assets and assign their references to the elements of the **tomAssets** array.

After the assets are created, the **main** method calls its **printAllAssets** method; so let's look at its definition. The **printAllAssets** method iterates through the elements of the array by using a **foreach** loop and calls the **printDescription** on each element of the array:

```
for (Asset asset : tomAssets) {
    System.out.println(lineSeparator);
    asset.printDescription();
}
```

When you call the **printDescription** method on the asset object, the runtime looks up the object type that the asset currently holds. During the first iteration, the asset refers to the object of type **SavingsAccount**—remember the array element at index 0 holds the reference to the **tomSavingsAccount** object. Therefore, the **printDescription** method defined in the **SavingsAccount** class would be called. During the second iteration, the asset refers to an object of type **CheckingAccount** and therefore the **printDescription** method defined in the **CheckingAccount** class would be called, and so on. Thus, the runtime calls an appropriate version of the overridden **printDescription** method, depending on the object type it refers to. This is called *runtime polymorphism*—the runtime decides which implementation to call.

Finally, the **main** method calls the **printNetWorth** method, which computes the total value of all the assets in the heterogeneous collection and prints it to the console:

```
float total = 0;
for (Asset asset : tomAssets) {
    total += asset.getNetWorth();
}
```

The method iterates through the entire collection, calling the overridden **getNetWorth** method on each object; it adds the value returned by each object in the loop and finally prints the total on the console.

To understand further how the runtime decides which implementation of the method to call, look the diagram shown in Figure 4-7.

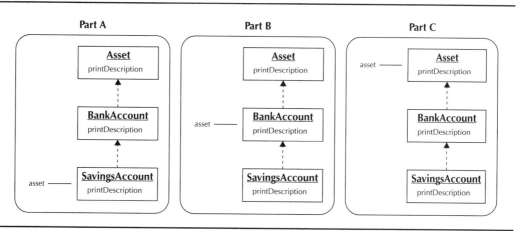

FIGURE 4-7. *Understanding runtime polymorphism*

The diagram in Figure 4-7 illustrates three situations. Each situation depicts three objects of type **Asset**, **BankAccount**, and **SavingsAccount**. Each object has a method called **printDescription**. Therefore, the method is overridden in the class hierarchy. The asset is a reference to these objects that invokes the **printDescription** method on each. The asset is of type **Asset**, which is the base class in the hierarchy. Now, consider the situation in Part A of the diagram. The asset in this situation is holding a reference to the **SavingsAccount** type. Therefore, when we execute the code **asset.printDescription**, it will invoke the **printDescription** method defined in the **SavingsAccount** class. Now, consider Part B. In this case, the asset refers to the **BankAccount** object type and therefore the statement **asset.printDescription** will invoke the method defined in the **BankAccount** class. Finally, in Part C, the asset holds the reference to the **Asset** class and therefore the statement **asset.printDescription** will invoke the method defined in the **Asset** class.

NOTE
*When your invocation starts in a superclass, the subclass implementation is not called. However, when an invocation starts in a subclass, the invoked method can invoke a superclass implementation by using the **super** keyword, as shown in the earlier program examples.*

Although we discussed this earlier, I'll reiterate for the current context: If the referred object does not implement the called method, the program flow automatically falls to the superclass implementation. Thus, if the **SavingsAccount** does not define a **printDescription** method and if the asset refers to an object of the **SavingsAccount** type, as shown in Part A of the diagram, the runtime will invoke the corresponding implementation in the **BankAccount** class, and if this, too, does not define the called method, the runtime will execute the corresponding method in the base class **Asset**. This is known as late binding because the method to be invoked is bound to a particular object at runtime.

Detecting the Object Type

In the program shown in the previous section, you saw how to create and traverse a heterogeneous collection. Now, what if you want to detect the type of element held by a specific location in the collection? To understand the need for doing so, consider a situation where the banks have raised the interest rate on all savings accounts to 4.5 percent from the current rate of 3 percent. Now we need to find all the objects in our heterogeneous collection that hold a reference to the **SavingsAccount** type. Therefore, we need a way to detect the type of object held by each element of the array. This is done with the help of the **instanceof** operator, as illustrated in the following code snippet:

```
private void raiseSavingsInterest() {
    for (Asset asset : tomAssets) {
        if (asset instanceof SavingsAccount) {
            ((SavingsAccount) asset).setInterestRate(4.5f);
            break;
        }
    }
}
```

The **raiseSavingsInterest** method iterates through all the elements of the collection, checking each retrieved object for its type. We use the **instanceof** operator to check whether the variable on its left side is of the type mentioned on its right side. If yes, it returns true; otherwise, it returns false. Once we locate an object of type **SavingsAccount**, we call the **setInterestRate** method on the located object to set the new interest rate. However, this requires a typecast on the **asset** variable. Note that **asset** is of type **Asset** and that **SavingsAccount** is a subclass of **Asset**. Typecasting from a superclass to a subclass does not happen automatically. Therefore, an explicit typecast to the **SavingsAccount** type is required before the desired set method can be called. After performing the desired operation, we break the loop because in our case it is not necessary to iterate through the rest of the records in the array—we know that we have only one **SavingsAccount** in our entire **Asset** collection.

Now, consider a situation where we want to compare the given reference with multiple types in an inheritance hierarchy. For this, we may create a loop as follows:

```
for (Asset asset : tomAssets) {
    if (asset instanceof Asset) {
        // do something with Asset
        System.out.println("Asset found");
    } else if (asset instanceof BankAccount) {
        // do something with bank account
        System.out.println("Bank Account found");
    } else if (asset instanceof SavingsAccount) {
        // do something with savings account
        System.out.println("Savings Account found");
    }
}
```

This is not going to give the desired results—but why? We compare the desired reference first with the base class type. Because any subclass object is of the type base class too, this comparison will always return true. This means your code will never execute the two **else if** clauses. Now, modify the code as shown here:

```
for (Asset asset : tomAssets) {
    if (asset instanceof SavingsAccount) {
        // do something with savings account
        System.out.println("Savings Account found");
    } else if (asset instanceof BankAccount) {
        // do something with bank account
        System.out.println("Bank Account found");
    } else if (asset instanceof Asset) {
        // do something with Asset
        System.out.println("Asset found");
    }
}
```

This time, we first compare the asset variable with the **SavingsAccount** type. If this comparison is found to be true, the comparison to the superclasses **BankAccount** and **Asset** will not be performed.

NOTE
The general rule is that if you want to detect an object type in an inheritance hierarchy, start with the lowermost subclass and then move up the hierarchy to the base class.

Typecasting Rules on Inheritance Hierarchies

As shown in the earlier examples, a typecast to a superclass is implicit; however, a typecast to a subclass must be explicit. Here's a summary of the typecasting rules for inheritance hierarchies:

- Casting "up" the class hierarchy is always permitted. This means you may typecast a subclass variable to its superclass without using the **cast** operator. In other words, a cast from a subclass to a superclass is implicit.

NOTE
How the compiler resolves methods on inheritance hierarchies was described earlier; due to this, developers do not need to worry about how method calls are resolved.

- Casting "downward" must be explicit. When typecasting a variable of a superclass to its subclass, you must do so explicitly by using the **cast** operator. The **cast** object type is checked at runtime. If the runtime does not find an object of the **cast** type during program execution, a runtime exception is generated. Exceptions are discussed in Chapter 8.
- The compiler must be satisfied with the cast. If you try to cast an object of one type to another that does not fit in the inheritance hierarchy, the compiler will definitely complain about the invalid cast. The casting is always permitted within the classes belonging to a single-inheritance hierarchy but not across two different hierarchies.

Preventing Method Overriding

When you create an inheritance hierarchy, sometimes you may want to ensure that the methods in your classes are not overridden by their subclasses. This is achieved with the use of the **final** keyword in front of the method name. For example, in our class hierarchy, you could make the **getId** method final so that no subclass can override its implementation. To make it final, you would use the following declaration:

```
public final int getId() {
```

When you do so, the subclasses **SavingsAccount** and **CheckingAccount** will not be able to override the definition of the **getId** method in their implementations. The attempt to override the **final** method will be detected at compile time and your code will not compile.

Preventing Subclassing

Sometimes, you may want to make sure your classes cannot be further subclassed. For example, it makes perfect sense not to allow anybody to subclass the **SavingsAccount** or **CheckingAccount** class. You do this by declaring the class itself as **final**.

TIP
*JDK libraries declare several classes, such as String, Math, Boolean, Double, Integer, Float, Long, Short, StringBuffer, System, Void, Character, Byte, and so on, as **final**. Therefore, you will not be able to extend these classes in your applications.*

To make our **SavingsAccount** class "final," just add the **final** keyword in its declaration, as shown here:

```
final class SavingsAccount {
```

Now, the compiler will give a compilation error if somebody tries to subclass this class further.

> **TIP**
> *So far you have seen the use of method overriding. An overridden method has the same signature as its corresponding base class method. So the question is, can we override the fields of a class the way we override a method? Yes, we can indeed do so. In such situations, to access the superclass variable, also known as the shadowed variable or simply a member, we would use the same super keyword we used for calling the superclass overridden method. Thus, a superclass variable can be accessed with the syntax super.variableName. You would very rarely use this feature because in your own created class hierarchies you would certainly avoid using the same name for fields in different classes to avoid ambiguity.*

Summary

The inheritance feature of object-oriented programming allows for code reuse. Java supports inheritance with the help of the **extends** keyword. In this chapter, you learned to extend the functionality of the existing classes using the inheritance feature. When a class is extended from another class, we say that the newly defined class is a subclass of the existing class and that the existing class is a superclass of the newly created class. Java supports single inheritance but not multiple inheritance, as other languages such as C++ do. However, the single-level inheritance may be extended to multiple levels, to any depth. An inherited class inherits the properties of its parent that have been declared using the **public** access modifier. You will study the implications of other access modifiers in upcoming chapters. Thus, its children inherit all the public methods and attributes of the base class. A child can override the definition of its parent's method. This is called *method overriding* or *compile time polymorphism*.

You may also declare an array of objects of the base type and assign elements of subclasses to it. This is called a *heterogeneous collection* because the objects that an array holds differ in their types. You can traverse the elements of such a heterogeneous collection by using a reference variable of the base class type. When you invoke a method on an object referred by the element of the array, the runtime resolves the object reference and calls an appropriate method, depending on the object type. This is known as *runtime polymorphism*.

It is possible to detect the type of object that a heterogeneous array element refers to by using the **instanceof** operator. You may need to provide an appropriate typecast when you use a reference of the base element type to access elements of the subclass type. When a subclass reference is used for accessing the elements of the base class type, no cast is required—it is implicit. However, whenever a base class variable type accesses an object of the subclass type, an explicit cast is required. You can prevent method overriding and subclassing with the use of the **final** keyword. In the next chapter, you will learn more features of inheritance—the object-creation process; the use of the **super**, **this**, and **final** keywords; and the member visibility rules.

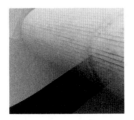

CHAPTER
5

Object Creation and
Member Visibility

n the last chapter, we covered inheritance in Java. Inheritance allows you to extend the functionality of existing classes. In this chapter, you learn what happens when a subclass is instantiated. Without explicitly creating a superclass object, how can a subclass object access its members? You learn the object-creation process during the instantiation of a subclass. The main motive behind understanding this is to gain control over the object-initialization process. You will understand how to call an appropriate constructor of each of the superclasses in the hierarchy to initialize the fields of the corresponding superclass. Sometimes, you may want to prevent others from inheriting your classes. You learned the use of the **final** keyword in the previous chapter to control this. In this chapter, you further your study of the **final** keyword to gain an in-depth knowledge of its use. In the previous chapter, you saw the use of **public** and **private** modifiers to control the visibility of a member. In this chapter, you will come to understand the need for controlling this visibility and also learn two more modifiers that give you finer control over member visibility. An in-depth study of all the visibility rules is also provided.

In particular, you will learn the following in this chapter:

- How superclass objects are created when you instantiate a subclass
- Deciding which superclass constructor is used during its instantiation
- More about the **super** and **this** keywords
- Declaring **final** classes, methods, and variables
- Understanding **public**, **protected**, **private**, and **default** access modifiers

Instantiating a Subclass

In the previous chapter, you learned to create a single-level class hierarchy of an arbitrary depth. We created an asset management system in that chapter, and the top-level class in this system was **Asset**. We derived several classes from **Asset** to represent various real-life assets. I stated that when you instantiate a class at the bottom of the hierarchy, all its superclasses get instantiated. We verified this with a concrete example. Now, you will learn about the object-creation process in-depth.

You learned in Chapter 3 that every class has a constructor—either the one provided by the compiler by default or a user-defined one. When the class is instantiated, the runtime allocates memory for it and then calls its constructor. The constructor has a special job—to see that the object is built properly. Each class can initialize its own data members. Although a subclass can initialize the members of its superclass (except for **private** and **static** members), it is best that we leave this functionality to each individual class involved in the hierarchy so as to maintain tight encapsulation in the classes.

Now, when you instantiate a subclass, it can obviously initialize its own data members; but then who is responsible for initializing the members of its superclass? For this reason, it is essential that every object-creation process calls its superclass constructor to get an opportunity to initialize its own data members. Likewise, calling each of the superclass constructors in the hierarchy right up to the top-level class will ensure that all the data members in the entire object hierarchy can be properly initialized. Therefore, the compiler enforces a constructor call for every superclass of a derived class. In the next section, we study this object-creation process with a code example.

CAUTION
An inherited class inherits all the fields and methods of its base class, except for its constructors. The constructors are strictly used by that base class only.

The Object-Creation Process

Suppose you have implemented inheritance in an application a few levels deep. Now, when you instantiate a class at the bottom of this inheritance hierarchy, what happens to its parents? Are the objects of each parent class in the class hierarchy created? If so, are each of these objects initialized properly? Who does the initialization, if any? Understanding the object-creation process will answer these questions and any others that may have come to your mind in the discussions so far. With a good knowledge of how objects are constructed, you are able to create objects with any desired state.

In our asset management system from Chapter 4, we created an inheritance hierarchy consisting of classes—**Asset**, **BankAccount**, and **SavingsAccount**. After instantiating a **SavingsAccount** class, we called the various setter methods in each of its superclasses to initialize the derived data members of each superclass. If there are many fields, you need to call several setter methods. With an understanding of the object-creation process, you will find a better way to initialize all these derived data members with an implicit call to the constructor of each superclass.

To better understand the object-creation process, let's begin with a simple case of two-level inheritance, where you have just a base class and its derived class. When you create an instance of a derived class, it contains an object of its base class. This base class object is the same as the one you would have created by directly instantiating the base class itself. The derived class object is just a wrapper on this base class object. It is essential that the base class object be properly initialized. This can be ensured only if you know for sure that during the object-creation process the constructor of the base class is called—remember from our previous discussions that a class constructor has all the appropriate knowledge and privileges to perform its initialization. Thus, the compiler automatically inserts calls to the base class constructor in the derived class constructor provided you do not call **super** explicitly.

To explain the object-creation process, we will use the inheritance hierarchy defined in our asset management system from the previous chapter. The extracted part of the class hierarchy is shown in Figure 5-1. Each of the three classes in this figure has an additional operation defined— and that is the class constructor. The **printDescription** method of the original **Asset** class is removed for simplicity. The constructor in all three cases does not take any arguments. The purpose of this no-arguments construct is to announce whenever the corresponding class is instantiated.

To keep things simple and focus on the aspects of object creation, we cover only the implementation code for the no-arguments constructor for each of these classes. The constructor prints a message to the user whenever the class is instantiated. The main program creates an

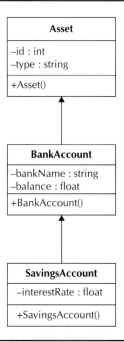

FIGURE 5-1. *Multilevel inheritance hierarchy*

object of **SavingsAccount**. This, in turn, creates objects of its superclasses, as you will see very shortly when you study the output of the program. The complete program is given in Listing 5-1.

Listing 5-1 *Object-Creation Process*

```java
class Asset {

    private int id;
    private String type;

    public Asset() {
        System.out.println("Creating Asset ...");
    }
}

class BankAccount extends Asset {

    private String bankName;
    private int accountNumber;
    private float balance;
```

```
    public BankAccount() {
        System.out.println("Creating BankAccount ...");
    }
}

class SavingsAccount extends BankAccount {

    private float interestRate;

    public SavingsAccount() {
        System.out.println("Creating SavingsAccount ...");
    }
}

public class ObjectCreationProcess {

    public static void main(String[] args) {
        SavingsAccount tomSavingsAccount = new SavingsAccount();
    }
}
```

As seen in Listing 5-1, the **main** method simply creates an instance of the **SavingsAccount** class. After that, the instances of all its parent classes will be created. This can be seen from the program output, shown here:

```
Creating Asset ...
Creating BankAccount ...
Creating SavingsAccount ...
```

As you can see from the output, the Java runtime first calls the **Asset** class constructor, followed by **BankAccount** class constructor, and finally the **SavingsAccount** class constructor. This means that the object of the topmost superclass, also known as the *base* class, is constructed first, followed subsequently by all its subclasses in the order they are defined in the class hierarchy. This is also known as *constructor chaining.*

In the preceding object-creation process, the runtime implicitly calls the no-arguments compiler-provided default constructor of each of the involved classes. As a matter of fact, the definition of the **SavingsAccount** constructor would be as follows:

```
public SavingsAccount() {
    super();
    System.out.println("Creating SavingsAccount ...");
}
```

Here, the compiler has added a call to **super** as the first statement in the constructor body. This is a hidden call provided by the compiler. The compiler provides this as long as you do not write any explicit call to another constructor, which can be provided by either the **super** or **this** keyword. The use of the **this** keyword in calling another constructor defined within the same class is discussed later in this chapter.

NOTE
*The one essential way in which constructors differ from methods is that the first statement of every constructor is either a call to the constructor of its superclass (using **super**) or a call to another constructor in the same class (using **this**). If you use **super** or **this**, it must be the first statement in the constructor body; otherwise, the compiler throws an error stating that **super** or **this** must be the first statement. This is required so that the data members of the superclass are properly initialized before their use.*

As you saw earlier, the real purpose of the constructor is for object initialization. Therefore, you would write your own constructor that provides initialization code. So, during the subclass-creation process, how do you call this constructor of a super class? You use the **super** keyword to do this. If you have more than one constructor defined for a class, you will be able to use the same **super** keyword to call any one of them. Generally, you provide multiple constructors to provide different initializations in each constructor for different situations.

Calling the super Constructor

To understand how the **super** keyword is used for calling the superclass constructors, let's add the constructors to our class hierarchy from Figure 5-1. The modified class hierarchy is shown in Figure 5-2.

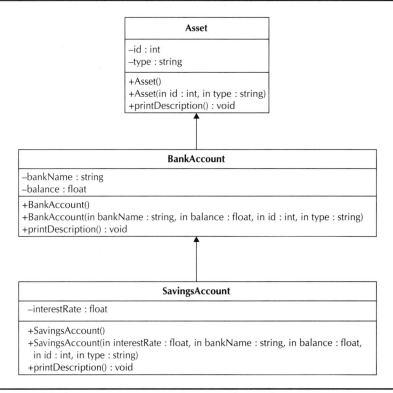

FIGURE 5-2. *Modified asset management inheritance hierarchy*

Each class now has two constructors—one with no arguments and the other with a few arguments. Look at the **SavingsAccount** constructor with five arguments. The **SavingsAccount** has a total of five fields—one of its own and the other four inherited. Therefore, to fully initialize an object of the **SavingsAccount** type, you need to accept the values of these five fields from the user. The values for the inherited fields will be passed to the superclass constructor. The superclass **BankAccount** constructor takes four arguments—two are used for initializing its own fields and two are passed to the **Asset** class constructor. Now, let's look at the program that makes calls to these user-defined superclass constructors. The code is given in Listing 5-2.

Listing 5-2   *Program Illustrating Calls to Custom super Constructors*

```
class Asset {

    private int id;
    private String type;

    public Asset() {
        System.out.println("Creating Asset ...");
    }

    public Asset(int id, String type) {
        this.id = id;
        this.type = type;
    }

    public void printDescription() {
        System.out.println("Asset ID: " + id);
        System.out.println("Asset type: " + type);
    }
}

class BankAccount extends Asset {

    private String bankName;
    private int accountNumber;
    private float balance;

    public BankAccount() {
        System.out.println("Creating BankAccount ...");
    }

    public BankAccount(String bankName, int accountNumber, float balance,
            int id, String type) {
        super(id, type);
        this.bankName = bankName;
```

```java
        this.accountNumber = accountNumber;
        this.balance = balance;
    }

    public void printDescription() {
        super.printDescription();
        System.out.println("Name: " + bankName);
        System.out.println("Account #: " + accountNumber);
        System.out.println("Current balance: $" + balance);
    }
}

class SavingsAccount extends BankAccount {

    private float interestRate;

    public SavingsAccount() {
        System.out.println("Creating SavingsAccount ...");
    }

    public SavingsAccount(float interestRate, String bankName,
            int accountNumber, float balance, int id, String type) {
        super(bankName, accountNumber, balance, id, type);
        this.interestRate = interestRate;
    }

    public void printDescription() {
        System.out.println("A savings account");
        super.printDescription();
        System.out.println("Interest rate (%): " + interestRate);
    }
}

public class SuperConstructorApp {

    public static void main(String[] args) {
        String lineSeparator = "-------------------";
        SavingsAccount tomSavingsAccount = new SavingsAccount();
        SavingsAccount jimSavingsAccount = new SavingsAccount(4.0f, "AMEX",
                        2015, 500.00f, 2005, "Bank Account");
        System.out.println(lineSeparator);
        System.out.println("Tom's Savings Account");
        tomSavingsAccount.printDescription();
        System.out.println(lineSeparator);
        System.out.println("Jim's Savings Account");
        jimSavingsAccount.printDescription();
        System.out.println(lineSeparator);
    }
}
```

Let's begin our discussion with the **SuperConstructorApp** class, because this is where the program execution begins. In the **main** method, we first construct an object of **SavingsAccount** class by calling its no-arguments constructor. This creates an uninitialized (or, to be more precise, an initialized object with default values set by the compiler) object of the **SavingsAccount** class, as in the earlier example.

The second statement in the **main** method then constructs another object of the **SavingsAccount** type by calling its constructor that takes arguments. Look at the definition of this constructor, shown here:

```
public SavingsAccount(float interestRate, String bankName,
        int accountNumber, float balance, int id, String type) {
    super(bankName, accountNumber, balance, id, type);
    this.interestRate = interestRate;
}
```

The first statement in the constructor is a call to **super** that takes four arguments. This results in calling the constructor of the **BankAccount** class, which is the superclass of the **SavingsAccount** class. The next statement initializes the value of the local field **interestRate**. Now, look at the definition of the **BankAccount** class constructor, shown here:

```
public BankAccount(String bankName, int accountNumber, float balance,
        int id, String type) {
    super(id, type);
    this.bankName = bankName;
    this.accountNumber = accountNumber;
    this.balance = balance;
}
```

The first statement in the constructor body is a call to **super** that takes two arguments. This results in calling the constructor of the **Asset** class. The remaining three statements initialize the fields of **BankAccount** class. Finally, look at the constructor of the **Asset** class:

```
public Asset(int id, String type) {
    this.id = id;
    this.type = type;
}
```

It uses the two arguments to initialize its state. From the preceding discussions, you can see how the user-defined constructors of superclasses are called within the constructor of the current class.

NOTE
*If you do not provide an explicit call to **super** with arguments, the compiler provides a call to **super** with no arguments, which results in calling a no-arguments constructor of the superclass. If you don't provide a no-arguments constructor, the compiler makes a call to the default no-arguments constructor, which it provides itself. This happens only if you have not defined any other constructor for the class; otherwise, the compiler throws an error.*

CAUTION
The compiler does not provide a no-arguments constructor if you provide any other constructor (a constructor with no arguments or a constructor having arguments) of your own.

The program output is shown here:

```
Creating Asset ...
Creating BankAccount ...
Creating SavingsAccount ...
-------------------
Tom's Savings Account
A savings account
Asset ID: 0
Asset type: null
Name: null
Account #: 0
Current balance: $0.0
Interest rate (%): 0.0
-------------------
Jim's Savings Account
A savings account
Asset ID: 2005
Asset type: Bank Account
Name: AMEX
Account #: 2015
Current balance: $500.0
Interest rate (%): 4.0
-------------------
```

Next, we discuss a new term, *method overloading,* before delving deeper into the constructor-calling process.

Method Overloading

In our example of the previous sections, the classes **Asset**, **BankAccount**, and **SavingsAccount** defined two constructors. Both constructors obviously have the same name. They simply differ in the number of arguments they accept. This feature is called *method overloading,* where two methods defined in a class have the same name. They must, however, differ from each other in some aspect so that the compiler knows which version to use for binding. Before discussing these aspects and covering the rules of method overloading, let's add another constructor to our **SavingsAccount** class to see the purpose behind method overloading.

In our example, we defined two constructors for the **SavingsAccount** class—one with no arguments and the other one with several arguments. The one with no arguments initialized the savings account object with null strings and zeroes, which does not make sense in real life. The other constructor required lots of arguments, so if you are constructing several objects, you will need to type in all these arguments in each call to the constructor. When you create a bank account, typically the bank name and the account number are sufficient information to be captured from the user. The rest of the values (the object's state) may be generated internally in the program. Therefore, it would be sufficient to have a constructor that takes only two parameters. The definition of such a constructor is given in the following code snippet:

```
public SavingsAccount (String bankName, int accountNumber) {
    this (5.0f, bankName, accountNumber, 0, 10001, "Bank Account");
}
```

As before, this definition indicates a constructor declaration because the method name is the same as the class name and the method does not return anything. The constructor takes only two arguments—the ones we want. In the body of the constructor, the one and only statement is a call to **this**. Earlier we used **this** keyword to refer to the fields of the current class. In this case, the **this** keyword is used to call a constructor belonging to the same class. Thus, we put opening and closing parentheses after this call with the required number of parameters embedded within. The call to **this** contains six parameters, which results in calling the constructor that takes six parameters. The two parameters are supplied by the caller of the **this** constructor. The rest of the parameters are hard-coded and could be generated internally in the **SavingsAccount** class. Now, to call this constructor, the developer uses the following:

```
SavingsAccount anitaSavingsAccount = new SavingsAccount("HSBC", 1022);
System.out.println("Anita's Savings Account");
anitaSavingsAccount.printDescription();
System.out.println(lineSeparator);
```

Add this code to the earlier **main** method and the previously defined two-argument constructor to the **SavingsAccount** class. Run the application; you will get the details of Anita's savings account printed to the console, as follows:

```
-------------------
Anita's Savings Account
A savings account
Asset ID: 10001
Asset type: Bank Account
Name: HSBC
Account #: 1022
Current balance: $0.0
Interest rate (%): 5.0
-------------------
```

Note how the savings account object is properly initialized with the desired values. You can easily see that this simplifies our object-creation process because we need to supply only a few parameters. It's very common for a constructor with fewer parameters to call a constructor with more parameters, supplying default values. For this usage, the constructors with fewer parameters will frequently consist of only the **this** call. The compiler matches **this** with a constructor with the appropriate number and types of parameters and then calls it.

CAUTION
*A call to the **this** constructor must be the first statement in the implementation of the constructor. It cannot appear anywhere else. Therefore, you can have only one call to **this**, which must be the first statement in the method body. If you call **this**, you cannot call **super** because **super** cannot appear anywhere else other than the first statement.*

Note that method overloading need not be restricted to compiler declarations. It can be applied to any other method of the class. For example, you may want to create another variation of the **printDescription** method that takes a few parameters. In that case, you overload the **printDescription** method. As you read further in this book, you will come across many examples of method overloading. For the time being, though, we'll just cover the rules of method overloading.

Rules of Method Overloading

The overloaded method must differ from the existing method in the number of parameters and/or the order of parameters. In the case of two methods where the number of parameters is the same and they are all of the same type in each of the methods, rearranging the parameters into a different order results in an overloaded method. While differentiating between the two overloaded methods, the compiler ignores their return types and the exceptions thrown (see Chapter 8 for more on exception handling). Therefore, if the two overloaded methods only differ in their return types or exceptions thrown, you will get a compilation error.

Creating a Copy Constructor

One more benefit of constructor overloading is the ability to create a copy constructor, which allows you to create an object copy from the values of another similar object. This gives you two independent objects to work with, and changes made to one will not affect the other.

The example shown in Listing 5-3 explains how to write a copy constructor.

Listing 5-3   *Program Illustrating How to Write a Copy Constructor*

```java
public class TimeOfDay {

    private int hour, mins;

    public TimeOfDay(int hour, int mins) {
        this.hour = hour;
        this.mins = mins;
    }

    public TimeOfDay(TimeOfDay other) {
        this(other.hour, other.mins);
    }

    public String toString() {
        return (this.hour + ":" + this.mins);
    }

    public static void main(String[] args) {
        TimeOfDay currentTime = new TimeOfDay(12, 30);
        TimeOfDay copyOfCurrentTime = new TimeOfDay(currentTime);
        System.out.println("Original: " + currentTime.toString());
        System.out.println("Copy: " + copyOfCurrentTime.toString());
    }
}
```

The class **TimeOfDay** defines two constructors—one that takes two arguments of the integer type and one that takes an object reference of the same type. The first constructor accepts the values of **hour** and **mins** from the user and initializes the created object's state with these values. The second constructor calls this two-argument constructor with the help of the **this** keyword, passing the state of the object that is passed to it as a parameter. The main program creates two objects using these two constructors and prints their state on the user's console to verify that both have the same state.

To print the state of the **TimeOfDay** object, we override the **toString** method of the **Object** class. Remember that every class in Java inherits from **Object**, which is a top-level class. In the overridden **toString** method, we format a string containing the state values of the current object and return it to the caller.

NOTE
*The default implementation of the **toString** method returns an object reference. Many times, developers override this method to print the object's state in the desired format.*

The next section summarizes what you have learned so far in constructor calling.

Invoking Constructors: Summary

So far, we have overloaded constructors to provide default values to some of the fields of a class, to provide a different initialization, and to create a copy constructor. Here are the key points to remember:

- To invoke a parent constructor, you must place a call to **super** in the first line of the constructor. Calling **super** after the first statement results in an error.

- The parameters you pass to **super** decide which specific implementation of the parent class constructor is called.

- The first statement in the constructor may be a call to **super** or **this**. You use **super** to call the superclass constructor and you use **this** to call some other constructor defined within the same class.

- If no **this** or **super** call is used in a constructor, the compiler adds an implicit call to **super()**, which calls the parent "no-arguments" constructor. The no-arguments constructor may be implicit or explicitly declared. If no such constructor is available in the parent constructor, the compiler generates an error.

- The compiler does not provide a no-arguments default constructor if you write your own constructor (either a no-arguments constructor or a constructor with arguments).

The final Keyword

So far we have discussed how to inherit from an existing class. However, what if you do not want anybody to inherit from your custom class? You can restrict other developers from extending your classes with the help of the **final** keyword. In Chapter 4, I briefly touched upon the use of the **final** keyword. In this chapter we'll go into more detail.

The **final** keyword can be applied to a class, a method, or a variable. In general, the use of the **final** keyword restricts further extensions or modifications. We discuss the application of the **final** keyword in all three cases in the following sections.

The final Classes

In some situations you would not want other developers to extend the classes you have created. For example, in the Java libraries, the **String** class cannot be extended. This is done to provide better memory management. **String**s are *immutable* objects, which means their contents cannot be modified once they are declared.

Now, consider the following two declarations:

```
String s1 = "abc";
String s2 = "abc";
```

Both **s1** and **s2** refer to the same immutable string. Therefore, it makes little sense maintaining two copies of the same object. The JVM creates all string literal objects in a dedicated memory pool and allocates the same reference to all the strings having the same value. Therefore, making the **String** class **final** makes sense so that Java's creators have ultimate control over the memory allocation used by the **String** type variables. Allowing developers to subclass **String** may result in independent strings having the same contents.

To make a class "final," you use the **final** keyword as a prefix in the class declaration, as follows:

```
public final class MyClass {

    ...;
}
```

Now, if you attempt to declare another class that extends the **final** class, as shown next, the compiler will generate an error during compilation:

```
public class YourClass extends MyClass {

    ...;
}
```

Declaring your classes **final** ensures that others cannot extend them. In our assets management software, we may want to make the **SavingsAccount** and **CheckingAccount** classes **final** if we are sure there is no need for anybody to extend them further.

The final Methods

Just the way you create **final** classes, you create **final** methods that cannot be overridden in the subclasses. To explain the purpose behind this, let's look at an example. In Java, the **Object** class includes methods such as **wait** and **notify**. These are system-level methods that implement core language capabilities. If Java allowed users to substitute these methods with their own overridden implementations, the semantics of the language itself would be altered. Therefore, these methods are declared as **final**.

If you do not want a subclass of your class to override your method implementation, you mark the method as **final**. The following code snippet shows a declaration of a **final** method:

```
public class MyClass {

    . . .
    public final void myMethod() {
    . . .;
    }
}
```

The method **myMethod** has been declared **final** and cannot be overridden in a subclass of **MyClass**. For example, the following declaration will generate a compile-time error:

```
public class YourClass extends MyClass {

    . . .
    public void myMethod() {
    . . .;
    }
}
```

NOTE
*Because the **private** and **static** methods cannot be overridden in a subclass, they are always implicitly **final**.*

There are three benefits to making a method **final**. The first benefit, as you have seen so far, is to explicitly prevent overriding it in a subclass. As mentioned earlier, there is a very valid reason not to allow the **wait** and **notify** methods of the **Object** class to be overridden in the subclasses.

The second benefit is that it tells the compiler that for a call to this method, dynamic binding isn't necessary, which potentially results in a slightly more efficient code. Static binding is always more efficient than dynamic binding. In the case of static binding, the method call is resolved at compile time, whereas in case of dynamic binding, the runtime resolves the method call.

The third benefit also results in better efficiency—marking a method **final** allows the compiler to turn any call to that method into an *inline* call. When the compiler sees a **final** method call, it can, at its discretion, skip the normal approach of inserting code via the method call mechanism. A *call mechanism* consists of pushing the method arguments on the stack, jumping to the method code, executing it, hopping back to the caller, cleaning off the stack arguments, and finally dealing with the returned value. Instead of this, the compiler now can replace the method call with a copy of the actual code in the method body. This is called *inlining* and eliminates the overhead of a method call. However, if the method is big, the benefit of saving time in calling and returning from a method will be dwarfed by the amount of time spent inside the method. Therefore, generally small methods benefit from inlining. The inlining benefits are not necessarily restricted to the size of the method, however, because inlining a method often leads to further optimizations, such as the elimination of dead code or more inlining.

NOTE
Java does not allow you to explicitly mark a method as an inline method. The compiler, at its own discretion, may inline the methods marked "final" in your code.

The final Variables

A variable declared with the **final** keyword is treated as a constant. Any attempt to change its value in the program causes a compile-time error. The following code snippet shows a declaration of a **final** variable:

```java
public class Math {

    public final double PI = 3.14;
    ...
}
```

The variable **PI** is declared as **final**. It is assigned a value of 3.14. The value assigned to **PI** remains constant throughout the program and cannot be altered by any further program statement.

> **NOTE**
> *By Java's coding conventions, all final variables should appear in uppercase letters with components separated by underscore characters.*

A **final** variable need not be initialized at the time of declaration. The program may initialize the variable elsewhere after its declaration. However, such initialization must be performed only once. A **final** variable that is not initialized at the time of its declaration is called a *blank **final** variable*.

> **NOTE**
> *A blank **final** variable provides much more flexibility in the use of the **final** keyword. For example, **final** fields inside a class can take a different value for each object and yet retain its immutable quality.*

The following code snippet illustrates this:

```java
public class Student {

    public final int ID;

    public Student() {
        ID = createID();
    }
    public int createID() {
        return ... // generate new ID
    }
    ...
}
```

Here, we declare a **final** variable called **ID** in the **Student** class. The variable is not initialized at the time of its declaration. The class constructor initializes this **final** variable.

CAUTION
*A blank **final** variable must be initialized in a constructor because it is called only once during the object life cycle. If a final variable is initialized in a constructor, it must be initialized in all overloaded constructors.*

The final Variables of the Class Type

Earlier we created and used variables of the class type that hold references to the objects of those class types. Now, we'll cover an important situation in which such a variable of the class type is declared **final**. Look at the program in Listing 5-4.

Listing 5-4   *Understanding the Use of the final Class Type Variables*

```
class Point {

    private int x, y;

    public Point(int x, int y) {
        this.x = x;
        this.y = y;
    }

    public void setX(int x) {
        this.x = x;
    }

    public void setY(int y) {
        this.y = y;
    }
}

class Circle {

    private final Point CENTER_POINT = new Point(0, 0);

    public void drawCircle() {
        CENTER_POINT.setX(10);
        CENTER_POINT.setY(10);
        // CENTER_POINT = new Point(50, 50); // illegal assignment
    }
}
```

In this program, we declare two classes: **Point** and **Circle**. The **Point** class declares two private variables: **x** and **y**. The **Circle** class declares a **final** variable called **CENTER_POINT** of type **Point**, as follows:

```
private final Point CENTER_POINT = new Point(0, 0);
```

The **final** variable **CENTER_POINT** is initialized to a **Point** object having its **x** and **y** coordinates set to (0,0). Note that **CENTER_POINT** holds a reference to a **Point** object having the value (0,0). This represents the center of the circle. Now, the question is, can we change these coordinates to change the circle's center before drawing a new circle? In the **drawCircle** method, we call the **setX** and **setY** methods of the **Point** class to change the values of the **x** and **y** fields, as shown here:

```
public void drawCircle() {
    CENTER_POINT.setX(10);
    CENTER_POINT.setY(10);
}
```

If we compile this code, it will compile without any errors because the **CENTER_POINT** variable, which is of the constant type, points to a **Point** object that has its state initially set to (0,0). The contents of the **Point** object—that is, (0,0) —are themselves not constant and therefore can be modified.

TIP
*If a **final** variable holds a reference to an object, the reference must remain constant, not the object. You can change the object's state by invoking mutator methods on it.*

Now, consider the case where you try to assign another **Point** object to the **CENTER_POINT** variable, as follows:

```
CENTER_POINT = new Point(50, 50); // illegal assignment
```

Compiling this statement results in a compilation error because the **CENTER_POINT** object should always point to the fixed object reference to which it is initialized. It cannot refer to any other instance of the **Point** class.

TIP
*A **final** variable of the class type cannot refer to any object other than the object reference to which it has been set.*

Important Points Related to the *final* Keyword

Here is a summary of the important points you should keep in mind when using the **final** keyword:

- You cannot subclass (extend) a **final** class.
- You cannot override a **final** method.
- A **final** variable that is a field of a class is a constant.
- A blank **final** variable (field) is a variable that is declared "final" but not initialized.

- A blank **final** variable (field) must be initialized in a constructor. If the variable is initialized in a constructor, you must initialize it in all the overloaded constructors of the class.
- A blank **final** variable (field) can be set only once.
- A blank **final** variable (field) must be set before it is used anywhere.

Understanding Member Visibility Rules

In the examples so far, you have seen the use of the **public** and **private** keywords. These are access modifiers that control the visibility of fields, methods, and classes in the scope of the entire application. Why would you really worry about the visibility of these members? All this time, we have been talking about data hiding and encapsulation in object-oriented design. Defining visibility rules for the members helps achieve these goals. To explain how, let's look at an example. Consider a situation where you are running a game in a Java applet downloaded from, say, www.zapak.com, and at the same time you are purchasing this book from the Amazon website. Just imagine what would happen in this situation if there were no visibility restrictions provided in Java. In this case, the credit card information you input on the Amazon site may become visible to the game downloaded from the Zapak site. Obviously, you won't like this—there should be some mechanism that protects the visibility of the members of one application from another application. This mechanism in Java involves the creation of *namespaces*. When a Java runtime loads a class (an internal class called **ClassLoader** is responsible for this), it does so in a namespace, which is made unique depending on its origin. A namespace is a set of unique class names loaded by a particular **ClassLoader**; each class name is bound to a specific **Class** object. Thus, the classes loaded from the Amazon site would be put in a different namespace than the classes loaded from the Zapak site. This not only allows information hiding but also helps in avoiding name collisions; therefore, the classes belonging to two different namespaces can have the same name.

Many times, you will also want to control the member's visibility within different parts of the same application. For example, the sensitive employee data should not be made visible to outsiders browsing the company website. Java provides this kind of security (or the access control of members) with the help of **private**, **protected**, **public**, and default modifiers.

Naturally, you need to define a namespace for achieving this kind of security. A namespace defines a boundary area within which access of a containing member is restricted. Java defines such namespaces by using the concept of *package*. Earlier, you used the Java packages **java.util** and **java.awt**. The members defined in the **java.util** package may be made available to other members within the same package and made inaccessible to members within the **java.awt** package. But who does this? When you create classes, your job is to create only appropriate logical packages in your application and define the desired visibility of each code member. The rest is taken care of by the JVM. So let's discuss how to define this visibility. Four possible values control the visibility or the access level of the entities in your program:

- **private** If an entity is declared with a **private** modifier, it will be accessible only to the code that is contained within the class that defines the entity.
- **protected** The entity can only be accessed by code that is contained
  - within the class that defines the entity,
  - by classes within the same package as the defining class,
  - or by a subclass of the defining class, regardless of the package in which the subclass is declared.

- **default (or package)** The entity can be accessed by code that is contained
  - within the class that defines the entity
  - or by a class that is contained in the same package as the class that defines the entity.
- **public** The entity can be accessed by code in any class.

These visibility modes are specified with specific keywords: **public, protected**, and **private**. If any of these keywords are not used as qualifiers, the entity is given a default visibility (that is, package-private or friendly). The four access modifiers and the resulting corresponding visibility are summarized in Table 5-1.

Note that there is no modifier called "default." If you do not specify any of the modifiers explicitly, the default is assumed.

To understand these accessibility rules, you must first understand the levels at which this visibility is tested. Accessibility is decided at five different levels:

- **Same class** Check whether the element is accessible to the code defined within the same class where the element is declared.
- **Same package subclass** The classes are grouped together in a package. You test the visibility for access within a subclass declared in the same package.
- **Same package nonsubclass** You test the visibility within a class that belongs to the same package but does not inherit from the declaring class.
- **Different package subclass** You test the visibility within a class that inherits from a class belonging to a different package.
- **Different package nonsubclass** In this case, the class neither derives from the declaring class nor belongs to the same package as the declaring class.

Now we'll focus our attention on the accessibility criteria set by each of the modifiers.

Modifier	Same Class	Same Package		Different Package	
		Subclass	**Nonsubclass**	**Subclass**	**Nonsubclass**
public	Yes	Yes	Yes	Yes	Yes
private	Yes	No	No	No	No
protected	Yes	Yes	Yes	Yes	No
Default (package-private)	Yes	Yes	Yes	No	No

TABLE 5-1. *Access Modifiers and the Scope of Variables*

The public Modifier

A **public** modifier makes the corresponding element truly public—that is, it is accessible to everybody. You would use this modifier only if you wish to make the member of a class publicly available (note that this is considered bad design and defeats the encapsulation principle of object-oriented design). Making the members visible to every other piece of code in your application makes them vulnerable to both accidental and intentional modifications, thus resulting in runtime errors in your application. You would, however, declare your classes **public** so that they can be instantiated by an outsider. To understand the accessibility rules of a public member, look at the program in Listing 5-5.

Listing 5-5 *Program Illustrating public Modifier Visibility*

```
package mypackage;

public class MyClass {

    public int count;

    public void setCount(int count) {
        this.count = count;
    }
}

class DerivedClass extends MyClass {

    void someMethod() {
        count = 10;
        setCount(5);
    }
}

class NonDerivedClass {

    void someMethod(int count) {
        MyClass obj = new MyClass();
        obj.count = 10;
        obj.setCount(5);
    }
}
```

The class **MyClass** declares a public field called **count** and a public method called **setCount**. The **DerivedClass**, which inherits **MyClass**, defines a method called **someMethod**. The method has access to both the **count** and **setCount** members of **MyClass**. The **NonDerivedClass** does not inherit from **MyClass**; however, it belongs to the same package, **mypackage**. The **someMethod** within this class creates an object of **MyClass** and accesses its public field **count** and also invokes the public method **setCount**. Both members, as expected, are available to the code within **NonDerivedClass**.

Now, let's consider the accessibility of these members from the classes belonging to another package. This is shown in Listing 5-6.

Listing 5-6 *Accessing Public Members Through Another Package*

```
package myanotherpackage;

import mypackage.MyClass;

class DerivedClass extends MyClass {

    void someMethod() {
        count = 10;
        setCount(5);
    }
}

class NonDerivedClass {

    void someMethod(int count) {
        MyClass obj = new MyClass();
        obj.count = 10;
        obj.setCount(5);
    }
}
```

Note that you must write this code in another .java file to declare another package called **myanotherpackage**. You import the definition of **MyClass** by using the **import** statement to resolve its references within the current program. The **DerivedClass** in this new package defines a method called **someMethod** that, as you can see, has access to both the public members of **MyClass**. The **NonDerivedClass** creates an object of **MyClass**, as in the earlier case, and accesses the two public members.

The preceding accessibility can easily be understood by examining Figure 5-3.

An upward arrow extending from the derived class to the base class indicates the inheritance. An X on this arrow indicates that the corresponding class is not a derived class. The **NonDerivedClass** in both packages does not inherit **MyClass**.

Therefore, as stated earlier, the identifier declared with the **public** attribute is truly public.

The private Modifier

The **private** modifier is really useful when you want to make a member accessible only to the class to which it belongs. An example of this might be a variable that stores a Social Security number or a credit card number. Consider a **CreditCard** class in an application that defines a field to store a credit card number. This variable should be accessible only to the code defined in the **CreditCard** class and not anywhere outside. You would declare this kind of field with a **private** modifier.

To understand the visibility of a private member, change the **public** keyword to **private** for the **count** and **setCount** declarations in the **MyClass** definition of Listing 5-5. If you compile the code, both files will not compile, giving you a compilation error wherever you try accessing the

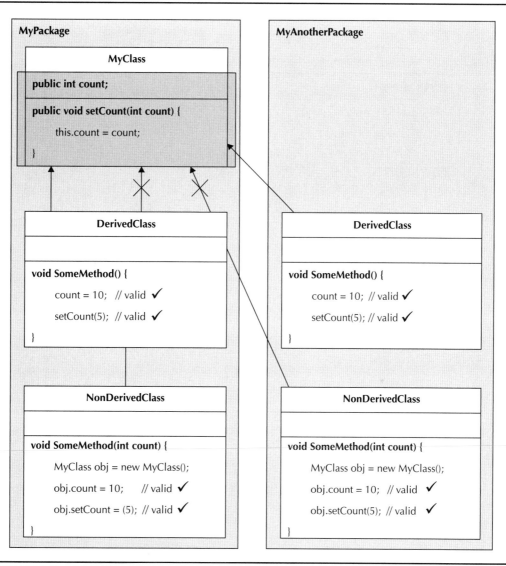

FIGURE 5-3.   *Visibility of public identifiers*

count and **setCount** members. The scope of a **private** identifier can be understood by examining Figure 5-4.

The protected Modifier

Going back to our asset management example, we have defined several classes that lie in a single hierarchy. The **Asset**, **BankAccount**, and **SavingsAccount** classes belong to one such inheritance hierarchy. The asset management software may contain another inheritance hierarchy containing classes responsible for accounting. The two inheritance hierarchies may

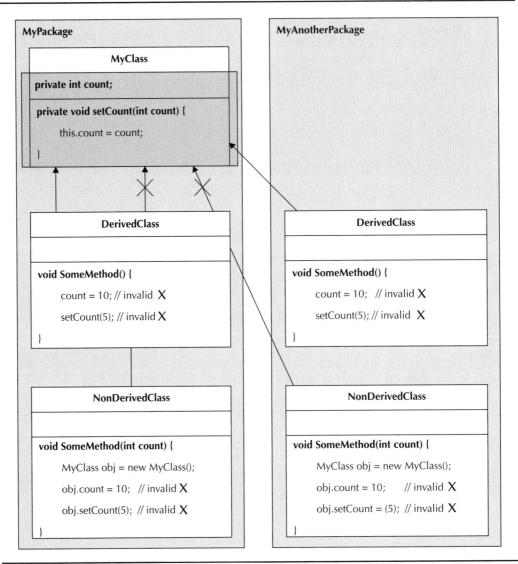

FIGURE 5-4. *Visibility of private identifiers*

be arranged in two different Java packages—say, **asset** and **accounting**, respectively. A certain class defined in the **accounting** package would need access to the net worth of an asset defined in the **asset** package. If this class derives from a class defined in the **asset** package, it would have access to the entities defined in the base class, provided those are declared **protected**.

To understand the visibility of protected members, change the **public** modifier of the **count** and **setCount** members in **MyClass** of Listing 5-5 to **protected**. The class **MyClass** compiles without error. Both the **DerivedClass** and **NonDerivedClass** belonging to **MyPackage** have access to the protected **count** and **setCount** members. However, the NewClass.java file will not compile. It would produce **NonDerivedClass** compilation errors on the statements shown in the following code snippet:

```
package myanotherpackage;

import mypackage.MyClass;

class DerivedClass extends MyClass {

    void someMethod() {
        count = 10;
        setCount(5);
    }
}

class NonDerivedClass {

    void someMethod(int count) {
        MyClass obj = new MyClass();
        obj.count = 10; //this does not compile
        obj.setCount(5); //this does not compile
    }
}
```

The visibility of a protected modifier (identifier) can be seen in Figure 5-5.

Thus, a **protected** variable is accessible to a subclass, regardless of its package declaration, and also to all classes belonging to the same package. It is not accessible to a class belonging to another package and that does not inherit from the defining class.

Lastly, we look at the default scope visibility.

The Default Modifier

When you do not apply any of the modifiers (**private, protected,** or **public)** to an entity, it gets the default visibility. An entity defined with a default visibility will be accessible within the class defining it and to all the classes that belong to the same package, but it is not accessible to any class in a different package.

To understand the visibility rules for a default modifier, remove the modifier in the declarations of the **count** and **setCount** members of **MyClass** of Listing 5-5. The MyClass.java file compiles without errors, indicating that both **DerivedClass** and **NonDerivedClass** belonging to **mypackage** have access to these members. The NewClass.java file, however, will not compile, giving errors, on the statements shown in the following code:

```
package myanotherpackage;

import mypackage.MyClass;

class DerivedClass extends MyClass {

    void someMethod() {
        count = 10; //this does not compile
        setCount(5); //this does not compile
    }
```

```
}

class NonDerivedClass {

    void someMethod(int count) {
        MyClass obj = new MyClass();
        obj.count = 10; //this does not compile
        obj.setCount(5); //this does not compile
    }
}
```

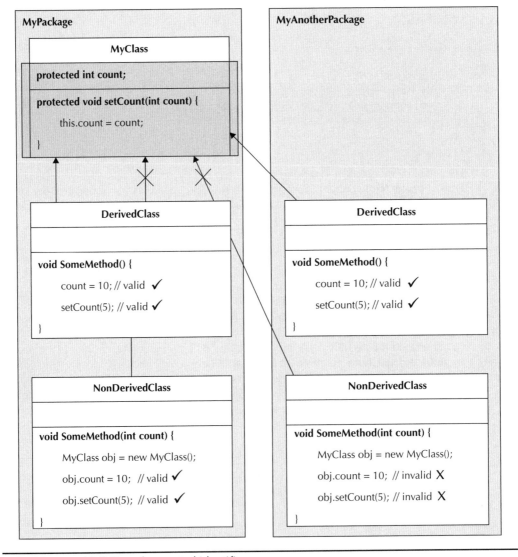

FIGURE 5-5. *Visibility of protected identifiers*

To understand the default access modifier, consider Figure 5-6.

Thus, an identifier having default scope is accessible to any class within the same package and not to any other class belonging to another package.

Now that you have seen the various visibility criteria for the entities and understand Java packages, let's look at the rules that must be applied when using inheritance.

A Few Rules on Inheriting

A member that is inherited in a subclass cannot have a weaker access privilege than the access privilege originally assigned to it. It can have only a stronger access privilege. The weakest type

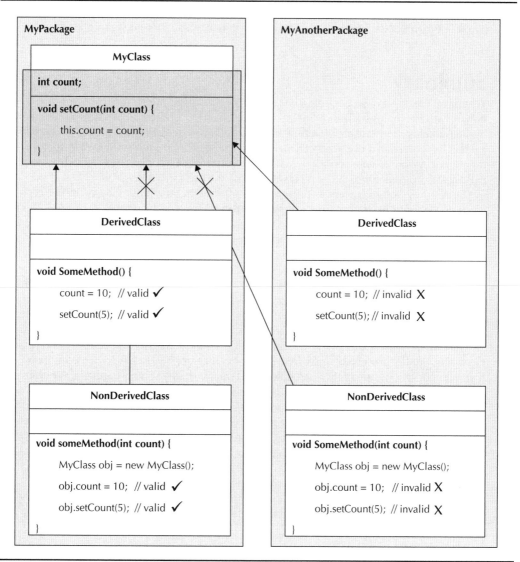

FIGURE 5-6. *Visibility of default identifiers*

of access is private and the strongest is public. This rule applies only to the methods of a class and not to its fields.

A field with the same name declared in a subclass is treated as a shadowed variable in the subclass that essentially hides the corresponding declaration in the base class. This rule can be exemplified using the following cases:

- A method declared public in a superclass also must be public in all subclasses.

- A method declared protected in a superclass must either be protected or public in subclasses; it cannot be private nor have a default scope.

- A method declared without access control (no modifier was used) cannot be declared private in a subclass.

- A member declared private is not inherited at all, so there is no rule for it.

Summary

When you create an object of a subclass, all its parent objects are created. The construction process begins with the topmost class in the inheritance hierarchy and continues down the line until the desired subclass is instantiated. During the construction of all these parent objects, a constructor of each of the instantiated classes is called. A class may declare more than one constructor. You use the **super** keyword to gain control over which constructor of a superclass is called. If you want to call another constructor of the same class, you use the **this** keyword.

Sometimes, you may want to prevent others from inheriting your classes. In this case, you use the **final** keyword in front of the class declaration to prevent its further derivation. The **final** keyword can also be applied to methods and variables. A method that is declared using the **final** keyword cannot be overridden in a subclass. A **final** variable is a program constant, and its value cannot be changed during program execution. A variable declared as **final** can be initialized only once during program execution (that is, when it is declared or in a constructor). If the variable is not initialized at the time of declaration, it is known as a blank **final** variable. A blank **final** variable must be initialized in a constructor because the constructor is called only once during program execution; all other methods may be called multiple times. If you initialize a **final** variable in a constructor, you must provide this initialization in all the overloaded constructors.

To control the visibility of the various identifiers during program execution, Java provides three keywords: **public**, **protected**, and **private**. These can be applied to a field, a method, or a class. If you do not specify any of these modifiers, a default visibility scope is applied. A **public** identifier, as its name suggests, is truly public and is accessible within the entire scope of the executing program. A **private** identifier, on the other hand, is privately accessible only within the class to which it belongs. A **protected** identifier is accessible within the package to which it belongs and all its subclasses, regardless of the package they belong to. A protected identifier cannot be accessed from a class declared in another package and that does not derive from the declaring class. Default access makes the identifier visible to all the classes within the defining package, but prevents its access from all derived and nonderived classes defined in a different package.

At this point, you have learned a good number of the features of a Java **class**. In the next chapter, you will learn some more advanced features of a Java class.

CHAPTER
6

Static Modifier
and Interfaces

n the previous chapters, you studied several important aspects of object-oriented programming. You learned to declare and use a class, extend its functionality with the help of inheritance, and so on. Java allows multiple levels in an inheritance hierarchy. You learned how the superclass objects are constructed when a subclass object is created. You also learned the use of the **super** keyword in calling the superclass methods and using superclass fields in subclasses. The access to the various members of a class is controlled using the access modifiers. You learned about all such available access modifiers that control the visibility of members. To restrict inheritance, you use the **final** keyword. You learned how to create **final** variables, methods, and classes.

In this chapter, you learn some more stuff related to classes and another important construct—interfaces.

In particular, you will learn the following:

- Understanding static fields, methods, and initializers
- Defining and extending interfaces
- Implementing multiple interfaces
- Abstract classes

The static Keyword

You have already seen the use of the **static** keyword in our Java programs. In fact, the first program you encountered in Chapter 2 uses the **static** keyword, where it was applied to the **main** method. The **static** keyword can also be applied to the fields of a class. The only other application of the **static** keyword is to create initializers. This chapter covers the use of the **static** keyword in all three cases—that is, used with fields, methods, and initializers—and their importance in practical situations. We'll start by discussing fields.

The Static Fields

A class field may be marked as **static**. But why would you do so? Suppose you have created an application that uses several of your own classes. The application user can create several objects of these classes during runtime. Therefore, you may want to know how many objects of each type a user has created in a typical session to get an understanding of the memory usage of your application. In this case, a static field will help in maintaining the count of number of objects created.

Another good application of a static field would be to create a truly global variable. As you already know, Java does not allow you to create any declarations outside the class definition (C++ allows you to create global variable declarations). However, you are able to create a globally accessible variable within your application using the **static** keyword. One more useful application of a static field declaration is to create an application-level programming constant. You will learn all these techniques in this section.

A static field is associated with the class definition itself. It is shared among all the instances of the class. This means that when a class is instantiated, no separate memory allocation will occur for a static field. The memory allocation for a static field happens only once, and that is when the class loads. When JVM loads the class definition into memory, it allocates space for all the static fields of a class. This memory space (that is, the fields) will be shared among all the objects of a class that are created throughout the life of the program. Conversely, all nonstatic fields will have their own memory allocation in each instance of the class. Therefore, when you have more than one instance of a class, each object will have an independent memory allocation for all its nonstatic fields. In other words, all nonstatic variables are copied into the newly created instance in memory.

Thus, in the case of a nonstatic variable, if you modify its value for a particular instance, the changes will remain local to that object and are not reflected in other instances of the class. However, for a static field, because only one allocation is shared among all the instances, any changes to it will be visible to all the instances of the class. An important application of this would be when you want to keep a count on how many instances of a class have been created by the running application. Let's look at this usage with the help of an application.

Consider a game that allows a player to create multiple balls during game play. Such an application would probably declare a class called **Ball**. As a game strategy, the application might keep track of the number of balls created by the player during the entire span of the game. Therefore, the static field would come in handy for counting the number of ball instances. This is illustrated in the program shown in Listing 6-1.

Listing 6-1 *Program Illustrating the Use of a Static Field*

```
class Ball {

    private static int count = 0;

    public static int getCount() {
        return count;
    }

    public Ball() {
        count++;
    }
}

public class BallGame {

    public static void main(String[] args) {
        for (int i = 0; i < 10000; i++) {
            int number = (int) (Math.random() * 10);
            if (number == 5) {
                new Ball();
            }
        }
        System.out.println("No of balls created: " + Ball.getCount());
    }
}
```

The class **Ball** declares one static attribute called **count**. The initial value of this attribute is 0:

```
private static int count = 0;
```

The class constructor increments the **count** value. Recall that each static field gets its own memory allocation, which is shared among all the instances of a class. Therefore, when the class constructor increments the **count** field, its shared value is incremented and thus it tracks every instantiation of a class. This is shown in Figure 6-1.

The **BallGame** class provides the **main** method in which you instantiate the **Ball** class. To simulate the situation that a player may create any number of balls, we use a randomizer in the program to set the number of balls. The randomizer generates a random number in the range 0 to 10. The program runs 10,000 iterations, creating a random number in each. When the generated random number equals 5, a **Ball** is created. At the end of the loop, we print the total number of balls created on the user console. The number of balls is retrieved using a getter method on the **count** field. Note that the getter method **getCount** is declared **static** and is called by using the syntax *ClassName.methodName*.

Accessing Static Fields Through Object References

In the previous section, we accessed the static method **getCount** by using the class name. Can we call this method on an object reference? Yes, we can. To understand how this is done and what it means, look at the following statement:

```
System.out.println(new Ball().getCount());
```

Here, we first create an instance of **Ball**. The class constructor would increment the **count** by 1. After the object is fully constructed, the runtime calls its **getCount** method. Thus, the count value printed to the console also includes the currently created object.

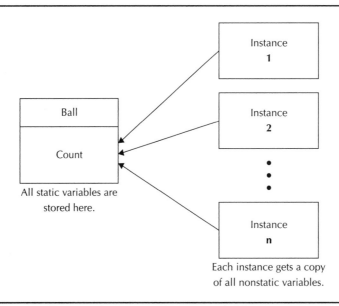

FIGURE 6-1. *Memory allocation for static and nonstatic fields*

Inheriting Static Fields

In Chapter 4, you learned about inheritance. The same way the class fields and methods are inherited by a subclass, the static fields of a class will be inherited in a subclass. Consider the following class declaration:

```
class RedBall extends Ball {

}
```

Here, **RedBall** simply inherits the **Ball** class, thereby inheriting all its members. Now, if we instantiate **RedBall** and get the ball count by using the following statement, we find that the **count** variable belonging to the **Ball** class is incremented during the construction of the **RedBall** object:

```
System.out.println(new RedBall().getCount());
```

This confirms that all static fields are also inherited by the subclasses.

Creating a Truly Global Variable

According to the best practices of object-oriented design, the fields of a class should always be made **private**. Now, what would happen if we declare them **public**? Well, the answer is simple. Any code outside the class definition would be able to access and modify these fields. Although this is considered bad design, making the static fields public allows us to create a truly global variable. For example, modify the declaration of the **count** field in our earlier program as follows:

```
public static int count = 0;
```

Now, we are able to access this **count** field anywhere in the code with the statement **Ball.count**. There is no need for a getter method.

CAUTION
*According to good programming practices recommended by Sun (now Oracle), instance variables should always be declared private. The problem with public non-**final** variables is that they can be changed by anyone who uses the enclosing class without you knowing. Using getters and setters gives you a chance to monitor/verify any reads or writes of that data, thus leading to more reliable programs. As you'll recall from the wallet example in Chapter 3, we do not let the cashier take the money out of our wallet; rather, we give it to him. We do this because we always want the chance to check for ourselves that the correct amount is taken out.*

TIP
*It is okay to declare class variables **public** when they are used as constants and marked **final**.*

Creating Application Constants

From the previous section, you know how to create an application global variable declaration. You also learned the use of the **final** keyword in Chapter 4. If you make your global variable declaration **final**, it will create a constant that cannot be modified throughout the application. The following statement shows how to create such a constant:

```
class Constants {

    public final static double PI = 3.14;
}
```

The variable **PI**, which is declared **static**, is accessible without creating an instance of the **Constants** class. The variable is initialized to a value of 3.14 at the time of declaration. Because it is declared **final**, its value cannot be modified further in the application. Thus, you have successfully created an application constant. To use this constant in your code, you would use the syntax **Constants.PI**. The visibility of this constant in your program code is decided by the access modifier applied to its declaration, which in this case is **public**. This constant can be accessed anywhere in your program code as long as the code has access to the class **Constants**.

If you read the web chapter "Syntax Reference 1: Java Language Constructs," you learned about the coding convention for declaring constants. To reiterate, the names of variables declared as class constants should be all uppercase, with words separated by an underscore character. You should avoid the use of ANSI constants in your program code as your own constants for ease of debugging.

Some Important Notes on Static Fields

Here's a summary of the observations made so far on static fields:

- A static field belongs to a class and not to an object (that is, an instance of a class).

TIP
For this reason, a static field is also called a class field/attribute *or simply a* class variable. *The nonstatic fields belong to an instance of a class and are therefore referred to as* instance variables.

- Static variables are *initialized only once,* at the start of the execution.
- All static fields are initialized before the initialization of any instance variables.
- A static field can be *accessed directly* via its class name and doesn't need any object reference.

The Static Methods

In general, methods may be classified under two categories: the ones whose behavior depends on the state of the object on which they are defined, and the ones that do not depend on the state of the object. Consider the example of the ball game described in the previous section. A player may be given the choice to select the color of the balls. This color choice will be applied to all the balls he creates during the game. Thus, if we define a **setDefaultColor** method for setting the color of a ball, the method may be attached to the **Ball** class rather than every object of the **Ball** type. Such a method is defined using the **static** keyword, as will be explained further. Now, consider a method that sets the velocity of the motion for a ball. The velocity will obviously depend on the current state of the game and will be independently set for each ball on the board game. Therefore, we'll want to define a method called **setVelocity** that operates on an instance of a **Ball** class. This type of method is a nonstatic method—a method that does not use the **static** keyword. We discuss both types of methods in this section. First, though, let's look at a few more situations where the methods need to be declared with the **static** keyword.

Sometimes you may want to execute program code without creating a class instance. A typical example of this is the declaration of the **main** method in your program code, as shown here:

```
public static void main(String[] args)
```

Because the program execution begins with the **main** method, you need to run it before you can create an instance of your application class. Therefore, the method is declared using the **static** keyword.

Another example is the use of mathematical functions. To compute an exponential or a logarithm, you would want to call the appropriate function directly instead of creating a class instance and then invoking a method on that instance. For example, Java libraries define a class called **Math** in the **java.lang** package. The **Math** class has several mathematical functions defined in terms of the class methods. All these methods are declared **static** so that they can be invoked without instantiating the **Math** class. For example, to determine a logarithm of a given number, you would use the method **log**, which is invoked as follows:

```
System.out.println(Math.log(5.0));
```

This statement would print the log of 5.0 on your terminal. To determine the square root of a given number, you would use the following:

```
System.out.println(Math.sqrt(5.0));
```

Both the **log** and **sqrt** methods of the **Math** class are static and can therefore be invoked without an instance of the **Math** class being created.

Now that we have discussed the need for static methods, let's go back to our ball game example. Listing 6-2 is an enhanced ball game that creates a random number of balls on each run. Out of the total number of balls created, a randomly selected number of them will be red and the rest green. Each ball has a constant radius, which is also set randomly on each run. As you can imagine, the radius is an appropriate candidate for creating a class field (static) with corresponding getter/setter static methods. Because the color of each ball is randomly set, it becomes the instance property (nonstatic). Finally, we set the velocity of motion for each ball after it is created. Setting the velocity of the ball will be an instance method (nonstatic) because it operates on an individual object. Examine the code in Listing 6-2 to understand the implementation of both static and nonstatic fields and methods.

Listing 6-2   *Modified Ball Game Program*

```
import java.awt.Color;

class Ball {

    private static int count = 0;
    private static int redBallCount = 0;
    private static int greenBallCount = 0;
```

```java
        private static int radius = 0;
        private Color defaultColor;

        public static int getRedBallCount() {
            return redBallCount;
        }

        public static int getGreenBallCount() {
            return greenBallCount;
        }

        public static int getRadius() {
            return radius;
        }

        public static void setRadius(int radius) {
            Ball.radius = radius;
        }

        public Ball(Color color) {
            count++;
            if (color == Color.RED) {
                this.defaultColor = Color.RED;
                redBallCount++;
            } else {
                this.defaultColor = Color.GREEN;
                greenBallCount++;
            }
        }

        public void setVelocity(double v) {
            String strColor = null;
            if (defaultColor == Color.RED) {
                strColor = "Red";
            } else {
                strColor = "Green";
            }
            System.out.printf("Ball #%d:%-10s  velocity set to %.02f%n",
                    count, strColor, v);
        }
    }

public class EnhancedBallGame {

    public static void main(String[] args) {
        int numberOfBalls = (int) (Math.random() * 10);
        int radius = (int) (Math.random() * 20) + 1;
        Ball.setRadius(radius);
        System.out.printf("Creating %d balls of radius %d%n",
                numberOfBalls, Ball.getRadius());
```

```
    for (int i = 0; i < numberOfBalls; i++) {
        int number = (int) (Math.random() * 2);
        if (number == 0) {
            new Ball(Color.RED).setVelocity(Math.random() * 10);
        } else {
            new Ball(Color.GREEN).setVelocity(Math.random() * 10);
        }
    }
    System.out.println("Number of red balls created: "
            + Ball.getRedBallCount());
    System.out.println("Number of green balls created: "
            + Ball.getGreenBallCount());
    }
}
```

The **Ball** class declares several fields—**count**, **redBallCount**, **greenBallCount**, **radius**, and **defaultColor**. The first four are static and the last one is nonstatic. The **defaultColor** field holds the color value of each individual ball and is therefore set to be an instance variable. The **count** field, as in the earlier example, tracks each ball that's created and at the end holds the total number of balls. The **redBallCount** and **greenBallCount** fields hold the total number of red and green balls created, respectively. The **radius** field is common to all balls and is therefore declared **static**. The class defines the desired getter/setter methods on these fields.

The class constructor takes one parameter of the **Color** type. Note that **Color** is a Java-supplied class defined in the **java.awt** package. The **Color** class defines several static fields to represent different colors. The constructor increments the static field **count** to account for the newly created object. The value of the input argument is copied into the **defaultColor** field. If this input argument is of type **Color.RED**, we increment the count of red balls; otherwise, we increment the count of green balls. Both these counts are static fields and therefore their values are retained during each instantiation of the **Ball** class.

Finally, the **Ball** class declares one nonstatic method called **setVelocity** that takes one parameter representing the velocity value to be set. This method simply prints the value of the velocity along with the ball number on which the velocity is set to the user's console. We also print the color value of each ball.

In the **main** method of the **EnhancedBallGame** class, we set the number of balls to be created using the randomizer from earlier:

```
int numberOfBalls = (int) (Math.random() * 10);
```

We set the radius for all the balls to be created by using the randomizer once again:

```
int radius = (int) (Math.random() * 20) + 1;
Ball.setRadius(radius);
```

Here, **setRadius** is a static method of the class that sets the value of the static field **radius**. This value will be common to all instances of the **Ball** class.

Next, we create the balls by setting up a **for** loop:

```
for (int i = 0; i < numberOfBalls; i++) {
```

We select between a red and green ball by once again using the randomizer:

```
int number = (int) (Math.random() * 2);
if (number == 0) {
    new Ball(Color.RED).setVelocity(Math.random() * 10);
} else {
    new Ball(Color.GREEN).setVelocity(Math.random() * 10);
}
```

We use the **new** keyword to instantiate the **Ball** class. We call the class constructor by sending either the red or green color value to it. After the class is instantiated, we call the **setVelocity** nonstatic method on the created instance to set the velocity of the created ball. The velocity value is set again using the randomizer.

After all the balls have been created, the program prints a tally of the red and green balls. A typical output is shown next. Note that this output varies on each run.

```
Creating 7 balls of radius 20
Ball #1:Green         velocity set to 5.82
Ball #2:Green         velocity set to 1.11
Ball #3:Green         velocity set to 1.05
Ball #4:Red           velocity set to 6.79
Ball #5:Green         velocity set to 7.33
Ball #6:Green         velocity set to 8.88
Ball #7:Red           velocity set to 1.23
Number of red balls created: 2
Number of green balls created: 5
```

The next section covers the restrictions imposed on the code that can be put in a static method.

Access Restrictions in Static Methods

Because a static method is invoked without a class instance, you cannot use a **this** or **super** reference in the static method. That is to say, it is illegal to reference any of the class fields or methods using a **this** reference within a static method. However, a static method can access the class members (both fields and methods). A *class member* is a member of the class that is declared using the **static** keyword. As you have seen so far, both fields and methods can be declared with the **static** keyword. Such static fields and methods are accessible to the code defined in a static method. The nonstatic fields are bound to a class instance and therefore cannot be accessed in the body of a static method. To understand these code restrictions in a static method, look at the code snippet in Listing 6-3.

Listing 6-3   *Access Restrictions in Static Methods*

```
class StaticMemberTestApp {

    private static int i;
    private int j;

    public static void staticMethod() {
        // do something
    }
```

```
    public void nonStaticMethod() {
        // do something else
    }

    public static void main(String[] args) {
        i = 5;
        j = 10; // this does not compile
        staticMethod();
        nonStaticMethod(); // this does not compile
    }
}
```

The **StaticMemberTestApp** class declares two fields: The variable field **i** is declared static whereas the variable **j** is nonstatic. The **main** method, which itself is static, modifies the value of **i**, which is legal. However, accessing **j** in the body of the **main** method generates a compile-time error. Note that a static method cannot access a nonstatic attribute within its body. Similarly, the class declares two methods: one static and one nonstatic. The **staticMethod** is a class method (static) and is called within the body of the **main** method without producing any compile-time errors. However, calling the **nonStaticMethod**, which is an instance (nonstatic) method, within the body of the **main** method generates a compile-time error.

Another important code restriction is that a static method cannot be overridden in a subclass. This is illustrated in the code snippet in Listing 6-4.

Listing 6-4   *Overriding Methods*

```
class MyClass {

    public static void staticMethod() {
        // do something
    }

    public void nonStaticMethod() {
        // do something
    }
}

class MySubClass extends MyClass {

    public void staticMethod() // this does not compile
    {
        // overrides base class implementation
    }

    public void nonStaticMethod() {
        // overrides base class implementation
    }
}
```

The class **MyClass** declares two methods: one static and one nonstatic. The class **MySubClass** inherits **MyClass**. The class **MySubClass** now attempts to override the two methods inherited from its parent. Overriding the **staticMethod**, which is declared using the static qualifier in the base class, generates a compile-time error. Overriding a nonstatic method (that is, **nonStaticMethod**) is permitted.

Some Important Notes on Static Methods

Here are a few important points about static methods:

- A static method is invoked via a class reference. You can use an object reference to invoke a static method; however, this is generally not considered good style.

- The special method **main** is declared static so that we do not need to create an instance of the class to which it belongs while starting the application.

- A static method cannot use **this** and **super** in its body.

- A static method can access static fields and methods of the class.

- A static method cannot access nonstatic fields and methods of the class.

- A static method cannot be overridden in a subclass.

The Static Initializers

We use constructors to initialize nonstatic fields of a class. The constructors are called at the time of object creation and complete the initializations defined in them before the object becomes ready to use. You may use the same constructors to initialize static fields of the class. Initializing the static fields in a constructor means that you have to wait until the time of object creation. In certain situations, you will want to initialize the static fields before a class is instantiated. Consider the situation where you have defined a class called **GoogleConnector** that provides a connection to the Google website. When the user of this class instantiates it, he would naturally expect that the connection is already made and readily available to his code. If connection-making code is written in the class constructor, at times the connection may fail and the created object would not have access to the Google site. Ideally, if we make this connection while loading the class, it will be available to all its created objects. Java allows us to perform these initializations of static fields in what is called a *static initializer* or simply a *static constructor.*

A static initializer block resembles a method with no name, no arguments, and no return type. The name is not required because there is no need to refer to it from outside the class definition. Therefore, it is like an anonymous method. Whereas a typical class constructor may contain arguments, a static block cannot have any arguments. Because the static block is executed automatically during the class load time, the arguments to it will not make any sense, and therefore no arguments are allowed. Finally, like a constructor, the static block has no return type.

In our **ExtendedBallGame** from the previous section, we defined a static field called **radius**. We initialized it to zero at the time of its declaration. Alternatively, we could have defined a static initializer, as follows, to initialize the static field:

```
static {
    radius = 5;
}
```

Now, every ball object will have a default radius of 5 that can be set to another value by calling the **setRadius** method elsewhere in the object code.

NOTE
A static block can access only the static members of the class and does not have access to its nonstatic members because no instance of the class is available when the code defined in the static block executes.

Advantages of a Static Initializer

Although the example in the preceding section illustrates a simple case where a static block is used for initializing a single static field, which could be done by other ways, too, its real purpose lies in the initialization and allocation of resources that are required throughout the life of the class. Here are a few examples:

- A **Modem** class may perform initializations of its registers in a static block.
- A device driver may register the required natives in a static block.
- In some situations, initialization of a static field may require some prior computations. For example, a digital key signature algorithm may require a random-seed value based on the current time. This would require reading the current time and performing some computations before the seed is generated. Such code may be executed in a static block so that when the class is loaded, the seed for the key generator is readily available.
- Sometimes you may want to audit whether anybody has loaded a class that has access to sensitive information, as is typical in banking and military applications. A static block can be used for logging such activities.
- For a typical database application, you may generate prepared SQL statements in a static block.
- In singletons, you may declare private static members that are initialized in a static block only once. (The singleton is a design pattern that implements the mathematical concept of a singleton by restricting the instantiation of a class to one object.)

Multiple Static Blocks

A static block is executed only once when the class is loaded. Your class may contain multiple static blocks. These are executed in the order in which they appear in the class. This can be useful in organizing the multiple logical initializations your class may require in a sequential order. Consider a class that creates a Sudoku puzzle. Creating a puzzle requires certain steps to be executed in sequence. The class definition to implement this may look like the following:

```
class Puzzle {

    static {
        // Initialize random number generator
    }

    static {
        // Formulate Sudoku solution board
    }
```

```
static {
    // Make puzzle
}
// Rest of the class code presents the generated puzzle to the user
}
```

The three static blocks execute in the sequence they are specified. Thus, first the random number generator will be initialized, followed by the formulation of the Sudoku solution board, and lastly the code that generates puzzle will be executed. When all three blocks execute successfully, a puzzle will be ready for the user.

Another example would be the **GoogleConnector** class we discussed earlier. This class might first initialize a modem, followed by making a Wi-Fi connection and then a network connection to the Google site. These three operations can be arranged in three independent static blocks and called sequentially in the given order in the class definition. Other places where you would use multiple static blocks include loading a database driver, followed by a connection to a database, and loading resource bundles for internationalization in a specific sequence. Be aware that loading expensive resources in a static block may not always be a good idea. What's more, handling failures in a static block is usually difficult, as explained later in the chapter.

An Alternative to a Static Initializer

Instead of using a static block as discussed in the previous section, you can initialize your static fields by defining a private static method. Let's look at how to do this in our **ExtendedBallGame** example. The game has a static field called **radius**. We could initialize this field using the following code snippet:

```
private static int radius = initClassVariables();

private static int initClassVariables() {
    // some computations to determine radius
    int radius = 5;
    return radius;
}
```

Defining a method like this for initialization is really useful if you have to reinitialize your objects later in the code. You may then simply call this private class method whenever a re-initialization is desired. For example, in our ball game, when two balls touch each other, we may want to create a bigger ball out of the two balls by merging them into a single ball. Thus, the initialization method gives us more flexibility in coding as compared to a static initialization block.

Some Important Notes on Static Initializers

Here are a few important points on using static blocks to keep in mind while coding these initializers:

- The JVM sets a limit of 64K on the size of a static initializer block. Therefore, you cannot put lot of code in this block.

- You cannot throw checked exceptions from a static initializer. The exceptions are discussed in Chapter 8 on exception handling.

- You cannot use the **this** keyword in a static block because no instance has been created so far.

- You cannot call **super** explicitly in a static block. Static blocks are loaded when the class is loaded, and **super** is called whenever object creation takes place. Therefore, it is built into a nonstatic initializer (that is, a constructor). That's why including it in a static block results in generating a compile-time error.
- There is no return type for a static block.
- Testing the code in a static block is usually considered a nightmare by developers.

CAUTION
*Although exceptions are discussed in depth in Chapter 8, we will briefly discuss here how to handle exceptions in static blocks. In our earlier programs, the methods catch and handle exceptions using a **try-catch** block. In static blocks, we cannot use **try-catch**. Therefore, one option is to log an exception and then throw a **RuntimeException** to end the current thread. Another option would be to call the **System.exit()** method. This, however, is not desirable in a managed environment such as a Servlet. This option is typically used in Java applications where the static block performs some critical operation without which the program cannot be run successfully—for example, loading the database driver. A third option would be to set a flag indicating the failure. The class constructor can then check the condition of the flag and throw an exception if desired. Lastly, if the operation in a static block is not really critical, we can just log the exception entry and continue.*

Interfaces

As mentioned earlier, Java does not support multiple inheritance—in other words, a class cannot have two or more superclasses. Multiple inheritance has its own advantages and disadvantages. Java achieves some of the benefits of multiple inheritance through interfaces. So what is an interface? An *interface* is a device or system that unrelated entities use to interact with each other. When you drive a car, you interact with a machine—two totally unrelated entities. These two entities interact through a well-defined interface for steering, throttling, and braking. The English and French languages may be considered an interface for communication between two people—not totally unrelated entities in this case. A remote control is an interface between a viewer and a television set. In the military, the interface between officers of different rank is the enforced protocol of behavior. Java interfaces are analogous to such protocols; they provide an agreed-upon behavior between objects of different types or of the same type.

NOTE
Other object-oriented languages also provide the functionality of Java's interfaces. For example, C++ provides an equivalent interface through its declaration of abstract base classes; Objective-C provides similar functionality through its protocols, and so on.

Interfaces may be considered a standard framework for accessing classes. They provide a separation between behavior and implementation. We will cover this point in more depth when we discuss a concrete, real-life example in the next section.

TIP
Object-oriented languages have a concept of composition, *where an object of a different type is composed within another object by holding a reference to the other object. Interfaces allow a kind of behavioral composition with the restriction that they do not allow the classes that implement them to inherit implementation from multiple classes. Both composition and inheritance allow you to place other objects inside your new class. Composition does this explicitly whereas inheritance does it implicitly. Composition is used when you want the features of an existing class inside your new class but not its interface. To do this, you embed private objects of existing classes inside your new class.*

So what does an interface look like? An interface has a structure similar to a class. It contains methods and fields. However, none of the methods of an interface can contain implementation code, and all fields must be declared **final**. Therefore, the methods defined in an interface provide only the signatures, and all the fields are program constants. You need to define a class in your program that provides the implementations of the methods declared in an interface. A class can implement multiple interfaces, and an interface can have multiple super-interfaces. You will learn more about this as you continue reading this section.

Although there seems to be a lot of similarity between interfaces and multiple inheritance, there are some subtle important differences:

- A class can inherit the fields of a superclass, but it inherits only the constants from an interface (note that an interface does not allow field declarations).

- A class can inherit method implementations from a superclass, but it cannot inherit method implementations from an interface because there are none in an interface.

- In the case of multiple inheritance, all involved classes in the hierarchy are somehow related to each other; in the case of interfaces, the classes that implement them may or may not be related through the class hierarchy.

Now that you know what an interface is, the next question is where to use it. Therefore, let's discuss the various uses of an interface:

- Interfaces are useful in capturing similarities between unrelated classes without the need to force a relationship between them in the class hierarchy. Think of an **Employee** class and a **Stock** class—both require a print functionality whereby the user can print its description. Thus, we could create an interface called **Printable** that has a **Print** method (besides other methods for the printer, page settings, and so on). Both the **Employee** and **Stock** classes will implement this **Printable** interface to provide a common functionality, but otherwise the classes are unrelated.

- Interfaces allow you to define behavior that one or more classes are expected to implement. In the **Printable** interface example, **Print**, **PageSetting**, **PrinterSetting**, and so on, would be the methods of the **Printable** interface that define the behavior for various classes.

■ Interfaces allow you to hide the implementation details of an object. For example, as discussed earlier, to drive a car, you need not be concerned with how the fuel is ignited in the engine's cylinders. Many times, you can provide anonymous objects to the user by revealing only the object's programming interface.

NOTE
*All methods in an interface are **public** and **abstract** by default. A method is said to be "abstract" when no implementation is provided for it.*

NOTE
Interfaces with no methods are known as marker interfaces. *A known example of this is the **Serializable** interface defined in the Java API. To save an object to a file or to send it across a network connection, the object's class must implement this interface. The **writeObject** method in the **ObjectOutputStream** class of the Java API accepts a parameter of type **Object**, which is also an instance of **Serializable**.*

A Real-life Example of an Interface

Suppose you are asked to develop communication software such as an FTP (File Transfer Protocol) or Telnet program that uses a modem. Your program must work with a variety of different modems. Although all the modems provide the same functionality, their implementations are quite different. Obviously, it would be inadvisable to create multiple versions of your application to interface with each of the modems available on the market because the code maintenance and application upgrades would be too much work. For this reason, you would develop an interface that specifies the method signatures your application uses for interfacing with the modem. This would provide a uniform programming interface to all the modems. This way, the application that uses a modem would not break even if the implementations in the methods of the modem change in future. Typically, you would have open, close, read, and write operations that your application would invoke on a modem. Your interface would declare these methods as follows:

```
interface Modem {

    public boolean open();
    public boolean close();
    public int read ();
    public int write(byte[] buffer);
}
```

NOTE
This is an extremely simplified view of the kind of API a modem might present. An interface for a modem in real life would have several more methods.

You will provide different implementations for the methods declared in the **Modem** interface for each of the supported modems.

To implement an interface, you use the following notation:

```
public class HayesModem implements Modem {

    public boolean open() {
        // implementation
    }
    public boolean close() {
        // implementation
    }
    public int read () {
        // implementation
    }
    public int write(byte[] buffer) {
    // implementation
    }
}
```

The class **HayesModem** declaration uses the **implements** keyword to implement the **Modem** interface. In the class definition, you need to provide an implementation for each method defined in the **Modem** interface.

NOTE

*If you do not implement all the methods of the interface, the class becomes **abstract**. Abstract classes are discussed later in this chapter.*

To support another modem, you would create another class (say, **IntelModem**). You would define this class as follows:

```
public class IntelModem implements Modem {

    public boolean open() {
        // implementation
    }
    public boolean close() {
        // implementation
    }
    public int read () {
        // implementation
    }
    public int write(byte[] buffer) {
        // implementation
    }
}
```

The method implementations in this class would be different from the implementations provided in **HayesModem** class. Each implementation would be specific to the modem manufacturer. Once you create such classes specific to each modem manufacturer, you can develop your application software that interfaces easily with each of these modems. To use the **HayesModem** class, you would use code similar to the following:

```
Modem modem = new HayesModem();
modem.open();
modem.write(buffer);
modem.read();
modem.close();
```

Note that you instantiate the **HayesModem** class and assign the object reference to a variable of type **Modem**. Remember from earlier chapters that an object reference can be assigned to its superclass without explicit typecasting. The **Modem** interface is a super-interface here. The **HayesModem** class implements **Modem** and therefore the assignment of an object reference from type **HayesModem** to the **Modem** interface is permitted.

Now, to interface your application with an Intel modem, you would use the following code:

```
Modem modem = new IntelModem();
modem.open();
modem.write(buffer);
modem.read();
modem.close();
```

The only difference between the earlier code and this code is in the class instantiation. In the earlier case we use **HayesModem** and in the latter case we use **IntelModem**. The rest of the code remains the same. This is the greatest advantage of creating interfaces—you don't need to change much of the code even when you change modems. This makes it easier to write an application that works with a lot of different modems. Here, you can see that your initial concern for how to provide a different implementation for each modem and yet maintaining a single interface to access them is easily resolved using an interface.

Understanding Interface Syntax

An interface uses syntax similar to that of a class declaration. The format of the interface syntax is shown here:

```
Modifiers_opt interface InterfaceName extends_opt InterfaceName(s) {

    InterfaceBody_opt
}
```

A typical interface declaration looks like the following:

```
interface PrimaryColors {

    int RED = 0xFF0000;
    int GREEN = 0x00FF00;
    int BLUE = 0x0000FF;
}
```

The interface is defined using the **interface** keyword. The interface has a name that follows the standard naming conventions for a class declaration. The *Modifiers* control its visibility, which can be either public or default. Therefore, you either specify this field as public or none. If you use a public modifier, you must put your interface definition in a separate compilation unit (a .java file). As in the case of classes, a public access modifier allows the interface to be accessed outside of the package in which it is declared.

NOTE
The Java Language Specifications lists the following values as the allowed values for **Modifiers**—**Annotation, public, protected, private, abstract, static,** *and* **strictfp***. The* **protected** *and* **private** *modifiers can be applied only to member interfaces within a directly enclosing class declaration. You learn more about this in Chapter 7.*

The **extends** keyword has a similar meaning as in the case of a class declaration. An interface may extend another interface. When an interface extends another interface, it adds a few more constants and/or method declarations to the existing interface. However, it is not allowed to provide an implementation for any of the new methods or the methods inherited from an existing interface.

CAUTION
Because none of the methods in an interface are implemented, the interface itself is considered abstract by default. Because every interface is implicitly abstract, the **abstract** *modifier is obsolete and should not be used in new programs.*

In the interface body, you declare constants and method signatures. An interface is allowed to declare constants but not variables. The declaration of a method signature in an interface is also called *abstract method declaration*. Because these methods do not contain any implementation, they are called abstract.

CAUTION
You cannot apply the following modifiers to the interface methods: **private, protected, transient, volatile,** *and* **synchronized***.*

Understanding Interfaces Through an Example

To illustrate how to declare and implement an interface, let's look at a concrete example. Suppose we are asked to represent different kinds of vehicles in our application software. A vehicle could run on gasoline or electric batteries. Therefore, we will have two different classes of vehicles. Each type would have its own fuel-efficiency measure. For gas vehicles, it is the gasoline consumed per mile, and for electric vehicles it is the kilowatts (KW) of power consumed per mile. Because this is common functionality and must be implemented by every type of car, including those that will come on the market in the future, let's create a standard interface that every vehicle will implement. We'll call this interface **MileageEfficiency**. Any vehicle that implements this interface will get a standard set of methods for obtaining the vehicle's efficiency. To keep things short and simple, we'll define this interface with a single method, as follows:

```
interface MileageEfficiency {

    public float getMilesPerGallon();
}
```

The **GasVehicle** and **ElectricVehicle** classes we will be writing shortly will implement this interface and provide an appropriate implementation for its sole method—**getMilesPerGallon**. The complete program is given in Listing 6-5.

Listing 6-5   *A Program Illustrating Interfaces*

```
interface MileageEfficiency {

    public float getMilesPerGallon();
}

class GasVehicle implements MileageEfficiency {

    private float fuelConsumed;
    private float tripCounter;

    public float getMilesPerGallon() {
        return tripCounter / fuelConsumed;
    }

    public void makeTrip() {
        tripCounter = 100;
        fuelConsumed = 8.5f;
    }
}

class ElectricVehicle implements MileageEfficiency {

    private float kwPowerConsumed;
    private float tripCounter;

    public float getMilesPerGallon() {
        return tripCounter / kwPowerConsumed;
    }

    public void makeTrip() {
        tripCounter = 100;
        kwPowerConsumed = 5.6f;
    }
}
```

```
public class TestDrive {

    public static void main(String[] args) {
        GasVehicle gasolineVehicle = new GasVehicle();
        gasolineVehicle.makeTrip();
        System.out.printf(
                "Efficiency of Gas Vehicle (miles/gallon): %.02f%n",
                gasolineVehicle.getMilesPerGallon());
        ElectricVehicle electricVehicle = new ElectricVehicle();
        electricVehicle.makeTrip();
        System.out.printf(
                "Efficiency of Electric Vehicle (miles/kw): %.02f%n",
                electricVehicle.getMilesPerGallon());
    }
}
```

Both the **GasVehicle** and **ElectricVehicle** classes define the **MileageEfficiency** interface and provide their own unique implementation for the method **getMilesPerGallon**. Both classes also define a method called **makeTrip** that records the fuel consumed and the distance traveled on a trip. The **TestDrive** class defines a **main** function that creates an instance of both the vehicles, makes a trip on each, and prints the fuel efficiency after the trip. When we run the program, we see the following output:

```
Efficiency of Gas Vehicle (miles/gallon): 11.76
Efficiency of Electric Vehicle (miles/kw): 17.86
```

Note that the **MileageEfficiency** interface we have created can be applied to any other vehicle type that may come in the future. You will see this when we create a hybrid vehicle in the next section.

Extending Interfaces

It is possible to extend an existing interface. The purpose behind doing so is to add more declarations, both constants and methods, to an existing interface. This helps in not breaking the existing applications that have implemented the earlier interface. We will now extend our **MileageEfficiency** interface from the previous example to provide a new way to compute the fuel efficiency of the newly introduced hybrid cars on the market that use both gasoline and electric batteries. We define this new interface as follows:

```
interface ExtendedMileageEfficiency extends MileageEfficiency {

    public float getFuelEfficiency();
    public float getElectricEfficiency();
}
```

To extend an existing interface, we use the keyword **extends**, just the way we did for extending class definitions. The interface declares two new methods: one for computing the fuel efficiency of the car and the other one for the battery consumption. The **getMilesPerGallon** method of the base interface will have an altogether different implementation that uses these two efficiencies to return a newly computed efficiency to the user. The declaration of the **HybridVehicle** class that implements this interface and the test program that creates an instance of this hybrid car are given in Listing 6-6.

Listing 6-6   *Modified Test Drive Program*

```
interface MileageEfficiency {

    public float getMilesPerGallon();
}

interface ExtendedMileageEfficiency extends MileageEfficiency {

    public float getFuelEfficiency();

    public float getElectricEfficiency();
}

class GasVehicle implements MileageEfficiency {

    private float fuelConsumed;
    private float tripCounter;

    public float getMilesPerGallon() {
        return tripCounter / fuelConsumed;
    }

    public void makeTrip() {
        tripCounter = 100;
        fuelConsumed = 8.5f;
    }
}

class ElectricVehicle implements MileageEfficiency {

    private float kwPowerConsumed;
    private float tripCounter;

    public float getMilesPerGallon() {
        return tripCounter / kwPowerConsumed;
    }

    public void makeTrip() {
        tripCounter = 100;
        kwPowerConsumed = 5.6f;
    }
}

class HybridVehicle implements ExtendedMileageEfficiency {
```

```java
    private float tripCounter;
    private float fuelConsumed;
    private float kwPowerConsumed;

    public float getFuelEfficiency() {
        return tripCounter / fuelConsumed;
    }

    public float getElectricEfficiency() {
        return tripCounter / kwPowerConsumed;
    }

    public float getMilesPerGallon() {
        return 0.8f * getFuelEfficiency() + 1.12f % getElectricEfficiency();
    }

    public void makeTrip() {
        tripCounter = 100;
        fuelConsumed = 4.1f;
        kwPowerConsumed = 3.4f;
    }
}

public class EnhancedTestDrive {

    public static void main(String[] args) {
        GasVehicle gasolineVehicle = new GasVehicle();
        gasolineVehicle.makeTrip();
        System.out.printf(
                "Efficiency of Gas Vehicle (miles/gallon): %.02f%n",
                gasolineVehicle.getMilesPerGallon());
        ElectricVehicle electricVehicle = new ElectricVehicle();
        electricVehicle.makeTrip();
        System.out.printf(
                "Efficiency of Electric Vehicle (miles/kw): %.02f%n",
                electricVehicle.getMilesPerGallon());
        HybridVehicle hybridVehicle = new HybridVehicle();
        hybridVehicle.makeTrip();
        System.out.printf(
                "Efficiency of hybrid Vehicle "
                + "(miles/EnergyConsumed): %.02f%n",
                hybridVehicle.getMilesPerGallon());
    }
}
```

The class **HybridVehicle** implements the newly declared interface **ExtendedMileageEfficiency** and provides the implementation of its two methods, along with the implementation of the inherited **getMilesPerGallon** method. The **main** method creates an instance of the hybrid vehicle, makes a trip, and then prints the car's efficiency.

NOTE
The actual computation of this hybrid efficiency would be more complicated than the simplistic calculations made here to illustrate the concept.

By this time, you have certainly started realizing (and appreciating) the use of interfaces. The interface we initially created provided a standard notation to the developer to compute the fuel efficiency of different types of cars. Later on, when the technology has been enhanced and new types of cars are introduced on the market, we could extend our existing interface and yet retain the same interface method **getMilesPerGallon** to compute the efficiency of the new cars. For a developer, the consistent interface he sees while writing an application is the greatest advantage to using interfaces.

NOTE
An interface can extend another interface but it cannot implement any interface.

Implementing Multiple Interfaces

In the previous section, we created a standard interface to get the fuel efficiency of a car. A car has many such standard functions that could be defined in terms of interfaces. For example, we could define interfaces for steering, braking, refilling, and so on. We'll now create one such interface for tracking the remaining battery life of electric and hybrid vehicles. Obviously, this interface is of no use to a car that runs on gasoline. Therefore, only electric and hybrid cars will implement our new interface. Let's call this interface **BatteryLifeTracker**. The interface definition is shown in the following code snippet:

```
interface BatteryLifeTracker {

    final int MAX_NUMBER_OF_RECHARGES = 300;

    public void chargeBattery();

    public int getRemainingLife();
}
```

The **BatteryLifeTracker** interface defines a constant that specifies the maximum number of times the car battery can be charged. It also defines a standard interface method called **chargeBattery** that increments the charge counter. The **getRemainingLife** method returns the number of times the battery can still be charged before it is rendered useless.

Both **ElectricVehicle** and **HybridVehicle** classes implement this interface. The class declaration now looks like this:

```
class ElectricVehicle implements MileageEfficiency, BatteryLifeTracker {
```

Note that the two interface names are separated with a comma. As a matter of fact, we could have any number of interfaces listed here, each separated with a comma. For each interface, we must implement all its methods within the class body.

Both **ElectricVehicle** and **HybridVehicle** now declare a static counter called **numberOfRecharges** to keep record of how many times the battery has been charged:

```java
private static int numberOfRecharges;
```

The implementations of the **chargeBattery** method in these classes simply increment this charge count. The implementation of the **getRemainingLife** method returns the difference between the total charge count and the number of times the battery has been charged so far. The **main** method prints this useful battery life information for both the cars. The complete program is given in Listing 6-7.

Listing 6-7   *Implementing Multiple Interfaces*

```java
interface MileageEfficiency {

    public float getMilesPerGallon();
}

interface ExtendedMileageEfficiency extends MileageEfficiency {

    public float getFuelEfficiency();

    public float getElectricEfficiency();
}

interface BatteryLifeTracker {

    final int MAX_NUMBER_OF_RECHARGES = 300;

    public void chargeBattery();

    public int getRemainingLife();
}

class GasVehicle implements MileageEfficiency {

    private float fuelConsumed;
    private float tripCounter;

    public float getMilesPerGallon() {
        return tripCounter / fuelConsumed;
    }

    public void makeTrip() {
        tripCounter = 100;
        fuelConsumed = 8.5f;
    }
}

class ElectricVehicle implements MileageEfficiency, BatteryLifeTracker {
```

```java
    private float kwPowerConsumed;
    private float tripCounter;
    private static int numberOfRecharges;

    public float getMilesPerGallon() {
        return tripCounter / kwPowerConsumed;
    }

    public void makeTrip() {
        tripCounter = 100;
        kwPowerConsumed = 5.6f;
    }

    public void chargeBattery() {
        numberOfRecharges++;
    }

    public int getRemainingLife() {
        return MAX_NUMBER_OF_RECHARGES - numberOfRecharges;
    }
}

class HybridVehicle implements ExtendedMileageEfficiency, BatteryLifeTracker {

    private float tripCounter;
    private float fuelConsumed;
    private float kWPowerConsumed;
    private static int noOfRecharges;

    public float getFuelEfficiency() {
        return tripCounter / fuelConsumed;
    }

    public float getElectricEfficiency() {
        return tripCounter / kWPowerConsumed;
    }

    public float getMilesPerGallon() {
        return 0.8f * getFuelEfficiency() + 1.12f % getElectricEfficiency();
    }

    public void makeTrip() {
        tripCounter = 100;
        fuelConsumed = 4.1f;
        kWPowerConsumed = 3.4f;
    }

    public void chargeBattery() {
        noOfRecharges++;
    }
```

```
      public int getRemainingLife() {
          return MAX_NUMBER_OF_RECHARGES - noOfRecharges;
      }
  }

public class FurtherEnhancedTestDrive {

    public static void main(String[] args) {
        GasVehicle gasolineVehicle = new GasVehicle();
        gasolineVehicle.makeTrip();
        System.out.printf(
                "Efficiency of Gas Vehicle (miles/gallon): %.02f%n",
                gasolineVehicle.getMilesPerGallon());

        ElectricVehicle electricVehicle = new ElectricVehicle();
        electricVehicle.makeTrip();
        System.out.printf(
                "%nEfficiency of Electric Vehicle (miles/kw): %.02f%n",
                electricVehicle.getMilesPerGallon());
        for (int i = 0; i < 78; i++) {
            electricVehicle.chargeBattery();
        }
        System.out.printf("The battery can be charged %d more times%n",
                electricVehicle.getRemainingLife());

        HybridVehicle hybridVehicle = new HybridVehicle();
        hybridVehicle.makeTrip();
        System.out.printf(
                "%nEfficiency of hybrid Vehicle "
                + "(miles/EnergyConsumed): %.02f%n",
                hybridVehicle.getMilesPerGallon());
        for (int i = 0; i < 15; i++) {
            hybridVehicle.chargeBattery();
        }
        System.out.printf(
                "The battery can be charged %d more times%n",
                hybridVehicle.getRemainingLife());
    }
}
```

When we run the program, the following output is produced:

```
Efficiency of Gas Vehicle (miles/gallon): 11.76

Efficiency of Electric Vehicle (miles/kw): 17.86
The battery can be charged 222 more times

Efficiency of hybrid Vehicle (miles/EnergyConsumed): 20.63
The battery can be charged 285 more times
```

Combining Interfaces

Java does not allow you to extend a class from more than one class. However, you can create an interface that extends one or more interfaces. For example, we could add a new interface that provides a method for computing the efficiency of a car irrespective of whether it runs on gasoline or a battery. Such an interface is declared as follows:

```
interface EfficiencyCalc extends MileageEfficiency, BatteryLifeTracker {

    public float getCarEfficiency();
}
```

Any class that implements **EfficiencyCalc** has to provide the implementation not only for the **getCarEfficiency** method but also for all the inherited methods of **MileageEfficiency** and **BatteryLifeTracker**. Implementing multiple interfaces like this allows them to inherit the behavioral protocols of the parent interfaces.

A Few Important Points on Interfaces

Here are a few important points you should keep in mind concerning interfaces:

- An interface is very similar to a class, except that it can have only fields that are implicitly public and static and method declarations that are implicitly public and abstract.
- The Java API documentation lists interfaces like classes.
- The interfaces compile to a .class file and get loaded by the same process that loads classes.
- You can create a reference variable whose type is the interface name. Only the methods defined in an interface will be visible through this reference.
- Any constants defined by an interface can be accessed without a prefix from code within the class because implementing the interface makes them part of the implementing class.

Abstract Classes

For an interface containing several methods, a developer can provide the implementation for some of the methods in a class that implements the interface. However, the developer may not be in a position to implement *all* the methods of the interface and might leave that task to a colleague or senior developer to perform at a later time. In such a case, compiling the class would result in compile-time errors. This situation can be remedied by declaring the class as **abstract**, and you create an abstract class using the **abstract** keyword.

Let's consider the case where a developer implementing our **HybridVehicle** class does not know the implementation of the **getMilesPerGallon** method, which requires a few computations that may not be known at the time of code development. In such a situation, the developer can provide the implementation of all other methods of the two interfaces, except for the **getMilesPerGallon** method. The class **HybridVehicle** must now be declared **abstract**, as follows:

```
abstract class HybridVehicle
    implements ExtendedMileageEfficiency, BatteryLifeTracker {
```

The code will now compile; however, the developer will not be able to create an instance of **HybridVehicle** anywhere in the program. To create an instance of **HybridVehicle**, he will probably extend this class further and provide the implementation of the **getMilesPerGallon** method in the new class.

A typical use of abstract classes is seen in our earlier example of the **Modem** interface. In the **Modem** interface, we declared four methods: **open**, **close**, **read**, and **write**. We could add one more method called **init** to this interface. The purpose of the **init** method, as the name suggests, is to initialize the modem. The new interface is shown in the following code snippet:

```
interface Modem {

    public boolean open();
    public boolean close();
    public int read ();
    public int write(byte[] buffer);
    public void init();
}
```

Because the implementation of the **read** and **write** methods is mostly the same for all the modems, we can provide these implementations for the benefit of modem manufacturers. However, the implementation of the **open**, **close**, and **init** methods will differ for each manufacturer. In particular, the **init** method that initializes the modem hardware will surely vary from manufacturer to manufacturer. Therefore, we may create a new class, **AbstractModem**, that provides the implementation of the **Modem** interface except for the implementations of **open**, **close**, and **init** methods. This class must be declared **abstract** because it does not provide the implementations of all the methods of the implementing interface. The class definition is shown here:

```
abstract class AbstractModem implements Modem {

    public int read() {
        int bytesRead = 0;
        // some implementation
        return bytesRead;
    }

    public int write (String buffer) {
        int bytesWritten = 0;
        // some implementation
        return bytesWritten;
    }
}
```

Thus, the abstract classes allow you to provide the partial implementation of the implementing interface and leave the rest of the implementation to another developer. Because the **abstract** class has some missing implementation, an abstract class cannot be instantiated. The following statement would generate a compile-time error:

```
Modem modem = new AbstractModem(); // generates compile-time error
```

NOTE

An interface is abstract by nature because all its methods are abstract. Some people think of an abstract class as a mixture of a concrete class and an interface. Some people prefer using abstract classes as a way of defining a behavioral protocol for interfaces.

NOTE

Abstract classes cannot be instantiated, but they can be subclassed.

Here are some important differences between an interface and an abstract class:

- An interface contains only the method signatures whereas an abstract class may have some of its methods implemented.

- All of an interface's methods are public by default. You cannot apply any other access modifiers to the methods declared in an interface. In an abstract class, the implemented methods can have access modifiers applied to them in their declarations. For this, the methods have to be public in an interface. Declaring them **protected** or **private** would result in an error. In an abstract class, you can apply a **protected** modifier to an implemented method but you cannot make it **private**.

- An interface can extend multiple interfaces. An abstract class cannot be extended from more than one abstract class.

- All methods in an interface are implicitly abstract. An abstract class may have a few concrete methods.

- An interface does not have a constructor. An abstract class may declare a constructor.

Summary

This chapter covered several important features of class declarations in Java. You saw the use of the **static** keyword in classes. The **static** keyword can be applied to methods and fields of a class. A method that is declared **static** can be invoked without the enclosing class being instantiated. A static field behaves like a program constant.

Java provides interfaces to incorporate the benefits offered by multiple inheritance in other languages. An interface consists of method signatures (with no implementations) and only **final** variables. A class uses an interface with the help of an **implements** keyword. The implementing class must provide implementation for all methods of the implemented interface; otherwise, the class becomes abstract. An interface can extend another interface. A class may implement multiple interfaces.

An abstract class implements some of the methods of the interface it inherits. An abstract class cannot be instantiated; however, another class can extend it. You create abstract classes when you do not know the implementation of some of the interface methods at the time of development.

In the next chapter, we define and use an inner class and discuss the many aspects of it.

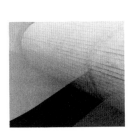

CHAPTER
7

Nested Classes

n the previous chapter we covered the use of static fields, methods, and initializers. You learned an important feature of Java language—the interfaces. In this chapter, you will learn another powerful feature of classes—that is, nested or inner classes. As the name suggests, you can embed a class declaration within another class. This gives you the power to hide your classes within an outer class. Embedding a class within another class has many more repercussions than simply hiding it from the outside world. An inner class may be declared not just within a class definition, but also within a method of a class or even in the parameter to a method. Such classes can also be anonymous. Given these possible combinations, it becomes a challenge to define the visibility rules for various identifiers included in such classes. Fortunately, you do not have to define these rules; the creators of Java have already done that. You simply need to learn the various rules, and that's what you will be doing in this chapter.

In particular, you will learn about the following:

- Nested (inner) classes
- Local classes
- Anonymous classes

Nested Classes

So far in this book, you have seen several examples of class declarations. We have defined fields and methods within a class declaration. So how about declaring a class within another class? Java allows us to have such a declaration. A class defined within another class is called a *nested* class. Why would you declare a nested class? There is more than one reason to do so, as we will discuss shortly. But first, here is the structure of the nested inner class declaration:

```
class OuterClass {

    ...
    static class StaticNestedClass {

        ...
    }
    class InnerClass {

        ...
    }
}
```

The **OuterClass** defines two inner classes: **StaticNestedClass** and **InnerClass**. The **StaticNestedClass** is declared with the **static** modifier, whereas the **InnerClass** is nonstatic. You learned the use of the **static** keyword in the previous chapter. The static and nonstatic inner classes have different significance and are therefore categorized separately. Two additional types of inner classes are local and anonymous. You will learn about all these different types of inner classes as you read this chapter. First, though, we'll discuss the purpose of using nested classes.

Why Use Nested Classes?

There are several compelling reasons for using nested classes:

- They allow logical groupings of related classes.
- They provide increased encapsulation.
- They lead to more readable and maintainable code.

Sometimes a class may be useful to only one other class. A typical example of this is the event listener classes defined in Java for its GUI components (the event listener classes are dealt with in greater detail in Chapter 13). For instance, let's say you use a command button in several applications. When the user clicks the button, the application executes a certain piece of code specific to that application. You may now declare a class that defines a method to process the click action initiated by the user. As such, a class may not have any significance outside the declaring class and therefore may be declared "inner." As another example, suppose that you are required to filter out all the odd numbers in a randomly generated array of integers. This filtering may be done on several random arrays. In such a situation, you would create a class that defines filtering methods. Such a class would have not much value outside the class that creates random arrays—meaning that it is not really reusable outside the random array-generation class. This filtering class would be an ideal candidate for creating an inner class. (We create this filtering class in the next section.)

The second useful benefit of creating nested classes is that it allows increased encapsulation. Consider that the **HayesModem** class from Chapter 6 is required to create an object for processing the internal read buffer. If you create a class outside the definition of **HayesModem**, you would need to provide the getter/setter methods on the read buffer attribute of the **HayesModem** class, making it accessible to the other code in the application. You may not want to do this—that is, to expose the private read buffer to the outside code. Therefore, you could create an inner class within the definition of the **HayesModem** class. This class would have access to all the private members of the **HayesModem** class, thus keeping them protected from exposure to the outside world. This inner class may also be declared **private** to hide it from the outside world. As you can see, this increases encapsulation—the data and the methods that operate on them are kept together.

Lastly, the use of inner classes make the code more readable and maintainable. Just imagine if the event listener and the filtering classes we just discussed were declared as outside classes. In this case, the definitions of these classes could be made anywhere in the project, and the project itself may consist of hundreds of Java files. Thus, you could easily get lost in searching for class definitions in a large project. Creating and keeping these classes embedded in a top-level class where they are used makes the code more readable and maintainable.

Classifications of Nested Classes

The nested classes are classified as follows:

- static
- nonstatic (or inner)
  - local
  - anonymous

To create a static nested class, you use the **static** keyword in front of the class declaration, the same way you declare a static field or a method within the enclosing class. Just like a static method cannot refer to the nonstatic members of the enclosing class, a static inner class cannot refer to the nonstatic members of its enclosing class. To refer to the nonstatic members, it has to use an object reference to the enclosing class. To access a static nested class, you need to use its fully qualified name, using the syntax ***OuterClassName.StaticNestedClassName***. To create an object of a static nested class, use the following syntax:

```
OuterClassName.StaticNestedClassName ClassObjectName =
            new OuterClassName.StaticNestedClassName();
```

From this syntax, you can see that a static nested class is just like any other top-level class. It is simply nested in another top-level class for packaging convenience.

As mentioned earlier, the nonstatic nested classes are also called inner classes. An inner class is associated with an instance of its enclosing class. It has direct access to the outer class's fields and methods. An inner class cannot define any static members because it is always associated with an instance. An instance of an inner class can exist only within an instance of its outer class. You may create multiple instances of the same inner class within a single instance of the enclosing class. To create an instance of the inner class, you must have an object of the outer class. The following code snippet illustrates this:

```
InnerOddsIterator iterator = this.new InnerOddsIterator();
while (iterator.hasNext()) {
    int returnValue = iterator.getNext();
```

This code snippet is taken from the program we will discuss later in this section. The **InnerOddsIterator** class is an inner class. To create an instance of this class, we use the call **this.new**, where **this** refers to the instance of the current class. The **new** keyword instantiates the class specified on its right side. The reference to the instance of the inner class is held in the **iterator** variable. We will use this variable to access the members of the inner class. Both **hasNext** and **getNext** are the methods of this inner class.

The last two types of nested classes—that is, local and anonymous—fall under the category of inner classes. An inner class defined within the body of a method is called a *local inner* or simply a *local class*. The scope of a local class is restricted to the method's scope. An anonymous inner class is an inner class declared within the body of a method without a name given to it. You will use anonymous classes while studying the building of a GUI in Chapter 13.

Now that you have seen the benefits of using inner classes and their classifications, let's look at a concrete example of using inner classes.

Demonstrating the Use of Inner Classes

Suppose you are required to create an application that generates a random list of odd numbers. The list itself should consist of a random number of entries. For this, you will first generate a fixed number of integers. You will then iterate through these entries to filter out only the odd numbers. You would define this filtering functionality in an inner class because this functionality would be of little use outside the scope of the current application. The purpose of declaring a class rather than a method is the ability to use this class for creating multiple lists within the application. The complete program for generating a random list of odd numbers is given in Listing 7-1.

Listing 7-1   *A Filtering Program That Uses an Inner Class*

```
public class DynamicOddsGenerator {

    private final static int SIZE = 25;
    private int[] arrayOfInts = new int[SIZE];

    public DynamicOddsGenerator() {
        for (int i = 0; i < SIZE; i++) {
            arrayOfInts[i] = (int) (Math.random() * SIZE);
        }
    }

    public void printOdds() {
        InnerOddsIterator iterator = this.new InnerOddsIterator();
        while (iterator.hasNext()) {
            int returnValue = iterator.getNext();
            if (returnValue != -1) {
                System.out.print(returnValue + " ");
            }
        }
        System.out.println();
    }

    //inner class implements the Iterator pattern
    private class InnerOddsIterator {

        private int next = 0;

        public boolean hasNext() {
            return (next <= SIZE - 1);
        }

        public int getNext() {
            int retValue = arrayOfInts[next++];
            if (retValue % 2 == 1) {
                return retValue;
            }
            return -1;
        }
    }

    public static void main(String s[]) {
        DynamicOddsGenerator numbers = new DynamicOddsGenerator();
        numbers.printOdds();
    }
}
```

The program first declares an array of 25 integers:

```
private final static int SIZE = 25;
private int[] arrayOfInts = new int[SIZE];
```

The constructor fills this array with randomly generated numbers:

```
for (int i = 0; i < SIZE; i++) {
    arrayOfInts[i] = (int) (Math.random() * SIZE);
}
```

Some of the numbers in the array will be odd and some will be even. The **printOdds** method prints all the odd numbers stored in this array. The method first creates an instance of an inner class that provides this filtering functionality:

```
InnerOddsIterator iterator = this.new InnerOddsIterator();
```

The **InnerOddsIterator** is an inner class that implements the Iterator design pattern and provides the **hasNext** and **getNext** methods. The **hasNext** method checks whether you have reached the end of the list and thus is used in the loop termination condition:

```
while (iterator.hasNext()) {
```

NOTE
Iterator is one of the patterns defined in Design Patterns: Elements of Reusable Object-Oriented Software, *by the "Gang of Four": Erich Gamma, Richard Helm, Ralph Johnson, and John M. Vlissides).*

The **getNext** method returns the number only if it is odd; otherwise, it returns –1:

```
int returnValue = iterator.getNext();
if (returnValue != -1) {
    System.out.print(returnValue + " ");
}
```

The **InnerOddsIterator** class is declared with a **private** modifier with the intention of keeping it totally private to the enclosing class:

```
private class InnerOddsIterator {
```

TIP
*Generally, you will not declare the inner classes **public** unless you really find a valid reason for using an object of an inner class outside the scope of the enclosing class.*

NOTE
*An inner class is just a member of an outer class and therefore can be declared **private**, **public**, **protected**, or **package private** (default). An outer class can only be declared **public** or **package private**. The same rules apply to the declaration of interfaces, as you learned in Chapter 6.*

The inner class declares a private field called **next**:

```
private int next = 0;
```

The **hasNext** method returns the next index in the array provided you have not crossed the limits of the array:

```
public boolean hasNext() {
    return (next <= SIZE - 1);
}
```

The **getNext** method checks whether the element value at the current index is an odd number. If so, it returns this number; otherwise, it returns –1 to the caller. Note that **SIZE** is a static constant defined in the outer class and is accessed within the body of the inner class.

The **main** method defined in the outer class simply instantiates it and invokes the **printOdds** method on it:

```
DynamicOddsGenerator numbers = new DynamicOddsGenerator();
numbers.printOdds();
```

Some typical output is shown here:

```
1 19 11 13 19 7 5 15 13 23 5
```

Note that every time you run the program, you will get a different list of odd numbers. The number of generated entries will also vary on each run.

NOTE
Inner classes were added in JDK1.1.

Accessing an Inner Class from the Outside

If an inner class is declared with a **public** access modifier, it can be instantiated from outside the scope of its enclosing class. This is illustrated in the program shown in Listing 7-2.

Listing 7-2 *A Program Illustrating Inner Class Visibility*

```
class Outer {

    private int counter=0;
    public class Inner {

        public void someMethod() {
            counter++;
        }
    }
}
```

```
        public int getCount(){
            return counter;
        }
    }
public class InnerClassExample {

    public static void main (String[] args) {
        Outer outer = new Outer();
        Outer.Inner inner = outer.new Inner();
        inner.someMethod();
        System.out.println ("Counter: " + outer.getCount());
        inner.someMethod();
        System.out.println ("Counter: " + outer.getCount());
    }
}
```

In the application's **main** method, the program creates an instance of the **Outer** class. To create an instance of the **Inner** class that is embedded in the definition of the **Outer** class, you use the following statement:

```
Outer.Inner inner = outer.new Inner();
```

Note that this statement uses the following syntax for a fully qualified name to create a variable of the **Inner** class type:

```
OuterClassName.InnerClassName
```

The **new** operator creates an instance of the **Inner** class. Once the program obtains an instance of the **Inner** class, it calls its **someMethod** twice and prints the value of the **private** variable **counter** in each case. Because a **private** variable cannot be accessed directly from outside the scope of the declaring class, the program uses the public **getCount** method to access this variable. If you run this application, you will see the following output:

```
Counter: 1
Counter: 2
```

Note that the value of the **counter** variable changes after each invocation of **someMethod**.

Accessing Shadowed Variables

When a variable declared within a certain scope (block, method, or inner class) has the same name as a variable declared in an outer scope, we say that the outer variable is *shadowed*. An inner class may declare a variable having the same name as the one defined in the outer class. The program in Listing 7-3 shows you how to differentiate between the shadowed and the original variables.

Listing 7-3   *A Program Illustrating Shadowed Variables in Inner Classes*

```
class Outer {

    private int size = 10;
    public class Inner {

        private int size=20;
        public void someMethod (int size) {
            System.out.println ("Method parameter (size): " + size);
            System.out.println ("Inner size: " + this.size);
            System.out.println ("Outer size: " + Outer.this.size);
        }

    }
}
public class ShadowedVariableExample {

    public static void main (String[] args) {
        Outer outer = new Outer();
        Outer.Inner inner = outer.new Inner();
        inner.someMethod(5);
    }
}
```

The **Outer** class declares a field called **size**. The **Inner** class declares a field with the same name. The **Inner** class defines a method called **someMethod**. This method takes a local parameter having the name **size**. In the method implementation, we now have to differentiate between these three variables having the same name **size**. If you use the field name **size** as is, without any qualifier, as shown in the following statement, it will refer to the method argument:

```
System.out.println ("Method parameter (size): " + size);
```

If you use the qualifier **this** in front of the field name, it refers to the field declared in the current class field, as shown in the statement here:

```
System.out.println ("Inner size: " + this.size);
```

To access the **size** variable declared in the **Outer** class, you need to use the notation **Outer.this.size**. This is shown in the following program statement:

```
System.out.println ("Outer size: " + Outer.this.size);
```

To verify these statements, in the application's **main** method, we invoke the **someMethod** method of the **Inner** class. The program output is shown here:

```
Method parameter (size): 5
Inner size: 20
Outer size: 10
```

You can compare the output with the values assigned to the three variables in the program code.

Important Points to Note

Here's a summary of some important points on the use of inner classes:

- The name of the inner class must differ from the name of its enclosing outer class.
- When you compile the outer class, the compiler generates a separate .class file for each of its inner classes. The name of the .class file is ***OuterClassName$InnerClassName***.
- The inner class can use both the class and instance variables of enclosing classes and local variables of enclosing blocks.
- The inner class may be declared using any of the available access modifiers. A private inner class can only be accessed within the outer class scope.
- An inner class can be an interface. Another inner class then implements this interface.
- An inner class can be abstract.
- An inner class that is declared **static** automatically becomes a ***TopLevel*** class.
- You cannot declare a **static** member inside an inner class unless the inner class itself is declared **static**.
- An inner class that wants to use a static variable must be declared **static**.
- The **static** keyword can be applied to an inner class and not to an outer class.

Member Classes

A nonstatic class defined within a class is called a *member* class of the enclosing class. A member class is commonly used as a helper class to the enclosing class. A member class can access the instance fields of the enclosing class, whereas a nested top-level class cannot do so. To refresh your memory, a nested top-level class is an inner class declared with a static modifier. Therefore, if you want objects of an inner class to have access to the fields of the enclosing class, you will declare it as a member class rather than as a nested top-level class. All objects of a member class will have access to the same field of the enclosing class.

Here are the main features of member classes:

- Every instance of a member class is internally associated with an instance of its outer class.
- The methods of a member class can implicitly refer to the fields defined by the enclosing class, including those that are declared **private**.

Local Classes

A class declared within a block of Java code is called a *local* class. Typically, such a block would be a method, but local classes may also be declared within static initializers and constructors of a class. A local class declared within the constructor of the enclosing class is shown in Listing 7-4.

Listing 7-4 *A Program Demonstrating Local Class Declarations*

```
public class OuterClass {

    public OuterClass() {
        class Local {

            public Local() {
                // local class constructor code here
            }
        }
        new Local();
    }

    public void instanceMethod() {
        new OuterClass();
    }
}
```

The constructor instantiates the **Local** class and uses this object within its scope. The **instanceMethod** is the member method of the **OuterClass** that creates an instance of it. During this instantiation, a copy of the **Local** object would be created within the scope of the constructor.

Defining an Inner Class within Method Scope

The inner class may also be defined within a method. In this case, the visibility of the inner class is restricted to the method scope. The use of an inner class declaration within a method body is illustrated with a trivial example in Listing 7-5.

NOTE
The classic example of using inner classes within a method is the implementation of event listeners. GUI building is discussed in Chapter 13, where we'll discuss a practical use of the inner anonymous classes within a method declaration.

Listing 7-5 *Declaring Inner Classes Inside a Method*

```
class Outer {

    private int a = 20;
    public void someMethod(final int b) {
        class Inner {
```

```
            int c = 30;
            public void innerMethod() {
                System.out.println("Formal parameter (B): " + b);
                System.out.println("Outer Class variable (A): " + a);
                System.out.println("Inner Class variable (C): " + c);
            }
        }
        new Inner().innerMethod();
    }
}
public class InnerClassWithinMethodExample {

    public static void main(String[] args) {
        Outer outer = new Outer();
        outer.someMethod(10);
    }
}
```

The **Outer** class defines a method called **someMethod** that takes a parameter of type **int**. Within the method body, we declare an inner class called **Inner**. The inner class declares a local variable, **c**, and defines a method called **innerMethod**. The method implementation accesses the formal parameter passed to the enclosing method and also the variables declared in the **Outer** and **Inner** classes. The **main** method of the application creates an instance of the **Outer** class and calls **someMethod** on it. **someMethod** in turn creates an **Inner** object and calls the method **innerMethod** on it. This outputs the three values, shown next, on the screen:

```
Formal parameter (B): 10
Outer Class variable (A): 20
Inner Class variable (C): 30
```

Note that the formal parameter to **someMethod** is declared using the **final** qualifier. An inner class can access the formal parameter only if it is declared **final**.

CAUTION
*A compile-time error is generated if a method within an inner class defined in the method body tries to access a formal method parameter that is not declared **final**. This is required to ensure that the method is not allowed to modify the value of the variable specified in the formal parameter.*

A Few Important Points on Local Classes
Here's a list of the important features of local classes:

- A local class is only visible and usable within the block of code in which it is defined.
- In addition to accessing fields defined by the containing class, local classes can access any local variables, method parameters, or exception parameters that are in the scope of the local method definition, provided they are declared with the **final** specifier.

■ Local classes cannot use the **new** and **super** keywords.

■ Local classes cannot contain fields, methods, or classes that are declared **static**. Because nested interfaces are implicitly static, local classes may not contain nested interface definitions.

■ Local classes cannot be declared with the modifiers **public**, **protected**, **private**, and **static**. These modifiers are used only on members of classes and are not allowed on local class declarations.

■ A local class cannot have the same name as any of its enclosing classes.

■ Interfaces cannot be defined locally.

■ A local class can use any **final** local variables or method parameters that are visible from the scope in which they are defined.

Anonymous Classes

A local class without a name is called an *anonymous* class. If you need only a single instance of a local class, you will create an anonymous class. Typically, a local class has a name and thus a declaration. You instantiate this class using its name. This process is meaningful if you are going to make multiple objects of the class. For a single object, you need not name the class. A typical use of this is found in the implementation of event listener methods in Chapter 16. To give you an idea of how it looks, consider the following code fragment:

```
button.addActionListener(new ActionListener() {

    public void actionPerformed(ActionEvent e) {
      System.out.println("The button was pressed!");
    }
});
```

Here, **ActionListener** is an interface that declares a sole method called **actionPerformed**. We create a new object of an anonymous class that implements the **ActionListener** interface. The object of this anonymous class is passed as a parameter to the **addActionListener** method on the button object.

Another classic example of the use of anonymous classes involves creating threads. The following small code snippet demonstrates this:

```
new Thread(new Runnable() {

  public void run() {
    try {
      while (true) {
        sleep(1000); System.out.print(".");
      }
    } catch(InterruptedException ex) {}
  }
}).start();
```

Here, we create an object of an anonymous class that implements the **Runnable** interface. The **Runnable** interface has a sole method called **run** that is implemented in the preceding code. The **new Thread** code creates a **Thread** object by taking the previously created anonymous object as a parameter. Rather than assigning the created **Thread** object to a variable, we directly invoke its **start** method, and in this particular case we do not need to refer to the created **Thread** object further in our program code. Thread programming is covered in depth in Chapter 17.

Another classic example of the use of anonymous classes is in Java's Collection Framework, which is covered in more detail in Chapter 16. The following example shows how to use a **Vector** for storing a list of friends:

```
Vector friendsList = new Vector(4) { // defining anonymous inner class
    {
        add("Sam");
        add("Smith");
        add("Anthony");
        add("Lisa");
    }
};
```

And here is one more example of the use of anonymous classes. The program in Listing 7-6 lists all the .txt files in the folder specified on the command line. You learn file handling in more detail in Chapter 9 and Chapter 10. Right now, however, simply examine how the anonymous class based on the implementation of the **FilenameFilter** interface is used.

Listing 7-6   *A Program Demonstrating the FileNameFilter Inner Class*

```
import java.io.*;

public class FileNameFilterExample {

    public static void main(String[] args) {
        File folder = new File(args[0]);
        String[] list = folder.list(new FilenameFilter() {

            public boolean accept(File folder, String fileName) {
                return fileName.endsWith(".txt");
            }
        });
        for (int i = 0; i < list.length; i++) {
            System.out.println(list[i]);
        }
    }
}
```

CAUTION
An important point to note in the creation of anonymous classes is that generally they should not be overly complex. If they are, they will clutter the enclosing class, making the code unreadable. So use them judiciously and only for small definitions.

Creating Anonymous Classes

In the previous section, you saw a few examples of how to use anonymous classes. Here is the syntax for creating them:

 new *ClassName*(*ArgumentList*_{opt}) {

    *classBody*_{opt}

}

or

 new *interfaceName*() {

    *interfaceBody*_{opt}

}

> **NOTE**
> *Anonymous classes cannot define constructors because they do not have names.*

Restrictions on the Use of Anonymous Classes

Here are the restrictions that apply to the use of anonymous classes:

- An anonymous class cannot have a constructor because there is no name associated with it.
- An anonymous class cannot define static fields, methods, or classes.
- You cannot define nested interfaces in an anonymous class because these interfaces are implicitly static.
- You cannot define an interface anonymously.
- Like local classes, anonymous classes cannot be made **public**, **private**, **protected**, or **static**. In fact, in the definition of the anonymous class syntax, there is no provision for specifying any modifiers in their declarations.

Compiled Anonymous Classes

Given that an anonymous class does not have a name, what is the name assigned to its .class file? The compiler produces two files when you compile a class containing an anonymous class. These are named ***EnclosingClassName.class*** and ***EnclosingClassName$1.class***. In the case of having more than one anonymous class in the same enclosing class, the compiler produces the corresponding .class files for each anonymous class by assigning a unique number to it after the $ sign.

Guidelines on Using Anonymous Classes

Finally, here are some tips on where to use local classes and where to use anonymous classes. In general, you should consider using an anonymous class instead of a local class under the following conditions:

- The class has a very short body.
- Only one instance of the class is needed.
- The class is used right after it is defined.
- The name of the class does not make the code any easier to understand.

Summary

A class definition may be embedded within another class. Such a class is called an *inner* class. An inner class can access the variables defined in its enclosing outer class. An inner class may be defined within the body of a class method. The rules on the use of inner classes were discussed in this chapter.

Local classes are declared within a block of code and are visible only within that block, just as any other method variable. A local class without a name is called an *anonymous* class. An anonymous class is used when only a single instance of a class is required, and it also makes code more readable.

In the next chapter, you learn how to handle compile-time and runtime errors in your program.

CHAPTER
8

Exception Handling

ooking at Murphy's Law, "If anything simply cannot go wrong, it will anyway," you know that you should always prepare yourself for the worst-case scenario. Things don't always turn out how you expect them to, and if anything can go wrong, it probably will. When this happens in real life, there may not be a remedial solution. Fortunately, in programming, if anything goes wrong, there is always a remedial action for you to take—this is called *exception handling*. When something goes wrong in your program, you say that an *exception* occurred. When you take a remedial action on it, you say that you *handled* the exception. Here is a famous quote by Douglas Adams:

> *The major difference between a thing that might go wrong and a thing that cannot possibly go wrong is that when a thing that cannot possibly go wrong goes wrong, it usually turns out to be impossible to get at or repair.*

To substantiate this quote in this chapter on exception handling, let's look at the most infamous computer bug in history. Due to an error in the software design, Ariane 5 Flight 501, which took place on June 4, 1996, failed within 40 seconds with a loss of a half-billion dollars. The reason? A tiny software bug. It occurred due to an exception thrown by some code that had originally been written for the earlier version of the rocket, Ariane 4. This particular routine, which could not be taken out easily, was left running although it was not really needed during flight. The code computed a big number that it tried to store in a short data type, causing an overflow condition. The program did not have a handler to catch this situation. Even an empty error handler would have probably saved the situation. But in the absence of an error handler, the error propagated to the operating system, which terminated the program. Unfortunately, the program was the guidance program for the rocket. All other computers on the flight had the same code and all of them crashed. Without any guidance, the rocket destroyed itself, which it was supposed to do in such a case.

From this story, you can certainly see the importance of exception handling. The proper use of exception handling can answer three basic questions:

- What went wrong?
- Where did it go wrong?
- Why did it go wrong?

The type of exception informs you of "what" went wrong. The exception stack trace tells you "where," and the exception message answers "why." To make the best use of exceptions, you need to follow three recommended rules:

- Be specific.
- Throw early.
- Catch late.

As you read this chapter, you will learn the "what," "where," and "why" as well as the importance of the three rules. So keep reading!

You have likely experienced errors while running many off-the-shelf applications on your machine. When an application error occurs, probably the application terminates abnormally and you have to redo everything you have done so far after restarting the application. An application error may occur due to several conditions, some of which may be beyond your control. For example, a network connection may get disrupted or a file that the application is trying to open may not exist. The application may try to access an out-of-bounds memory location, or the .class file the application needs may be missing. An application can fail under several such conditions. This chapter teaches you the intricacies of exception handling.

In particular, you will learn the following:

- What is meant by an exception
- The **try/catch/finally** constructs for catching and processing exceptions
- Exception classifications
- Throwing exceptions to the caller
- Creating your own exception classes
- Learning rules for exception declarations in overridden methods
- Obtaining and analyzing the stack trace
- Some guidelines for efficient exception processing

What Is an Exception?

When a running Java application fails, it creates an exception object encapsulating the error condition and throws it back to the running code. The executing program can now introspect the exception object, which is simply a Java object, to analyze the cause of the exception and take a corrective action. If no corrective action is taken, the program may terminate abnormally. In a multithreaded program, the thread that generated the unhandled exception may terminate while the other threads in the application continue running.

Error Types

Errors may be classified as fatal or non-fatal. The fatal errors are the ones that need to be terminated when the application cannot continue to function properly. These are sometimes also called *hard errors*. A typical example of this type of error is **OutOfMemoryError**. This is a serious problem, and application recovery in such a situation may not be viable. Generally, these types of fatal errors are thrown by the methods of the Java API—or by the Java Virtual Machine itself.

The other types of errors, known as *non-fatal,* may not be so serious, and application recovery in most cases is possible. As examples of this type of error condition, consider the case where your application tries to open a file. If the file is not locatable, the application will allow you to reenter the filename, along with the appropriate path, and reattempt to open the file. If the file is corrupted, the program may give you an opportunity to open another copy or to open an altogether different file. Consider another example: When you open a website in your browser, if the site is currently unavailable, the browser allows you to open another site. One more example: If an application is performing some mathematical computation on some input data and the data is out of range, the application detects the condition during computation and allows you to reenter the data before performing the computations one more time.

In all these cases, the error conditions do not cause the application to terminate. These are aptly called *non-fatal errors*. They occur in a running application, and a corrective measure is taken to prevent an application crash. There is another class of non-fatal errors that occur due to mistakes made by a programmer. For example, a **NullPointerException** is a typical error that is generated by error-ridden application code.

In this chapter, you learn the facilities provided in the Java programming language to capture these non-fatal error conditions and take corrective actions. These types of errors are more often called *exceptions,* and the corrective actions are referred to as *exception handling.*

The Non-fatal Errors

As you just learned, non-fatal errors are generally caused by inherent mistakes made by programmers. We typically call these mistakes *program bugs.* Whatever you do, these non-fatal errors or exceptions will always occur in your application—and when you least expect them. Fortunately, Java provides a mechanism to take preventive action against such unforeseen errors. Before I discuss this mechanism, let's first look at why such errors occur in the first place and why it is necessary to catch them. Consider an installer for a new software application. This new software may depend on some other software for its operation. For example, installing NetBeans requires that Java SE be preinstalled on your machine. The NetBeans installer therefore looks for Java SE on the machine where NetBeans is being installed. After searching the default directories, if it does not find Java SE, it raises an exception, prompting the user to specify the Java installation folder. If this error is not processed as indicated, the installer will terminate. By providing the error handler, the installer application gives the user an opportunity to try another folder. Consider another example: software that monitors the cabin pressure in an airplane. When the cabin pressure drops below a predetermined threshold, the oxygen masks automatically drop down. The drop in cabin pressure generates an exception, which is then processed gracefully, thus saving us from an application crash (perhaps even an airplane crash) and providing us with needed oxygen.

We'll now look at a simple program that demonstrates a typical mistake made by a programmer that causes a program error at runtime. Later, you'll learn how to handle this error condition. For this example, suppose you are writing software for recording the names of all the visitors who come by your exhibition booth. You expect a maximum of 100 visitors per day. Therefore, you allocate space for storing the names of 100 visitors—basically declaring an array of 100 strings. Most likely, you will also declare a constant set to 100 and use this in the rest of your application code. In the future, you can adjust the value of this constant to accommodate the growing needs of the software. Your application also needs to print the list of all those who visited your booth at the end of the day. The code for this program is shown in Listing 8-1.

Listing 8-1   *A Visitor Roster Application*

```java
import java.util.Random;

public class VisitorRoster {

    private final int MAX_CAPACITY = 100;
    private String[] visitors;

    public static void main(String[] args) {
        VisitorRoster roster = new VisitorRoster();
        roster.init();
        roster.registerVisitor();
        roster.printVisitorList();
    }
```

```
    private void init() {
        visitors = new String[MAX_CAPACITY];
    }

    private void registerVisitor() {
        Random r = new Random();
        System.out.println("Registering visitors");
        for (int i = 0; i < MAX_CAPACITY; i++) {
            visitors[i] = Long.toString(Math.abs(r.nextLong()), 36);
        }
    }

    private void printVisitorList() {
        System.out.println("\nToday's Visitors:");
        int i = 0;
        while (i <= MAX_CAPACITY) {
            System.out.println("Visitor ID # " + visitors[i++]);
        }
    }
}
```

The **VisitorRoster** class declares a string array called **visitorList** to store the visitor IDs. The **MAX_CAPACITY** constant decides the size of this array. For brevity, we have set this to 100. In a real-life scenario, this would be probably 1000 or more. The **main** function creates an instance of the application class and calls its **init** method to allocate the array. The **registerVisitor** method adds some randomly generated IDs to the array. Finally, the **printVisitorList** method dumps all the elements of the array onto the user console. Now, a common mistake made by inexperienced developers is to set the **while** condition as "less than or equal to" **MAX_CAPACITY**. Instead, this should simply be less than **MAX_CAPACITY**. Let's see what happens when we run this program with this condition. The program output is shown here:

```
Recording visitors
Today's Visitors:
    . . .
Visitor ID # 1v3qp79jupnvf
Visitor ID # 35nwc3u2w9zh
Visitor ID # 15z1o2bzl6di3
Visitor ID # deicu0zzg9cw
Exception in thread "main" java.lang.ArrayIndexOutOfBoundsException: 100
        at VisitorRoster.printVisitorList(VisitorRoster.java:35)
        at VisitorRoster.main(VisitorRoster.java:16)
Java Result: 1
```

The program printed the IDs of 100 visitors properly. However, it terminated abruptly when it tried to print the name of the 101st visitor, which of course does not exist. The program prints an error message on the console before terminating. The message specifies the type of error, which is **ArrayIndexOutOfBoundsException**. From the name, one can deduce easily that the error was caused because an invalid index value was used while accessing an element of the array. The message also tells the index value, which is 100. In addition, the error message indicates the methods along with the line numbers where the error originated and how it propagated throughout the program code.

You can easily catch and handle such errors in your programs so that they do not terminate abnormally. When a program terminates abnormally, typically it dumps some undecipherable messages to the user terminal. Worse is the case where GUI applications terminate abnormally and switch to a console mode, thus totally confusing the user. You better take care of such exceptions in your programs in order to provide a rich user experience.

The try-catch Statements

To catch such exception conditions in your program, Java provides a construct called the **try-catch** block. The susceptible code that may generate an exception at runtime is enclosed in a **try** block, and the exception-handling code is enclosed in a **catch** block. The syntax of a **try-catch** block is shown here:

```
try {
     blockStatements_opt
} catch ( ExceptionType exceptionObjectName ) {
     blockStatements_opt
}
```

A **try-catch** block in your program code looks like this:

```
try {
    // code that may generate a runtime or some kind of exception
} catch (Exception e) {
    // your error handler
}
```

If an exception occurs while the code in the **try** block is being executed, the Java runtime creates an object of the **Exception** class, encapsulating the information on what went wrong, and transfers the program control to the first statement enclosed in the **catch** block. The code in the **catch** block analyzes the information stored in the **Exception** object and takes the appropriate corrective action.

The exception in the previous example can be handled gracefully by putting the susceptible **printVisitorList** method in a **try-catch** block, as shown here:

```
try {
     roster.printVisitorList();
} catch (Exception e) {
    System.out.println("Quitting on end of list");
}
```

Now, when you run the program, you will get a more graceful quit message on the terminal at the end of the list. The partial output is shown here:

```
...
Visitor ID # gc051hh3hba7
Visitor ID # i98ivsnwunp4
Visitor ID # rapll6ouc0m6
Quitting on end of list
```

Unfortunately, this error message appears on the terminal in any iteration of the **while** loop if an error occurs in that iteration, and not necessarily only at the end of the list.

You will learn how to handle errors in a better way in your exception handlers as you progress further in this chapter.

Classifying Exceptions

As you saw in the preceding example, the Java runtime always passes an **Exception** object to your exception handler. Because the types of exceptions or runtime errors that can occur in your application can be very large, it will be difficult to assimilate the information provided by a single **Exception** object. Therefore, the **Exception** class is categorized into several subclasses. Figure 8-1 shows the high-level view of the **Exception** class hierarchy.

At the top of the class hierarchy you have the **Throwable** class. All other exception classes, including your own designed exception classes, inherit from the **Throwable** class. Both **Error** and **Exception** are subclasses of **Throwable**. The **Error** class denotes the fatal errors, and the **Exception** class denotes the non-fatal errors, discussed earlier. We will be focusing on the **Exception** class hierarchy, which has several subclasses, each meeting a specific situation. For example, the class **ArrayIndexOutOfBoundsException** is used for designating an illegal access to an array element, whereas the class **ArithmeticException** describes an exception that may occur during an arithmetic operation.

The purpose behind creating this exception hierarchy is to give you the option of treating various exception cases differently and to allow specialized information to reside in exception classes specific to particular situations.

Several subclasses of the **Exception** class are provided for this purpose so that you can catch a specific type of exception. For each specific type of exception you want to capture, you have to write a separate **catch** block. Thus, your code will consist of multiple **catch** blocks when you want to handle different types of exceptions differently. The order in which these blocks are defined in your code is also important. When the code inside a **try** block throws an exception, its **catch** clauses are examined in their order of appearance in the source file. Your program should first try to catch an exception of a subclass type. If no such subclass exceptions are

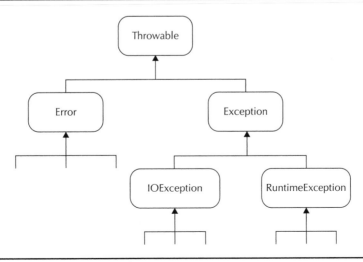

FIGURE 8-1.   *Exception class hierarchy*

handled, eventually your code provides an exception handler for the most generic **Exception** class. The syntax for incorporating this feature is shown here:

```
try {
    blockStatementsopt
} catch ( ExceptionType1 exceptionObjectName1 ) {
    blockStatementsopt
}
    ...
} catch ( ExceptionTypeN exceptionObjectNameN ) {
    blockStatementsopt
}
```

A typical **try** with multiple **catch** blocks looks like this:

```
try {
    // code that may generate a runtime exception
} catch (ReadOnlyBufferException e1) {
    // your error handler
} catch (UnsupportedOperationException e2) {
    // your error handler
} catch (Exception e) { // other catch blocks
    // your error handler
}
```

Java SE 7 has added new syntax for catching multiple exception types in the same **catch** clause, as shown here:

```
try {
    // code that may generate a runtime exception
} catch (ReadOnlyBufferException | UnsupportedOperationException e1) {
    // your error handler
}
```

When you use this syntax, you provide a common error handler for all these types of exceptions.

NOTE
A subclass exception must be handled before its superclass exception.
If you write an **Exception** *handler block as the first block in your*
multiple-exception-handler code, this would always get called
whenever an exception occurs and the code provided in other
exception handlers would never get called. The compiler catches this
error and complains about "unreachable code."

Let's now look at an example where the running code generates multiple types of exceptions. Rather than providing a generic exception handler to catch all types of exceptions, we provide an exception handler for each type of exception that may be generated by the running code. The application asks the user to enter a valid URL, opens it in the program using the built-in **URL** class, and dumps its contents (albeit in simple text format, for simplicity) to the user console. Now, what kinds of errors can you envision in this simple application? At the simplest level, the user might not enter any URL, the entered URL might be invalid, the user might forget to specify the protocol, there might be an error opening the URL, and the data reading might generate I/O errors—there could be any number of unforeseen errors. Our program will try to safeguard against all these errors, and if an error occurs, it will take corrective action to ensure against a program crash. Listing 8-2 illustrates this use of multiple exception handlers.

Listing 8-2   *Program Illustrating Multiple Exception Handlers*

```java
import java.io.*;
import java.net.*;

public class MultipleExceptionsExample {

    public static void main(String[] args) {
        String urlStr = null;
        while (true) {
            try {
                System.out.print("Enter url: ");

                BufferedReader reader = new BufferedReader(
                  new InputStreamReader(System.in));

                urlStr = reader.readLine();

                if (urlStr.length() == 0) {
                  System.out.println("No url specified:");
                  continue;
                }

                System.out.println("Opening " + urlStr);

                URL url = new URL(urlStr);

                reader = new BufferedReader(new InputStreamReader(
                    url.openStream()));

                System.out.println(reader.readLine());
                reader.close();
            } catch (MalformedURLException e) {
                System.out.println("Invalid URL " + urlStr + ": "
                    + e.getMessage());
            } catch (IOException e) {
                System.out.println("Unable to execute " + urlStr + ": "
                    + e.getMessage());
            } catch (Exception e) {
                System.out.println(e.getMessage());
            }
        }
    }
}
```

Note that the application uses certain classes from the **java.io** and **java.net** packages, which are discussed in depth in Chapter 9 and Chapter 20. To understand the current application, you do not need a deep understanding of these classes. We will focus mainly on what happens when the execution of the code within these classes generates errors at runtime.

The **main** method defines an infinite loop to accept the user input endlessly. The user is asked to enter a desired URL. The program reads the input using the following lines of code:

```
BufferedReader reader = new BufferedReader(new InputStreamReader(System.in));
urlStr = reader.readLine();
```

The **BufferedReader** class is discussed in Chapter 9, and **InputStreamReader** is discussed in Chapter 10. It suffices to say here that these lines of code read a line of input from the keyboard (until the ENTER key is pressed) and assigns it to the **urlStr** variable. The program then checks whether the user indeed input some string with the following statement:

```
if (urlStr.length() == 0) {
    System.out.println("No url specified:");
    continue;
}
```

This takes care of one of the error conditions mentioned earlier. If there is no input, the program simply loops back and asks the user to reenter the URL. Next, we try to establish a connection to this URL using the following statement:

```
URL url = new URL(urlStr);
```

At this time, if the URL is invalid, it will generate an error. This is caught in the following exception handler:

```
catch (MalformedURLException e) {
    System.out.println("Invalid URL " + urlStr + ": " + e.getMessage());
}
```

The following output shows what happens when an invalid URL is entered:

```
Enter url: google.com
Opening google.com
Invalid URL google.com: no protocol: google.com
```

Because we forgot to input the protocol, let's try one more time by entering a protocol, as follows:

```
Enter url: ttp://google.com
Opening ttp://google.com
Invalid URL ttp://google.com: unknown protocol: ttp
```

Oops! This time we missed the **h** in **http**. The same exception handler has trapped the error, this time giving another message (unknown protocol), which again is an appropriate one. Now, let's enter the URL one more time without any mistakes. The output is as follows:

```
Enter url: http://google.com
Opening http://google.com
<!doctype html><html><head><meta http-equiv="content-type" content="text/html;
charset=ISO-8859-1"><title>Google</title><script>window.google={kEI:"BK9TTbv
XJIjfcbD5sOEI",kEXPI:"28317,28600,28641,28722",kCSI:{e:"28317,28600,28641,28
722",ei:"BK9TTbvXJIjfcbD5sOEI",expi:"28317,28600,28641,28722"},ml:function()
{},kHL:"en",time:function(){return(new Date).getTime()},log:function(c,d,
```

Wow! We got the contents of the Google home page. Now, the question is, why did we include another exception handler, **IOException**?

```
catch (IOException e) {
    System.out.println("Unable to execute " + urlStr + ": " + e.getMessage());
}
```

To understand this, try the following URL:

```
Enter url: http://google.com:81
```

You will get the following output:

```
Opening http://google.com:81
Unable to execute http://google.com:81: Connection timed out: connect
```

This time the program executed the code in the **IOException** handler. Finally, why do we have the most generic exception handler at the end?

```
catch (Exception e) {
    System.out.println(e.getMessage());
}
```

This is to account for all remaining unforeseen errors. This takes care of all the errors mentioned earlier, thus ensuring the program runs without crashing.

Combining Exception Handlers

Look at the following code segment that contains multiple exception handlers:

```
try {
    // Say some file parser code here...
} catch (IOException ex) {
    // log and rethrow exception
} catch (ParseException ex) {
    // log and rethrow exception
} catch (ClassNotFoundException ex) {
    // log and rethrow exception
}
```

The code parses the contents of a given file. The process may generate different types of exceptions, such as **IOException**, **ParseException**, and **ClassNotFoundException**. Each exception handler for these errors logs the exception and re-throws another exception to the caller. We discuss this re-throwing business later in the chapter. What is important here is that all exception handlers execute the same piece of code. So why not combine them? Java SE 7 facilitates this. Here's what the new code looks like:

```
try {
    // Say some file parser code here...
} catch (IOException ex | ParseException ex |
    ClassNotFoundException ex) {
    // log and rethrow exception
}
```

Here, all those exception handlers that have common code are combined by using a logical OR operator between their exception types. This makes the code simpler. However, this feature works only on Java SE 7 and above. If you want to take different actions for different exceptions, you do not have a choice other than to provide individual exception handlers, as stated earlier.

How Runtime Matches catch Blocks

Whenever an exception occurs in running code, the search for the first matching **catch** block begins and the rules listed here are followed:

- A thrown exception object is caught by the **catch** block that specifies the class of the occurred exception or its superclass.

- In the case of multiple **catch** blocks, these are evaluated sequentially in the order they are specified by applying the first rule. If a **catch** block is found, the rest of the **catch** blocks are ignored.

- A certain **catch** block will never be executed if a **catch** block containing its superclass is listed prior to it. In such situations, a compile-time error is generated.

- The compiler forces the programmer to handle all checked exceptions. In other words, you must provide error handling for all exceptions except for the **RuntimeException** and its subclasses.

- If the **try** block never throws an exception specified in the **catch** list, the compiler generates an error.

The finally Statement

In the program example discussed in the previous section, we made a URL connection to read the home page contents from the user-specified URL. We closed this connection by calling the **close** method on the stream object. Now, consider some slightly low-level code that makes a socket connection to another machine on the network and reads/writes data using this socket. During this entire communication, if an exception occurs, our exception handler handles the exception. If the communication was successful, our program would usually close the socket before proceeding with the next program statement. However, the socket closing is required even if an exception occurs at runtime. For example, even though we may be able to make a successful socket connection, an exception might occur during the read/write operations. Obviously, the socket needs to be closed in this case too. To take care of such situations, Java provides a construct called **finally**. The **finally** block does this trick. We execute the socket-close operation in the **finally** block. The structure of a **finally** block is illustrated in Figure 8-2.

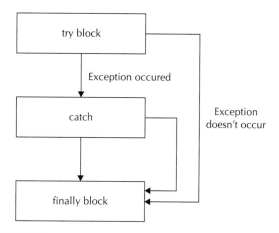

FIGURE 8-2. *The try/catch/finally program flow*

And the syntax of the complete **try/catch/finally** block is as shown here:

```
try {
     blockStatements opt
} catch ( ExceptionType  exceptionObjectName ) {
     blockStatements opt
}
finally {
     blockStatements opt
}
```

Typical **try/catch/finally** code is shown here:

```
try {
     // code that may generate a runtime exception
} catch (SubclassException e1) {
     // your error handler
} catch (SubclassException e2) {
     // your error handler
} catch (Exception e) {
     // your error handler
} finally {
     // this code is always executed
}
```

The code to be tested is enclosed in the **try** block. If an exception occurs during execution, an appropriate exception handler is called. After the exception is processed, the program calls the **finally** block and executes the code in it. What happens if you have not provided the handler for the type of exception that occurs in the running program? The code in the **finally** block still executes. What happens if the code under test does not generate an exception? In this case, too, the code in the **finally** block is called and executed. It means that the **finally** block code is always executed.

From this discussion, you can see that the ideal place for closing the socket connection would be the **finally** block. By placing the socket- or stream-close code in the **finally** block, we ensure that the socket or stream is always closed regardless of communication success or failure.

NOTE
*A **finally** block is typically useful for cleanup code or any mess created in the **try** block, especially when recovering resources in use.*

Guidelines on the Use of the finally Block

You may have a **finally** block in conjunction with a **try** block without a **catch** block. In other words, it is possible to eliminate the **catch** block totally in your program code. The syntax for this is shown here:

```
try {
        blockStatements_opt
} finally {
        blockStatements_opt
}
```

In such a case, your code would have the following structure:

```
try {
    // some code
} finally {
    // free resources
}
```

This is typically used for freeing resources used in the **try** block. It would always be executed regardless of whether or not the code in the **try** block generates an error. Now, if an error occurs in the code specified in the **try** block, the program tries to find an appropriate exception handler in the code; however, because no handler is found, the current thread terminates. Before terminating the thread, the program executes the **finally** clause specified in your code. After this, it also executes the **uncaughtException** method in the **ThreadGroup** object to which the current thread belongs.

The fact that the **Exception** object is thrown to the outer code can be used to our advantage in separating out the error-handling code from the resource-freeing code. This is shown in the following code block:

```
try {
    try {
        // some code
    } finally {
        // free resources
    }
} catch (Exception e) {
    // handle exceptions
}
```

If an exception occurs in the inner **try** block, it is caught in the exception handler provided by the outer **try** block. Thus, the code in the **finally** block becomes solely responsible for cleaning up resources while the code in the **catch** block takes the responsibility of handling exceptions. In fact, if the code in the **finally** block were to generate an exception, it would also be caught and handled in the **catch** block.

There is one design flaw in Java's **finally** syntax. The **finally** block allows you to include one of the jump statements, such as **break**. If the **finally** block is entered from a **throw** statement, which is discussed later in the chapter, the execution of a **break**, **continue**, or **return** statement in the **finally** block overrides the **throw** statement and aborts the error handling. Note that the **finally** block does not have access to the **Exception** object and therefore cannot determine whether it has been entered as a result of a **throw** statement or due to another cause.

NOTE
*C# takes care of this flaw in Java by prohibiting the use of any jump statements in a **finally** block.*

Another important point you should note here is that the **finally** block cannot handle errors. As stated earlier, it does not have access to the **Exception** object or any of the objects referenced by it. Therefore, it cannot log an error, diagnose it, or apply any corrections. It does not even know whether it was entered normally or as a result of an error. The philosophy behind a **finally** block is to free the resources and clean up any mess that the code might have created. It is typically used to achieve unconditional error cancellation.

CAUTION
*When a **return** statement is executed in your code, the **finally** block is never executed.*

CAUTION
*If an exception occurs in the **finally** block, the original exception generated in the corresponding **try** block is lost.*

Rules for Using the try/catch/finally Block

Before we move on to study the exception types, here's a quick summary of the rules for exception-handling code:

- A **try** block can have zero or more **catch** blocks, but only one **finally** block.
- The **catch** blocks and a **finally** block must always appear in conjunction with a **try** block.
- A **catch** or **finally** block must follow every **try** block.
- In case of multiple exception handlers, the order starts with the most specific exception at the top.

The try-with-resources Statement

So far, we have used the **finally** block for cleaning up resources. Java SE 7 has added a new syntax to the **try** block to provide an easier way of cleaning resources. With this new syntax, you open the resources that require automatic cleaning in the **try** statement. For example, if your code requires a file, you can now open it using the syntax

```
try (expression) {
    blockStatements_opt
}
```

where ***Expression*** could be **InputStream fis = new FileInputStream(source)**.

Your code would look like this:

```
try (InputStream fis = new FileInputStream(source)) {
    ...
}
```

After you are done with this input stream, do not bother closing it. The Java runtime will automatically close it. Thus, there is no need to add a **finally** block if this is the only resource in your code that requires cleanup. You may include multiple resources in the **try** block, each separated by a semicolon. This is illustrated in the program in Listing 8-3.

Listing 8-3 *Program Demonstrating the try-with-resources Syntax*

```
import java.io.*;
public class FileCopy {

    public static void main(String[] args) {
        try
            (InputStream fis = new FileInputStream(new File("src.txt"));
            OutputStream fos = new FileOutputStream(new File("dest.txt"))) {
                byte[] buf = new byte[8192];
                int i;
                while ((i = fis.read(buf)) != -1) {
                    fos.write(buf, 0, i);
                }
        } catch (Exception e) {
            e.printStackTrace();
        }
    }
}
```

Once again, do not worry about the file-handling code. We cover that in a later chapter. Just focus on the **try-with-resources** syntax. Here, we open two files in the **try** block. We do not close these files anywhere in the program and also do not provide a **finally** block. The files will be automatically closed at the end of the **main** method.

Likewise, you may allocate multiple resources in the **try** block. The only restriction is that each such resource must implement the **java.lang.AutoCloseable** interface. Note that this feature works only for Java SE 7 and above.

Checked/Unchecked Exceptions

In Java, exceptions are broadly classified as checked and unchecked. Sometimes, the checked exceptions are also called *compile-time exceptions* because your code would not compile if you do not handle a checked exception. All unchecked exceptions need not be caught in the program, and the code would compile even when they are not caught. Refer once again to Figure 8-1 for the Exception class hierarchy. All exceptions that come under **IOException** (including **IOException** itself) are called checked exceptions. All other exceptions that come under **RuntimeException**, including itself, and all subclasses of **Error**, including itself, are unchecked exceptions and do not require you to provide a handler in your code. When a checked exception occurs in a method, the method must either catch the exception and take the appropriate action, or pass the exception on to its caller. Thus, checked exceptions force programmers to deal with an exception that may be thrown at runtime. Examples of checked exceptions include **NoSuchFieldException**, **ClassNotFoundException**, and **NoSuchMethodException**. In the program in Listing 8-3, we used file handling and network programming. The use of these classes forced us to provide exception handlers. These are examples of checked exceptions.

In case of unchecked exceptions, the compiler does not force the programmer to catch the exception or to declare it in a **throws** clause (discussed later). The programmer need not even know that the exception could be thrown at runtime. Examples of unchecked exceptions are **IndexOutOfBoundsException**, **ArrayIndexOutOfBoundsException**, **ClassCastException**, and **ArithmeticException**.

NOTE
Although the compiler does not force you to provide a handler for unchecked exceptions, you could still provide one, if you want to.

The throws Construct

Due to the requirement to handle checked exceptions, you may have to insert the exception handler in your program at several places. This distribution of exception handlers throughout your program may clutter your code and make you lose focus on your core program logic. Also, in some situations, you may not want to handle an exception in the place where it is thrown. This is as good as saying, "I have generated an error. I do not know what to do with it, so I am passing along the details so you can take care of it." Java enables you to centralize your exception-handling code. With this facility, a method encapsulating the suspect code may simply pass on the exception information to its caller and without worrying about handling the exception. The caller, in turn, can pass on the generated exception information to its caller, and so on. Ultimately, the topmost calling method must handle the exception; otherwise, the result is a compilation error (because a checked exception is not caught anywhere in the program). This feature is provided with the help of the **throws** keyword.

Let's look at the example shown in Listing 8-4 so you can better understand this feature.

Listing 8-4   *Distributed Exception Handlers*

```
import java.io.*;
import java.net.*;

public class CentralizedExceptionHandlerApp {

    private static BufferedReader reader = null;
```

```
public static void main(String[] args) {
    String urlStr = null;
    try {
        CentralizedExceptionHandlerApp app =
                new CentralizedExceptionHandlerApp();
        app.openDataFile("data.txt");
        app.readData();
        reader.close();
    } catch (IOException e) {
        System.out.println("Error closing file");
    } catch (Exception ex) {
        System.out.println("Unknown error: " + ex.getMessage());
    }
}

void openDataFile(String fileName) {
    try {
        reader = new BufferedReader(new FileReader(fileName));
    } catch (FileNotFoundException e) {
        System.out.println("Specified file not found");
    }
}

void readData() {
    String str;
    try {
        while ((str = reader.readLine()) != null) {
            int n = Integer.parseInt(str);
            System.out.println(n);
        }
    } catch (IOException e) {
        System.out.println("Error while reading data");
    } catch (NumberFormatException ne) {
        System.out.println("Invalid number format, skipping rest");
    }
}
}
```

As with an earlier example, you have not learned about certain classes in this example so far in the book. Of course, if you are interested in them, you can always refer to javadocs (which by now you know how to use). Even if you do not want to learn more about these classes, you should still be able to learn the point of this example.

A quick look at the program tells you that the **CentralizedExceptionHandlerApp** class has three methods: **main**, **openDataFile**, and **readData**. All three methods have some sort of exception-handling code. If you do a little more observation, you will also realize that almost 50 percent of the total source code consists of exception handling. So why not gather all the exception handling into one place and make our methods cleaner? The modified program is given in Listing 8-5.

Listing 8-5 *Centralizing Exception-Handling Code*

```java
import java.io.*;
import java.net.*;

public class ModifiedCentralizedExceptionHandlerApp {

    private static BufferedReader reader = null;

    public static void main(String[] args) {
        String urlStr = null;
        try {
            ModifiedCentralizedExceptionHandlerApp app =
                    new ModifiedCentralizedExceptionHandlerApp();
            app.openDataFile("data.txt");
            app.readData();
            reader.close();
        } catch (FileNotFoundException e) {
            System.out.println("Specified file not found");
        } catch (IOException e) {
            System.out.println("Error closing file");
        } catch (NumberFormatException ne) {
            System.out.println("Invalid number format, skipping rest");
        } catch (Exception ex) {
            System.out.println("Unknown error: " + ex.getMessage());
        }
    }

    void openDataFile(String fileName) throws FileNotFoundException {
        reader = new BufferedReader(new FileReader(fileName));
    }

    void readData() throws IOException, NumberFormatException {
        String str;
        while ((str = reader.readLine()) != null) {
            int n = Integer.parseInt(str);
            System.out.println(n);
        }
    }
}
```

Examine this code and you will realize that the two methods, **openDataFile** and **readData**, do not contain any exception handlers. However, the code within these methods may still generate errors at runtime. So, who handles those? Note the use of the **throws** keyword in their declarations. The **openDataFile** method is declared to throw a **FileNotFoundException**. This means that if such an error occurs in the body of this method, it will be thrown to its caller, asking the caller to take care of it, if it wants to do so. Similarly, the method **readData** throws two types of exceptions: **IOException** and **NumberFormatException**. If these errors occur at runtime, they will be passed on to the caller for further processing. Now, let's look at the **main** method. Here, you will find several **catch** blocks. In fact, some of these **catch** blocks came from our earlier definitions of the **openDataFile** and **readData** methods. Therefore, the errors thrown by these methods are now handled in the **main** method. This makes your code cleaner. It allows you to centralize exception handling and pass on the exception-handling responsibility to somebody higher up the calling stack.

Throwing Multiple Exceptions

You may cause a method to throw more than one type of exception by listing all the desired exception types in the **throws** clause, separated by commas. This is what you have seen in the modified definition of our **readData** method from the previous example:

```
void readData () throws IOException, NumberFormatException {
```

Here, the method **readData** throws two types of exceptions to its caller. Therefore, it need not provide exception handlers for either of these two types. However, if the code inside **readData** can generate an exception of any other type, which is also a checked exception, **readData** must provide an internal exception handler. The exceptions of the unchecked type need not be caught but may result in abnormal program termination.

This indicates that a method may handle some of the errors itself and leave the handling of specialized exceptions to its caller.

User-defined Exceptions

Sometimes you may find that the exception messages given by the standard exception classes are not intuitive, and it may be necessary to provide more elaborate messages to the application user. In some other situations, you may want to capture the application errors and inform the user of them. An application error could simply be an abnormal condition that needs to be reported to the user and would not result in an application shutdown. To illustrate this point, we will develop an application in this section that reports the weather conditions to the user. Consider the case where a tourist agency sends the enrolled tourists to their desired locations. Once they are on their tour, each one reports the weather condition at their location. The agency simply logs the report sent by each tourist. The current temperature determines the weather condition at that time. If the temperature is more than 60°F, we generate a too-hot exception and if the temperature is less than 10°F, we generate a too-cold exception. For the in-between range, no exception is generated. The implementation of this scenario is shown in Listing 8-6.

Listing 8-6   *Program Demonstrating Custom Exceptions*

```
public class Tourist {

    public static void main(String[] args) {
        for (int i = 0; i < 10; i++) {
            Tourist person = new Tourist();
            try {
                person.takeTour();
                System.out.printf(
                    "Tourist %d say: This is cool%n", i + 1);
            } catch (TooHotException hx) {
                System.out.printf(
```

```
                        "Tourist %d say: %s%n", i + 1, hx.getMessage());
                    continue;
                } catch (TooColdException hx) {
                    System.out.printf(
                        "Tourist %d say: %s%n", i + 1, hx.getMessage());
                    continue;
                } finally {
                    System.out.println();
                }

            }
        }

    void takeTour() throws TooHotException, TooColdException {
        int temperature = (int) (Math.random() * 100);
        System.out.println("temperature = " + temperature);
        if (temperature > 60) {
            throw new TooHotException("Too hot here");
        } else if (temperature < 10) {
            throw new TooColdException("Too cold here");
        }
    }

    class TooColdException extends Exception {

        public TooColdException(String message) {
            super(message);
        }
    }

    class TooHotException extends Exception {

        public TooHotException(String message) {
            super(message);
        }
    }
}
```

Besides the main application class **Tourist**, the program defines two classes: **TooColdException** and **TooHotException**. Both these classes extend **Exception** classes and provide a constructor that takes a **String** type argument. The **Tourist** class declares a method called **takeTour**. The method is declared to throw the two aforementioned exceptions to its caller for it to handle them. In the method, we set the current temperature to a random value in the range of 0 to 100. We check this value against the preset values of 60 and 10. If the temperature exceeds 60°F, we throw an object of **TooHotException** to the caller using the following statement:

```
if (temperature > 60) {
    throw new TooHotException("Too hot here");
```

Note how the object is constructed. We use the **new** keyword, as usual, to create the object and then pass this instance to the caller of this method by using the **throw** keyword. Likewise, if the temperature is lower than 10°F, we throw a **TooColdException** to the caller.

In the **main** method, we create 10 tourists, and for each created tourist we call its **takeTour** method. In the exception handler, we create an appropriate message. In case of no exceptions, we create a "cool weather" message. In each iteration, we print the message and clear the buffer for the next tourist.

Partial output on a sample run of the application is shown here:

```
temperature = 37
Tourist 1 say: This is cool
temperature = 97
Tourist 2 say: Too hot here
temperature = 97
Tourist 3 say: Too hot here
temperature = 12
Tourist 4 say: This is cool
```

The throw Statement

As seen in the previous section, you need to construct an instance of a user-defined exception; the Java runtime cannot detect and create instances of user-defined exceptions. Thus, a user-defined exception is handled at the place of its occurrence. But what if you want to centralize the entire exception handling, including the user-defined application-specific exceptions, as explained earlier? In such a case, there has to be some mechanism of passing the exception to a caller. As seen earlier, the Java runtime takes care of this for the system-generated exceptions. For user-defined exceptions, Java provides the **throw** keyword, which allows the exception to be passed to its caller. The **throw** statement is not restricted to user-defined exceptions and can be used for both user-defined and system-generated exceptions, as explained further in this chapter.

TIP
*The **throws** clause declares that a method passes the exception generated during its execution to its caller, whereas the **throw** statement explicitly creates or obtains an **Exception** object and passes it to its caller.*

Re-throwing Exceptions

An exception event handler that receives an exception object is allowed to throw the received **exception** object to its caller. This may be done after the exception handler either has processed the exception or has decided not to process it at all. The JLS syntax for this is

```
try {
    blockStatementsopt
} catch ( ExceptionType exceptionObjectName ) {
    blockStatementsopt
    throw ( exceptionObjectName )
}
```

where *exceptionObjectName* for **catch** and **throw** is the same.

Here is how this will be done in your code:

```
try {
    // some arithmetic operation
} catch (ArithmeticException e) {
    // e may be partially processed here
    e.getMessage();
    throw (e);
}
```

The **catch** block partially processes the **ArithmeticException** object. It prints the message associated with the received exception object. After processing the exception object, it calls the **throw** method with exception object **e** as its parameter. The caller receives the exception object and may use it for further diagnosis.

Rather than throwing the received exception object, you may like to create your own exception object with a custom message and throw it to the caller. You have already seen how to do this by declaring your exception class. However, there is a better way, which is shown in the following code snippet:

```
try {
    // numerical processing code
} catch (ArithmeticException e) {
    Throwable ae = new ArithmeticException("Attempt to divide by zero");
    ae.initCause(e);
    throw(ae);
}
```

The exception handler now creates an instance of the original exception type and sets a custom message in it. The original exception is then embedded into the new object by calling the **initCause** method. Finally, the newly constructed object is thrown to the caller. The caller now has an exception object that contains a custom message created by the method in which an exception is generated, along with the cause of the exception. To retrieve the custom message, the caller calls the **getMessage** method on the received exception object. To get further information about the exception, the caller calls the **getCause** method on the exception object, as shown in the following code snippet:

```
System.out.println(e.getMessage());
System.out.println(e.getCause().getMessage());
```

The first statement prints the custom message to the console, whereas the second one prints the original error message.

CAUTION
*The **initCause** and **getCause** methods were introduced as of J2SE 1.4.*

The method of wrapping the original exception object into a custom object and throwing it to the caller is also sometimes called *exception chaining*. The exceptions are chained and passed to the caller.

Difference Between the throw and throws Keywords

As you can make out from the preceding discussions, the **throw** keyword (note the singular form) is used to force an exception. It can also be used to pass a customized message to the error-handling code. For example, the following statement throws a custom message in the **ArithmeticException**:

```
new ArithmeticException("Attempt to divide by zero");
```

The **throws** keyword is used when we know that a particular exception may be thrown or whenever we want to pass a possible exception.

The final Re-throw in Java SE 7

You have seen so far that to throw an exception higher up the caller hierarchy, your method must declare that exception type in the **throws** clause of its declaration. Now, consider a situation where your method may want to throw two different types of exceptions, as shown in the following code snippet:

```
public void compute() throws IOException, ParseException {
    try {
        // code which may generate IOException, ParseException
    } catch (Exception e){
        throw e;
    }
}
```

However, this code will not compile because we are trying to throw a more generic exception. For the code to compile, we will need to add the **Exception** type in the **throws** clause. This, too, will not compile if the **compute** method overrides a method that does not declare throwing the **Exception** type (this is explained in the next section). Java SE 7 solves this problem when we add a **final** keyword in the **catch** block, as follows:

```
catch (final Exception e){
```

Using the **final** keyword in the **catch** block allows us to throw the exact exception subtype that occurred. For example, if **IOException** occurs, then **IOException** would be thrown; if **ParseException** occurs, then **ParseException** would be thrown. The **final** keyword allows us to throw the exact exception that occurred without the need to add the **Exception** type to the method signature.

Declaring Exceptions in Overridden Methods

In Chapters 4 and 5, you saw the benefits of creating inheritance hierarchies to produce highly structured code. When you extend the classes, you override some of their methods in their subclasses. What if some of these methods are already declared to throw a few exception types? When you override these methods, you must observe certain rules:

- An overriding method must throw exceptions of the same type as the exceptions being thrown by the overridden method.
- An overriding method may throw exceptions that are subclasses of the exceptions being thrown by the overridden method.

- An overriding method cannot throw a superclass exception of an exception declared by an overridden method.
- In case of an overridden method throwing multiple exceptions, an overriding method must throw a proper subset of exceptions thrown by the overridden method.

To explain these rules, we'll look at a few code snippets. Here's the first:

```
class WebBrowser {

    public void makeConnection() throws IOException {
    }
}

class HTMLWebBrowser extends WebBrowser {

    public void makeConnection() throws ProtocolException {
    }
}

class RichTextWebBrowser extends HTMLWebBrowser {

    public void makeConnection() throws Exception {
    }
}
```

The **HTMLWebBrowser** class that inherits **WebBrowser** overrides the **makeConnection** method. This overridden method throws **ProtocolException**, which is a subclass of **IOException**. This satisfies the second rule in the list and is therefore permitted. The class **RichTextWebBrowser**, too, overrides the **makeConnection** method in its implementation. However, it tries to throw an **Exception** type, which violates the third rule and therefore won't compile. This explains why earlier I said that throwing the **Exception** type would not compile the code, causing us to use the **final** keyword in the **catch** block, which is a Java SE 7 feature. To explain the other rules, let's make some slight modifications to the earlier code snippet, as shown here:

```
class WebBrowser {

    public void makeConnection() throws IOException, RuntimeException {
    }
}

class HTMLWebBrowser extends WebBrowser {

    public void makeConnection() throws ProtocolException, EOFException,
            ArithmeticException, SecurityException {
    }
}
```

```
class RichTextWebBrowser extends HTMLWebBrowser {

    public void makeConnection() throws ProtocolException, SecurityException {
    }
}
```

Now, the **makeConnection** method in the base class throws two types of exceptions: **IOException** and **RuntimeException**. The overridden **makeConnection** method in the **HTMLWebBrowser** class throws four different types of exceptions. All these are the subtypes of either **IOException** or **RuntimeException**, thus adhering to the second rule. The **makeConnection** method of **RichTextWebBrowser** overrides the corresponding method of **HTMLWebBrowser**, but throws only a subset of exception types thrown by the overridden method. This satisfies the fourth rule and would thus compile without errors.

CAUTION

If a superclass method throws no exceptions, neither can the subclass method.

The situation stated in the nearby Caution can be overcome with a simple trick. You have seen how to construct and throw a custom exception object. In situations where you are not allowed to throw a checked exception, you can wrap a checked exception into an object of **RuntimeException** and throw it to the caller. This is illustrated in the program in Listing 8-7.

Listing 8-7 *Wrapping RuntimeException*

```
import java.net.*;

public class CustomBrowser {

    public static void main(String[] args) {
        HTMLWebBrowser app = new HTMLWebBrowser();
        try {
            app.makeConnection();
        } catch (Exception e) {
            System.out.println (e.getMessage());
        }
    }
}

class WebBrowser {

    public void makeConnection() {
    }
}

class HTMLWebBrowser extends WebBrowser {
```

```
public void makeConnection() throws RuntimeException {
    try {
        URL url = new URL("http://www.oracle.com");
    } catch (MalformedURLException e) {
        RuntimeException ae = new RuntimeException("Invalid url");
        ae.initCause(e);
        throw ae;
    }
}
}
```

The **makeConnection** method of the **HTMLWebBrowser** class knows that its code may generate an error at runtime; however, it would like its base class to take care of the error handling. The **makeConnection** method of the base class (**WebBrowser**) also does not process or throw an exception up the hierarchy. To overcome this problem, you can always create an object of **RuntimeException** in the overridden method, wrap the generated exception in it, and throw it up the hierarchy. The following three lines of code do this:

```
RuntimeException ae = new RuntimeException("Invalid url");
ae.initCause(e);
throw ae;
```

This trick works, and the compiler does not complain on the overridden method declaration. You may now process the custom exception object anywhere up the hierarchy. In our case, the exception is caught and processed in the **main** method.

Printing a Stack Trace

In some of the earlier examples in this chapter, you might have noticed that in the exception handler we used the following statement:

```
e.printStackTrace();
```

This statement prints a stack dump to the user console. Although, typically, this is used for getting the stack dump in case of errors, it can also be used in other situations where there are no errors. With J2SE 1.4 onward, this better way of analyzing a stack trace is available. For example, when you have a recursive function call in your program, such as a program that generates Fibonacci numbers, you may want to study how many times and when the recursive method is called. To get a stack trace, you construct a **Throwable** object and call its **getStackTrace** method. This is illustrated in the program given in Listing 8-8.

Listing 8-8   *Analyzing a Stack Trace*

```
public class FibonacciGenerator {

    public static void main(String[] args) {
        generate(3);
    }
```

```
    public static int generate(int n) {
        Throwable t = new Throwable();
        StackTraceElement[] frames = t.getStackTrace();
        for (StackTraceElement frame : frames) {
            System.out.println("Calling: " + frame.getMethodName());
        }
        if (n <= 2) {
            return 1;
        } else {
            return generate(n - 1) + generate(n - 2);
        }
    }
}
```

The program in Listing 8-8 computes and prints a Fibonacci number for a specified input. The recursive function **generate** does this. In each call to the function, it obtains a stack trace and prints the called method name to the console. The **getStackTrace** method returns an array of **StackTraceElements**. The program iterates through this array to print the method names pushed on the stack. The program output is shown for the case when the Fibonacci number for value 3 is computed:

```
Calling: generate
Calling: main
Calling: generate
Calling: generate
Calling: main
Calling: generate
Calling: generate
Calling: main
```

Note that the **generate** function calls itself twice recursively. Therefore, you will see multiple calls to **generate** between every two calls to the **main** function.

Thus, using this stack trace facility, you can get the stack dump anytime in your program and you do not have to necessarily wait for an exception to occur in the code.

TIP
*In J2SE 5.0 onward, you can obtain a stack trace of all the running threads by calling the **getAllStackTraces** static method of the **Thread** class.*

Asynchronous Exceptions

Before we conclude this chapter, let's discuss one more type of exception. The exceptions you have seen so far are synchronous in nature, in the sense that you know the point in the program where they occur and when they happen, and you process them immediately in the same thread. Contrary to this, an asynchronous exception may occur at any point in the execution of a program. For example, an internal error generated by the JVM is a type of asynchronous exception—you don't know when will it occur. Similarly, when you execute a **stop** method of the **Thread** or

ThreadGroup class (threads are discussed later, in depth), you cause an asynchronous exception in another thread. Handling such exceptions is nontrivial and beyond the scope of this book.

Guidelines for Using Exceptions

We have discussed several features of exception handling so far. Now, we'll look at some guidelines on how to use exception handling efficiently in your program code.

Use exception handling judiciously. Wherever your program code can perform a simple check to avoid errors, do it rather than waiting for the exceptions to occur. In other words, do not use exception handling unless you are required to do so. Let's suppose you have written a stack class and have written a method, **pop**, that pops an element from the stack. Before you perform a pop operation on the stack, you must confirm that the stack is not empty. A simple check will reveal this condition, and doing so will be more efficient than letting an exception occur in the running code. Another example would be checking the number of command-line arguments passed to your program. It would be more efficient to ensure that the user has indeed supplied the required number of parameters rather than letting an exception occur in the running code. In situations similar to our earlier example where an **ArrayIndexOutOfBoundsException** occurred, the real fix for the array access exception is not to handle the exception, but to fix the code.

Some developers put the **try/catch** block on every possible statement in the program code. This results in cluttering the code with several **try/catch** blocks and obscures the program's main logic. Organize all the suspected statements in a single **try** block and provide multiple handlers to this **try** block. If you prefer, you may throw the exceptions to the caller and centralize all the exception processing, as discussed earlier in this chapter.

Because Java makes it mandatory to handle all the checked exceptions, oftentimes programmers tend to provide an empty exception handler like the one shown here:

```
try {
    // do something
} catch (Exception e) {} // do not do this.
```

Never do this, because if an exception occurs at any time, it will be silently ignored. Ignoring an exception would result in an unpredictable program state, which would be difficult to diagnose and fix.

Another important question that comes to the programmer's mind is, Should I handle the exception or pass it on to somebody else? Whenever possible, handle the exception. It is always better to handle the exceptions near the place where it occurs initially. If you feel that centralizing the exception handling can improve the code readability, feel free to pass the exception to the caller.

Also, it is important that you make best use of the exception hierarchy. Wherever possible, provide the handlers for the subclass exceptions rather than the most generic exception. If the existing exception class does not adequately describe the exception in your problem domain, create your own exception class.

Lastly, and most important, do not forget the golden rules defined at the beginning of the chapter:

- Be specific.
- Throw early.
- Catch late.

Summary

This chapter discussed several aspects of exception handling in a Java program. A running program may encounter errors and may even crash. As a developer, you can minimize the occurrence of such situations by providing the exception-handling code in your program. The exceptions can be of two types: fatal and non-fatal. The fatal errors are usually beyond your control and typically result in an application crash. The non-fatal errors are under your control, and you can provide the appropriate exception handlers in your code to deal with exceptions when they arise.

Java provides **try/catch/finally** constructs to support exception handling. Because there can be several types of errors, Java has neatly classified them into logical classes. The entire exception hierarchy runs into several classes, all of which derive from the **Throwable** class. You can choose an appropriate subclass to handle an individual situation in your program. Java allows you to provide multiple handlers for a single **try** block in which you write the susceptible code. In situations where you are not able to find a built-in subclass that adequately describes your exception situation, you are allowed to provide your own exception class.

Java further classifies the exceptions into two types: checked and unchecked. All checked exceptions must be handled in your program code. This may clutter the code with several exception handlers. In such cases, you can centralize the exception-handling code by using the **throw** and **throws** constructs in your program code. The **throw** statement enables you to pass an exception object to the caller. The **throws** clause marks the specified method, indicating that the method will throw the exception of the specified type to its caller. Therefore, the caller must provide a handler for it.

When a subclass overrides a method that throws exceptions, it must observe certain rules. This chapter discussed those rules in depth. When an exception occurs, you can print a stack trace to see what went wrong. In J2SE 1.4 onward, you can obtain this stack trace even if there is no generated exception. Finally, the chapter concluded with a few guidelines for efficient coding of exception mechanisms in your programs.

In the next chapter, you learn I/O programming.

CHAPTER
9

Java I/O

S o far we have focused on Java language syntax, classes, interfaces, arrays, and other language-related stuff. Most of the programs discussed in earlier chapters used classes from the **java.lang** package, which were implicitly imported in the code. In a few programs, we used the classes from other packages such as **java.util**, **java.awt**, **java.net**, and **java.io**. Now that the language syntax is mostly covered, we will discuss the classes from these and other packages provided in Java libraries. One such important set of classes comes in the **java.io** package. This is one of the core packages of the Java language and was a part of JDK 1.0. These classes facilitate the input/output functionality in your programs. Typical examples of such functionalities include reading from the keyboard, sending some output to the console, storing data in a disk file, chatting with another user using peer-to-peer networking, transferring files, browsing the Web, and so on. Thus, the I/O classes are used in a wide range of applications, including the latest innovations such as voice and video calls, peer-to-peer gaming, and more.

In this chapter and the next, you will be introduced to several I/O classes. The **java.io** and **java.nio** packages define several useful classes that cannot be fully covered in a single chapter, so the discussion of I/O classes has been split accordingly. This chapter covers most basics of I/O, and the next chapter covers more advanced features, including all the latest updates. In particular, you will learn the following in this chapter:

- The stream classes
- The binary and character-oriented streams
- Accessing and manipulating the file system
- Reading and writing objects

Input/Output Streams

You may not have realized this, but you have already used some functionality of I/O classes in the previous chapters. In many of our programs, we used **System.out.println** to output a message to the user console. You learned earlier that **println** is a method executed on the **out** object. The **out** object is of type **OutputStream**, which is an abstract class. It is the superclass of all classes representing an output stream of bytes. A stream accepts bytes and sends them to some sink, as explained later in the section. Likewise, to read input from the user, we used the **System.in.read** method. The **in** is an object of type **InputStream**. Both **InputStream** and **OutputStream** belong to the family of I/O classes. The **System** class, which is defined in the **java.lang** package, contains three static fields, called **in**, **out**, and **err**. The **in** is of type **InputStream**, whereas **out** and **err** are of the **PrintStream** type, which is a subclass of **OutputStream**.

Java defines the functionality of its various I/O classes through streams. A *stream* is an abstraction and can be thought of as a flow of data from a source to a sink. A stream can be classified in two ways. A *source* stream, also called an *input* stream, initiates the flow of data. A *sink* stream, also called an *output* stream, terminates the flow of data. Source and sink streams are also called *node* streams. A stream is just a continuous flow of data. Like an array that holds some data, a stream does not have the concept of a data index. You cannot move back and forth in a stream. The data can only be accessed sequentially.

A stream either consumes or provides information. A stream is usually linked to a physical device. It provides a uniform interface to a device for data flow. In the case of an input stream, the device to which it connects may be a physical disk, a network connection, a keyboard, and so on. In the case of an output stream, it may be connected to a console, a physical disk, a network connection, and so on. Thus, when you use the input/output stream classes, your program code becomes independent of the device to which the stream connects. Examples of source streams are files and memory buffers. A printer or a console can represent a stream destination.

The streams in Java are of two types: byte and character oriented. The byte streams operate on bytes of data, whereas the character-oriented streams operate on characters, typically a Unicode character set. JDK 1.0 provided only byte-oriented streams. JDK 1.1 introduced character-oriented streams. Because the underlying mechanism for streams is still byte oriented, JDK 1.1 also introduced bridge classes to convert a byte stream into a character stream, and vice versa.

The I/O Class Hierarchy

Java provides a rich set of classes for I/O. A high-level class diagram for the I/O class library is shown in Figure 9-1.

All classes in Java inherit from the **Object** class, and so do the various I/O classes. The **InputStream** and **OutputStream** classes operate on byte data. The **Reader** and **Writer** classes work on characters. The **java.io.File** class provides the interface to physical files. Java SE 7 introduced the **java.nio.file.Path** class, which is considered the equivalent of **java.io.File** in the new API and provides much more sophisticated functionality.

The byte-oriented files work on 8-bit code and the character-oriented files work on 16-bit Unicode. We'll begin with the byte-oriented files. Both **InputStream** and **OutputStream** are abstract classes from which the various byte-stream-oriented classes derive their functionality. The **InputStream** class is a base class for all the input-related classes, and the **OutputStream** class is a base class for all output-related classes. These two classes provide several methods, such as **read**, **write**, **readInt**, **writeInt**, **readFloat**, **writeFloat**, and more, for reading and writing. The subclasses provide the implementations of these methods. Examples of these subclasses are **ByteArrayInputStream**, **FileInputStream**, **ObjectOutputStream**, and **PipedOutputStream**.

The Byte Streams

Let's discuss the various **InputStream** derived classes first. Figure 9-2 shows a few subclasses of **InputStream**.

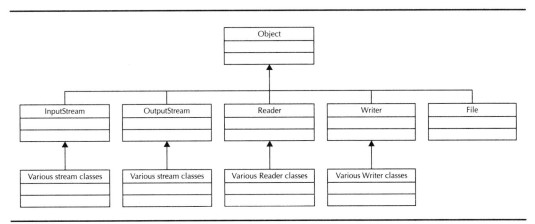

FIGURE 9-1. *The top-level I/O class hierarchy*

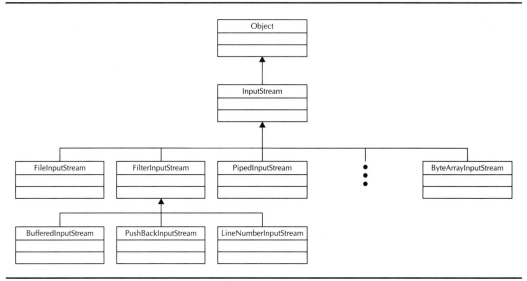

FIGURE 9-2. *Hierarchy of input stream classes*

As mentioned earlier, the number of classes in the Java I/O package is too large to cover all of them in a book like this. Therefore, we will take a more practical approach and discuss these classes through programming examples. The first programming example teaches you how to open a file, read its contents byte by byte, and then close the file. This program determines the length of the specified file in terms of the number of bytes it contains. Note that we are currently focusing on byte-oriented files. When we deal with a text file, we will use character-oriented stream classes, where each character (Unicode) consists of two bytes of data.

Determining File Length

The simplest way to determine the length of a physical file is to open it in binary mode. When you use the byte-oriented classes based on **InputStream** and **OutputStream**, the file will be opened in binary mode. When you use the character-oriented classes based on **Reader** and **Writer**, the file will be opened in character mode.

After opening the file, we read its contents a byte at a time until the end-of-file marker is reached. On every read operation, we increment a counter and then get the file length in the counter when the program terminates.

The program for determining the length of a file is given in Listing 9-1.

Listing 9-1 *File Length Program*

```
import java.io.*;

public class FileLength {

    public static void main(String[] args) {
        int count = 0;
```

```
            InputStream streamReader = null;
            if (args.length < 1) {
                System.out.println("Usage: java FileLength <filename>");
                System.exit(0);
            }
            try {
                streamReader = new FileInputStream(args[0]);
                while (streamReader.read() != -1) {
                    count++;
                }
                System.out.println(args[0] + " length = " + count);
                streamReader.close();
            } catch (FileNotFoundException fe) {
                System.out.println("File " + args[0] + " was not found");
                System.exit(0);
            } catch (IOException ie) {
                System.out.println("Error reading file");
            } finally {
                try {
                    streamReader.close();
                } catch (Exception e) {
                    e.printStackTrace();
                }
            }
        }
    }
}
```

The various I/O classes are defined in the **java.io** package. Thus, to use I/O, you need to import the **java.io** package at the top of your source program:

```
import java.io.*;
```

The **main** function accepts the command-line arguments. When you run the program, you will need to specify the name of some file on the command line. The program determines the length of this file and prints this value on the user console.

The command-line parameters are passed as arguments to the **main** method:

```
public static void main(String[] args) {
```

The **args** argument in the preceding program is an array of **String** objects, where **args[0]** represents the first command-line argument, **args[1]** represents the second command-line argument, and so on.

In the **main** method, we first check whether any command-line parameters are specified while invoking the application. We do this by checking the length of the **args** array:

```
if (args.length < 1) {
```

If there are no command-line arguments, the program prints a message to the user on how to run the application:

```
System.out.println("Usage: java FileLength <filename>");
```

The angular brackets around **filename** indicate that this is an optional parameter specified on the command line. If you do not specify this parameter, the program still runs.

After printing the message, we terminate the application gracefully by calling the **exit** method of the **System** class:

```
System.exit(0);
```

The parameter **0** (zero) is typically interpreted as an indication to the JVM that the program has terminated with success.

TIP
*Refer to javadocs to learn more about the **System** class.*

Assuming that the user specifies a command-line argument, the program will now proceed with the next statement:

```
try {
    streamReader = new FileInputStream(args[0]);
```

This statement creates an instance of the **FileInputStream** class by passing the first command-line argument as a parameter to it. The **FileInputStream** class constructor opens the file specified as a parameter for reading. The file is opened in binary mode. On success, it returns a reference to the open file; we store this reference in a variable (in our example, it is called **streamReader**). Note that this variable is of type **InputStream**, which is a superclass of **FileInputStream**.

TIP
*This may be a good time to look up the different constructors of the **FileInputStream** class in javadocs.*

As mentioned in the chapter on exception handling, opening a file is a checked operation and must be enclosed in a **try/catch** block. The file-opening operation may generate a **FileNotFoundException** at runtime, which must be caught in the program:

```
} catch (FileNotFoundException fe) {
    System.out.println("File " + args[0] + " was not found");
}
```

NOTE
*As discussed in Chapter 8, the **Exception** object provides detailed information on the type and cause of an exception. You should use this information in your code to generate an appropriate message to the user. In the current program, we provide different types of messages in each of the three exception handlers.*

After opening the file successfully, we call the **read** method of the **FileInputStream** class:

```
while (streamReader.read() != -1) {
    count++;
```

The statement **streamReader.read()** reads a byte from the stream and increments the file pointer to the next position.

NOTE
*If you look up the documentation of the **read** method in javadocs, it says that it returns an **int**. The method, no doubt, reads a byte, but returns it in **int** format. The file pointer is incremented by one—a byte length.*

The file pointer indicates the current position in the stream for reading or writing. When the file pointer reaches the end-of-file, the read operation returns –1 to the caller. Therefore, in our **while** loop, the test condition checks for this –1. For each byte read, we increment the **count** variable by 1. The **count** variable has been set to 0 at the start of the program. When the **while** loop terminates, the **count** contains the number of bytes read, which is the length of the specified file.

The **read** operation is also a checked operation, and you must provide an appropriate error handler for it. The **read** operation may generate an **IOException**. Therefore, we provide a corresponding **catch** block:

```
} catch (IOException ie) {
    System.out.println("Error reading file");
}
```

In this exception handler, like the earlier one, we do not dig into the details provided in the exception object; instead, we simply print a custom message to the user.

After reading the file fully, we print the **count** value to the user:

```
System.out.println(args[0] + " length = " + count);
```

Note that we must close all open files. We close the file in the **finally** block as follows:

```
} finally {
    try {
        is.close();
    } catch (Exception e) {
        e.printStackTrace();
    }
}
```

Remember from our discussions in Chapter 8 that the **finally** block is always executed regardless of whether or not an exception occurs in the running code. This ensures that the file is always closed regardless of what happens earlier in the running program. Note that calling the **close** method does not guarantee file closure; it just ensures an attempt is made to close the file. It is still possible the file may not close. The **close** operation itself may generate an exception. We catch this and print a detailed message to the user by calling the **printStackTrace** method on the exception object.

Some typical program output is shown here:

```
C:\360\ch09\>java FileLength build.xml
build.xml length = 69
```

This execution assumes that the build.xml file is available in the same folder as the one where the FileLength.class file is stored. Alternatively, you may specify a relative path with respect to the current folder of program execution or give an absolute path to the file.

The InputStream Methods

The **read** method we used in the previous program is in fact defined in the **InputStream** class. The **FileInputStream** class that extends from the **InputStream** class inherits this method. The **InputStream** class defines several other important methods, which are inherited and implemented in its subclasses. We will now discuss some of the most frequently used methods of the **InputStream** class.

In the previous example, we used the **read** method, which did not take any arguments. This method reads one byte at a time. Two more variations of the **read** method are available in the **InputStream** class. These methods take one or more arguments. The following **read** method takes a byte array as an argument:

```
public int read(byte[] b) throws IOException, NullPointerException
```

The method reads the number of bytes equal to the length of the byte array. The data read is stored in the byte array. It returns the number of bytes read, which could be less if the end-of-file is reached earlier. The method throws two different types of exceptions. If the first byte cannot be read for any reason other than the end-of-file condition, it throws an **IOException**. In particular, executing this call on an already closed input stream causes this exception to be thrown. If the argument **b** is null, the method throws a **NullPointerException**.

The following **read** method takes three arguments:

```
public int read(byte[] b, int off, int len)
        throws IOException, NullPointerException
```

The first parameter specifies the byte array in which the data will be stored. The second argument, **off**, specifies the offset in the byte array where the first byte read will be stored. The third parameter, **len**, specifies the number of bytes to read. The method returns the number of bytes actually read. The method throws two types of exceptions, like in the earlier case, for the same reasons.

```
public int available() throws IOException
```

This method returns an estimate of the number of bytes that can be read from this input stream without blocking, or it returns 0 when it returns the end of the input stream.

NOTE
*The phrase "without blocking" is important in the definition of **available** method. A stream may flow continuously and keep on acquiring newer data as time advances. When we say that the method returns an estimate of the count without blocking, this means that the receiver can receive the stated number of bytes in a single subsequent read call.*

TIP
*The **java.nio** package, introduced since J2SE 1.4.2, solves the issues of blocking calls by providing buffers and channels. This package is discussed in the next chapter.*

Our next method, **skip**, has the following signature:

```
public long skip(long n) throws IOException
```

The **skip** method is useful if you want to skip and discard some bytes of data from the input stream. The number of bytes to discard is specified by the parameter **n** to the **skip** method. As you'll recall from earlier, streams are sequential. Therefore, by calling the **skip** method, we can simply jump ahead in the buffer, but we cannot come back to read whatever we skipped.

The **close** method closes the input stream:

```
void close()
```

Note that the garbage collector does not close an open stream on its own. Therefore, to reclaim the resources, we must always explicitly close the stream we have opened previously.

TIP
*The **InputStream** class provides a few additional methods, such as **mark**, **reset**, and **markSupported**. I encourage you to open the javadocs to learn the use of these methods. Whenever you encounter a new class, it is a good practice to open the javadocs to check out what the class offers you.*

The OutputStream Class

Similar to the **InputStream** class, the abstract **OutputStream** class is a superclass of all classes representing an output stream of bytes. A few examples of these subclasses are **ByteArrayOutputStream**, **FileOutputStream**, **FilterOutputStream**, **ObjectOutputStream**, and **PipedOutputStream**. Similar to **FileInputStream**, the **FileOutputStream** class provides a real implementation of the **OutputStream** class. We will be using the **FileOutputStream** class and its methods in our next example, which is a file-copy program that copies the contents of the specified file to another file.

File Copy Utility

The File Copy program accepts two command-line parameters and copies the contents of the file specified by the first parameter to the filename specified in the second parameter. If the file listed in the second parameter does not exist, it creates a new file. On the other hand, if the file does exist, its contents are destroyed before the copy operation. Listing 9-2 provides the code for the File Copy program.

Listing 9-2   *A File Copy Utility*

```
import java.io.*;

public class FileCopy {

    public static void main(String[] args) {
        int numberRead = 0;
        InputStream readerStream = null;
        OutputStream writerStream = null;
```

```
        byte buffer[] = new byte[512];
        if (args.length < 2) {
            System.out.println("Usage: java FileCopy file1 file2");
            System.exit(0);
        }
        try {
            readerStream = new FileInputStream(args[0]);
        } catch (FileNotFoundException fe) {
            System.out.println(args[0] + " not found");
            System.exit(0);
        }

        try {
            writerStream = new FileOutputStream(args[1]);
        } catch (FileNotFoundException fe) {
            System.out.println(args[1] + " not found");
            System.exit(0);
        }
        try {
            while ((numberRead = readerStream.read(buffer)) != -1) {
                writerStream.write(buffer, 0, numberRead);
            }
        } catch (IOException ioe) {
            System.out.println("Error reading/writing file");
        } finally {
            try {
                readerStream.close();
                writerStream.close();
            } catch (Exception e) {
                e.printStackTrace();
            }
        }
        System.out.println("1 file copied!");
    }
}
```

The **main** method declares a byte buffer with a size of 512:

```
byte buffer[] = new byte[512];
```

This **buffer** array is used for reading and writing the file data during the copy process. We could have read one byte at a time, like in the previous example, and written each read byte to the new file. However, this would slow down the entire copy process for reasons given shortly. It is always advisable to read and write a chunk of data at a time. For this, we created a buffer with a size of 512. Generally, buffers are allocated in multiples of 512—a typical value for disk sector size. A disk organizes its data in sectors of 512 bytes or multiples thereof. Reading a single byte of data or one full sector of data requires the same amount of disk I/O processing time. Therefore, it is always efficient for a disk I/O to read/write a sector of data. Creating a buffer of 512, like in our program, results in efficient disk I/O operations.

TIP
*The **java.io** package also defines classes that provide in-built buffering. These are discussed later.*

As before, the program now checks for the number of arguments by checking the length of the **args** array:

```
if (args.length < 2) {
    System.out.println("Usage: java FileCopy file1 file2");
    System.exit(0);
}
```

Next, we open an input stream on the file specified by the first command-line argument:

```
readerStream = new FileInputStream(args[0]);
```

To open the output stream on the file specified by the second command-line argument, we instantiate the **FileOutputStream** class:

```
writerStream = new FileOutputStream(args[1]);
```

Next, we set up a **while** loop for reading and writing files:

```
while ((numberRead = readerStream.read(buffer)) != -1) {
    writerStream.write(buffer, 0, numberRead);
}
```

We use the previously discussed overloaded **read** method of the **InputStream** class, which accepts the **byte array** argument. The method returns the number of bytes read. If this number equals –1, it indicates that we have reached the end-of-file (EOF) condition. The number read usually equals the buffer length, but may be less if the EOF condition occurs before the buffer is completely filled. Because the buffer length is 512 bytes, we would be reading 512 bytes in each read operation, except for the last read, which may return a number less than 512.

We use the **write** method of the **OutputStream** class to write the buffer contents to the file specified by the **writerStream** object. The second parameter of the **write** method specifies the offset in the buffer from where the data should be written. This is always 0 in our case. The third parameter specifies the number of bytes to write from the buffer. This is the number returned by our **read** method.

As before, we attempt to close both the files in the **finally** block, regardless of the outcome of the file-copy process:

```
readerStream.close();
writerStream.close();
```

As in the earlier example, we need to enclose all the file operations in a **try-catch** block and provide error handlers for file-not-found and I/O errors.

To run this program, you would use the following command line:

```
C:\360\ch09\>java FileCopy filename1 filename2
```

Remember that the file-copy program will destroy the contents of the file specified by **filename2** if it exists. In the preceding command, the file specified by **filename1** must be present in the current working folder from where the **FileCopy** program is executed. The newly created file will be available in the same working folder. You may alternatively specify relative or absolute folders (path of file) for either or both filenames.

The OutputStream Methods

The **OutputStream** class defines three overloaded **write** methods:

```
public abstract void write(int b) throws IOException
public void write(byte[] b) throws IOException
public void write(byte[] b, int off, int len) throws IOException
```

The first method writes the byte specified in its parameter to the output stream. The byte to be written is stored in the eight low-order bits of the argument **b**. The 24 high-order bits of **b** are ignored. The subclasses of **OutputStream** must provide an implementation for this method.

The second method writes the entire buffer specified in its parameter, and the third method writes the buffer contents specified by the first parameter, starting at an offset in the buffer specified by the second parameter, and the number of bytes specified by the third parameter. Note that the actual contents written to the file could be less than the number specified if an error occurs during writing.

The **flush** method flushes the contents of the buffer to the output stream:

```
public void flush() throws IOException
```

This method is useful if you want to force an immediate write of the file buffer. If you do not flush the buffer using the **flush** method, the operating system will at some suitable time write the buffer to the physical file. In the case of multiuser applications, flushing the buffer immediately becomes important for maintaining the consistency of data between different threads or users. Generally, a word processing program such as Microsoft Word flushes your edits into a temporary file periodically so that if the program crashes for some reason, your edits are not completely lost. The explicit save operation by the user flushes all edits to the original file.

We have already used one of the constructors of the **FileOutputStream** class that takes one **String** argument specifying the name of the file to be opened. Another important variation of the constructor is the one that takes two parameters, as specified here:

```
public FileOutputStream(String name, boolean append)
      throws FileNotFoundException
```

The first parameter specifies the filename, as in the earlier case. The second parameter, if set to **true**, indicates that the file should be opened in *append* mode. Any data you write to a file opened in append mode will be added to the tail of the file. Thus, the original contents would be kept intact. In other words, the file is not overwritten when it is opened in append mode. The method throws the **FileNotFoundException** if the file exists but refers to a folder rather than a regular file, does not exist but cannot be created, or cannot be opened for any other reason. The method may also throw a **SecurityException** if a security manager exists and its **checkWrite** method denies write access to the file.

Character Streams

Just the way binary streams operate on binary files, the character streams operate on character files—that is, text files such as .txt, .odt, and .docx. Just the way you have several real (fully implemented) subclasses of input and output byte stream types, you have several real classes of

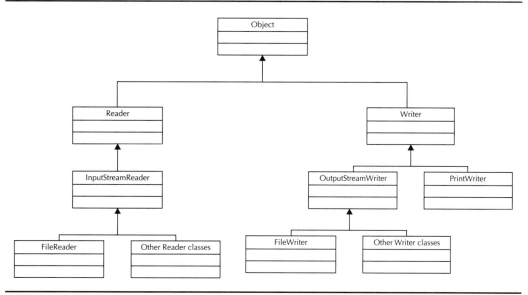

FIGURE 9-3. *Reader/Writer class hierarchy*

input and output character stream types. The high-level class hierarchy for character stream classes is given in Figure 9-3.

The **Reader** and **Writer** classes act as super classes for the rest of the classes in this category. Several **Reader/Writer** subclasses are available that match the corresponding byte stream classes in functionality, except they work on character streams rather than byte streams.

To explain some of these classes, let's look at some program examples.

File Viewer Utility

Let's write a utility called File Viewer that accepts the name of a character file on the command line and displays its contents to the user console. The complete program for the file viewer is given in Listing 9-3.

Listing 9-3 *The File Viewer Utility*

```
import java.io.*;

public class FileView {

    public static void main(String[] args) {
        int numberRead = 0;
        FileReader reader = null;
        PrintWriter writer = null;
        char buffer[] = new char[512];
        if (args.length < 1) {
            System.out.println("Usage: java FileView filename");
```

```
        System.exit(0);
    }
    try {
        reader = new FileReader(args[0]);
        writer = new PrintWriter(System.out);
        while ((numberRead = reader.read(buffer)) != -1) {
            writer.write(buffer, 0, numberRead);
        }
    } catch (FileNotFoundException fe) {
        System.out.println(fe.getMessage());
        System.exit(0);
    } catch (IOException ioe) {
        System.out.println("Error reading/writing file");
    } finally {
        try {
            reader.close();
            writer.close();
        } catch (Exception e) {
            e.printStackTrace();
        }
    }
    }
}
```

The file viewer accepts one command-line argument; if it is missing, the user is informed about the proper usage of the file viewer utility. After accepting the correct number of arguments from the user, the program opens the specified file by instantiating the **FileReader** class:

```
reader = new FileReader(args[0]);
```

The program opens an output stream on the user console using the following statement:

```
writer = new PrintWriter(System.out);
```

Note that **System.out** refers to the output stream where the system by default outputs its contents. We create an instance of the **PrintWriter** class on top of this output stream. The **PrintWriter** class provides methods for writing primitive data and user-defined types. It is very useful in outputting text-based data in a formatted way. For instance, it can write **int**, **long**, and other primitive data types as text rather than as their byte values. The overloaded **print** method accepts a **boolean**, **char**, **int**, **float**, **double**, **long**, or other as an argument and prints its value in the text format. These methods take the form shown here:

```
public void print(int i)
public void print(long l)
public void print(float f)
public void print(double d)
...
```

The class also provides the **println** version of all these methods, which prints a newline character immediately following the specified data type. Thus, by using this class, we are not required to convert primitive data types to text for printing to the console or any writer instance.

The **PrintWriter** class also contains a powerful **format** method that allows us to print a list of arguments of various data types in a specified format string and their locale. For those who are more conversant in C language programming, the **PrintWriter** class also provides a method called **printf** (same as the C language method) that offers the same functionality as the **format** method.

NOTE
*In relation to Java Design Patterns, the **PrintWriter** class implements a Decorator pattern that wraps the stream and reader/writer classes.*

Next, we set up a loop for reading and writing files until the end-of-file (EOF) condition is reached on the input stream:

```
while ((numberRead = reader.read(buffer)) != -1) {
    writer.write(buffer, 0, numberRead);
}
```

The **read** method of the **FileReader** class reads the file contents into the buffer specified in its argument. It normally returns the number of characters read and returns –1 on the EOF condition. The number of characters read usually equals the buffer length, except for the last read operation, which returns a lesser number because the EOF condition is reached.

The **write** method of the **PrintWriter** class writes the buffer contents to the output stream. The second parameter of the **write** method specifies the offset in the buffer from where the writing should begin. The third parameter of the **write** method indicates the number of characters to write from the buffer.

NOTE
*The **PrintWriter** class automatically encodes using ISO-8859-1. The ISO-8859 series defines 13 character encodings representing several languages; each encoding can have up to 256 characters. ISO-8859-1 (Latin-1) comprises the ASCII character set, characters with diacritics, and additional symbols.*

After the **while** loop terminates, we close both the files by calling the **close** method on the two instances in the **finally** block.

As in the earlier cases, all operations on files are enclosed in a **try-catch** block, and we provide appropriate exception handlers for the checked exceptions. To run the program, you would use the following command line:

```
C:\360\ch09\>java FileView filename
```

The program dumps the contents of the file specified by **filename** to the user console. The file specified by the **filename** parameter must be available in the current working folder from where the File Viewer utility is executed. Alternatively, you could specify a relative or absolute path to the file.

Buffered Readers/Writers

In the previous example, we declared our own character buffer for reading/writing the file. Java provides the **BufferedReader** and **BufferedWriter** classes, which provide the in-built buffers. Remember that reading a single byte or 512 bytes at a time requires the same amount of I/O processing. Therefore, buffering characters makes file reading and writing more efficient.

When you use these classes, you may specify the size for the buffer; otherwise, a default size is used that is adequate for most purposes. If you have a lot of system memory, you may allocate a larger buffer to provide data caching so as to avoid frequent reads and writes from and to a physical disk.

The BufferedReader Class

Typically, you would construct an instance of the **BufferedReader** class as follows:

```
BufferedReader reader = new BufferedReader(new FileReader("filename"));
```

We first construct an instance of the **FileReader** class by specifying the name of the file to be opened in its parameterized constructor. We use this instance of the **FileReader** class as a parameter to **BufferedReader** during its instantiation. Once the **reader** object is constructed, you may call its various overloaded **read** methods to read the file contents. A typical method for reading the file line by line is the **readLine** method:

```
public String readLine() throws IOException
```

The **readLine** method reads one line at a time from the input stream and returns it to the caller as a **String** object. A line is terminated by either a linefeed ('\n'), a carriage return ('\r'), or a carriage return followed immediately by a linefeed. The returned string does not include the line-termination character. It returns **null** on reaching the end of the stream.

The BufferedWriter Class

Similar to the **BufferedReader** class, Java provides a **BufferedWriter** class for efficient writing to the files. You construct an instance of **BufferedWriter** as follows:

```
BufferedWriter writer = new BufferedWriter(new FileWriter("foo.out"));
```

This creates a file called foo.out if it does not already exist; if the file exists, its contents will be overwritten. After the file is opened for writing, the **BufferedWriter** creates a wrapper on it to provide efficient write operations that can accept the data to be written in a character array format or a string. It also provides a **newline** method that writes a newline character to the output stream.

Now that we have discussed both binary and character stream files, let's discuss when to use each type.

Binary Versus Character Streams

If you are working with binary data such as images and sounds, you need to use binary mode files. For other purposes, you would use character streams, as in the reader and writer classes described earlier. These reader/writer classes offer you the following benefits:

- They handle any character in the Unicode character set; the byte streams are limited to ISO Latin-1 eight-bit bytes.

- Programs that use character streams can easily be internationalized because they do not depend on a specific character encoding.

- Because character stream classes use internal buffering, inherently they are more efficient than byte streams.

In general, use the **FileInputStream** and **FileOutputStream** classes to read and write binary data from and to image files, sound files, video files, configuration files, and so on. These classes can also be used to read/write ASCII-based text files. To read/write modern Unicode-based text files, use the **FileReader** and **FileWriter** classes.

Chaining Streams

In the previous section, you saw how a **BufferedReader** instance is opened on top of a **FileReader** object. This is called *wrapping* or *chaining streams.* Very rarely, a program uses a single stream object. Generally, several stream objects (in a series) are chained to process the data more efficiently. The Java I/O libraries provide several such wrappings. The wrappings help in processing and managing the data more efficiently by providing the additional convenience methods in the subclasses. Connecting several stream classes together helps in getting the data in the required format. Each class performs a specific task on the data and forwards it to the next class in the chain. A typical example of this could be a data-backup utility. Such a program would chain several streams to compress, encrypt, transmit, receive, and finally store the data in a remote file.

Figure 9-4 shows one such wrapping for an input stream.

Here, we first open the **FileInputStream** on a physical data source. The output of this is buffered in the **BufferedInputStream** object. We wrap this with a **DataInputStream** for convenient handling of primitive data types. The **DataInputStream** class provides several read methods, such as **readByte**, **readChar**, **readDouble**, and so on, that operate on primitive data types. A similar wrapping is provided for writer classes, as illustrated in Figure 9-5.

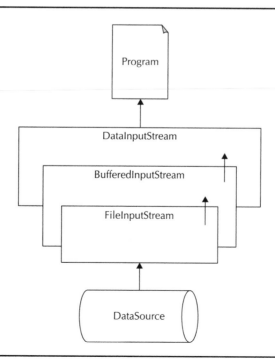

FIGURE 9-4.   *Chaining input stream classes*

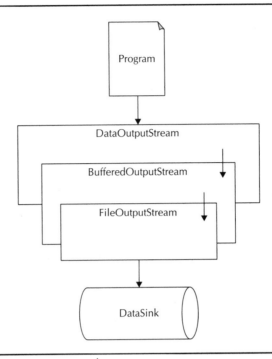

FIGURE 9-5. *Chaining output stream classes*

In this case, the program writes data to a **DataOutputStream** by using its **write** methods that accept primitive data types. The data written is buffered in a **BufferedOutputStream** object for efficient disk writing. Finally, the data is written out to a physical device using the **FileOutputStream** object.

We'll now look at how this wrapping helps in writing efficient file I/O programs.

The Line Count Program

The Line Count program counts the number of lines in the specified text file. Java provides a class called **LineNumberReader** for this purpose. The **LineNumberReader** class wraps the **BufferedReader** class, which in turn wraps the **Reader** class.

The code for the Line Count program is given in Listing 9-4.

Listing 9-4 *Program for Counting the Number of Lines in a File*

```
import java.io.*;

public class LineCounter {

    public static void main(String[] args) {
        LineNumberReader reader = null;
        if (args.length < 1) {
```

```
        System.out.println("Usage: java LineCounter <filename>");
        System.exit(0);
    }
    try {
        reader = new LineNumberReader(new FileReader(args[0]));
        while (reader.readLine() != null) {
        }
        System.out.println(
                "Line number of the last line in the file is: "
                + reader.getLineNumber() + 1);
    } catch (FileNotFoundException fe) {
        System.out.println(fe.getMessage());
    } catch (IOException e) {
        System.out.println("Error reading file");
    } finally {
        try {
            reader.close();
        } catch (Exception e) {
            e.printStackTrace();
        }
    }
    }
}
```

The **main** method takes one command-line argument that specifies a text file. The program counts the number of lines in this text file and prints that number to the user console. The **main** method checks the appropriate usage of the command line and prints an appropriate message to the user if the command-line parameters are missing.

We open the file for reading by constructing a **LineNumberReader** class instance as follows:

```
reader = new LineNumberReader(new FileReader(args[0]));
```

After obtaining the **reader** object, the program simply reads the file line by line, ignoring the contents read:

```
while (reader.readLine() != null) {
}
```

The **readLine** method returns **null** after reaching the end-of-file. At this time, it will have the count of the total number of lines in the file, which we print to the user's console:

```
System.out.println(
        "Line number of the last line in the file is: "
        + reader.getLineNumber() + 1);
```

We now close the file by calling the **close** method in the **finally** block. The entire file-handling code is enclosed in a **try-catch** block, and we provide appropriate exception handlers for all the required checked exceptions.

Some typical program output is shown here:

```
C:\360\ch09>java LineCounter Build.xml
Number of lines: 69
```

NOTE
The Line Count *program may also take a binary file as input and give you legitimate output. The reason behind this is how the* **readLine** *method operates. If you open the javadocs for the* **LineNumberReader** *class, you'll see that this method reads a line of text. However, this could be a line containing non-ASCII data. The documentation also says that a line is considered to be terminated by any of the following: a linefeed ('\n'), a carriage return ('\r'), or a carriage return followed immediately by a linefeed. Thus, when you run this program on a non-ASCII data file, it counts the numbers of lines, as defined, and gives you legitimate output.*

Let's look at another example to further illustrate the use of reader/writer classes.

File Concatenation

The File Concatenation program, as the name suggests, concatenates the contents of a given number of files. We specify the files on the command line as a variable argument list. The output of the program will be a new file that is a sequential combination of all the input files. In this example, you learn a new language feature (introduced in J2SE 5.0) called *varargs*, which are variable arguments to a method. The code for the File Concatenation program is given in Listing 9-5.

Listing 9-5 *Concatenating Files*

```java
import java.io.*;

public class Concatenate {

    public static void concenateFile(String... fileName) {
        String str = null;

        try (BufferedWriter writer = new BufferedWriter(
                    new FileWriter("CombinedFile.txt"));) {
            for (String name : fileName) {
                try (BufferedReader reader =
                            new BufferedReader(new FileReader(name));) {
                    while ((str = reader.readLine()) != null) {
                        writer.write(str);
                        writer.newLine();
                    }
                } catch (IOException e) {
                    System.out.println("Error reading/writing file");
                }
            }
        } catch (Exception e) {
            e.printStackTrace();
        }
    }
}
```

```
public static void main(String[] args) {
    if (args.length < 0) {
        System.out.println("Usage: java Concatenate file1 file2");
        System.exit(0);
    }
    concenateFile(args);
    System.out.println("Successfully created CombinedFile.txt");
}
}
```

The File Concatenation program accepts a variable number of arguments on the command line. The arguments specify the files to be concatenated. First comes the content of the file, as specified by the first argument. To this the contents of the file specified by the second argument are appended, and so on. The resultant output is stored in a file named CombinedFile.txt. The original files remain unchanged.

After checking the valid input on the command line, the **main** function calls the **concenateFile** method by sending it the variable list of arguments:

```
public static void concenateFile(String... fileName) {
```

Note how this list is specified. The ellipsis indicates that the number of arguments is variable. Each argument is of type **String**. This varargs (variable arguments) feature allows a developer to declare that a method can take a variable number of parameters for a given argument.

CAUTION
The varargs must be the last argument in the formal argument list.

The compiler converts this list of variable arguments to an array. Inside the method, we iterate through this variable arguments list by using a **foreach** loop:

```
for (String name : fileName) {
```

In each iteration, we open a **FileReader** on the specified file, read its contents a line at a time, and keep on writing to a previously created **writer** instance:

```
try (BufferedReader reader = new BufferedReader(new FileReader(name));) {
    while ((str = reader.readLine()) != null) {
        writer.write(str);
        writer.newLine();
    }
}
```

Note that we use the **try-with-resources** syntax of Java SE 7 to open the files. This reduces the exception-handling code substantially. Also, we do not have to worry about closing the resources. A typical program run is shown here:

```
C:\360\ch09>java Concatenate catalog1.txt catalog2.txt catalog3.txt
C:\360\ch09>
```

Note that the program does not output anything to the console. Instead, it creates a CombinedFile.txt file in the current folder. The newly created file will contain the concatenation of the three specified input files.

Accessing the Host File System

We'll now discuss another important class in the I/O package. The **java.io.File** class provides an abstract representation of a file or directory on the host file system. As mentioned previously, Java SE 7 introduced a new class called **Path** in the **java.nio.file** package. This class provides more sophisticated functionality than the **File** class. This does not, however, reduce the importance of the **File** class, and it is recommended that you study this class in the javadocs. The **java.nio** package is discussed in the next chapter. However, we will use the newly introduced **Path** class for the program in this section. Our program will accept a path on the command line and list out all the files found in the specified path.

The Directory Listing Program

The Directory Listing program accepts an argument on the command line. The program prints the names of all the files under the path specified in this argument to the system console. The full program is given in Listing 9-6.

Listing 9-6   *Listing Files in a Directory*

```java
import java.nio.file.*;
import java.io.*;
public class DirListing {

    public static void main(String[] args) {

        if (args.length < 1) {
            System.out.println("Usage: DirListing DirectoryName");
            System.exit(0);
        }

        Path dirPath = Paths.get(args[0]);
        DirectoryStream<Path> directory = null;
        try {
            directory =  Files.newDirectoryStream(dirPath);

            for (Path p : directory) {
                System.out.println(p.getFileName());
            }
        } catch (Exception ie) {
            System.out.println("Invalid path specified:" + args[0]);
        } finally {
            try {
                if (directory != null) {
                directory.close();
                }
            } catch (IOException ie) {
                ie.printStackTrace();
            }
        }
    }
}
```

Note that at the top, we import classes from the **java.nio.file** package. After confirming that the user has input an argument on the command line, we construct a **Path** object by calling the static **get** method of the **Paths** class:

```
Path dirPath = Paths.get(args[0]);
```

After this, we declare a **directory** variable of type **DirectoryStream**, as follows:

```
DirectoryStream<Path> directory = null;
```

This declaration uses generics, which is discussed in Chapter 12. We initialize this variable by calling the **newDirectoryStream** method of the **Files** class on the previously created **dirPath** object:

```
directory = Files.newDirectoryStream(dirPath);
```

Now, we can print the names of all the files from this **directory** stream using a **foreach** loop, as follows:

```
for (Path p : directory) {
    System.out.println(p.getFileName());
}
```

In the **finally** block, we close the opened stream.

You can run the program by specifying a desired path on the command line, and you will see the list of files printed to your console.

Filtering the Directory Listing

In the preceding example, all the files present in the specified directory are listed on the console. With a little modification to this program, we could filter out the files of a specified type in our output. For example, we might want to list out only the files with .doc extension from the specified directory. We can add such filters easily in our program by making the following modification in the initialization of the **directory** object:

```
directory = dir.newDirectoryStream("*.{doc}");
directory = Files.newDirectoryStream(dirPath, "*.{docx}");
```

The **newDirectoryStream** method now takes a filter string as an argument. Thus, when we retrieve elements from the created stream, we get only the files with the extension .doc. You can create your own filter, as shown in the following example, which returns files having a size greater than 8,192 bytes:

```
DirectoryStream.Filter<Path> filter = new DirectoryStream.Filter<Path>() {
    public boolean accept(Path file) throws IOException {
        return (Files.size(file) > 8192L);
    }
};
```

To use this filter while listing the files in the directory, you would use the following code:

```
directory = Files.newDirectoryStream(dirPath, filter);
```

TIP
*Prior to Java SE 7, you would have used the **FilenameFilter** class to perform such a filtering. This class has not been deprecated in Java SE 7 and therefore you can still continue using it.*

Reading/Writing Objects

The Java I/O library provides classes that allow you to read or write a user-defined object from or to a stream. The two classes, **ObjectInputStream** and **ObjectOutputStream**, provide this functionality. Java also defines an interface called **Serializable**. If you want to read/write objects, the class representing the desired object must implement this interface. The **Serializable** interface does not have any methods, so its implementation remains null.

Let's illustrate the use of these classes with an example. Suppose you have created a **Student** class to hold a student's ID as well as the student's first and the last names. You now want to create a student database holding the data for the various students in the class. Your program should also be able to retrieve this data. The program shown in Listing 9-7 does just this.

Listing 9-7   *Program Illustrating Object Serialization*

```java
import java.io.*;

public class ObjectSerializationApp {

    public static void main(String[] args) {
        ObjectOutputStream objectWriter = null;
        ObjectInputStream objectReader = null;
        try {
            objectWriter = new ObjectOutputStream(
                new FileOutputStream("student.dat"));
            objectWriter.writeObject(new Student(1, "John", "Mayor"));
            objectWriter.writeObject(new Student(2, "Sam", "Abel"));
            objectWriter.writeObject(new Student(3, "Anita", "Motwani"));

            System.out.println("Printing list of students in the database:");
            objectReader = new ObjectInputStream(
                new FileInputStream("student.dat"));
            for (int i = 0; i < 3; i++) {
                System.out.println(objectReader.readObject());
            }
        } catch (Exception e) {
            e.printStackTrace();
        } finally {
            try {
                objectWriter.close();
                objectReader.close();
            } catch (IOException ie) {
                ie.printStackTrace();
```

```
                }
            }
        }
    }
}

class Student implements Serializable {

    private String firstName;
    private String lastName;
    private int id;

    public Student(int id, String firstName, String lastName) {
        this.id = id;
        this.firstName = firstName;
        this.lastName = lastName;
    }

    public String toString() {
        return ("ID:" + id + " " + firstName + " " + lastName);
    }
}
```

Let's first discuss the **Student** class. The class implements the **Serializable** interface:

```
class Student implements Serializable {
```

As mentioned earlier, the **Serializable** interface does not have any methods to implement and is therefore known as a *marker interface*. The class constructor takes three arguments and stores their values in instance variables. The **Student** class overrides the **toString** method to provide its own string representation.

The **main** method of the **ObjectSerializationApp** class constructs an instance of **ObjectOutputStream**, as follows:

```
objectWriter = new ObjectOutputStream(new FileOutputStream("student.dat"));
```

Note that this statement creates a new file called student.dat. If the file with this name already exists, it will overwrite its contents. Once an instance of the **ObjectOutputStream** is obtained, you can call its **writeObject** method to write any serializable object to it. The program constructs and writes three student objects to the student.dat file using the following statements:

```
objectWriter.writeObject(new Student(1, "John", "Mayor"));
objectWriter.writeObject(new Student(2, "Sam", "Abel"));
objectWriter.writeObject(new Student(3, "Anita", "Motwani"));
```

After writing objects, the output file is closed via a call to its **close** method. The program then reopens the student.dat file by constructing an **ObjectInputStream** object around it:

```
objectReader = new ObjectInputStream(new FileInputStream("student.dat"));
```

The program then reads the three objects from this file and prints their string representation using the following **for** loop:

```
for (int i = 0; i < 3; i++) {
    System.out.println(objectReader.readObject());
}
```

The method **readObject** returns a **Student** object, which is printed to the console by calling the implicitly overridden **toString** method. When you run the program, you'll see the following output on your console:

```
C:\360\ch09>java ObjectDemo
Printing list of students in the database:
ID:1 John Mayor
ID:2 Sam Abel
ID:3 Anita Motwani
```

You can also check for the presence of the newly created student.dat file in your current folder.

Summary

The **java.io** package provides several useful classes to facilitate I/O operations in your Java applications. All I/O classes are based on streams, which are an abstraction to a data flow from a source to a sink. The streams can be byte or character oriented. The byte streams are based on the **InputStream** and **OutputStream** classes. The character-oriented streams derive from the **Reader** and **Writer** classes. Both byte- and character-oriented streams define several subclasses to provide a wide range of functionality. You learned to use several I/O subclasses to operate on both byte and character streams. Besides these, Java also provides a **File** class that provides an abstraction to a physical file. The **File** class is useful when you want to work on system files. Java 7 provides another equivalent class called **Path**, which has more sophisticated functionality when compared to the **File** class. You learned to use this class via concrete examples. Finally, we covered the technique of reading and writing user-defined objects from and to a stream. In the next chapter, you learn more I/O classes and advanced I/O manipulation techniques. The next chapter also covers additions within the new versions of Java SE.

CHAPTER
10

Advanced I/O

he previous chapter introduced you to several classes defined in the **java.io** package and a few from the **java.nio** package. This chapter continues the discussion on the remaining I/O classes and more advanced features of the I/O libraries. To give you a feel of the exhaustiveness of this package, the class hierarchy is shown in Figure 10-1.

As you can see from this figure, the Java I/O libraries contain several classes that inherit **InputStream** and **OutputStream**. These classes decorate the **InputStream** and **OutputStream** based on the well-known Decorator design pattern. You studied the use of some of these classes in the previous chapter. This chapter covers many more classes from this list and provides practical examples using them. Besides the wrapper classes on streams, Figure 10-1 shows other classes that deal with physical files on the disk. You learn about these classes too in this chapter. Additionally, this chapter covers the newly introduced classes in Java 7.

In particular, you will learn the following in this chapter:

- Byte-oriented stream classes
- The **PushbackInputStream** class
- The **SequenceInputStream** class
- The **PrintStream** class

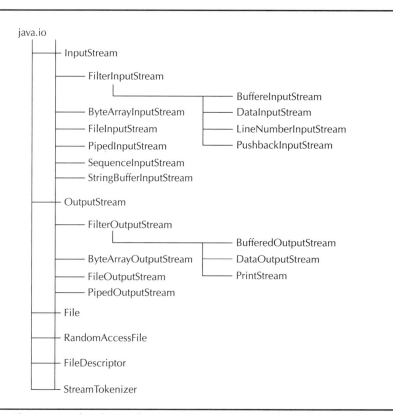

FIGURE 10-1. *The java.io class hierarchy*

- Character-oriented stream classes
- The **CharArrayReader/CharArrayWriter** classes
- The **Console** class
- The **StreamTokenizer** class
- Object-oriented streams
- The **Externalizable** interface
- Serializing nested objects
- Maintaining object versions

The Byte-Oriented Stream Classes

In the last chapter, you got an introduction to byte-oriented stream classes, where you used the **FileInputStream** and **FileOutputStream** classes. As you can see from Figure 10-1, there are several more classes in this category. Although it is not possible to cover all these classes in this book, we will look at how to use some of them in practical situations so that you are able to use the rest in your applications. We begin with the **ByteArrayInputStream/ByteArrayOutputStream** and **DataInputStream/DataOutputStream** classes. As the names suggest, the first two classes operate on a byte array and the latter two operate on object data—rather than primitive data types. These are obviously the decorator classes that wrap the **InputStream/OutputStream** base classes. Let's discuss the purpose behind having them in the first place.

In many situations, you have the data available in byte arrays. For example, when you transmit and receive data over a modem, the data is available in modem buffers, which are basically the byte arrays. Consider the case of the NYSE and NASDAQ. These stock exchanges stream trade data in real time to brokers. Trade data consists of scrip code, trade time, bid price, offer price, volume, the high, low, and opening prices, as well as a few more fields. This data is transmitted over a socket connection to the client machine. The exchange server writes this data to a modem buffer. The data is sent in raw binary format in order to save bandwidth. In this case, you would use a **ByteArrayOutputStream** class to write the data to its internal buffer. This class deals with only raw binary data. To provide the abstraction to higher data types, you would use the **DataOutputStream** class, which is a wrapper on the **ByteArrayOutputStream** class. The **DataOutputStream** contains many methods to write the primitive data types. By chaining the data output stream to a byte array output stream, you can write the binary form of the trade data into a byte array and then send the entire array in a single packet to the remote machine. At the client end, you would use **ByteArrayInputStream** to buffer the data retrieved from a socket connection. You would then use the **DataInputStream** class to convert the raw data to primitive data types.

CAUTION
*The **DataInputStream** and **DataOutputStream** go together. If the data is written using any other output stream class, the **read** methods of the **DataInputStream** will not be able to successfully read the data.*

In general, whenever you want to extract data values of different types from an array of bytes, you would use these **InputStream**-derived classes. The **LiveData** application we will discuss shortly uses such a data buffer; it contains an integer, a character array, a few **double** values, and a **long** data type. In C++, you would use memory pointers to reference different parts of the array and perform casting on a group of bytes to extract the data of a particular type. In Java, this type of direct memory referencing is not permitted. And that's where these **InputStream**-derived classes come in handy.

TIP
*None of the methods of the **ByteArrayInputStream** class throw an **IOException**. This is because the data comes from an array rather than an actual I/O device.*

NOTE
Java uses big-endian *notation for number representation. This means that for any primitive data value longer than one byte, the most significant byte is at the lowest address (in other words, big end first.) Thus, in an output stream of **int** values, the high order byte goes out first, and in an input stream the high order byte arrives first. JVM preserves this order on all underlying platforms, including Intel, which uses the reverse representation known as* little-endian. *When you use the **InputStream**-derived classes, you do not have to worry about these internal representations, and your Java application is assured to work correctly on any platform. Therefore, our stock exchange server and the client could be running on different platforms, yet proper data transfers are guaranteed between the two machines.*

We will now discuss the **LiveData** program mentioned earlier to illustrate the use of these classes. The complete program is given in Listing 10-1.

Listing 10-1   *Stock Trade Data Streaming*

```java
import java.io.*;
import java.text.SimpleDateFormat;
import java.util.*;

public class LiveData {

    private ByteArrayOutputStream outStream;

    public static void main(String args[]) throws IOException {
        LiveData app = new LiveData();
        app.createData();
        app.readData();
    }

    public void createData() {
        try {
            outStream = new ByteArrayOutputStream();
            DataOutputStream writer = new DataOutputStream(outStream);
            for (int i = 0; i < 10; i++) {
                Trade lastTrade = new Trade(i);
```

```java
                writer.writeInt(lastTrade.scripCode);
                writer.write(lastTrade.time);
                writer.writeDouble(lastTrade.bid);
                writer.writeDouble(lastTrade.offer);
                writer.writeDouble(lastTrade.high);
                writer.writeDouble(lastTrade.low);
                writer.writeLong(lastTrade.quantity);
            }
        } catch (Exception e) {
            System.out.println("Error while writing data to buffer");
        }
    }

    private void readData() {
        byte[] timeBuffer = new byte[8];
        StringBuilder sb = new StringBuilder();
        Formatter formatter = new Formatter(sb, Locale.US);
        ByteArrayInputStream inStream =
                new ByteArrayInputStream(outStream.toByteArray());
        DataInputStream reader = new DataInputStream(inStream);
        try {
            for (int i = 0; i < 10; i++) {
                int scripCode = reader.readInt();
                reader.read(timeBuffer);
                String time = new String(timeBuffer);
                double bid = reader.readDouble();
                double offer = reader.readDouble();
                double high = reader.readDouble();
                double low = reader.readDouble();
                long volume = reader.readLong();

                formatter.format("ScripCode: %2d"
                        + "\tTime: %s "
                        + "\tBid:$ %05.2f"
                        + "\tOffer:$ %05.2f"
                        + "\tHigh:$ %05.2f"
                        + "\tLow:$ %05.2f"
                        + "\tVolume: %d",
                        scripCode, time, bid, offer, high, low, volume);
                System.out.println(sb);
                sb.delete(0, sb.length());
            }
        } catch (Exception e) {
            System.out.println("Error while reading data");
        }
    }

    private class Trade {

        private int scripCode;
        private byte[] time;
```

```
            private double bid, offer, high, low;
            private long quantity;

            public Trade(int i) {
                scripCode = i + 1;
                time = now("hh:mm:ss").getBytes();
                bid = Math.random() * 100;
                offer = Math.random() * 100;
                high = Math.random() * 100;
                low = Math.random() * 100;
                quantity = (long) (Math.random() * 100000000);
            }

            private String now(String dateFormat) {
                Calendar cal = Calendar.getInstance();
                SimpleDateFormat sdf = new SimpleDateFormat(dateFormat);
                return sdf.format(cal.getTime());
            }
        }
    }
}
```

The **main** function in the **LiveData** class creates an application instance and calls its two methods: **createData** and **readData**. The **createData** method creates a few random trades and writes this data to an output stream. The **readData** method reads this data from a byte array obtained from the preceding output stream and prints the data in proper format on the user console.

NOTE
*In practical reality, the **createData** method would belong to a server process and the client program would contain the **readData** method. The idealistic simulation of this stock server would require the use of threads. Because we have not covered thread programming so far in this book, we will have both **create** and **read** functions within the same application.*

The **createData** method creates an instance of **ByteArrayOutputStream** and copies its reference to a class variable for use by the **readData** method:

```
outStream = new ByteArrayOutputStream();
```

We build a **DataOutputStream** object on top of this output stream:

```
DataOutputStream writer = new DataOutputStream(outStream);
```

Using this object reference, we are now able to write data to the underlying byte array using the higher-level primitive data type **write** methods. We create 10 instances of the **Trade** class and write its fields using the methods **writeInt**, **writeDouble**, and so on:

```
for (int i = 0; i < 10; i++) {
    Trade lastTrade = new Trade(i);
    writer.writeInt(lastTrade.scripCode);
    writer.write(lastTrade.time);
    writer.writeDouble(lastTrade.bid);
```

The **Trade** class constructor assigns some random values to its fields during instantiation. The **readData** method creates an instance of the **ByteArrayInputStream** on the byte array obtained from the **out** stream:

```
ByteArrayInputStream inStream =
                new ByteArrayInputStream(outStream.toByteArray());
```

We open the **DataInputStream** on top of it to read the data by using the higher-level data-read functions:

```
DataInputStream reader = new DataInputStream(inStream);
```

Note the use of various **read** methods, such as **readInt**, **readDouble**, and so on. Some partial program output is shown here:

```
ScripCode:  1     Time: 04:53:41  Bid:$ 82.92  Offer:$ 49.41  High:$ 45.25
                  Low:$ 52.26     Volume: 4882176
ScripCode:  2     Time: 04:53:41  Bid:$ 48.84  Offer:$ 00.18  High:$ 78.27
                  Low:$ 71.53     Volume: 31719488
ScripCode:  3     Time: 04:53:41  Bid:$ 17.35  Offer:$ 29.33  High:$ 42.93
                  Low:$ 98.08     Volume: 88175262
ScripCode:  4     Time: 04:53:41  Bid:$ 05.96  Offer:$ 65.09  High:$ 91.19
                  Low:$ 15.66     Volume: 16592232
```

TIP
*To save the contents of the **out** buffer in the **OutputStream** class to a physical file, you call its **writeTo** method as shown here:*

```
FileOutputStream f = new FileOutputStream("test.txt");
out.writeTo(f);
f.close();
```

Note that we do not close the files. Because the files are based on byte arrays, which do not persist beyond the application's life, it does not make sense to close the files. We need to maintain the reference to these resources ourselves, and that is why we declare the **out** variable in our program as an instance variable.

The PushbackInputStream Class

The **PushbackInputStream** class comes under the category of **FilterInputStream** classes. The **FilterInputStream** has four subclasses, as shown earlier in Figure 10-1. Imagine this class as providing the structure of the pipe for the flow of data. Its subclasses then extract the data into small, usable bits. Out of these four subclasses, we have already used **DataInputStream** in the previous program. We will use the **PushbackInputStream** in this section, and the other two later in this chapter.

The **PushbackInputStream** class is used when you want to look ahead in the read buffer to see what the next character is. It creates a one-byte input buffer that allows the input stream to retreat one byte after it has been read, which enables you to test the next byte before taking any action. The typical application of this comes in lexical analysis of compiler construction. Rather than taking on this traditional example, we will discuss another application that effectively uses this class. Suppose we are developing a print calculator where the user inputs a number (let's say the purchase price of an item) on the keypad. If this purchase price contains zero cents, we want to print ** in place of 00 in the item's price. Thus, if the purchase price is $5.00, the calculator should print $5.**, and if the purchase price is $249.00, it will print $249.**. For any other value after the decimal point, the value is printed "as is." Thus, the prices $36.02 and $78.85 would be printed as normal. Look at the program in Listing 10-2 to see how this conversion is done.

Listing 10-2 *The Print Calculator*

```java
import java.io.*;

public class PrintCalc {

    public static void main(String args[]) {
        PrintCalc app = new PrintCalc();
        try {
            app.readAndPrint();
        } catch (IOException e) {
            System.out.println("Error encountered during printing");
        }
    }

    private void readAndPrint() throws IOException {
        PushbackInputStream f = new PushbackInputStream(System.in, 3);
        int c, c1, c2;
        while ((c = f.read()) != 'q') {
            switch (c) {
                case '.':
                    System.out.print((char) c);
                    if ((c1 = f.read()) == '0') {
                        if ((c2 = f.read()) == '0') {
                            System.out.print("**");
                        } else {
                            f.unread(c2);
                            f.unread(c1);
                        }
                    } else {
                        f.unread(c1);
                    }
                    break;

                default:
                    System.out.print((char) c);
                    break;
            }
        }
        f.close();
    }
}
```

The **readAndPrint** method reads the number from the keypad, which in our case is the system keyboard, and sends the formatted output to the printer, which in our case is a system console, after making adjustments for zero cents. We first create an instance of **PushbackInputStream** on the **System.in** stream:

```
PushbackInputStream f = new PushbackInputStream(System.in, 3);
```

The second argument to the constructor sets the buffer size for rollback, which is one byte by default. Therefore, if we use a constructor without the second parameter, we are able to push back only the last read byte.

Next, we set up a loop for reading the keyboard until the user hits the q key on the keypad:

```
while ((c = f.read()) != 'q') {
```

We now test the input character for a period (or dot). If the character is not a dot, we print the character on the console in the **default** case of the **switch** statement. If a dot is found, we print it on the console and start looking for the "00" character sequence. If this sequence is found, the program prints ****** to the console:

```
if ((c1 = f.read()) == '0') {
    if ((c2 = f.read()) == '0') {
        System.out.print("**");
```

If some other character follows the first read 0, the program puts both the characters back in the buffer by calling the **unread** method twice:

```
f.unread(c2);
f.unread(c1);
```

If the first read character itself does not equal 0, we simply put it back in the buffer:

```
else {
    f.unread(c1);
}
```

The **unread** method pushes back a byte by copying it to the front of the pushback buffer. There are other variations (overloaded) of the **unread** method available that push back a byte array or a portion of a byte array. Please refer to the javadocs to learn about these methods.

Here is some sample output:

```
$500.00
$500.**
$245.02
$245.02
$549.78
$549.78
$1024.00
$1024.**
$245.0089
$245.**89
q
```

The odd-number lines show the user input and the even-number lines indicate the program-generated print number. Note the output for $500.00 and $1024.00, where 00 is replaced with **. The other numbers are printed as is. What about the last input, $245.0089? Here the two zeroes are replaced with the two asterisks. I assume a typical physical calculator would not permit entry beyond two decimal digits. As an exercise for the interested reader, you can impose this restriction in the software by modifying the application.

TIP
*There is class called **PushbackReader** that works on character streams, allowing you to push characters back into the stream.*

The SequenceInputStream Class

The **SequenceInputStream**, as the name indicates, provides a logical concatenation of other input streams. The construction of a **SequenceInputStream** is different from the other **InputStream** classes. The constructor either takes two arguments of the **InputStream** type or a list of **InputStream** objects contained in an **Enumeration** (**java.io.Enumeration**), which is basically an indexed list of items. Refer to the javadocs to learn more about the **Enumeration** interface. The two constructors are shown here:

```
SequenceInputStream(InputStream first, InputStream second);
SequenceInputStream(Enumeration streamEnum);
```

The **SequenceInputStream** class allows you to read multiple files in sequence and converts them into a single stream. The only methods available for this class are **read** and **close**. The **read** method fulfills the requests from the first input stream until it runs out of contents; it then switches over to the next one in the list, and so on, until it reaches the end-of-file (EOF) on the last listed file. An immediate application of this that comes to mind is combining multiple files into a single file. Recall the EOD (end-of-day) data files provided by the stock exchanges, discussed earlier. These are supplied on a daily basis. Suppose we want to perform some technical analysis on the historical data of a stock traded on the exchange? We need to combine these daily data files into a monthly or, rather, yearly data file for creating historical technical charts. We would use the **SequenceInputStream** class for this purpose, as demonstrated in the next application. Another reason to use this class is to create one input stream from multiple inputs and pass the new stream to another class that has more data-manipulation methods available. For example, we could use the **DataInputStream** class on our combined EOD prices file to retrieve the data in a format needed by a charting application. Listing 10-3 shows the code for the **FileMerger** application.

Listing 10-3 *A File Merge Utility Demonstrating the Use of SequenceInputStream*

```
import java.io.*;
import java.util.*;

public class FileMerger {

    private Vector listOfFileNames = new Vector();
    private Vector fileList = new Vector();
```

```java
public static void main(String args[]) throws IOException {
    FileMerger app = new FileMerger();
    app.getFileNames();
    if (!app.createFileList()) {
        System.exit(0);
    }
    app.mergeFiles();
}

private void getFileNames() {
    String fileName = "";
    System.out.println("Enter file names (one on a line): ");
    BufferedReader reader =
            new BufferedReader(new InputStreamReader(System.in));

    while (true) {
        try {
            fileName = reader.readLine();
        } catch (IOException e) {
            System.out.println("Error reading keyboard");
        }
        if ((fileName.equals("over"))) {
            break;
        }
        listOfFileNames.add(fileName);
    }
}

private boolean createFileList() {
    Enumeration list = listOfFileNames.elements();
    while (list.hasMoreElements()) {
        String fileName = (String) list.nextElement();
        InputStream inputStream = null;
        try {
            inputStream = new FileInputStream(fileName);
        } catch (FileNotFoundException fe) {
            System.out.println("File not found: " + fileName);
        }
        fileList.add(inputStream);
    }
    return true;
}

private void mergeFiles() throws FileNotFoundException {
    try (
            OutputStream outStream =
                    new FileOutputStream("monthlyDataFile.txt");
            SequenceInputStream inputStream =
                    new SequenceInputStream(fileList.elements());) {
        byte[] buffer = new byte[4096];
```

```
            int numberRead = 0;
            while ((numberRead = inputStream.read(buffer)) != -1) {
                outStream.write(buffer, 0, numberRead);
            }
        } catch (IOException e) {
            System.out.println("Error reading/writing file");
        }
        System.out.println(
                "Created monthlyDataFile.txt "
                + "in your current folder");
    }
}
```

The **FileMerger** class declares two variables of the **Vector** type. Because we have not covered this very useful class previously, I strongly recommend you open javadocs to study it in greater detail—you will use it quite often in your applications. We have covered arrays previously. As you'll recall, before using an array, we need to declare its size, which cannot be changed later in the program. The **Vector** class, on the other hand, implements a growable array of objects. Its elements can be accessed using an integer index, just the way we access array elements. The size of the **Vector** can grow or shrink dynamically as we add or remove elements from it. In our program, we accept a variable number of files from the user for concatenation. Therefore, we cannot use a fix-sized array for this application (using Java arrays would be awkward because we would need to keep creating new ones as the size changes). We declare two **Vector** variables, as follows:

```
private Vector listOfFileNames = new Vector();
private Vector fileList = new Vector();
```

The **listOfFileNames** vector stores the string objects with the names of the files to be merged. The **fileList** vector holds the open stream objects pertaining to each filename from the **listOfFileNames** array.

The **main** function creates an application instance and calls its **getFileNames** method. This method requests the user to enter the filenames, one on each line. To get the filename from the keyboard, we open a stream object on the keyboard as follows:

```
BufferedReader reader = new BufferedReader(new InputStreamReader(System.in));
```

NOTE
*We wrap **System.in** with a **BufferedReader** class, which you will learn about later in this chapter. The **BufferedReader** class provides a method called **readLine** that eases reading a line of text from the underlying stream.*

Next, the program sets an infinite loop for getting the filenames from the user. The **readLine** method reads one line of text. If this text equals "over," we terminate the loop. Note how the input **fileName** is compared to the string "over" by calling the **equals** method of the **String** class.

Once again, you are encouraged to open the javadocs to learn the various string-manipulation methods defined in the **String** class. We add each entered filename to the **Vector** by calling its **add** method:

```
listOfFileNames.add(fileName);
```

After receiving the filenames from the user, the program tries to open these files by calling its **createFileList** method. The method first obtains the list of filenames in an **Enumeration**. The **Enumeration** interface provides two methods: **hasMoreElements** and **nextElement**. These two methods have obvious meanings, as conveyed by their names. We set up a loop to iterate through the entire list:

```
while (list.hasMoreElements()) {
```

We read each element in the list object using the following statement:

```
String fileName = (String) list.nextElement();
```

Note that the list holds its elements using an **Object** reference. We need to typecast this to a desired type, which in this case is the type **String**. We now attempt to open the file having the specified name and add it to the **fileList** vector array:

```
inputStream = new FileInputStream(fileName);
fileList.add(inputStream);
```

After successfully opening all the listed files, the program proceeds with the file merger by calling its **mergeFiles** method. In the case of an error while opening any of the files, the program simply quits.

The **mergeFiles** method declares a variable of type **OutputStream** and creates a file called monthlyDataFile.txt using the following statement:

```
OutputStream outStream = new FileOutputStream("monthlyDataFile.txt");
```

Because we are going to merge all daily data files into a monthly file, we've named the output file accordingly to indicate that it is going to contain a month's worth of data. You may use any other name you choose.

Next, we build a **SequenceInputStream** object:

```
SequenceInputStream inputStream =
                new SequenceInputStream(fileList.elements());) {
```

The class constructor receives a set of filenames in an **Enumeration**, which is constructed by calling the **elements** methods of the **fileList** vector. After this, the program simply reads from the **inputStream** object an array of bytes and writes it to the previously created output file:

```
while ((numberRead = inputStream.read(buffer)) != -1) {
    outStream.write(buffer, 0, numberRead);
}
```

Note that this will read all the files added into the **SequenceInputStream** object. The output file now contains the concatenation of all the listed files.

Note that we use the **try-with-resources** syntax of Java SE 7 to open the files; thus, an explicit close on these files is not required.

Some typical sample output is shown here:

```
Enter file names (one on a line):

EQ210211.csv
EQ220211.csv
EQ230211.csv
EQ240211.csv
over
Created monthlyDataFile.txt in your current folder
```

If you examine the contents of the output file, you will notice that each file is specified in the sequence in which it was added to the vector.

The PrintStream Class

This is a very convenient class that has the ability to print representations of various data values, such as all primitive types. During printing it converts all characters into bytes using the platform's default character encoding.

TIP
What is character encoding? You must have heard about Morse Code, which has been in use worldwide for a long time. Morse Code maps textual information as a series of on/off tones, lights, or clicks. The skilled listener or observer interprets the original text without any special equipment. This is called character encoding. Several character encoding standards are in place today, including ISO 8859-1 (Western Europe), ISO 8859-2 (Western and Central Europe), ISO 8859-8 (Hebrew), and HKSCS (Hong Kong). Unicode, which you have certainly heard of, is one such character encoding. Java supports a variety of encoding standards. Such encoding systems map each character in a given repertoire to a certain sequence of natural numbers, octets, or electrical pulses to facilitate the data transmission of textual information through networks and stores them in computers.

The **PrintStream** class has several versions of an overloaded **print** method that accept a primitive data type as an argument. These methods include **print (boolean)**, **print (char)**, and **print (double)**. The corresponding **println** methods are also provided for your convenience; these print a newline at the end. The class also provides a C-style **printf** method that includes the format specifiers for the various data types in its placeholders. Unlike other output streams, this class does not throw an **IOException**. Calling its **checkError** method checks for exceptions. Optionally, a **PrintStream** can be created to flush automatically. For this, you would use the following constructor:

```
PrintStream (OutputStream out, Boolean autoFlush)
```

If **autoFlush** is enabled, the **flush** method will be automatically invoked after a byte array is written, a newline character (or '**\n**') is written, or one of the **println** methods is invoked.

NOTE
*The **System.out** object we've used several times so far for outputting to the console is of type **PrintStream**.*

The Character-Oriented Stream Classes

As the name suggests, character-oriented stream classes operate on characters. Java uses Unicode to store strings. You'll recall that Unicode is one of the encoding formats; Java supports a wide variety of encoding formats, all of which can be configured when reading/writing textual information with the reader/writer classes.

In the previous chapter, we looked at a few classes in this category. Let's continue our discussion by looking at a few more classes in this category.

The CharArray Reader/Writer Classes

Earlier in this chapter, we studied the **ByteArray** input/output classes, which operate on binary data. The corresponding equivalents of these classes that operate on character data are the **CharArrayReader** and **CharArrayWriter** classes. Like their binary counterparts, these classes operate on a buffer; however, this time the buffer is a character buffer rather than a byte buffer. Note that a character in Java consists of two bytes. Thus, each element of the character array takes up two bytes of space to represent a given character. Except for this difference, the two types of classes—**ByteArray** and **CharArray**—provide very similar functionality to each other. Like a **ByteArrayOutputStream** class, the **CharArrayWriter** class implements a character buffer that can grow dynamically. The **CharArrayReader** creates a reader on the existing buffer to read the characters stored in it. You have previously used the **String** class. This class provides an important method called **toCharArray** that returns a character array containing the elements of the string. Using this method, you will be able to construct an instance of **CharArrayReader** as follows:

```
CharArrayReader reader = new CharArrayReader(str.toCharArray());
```

Once an instance of **CharArrayReader** is obtained, you can use it for accessing the individual characters of the string to perform further operations on it.

The Console Class

So far we have been using **System.out** to print messages to the console. Java SE 6 added a **Console** class to enhance and simplify command-line applications. It provides a C-style **printf** method that allows the use of format specifiers in the output string. Most importantly, it provides a method for reading passwords that disables console echo and returns a **char** array. Both these features are very important for ensuring security, as explained shortly.

No public constructor is available for the **Console** class. You can obtain an instance of **Console** by calling the **console** method of the **System** class. It returns you a reference to the **Console** object. When you start the JVM from a command line, the console typically will be connected to the keyboard and the display, unless you have explicitly redirected these to other streams.

CAUTION
*A **Console** might not be available under some situations. For example, if you execute the program statement **System.console()** in a NetBeans IDE (as well as in some other IDEs), it returns a **null** object for the **Console**, because NetBeans provides its own window for the console output. Likewise, if a JVM is started by a background job scheduler, it will typically not have a console.*

The program shown in Listing 10-4 illustrates the use of the **Console** class. This program provides a secure login for a console-based application.

Listing 10-4   *Accepting a Secure Login in a Command-Line Application*

```java
import java.io.Console;
import java.util.Arrays;

public class ConsoleApp {

    private static final int MAX_LOGINS = 3;

    public static void main(String[] args) {
        ConsoleApp app = new ConsoleApp();
        if (app.login()) {
            System.out.println("Thanks for logging in!");
        } else {
            System.out.println("Login failed!");
        }
    }

    private boolean login() {
        Console console = System.console();
        boolean isAuthenticated = false;

        if (console != null) {
            int count = 0;
            do {
                char[] pwd = console.readPassword("[%s]", "Password:");
                isAuthenticated = authenticate(pwd);
                // delete password from memory
                Arrays.fill(pwd, ' ');
                console.writer().write("\n");
            } while (!isAuthenticated && ++count < MAX_LOGINS);
        }
        return isAuthenticated;
    }

    private boolean authenticate(char[] passwd) {
        char[] secret = {'M', 'c', 'G', 'R', 'A', 'W', 'H', 'I', 'L', 'L'};
        if (java.util.Arrays.equals(passwd, secret)) {
            java.util.Arrays.fill(passwd, ' ');
            System.out.println("Authenticated\n");
            return true;
        } else {
            System.out.println("Authentication failed\n");
        }
        return false;
    }
}
```

The **main** method creates an application instance and calls its **login** method before proceeding with the rest of the application's functionality. The **login** method obtains the **Console** object by calling the **console** method of the **System** class:

```
Console console = System.console();
```

This object would be **null** if we run the application in NetBeans. In such a situation, we return **false** to the caller, which eventually terminates the application. We give three attempts to the user to enter the correct password. We read the password using the following statement:

```
char[] pwd = console.readPassword("[%s]", "Password:");
```

The preceding statement prints a prompt on the user's console. The user-entered password is returned in the **pwd** character array. The **authenticate** method verifies the entered password with the system-stored password. Immediately after obtaining the result of this verification, we clear the character buffer with spaces:

```
Arrays.fill(pwd, ' ');
```

Now, two important things are happening here in regard to security. First, the **readPassword** does not echo the characters typed; therefore, even if someone is looking over the user's shoulder, the password is not revealed. Second, the password is cleared from system memory immediately after its use. If we had stored this password in a **String** variable, nullifying the **String** object still might have left the password string in the pool, thus making it available to a malicious resident program. Clearing the character buffer ensures that the password is removed from system memory. The idea behind the character array is that a primitive array can be deterministically cleared from memory, as opposed to a **String** or other container, thereby minimizing the time the sensitive data is active in the memory.

Finally, let's look at the implementation of the **authenticate** method. This is just a stub. The method stores the secret password in a character array. In reality, we would store an encrypted password, or rather the hash of the password, in a database. The **equals** method of the **Arrays** class compares its two arguments for equality. Depending on the outcome of this comparison, we print an appropriate message to the caller and return a **boolean** value to the caller.

The StreamTokenizer Class

The **StreamTokenizer** is another very useful class that parses an input stream into tokens. This class is not derived from **InputStream** or **OutputStream**. Yet, it is classified under the I/O library. The reason behind this is that it works only with **InputStream** objects. It tokenizes an underlying stream or even a **Reader** into tokens. Here's what we mean by tokenizing: The sentence "Mary had a little lamb" contains five tokens, because each word is considered a token.

TIP
The process of breaking a file's contents or a computer language program into tokens for further processing is called lexing.

Once a given input stream is tokenized, you use the **nextToken** method in a loop to iterate through all the tokens. For each token, you can find its kind, value, and so on, with the help of several predefined fields or attributes. For example, the **ttype** field indicates the type of token read, which can be a word, number, or end-of-line. The **sval** field indicates the string value of a token, and the **nval** field indicates its numeric value. You will learn to use these fields in the next program. Before starting the loop, we can set the syntax table to customize what is recognized and what is ignored; otherwise, we can simply use the default rules. The class recognizes identifiers, numbers, quoted strings, and C/C++-style comments.

The use of this class is illustrated in the program shown in Listing 10-5.

Listing 10-5   *Utility to Count Words and Numbers*

```java
import java.io.*;

public class WordAndNumberParser {

    public static void main(String args[]) throws IOException {
        if (args.length < 1) {
            System.out.println("Usage: java WordAndNumberParser <filename>");
            System.exit(0);
        }
        WordAndNumberParser app = new WordAndNumberParser();
        app.parseFile(args[0]);
    }

    private void parseFile(String fileName) {
        int wordCount = 0;
        int numberCount = 0;
        try (FileReader reader = new FileReader(fileName);) {
            StreamTokenizer tokenizer = new StreamTokenizer(reader);
            tokenizer.slashSlashComments(true);
            tokenizer.slashStarComments(true);
            while (tokenizer.nextToken() != StreamTokenizer.TT_EOF) {
                if (tokenizer.ttype == StreamTokenizer.TT_WORD) {
                    wordCount++;
                } else if (tokenizer.ttype == StreamTokenizer.TT_NUMBER) {
                    numberCount++;
                }
                if (tokenizer.sval != null
                        && tokenizer.sval.equals("DataInputStream")) {
                    System.out.println(tokenizer.toString());
                }
            }
        } catch (FileNotFoundException fe) {
            System.out.println("File not found: " + fileName);
            return;
        } catch (IOException ioe) {
            System.out.println("Error parsing file");
        }
        System.out.println("Number of words: " + wordCount);
        System.out.println("Number of numerals: " + numberCount);
    }
}
```

The **main** function, after checking for the proper invocation, creates an application instance and calls its **parseFile** method. The **parseFile** method creates a **StreamTokenizer** instance by first opening the given file using the character-oriented reader classes discussed earlier:

```
FileReader reader = new FileReader(fileName);
StreamTokenizer tokenizer = new StreamTokenizer(reader);
```

Note that we use the **try-with-resources** syntax of Java SE 7 for opening the file. Before parsing the file, we set the following constraints:

```
tokenizer.slashSlashComments(true);
tokenizer.slashStarComments(true);
```

The **tokenizer** now ignores both styles of Java comments (that is, single and multiline). The **tokenizer** ignores all the tokens inside these comments. We now set up a **while** loop to iterate through all the tokens in the file:

```
while (tokenizer.nextToken() != StreamTokenizer.TT_EOF) {
```

For each token, we check whether it is an alphanumeric word or a number by comparing its **ttype** field with the predefined constants:

```
if (tokenizer.ttype == StreamTokenizer.TT_WORD) {
    wordCount++;
} else if (tokenizer.ttype == StreamTokenizer.TT_NUMBER) {
    numberCount++;
}
```

Accordingly, the program increments the two counters. Within the loop, we also check whether the current token equals the identifier **DataInputStream**. If so, we print the line number on which the token is found:

```
if (tokenizer.sval != null
        && tokenizer.sval.equals("DataInputStream")) {
    System.out.println(tokenizer.toString());
}
```

After the loop terminates, the program prints the word and number count to the console. A sample, typical output run on the same program listing (that is, Listing 10-5) is shown here:

```
Token[DataInputStream], line 34
Number of words: 82
Number of numerals: 5
```

The output shows the word **DataInputStream** occurred in one place, on line number 34. The number of words in the entire file is 82, and the number of numerals is five. We can modify the contents of the comments in the input file to confirm that the tokenizer indeed ignores the comments. Note that the actual output will vary depending on your input file.

The Object-Oriented Streams

In the last chapter, you saw how to store and retrieve the objects. We'll now look at a few more techniques for storing and retrieving objects.

The Externalizable Interface

The previous chapter covered the use of the **Serializable** interface for persisting the object state. We'll now look at the **Externalizable** interface, which provides control over the serialization process. If an object implements the **Serializable** interface, all its fields get persisted unless they are marked with the **transient** keyword or are declared **static** in the class. The **transient** keyword was designed to meet this specific requirement of allowing the object's field containing sensitive data not to persist. The class may hold some sensitive data, such as credit card number, encryption key, and so on, in its fields. Also, the class may declare a few instance fields for its own internal workings and may also contain declarations of some temporary variables. Obviously, you won't want to transmit such data over the network or even store it to disk. You would mark such fields with the **transient** keyword. When you save or transmit such an object, its entire other state will be transmitted or saved. Likewise, the fields that are marked with the **static** keyword are not serialized; this is because such fields belong to the class and not to an object.

In some situations, you may want to provide your own way to persist the object state, other than the default algorithm used by the JVM. For example, if your object is of type **Customer** and contains credit card numbers in one of its fields, you will not want to save this number as is. Instead, you would encrypt this field before the **Customer** object is saved to persistent storage or transmitted over the network. This is where the interface **Externalizable** comes in handy. This interface has two callback methods: **readExternal** and **writeExternal**. Before the object is persisted, the runtime calls these two methods. You can perform operations such as encryption and decryption in these two methods. Also, you need to write code to persist whatever fields you want to save.

The **Serializable** interface uses the default runtime mechanism to implement the object serialization, whereas the **Externalizable** interface mandates that the class handle its own serialization. This means that you need to decide which fields to write (and read) and in what order. You implement this in the **writeExternal** (and corresponding **readExternal**) method.

TIP
*Because implementing the **Externalizable** interface mandates that you write code for serializing the desired fields of the class, the rest of the class fields need not be marked **transient**.*

A program that illustrates the use of the **Externalizable** interface is given in Listing 10-6. Note that the program uses Java's security API. You need not worry about the security code while learning the importance of the **Externalizable** interface.

Listing 10-6 *Program Illustrating the Externalizable Interface*

```
import java.io.*;
import javax.crypto.*;
import javax.crypto.spec.SecretKeySpec;

public class ExternalizableTestApp {

    public static void main(String args[]) throws IOException {
        try {
            Customer customer = new Customer(1, "1234-5678-9876");
            System.out.println("Before saving object: ");
```

```
            System.out.println(
                    "ID:" + customer.getId()
                    + "  CC:" + customer.getCreditCard());
            ObjectOutputStream outStream = new ObjectOutputStream(
                    new FileOutputStream("customer.dat"));
            outStream.writeObject(customer);
            outStream.close();
            ObjectInputStream inputStream = new ObjectInputStream(
                    new FileInputStream("customer.dat"));
            customer = (Customer) inputStream.readObject();
            System.out.println("After retrieving object: ");
            System.out.println("ID:" + customer.getId()
                    + "  CC:" + customer.getCreditCard());
            inputStream.close();
        } catch (Exception ex) {
            ex.printStackTrace();
        }
    }
}

class Customer implements Externalizable {

    private int id;
    private String creditCard;
    private static Cipher cipher;
    private static SecretKeySpec skeySpec;

    static {
        try {
            createCipher();
        } catch (Exception e) {
            e.printStackTrace();
            System.exit(0);
        }
    }

    public String getCreditCard() {
        return creditCard;
    }

    public int getId() {
        return id;
    }

    public Customer() {
        id = 0;
        creditCard = "";
    }
```

```java
    public Customer(int id, String ccNumber) {
        this.id = id;
        this.creditCard = ccNumber;
    }

    public void writeExternal(ObjectOutput out) throws IOException {
        try {
            out.write(id);
            encrypt();
            out.writeUTF(creditCard);
            System.out.println("After encryption: ");
            System.out.println("ID:" + id + "  CC:" + creditCard);
        } catch (Exception ex) {
            ex.printStackTrace();
        }
    }

    public void readExternal(ObjectInput in)
            throws IOException, ClassNotFoundException {
        try {
            id = in.read();
            String str = in.readUTF();
            decrypt(str);
        } catch (Exception ex) {
            ex.printStackTrace();
        }
    }

    private static void createCipher() throws Exception {
        KeyGenerator kgen = KeyGenerator.getInstance("AES");
        kgen.init(128);
        // Generate the secret key specs.
        SecretKey skey = kgen.generateKey();
        byte[] raw = skey.getEncoded();
        skeySpec = new SecretKeySpec(raw, "AES");
        // Instantiate the cipher
        cipher = Cipher.getInstance("AES");
    }

    private void encrypt() throws Exception {
        cipher.init(Cipher.ENCRYPT_MODE, skeySpec);
        byte[] buff = cipher.doFinal(creditCard.getBytes());
        creditCard = new String(buff);
    }

    private void decrypt(String str) throws Exception {
        cipher.init(Cipher.DECRYPT_MODE, skeySpec);
        byte[] buff = cipher.doFinal(str.getBytes());
        creditCard = new String(buff);
    }
}
```

The **main** function creates an instance of the **Customer** object:

```
Customer customer = new Customer(1, "1234-5678-9876");
```

The first parameter to the **Customer** constructor is the customer ID, and the second parameter is the credit card number. We will be saving this customer information to a disk file. However, before saving the customer instance, we must encrypt the credit card information so that anybody with access to the disk file will not be able to steal the customer credit card information. The **main** function creates the customer.dat file for writing the customer data and then writes the **Customer** object by calling its **writeObject** method:

```
ObjectOutputStream outStream = new ObjectOutputStream(
    new FileOutputStream("customer.dat"));
outStream.writeObject(customer);
```

Before the object is serialized, the **Customer** object ensures that its credit card field is encrypted, as explained shortly. After saving the object, the program closes the data file and reopens it for reading the saved information:

```
ObjectInputStream inputStream = new ObjectInputStream(
    new FileInputStream("customer.dat"));
```

The **readObject** method now reads back the stored information and re-creates the customer object:

```
customer = (Customer) inputStream.readObject();
```

Before the object is fully initialized, it ensures that its credit card information is decrypted. The program prints the object's state to the user console before saving it to disk and after retrieving it from disk. When we run the program, the following output is shown:

```
Before saving object:
ID:1   CC:1234-5678-9876
After encryption:
ID:1   CC:\MT?s?/?X|[YQ.
After retrieving object:
ID:1   CC:1234-5678-9876
```

The output also shows the intermediate state after the credit card field is encrypted. Now, let's look at the implementation of the **Customer** class. This class implements the **Externalizable** interface:

```
class Customer implements Externalizable {
```

As part of the implementation, it must implement the two interface methods **writeExternal** and **readExternal**. We'll look at the **writeExternal** method first:

```
public void writeExternal(ObjectOutput out) throws IOException {
    try {
        out.write(id);
        encrypt();
        out.writeUTF(creditCard);
```

In this method, we first write the **id** field to the output stream. The **encrypt** method encrypts the **creditCard** field of the **Customer** class. After encryption, the program writes it to disk by calling the **writeUTF** method of the output stream. If we examine the contents of the disk file, we'll find only the encrypted version of the credit card information stored in the file.

The **readExternal** method provides the decryption of the **creditCard** field:

```
public void readExternal(ObjectInput in)
        throws IOException, ClassNotFoundException {
    try {
        id = in.read();
        String str = in.readUTF();
        decrypt(str);
```

The method first reads the **id**, followed by the encrypted credit card information. The **decrypt** method decrypts this information and copies the plain text to the **creditCard** field of the **Customer** object. Thus, the program always sees the plain text (the unencrypted version) of the credit card information. However, the stored data always contains the encrypted version of this field. The **readExternal** and **writeExternal** methods do this trick transparently.

NOTE
*The rest of the code in the **Customer** class uses the security API. Explaining this code is beyond the scope of this book. Be sure to refer to the security API in Java documentation for further details.*

Nested Objects Serialization

A **Serializable** object may contain references to other objects. You may be wondering if you serialize an object, whether the nested objects are also serialized. The answer is yes—the nested objects will also be serialized (unless they are marked **transient**) along with the top-level object, provided that all the concerned objects implement the **Serializable** or **Externalizable** interface. Listing 10-7 provides an example to illustrate this feature.

Listing 10-7 *Serializing Nested Objects*

```
import java.awt.Color;
import java.io.*;

public class NestedObjectsApp {

    public static void main(String args[]) {
        Line line = new Line();
        System.out.println("Before saving object:\n" + line);
        try (ObjectOutputStream outStream = new ObjectOutputStream(
                        new FileOutputStream("graph.dat"))) {
            outStream.writeObject(line);
        } catch (IOException ex) {
            System.out.println("Error writing object");
        }
        try (ObjectInputStream inStream = new ObjectInputStream(
                        new FileInputStream("graph.dat"));) {
```

```
            line = (Line) inStream.readObject();
        } catch (IOException ioe) {
            System.out.println("Error reading object");
        } catch (ClassNotFoundException cfe) {
            System.out.println("Casting error");
        }
        System.out.println("\nAfter retrieving object:\n" + line);
    }
}

class Point implements Serializable {

    protected int x;
    protected int y;

    public Point(int x, int y) {
        this.x = x;
        this.y = y;
    }
}

class ColorPoint extends Point implements Serializable {

    private Color color;

    public ColorPoint(int x, int y, Color color) {
        super(x, y);
        this.color = color;
    }

    @Override
    public String toString() {
        return "Point{" + "x=" + x + " y=" + y + '}'
                + "  ColorPoint{" + "color=" + color + '}';
    }
}

class Line implements Serializable {

    private ColorPoint startPoint = new ColorPoint(0, 0, Color.red);
    private ColorPoint endPoint = new ColorPoint(10, 10, Color.blue);

    @Override
    public String toString() {
        return "StartPoint=" + startPoint + "\nEndPoint=" + endPoint;
    }
}
```

The program declares a class called **Point** having fields **x**, **y**. The class is serializable. The **ColorPoint** class inherits the **Point** class and declares a **Color** field. This, too, is serializable. The **Line** class declares two fields of the **ColorPoint** type and initializes them.

The **main** function creates a **Line** object and prints its initial state. It then serializes the created object to a disk file and closes it. The program reopens the file, reads the data into a **Line** object, and prints its state. When you run the program, you will notice that the original state of the **Line** object is restored. It indicates that when you save an object, all its nested objects are also saved along with their inherent states. The program output is given here:

```
Before saving object:
StartPoint=Point{x=0 y=0}   ColorPoint{color=java.awt.Color[r=255,g=0,b=0]}
EndPoint=Point{x=10 y=10}   ColorPoint{color=java.awt.Color[r=0,g=0,b=255]}

After retrieving object:
StartPoint=Point{x=0 y=0}   ColorPoint{color=java.awt.Color[r=255,g=0,b=0]}
EndPoint=Point{x=10 y=10}   ColorPoint{color=java.awt.Color[r=0,g=0,b=255]}
```

Versioning Objects

We have covered how to persist the object state to a disk file. In many situations, the classes in a program evolve over time. When a class definition changes, the object's data saved with previous versions of the class becomes mostly unreadable. Versioning objects can manage this kind of situation where you are trying to read from an older version of the class. We will demonstrate this problem with a typical example in a practical situation. Consider the program shown in Listing 10-8.

Listing 10-8 *Program to Serialize the Product Class*

```java
import java.io.*;

public class ProductWriter {

    public static void main(String args[]) throws IOException {
        Product p1 = new Product(100);
        ObjectOutputStream os = new ObjectOutputStream(
                new FileOutputStream("product.dat"));
        os.writeObject(p1);
        os.close();
    }
}

class Product implements Serializable {

    private float price;
    private float tax;

    public Product(float price) {
        this.price = price;
        tax = (float) (price * 0.20);
    }
}
```

The program declares a **Product** class that has two fields, **price** and **tax**, of type **float**. The **main** function constructs an instance of **Product** and saves it to a physical disk file. After the data is saved at a later time, we want to read this data from the disk file and use it in future applications. For this, we write a **ProductReader** class, as shown in Listing 10-9.

Listing 10-9   *Program to Read Serialized Product Data*

```
import java.io.*;

public class ProductReader {

    public static void main(String args[]) throws Exception {
        ObjectInputStream is = new ObjectInputStream(
                new FileInputStream("product.dat"));
        Product p1 = (Product) is.readObject();
        System.out.println(p1.toString());
    }
}
```

The program simply opens the previously created data file, reads its data into the **Product** object, and prints its contents. When we run the program, output similar to the following is shown:

```
Product@9304b1
```

Whatever is printed to the console is definitely not what we want. We want the product's price and tax to be printed to the console. Therefore, we will now override the default **toString** method of the **Product** class. The modified **Product** class definition is shown in Listing 10-10.

Listing 10-10   *Modified Product Class*

```
class Product implements Serializable {

    private float price;
    private float tax;

    public Product(float price) {
        this.price = price;
        tax = (float) (price * 0.20);
    }

    public String toString() {
        return ("Price:" + price + "  Tax:" + tax);
    }
}
```

Now, let's run the **ProductReader** application again. We'll see the following error printed to the console:

```
Exception in thread "main" java.io.InvalidClassException: Product; local class
incompatible: stream classdesc serialVersionUID = -4609301823165882715, local
class serialVersionUID = -3424249794808075076
```

This is because the **Product** state was saved with the previous version of the **Product** class. Java assigns a unique identifier (**serialversionUID**) to every serializable class during compilation. Thus, when we change the class definition, the object state information we had saved becomes incompatible with the new version of the class. This problem can be solved by adding the **serialversionUID** (which represents the stream unique identifier, or SUID) of the original class to the modified class definition. To determine the **serialversionUID** of a class, run the following command on the command prompt:

```
C:\360\ch10>serialver Product
Product:    static final long serialVersionUID = -3424249794808075076L;
```

The utility gives us the serial version UID of the specified class. Copy the following statement into the new class definition:

```
static final long serialVersionUID = -3424249794808075076L;
```

Note that the ID generated on your machine will differ from what's shown here. The modified **Product** class is shown in Listing 10-11.

Listing 10-11   *Product Class Having the Same Serial Version UID*

```java
class Product implements Serializable {

    private float price;
    private float tax;
    static final long serialVersionUID = -3424249794808075076L;
    public Product(float price) {
        this.price = price;
        tax = (float) (price * 0.20);
    }

    public String toString() {
        return ("Price:" + price + "  Tax:" + tax);
    }
}
```

Recompile the **Product** class and re-run your **ProductReader** application. You will see the following output:

```
Price:100.0  Tax:20.0
```

The new class now uses the **serialVersionUID** of the earlier class. The compiler in this case does not generate the new ID for the modified class. Thus, the objects created with earlier versions now remain compatible with the newer versions as far as serialization is concerned.

CAUTION
*If you modify the class fields, add a new field, or delete an existing field, the object's saved state will become incompatible with the earlier version of the class. The earlier objects will still be readable with the modified class definitions as long as you maintain the same **serialVersionUID** across the different versions of a class. Your program should take care of the newly added fields or the missing fields when you read the data stored in earlier versions.*

Summary

This chapter covered many important classes of the **java.io** package. The **PushbackInputStream** class allows you to read ahead in the buffer. This class is very useful in compiler construction and in general for parsing text documents. The **SequenceInputStream** class allows you to combine multiple streams into a single stream. The **PrintStream** class provides functions for printing primitive data types and also formatted strings. The data input/output stream classes facilitate the reading/writing of primitive data types.

Under the character-oriented streams, we covered four important classes. The **CharArray** reader/writer classes operate on character array data and are equivalent to **ByteArray** input/output stream classes that operate on byte data. The **Console** class provides several useful methods to output primitive data types to the user console. The **StreamTokenizer** class facilitates parsing the file contents into tokens. Besides numeric and alphanumeric data, it also recognizes both types of Java comments. Therefore, this class is very useful for parsing the source code.

Under the object-oriented streams, we discussed the use of the **Externalizable** interface. This interface allows you to control the object serialization process. When you serialize an object, all the referenced objects within it also get serialized. Thus, the entire object tree can be serialized and deserialized easily via the serialization mechanism.

Finally, this chapter described the problems encountered in object serialization when classes evolve over a period of time. Maintaining the same serial version ID across the different versions resolves this problem.

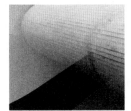

CHAPTER
11

Enums, Autoboxing, and Annotations

t this point in the book, you have learned many features of the Java language. Most of these features are part of the original language specification. The language itself has evolved substantially over last several years. Many new features have been added to the language throughout the various versions of Java SE. Java SE 6 and some of the releases prior to J2SE 5.0 did not add anything new to the language. We studied some of these features, such as enhanced **for** loops and varargs, in the previous chapters. We will now look at some more advanced features. Although the list is long, it is not exhaustive, and you will continue learning more language features in the chapters to follow.

In particular, this chapter covers the following features:

- Typesafe enumerations
- Primitive data type wrappers
- Bit manipulations using wrapper classes
- The NaN (Not-a-Number) infinity definitions
- Character manipulations using character class
- Autoboxing and unboxing
- Annotating your code
- Types of annotations
- Creating your own annotations
- Annotating your annotations

Typesafe Enumerations

Oftentimes, you need a fixed set of constants in your application. Examples might include the days of the week and the colors in a rainbow. To create such sets, you create integer patterns in your code. In this section, we discuss these integer patterns—how they are created and what their drawbacks are—before looking at the new **enum** construct.

Creating Integer Patterns for Enumerations

To declare enumerations for the colors of a rainbow, we would declare the following sort of **int** pattern:

```
public static final int COLOR_VIOLET = 0;
public static final int COLOR_INDIGO = 1;
public static final int COLOR_BLUE = 2;
```

Using such an **int** pattern poses many problems. In the first place, they are not typesafe. We could simply pass in any **int** value where a color in a rainbow is required. Even worse, we could do some arithmetic on these colors, which is obviously meaningless. Second, to avoid name collisions with other constants in our application, we need to prefix their names, which is why the COLOR prefix is used in this example. Third, such enumeration types are brittle in the sense that they are compiled on the client. Later on, if we change their order or simply add a new constant, the client would require a recompilation. If not recompiled, the client would behave unpredictably. Finally, if we print these constants in our program, what we get are simply integer values, which don't convey what they represent or their type.

NOTE
Sir Isaac Newton originally named only five primary colors (red, yellow, green, blue, and violet) in a rainbow. Later he added orange and indigo. Thus, even in such rare cases, the constants in an enumeration type could change.

The enum Type

The issues we just discussed are now resolved with the introduction of the **enum** type in J2SE 5.0. The **enum** type in Java is more enhanced compared to similar-looking enumerations in other languages. In most other languages, an enumeration is simply a list of named integer constants. In Java, **enum** is a full-fledged class and thus offers all the benefits of declaring a class, as discussed so far in this book. It allows you to add arbitrary methods and fields, to implement arbitrary interfaces, and much more. The objects of the **enum** type can be compared to each other and can be serialized—the serialization withstands arbitrary changes in the **enum** type. To illustrate these benefits, let's look at some concrete examples.

Listing Enumeration Constants

Suppose we want to create a list of the days in a week. We would do so with the following declaration:

```
enum WeekDays {

    MONDAY, TUESDAY, WEDNESDAY, THURSDAY, FRIDAY, SATURDAY, SUNDAY;
}
```

This declaration assigns integer ordinal values to the constants. Thus, MONDAY takes a value of 0, TUESDAY takes a value of 1, and so on. If we try to print a list of days in a **for** loop, the output would simply list these ordinal values. With the new facilities available in **enum**, we can overcome this problem easily by adding an overloaded **toString** method to the declaration. This can be seen in Listing 11-1.

Listing 11-1 *Enumerating the Days of the Week*

```
public class WeekDaysList {

    public static void main(String[] args) {
        System.out.println("Days of week:");
        for (DaysOfTheWeek day : DaysOfTheWeek.values()) {
            System.out.printf("%s ", day);
        }
        System.out.println();
    }
}

enum DaysOfTheWeek {
```

```
MONDAY, TUESDAY, WEDNESDAY, THURSDAY, FRIDAY, SATURDAY, SUNDAY;

@Override
public String toString() {
    //only capitalize the first letter
    String s = super.toString();
    return s.substring(0, 1) + s.substring(1).toLowerCase();
}
}
```

The **DaysOfTheWeek** enumeration, after declaring the seven constants pertaining to the days of the week, adds a definition of the overloaded **toString** method. Here, we obtain the string representation of each constant by calling **super.toString**. We then retain the first letter of the string and convert the rest into lowercase. The modified string is returned to the caller. In the **main** function, we iterate through all the elements of the **enum** using a **foreach** loop:

```
for (DaysOfTheWeek day : DaysOfTheWeek.values()) {
    System.out.printf("%s ", day);
}
```

The **values** method returns an array that contains a list of enumeration constants. When we print the element **day**, its **toString** method is called by default. Our overridden **toString** method prints each constant in its string format with only the first letter capitalized. The program output is shown here:

```
Days of week:
Monday Tuesday Wednesday Thursday Friday Saturday Sunday
```

This takes care of one of the problems mentioned earlier—the string representation of each enumeration constant is returned rather than its ordinal number (an integer).

Adding Properties to an Enumeration

To add a property to an enumeration constant, we would need to define its constructor.

NOTE
*The **enum** class has only a single protected constructor that cannot be invoked by a programmer.*

To illustrate, let's create an enumeration of apples. Apples come in several varieties. Each variety has a specific name and a price that may be different from the other varieties. A constructor for **Apple** will facilitate setting its price at the time of its construction. We can also define a method to retrieve the price of each apple. This program is shown in Listing 11-2.

Listing 11-2 *Adding Custom Properties to an Enumeration*

```
enum Apple {

    AURORA(10), BELMAC(12), CORTLAND(15), EMPIRE(8), GRAVENSTEIN(11);
    private int price;
```

```
    // Constructor
    Apple(int price) {
        this.price = price;
    }

    int getPrice() {
        return price;
    }
}

public class ApplesEnum {

    public static void main(String args[]) {
        System.out.println("Apple price list:");
        for (Apple apple : Apple.values()) {
            System.out.println(apple + " costs "
                    + apple.getPrice() + " cents.");
        }
    }
}
```

The **Apple** enumeration declares five different varieties:

```
AURORA(10), BELMAC(12), CORTLAND(15), EMPIRE(8), GRAVENSTEIN(11);
```

Each constant declaration now accepts a parameter. In fact, each time a constant is declared, its constructor is called, and this parameter is sent as an argument to the constructor. The constructor is declared the same way as for any other class declaration:

```
Apple(int price) {
    this.price = price;
}
```

The parameter **price** is copied to a **private** instance variable. Thus, when we declare the constant **AURORA**, its price will be set to its input parameter value, which is 10. Likewise, **BELMAC** gets a price of 12, and so on. We also define a **getPrice** method that returns this price to the caller.

In the **main** function, we print the name and price of each apple using a **foreach** loop:

```
for (Apple apple : Apple.values()) {
    System.out.println(apple + " costs " + apple.getPrice() + " cents.");
}
```

Note that the call to **apple** in this print statement calls its default **toString** method. The explicit call to **getPrice** returns the price of the specified instance.

NOTE
We could easily add more apple varieties to this enumeration and/or change the order of these varieties without breaking the client code. This solves the problem with the integer pattern for enumerations discussed earlier.

The ordinal and compareTo Methods

The two most useful methods of the **enum** class are **ordinal** and **compareTo**. The **ordinal** method returns the ordinal value of the current enumeration constant, which is its position in the list of constants. The first constant in the list takes an ordinal value of 0. Thus, MONDAY in the **DaysOfTheWeek** enumeration has an ordinal value of 0, TUESDAY has a value of 1, and so on. The **compareTo** method compares this enumeration with another object for its order in the enumeration. The method returns a negative integer, zero, or a positive integer, depending on whether the current object appears before, is equal to, or appears after the specified object. For example, if the current day instance is **DaysOfTheWeek.WEDNESDAY** and we compare it with **DaysOfTheWeek.SATURDAY**, the function returns a value of –3. If we compare it with **DaysOfTheWeek.MONDAY**, the return value is +2.

Attaching Methods to Enumerations

Suppose we want to convert a user-specified weight in pounds to a different unit of measure, such as kilograms, carats, or ounces. To convert pounds into kilograms, for example, we would multiply the given value by the constant 0.45359237. To convert pounds into carats, you would multiply the given value by the constant 2267.96185. Thus, we could be tempted to declare the following type of enumeration:

```
enum Converter {

    0.45359237, 2267.96185, 453.59237, 16, ..., ...
}
```

Now, we will need to remember that the first conversion factor converts the given pounds into kilograms, the second converts it into carats, the third converts it into grams, and so on. In the future, if we change this order or insert one more conversion factor between two existing ones, we cannot be assured that the conversions performed in the client application will be accurate for all measurement units. We can easily overcome this problem by using the class features of the **enum** declaration. For each constant, we define a conversion method. To understand how this is done, refer to the complete conversion utility given in Listing 11-3.

Listing 11-3 *Attaching a Method to an Enumeration Constant*

```
public class UnitsConverter {

    private static double numberToConvert = 0;

    public static void main(String[] args) {

        if (args.length == 0) {
            System.out.println(
                    "Usage: java UnitsConverter <weight in pounds>");
            System.exit(0);
        }
        numberToConvert = Double.parseDouble(args[0]);
        System.out.println("lbs " + args[0] + " equals:\n");
        for (Converter conv : Converter.values()) {
            System.out.printf("%s: %f%n",
```

```java
                        conv, conv.performConversion(numberToConvert));
        }
    }
}

enum Converter {

    KG("KG") {

        double performConversion(double f) {
            return f *= 0.45359237;
        }
    },
    CARAT("carat") {

        double performConversion(double f) {
            return f *= 2267.96185;
        }
    },
    GMS("gms") {

        double performConversion(double f) {
            return f *= 453.59237;
        }
    },
    OUNCE("ounce") {

        double performConversion(double f) {
            return f *= 16;
        }
    },
    STONE("stone") {

        double performConversion(double f) {
            return f *= 0.071428571429;
        }
    };
    private final String symbol;

    Converter(String symbol) {
        this.symbol = symbol;
    }

    @Override
    public String toString() {
        return symbol;
    }

    abstract double performConversion(double f);
}
```

In this code, we declare an enumeration called **Converter**. We also define an abstract method called **performConversion**, as follows:

```
abstract double performConversion(double f);
```

Each constant defined in the **Converter** will now have to implement this method. Look at the **KG** declaration, shown here:

```
KG("KG") {

    double performConversion(double f) {
        return f *= 0.45359237;
    }
},
```

The declaration implements the **performConversion** method, which multiplies the input number by a predefined constant. This constant value is the same as the one specified earlier to convert pounds into kilograms. The name of the constant is **KG**. Its instance is created by calling the constructor as follows:

```
KG ("KG")
```

The constructor takes a string argument that will be used in printing the name or the description of the respective constant. For this, we define a private constructor, as in the earlier case, that copies the input parameter into an instance variable. We also override the **toString** method, as in the earlier case, to return the appropriate name to the caller.

Likewise, we add the definitions of other conversions such as **CARAT**, **GMS**, **OUNCE**, and so on. In the **main** function, we simply iterate through all the elements of this **Converter** enumeration to print the conversions of a given value to different units. Typical program output is shown here:

```
lbs 5.0 equals:

KG: 2.267962
carat: 11339.809250
gms: 2267.961850
ounce: 80.000000
stone: 0.357143
```

In the future, if we want to add more conversion units, we can do so easily by adding a new constant definition anywhere we want. For example, to add a **troy ounce** conversion after the **ounce** conversion, we add the following constant declaration between the **ounce** and **stone** declarations:

```
TROYOUNCE("troy ounce") {

    double performConversion(double f) {
        return f *= 14.583333333;
    }
},
```

When you run the client program after this new addition is done, in the output you will see the given pounds converted into **troy ounce**.

NOTE
*Whenever we add a new constant in the **Converter** enumeration,
we need to provide the implementation of the **performConversion**
method because this method has been declared an **abstract** method
in the **Converter** enumeration. This makes the enumeration definition
foolproof.*

Serializing enum Types

Earlier you learned that objects of the **enum** type can be serialized and compared to each other. Suppose we create an enumeration for the colors used in a drawing program. Such an enumeration may look like this:

```
enum ColorPalette {

    RED, GREEN, BLUE
}
```

We can select the color green for the current drawing with the following declaration:

```
ColorPalette drawingColor = ColorPalette.GREEN;
```

We can now save the **drawingColor** object to a setting file by calling the **writeObject** method of the **ObjectOutputStream** class (refer to the previous chapter). The code might look like this:

```
ObjectOutputStream outStream = new ObjectOutputStream(
                                new FileOutputStream("Settings.dat"));
outStream.writeObject(drawingColor);
```

Later on, to read the settings from the Settings.dat file, we would use the following code:

```
ObjectInputStream inStream = new ObjectInputStream(
                                new FileInputStream("Settings.dat"));
System.out.println("Retrieved object: "
                    + (ColorPalette) inStream.readObject());
```

This prints GREEN to the terminal. Note that the message printed to the console is the string name of the constant rather than its ordinal value. The default implementation of the **toString** method of the **enum** class does this for you.

Earlier you learned that serialization withstands arbitrary changes in the **enum** type. So now, let's modify our definition of the **ColorPalette** enumeration as follows:

```
enum ColorPalette {

    RED, YELLOW, GREEN, MAGENTA, BLUE, VIOLET
}
```

Note that we have now added a new color (yellow) before green. If we read the previous Settings.dat file, GREEN is still printed to the console, although the ordinal value of GREEN has now changed. The trivial code for testing this is provided in Listing 11-4.

Listing 11-4   *Serializing Enumeration Constants*

```
import java.io.*;

public class EnumSerialization {

    public static void main(String[] args) {
        ColorPalette drawingColor = ColorPalette.GREEN;

        try {
            System.out.println("Saving color setting");
            ObjectOutputStream outStream = new ObjectOutputStream(
                    new FileOutputStream("Settings.dat"));
            outStream.writeObject(drawingColor);
            outStream.close();
            ObjectInputStream inStream = new ObjectInputStream(
                    new FileInputStream("Settings.dat"));
            System.out.println("Retrieved object: "
                    + (ColorPalette) inStream.readObject());
            inStream.close();
        } catch (IOException e) {
            System.out.println("Error reading/writing object");
        } catch (ClassNotFoundException cfe) {
            System.out.println("Class casting error");
        }
    }
}

enum ColorPalette {

    RED, GREEN, BLUE
}
```

We will now discuss the next vital addition to Java language that eases coding effort to a great extent—autoboxing.

Autoboxing

J2SE 5.0 introduced a new feature called *autoboxing* and *unboxing* that automatically converts between the primitive data types and their wrapper classes. To understand this feature and appreciate its importance, you need to understand the previously used wrapper classes.

Wrapper Classes

As you know, Java is highly object oriented. But what about its primitive data types? Are these objects? The answer to this question is no; the primitive data types in Java are not classes. Therefore, you lose the advantages that you have with classes when using the primitive data types. Here are some of the disadvantages:

■   The simple data types are not part of the **Object** hierarchy and therefore cannot be used as objects, as you would do with any other class in the **Object** hierarchy.

- You cannot pass a primitive data type to a Java method by reference; it is always sent by value.

- Two different methods in your program cannot refer to the same instance of a simple data type.

- Some classes can use only objects and cannot use simple data types. For example, the **Vector** class we covered previously cannot hold a list of numbers.

To overcome this and other limitations, Java provides type wrappers for all its primitive data types. The **Integer** class wraps an **int** data type, the **Float** class wraps a **float** data type, and so on. Each of the primitive data types is wrapped into a class having the same name as the data type but with the first letter capitalized. The exceptions are **char**, for which the wrapper class is called **Character**, and the **int** type, for which the wrapper class is **Integer**. All these wrapper classes are derived from the **Number** class.

Let's go over a few important fields and methods of these wrapper classes that you will use frequently. The **MAX_VALUE** and **MIN_VALUE** fields define the maximum and the minimum values for the data type being wrapped. The **parseInt** method (and the **parseXxx** methods for other data types) takes a string argument with an optional radix argument and returns the corresponding data type to the caller after converting the value specified in its argument. The **valueOf** method takes a primitive data type as its argument and returns an object of the corresponding wrapper class. The **toString** method returns the string representation of the value of the wrapped primitive data type. These classes also provide a **xxxValue()** method that returns the wrapped primitive type. For example, the **booleanValue** method of the class **Boolean** will return a **boolean** data type, and the **intValue** method of the class **Integer** will return an **int** variable.

TIP
For simple tasks, primitives are easy to use because you can use many of the operators on them, rather than calling methods.

To wrap a primitive type into one of these classes, you use the provided class constructor. Generally, each of these classes provides two constructors: one that takes a primitive type and one that takes a string as a parameter. For example, you can wrap an integer data type using any of the following statements:

```
Integer n1 = new Integer(5);
Integer n2 = new Integer("10");
```

In the first statement, an integer argument is used, and in the second statement a string argument is used.

You can retrieve and print the value contained in these two objects by using the following program statements:

```
int i1 = n1.intValue();
int i2 = n2.intValue();
```

The **intValue** method returns an integer representation of the contained number; the **println** method converts this to a string and prints it to the console.

Because **n1** and **n2** are objects, you can compare them for equality. For example, the following program statement prints **false** on comparing the two objects:

```
System.out.println(n1 + " = " + n2 + " is " + n1.equals(n2));
```

However, if you had set the value of **n2** equal to the integer value held by **n1** (both being equal to, say, integer constant 5), will the comparison return true? Yes, the overloaded **equals** method compares the values of the objects and returns **true** if they are equal, even though the two objects are different. The **Integer** class also provides a **compareTo** method that provides a better comparison between the two objects of its type. The method returns a value less than 0 if this integer is numerically less than the argument integer, and it returns a value greater than 0 otherwise; however, if the two **Integer** objects hold the same numeric value, it returns 0. The following comparison will print –1 to the terminal:

```
System.out.println (n1.compareTo(n2));
```

And the following comparison will print 1 to the terminal:

```
System.out.println (n2.compareTo(n1));
```

The **Integer** class also provides a very useful method called **parseInt** that parses an input string to extract its **int** representation. You may also specify the radix while parsing the string.

NOTE
Radix *is a Latin word meaning "root," which is considered a synonym for "base" in the arithmetical sense. For a decimal system, the radix is 10. For an octal system, it is 8.*

This is a **static** method of the class, so you call it without instantiating the class. When you execute the following two statements, the first statement prints 245 to the terminal and the second statement prints 255 to the terminal:

```
System.out.println("The string holds int value: "
                   + Integer.parseInt("245"));
System.out.println("The string holds int value: "
                   + Integer.parseInt("FF", 16));
```

Note that in the second statement, the second parameter specifies the radix that is used during parsing. Thus, the input string **FF** is considered as a hex number and its decimal value is printed to the terminal. If the given string cannot be parsed in the specified radix, the method will throw a **NumberFormatException**. For example, **Integer.parseInt ("FF", 10)** will throw an exception. You may specify a radix of your choice while parsing the string. The following statement parses the specified string using octal conversion and prints the corresponding decimal number 64 to the console:

```
System.out.println("The string holds int value: "
                   + Integer.parseInt("100", 8));
```

NOTE
You may specify a radix of your choice. For example,
Integer.parseInt("Jim", 27) *is a valid statement that returns an*
integer value of 14359. Here, the radix is 27. Thus, to convert
the string **"Jim"** *you evaluate it as* $J \times 27^2 + i \times 27^1 + m \times 27^0$.

CAUTION
The statement **Integer.parseInt("Java", 27)** *raises a*
NumberFormatException *error because the value of the*
expression evaluates to the maximum size that an integer
variable can hold.

The program given in Listing 11-5 summarizes our discussion in this section.

Listing 11-5   *Demonstrating Wrappers for Primitive Data Types*

```java
public class TypeWrapperApp {

    public static void main(String args[]) throws Exception {
        // object construction
        Integer n1 = new Integer(5);
        Integer n2 = new Integer("10");
        // object value
        System.out.println("n1 holds value: " + n1.intValue());
        System.out.println("n2 holds value: " + n2.intValue());
        // object equality
        System.out.println(n1 + " = " + n2 + " is " + n1.equals(n2));
        // object comparison
        System.out.println(n1 + " compared to " + n2 + " returns "
                + n1.compareTo(n2));
        System.out.println(n2 + " compared to " + n1 + " returns "
                + n2.compareTo(n1));
        // parsing a string
        System.out.println("The string holds int value: "
                + Integer.parseInt("245"));
        System.out.println("The string holds int value: "
                + Integer.parseInt("FF", 16));
        System.out.println("The string holds int value: "
                + Integer.parseInt("100", 8));
        System.out.println("The string holds int value: "
                + Integer.parseInt("Jim", 27));
    }
}
```

Here is the program output:

```
n1 holds value: 5
n2 holds value: 10
5 = 10 is false
5 compared to 10 returns -1
10 compared to 5 returns 1
The string holds int value: 245
The string holds int value: 255
The string holds int value: 64
The string holds int value: 14359
```

TIP

*Here are some features of these wrapper classes worth noting: All the methods of the wrapper classes are **static**; a wrapper class does not contain constructors; and the objects of the wrapper classes are immutable, which means that once a value is assigned to a wrapper class object, it cannot be changed.*

A Few Additions in J2SE 5.0

The type wrapper classes were provided in Java libraries since its first release. J2SE 5.0 made several useful additions to its methods. For example, the **Integer** class now provides methods for bit manipulations. The **rotateRight** method rotates the represented number to the right. The rotation is performed on the Two's Complement binary representation of the number. Thus, the rightmost bit that is rotated out reenters on the left side. Similarly, the **rotateLeft** method rotates the represented number to the left. The bit shifted out reenters on the right side. A **rotateRight** operation by one digit results in arithmetic division by two, and a **rotateLeft** operation results in multiplication by two. The following code snippet illustrates the use of these methods:

```
Integer n1 = new Integer(0x100);
Integer n2 = new Integer(0x1);
n1 = Integer.rotateRight(n1, 1);
n2 = Integer.rotateLeft(n2, 1);
```

The second parameter to the rotate operation specifies the number of bits by which the rotation is to be performed. If you rotate the number by 32, its value remains unaffected.

J2SE 5.0 also introduced a few bit-manipulation methods: The **bitCount** method returns the number of 1's in the Two's Complement binary representation of its input argument; the **numberOfLeadingZeros** and **numberOfTrailingZeros** methods return the count of leading and trailing zeros, respectively, as indicated by their names. The **toBinaryString** method returns a string containing the binary representation of the specified number. This representation does not print the leading zeros. Likewise, the **toHexString** and **toOctalString** methods return the hexadecimal and octal representations. You could also use the **toString** method to obtain a string representation of a number to any arbitrary radix. For example, the following code fragment prints the string "3333" to the console:

```
Integer n = new Integer(255);
System.out.println("Radix4: " + Integer.toString(n, 4));
```

Additional Functionality

The functionality of the wrapper classes mentioned so far applies to most of the wrapper classes in this category. A few wrapper classes provide additional functionality, as detailed in this section.

The **Double** class that wraps a **double** data type contains three fields: **NaN** (Not-a-Number), **POSITIVE_INFINITY**, and **NEGATIVE_INFINITY**. It also provides the **isNaN** and **isInfinite** methods to test for **NaN** and **Infinity** conditions. For example, the following two statements print **true** to the console in each case:

```
System.out.println(Double.isNaN(new Double(0 / 0.0)));
System.out.println(Double.isInfinite(new Double(1 / 0.0)));
```

CAUTION

*If you attempt 0/0 or 1/0, it is treated as integer division and results in a divide-by-zero **ArithmeticException**. This is the reason behind using 0.0 in the preceding expressions, which is a double number by its default representation.*

The **Character** class that wraps a **char** data type provides several utility methods to operate on character data. You can test whether the given character is a digit, a letter, a lowercase character, and so on. The simple program given in Listing 11-6 illustrates the use of some of these methods.

Listing 11-6 *Demonstrating the Unique Functionality of a Character Wrapper*

```
public class CharWrapper {

    public static void main(String args[]) throws Exception {
        int digitCount = 0, letterCount = 0, lcCount = 0, ucCount = 0,
                wsCount = 0;
        for (int i = 0; i < 0xFF; i++) {
            if (Character.isDigit(i)) {
                digitCount++;
            }
            if (Character.isLetter(i)) {
                letterCount++;
            }
            if (Character.isLowerCase(i)) {
                lcCount++;
            }
            if (Character.isUpperCase(i)) {
                ucCount++;
            }
            if (Character.isWhitespace(i)) {
                wsCount++;
            }
        }
        System.out.println("No of digits: " + digitCount);
        System.out.println("No of letters: " + letterCount);
```

```
        System.out.println("No of lower case letters: " + lcCount);
        System.out.println("No of upper case letters: " + ucCount);
        System.out.println("No of white space characters: " + wsCount);
    }
}
```

The program tests each character in the numeric range 0 to 255 for a digit, a letter, a lowercase letter, an uppercase letter, and a white space. It counts the occurrence of each of these types and finally prints the result to the user console.

When we run the program, we see the following output:

```
No of digits: 10
No of letters: 116
No of lower case letters: 60
No of upper case letters: 56
No of white space characters: 10
```

Extended Support for Unicode Code Point

Unicode characters that occupy 16 bits have now been extended to 32 bits to accommodate more characters. Thus, now the characters range from 0 to 0x10FFFF. The characters having values greater than 0xFFFF are called *supplemental characters*. Let's again run the program given in Listing 11-6, but this time modifying the loop count to 0x10FFFF, as follows:

```
for (int i = 0; i < 0x10FFFF; i++) {
```

The program output after this modification is shown here:

```
No of digits: 268
No of letters: 90547
No of lower case letters: 1415
No of upper case letters: 1190
No of white space characters: 27
No of digits: 420
No of letters: 100520
No of lower case letters: 1918
No of upper case letters: 1478
No of white space characters: 26
```

The output will vary depending on your OS and the selected character set.

The new **Character** class has overloaded many of its existing methods that operate on the **char** type (which is a 16-bit number) to use an **int** type (which is 32 bits wide). Besides these, the **Character** class has also introduced several new methods that allow you to work on the new Unicode character set.

TIP
You can obtain more information on the new Unicode character set at www.unicode.org.

The Void Wrapper

Lastly, let's discuss the wrapper on the **void** data type. The **Void** class has one field called **Type**. This field holds a reference to the **Class** object that represents the **void** type. You cannot instantiate the **Void** class. You can simply print its class type as follows:

```
System.out.println("The Class for Void is " + Void.TYPE);
```

This prints the following message to the terminal:

```
The Class for Void is void
```

Now, it's time to discuss the most important feature, which is why we went through all these wrapper classes. The new feature, called *autoboxing,* makes the use of wrapper classes totally redundant. However, an understanding of wrapper classes is required to appreciate the usefulness of autoboxing.

Autoboxing/Unboxing

You have just seen the use of type wrappers in wrapping the primitive data types. Beginning in J2SE 5.0, you will not have to explicitly perform such wrapping. The wrapping/unwrapping is now implicit and automatic.

For example, to wrap an integer constant 100 into an **Integer** type, prior to J2SE 5.0 you would use the following code:

```
Integer a = new Integer(100);
```

Now, with the autoboxing feature introduced in J2SE 5.0, you can achieve the same with the following code:

```
Integer a = 100;
```

Here, the number 100 is encapsulated into an **Integer** type and assigned to the variable **a**. There is no need to use the **new** keyword.

To unwrap the contents of **Integer**, prior to J2SE 5.0, you would have used the following statement:

```
int ii = a.intValue();
```

Now, you would simply type the following:

```
int ii = a;
```

Very neat and clean, isn't it?

The process of wrapping a primitive data type into its corresponding type wrapper class is called *autoboxing,* and the opposite process of extracting the wrapped primitive type from an object is called *unboxing.*

This implicit boxing/unboxing works in all situations wherever such an action is necessary. For example, you can freely mix the objects and the primitive types in an arithmetic expression. Consider the following code fragment:

```
Integer a = new Integer(100);
int b = 200;
Integer c = a + b;
```

This code compiles without errors and produces the expected result of **c** equals 300. Note that the expression **a + b** adds an **int** variable and an **Integer** object. In this case, the **Integer** object **a** is implicitly converted to an **int** type. The program then performs the addition of two **int** data types and assigns this to variable **c** of type **Integer**. During assignment, the autoboxing converts the **int** type to the **Integer** type.

The autoboxing/unboxing also applies to method parameters and the return type. For example, consider the following method declaration:

```
private static Integer adder(Integer a, Integer b) {
    return a + b;
}
```

The method takes two arguments of type **Integer** and returns an **Integer** result. You may call this method with the following statement:

```
int result = adder (100, 200);
```

You are passing **int**-type parameters rather than **Integer** objects to the method. Inside the method, these parameters are converted to **Integer** objects. In the evaluation of the expression **a + b**, the objects are unboxed into **int** types. The **return** statement boxes the result into an **Integer** type. The returned value is unboxed and assigned to **result**, which is an **int** type variable. This entire process is demonstrated in the trivial example shown in Listing 11-7.

Listing 11-7   *Demonstrating Autoboxing/Unboxing*

```
public class Autobox {

    public static void main(String args[]) throws Exception {
        System.out.println
            ("Demonstrating power of autoboxing/unboxing");
        Integer a = 100;
        int b = 200;
        int c = a + b;
        System.out.println
            ("Autoboxing in action: arithmetic expressions");
        System.out.printf("%d + %d = %d%n%n", a, b, c);
        System.out.println("Autoboxing in action: "
            + "method parameters and return types");
        System.out.printf("%d + %d = %d%n", a, b, adder(a, b));
    }

    private static Integer adder(Integer a, Integer b) {
        return a + b;
    }
}
```

TIP
The autoboxing/unboxing feature now frees you completely from using the tedious wrapper classes.

We'll now discuss the next important addition to the Java language—annotation and Annotation types.

Annotations

One of the major goals of any IDE such as NetBeans or Eclipse is to enhance ease of development. The IDE generally provides the boilerplate code for many types of applications so that the developer can focus on the core functionality of the application. However, having source code that does not contain any boilerplate code makes it easier to maintain and create a bug-free application. Annotations help achieve this goal by facilitating the tool vendors in generating the boilerplate code. Besides this, annotations help in code analysis and checking. Other uses of annotations include documenting your code for the benefit of fellow developers and providing vital runtime information to testing tools. You'll learn all these benefits as you read this section.

Annotations are like meta-tags—a data about data. One such annotation (meta-tag) you have already come across in Java's documentation is **@Deprecated**. J2SE 5.0 added many more annotations, as well as added the facility for creating your own annotations. This section covers the built-in annotations and how to create your own annotations.

An annotation is a mechanism in the Java language that allows developers to attach information to different parts of their code. Two instances of annotations you might have noticed while surfing through Java's documentation are **@Override** and **@Deprecated**. Annotations do not become a part of your code in the sense that they do not alter the code behavior at runtime. They also do not change the code semantics. They are helpful in indicating whether your methods are dependent on other methods, whether your methods are incomplete, whether your classes have references to other classes, and so on. They simply help tool vendors to assist you in writing error-free code. Deployment tools such as the EJB (Enterprise JavaBeans) deployer can also use annotations to achieve error-free deployment.

We will discuss the annotations relevant to the Java language and not consider the ones used by deployment tools.

Built-in Annotations

In this section we cover the following three built-in annotations:

- **@Deprecated**
- **@Override**
- **@SuppressWarnings**

The @Deprecated Annotation

The Java API over the years has deprecated quite a few classes and methods. This means new methods and classes have been added that provide a better way to achieve the same task; therefore, the deprecated classes and methods need not be used any more by developers. Such entities are marked with the **@Deprecated** annotation. One such class is **StringBufferInputStream**. Let's see what happens when we use this class in the program code given in Listing 11-8.

Listing 11-8 *Demonstrating the @Deprecated Annotation*

```
public class DeprecatedAnnotation {

    public static void main(String[] args) {
        java.io.StringBufferInputStream in =
            new java.io.StringBufferInputStream("A sample string");
    }
}
```

We compile this code with the following command line:

```
javac -Xlint:deprecation DeprecatedAnnotation.java
```

The compiler output is shown here:

```
DeprecatedAnnotation.java:9: warning: [deprecation] StringBufferInputStream
in java.io has been deprecated

java.io.StringBufferInputStream in =
        ^
DeprecatedAnnotation.java:10: warning: [deprecation] StringBufferInputStream
in java.io has been deprecated
new java.io.StringBufferInputStream("A sample string");
        ^
2 warnings
```

The compiler generates two warnings, showing us the lines in our program where we have used the deprecated class. You can even use this **@Deprecated** annotation in your own code for marking the elements you want to phase out eventually. Consider the code shown in Listing 11-9.

Listing 11-9 *Using the @Deprecated Annotation*

```
public class DeprecatedAnnotationDemo {

    public static void main(String[] args) {
        MyTestClass testObject = new MyTestClass();
        testObject.doSomething();
        testObject.doSomethingNew("Bowling");
    }
}

class MyTestClass {
```

```
@Deprecated
 public void doSomething() {
 }

 public void doSomethingNew(String SomeFun) {
 }
}
```

Here, we have defined a class called **MyTestClass** with two methods. In this scenario, we initially have only one method in this class, called **doSomething**. Later on, though, we decide to provide a better implementation for this method, which requires sending a **String**-type parameter to the method. Therefore, we write another method called **doSomethingNew** that takes a **String** parameter. In this test application, we call both the old and new methods. Now, when we compile this code, the compiler generates the following output:

```
javac -Xlint:deprecation DeprecatedAnnotationDemo.java
DeprecatedAnnotationDemo.java:10: warning: [deprecation] doSomething() in
MyTest Class has been deprecated
testObject.doSomething();
          ^

1 warning
```

Note that the **-Xlint** switch is used on the command line to get warning errors on deprecated elements. In this situation, the compiler gave us the warning that the **doSomething** method has been deprecated. This is how you'll use the **@Deprecated** annotation in your classes to mark any methods you do not want your developers to use in their future code while ensuring at the same time that their existing code does not break. Note that this **@Deprecated** annotation can also be applied to classes like the one we've seen for the **StringBufferInputStream** class. This is the mechanism Java uses to discourage developers from using certain classes and methods in their future code.

The @Override Annotation

The **@Override** annotation indicates that the annotated method is required to override a method in its superclass. If it does not do so, the compiler will flag an error. We discuss the importance of this annotation after looking at the code in Listing 11-10.

Listing 11-10   *Demonstrating the @Override Annotation*

```
public class OverrideAnnotationDemoApp {

    public static void main(String[] args) {
        Cat c = new Cat();
        c.saySomething();
    }
}

class Animal {
```

```
    void saySomething() {
        System.out.println("Animal talking");
    }
}

class Cat extends Animal {

    @Override
    void saySomething() {
        System.out.println("meow... meow");
    }
}
```

Here, the **Animal** class defines one method called **saySomething**. **Cat** is a subclass of **Animal** that redefines the method's implementation. In the subclass definition, we mark this method with the **@Override** annotation. When we compile this code, it compiles without any warnings and errors, which is good. Now let's take out the **@Override** line from the source and recompile the code. It again compiles without any errors. So what's the use of the **@Override** annotation? To find out, let's now modify the method name in the **Cat** definition to **saySomethng**—a simple spelling mistake. Now, let's once again compile the code. The code compiles without errors. However, when we run the code, we see the following output:

```
Animal talking
```

What happened here? We were expecting the cat to say "meow... meow." Such types of errors are hard to find, and programmers have spent many sleepless nights on such trivial-looking errors. Okay, now let's add the **@Override** annotation, as before, and recompile the code. Now the compiler throws the following error to the terminal:

```
OverrideAnnotationDemoApp.java:22: method does not override or implement a
method from a supertype
@Override
^
1 error
```

Now, we would probably know that we do not have an overridden method that matches the signature of a method in its superclass. We can easily save ourselves a lot of valuable time by marking those methods we are overriding in a subclass with the **@Override** annotation.

The @SuppressWarnings Annotation

The use of this annotation tells the compiler not to spit out the specified warnings in its output. To understand its use, let's go back to our **DeprecatedAnnotationDemoApp** program. The compilation of this program gives us the method deprecation warning we observed earlier. Now, add the following line before the **main** function declaration:

```
@SuppressWarnings({"deprecation"})
public static void main(String[] args) {
```

Save the file and recompile the code. The deprecation warning error vanishes from the output. You can use this feature judiciously to avoid cluttering the compiler output with unwanted messages.

Having seen the built-in simple annotations, it is time now to create your own annotations. Why would you create your own annotations? As you must have noticed, the built-in annotations allow you to do so little that, for all practical purposes, you would want to create your own. In the following section, you learn the entire process of creating your own annotations and see why doing so is important. You also learn how to annotate your annotations.

Declaring Annotations

To facilitate the creation of a custom annotation, Java language has added a new type—the **annotation** type. It looks like an ordinary class, but it has some unique properties. The definition looks like an interface definition, except that the **interface** keyword is preceded by an @ sign. The annotations can be of three different types—one without any elements, one with a single element, and one with multiple elements. You will learn how to create all three types of annotations in this section. First, we'll start with a simple case of an annotation with no members.

Marker Annotations

This type of annotation does not have any elements. The following statement illustrates how to declare such an annotation:

```
public @interface WorkInProgress {}
```

To use this in code, we would use the following syntax:

```
@WorkInProgress
public static float computeTax (float amount, float rate) {
    // to be implemented
    return 0;
}
```

The **@WorkInProgress** annotation would probably be used to indicate to our fellow developers that the annotated method is yet to be implemented.

Single-Value Annotations

At this point, we might want to add what is yet to be done in the method's implementation. For this, we'll create another annotation, called **Task**, as shown here:

```
@interface Task {

    String value();
}
```

We can now annotate the **computeTax** method as follows:

```
@Task("Implement tax computations")
```

These types of annotations are called *single-element* annotations because they take only a single-value type. (We also have multivalue types of annotations that have multiple data members.)

In case of a single-element annotation, the data member is specified with the word **value**. The syntax for specifying a member is similar to declaring a method. A few restrictions apply to member declarations—these are discussed later. For now, let's see what happens if we use any word other than **value** in the preceding definition. The new definition looks like this:

```
@interface Task {

    String description();
}
```

We now need to annotate our method using the following syntax:

```
@Task(description = "Implement tax computations")
```

Note that this time, we had to explicitly spell out the member name—**description**. In the earlier case, where we used the default name **value**, we specified only the target string, omitting the member name. If we don't do so, the compiler will generate an error during compilation.

Multivalue Annotations

Now let's add a few more data members to our **Task** annotation:

```
@interface Task {

    String description();

    String targetDate();

    int estimatedHours();

    String additionalNote();
}
```

The **description** member instructs the developer about the nature of the task. The **targetDate** member sets the expected deadline. The **estimatedHours** member specifies the number of man-hours required to complete the job, and the **additionalNote** member may be used to specify any additional instructions to the developer. We can now annotate our method as follows:

```
@Task(description = "Implement tax computations",
targetDate = "Jan 1, 2012",
estimatedHours = 50,
additionalNote = "This implementation is critical for the final launch")
```

See how all four members are specified using **data=value** syntax? These types of annotations are called *multivalue* annotations.

Setting Default Values

We are now allowed to specify the default values for any of the data members. We do so by using the **default** keyword. For example, in the modified definition of **Task** shown here, we have set the default **targetDate**:

```
@interface Task {

    String description();
```

```
    String targetDate() default "Jan 1, 2012";

    int estimatedHours();

    String additionalNote();
}
```

When we annotate our code using this modified **Task** annotation, we need not specify the **targetDate** member unless we want to assign a different value to it.

Custom Annotation Program
The full program that contains the concepts discussed thus far is given in Listing 11-11.

Listing 11-11   *Creating Our Own Annotation*

```
public class CustomAnnotation {

    @WorkInProgress
    @Task(description = "Implement tax computations",
    targetDate = "Jan 1, 2012",
    estimatedHours = 50,
    additionalNote = "This implementation is critical for the final launch")
    public static float ComputeTax(float amount, float rate) {
        return 0;
    }
}

@interface WorkInProgress {
}

@interface Task {

    String description();

    String targetDate();

    int estimatedHours();

    String additionalNote();
}
```

Rules for Defining Annotation Types
To summarize our discussion about creating annotations, here are the rules for defining annotation types:

- An annotation declaration starts with **@interface**, followed by the annotation's name.
- To create parameters for an annotation, you declare methods in its type.
- Method declarations should not contain any parameters.
- Method declarations should not contain any **throws** clauses.

- Return types of the method should be one of the following:
    - Primitive
    - String
    - Class
    - Enum
    - An array of the preceding types

Annotating an Annotation

When you create your own annotations, their purpose may not be always self-evident. You might want to supply some sort of metadata (another annotation) on your newly created annotation type so that a tool can introspect and reveal this intended functionality or a compiler can enforce the intended functionality during compilation. The Java language defines four annotation types for this purpose:

- **Target**
- **Retention**
- **Documentation**
- **Inherited**

These are called *meta-annotations* and are used for annotating your annotations. We discuss each one in detail in this section.

The Target Annotation

The **Target** annotation specifies which elements of your code can have annotations of the defined type. A concrete example will help explain this concept. Add the **Target** annotation to the **Task** annotation we defined earlier, as shown here:

```
@Target(ElementType.METHOD)
@interface Task {

    String description();
    ...
}
```

Now, the **Task** annotation can only be applied to a method. Let's verify this. Modify the **CustomAnnotation** class defined earlier to add a private **taxID** field. Apply the **Task** annotation to this field. The modified class definition is shown here:

```
public class CustomAnnotation {

    @Task(description = "Assign ID",
    estimatedHours = 0,
    additionalNote = "The IDs are available from IRS")
    private int taxID;
```

```
@WorkInProgress
@Task(description = "Implement tax computations",
estimatedHours = 50,
additionalNote = "This implementation is critical for the final launch")
public static float ComputeTax(float amount, float rate) {
    return 0;
}
}
```

When you compile this code, the compiler throws an error indicating that the annotation type is not applicable to this kind of declaration, where you have defined the **taxID** field. The application of the **Task** annotation on the **ComputeTax** method compiles without errors.

Here are the other types of targets that can be specified in place of **ElementType.METHOD**:

- **ElementType.TYPE**—Can be applied to any element of a class
- **ElementType.FIELD**—Can be applied to a field
- **ElementType.PARAMETER**—Can be applied to method parameters
- **ElementType.CONSTRUCTOR**—Can be applied to constructors
- **ElementType.LOCAL_VARIABLE**—Can be applied to local variables
- **ElementType.ANNOTATION_TYPE**—Indicates that the declared type itself is an annotation type

The Retention Annotation

This annotation sets the visibility of the annotation to which it is applied. The visibility can be set for three different levels: compilers, tools, and runtime. The visibility is set with the help of another built-in annotation called **@Retention**. You set the annotation visibility using the following syntax:

```
@Retention(RetentionPolicy.RUNTIME)
@interface Task {
```

As shown, the **@Retention** annotation precedes the annotation declaration. It has one field that is set to a predefined constant of the **RententionPolicy** enumeration.

The **RetentionPolicy** enumeration defines three constants—**SOURCE**, **CLASS**, and **RUNTIME**. If you select **SOURCE**, the annotation will be visible to the compiler and will not be available in the .class files and to the runtime. The compiler uses this annotation to detect errors and suppress warnings. After its use, the compiler discards the annotation. When you use the **CLASS** identifier, the annotation will be recorded in the .class file; however, the virtual machine (VM) need not retain it at runtime. This is the default policy. Lastly, if you use the **RUNTIME** identifier, not only is the annotation recorded in the .class file, but it is also made available to the runtime by the VM. Thus, a running program can introspect this annotation and display its values to the user. This feature is demonstrated in the example that follows.

Annotations at Runtime

The program presented here uses the introspection and reflection feature of the Java language. Let's briefly discuss this feature so that you will not have any difficulties in understanding how annotations are discovered at runtime. A more detailed treatment on introspection and reflection is available in Chapter 21.

When the JVM loads a class in memory, it creates an object of the **Class** type for the loaded class. This object contains all the details about the class, which are available in its source program. You obtain a reference to this **Class** object by calling the **getClass** method on an object loaded in memory. You can introspect the various methods of the loaded class by calling the **getMethods** method on the **Class** object. The method returns an array of **Method** objects. **Method** is a class that defines the physical representation of a method of a class. For example, the **getName** method of the **Method** class returns its name; the **getParameterTypes** method returns an array of **Class** objects that represent the formal parameter types; and the **getReturnType** method returns a **Class** object that represents the formal return type of the method. In the program that follows, we use the **getAnnotation** method to obtain the annotation, if any, associated with the method. With this little introduction to introspection and reflection, you are now ready to learn the runtime discovery of annotations. You are encouraged to refer to the javadocs API for a full treatment of introspection and reflection.

Let's now look at the program in Listing 11-12, which discovers the annotations on various elements at runtime.

Listing 11-12   *Discovering Annotations at Runtime*

```java
import java.lang.annotation.Retention;
import java.lang.annotation.RetentionPolicy;
import java.lang.reflect.Method;

@WorkInProgress
public class RuntimeAnnotation {

    @WorkInProgress
    @Task(description = "Implement tax computations",
    estimatedHours = 50,
    additionalNote = "This implementation is critical for the final launch")
    public static float ComputeTax(float amount, float rate) {
        return 0;
    }

    public static void main(String args[]) {
        try {
            RuntimeAnnotation obj = new RuntimeAnnotation();
            Class cls = obj.getClass();
            WorkInProgress annotation =
                    (WorkInProgress) cls.getAnnotation(WorkInProgress.class);
            System.out.println("Class " + cls.getName());
            if (cls.isAnnotationPresent(WorkInProgress.class)) {
                System.out.println("\tThis class is not fully implemented");
            }

            System.out.println("\nList of methods:");
            Method[] methods = cls.getMethods();
            for (Method method : methods) {
                System.out.println(method.getName());
```

```
                if (method.isAnnotationPresent(WorkInProgress.class)) {
                    System.out.println(
                            "\tThis method is not fully implemented");
                }

                if (method.isAnnotationPresent(Task.class)) {
                    Task annotationTask =
                            (Task) method.getAnnotation(Task.class);
                    System.out.printf("\tWhat TODO: "
                            + annotationTask.description()
                            + "%n\tTarget date: "
                            + annotationTask.targetDate()
                            + "%n\tEstimated hours: "
                            + annotationTask.estimatedHours()
                            + "%n\tNote: " + annotationTask.additionalNote()
                            + "%n");
                }
            }
        } catch (Exception e) {
            System.out.print(e.getMessage());
        }
    }
}

@Retention(RetentionPolicy.RUNTIME)
@interface WorkInProgress {
}

@Retention(RetentionPolicy.RUNTIME)
@interface Task {

    String description();

    String targetDate() default "Jan 1, 2012";

    int estimatedHours();

    String additionalNote();
}
```

Like in earlier cases, we declare two annotations—**WorkInProgress** and **Task**—both having the same definitions as in the earlier examples. However, we apply a retention policy on both with the following statement:

```
@Retention(RetentionPolicy.RUNTIME)
```

Thus, these annotations are now available at runtime, which is what we want for this demonstration. The main application class is **RuntimeAnnotation**. We apply the **WorkInProgress** annotation to it by preceding the class declaration with the **@WorkInProgress** annotation. In the class definition, first we define the method **ComputeTax**, to which we apply the two annotations—**WorkInProgress** and **Task**. Next, we define the **main** method. We do not apply any annotations to it because we have fully implemented this method. In the **main** method, we create an instance of **RuntimeAnnotation**. Now comes the important part of introspection and displaying the annotation information at runtime. To do this, the program obtains the type of the created object by calling its **getClass** method:

```
Class cls = obj.getClass();
```

NOTE
*The getClass method is defined in the **Object** class. It returns the runtime class of **this** object. Every object in Java has an associated class that is represented by a class called **Class**. The getClass method returns a reference to this **Class** object.*

The program now obtains the associated annotation by calling the **getAnnotation** method on the obtained **Class** object:

```
WorkInProgress annotation =
        (WorkInProgress) cls.getAnnotation(WorkInProgress.class);
```

The **getAnnotation** method takes one parameter that specifies the annotation class type. Therefore, the method retrieves the annotation of the specified type, and if it is not found, **null** is returned. The program now retrieves the class name by calling its **getName** method for display to the user:

```
System.out.println("Class " + cls.getName());
```

Next, we check whether this element (the class) has an annotation present by calling the **isAnnotationPresent** method on the **Class** object; if it does, we print an appropriate message to the user:

```
if (cls.isAnnotationPresent(WorkInProgress.class)) {
    System.out.println("\tThis class is not fully implemented");
}
```

We now introspect the class object **cls** to discover all the methods defined in it. This is done by calling the **getMethods** method on the **Class** object:

```
Method[] methods = cls.getMethods();
```

The method returns an array of **Method** objects. A **Method** is a class defined in the **java.lang. reflect** package and represents a method declaration in a class.

NOTE
*The process of retrieving the **Class** for an object and its methods and fields is called* introspection and reflection. *You introspect a class to obtain its details, and the class reflects upon itself by providing the methods **getMethods**, **getFields**, **getConstructors**, and so on.*

The method returns us the array of all the methods defined for the class. We iterate through this list by using a **foreach** loop:

```
for (Method method : methods) {
```

For each method, we print its name:

```
System.out.println(method.getName());
```

For each method, we check whether **WorkInProgress** annotation has been applied to it:

```
if (method.isAnnotationPresent(WorkInProgress.class)) {
    System.out.println("\tThis method is not fully implemented");
}
```

Next, we check whether the **Task** annotation has been applied:

```
if (method.isAnnotationPresent(Task.class)) {
```

If so, we get the various members of the **Task** annotation and print their values to the console:

```
Task annotationTask = (Task) method.getAnnotation(Task.class);
System.out.printf("\tWhat TODO: "
                  + annotationTask.description()
                  + "%n\tTarget date: " + annotationTask.targetDate()
                  + "%n\tEstimated hours: "
                  + annotationTask.estimatedHours()
                  + "%n\tNote: " + annotationTask.additionalNote()
                  + "%n");
```

NOTE
The annotation fields are retrieved using the method call *syntax.*
This method call cannot have any parameters.

When we run the application, we see the following output:

```
Class RuntimeAnnotation
        This class is not fully implemented

List of methods:
main
ComputeTax
        This method is not fully implemented
        What TODO: Implement tax computations
        Target date: Jan 1, 2012
        Estimated hours: 50
        Note: This implementation is critical for the final launch
wait
wait
wait
```

```
equals
toString
hashCode
getClass
notify
notifyAll
```

In the output, observe how the messages for the two annotations are printed and how the values of different members of the **Task** annotation are printed to the console.

TIP
*The real use, and one of the applications of the runtime discovery of annotations, comes in software testing. A test runner tool can run all of the class's annotated methods reflectively by calling **Method.invoke**. The **isAnnotationPresent** method can tell the tool which methods to run.*

The Documented Annotation

The **Documented** annotation indicates that an annotation with this type should be documented by the Javadoc tool. Javadoc is a documentation generator provided as a part of the JDK that helps in generating API documentation in HTML format from Java source code. In Syntax Reference 1, we discussed the use of /** ... */ for commenting the code. This is a Javadoc comment. Javadoc defines several tags, such as **@author**, **@version**, **@param**, **@return**, and so on. You use these tags to describe the corresponding elements.

By default, the Javadoc tool includes annotations in the generated document. Applying the **@Documented** annotation allows Javadoc-like tools to include the annotation type information in the generated documentation. Incidentally, this is a **Marker**-type annotation because it does not have any members. To understand how this works, add the **@Documented** annotation to the **WorkInProgress** and **Task** annotations we have created previously. Now, generate the documentation for the **RuntimeAnnotation** class by executing the following command on the command prompt:

```
c:\360\ch11>javadoc RuntimeAnnotation.java
```

Executing this **javadoc** command will generate quite a few HTML files in the current folder. Open the index.html file in your favorite browser and examine the documentation for the **ComputeTax** method, which uses both annotations. The output is shown in Figure 11-1.

As you can see in the output, both annotations are documented.

The Inherited Annotation

When a class is inherited, the subclass inherits all the nonprivate properties of its superclass. Does this happen in the case of annotations too? In other words, if a class is annotated, are the annotations of the parent class inherited by the subclass? Let's look at an example. Suppose we have a class called **Shape** that implements a few drawing primitives. The **Shape** class is not yet fully implemented, so we add the **@WorkInProgress** annotation we have been using so far. We'll now extend the **Shape** class to create a **Line** class. We would naturally expect and want the **Line** class to inherit the **WorkInProgress** annotation because this class is yet to be implemented.

Method Detail

Compute Tax

```
@WorkInProgress
@Task(description="Implement tax computations",
      estimatedHours=50,
      additionalNote="This implementation is critical for the final launch")
public static float ComputeTax(float amount,
                               float rate)
```

FIGURE 11-1. *Annotations documented by javadoc*

Does this happen naturally? No, this inheritance takes place only if the **WorkInProgress** annotation is annotated with **@Inherited**. To better understand this concept, let's look at the program in Listing 11-13.

Listing 11-13 *Inheriting Annotations*

```
import java.lang.annotation.*;

@WorkInProgress
class Shape {

    public void drawShape() {
    }
}

public class drawShape extends Shape {

    @Override
    public void drawShape() {
    }

    public static void main(String[] args) {
        Shape shape = new Shape();
        Class cls = shape.getClass();
        if (cls.isAnnotationPresent(WorkInProgress.class)) {
            System.out.println("Shape class does require some work");
            WorkInProgress progress = (WorkInProgress) cls.getAnnotation(
                    WorkInProgress.class);
            System.out.println(progress.doSomething());
        } else {
            System.out.println("Shape is fully implemented");
        }
        System.out.println();
```

```
        drawShape line = new drawShape();
        cls = line.getClass();
        if (cls.isAnnotationPresent(WorkInProgress.class)) {
            System.out.println("Line class does require some work");
            WorkInProgress progress = (WorkInProgress) cls.getAnnotation(
                    WorkInProgress.class);
            System.out.println(progress.doSomething());
        } else {
            System.out.println("Line is fully implemented");
        }
        System.out.println();
    }
}


@Retention(RetentionPolicy.RUNTIME)
@Documented
@Inherited
@interface WorkInProgress {

    String doSomething() default "\tDo what?";
}
```

The **WorkInProgress** annotation defines one property (**doSomething**) and is annotated with **Retention**, **Documented**, and **Inherited**. The **Shape** class is annotated with **WorkInProgress**. The **Line** class inherits the **Shape** class, but does not contain an explicit **WorkInProgress** annotation. In the **main** method of the **Line** class, we print the status of annotations by using the reflection mechanism discussed earlier. We create instances of both **Shape** and **Line** classes. We obtain the **Class** instances of both classes by using the **getClass** method of **Object**, as used previously. We check whether the annotation is present by calling the **isAnnotationPresent** method of **Class**. If the annotation is present, we print the value of **doSomething** to the user console; otherwise, we print the message that the class is fully implemented. When we run the program, we see the following output:

```
Shape class does require some work
        Do what?

Line class does require some work
        Do what?
```

From this output, we can clearly see that **Line** class has inherited the **WorkInProgress** annotation applied only to its parent class—**Shape**. Now, comment out the **@Inherited** annotation in the declaration of the **WorkInProgress** annotation. Run the program and you will see the following output:

```
Shape class does require some work
        Do what?

Line is fully implemented
```

The output now indicates that the **Line** is fully implemented, indicating that it does not have the **WorkInProgress** annotation in effect. It is assumed that the developer has implemented the **Line** class without first completing the **Shape** class—which may be true in some situations.

NOTE
It may not always be wise to inherit the annotations by default.
*For example, it is meaningless to inherit the **Task** annotation we used*
previously in the subclasses. Therefore, by default, the annotations are
*not inherited; you must apply the **@Inherited** annotation if you wish a*
particular annotation to be inherited by the subclasses of the class that
uses this annotation.

In general, these annotations are very useful in documenting your code, for compilers to generate appropriate warnings, and for runtime tools to provide better testing of an application.

Summary

This chapter presented many of the additions made to the Java language, beginning in J2SE 5.0. Now, it has the typesafe **enum** in its repertoire. The enumerations in Java differ from their equivalents in other languages. In Java, an enumeration is declared as a class and thus derives all the benefits of using classes in your programs. The enumeration is declared using the **java.lang.Enum** class. This class implements the **Serializable** interface, and objects of **Enum** can be serialized and deserialized without any extra piece of code to save and retrieve their state.

The chapter also described the type wrapper classes for primitive data types. Java provides a class for wrapping each of its primitive data types, thus extending the benefits of object-oriented programming in the use of primitive types. Although these classes were available in Java right from the start, their functionality was greatly enhanced in J2SE 5.0. The new classes now allow for bit and character manipulations, including support for extended Unicode. J2SE 5.0 has also added the autoboxing/unboxing feature, which allows implicit conversions between primitive types and their corresponding wrapper classes. The autoboxing feature makes the use of wrapper classes somewhat redundant.

Finally, the chapter described the annotation feature. Annotations are better structured and are therefore preferred over the conventional documentation methods that have been used for many years. You create annotations using the **@interface** keyword. You can apply annotations to classes, methods, fields, and other program elements. The compilers and tools can use these annotations. The annotation visibility may be set to the source, class, or runtime level. You learned how to retrieve the applied annotations at runtime using the introspection and reflection feature of Java.

In the next chapter, we cover another vital addition to the Java language—generics.

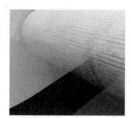

CHAPTER
12

Generics

n the previous chapter, you learned several new features introduced in the Java language beginning in J2SE 5.0. One important addition to the language we did not cover in the previous chapter is generics. As a matter of fact, the topic of generics is so vast it deserves a dedicated chapter to itself. Therefore, this chapter deals with the various aspects of generics.

In particular, you will learn the following in this chapter:

- Understanding what generics are
- Understanding why you would use generics
- Using built-in generic classes
- Creating your own generic types
- Understanding erasures and raw classes
- Creating bounded types
- Using wildcards
- Understanding bounded wildcards
- Using generics with multiple parameters
- Understanding typecasting between generic types
- Creating generic methods
- Declaring generic interfaces
- Restrictions in generics

Generics

Generics refers to a parameterized type. At this point, you have definitely heard about collections, and you have used some of their classes in previous chapters. The collection classes use generics. It is a very vast topic, as you will see shortly.

What Are Generics?

So what are generics? In a literal sense, a generic is a parameterized type. Generics enable you to create generalized classes, interfaces, and methods that can operate on any type of data specified as a parameter. You'll learn about the importance of this generalization in the following section. Many times, library developers use this feature extensively. One such example of generics is the classes defined in the **Collections** framework, which was introduced in J2SE 5.0 platform libraries.

 NOTE
*The **Collections** framework is discussed in depth in Chapter 16. You do not need to know everything about **Collections** to understand the material presented in this chapter.*

A typical example of a class defined in the **Collections** framework is the **java.util.LinkedList<E>** class. Note that the class declaration has angular brackets and a parameter, **E**, declared within them.

The parameter **E** is called the *type parameter* and represents the type of element stored in the list. This class is a generic type. You instantiate it by replacing the parameter **E** with an actual type, such as **String** or **Integer**. Developers do this kind of instantiation by specifying the desired type in their code. For example, if we wanted to create a **LinkedList** that stores only **Integer** values, we would make the following statement in our code:

```
LinkedList<Integer> list = new LinkedList<Integer>();
```

Declarations, such as **LinkedList<Integer>** or a **LinkedList<String>**, are called **parameterized** types.

Why Do We Need Generics?

Using generic types in our program code helps the compiler enforce better type checking on our code. Java has always been known as a very strongly typed language—something you have already observed in the previous chapters. Type safety is one of the key features of the Java language. This characteristic has been extended further with the help of generics. To explain how, let's look at an example. Suppose we want to maintain a list of famous quotes in an array of strings. Rather than maintaining the list in a fixed-size array, we will use the **ArrayList** class, where the list size can grow dynamically. The following code fragment illustrates how to create such a list:

```
void buildList() {
    listOfFamousQuotes = new ArrayList();
    listOfFamousQuotes.add(
                "Where there is love there is life - Mahatma Gandhi");
    listOfFamousQuotes.add(
                "A joke is a very serious thing - Winston Churchill");
    listOfFamousQuotes.add(
                "In the end, everything is a gag - Charlie Chaplin");
}
```

To print this list to the terminal, we would use the following code:

```
void printList() {
    Iterator listIterator = listOfFamousQuotes.iterator();
    while (listIterator.hasNext()) {
        String quote = (String) listIterator.next();
        System.out.println(quote);
    }
}
```

The **Iterator** interface, which is covered in Chapter 16, makes it easy to iterate through all the elements of a collection. The **next** method of the **Iterator** interface returns an **Object** type. We must typecast it before assigning it to a **String** type variable. If we do not typecast, the compiler throws an error.

Now, let's modify the preceding code to use the generic type: **ArrayList<E>**. We can create the list using the following code fragment:

```
private static ArrayList<String> listOfFamousQuotesTypechecked;
void buildCheckedList() {
    listOfFamousQuotesTypechecked = new ArrayList<String>();
```

```
     listOfFamousQuotesTypechecked.add(
             "Where there is love there is life - Mahatma Gandhi");
     listOfFamousQuotesTypechecked.add(
             "A joke is a very serious thing - Winston Churchill");
     listOfFamousQuotesTypechecked.add(
             "In the end, everything is a gag - Charlie Chaplin");
}
```

Note how the parameter **String** is used in the declaration of the variable **listOfFamousQuotesTypechecked**. Also note how the **String** parameter is specified in the instantiation of the **ArrayList** class. To iterate and print the elements of the list, we use the following code:

```
void printCheckedList() {
    Iterator<String> quoteIterator = listOfFamousQuotesTypechecked.iterator();
    while (quoteIterator.hasNext()) {
      String quote = quoteIterator.next();
      System.out.println(quote);
    }
}
```

The **quoteIterator** is declared as a parameterized type having the parameter type **String**. Note that now the **next** method does not require a typecast before assigning its return value to a **String** variable. This is because the compiler knows for sure that each element that it retrieves from the list is of type **String**. How does the iterator know this? We declared the **quoteIterator** of type **Iterator<String>**, indicating that each element retrieved by the iterator is the **String** type. The **quoteIterator** operates on **listOfFamousQuotesTypechecked**, which is a list of **String** objects. When you insert elements into this list, the compiler ensures that only the **String** type variables are added to the list. Therefore, the **quoteIterator** clearly knows that the elements over which it iterates are guaranteed to be of type **String**. With this information, the compiler itself is able to enforce the type checking rather than waiting for a running program to generate typecasting errors at runtime.

Because the **listOfFamousQuotesTypechecked** is declared with a parameter of type **String**, adding any other data type to the list will produce a compile-time error. For example, the following statement would result in a compile-time error:

```
listOfFamousQuotesTypechecked.add (100);
```

Let's now look at another use for generics. Suppose we want to write a method to remove all quotes by Winston Churchill from the list of quotes created earlier. Let's assume we are not using generics. In this case, we would write the method as follows:

```
void expurgate(Collection c, String strAuthor) {
    for (Iterator i = c.iterator(); i.hasNext();) {
        if (((String) i.next()).contains(strAuthor)) {
            i.remove();
        }
    }
}
```

Note that each element retrieved from the collection is typecast to the **String** type before the check for the author. If the list contains a data type other than **String**, the program will break with a **ClassCastException**. You can try this by adding an **Integer** object to the list using the following statement:

```
listOfFamousQuotes.add(100);
```

Now, compare the preceding method with the version that uses generics, shown next:

```
void expurgateCheckedList(Collection<String> c, String strAuthor) {
    for (Iterator<String> i = c.iterator(); i.hasNext();) {
        if (i.next().contains(strAuthor)) {
            i.remove();
        }
    }
}
```

Note how the **Iterator** is declared to receive a **String**-type parameter. In this case, we do not typecast the retrieved element before checking for the presence of the specified author name. Also, we are assured that the code will not break at runtime with a **ClassCastException** because all elements in the list are guaranteed to be of the **String** type.

A Sample Generics Program

So you can experiment with the concepts discussed thus far, the complete program is given in Listing 12-1.

Listing 12-1   *Using Built-in Generic Types*

```
import java.util.*;

public class FamousQuotes {

    private static ArrayList listOfFamousQuotes;
    private static ArrayList<String> listOfFamousQuotesTypechecked;

    public static void main(String[] args) {

        FamousQuotes app = new FamousQuotes();

        System.out.println("Without using generics\n");
        app.buildList();
        app.printList();
        System.out.println();

        System.out.println("With generic classes\n");
        app.buildCheckedList();
        app.printCheckedList();

        System.out.println("\nNon-generics version of expurgate\n");
        String strAuthor = "Winston Churchill";
        System.out.println("After removing quotes by " + strAuthor);
        app.expurgate(listOfFamousQuotes, "Winston Churchill");
        app.printList();
```

```
            System.out.println("\nGenerics version of expurgate\n");
            System.out.println("After removing quotes by " + strAuthor);
            app.expurgateCheckedList(listOfFamousQuotesTypechecked, strAuthor);
            app.printCheckedList();
        }

        void buildList() {
            listOfFamousQuotes = new ArrayList();
            listOfFamousQuotes.add(
                    "Where there is love there is life - Mahatma Gandhi");
            listOfFamousQuotes.add(
                    "A joke is a very serious thing - Winston Churchill");
            listOfFamousQuotes.add(
                    "In the end, everything is a gag - Charlie Chaplin");
//          listOfFamousQuotes.add(100); // add this to generate runtime error
        }

        void buildCheckedList() {
            listOfFamousQuotesTypechecked = new ArrayList<String>();
            listOfFamousQuotesTypechecked.add(
                    "Where there is love there is life - Mahatma Gandhi");
            listOfFamousQuotesTypechecked.add(
                    "A joke is a very serious thing - Winston Churchill");
            listOfFamousQuotesTypechecked.add(
                    "In the end, everything is a gag - Charlie Chaplin");
        }

        void printList() {
            Iterator listIterator = listOfFamousQuotes.iterator();
            while (listIterator.hasNext()) {
                String quote = (String) listIterator.next();
                System.out.println(quote);
            }
        }

        void printCheckedList() {
            Iterator<String> quoteIterator =
                    listOfFamousQuotesTypechecked.iterator();
            while (quoteIterator.hasNext()) {
                String quote = quoteIterator.next();
                System.out.println(quote);
            }
        }

        void expurgate(Collection c, String strAuthor) {
            for (Iterator i = c.iterator(); i.hasNext();) {
                if (((String) i.next()).contains(strAuthor)) {
                    i.remove();
                }
            }
        }
    }
```

```
void expurgateCheckedList(Collection<String> c, String strAuthor) {
    for (Iterator<String> i = c.iterator(); i.hasNext();) {
        if (i.next().contains(strAuthor)) {
            i.remove();
        }
    }
}
```

When you run the program, you see the following output:

```
Without using generics

Where there is love there is life - Mahatma Gandhi
A joke is a very serious thing - Winston Churchill
In the end, everything is a gag - Charlie Chaplin

With generic classes

Where there is love there is life - Mahatma Gandhi
A joke is a very serious thing - Winston Churchill
In the end, everything is a gag - Charlie Chaplin

Non-generics version of expurgate

After removing quotes by Winston Churchill
Where there is love there is life - Mahatma Gandhi
In the end, everything is a gag - Charlie Chaplin

Generics version of expurgate

After removing quotes by Winston Churchill
Where there is love there is life - Mahatma Gandhi
In the end, everything is a gag - Charlie Chaplin
```

Experiment in the code to see how generics help in detecting errors early.

What you have seen so far is just the tip of the iceberg. The real power of generics can be seen when you use different classes in Java's **Collections** framework, or for that matter any generalized classes created by others. Likewise, you may generalize your own classes so that others can experience the power of generics when they use your classes in their programs. Generics make the code more reliable in the face of runtime typecasting exceptions. You will understand this power as you read further in this chapter.

Type Safety

As we have seen so far, the primary use case for generics is to instruct the compiler to type check the contents of collections; this was the initial motive behind the design of generics. However, the use of generics is not restricted to the **Collections** framework. It is now applied to many other classes, such as **java.lang.ref**, several interfaces and classes of the **java.util.concurrent** package, and so on. These classes use generic types in their parameters; you specify the actual type during its use (*instantiation,* as it is called) in your source program. The compiler replaces the generic types with the real types during precompilation. Later on, we discuss this process further by looking at the intermediate files created by the compiler.

Before we conclude this section, let's briefly discuss static versus dynamic typing. Java uses static typing, also known as *strong* typing. The Java compiler checks whether proper data types are assigned to variables—remember the implicit typecast mandated by Java while assigning a variable to its subclass type. This puts more load on the programmer but enables catching the errors early. Contrast this with the dynamic (or *weak)* typing used by some languages such as Ruby and PHP, which allow different type values to be assigned to variables. Such a variable has a type of the last assigned value. It is argued by some people that this benefits the developers because they don't have to worry about getting the types correctly specified in the code, thus making development quicker. With test-driven development (TDD), any bad assignments can nevertheless be quickly discovered and fixed. Rather going further into the debate on the merits of static versus dynamic typing, let's focus on what is implemented in Java. Java uses static/strong typing, and the introduction of generics allows even stronger typing.

The type safety is just one of the benefits of using generics. You'll learn more benefits as you read on.

Creating a Parameterized Stack Type

So far, you have seen how to use the types created by others that use generics. Now, you will learn how to create your own parameterized type, something like an **ArrayList**. But first, let's discuss why you would create one. Consider a stack data structure in a program where you push and pop some data. Now, suppose you want to create a stack that operates only one particular data type. This means you would push and pop only the **Integer** data type or the **String** data type, as an example. The purpose behind creating such a type-safe stack is to safeguard against runtime errors when you push a certain data type and pop it to another type. You would want to make your stack type safe so that you can push and pop only one type of data. Trying to push any other type should generate a compile-time error.

Before going any further, let's look at the syntax for creating a parameterized type.

Declaration Syntax

You declare a parameterized type using the syntax

```
class ClassName <type> {
    . . .
}
```

where *type* is generally a single capital letter to distinguish it from the rest of the identifiers, which are generally more descriptive. Therefore, to declare a generic class called **Stack** that takes a single parameter, you would use the following declaration:

```
class Stack<T> {

    . . .
}
```

To instantiate the **Stack** class, you would use the following declaration:

```
Stack<Integer> integerStack;
```

In some situations, you might want to create a class that operates on more than one data type. For example, a map data structure requires two elements—the key and the corresponding value. An implementation of this in Java is the **HashMap** class, which is defined as

```
class HashMap<K, V> {

    . . .

}
```

where **K** specifies the type of keys maintained by this map and **V** specifies the type of mapped values. You would instantiate **HashMap** as follows:

```
HashMap<String, Integer> map1 = new HashMap<String, Integer>();
HashMap<Integer, String> map2 = new HashMap<Integer, String>();
```

In **map1**, the key is a **String** type and its value is an **Integer** type. In **map2**, the key is an **Integer** type and its value is a **String** type. Thus, while instantiating the class, a developer specifies the type of parameters.

The generic class can, however, take any number of parameters. The general syntax for a generic class is

```
class className <paramList> {...}
```

where **className** specifies the name of the generic class and **paramList** consists of one or more parameters separated by commas. Here is the general syntax for instantiating a generic class:

```
className <ArgumentList_opt> varName = new className < > (argList);
```

Now that we have looked at the syntax for creating a parameterized type, let's move to our example of a generic **Stack** class.

A Generic Stack Class

The definition of a generic **Stack** class is given in Listing 12-2.

Listing 12-2   *A Stack Class That Uses Generics*

```
class Stack<T> {

    protected T[] stack = (T[]) new Object[100];
    int ptr = -1;

    void push(T data) {
        ptr++;
        stack[ptr] = data;
    }

    T pop() {
        return (T) stack[ptr--];
    }
}
```

The **Stack** class takes one parameter, specified by the identifier **T**. The class declares a variable called **stack**, which is an array of **T** types:

```
protected T[] stack = (T[]) new Object[100];
```

NOTE
This is declared protected only for the reverse-engineering process discussed later; ideally, this should be private.

We initialize this to an array of the **Object** class having a size equal to 100. Note that this array is typecast to an array of **T** types. Next, we declare a **ptr** variable, which is our stack pointer. The **push** method takes one parameter called **data** of type **T**. Likewise, the **pop** method returns data of type **T**. This **T** type would be replaced with the actual data type during precompilation, as demonstrated shortly.

To instantiate the **Stack** class, we use the following declaration:

```
Stack<Float> floatStack;
```

When we use this declaration, the compiler replaces every occurrence of **T** in the **Stack** definition with **Float**. We will now use a reverse-engineering technique to gain some insight on this precompilation process.

Examining Intermediate Code

Compile the **Stack** class of Listing 12-2 using javac compiler. Now, run the javap utility on the generated class files with the following command:

```
C:\360\ch12>javap Stack
```

The output of this command is shown here:

```
Compiled from "Stack.java"
class Stack extends java.lang.Object{

    protected java.lang.Object[] stack;
    int ptr;
    Stack();
    void push(java.lang.Object);
    java.lang.Object pop();
}
```

The javap utility provides the reverse engineering on a .class file and produces the .java code. The screen output shows that our definition of the class variable **stack** of type **T[]** is now replaced with the following statement:

```
protected java.lang.Object[] stack;
```

Similarly, the **push** method, which we declared to take a parameter of type **T**, now takes a parameter of type **java.lang.Object** and the **pop** method, which did return a variable of type **T** but now returns an object of type **java.lang.Object**.

When we instantiate the **Stack** class with parameter of type **Integer**, we specify the real data type in place of the generic type **T**. The compiler now further replaces the declaration of the variable type **stack** and the parameter to the **push** method with the specified real data type. Thus, we would see the following two statements (provided only if we could examine the intermediate output):

```
protected Integer[] stack;
void push(Integer);
```

If you specify the **Float** data type at the time of instantiation, these two statements would be replaced with the following:

```
protected Float[] stack;
void push(Float);
```

These discussions explain how the compiler replaces the generic types with the real types at the precompilation stage.

> **NOTE**
> *The compiler erases all the angle bracket syntax and replaces the type variables with an **Object** type that can work with any other Java type at runtime. This feature is called erasure.*

> **TIP**
> *The compiler, when it erases the type information, does not create multiple classes for each instantiated real data type. It maintains the information on the real type in the bytecode and uses an appropriate typecast wherever necessary.*

> **NOTE**
> *The compiler treats each parameterization of a generic type as a truly different type at compilation. However, only one real type exists at runtime. For example, **Stack<Integer>** and **Stack<Float>** share the same plain-old Java class **Stack**. The **Stack** is called the raw type (class) of the generic **Stack<T>** class.*

Testing the Stack Class

The code for instantiating the **Stack** class with different data types is given in Listing 12-3.

Listing 12-3   *Testing the Generic Stack Class*

```
import java.math.*;

public class StackDemoApp {

    public static void main(String args[]) {
```

```java
        // long type stack
        System.out.println("Creating 'long' stack:");
        Stack<Long> longStack = new Stack<Long>();
        System.out.println("Pushing 5");
        longStack.push(5L);
        System.out.println("Pushing 10");
        longStack.push(10L);
        System.out.println("Emptying stack");
        System.out.println(longStack.pop());
        System.out.println(longStack.pop());
        System.out.println();

        // float type stack
        System.out.println("Creating 'float' stack:");
        Stack<Float> floatStack = new Stack<Float>();
        System.out.println("Pushing 5.0");
        floatStack.push(5.0f);
        System.out.println("Pushing 10.0");
        floatStack.push(10.0f);
        System.out.println("Emptying stack");
        System.out.println(floatStack.pop());
        System.out.println(floatStack.pop());
        System.out.println();

        // BigDecimal type stack
        System.out.println("Creating 'BigDecimal' stack:");
        Stack<BigDecimal> bigDecimalStack = new Stack<BigDecimal>();
        System.out.println("Pushing bigdecimal 12.5E+7");
        bigDecimalStack.push(new BigDecimal("12.5E+7"));
        System.out.println("Pushing bigdecimal 125");
        bigDecimalStack.push(new BigDecimal(125, MathContext.DECIMAL128));
        System.out.println("Emptying stack");
        System.out.println(bigDecimalStack.pop());
        System.out.println(bigDecimalStack.pop());
        System.out.println();

        // Stack without using generics
        Stack oldtypeStack = new Stack();
        oldtypeStack.push(10);
        oldtypeStack.push("test string");
        for (int i = 0; i < 2; i++) {
            String str = (String) oldtypeStack.pop();
            System.out.println(str);
        }
    }
}

class Stack<T> {
```

```
      private T[] stack = (T[]) new Object[5];
      private int ptr = -1;

      void push(T data) {
          ptr++;
          stack[ptr] = data;
      }

      T pop() {
          return (T) stack[ptr--];
      }
  }
```

In the **main** function, first we create a **Stack** that holds only the **Long** data type:

```
Stack<Long> longStack = new Stack<Long>();
```

Note how the **Long** data type is specified in both the declaration of the variable and the class instantiation. We push a few items on the stack by calling its **push** method. The **push** method takes a **long**-type parameter, which is automatically converted into a **Long** data type by the autoboxing feature (covered in the previous chapter). We pop these pushed items from the stack by calling its **pop** method. The **pop** method returns a **Long** data type that gets converted automatically into a **long** data type by the unboxing feature. If we try pushing any other data type onto this stack, a compile-time error is produced.

Next, we create a **float**-type stack for testing by executing the following statement:

```
Stack<Float> floatStack = new Stack<Float>();
```

To create a stack that holds **BigDecimal** numbers, we use the following statement:

```
Stack<BigDecimal> bigDecimalStack = new Stack<BigDecimal>();
```

Finally, the code demonstrates what happens when we do not use a generic type in the **Stack** creation. We now construct the stack the old way (without using generic types) and push two values onto it:

```
Stack oldtypeStack = new Stack();
oldtypeStack.push(10);
oldtypeStack.push("test string");
```

Note that the first value is of type **long** and the second is of type **String**. The compiler or the runtime will not generate any errors on these statements. Now, let's see what happens when we pop these values from the stack and try to use them somewhere in our code. We use a **for** loop to pop these two values:

```
for (int i = 0; i < 2; i++) {
    String str = (String) oldtypeStack.pop();
    System.out.println(str);
}
```

The code simply typecasts the popped value to a **String** and prints it to the console. The last pushed value is popped first; thus, we will see the message "test string" printed to the console.

However, when we pop the next value, a typecasting error occurs. Such runtime errors can be avoided only by the proper ordering of **push** and **pop** methods, remembering the type of data pushed and popped each time. By using generics, we are able to create a type-safe stack that catches errors at compile time.

In general, when data is stored in a data structure such as an array, stack, or list, only the programmer knows what types of objects are stored and is therefore responsible for proper typecasting when the stored objects are retrieved. If he makes a mistake in this typecasting, runtime errors are produced. Using generics will detect such errors at compile time, thus making the code more robust.

Bounded Types

In the previous section, you saw how to create a generic class to store any type of data. Now, what if you want to create a generic class that operates on a specified range of types? Using generics, you are able to restrict the range of data types on which your class can operate. These are called bounded types, because you bound the class with a certain range of data types to operate on. This is a typical use for generics, so let's look at how to create such a generic class.

In the previous section, we designed a **Stack** class that can operate on any data type, including a **String** type. What if we want to restrict **Stack** to operate only on numeric types? To place this restriction, we declare our generic **Stack** class as follows:

```
class NumberStack<T extends Number>
```

Here, the **NumberStack** class takes one parameter, called **T**, that extends **Number**.

NOTE
*In general, **T** may extend any other class where the inheritance hierarchy exists under it.*

Thus, the **NumberStack** class can operate on any data type that derives from the **Number** class, which is the superclass of all numeric data types in Java. We can create instances of the **NumberStack** class with the following kinds of declarations:

```
NumberStack<Long> longStack;
NumberStack<Float> floatStack;
```

The first statement creates an instance of the **NumberStack** class that operates on the **Long** data type, and the second statement creates an instance that operates on the **Float** data type. Now, what if we try the following?

```
NumberStack<Character> characterStack; // invalid
```

The compiler will throw an error indicating that the **Character** is not within the bounds of the class because **Character** does not inherit **Number**. We can, however, specify any other class that derives from **Number**. For example, the **BigDecimal** class inherits **Number**. Thus, the following declaration is valid:

```
NumberStack<BigDecimal> bigDecimalStack;
```

NOTE
*The **BigDecimal** class is defined in the **java.math** package and represents immutable, arbitrary-precision signed decimal numbers.*

Next, we write the **NumberStack** class itself. To restrict this class to using certain types of data, we do not have to do anything special in its implementation. We will use our previously defined **Stack** class and perform the necessary modifications to add the new restriction. The modified **Stack** class is shown here:

```
class NumberStack<T extends Number> {

    private Number[] stack = new Number[100];
    private int ptr = -1;

    void push(T data) {
        ptr++;
        stack[ptr] = data;
    }

    T pop() {
        return (T) stack[ptr--];
    }
}
```

Note that the only change we made was to replace the allocation of the **Object** array with a **Number**-type array:

```
private Number[] stack = new Number[100];
```

The rest of the class code remains the same.

Using Wildcards

Now, let's suppose we want to write a general method that dumps the entire contents of our **NumberStack** class from the previous example. We could write such a method easily, as follows:

```
static void dumpStack(NumberStack<Number> stack) {
    for (Number n : stack.stack) {
        System.out.println(n);
    }
}
```

The **dumpStack** method receives a parameter of type **Stack<Number>**. Note the parameter specified in the type declaration. Because **NumberStack** is a generic type, we specify the data type on which the **NumberStack** will operate. Because **Number** is the least common superclass of all the real types used in our **NumberStack** class definition, we use **Number** in the parameter declaration. Thus, we should be able to pass on a **NumberStack** object of any type to the **dumpStack** method. Wait a minute! This is not quite true, as you'll see shortly.

Now, let's instantiate the **NumberStack** class with **Number** as the real type and push a **Long** number on it:

```
NumberStack<Number> numberStack = new NumberStack<Number>();
numberStack.push(10L);
```

Let's dump this stack by calling our **dumpStack** method:

```
dumpStack(numberStack);
```

The code will compile and run without any errors. Now, let's consider our earlier instantiation of a **NumberStack** class that stores the **Long** numbers:

```
NumberStack<Long> longStack = new NumberStack<Long>();
```

Try dumping this stack using our **dumpStack** method:

```
dumpStack(longStack);
```

The compiler complains with the following error:

```
dumpStack(NumberStack<java.lang.Number>) in WildCardDemoApp cannot be applied
to (NumberStack<java.lang.Long>)
```

The **dumpStack** method expects a parameter of type **NumberStack<Number>**. In our method call, we pass an instance of **NumberStack <Long>**. You might think that because **Long** is a subclass of **Number**, this should be acceptable to the compiler. However, the main purpose of generics is to guard against such errors by providing type safety. Thus, the compiler rightly generates an error here. Now, how do we solve this problem so that our **dumpStack** method will work on any instance of the **NumberStack** class? To make this happen, we simply change the definition of the **dumpStack** method to the following:

```
static void dumpStack(NumberStack<?> stack)
```

Here, we have replaced the **Number** argument with a question mark (**?**). This is called a *wildcard.* It tells the compiler to accept an instance of the **NumberStack** class that operates on any permissible data type. If we recompile the code after making this change, it compiles without any errors. The full code, along with the code for the **NumberStack** class for testing, is given in Listing 12-4.

Listing 12-4   *Program Demonstrating the Use of Wildcards*

```
public class WildCardDemoApp {

    public static void main(String args[]) {
        System.out.println("Creating 'Long' stack:");
        NumberStack<Long> longStack = new NumberStack<Long>();
        longStack.push(5L);
        longStack.push(10L);

        System.out.println("Creating 'Number' stack:");
        NumberStack<Number> numberStack = new NumberStack<Number>();
```

```
            numberStack.push(10L);
            System.out.println("\nDumping 'Long' stack");
            dumpStack(longStack);
            System.out.println("\nDumping 'Number' stack");
            dumpStack(numberStack);
        }

        static void dumpStack(NumberStack<?> stack) {
            for (Number n : stack.getStack()) {
                System.out.println(n);
            }
        }
    }

    class NumberStack<T extends Number> {

        private Number stack[] = new Number[5];
        private int ptr = -1;

        public Number[] getStack() {
            return stack;
        }

        void push(T data) {
            ptr++;
            stack[ptr] = data;
        }

        T pop() {
            return (T) stack[ptr--];
        }
    }
```

When we run the program, we see the following output:

```
Creating 'Long' stack:
Creating 'Number' stack:

Dumping 'Long' stack
5
10
null
null
null

Dumping 'Number' stack
10
null
null
null
null
```

Note that the stack size is 5. In the first instance, we had pushed two values on the stack, and in the second instance we had pushed only one value on the stack. Therefore, the rest of the elements on the stack show a null value.

Bounded Wildcards

So far, you have learned about the bounded types and wildcards. A *bounded type* sets the restriction on a type used by a generic to a certain class hierarchy. A *wildcard* allows you to substitute any of the allowed types in the generic parameter type. In some situations, you may want to set both the upper and lower bounds on the range of classes used in generics. As an example of this, look at the class hierarchy in Figure 12-1.

The **JPasswordField** class derives from several superclasses. Suppose in your application you want to write a method to describe the features of a component that is an instance of **java.awt.Component** or any of its subclasses. You might also want to set up the restrictions on the component type that you pass to this method. For this, you could create upper and lower bounds for the range of components. For example, you may want to accept components only in the range of the **Container** and **JTextField** classes, which means the allowed classes would be **Container**, **JComponent**, **JTextComponent**, and **JTextField**.

To achieve this purpose, you may define a generic class called **CustomComponent**, as follows:

```
class CustomComponent<T>
```

While defining a generic, when you declare a type parameter such as **T** as in the preceding example, it can be substituted with any of the Java classes because all Java classes derive from **java.lang.Object**.

To restrict **T** to use a certain set of classes, you can use the **extends** clause, as shown here (remember our earlier example where we extended the **Number** class):

```
class CustomComponent<T extends Component>
```

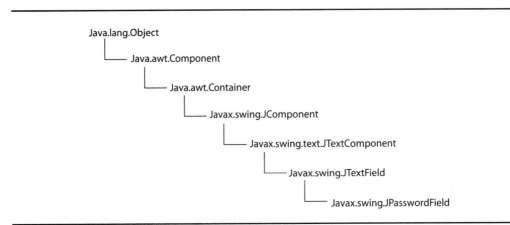

FIGURE 12-1. *A class hierarchy to illustrate bounded wildcards*

In this case, **T** can be substituted with **Component** or any of its subclasses. This, as you saw earlier, is called a *bounded* type. When you declare a method that takes a generic type as its parameter, you use the wildcard to allow the method to accept an object of any of the allowed classes in the specified hierarchy. The method declaration is made as follows:

```
void describeComponent(CustomComponent<?> component)
```

This method will accept a **CustomComponent** object that operates on **Component** or any of its subclasses. Now, if you want to restrict this parameter to operate on a certain type and its subclasses, you make the following declaration:

```
void describeComponent(CustomComponent<? extends JTextField> ref) {
    //...
}
```

Here, **JTextField** refers to the class shown in the hierarchy in Figure 12-1. Now, the method **describeComponent** will take a parameter of **CustomComponent** that operates on **JTextField** and its subclasses. This means you can input a parameter of the **JTextField** and **JPasswordField** types only. The **CustomComponent** that operates on **Component**, **Container**, **JComponent**, and **JTextComponent** will not be an acceptable parameter. This is called a *bounded wildcard*, where the lower bound is set to **JTextField**.

Just the way you set a lower bound, you can also set an upper limit by using the following syntax:

```
void describeComponent(CustomComponent<? super Container> ref) {
    ...
}
```

In this case, all the superclasses of **Container** will be acceptable parameters. Thus, the method can take a **CustomComponent** instance that operates on **Object** and **Component**. Note that **Container** itself is omitted, along with all its subclasses. To achieve the goal of restricting only the classes **Container**, **JComponent**, **JTextComponent**, and **JTextField**, you would declare your method as follows:

```
void describeComponent(CustomComponent<? super JPasswordField> ref) {
    //...
}
```

Note that **JPasswordField,** which is a superclass of **JTextField,** itself is omitted in the list of permissible objects. You would also need to declare **CustomComponent** as follows:

```
class CustomComponent<T extends Container>
```

This ensures that **CustomComponent** can accept only **Container** and its subclasses. Thus, with these two declarations, you are able to create upper and lower bounds for the range of classes that the **describeComponent** method can operate on.

Raw Types

In the FamousQuotes application from Listing 12-1, we created the list using the following statement:

```
ArrayList listOfFamousQuotes = new ArrayList();
```

Here, we did not specify a parameter to **ArrayList**, which takes one generic parameter, by its definition. When you use a generic type without parameters, it is called a *raw* type. The **ArrayList** class existed even prior to J2SE 5.0, where generics were introduced. By not allowing you to specify the parameters, code written prior to J2SE 5.0 is ensured to compile in new versions of Java. However, because the new compiler expects you to use generic types with parameters, it issues warnings thinking you have probably forgotten to substitute parameters for generic types with some actual types. When you compile FamousQuotes.java, you get following warning error:

```
FamousQuotes.java uses unchecked or unsafe operations.
Note: Recompile with -Xlint:unchecked for details.
```

If you do not want the new compiler to generate this warning, you have the following three choices:

- Use the **–source 1.4** switch during compilation. This compiles the code, considering it to be JDK 1.4 code. This means your code cannot contain generics or any other J2SE 5.0 features.
- Use the **@SuppressWarnings ("unchecked")** annotation discussed in Chapter 11. You may place this annotation just before the class declaration.
- Replace your raw type declarations to use **Object** as the actual type wherever a generic type is required, as in the following declaration:

```
ArrayList<Object> listOfFamousQuotes = new ArrayList<Object>();
```

The raw types are essentially created for backward compatibility.

More on Generic Types

In this section, we look at some more features of generics. We start with generic types that take more than one parameter. You learn how to use a built-in **HashMap** generic class that requires two parameters. You also learn what the restrictions are while casting a generic type, what happens during assignments and comparisons of two generic types, and what the generic methods are. Finally, you learn how to declare generic interfaces.

Class with Two Generic Parameters

The **HashMap** class is defined in J2SE 5.0 as follows:

```
class HashMap<K, V>
```

Here, **K** and **V** are the type parameters that can be substituted with any Java object at the time of instantiation. The **HashMap** class is used for storing key/value pairs. The **K** parameter specifies the key, and the **V** parameter specifies its value. Both **K** and **V** can be of any Java type. To illustrate how to use this two-parameter generic class, let's build a hashmap of the planets in our solar system. Each planet in our solar system has a fixed position. We will create a hashmap that defines the position as the key and the planet name as its value. This can then be used easily to find out which planet exists at what position. The PlanetMap program is given in Listing 12-5.

Listing 12-5 *Program Demonstrating the Use of a Two-Parameter HashMap Class*

```java
import java.util.*;

public class PlanetMap {

    public static void main(String args[]) {
        HashMap<Integer, String> mapOFPlanets =
                new HashMap<Integer, String>();

        mapOFPlanets.put(1, "Mercury");
        mapOFPlanets.put(2, "Venus");
        mapOFPlanets.put(3, "Earth");
        mapOFPlanets.put(4, "Mars");
        mapOFPlanets.put(5, "Jupiter");
        mapOFPlanets.put(6, "Saturn");
        mapOFPlanets.put(7, "Uranus");
        mapOFPlanets.put(8, "Neptune");

        System.out.println("Enter the desired position: ");
        Scanner scanner = new Scanner(System.in);
        int i = scanner.nextInt();
        System.out.printf("Solar system position %d is taken by %s%n",
                i, mapOFPlanets.get(i));
    }
}
```

We create our hashmap by instantiating the **HashMap** class:

```java
HashMap<Integer, String> mapOFPlanets = new HashMap<Integer, String>();
```

Note how the two parameters are specified in the declaration of the **mapOfPlanets** variables and the instantiation of the class **HashMap**. Although we want to store an integer value in the first parameter, we have specified an **Integer** wrapper class because the generic parameter needs to be a subclass of **Object** and cannot be a primitive type. We add the planets and their positions in the map as follows:

```java
mapOFPlanets.put(1, "Mercury");
mapOFPlanets.put(2, "Venus");
```

Note the first parameter is specified in integer format, which is autoboxed to the **Integer** type. Next, we ask the user to input a number. Calling the **get** method of the **HashMap** class retrieves the name of the planet at this position:

```java
System.out.printf("Solar system position %d is taken by %s%n",
    i, mapOFPlanets.get(i));
```

We could also use the same **HashMap** class to reverse the planet position and its name in the list. The purpose would be to enable the user to find out what the position is of a given planet. For this, we create our map as follows:

```
HashMap<String, Integer> mapOFPlanets = new HashMap<String, Integer>();
```

Note that we simply specify the first parameter to be of type **String** and the second parameter to be of type **Integer**. This is permitted because the **HashMap** class can take any Java object in either of its parameters. You can appreciate the flexibility that generics provides in defining the **HashMap** class. To build the list, we use the statements as follows:

```
mapOFPlanets1.put("Mercury", 1);
```

To retrieve the planet position once again, we use the **get** method, this time specifying a **String** as an argument.

Casting Types

An important point you must consider while using generic types is the casting of one type to another. It may seem obvious to perform a cast by merely considering the class hierarchy. But, in most situations such a cast will not be valid and will generate a compile-time error. Consider our earlier example of a **Stack** class. The class was defined as follows:

```
class NumberStack<T extends Number> {
```

You may now create two instances of the **NumberStack** class using the following declarations:

```
NumberStack<Long> longStack = new NumberStack<Long>();
NumberStack<Number> numberStack = new NumberStack<Number>();
```

The **longStack** operates on **Long** numbers and the **numberStack** operates on **Number**. Because **Long** is a subclass of **Number**, you might think that the following casting is valid:

```
numberStack = (NumberStack<Number>) longStack; // generates compile-time error
longStack = (NumberStack<Long>) numberStack; // generates compile-time error
```

Both statements generate a compile-time error. Any implicit or explicit typecasting, even within the same class hierarchy, is invalid.

Now, let's make another declaration:

```
NumberStack<Long> longStackNew = new NumberStack<Long>();
```

The following assignment statements will be valid:

```
longStack = longStackNew;
longStackNew = longStack;
```

In both situations, we have assignment variables of the same type, and the compiler knows that both variables refer to an instance of the **NumberStack** class that operates on a **Long** data type. Consider the declaration from our earlier PlanetMap example in Listing 12-5:

```
HashMap<String, Integer> mapOfPlanets = new HashMap<String, Integer>();
```

You may have another declaration, as follows:

```
HashMap<Integer, String> mapOfPlanetsNew = new HashMap<Integer, String>();
```

Now, if you attempt the following assignment, it will produce a compile-time error:

```
mapOfPlanets = mapOfPlanetsNew;
```

Although both **mapOfPlanets** and **mapOfPlanetsNew** are instances of the **HashMap** class, they operate on a different set of parameters and are therefore incompatible for the shown assignment.

TIP
Beginning in Java SE 7, you can replace the type argument required to invoke the constructor of a generic class with an empty set of type parameters, as long as the compiler can infer the type of arguments from the context. Thus, our previous declaration can now become the following:

```
HashMap<String, Integer> mapOfPlanets = new HashMap<>();
```

This pair of angle brackets (<>) is informally called the diamond.

Comparing and Assigning Generic Types

Consider the following simple generic type declaration for a universal data type that can hold any data type as its value. This is equivalent to a universal data type in PHP:

```
class UniverseType<T> {

    T a;

    UniverseType(T a) {
        this.a = a;
    }
}
```

The following two statements instantiate this class using **Float** and **Double** as actual parameters:

```
UniverseType<Float> f = new UniverseType<Float> (5f);
UniverseType<Double> d = new UniverseType<Double> (5.0);
```

Both **f** and **d** have been assigned the same numeric value of 5.0. Now, let's look at the various assignments and comparisons between these two objects. If you perform the comparison **f.equals(d)**, what will it return? It returns **false**, indicating that the two objects are not equal, even though they hold the same numeric value. What if you try an equality operation such as **if (f == d)**? Rather than getting a runtime error, you will get a compile-time error in this case because the two objects are incomparable. The object **f** operates on a **Float** and the object **d** operates on **Double**. Therefore, they cannot be compared. What if you try an assignment such as **f = d**? This, too, will generate a compile-time error because you are trying an assignment between two incompatible types. What if you try **d = f**? This looks like a promotion—assigning a float to a double. This, too, generates a compile-time error.

Generic Methods

A generic method takes parameters of a generic type or returns a generic value. Such a method may be defined in a generic or a nongeneric class. You have seen several examples of generic methods so far in this chapter. For example, the **push** and **pop** methods of our generic **Stack** class used type parameters and are therefore known as generic methods. The two definitions are reproduced here:

```
void push(T data) {...}
T pop() {...}
```

The **push** method uses a generic type argument, and the **pop** method returns a generic type value. The **dumpStack** method from our earlier example in Listing 12-4 is a generic method defined in a nongeneric class:

```
static void dumpStack(NumberStack<Number> stack) {
```

The generic method may be declared **static**, as in the case of **dumpStack**.

Declaring Generic Interfaces

The same way you create a generic class and method, you can create interfaces that operate on generic data types. A good example of this is the **Map** interface defined in the **Collections** framework. The interface is declared as follows:

```
public interface Map<K,V>
```

The **Map** interface uses two generic types. The implementing class will use these two types in its implementation. The **HashMap** class implements this interface. **HashMap** is declared as follows:

```
public class HashMap<K,V>extends AbstractMap<K,V>
        implements Map<K,V>, Cloneable, Serializable
```

The class implements the **Map** interface using the **implements** keyword. Besides this generic interface, it also implements the two nongeneric interfaces **Cloneable** and **Serializable**. Thus, a class can implement any number of generic and nongeneric interfaces in its declaration.

NOTE
*The declaration of the **HashMap** class also indicates that it inherits from the **AbstractMap** class. The **extends** word indicates this inheritance. The **AbstractMap** class itself is generic. Thus, a class can extend another generic class.*

Restrictions in Generics

When you use generics in your programs, you must obey certain restrictions that apply. In this section, we discuss these restrictions.

Creating Arrays

Look at our earlier generic **NumberStack** class, the partial definition of which is reproduced here:

```
class NumberStack<T extends Number> {

    private Number stack[] = new Number[100];
```

You might be wondering why we created a **Number** array. Couldn't we create an array of **T** types in the class constructor, as shown here?

```
public Stack () {
    stack = new T[100];
}
```

This is illegal. You cannot create an array of generic types. You could, however, create a variable of the generic array type and assign it to an array of real data types at runtime. To understand this, consider the following class declaration:

```
class NumberStack<T extends Number> {

    T stack[];

    Stack(T[] stack) {
        this.stack = stack;
    }
}
```

The class **NumberStack** declares an array of **T** types as its class variable. The class constructor receives a reference to an array of generic type **T** and assigns it to the class variable **stack**. The main program that uses this class can now create an array of real data types and assign it to **stack** at runtime, as shown here:

```
Double[] doubleArray = new Double[100];
NumberStack<Number> doubleStack = new NumberStack<Number>(doubleArray);
```

In this example, we create an array of **Double** and pass it as a parameter to the **NumberStack** constructor. Couldn't we create an array of generic types directly, as follows?

```
NumberStack<Double> doubleStack = new NumberStack<Double>[10]; // illegal
```

This is illegal because the creation of generic arrays is not permitted.

Instantiating Type Parameters

Consider our previous definition of **NumberStack**:

```
class NumberStack<T extends Number> {
```

The class uses one generic parameter, **T**. It is illegal to try to instantiate this parameter anywhere in the class definition. In other words, you cannot call **new T()** anywhere in the code. The generic parameters are replaced by the actual parameters during the precompilation stage. Therefore, creating an object of a generic type is not permitted.

Use of the static Keyword

To understand the restrictions on the use of the **static** keyword in generic classes, consider the following class definition:

```
class WordDefinition<W, M> {

    static W word; // illegal
```

```
M meaning; // allowed

W get() {
    return word;
}

static void showMeaning() {
    System.out.println(meaning); // illegal
}
}
```

The class **WordDefinition** defines a word and its meaning. It takes two generic parameters, **W** and **M**. We define two variables, **word** and **meaning**, in the class definition. Because these two variables are of the generic type, their actual types will only be defined at the time of class instantiation. Making these variables **static** produces a compile-time error because the variables of generic types are always treated as nonstatic and their real types are substituted during the precompilation stage.

Likewise, you cannot mark the **get** method as **static** because it returns a generic type, which is a nonstatic variable.

Similarly, a class method that is declared **static**, such as **showMeaning**, cannot use a variable of the generic type, as shown here:

```
System.out.println(meaning); // illegal
```

These restrictions on the use of **static** are easily understandable because the static variables and methods are always attached to the class implementation and not its instances.

Summary

Java has always been known as a very strongly typed language. Generics enable stricter type checking at compile time. J2SE 5.0 introduced the **Collections** framework, where several existing classes were reintroduced using generics. They made two important contributions to the existing classes. First, they added type checking to collection types at compile time, thus ensuring that the type of objects a collection can hold is restricted to the type passed to it. Second, they eliminated the need for typecasting when retrieving an element from a collection.

Generics were introduced in the Java language core features beginning with J2SE 5.0. A generic is a parameterized type. You use generics to help enforce better type safety in your programs. At the time of instantiation, you provide a real data type in the place of a generic type. The compiler erases the generic type from the source program and creates a raw Java class. The compiler does not generate multiple classes, each for the specified real type. Instead, it creates only one raw class and provides an appropriate typecast wherever required. The generic parameters can be bounded with both upper and lower limits. You use wildcards to specify that a generic method can accept any of the allowable real types. The generics feature is extensively used in the **Collections** framework. You will learn more about its use in Chapter 16.

We have covered many features of Java language so far. Now, it is time to move into real-world application development—which is the topic of the next chapter.

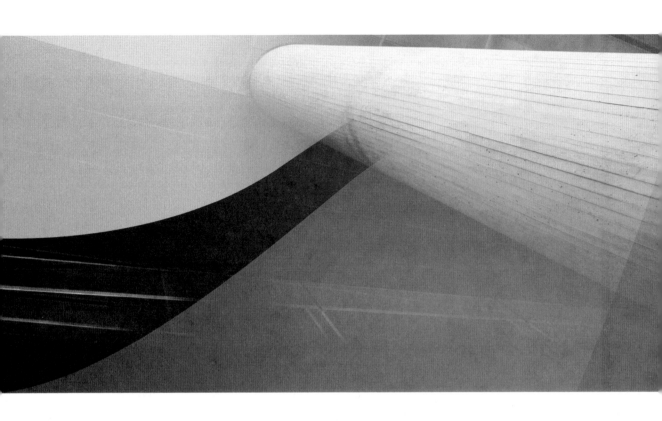

CHAPTER
13

Event Processing
and GUI Building

n all the earlier chapters, Java programs we discussed were console based. These console-based applications make it easier to focus on learning the language syntax. However, in real life, application users demand a better interface than the one provided in a console-based application. The graphical user interface (GUI) has been in existence now for a few decades, and your users will certainly expect one in the applications you develop. Practically all applications, from Microsoft Office to OpenOffice, provide a graphical interface. It is now time to learn how to develop a graphical interface in Java for your own applications. In this chapter, you learn how to create GUI-based applications in Java. Then, going forward, the rest of the chapters in this book will contain a mix of both console- and GUI-based applications.

A typical GUI-based application consists of a few windows, dialog boxes, and other elements and contains many controls such as labels, edit controls, list boxes, and so on. Java provides a rich set of controls to develop such GUI applications. Before you start learning to use these controls in your applications, it is necessary to understand the processing model for such applications. GUI programs are *event driven*. This means that after a GUI application is started, it simply waits for some event to occur. When an event occurs, event-handler code in the application gets executed. After the event handler finishes, the application once again waits for another event to occur. This process continues for the entire life of the program. A typical example is your word processing application. When you start such an application, a blank document window opens on your screen and the application simply waits for you to enter something on the keyboard. When you press a character key, it is displayed on the screen and then the program again waits for more input. Pressing a key is considered an event that is external to the word processing application. Understanding the key press and displaying the appropriate character on the screen is the event processing. As a developer, you need to learn the different types of external events that occur in your system, how to capture such events in your applications, and how to write event handlers for processing these events. In short, you must understand the event-processing model defined in Java in order to develop GUI-based applications.

In this chapter, you learn the Java event-processing model and a few of the controls you can use in your application. The next chapter focuses on placing these controls on your screen to create a pleasing and usable interface for your application. These two chapters together will prepare you for creating GUI applications.

In this chapter, you will learn the following:

- The delegation event model of Java
- Event sources and listeners
- Processing events
- Registering on multiple event sources
- Understanding event types and defining handlers
- Using adapter classes
- Using inner classes and anonymous classes in event handling
- Building GUI applications
- Using Swing components such as **JButton**, **JTextField**, and **JList**

Event Processing Model

When Java was introduced in 1995, it used the conventional event-processing model of that time, which was the same one used by Microsoft Windows. This model is known as the *hierarchical event model,* where events move up in a container hierarchy until they are consumed or eventually lost.

Hierarchical Event Model

JDK 1.0 used the hierarchical event model. In this model, an event propagates up the container hierarchy. To understand what *container hierarchy* means, we first need to discuss the concept of events.

In an event-driven programming model, each application defines an event queue. The **main** function within the application keeps scanning this queue for events. The operating system posts the events for the application in its queue. If an event is pending in the queue, the **main** function picks up the event and dispatches it to the appropriate event handler defined within the application.

Let's illustrate this with an example: Consider what happens when you click a button in an application displayed on your desktop. The operating system decides where the event should be dispatched, depending on the position of the mouse click on the screen. The event will be dispatched to the active application under the mouse click position. Next, the application determines the component at the mouse click position. If the component is unable to handle the event, the event is transferred to its parent container, which could be a dialog box or a window on which the button is placed. If this parent container also does not handle the event, the event is further transferred to *its* parent container. If this container also does not handle the event, it is further transferred to *its* parent, and so on. Thus, the event moves up the container hierarchy until it is handled somewhere in the application (see Figure 13-1).

Figure 13-1 shows a typical Windows desktop. The active application on the screen is Microsoft Word with its **Insert Hyperlink** dialog box opened up. The user has opened up another dialog box—called **Set Hyperlink ScreenTip**—that is subordinate to it. This dialog box has two buttons: **OK** and **Cancel**. Now, let's suppose the user clicks the OK button. Basically, as far as the operating system is concerned, the user has clicked the mouse on a certain location on the screen. The OS now has to determine what lies at this location. It finds out from the list of currently displayed applications that the current click position is on the OK button of the **ScreenTip** dialog box within **Microsoft Word**. It now dispatches the **click** event to Microsoft Word. The event gets added to the end of the event queue maintained by Word. The application, at some later time, will process this event. When it does so, it first finds out whether an event handler is available for the OK button. If the developer has not provided an event handler for the OK button, the event will be passed on to the **ScreenTip** dialog box, which is the **parent** container of the OK button. If this dialog box does not provide the event handler, the event is propagated to the next **parent** container, which is the **Insert Hyperlink** dialog box. If it, too, is unable to process the event, the event is passed on to the main application window (that is, the **parent** of the **Insert Hyperlink** dialog box). If the main application window is also unable to handle this event, the event is finally propagated to the desktop, where eventually it is lost as far as Microsoft Word is concerned.

Thus, in the hierarchical event model, the event propagates up the container hierarchy. The hierarchical event model, though simple enough, has several disadvantages:

- If none of the application containers in the hierarchy handle the event, the event is lost. This causes the consumption of unnecessary CPU cycles.

- If the container is not interested in a particular event, it still has to process all events occurring on its child components.

- A component at the top of the hierarchy (that is, a child component) may accidently consume an event that was not meant for it but rather for its parent component.

- If the component on which the event occurs wishes to consume the event, the component must be subclassed. For example, if you want to create a customized picture button, you need to subclass the **java.awt.Button** class and provide your own event handlers. This unnecessarily adds the creation of several subclasses in your code. Refer to javadocs for a list of subclasses created under **java.awt .Component** to provide for the custom event handling for each type of component.

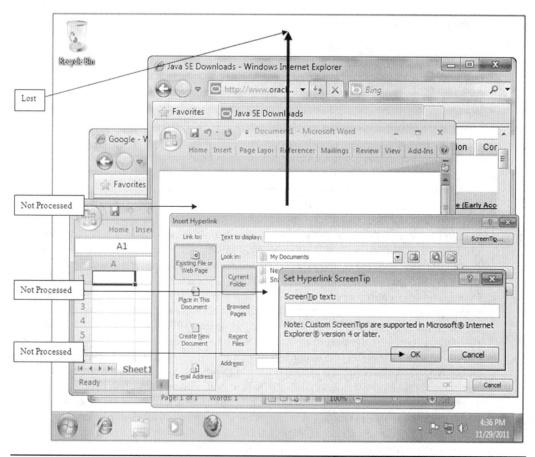

FIGURE 13-1. *Event propagation in the container hierarchy*

This model is now deprecated and not recommended for use in Java. (See the preceding sidebar for more information on this model. You'll also get a good understanding of event processing in general as well as an appreciation for the importance of the new event model.) The legacy code written in JDK 1.0 that uses this hierarchical event model still runs on a modern JVM. If you are interested in learning only the current event-processing model, you could certainly skip the sidebar without affecting your learning of GUI application development.

Due to several disadvantages of the hierarchical event model used in JDK 1.0, Java's event-processing model was changed in the very next version of the JDK. The new model is called the delegation event model and has been in effect since JDK 1.1. Therefore, only JDK 1.0 code does not support the new model. This new model solves most of the problems of the earlier event model and provides much better performance.

NOTE
Creating a sophisticated, multithreaded GUI toolkit could solve most of these problems, but this still remains a dream for many creators of GUI libraries, not just Java creators. Using events is still the preferred way for GUI development.

Delegation Event Model

The delegation event model is based on the concept that for every event, there is an event source and an event listener. This is illustrated in Figure 13-2.

In the delegation event model, we clearly define an event source and an event listener. An event source either generates an event on its own or is subject to the occurrence of an external event. The event source transmits such events to the event listeners. Rather than being transmitted up the container hierarchy, events are transmitted to preregistered event listeners. Any object may act as an event source, an event listener, or both. For example, a button, when clicked, acts as an event source and sends the **click** event to its registered listeners. A button may also change its

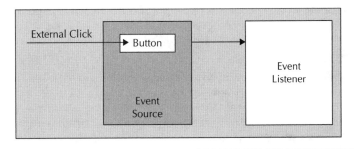

FIGURE 13-2. *Event source and a listener*

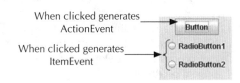

FIGURE 13-3. *Different event sources generating different types of events*

caption when another button somewhere in the window is clicked. In this case, the first button acts as a listener for the **click** event generated by the second button. Thus, a single component (a button in this case) can act as both a source and a listener of events.

The Event Source

An *event source* is a component that generates an event. Figure 13-3 shows two different types of event sources: a button and a radio button.

An event source generates an event subject to the occurrence of an external event. For example, when you click a **Button** control, a "mouse click" event occurs on the button. This is an external event; the button consumes this and transmits another event called **ActionEvent** to its listeners. The button, which acts as an event listener here, can decide what to do in reaction to an external event before sending an **ActionEvent** to its registered listeners. For example, it may send out an e-mail in its own event-processing code. For this, you would need to subclass the button.

When you click a radio button, once again a "mouse click" event occurs. The radio button, in turn, generates an **ItemEvent** and sends it to its listeners. The type of event generated is solely decided by the event source. We discuss the different event types later.

An event source may generate an event due to its own internal working. Depending on the result of some computation, a component may generate and transmit an event to the external world. For example, suppose an event source object is counting down to zero; when the count reaches zero, the object may generate and transmit an event to its listeners. Here's another example: When the temperature rises above a certain threshold, an alarm may be raised as an event.

The **JButton**, **JCheckbox**, **JTextArea**, and **JTextField** classes in the Swing package are a few examples of event sources. All classes that derive from **java.awt.Component** are candidate event sources in your application.

The Event Listener

For every event source there may be one or more registered listeners. The objects that are interested in the occurrence of a particular event will register themselves with the corresponding event source. This means that an interested event listener sends its own object reference to the event source. The event source copies this reference into its own storage and calls a specified callback method on the event listener whenever it generates an event. This is illustrated in Figure 13-4.

Figure 13-4 shows a button that generates an event to the external world whenever it is clicked. The figure also shows three more objects—**Listener1**, **Listener2**, and **Listener3**—that could be possible listeners for this event. Out of these three listener objects, the first two listener objects (**Listener1** and **Listener2**) have registered with the **button** event source. As the figure shows, the button object maintains a list of registered listeners. Now, when the user clicks the button, the button will generate an event that gets transmitted to **Listener1** and **Listener2**; however, it does not propagate to the **Listener3** object, which is not registered with the **button** event source for

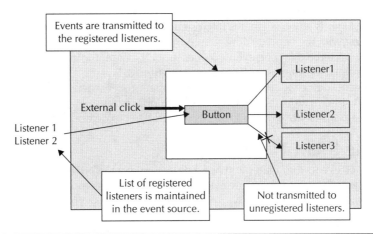

FIGURE 13-4. *Transmitting an event to the registered listeners*

the click event. The event source essentially calls a predefined callback method on each of the registered listeners. The listeners implement these callback methods to provide their own processing of the external event.

Thus, the event source is responsible for maintaining the list of registered event listeners and is also responsible for transmitting the appropriate event to these listeners whenever such an event is generated. The event source will not transmit an event to unregistered listeners. Therefore, the events are essentially transmitted to objects that are interested in that event. This saves lot of unnecessary processing of events by objects interested in them and thus takes care of one of the problems that exists in the earlier hierarchical event model (refer to the earlier sidebar).

Event Processing Sequence

The multiple listeners obviously register with the event source in a certain order. However, when an event is transmitted to the listeners, you cannot assume the order in which event listeners will receive it—there is no first-come-first-serve guarantee in the Java model. All the registered listeners will receive the event, but in an unpredictable order. It is possible that some event listeners may not receive the event at all, as explained next.

Whenever an event source generates an event, it transmits the event to the registered listener by calling a method of the listener object. Note that for this purpose, the event source holds the object reference to the registered listener. The event source uses this reference to call a method on it. This method receives a parameter that details the type of event and other relevant information (more details later). Thus, the event source keeps on calling the method on each and every registered listener. When the program returns after a method call on the first listener, the method on the second listener is called, and so on. Now, consider a situation where one of the listener methods is badly written (say, for example, the method creates an infinite loop). In this case, the methods on the remaining listeners cannot be called. This blocks further event propagation, and your application will stop responding to any future events. Fortunately, a separate event thread is created by the JVM to process these application events. This thread blocks in a malfunctioning method. However, the rest of the applications under the JVM continue to run and in effect will not cause the system to hang.

Registering on Multiple Event Sources

An event listener is an object that is interested in the occurrence of a particular external event and registers itself with the desired event source. A listener may be interested in more than one event occurring from more than one event source. In such a case, the event listener registers itself with all the desired event sources, as illustrated in Figure 13-5.

Each event source will transmit an event to the listener whenever it generates one. The event source sends information about itself in an event object transmitted to the listener. The event listener is responsible for investigating this event object to determine who sent the event.

Multiple Event Types

Java classifies events into multiple types. For example, an event may be classified as a mouse event, a keyboard event, a window event, and so on. As shown in Figure 13-6, whenever the mouse enters the component body, a **mouseEntered** event is generated. When the mouse exits the component body, a **mouseExited** event occurs. When you click the mouse on a component, a **mouseClicked** event occurs. Likewise, events are classified into different categories to simplify their processing.

For each event type, a distinct event object is generated. For example, for action events, an **ActionEvent** object is generated; for mouse click events, a **MouseEvent** object is generated; for mouse motion events, a **MouseMotionEvent** object is generated. Therefore, Java defines several classes for describing these event types.

A unique event handler is provided to handle each type of event. For example, an **actionPerformed** method is called for processing **ActionEvent**s, and an **itemStateChanged** method is called for processing **ItemEvent**s. We cover event handling in detail through several programming examples that follow. The important point to note here is that the events come in

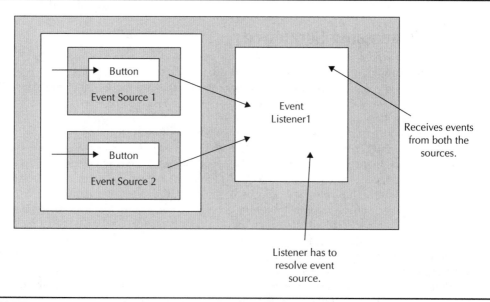

FIGURE 13-5. *An event listener registering with multiple sources*

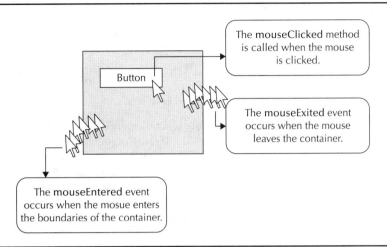

The **mouseClicked** method is called when the mouse is clicked.

The **mouseExited** event occurs when the mouse leaves the container.

The **mouseEntered** event occurs when the mosue enters the boundaries of the container.

FIGURE 13-6. *Classifications of mouse events*

different types because they carry different kinds of information, according to what they represent. The listeners also have different event-processing methods to match the different event types.

Building a GUI

In the early days of computing, all the applications were text based. The user would input data into the program from the console and generally receive the program output on the console itself. We have been using such console-based programs throughout this book. The current trend in computing is to create applications that have a graphical interface. The main two types of applications we see in today's world are browser based (HTML) and rich GUI applications based on Swing in Java or other libraries on other platforms. These GUI applications provide for easier human interaction. The graphical interface provides a rich experience to the application user. To create a graphical interface for an application, Java provides several classes. The important package supplied by Java in its early days was AWT (Abstract Windowing Toolkit). Although AWT is still available in the current versions of the JDK, its use in creating GUI applications was replaced by a toolkit called Swing. In this chapter, we use Swing classes to build GUI applications. Both packages provide several components, such as label controls (**javax.swing.JLabel**), buttons (**javax.swing.JButton**), list boxes (**javax.swing.JList**), and so on. The components in AWT use low-level API classes of the operating system, whereas Swing is mostly Java based. Therefore, Swing components are considered lightweight components. As far as developers are concerned, both Swing and AWT are platform independent; however, because parts of AWT use native widgets of the underlying platform, they are sometimes considered heavyweight components.

The Swing library is very vast, providing several components. To make learning easier, the programs in the following sections are simple. Each program introduces you to a certain set of components in the Swing library. By the end of the next chapter, you will have learned how to create powerful GUI applications that have real-life value.

Creating the User Interface

A graphical user interface requires a window. You create a window in your Java application by using the **JFrame** class provided in the Swing libraries. You display a window for your application by using the following code snippet:

```
JFrame frame = new JFrame();
frame.setVisible(true);
```

The **JFrame** class provides the windowing functionality. Typically, you subclass **JFrame** to add your application-specific functionality. Once a **JFrame** object is created, you call its **setVisible** method to show the window on the screen. By passing the **false** parameter to the **setVisible** method, you cause the window to be hidden from the screen. Note that hiding the window does not destroy it. A hidden window can be brought back to the screen by calling the **setVisible** method with the **true** parameter.

To create a user interface for your application, you need to place a few controls on the window. You place the controls by instantiating the various control classes provided in the Swing libraries and adding the created objects on the window. The added controls follow certain predefined placement rules, and a layout manager determines their positions. The layout manager is responsible for arranging the components based on predefined rules of placement. Java provides several layout managers for your use. We will be using a few layout managers in the programs that follow this section.

You can place various types of controls on a window. For example, to display simple text, you use a label control (an instance of **JLabel**). To accept user input, you use an edit control (an instance of **JTextField**). To show a list of items, you use a list box (an instance of **JList**), and so on. You learn the use of these controls and how to process events generated by them in the following sections.

Demonstrating the Button Control

In this section, we develop a simple application that displays a button with the caption "Show" (or "Hide") on a window. When you click the Show button, a message is displayed on the window and the button text itself changes to "Hide." When you click the button one more time, the message is hidden. The action is repeated for every click of the button. Additionally, we provide one more button, called Close. Clicking this button results in the application terminating. The user interface for the application is shown in Figure 13-7.

FIGURE 13-7. *Demonstrating the use of button controls*

The program that creates this interface and processes the button events is given in Listing 13-1.

Listing 13-1 *Building a GUI and Demonstrating a Button Control*

```java
import javax.swing.*;
import java.awt.event.*;

public class ButtonDemo {

    public static void main(String[] args) {
        MyFrame frame = new MyFrame("Button Demo");
        frame.setSize(200, 200);
        frame.setVisible(true);
    }
}

class MyFrame extends JFrame implements ActionListener {

    private JButton closeButton = new JButton("Close");
    private JButton messageButton = new JButton("Hide");
    private JLabel label = new JLabel(
                "Java Programming is easy", JLabel.CENTER);

    public MyFrame(String str) {
        super(str);
        add(messageButton, "North");
        add(closeButton, "South");
        add(label, "Center");
        messageButton.addActionListener(this);
        closeButton.addActionListener(this);
    }

    public void actionPerformed(ActionEvent evt) {
        if (evt.getSource().equals(messageButton)) {
            if (messageButton.getText().equals("Show")) {
                label.setVisible(true);
                messageButton.setText("Hide");
            } else {
                label.setVisible(false);
                messageButton.setText("Show");
            }
        } else if (evt.getSource().equals(closeButton)) {
            System.exit(0);
        }
    }
}
```

To use the Swing classes in an application, we first need to import the Swing package in our program, as follows:

```
import javax.swing.*;
```

Note that the Swing package is defined in the javax package. In early versions of the JDK, all Java packages were defined in the java package. Now, many packages are defined in the javax package. The Swing package is one of them.

To include the event-processing classes, we need to include the event package in our code, as follows:

```
import java.awt.event.*;
```

To create an application window for our application, we create a class called **MyFrame** that extends from **JFrame**:

```
class MyFrame extends JFrame implements ActionListener {
```

The class **MyFrame** also implements an interface called **ActionListener**, because it will be made responsible for handling the click events for the buttons placed on it. A button click causes an **ActionEvent** to be generated. A listener must implement the **ActionListener** interface and provide the implementation for the event-processing methods offered in the listener interface.

In the **MyFrame** class, we first create two buttons:

```
private JButton closeButton = new JButton("Close");
private JButton messageButton = new JButton("Hide");
```

A button is created by instantiating the **JButton** class. One of the class constructors takes a parameter of a **String** type that holds the text to be displayed on the button. The **JButton** class provides other constructors besides the one used here.

We create a label object for displaying some text to the user by instantiating the **JLabel** class:

```
private JLabel label = new JLabel("Java Programming is easy", JLabel.CENTER);
```

The **JLabel** constructor used here accepts two parameters. The first parameter specifies the text to be displayed on the label. The second parameter specifies the text alignment. Using the predefined constant in the **JLabel** class specifies the center alignment.

Next, we define a constructor for our **MyFrame** class:

```
public MyFrame(String str) {
```

The constructor takes a parameter of the **String** type. The contents of this parameter will be used for displaying the window title. The first statement in the constructor is a call to its super class constructor:

```
super(str);
```

Note from earlier chapters that a call to **super** must be the first statement in our constructor. The **super** call passes the **str** argument to its superclass constructor, which uses its value for constructing the window title.

We now add two buttons to our window:

```
add(messageButton, "North");
add(closeButton, "South");
```

The first button is added to the "North" region of the window, and the second button is added to the "South" region of the window. The window is considered to be divided into five different regions, as shown in Figure 13-8.

Note that each Swing component that can contain other components has a layout manager that decides how the contained components are arranged spatially. The default layout manager for a **JFrame** is **BorderLayout**. This layout manager splits the window into five different regions, as illustrated in Figure 13-8. Using this layout manager, we can place up to five visible components on the window. Placing an additional component in any region results in setting the earlier placed component behind the newly placed component, effectively hiding it from the user's view.

CAUTION
Since JDK 1.4, the five regions in a BorderLayout *are specified using a different set of constants, which you will study in the next chapter.*

We then add the label control to the center region of the window:

```
add(label, "Center");
```

After adding the components, we set the event listener for our buttons:

```
messageButton.addActionListener(this);
closeButton.addActionListener(this);
```

To add an action event listener for the button, we call its **addActionListener** method. This method takes one parameter that refers to the instance of the desired listener. In our case, we specify **this** as the parameter to the **addActionListener** method. The **this** parameter indicates the instance of the current object, which is **MyFrame**. Thus, the **MyFrame** object listens to and processes the action events generated by two buttons.

NOTE
If you forget to add a listener and the user clicks the button, the generated event is not processed at all. For a user, this means that nothing happens when he clicks the button; the rest of the application will still work as expected.

Next, we need to provide the implementation for all the abstract methods defined in the **ActionListener** interface. The **ActionListener** interface declares only one method, called

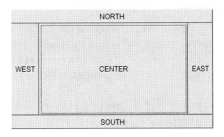

FIGURE 13-8. *Component positions in the default layout manager of JFrame*

actionPerformed, that receives one parameter of type **ActionEvent**. We provide its implementation as follows:

```
public void actionPerformed(ActionEvent evt) {
```

The Java runtime calls this **actionPerformed** method whenever the user clicks either of the two buttons in our application. The runtime passes an **ActionEvent** object to this method that contains the action details. We call its **getSource** method to check which button is clicked:

```
if (evt.getSource().equals(messageButton)) {
```

If the event was generated by the **messageButton**, we check its current label by calling its **getText** method:

```
if (messageButton.getText().equals("Show")) {
    label.setVisible(true);
    messageButton.setText("Hide");
```

If the current label is "Show," we show the label control by calling its **setVisible** method. We also set the new text for the **messageButton** by calling its **setText** method. The next time the user clicks the same button, the preceding **if** condition will fail. In this case, we execute the **else** clause, where we hide the label and set the button control text back to "Show."

If the user clicks the Close button, we call the **exit** method of the **System** class to close the application:

```
else if (evt.getSource().equals(closeButton)) {
    System.exit(0);
}
```

Finally, let's discuss the **main** method of our **ButtonDemo** class, which is the starting point of our application. In the **main** method, we create an instance of the **MyFrame** class:

```
MyFrame frame = new MyFrame("Button Demo");
```

The text that is passed to the constructor of the **MyFrame** class is displayed as a caption in our application window. We set the initial size for the window by calling its **setSize** method. The size is specified in terms of pixels:

```
frame.setSize(200, 200);
```

Finally, we show the window to the user by calling its **setVisible** method:

```
frame.setVisible(true);
```

To quit the application, click the **Close** button.

In this simple program, you learned the use of the **JLabel**, **JButton**, and **JFrame** classes. You also got a brief introduction to one of the layout managers, which places these controls on an instance of **JFrame**. This layout manager, called the **BorderLayout** manager, is the default for **JFrame**. You learn more about this layout manager in the next chapter.

Demonstrating the Edit Control

In this section, you learn to use a **JTextField** control. The **JTextField** control is nothing but an edit control you have used elsewhere. The **JTextField** control accepts a single line of text input

FIGURE 13-9. *An application interface for demonstrating the use of edit controls*

from the user. We create a simple integer adder using this control. Our application contains two **JTextField** controls. The user enters the two values to be added in these controls and clicks the addition operator button to see the result of the operation. The application GUI is shown in Figure 13-9.

The program that creates the user interface shown in Figure 13-9 and processes the application events is given in Listing 13-2.

Listing 13-2 *Demonstrating the Use of the Edit Control*

```java
import javax.swing.*;
import java.awt.event.*;
import java.awt.*;

public class TextFieldDemo {

    public static void main(String[] args) {
        MyFrame frame = new MyFrame("Integer Adder");
        frame.setVisible(true);
        frame.setSize(500, 100);
    }
}

class MyFrame extends JFrame implements ActionListener, WindowListener {

    private JTextField number1 = new JTextField();
    private JTextField number2 = new JTextField();
    private JButton adder = new JButton("+");
    private JLabel result = new JLabel("0.0", JLabel.RIGHT);

    public MyFrame(String str) {
        super(str);
        this.setLayout(new GridLayout(2, 4));
        add(new JLabel("Number1", JLabel.CENTER));
        add(new JLabel("Number2", JLabel.CENTER));
        add(new JLabel("Operator", JLabel.CENTER));
        add(new JLabel("Result", JLabel.CENTER));
        add(number1);
        add(number2);
        add(adder);
        add(result);
```

```
            adder.addActionListener(this);
            this.addWindowListener(this);
    }

    public void actionPerformed(ActionEvent evt) {
        if (evt.getSource().equals(adder)) {
            try {
                int num1 = Integer.parseInt(number1.getText());
                int num2 = Integer.parseInt(number2.getText());
                int answer = num1 + num2;
                result.setText(String.valueOf(answer));
            } catch (NumberFormatException ne) {
                System.out.println("Number parsing error "
                        + ne.getMessage());
            }
        }
    }

    public void windowActivated(WindowEvent e) {
    }

    public void windowClosed(WindowEvent e) {
    }

    public void windowClosing(WindowEvent e) {
        System.exit(0);
    }

    public void windowDeactivated(WindowEvent e) {
    }

    public void windowDeiconified(WindowEvent e) {
    }

    public void windowIconified(WindowEvent e) {
    }

    public void windowOpened(WindowEvent e) {
    }
}
```

As in the earlier example, we first import the required packages. The class **MyFrame** extends **JFrame** and implements the **ActionListener** interface to process the action events. Additionally, it implements the **WindowListener** interface for processing window events:

```
class MyFrame extends JFrame implements ActionListener, WindowListener {
```

In the earlier example, we used the Close button for closing the application window. If you click the close icon in the upper-right corner of the window, the window would normally disappear from the screen, but your application might not necessarily close. To close the application via the click of the window's close icon, you need to process window events.

TIP
*If you use the Java Desktop Application template in NetBeans to
create a Windows application, clicking the close window icon
will terminate it. This facility is provided by the NetBeans built-in
framework.*

A designated listener handles window events. You create a listener by implementing the
WindowListener interface. We discuss the various methods of the **WindowListener** interface after
discussing the rest of the program code.

In **MyFrame**, we create the two **JTextField** instances, as follows:

```
private JTextField number1 = new JTextField();
private JTextField number2 = new JTextField();
```

We also create a button and a label control. In the class constructor, we set the layout manager
to grid layout using the following statement:

```
this.setLayout(new GridLayout(2, 4));
```

In the grid layout, the container on which the components are placed is visualized as a grid
consisting of rows and columns. You create a grid layout manager by instantiating the **GridLayout**
class. The **GridLayout** class declares several constructors. The one used in our example takes two
arguments. The first argument specifies the number of rows in our imaginary grid, and the second
argument specifies the number of columns. When we add the components to this imaginary grid,
the first component is added in the first cell of the grid (that is, Row 1, Column 1). The second
component is added to Column 2 in Row 1, the third component to Column 3 in Row 1, and so
on until the first row is completely filled. The next component will now be added to Row 2,
Column 1, and so on. This continues until the second row is filled. If our imaginary grid has more
declared rows, the further components will be added in the next row, column-wise. In other
words, until a row is completely filled, no component will be added to the next unfilled row.

After setting the layout manager, we add the four label controls to this imaginary grid:

```
add(new JLabel("Number1", JLabel.CENTER));
add(new JLabel("Number2", JLabel.CENTER));
add(new JLabel("Operator", JLabel.CENTER));
add(new JLabel("Result", JLabel.CENTER));
```

Note how we have created the label control in the call to the **add** statement itself. Each label
control sets its own text and alignment. The text alignment in our case is "center" for all four controls.
These four controls now form the first line of our application user interface. Next, we add the two
JTextField controls—a button control and a label control—with the following program statements:

```
add(number1);
add(number2);
add(adder);
add(result);
```

These components now form the second line of our application interface. Finally, we add the
listener for handling the button events:

```
adder.addActionListener(this);
```

The event handler, in our earlier case, is the frame itself. Finally, we look at the implementation of the **actionPerformed** method. In this method, we check the event source by calling the **getSource** method of the **Event** class:

```
if (evt.getSource().equals(adder)) {
```

The **getSource** method returns an object reference, which is unique in the context of the frame. We compare this object reference with the reference to the **adder** object. If the comparison returns "true," it indicates that the adder button has been clicked. We now obtain the two operands entered by the user via the following two statements:

```
int num1 = Integer.parseInt(number1.getText());
int num2 = Integer.parseInt(number2.getText());
```

The **getText** method of the **TextField** class returns the current text contents. The text contents are returned as a **String** value. We need to convert this string into an integer value. We do this by calling the **parseInt** method of the **Integer** class, which is a wrapper of the **int** data type, as detailed in the previous chapter. **parseInt** is a static method of the **Integer** class and therefore can be invoked without instantiating the **Integer** class. The **parseInt** method takes a string argument as a parameter and converts it to an integer value.

We add the two numbers and assign this to the **result** label by calling its **setText** method:

```
int answer = num1 + num2;
result.setText(String.valueOf(answer));
```

We convert the integer value into a string by calling the **valueOf** static method of the **String** class.

Now, let's look at how the window events are processed by our application frame. First, we set the listener for window events using the following statement:

```
this.addWindowListener(this);
```

NOTE
*You need not give an explicit object reference (**this**) while calling the **addWindowListener** method.*

We want the **MyFrame** window object to process all its window events. Thus, we add the listener to **MyFrame** by specifying **this.addWindowListener**. The listener object is specified in the parameter list to the **addWindowListener** method. In our case, we want the **MyFrame** class itself to handle these events. Therefore, we pass the **this** parameter to the **addWindowListener** class. The **MyFrame** class must now implement the **WindowListener** interface and provide the implementation of all the abstract methods of the interface. The **WindowListener** interface declares several methods, such as **windowActivated**, **windowClosed**, and so on. Each of these methods is implemented with an empty body:

```
public void windowActivated(WindowEvent e) {
}
```

Note that unless all the methods declared in the interface are implemented, the class itself will become abstract. We provide the implementation for the **windowClosing** method as follows:

```
public void windowClosing(WindowEvent e) {
    System.exit(0);
}
```

Whenever the user clicks the close icon for the window, the **windowClosing** event is called. In this method, we call the **exit** method of the **System** class to close the application. This closes the application window and properly terminates it. You will be able to guess from the name of each of the methods in the **WindowListener** interface as to when it is called.

In this section, you learned a new control, **JTextField**, for accepting user input. You also studied how to process the window events by implementing the **WindowListener** interface. In addition, you got an introduction to the **GridLayout** manager, the full treatment of which is given in the next chapter. In the next section, you learn how to use a list box control.

Demonstrating the List Box Control

In this section, you learn to use one more Swing component, called **JList**. The **JList** component maintains a list of items such as strings. You can add and remove items to and from a **JList** through your program. We create two list boxes in our application and also provide two buttons, Add and Remove, on the application interface. Initially, one of the list boxes, we call it "source," is filled with a few items, and the other list box, we call it "destination," is empty. When you click the "add" button, a selected item from the source list box gets transferred to the destination list box. The transferred item is removed from the source. When you click the "remove" button, the selected item in the destination list box is transferred to the source list box. The application user interface is shown in Figure 13-10.

The full program that creates the user interface shown in Figure 13-10 and processes the various application events is given in Listing 13-3.

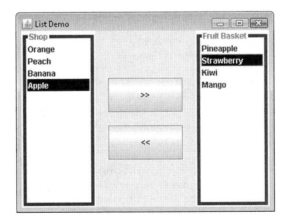

FIGURE 13-10.   *User interface to demonstrate the list box controls*

Listing 13-3 *Demonstrating the Use of List Box Controls*

```java
import javax.swing.*;
import java.awt.event.*;
import java.awt.*;

public class ListDemoApp {

    public static void main(String[] args) {
        MyFrame frame = new MyFrame("List Demo");
        frame.setBounds(20, 50, 400, 300);
        frame.setVisible(true);
    }
}

class MyFrame extends JFrame implements ActionListener {

    private DefaultListModel sourceModel;
    private DefaultListModel destModel;
    private JList source;
    private JList dest = new JList();
    private JButton addButton = new JButton(">>");
    private JButton removeButton = new JButton("<<");

    public MyFrame(String title) {
        super(title);
        addWindowListener(new WindowAdapter() {

            public void windowClosing(WindowEvent e) {
                System.exit(0);
            }
        });

        sourceModel = new DefaultListModel();
        sourceModel.addElement("Banana");
        sourceModel.addElement("Apple");
        sourceModel.addElement("Orange");
        sourceModel.addElement("Mango");
        sourceModel.addElement("Pineapple");
        sourceModel.addElement("Kiwi");
        sourceModel.addElement("Strawberry");
        sourceModel.addElement("Peach");
        source = new JList(sourceModel);

        source.setSelectionMode(ListSelectionModel.SINGLE_SELECTION);
        source.setBorder(BorderFactory.createTitledBorder
                (BorderFactory.createLineBorder(Color.DARK_GRAY, 5), ""
                    + "Shop", 0, 0, null, Color.RED));
        source.setSelectedIndex(0);
        source.setSelectionBackground(Color.BLACK);
        source.setSelectionForeground(Color.WHITE);
```

```
        destModel = new DefaultListModel();
        dest.setModel(destModel);
        dest.setSelectionBackground(Color.BLACK);
        dest.setSelectionForeground(Color.WHITE);
        dest.setBorder(BorderFactory.createTitledBorder
                (BorderFactory.createLineBorder(Color.DARK_GRAY, 5), ""
                + "Fruit Basket", 0, 0, null, Color.RED));

        // Building GUI
        JPanel panel = new JPanel();
        panel.setLayout(new GridLayout(4, 1, 20, 20));
        panel.add(new JLabel());
        panel.add(addButton);
        panel.add(removeButton);
        panel.add(new JLabel());
        this.setLayout(new GridLayout(1, 3, 20, 20));
        add(source);
        add(panel);
        add(dest);

        // Setting event handlers
        addButton.addActionListener(this);
        removeButton.addActionListener(this);
    }

    public void actionPerformed(ActionEvent evt) {
        if (evt.getSource().equals(addButton)) {
            if (source.getSelectedValue() != null) {
                String str = (String) source.getSelectedValue();
                if (str != null) {
                    destModel.addElement(str);
                    dest.setSelectedIndex(0);
                    sourceModel.removeElement(str);
                    source.setSelectedIndex(0);
                }
            }
        }
        if (evt.getSource().equals(removeButton)) {
            if (dest.getSelectedValue() != null) {
                String str = (String) dest.getSelectedValue();
                if (str != null) {
                    sourceModel.addElement(str);
                    source.setSelectedIndex(0);
                    destModel.removeElement(str);
                    dest.setSelectedIndex(0);
                }
            }
        }
    }
}
```

Like in earlier examples, in the **main** method we create an instance of the **MyFrame** class and make it visible to the user after setting the initial size for the window:

```java
MyFrame frame = new MyFrame("List Demo App");
frame.setBounds(20, 50, 400, 300);
frame.setVisible(true);
```

MyClass extends **JFrame** and implements **ActionListener** to process the events generated by the two buttons. We declare two private variables of type **DefaultListModel**. These are used for storing the data items in the two list boxes:

```java
private DefaultListModel sourceModel;
private DefaultListModel destModel;
```

After this, we create two variables of the **JList** type:

```java
private JList source;
private JList dest = new JList();
```

The variable **source** is not initialized, whereas the variable **dest** is initialized with an object reference of the **JList** type. This is done for the purpose of demonstrating the two different initialization techniques for list boxes and is discussed further.

We then create two button objects, as follows:

```java
private JButton addButton = new JButton(">>");
private JButton removeButton = new JButton("<<");
```

Now let's discuss the class constructor. The constructor takes a string parameter and passes it on to its superclass constructor. The string is displayed in the window title.

```java
public MyFrame(String title) {
    super(title);
```

Next comes the important code for creating an anonymous class. Remember in the previous example that our **MyFrame** class implemented the **WindowListener** interface by providing the empty implementation to the different methods declared in the interface. This was required; otherwise, the class would have become **abstract**. Only one method called **windowClosing** was implemented, with some useful implementation that terminates the application gracefully.

Many listener interfaces define several methods that may not be required by your application. However, whenever you implement an interface you must provide the implementation for all its methods (refer to Chapter 6). The designers of the Swing APIs came up with the idea of **Adapter** classes for event processing, which save you the trouble of implementing the various interface methods. A typical **Adapter** class implements a certain listener interface and provides empty implementation to all its methods. You simply need to extend your class from the **Adapter** class and override the desired methods to achieve whatever application functionality your application needs. This is exactly what we have done in the current application. Look at the following code snippet:

```java
addWindowListener(new WindowAdapter() {

    public void windowClosing(WindowEvent e) {
        System.exit(0);
    }
});
```

We call the **addWindowListener** method on the current object instance. (Note that the **this** object reference is implicit in the current context.) The **addWindowListener** requires an object reference as a parameter. The object reference refers to the object that will listen to window events generated by the current object. We create this object reference by instantiating the **WindowAdapter** class. Immediately following this instantiation, we write the code to override the **windowClosing** method. Note that we did not create a class that extends the **WindowAdapter** class. However, the compiler would generate a separate class for this **WindowAdapter** code. This class is anonymous because we have not named it. It is also treated as an inner class because its definition is available only within the context of the current class. Because the class is not named, we cannot create another instance at any other place in our program code. In the overridden method, we gracefully exit the application by calling the **exit** method of the **System** class.

After we have set the window listener for gracefully exiting the application on the click of the Close button, we now proceed to fill our source list box. We first create an instance of **DefaultListModel**:

```
sourceModel = new DefaultListModel();
```

We then add several items of the **String** type to the created data model:

```
sourceModel.addElement("Banana");
sourceModel.addElement("Apple");
. . .
```

We next create an instance of **JList** by passing the preceding data model as a parameter to its constructor:

```
source = new JList(sourceModel);
```

We set the selection mode for selecting the items from the **source** list box using the following program statement:

```
source.setSelectionMode(ListSelectionModel.SINGLE_SELECTION);
```

The list box allows the user to select multiple items. The various modes of selection are available as static constants in the **ListSelectionModel** class. We set the initial selection to the first item using the following statement:

```
source.setSelectedIndex(0);
```

We then create the data model for our other list box by instantiating the **DefaultListModel** class:

```
destModel = new DefaultListModel();
```

We set the data model for the **dest** list box by calling its **setModel** method:

```
dest.setModel(destModel);
```

TIP
Setting the model allows you to replace the contents of a list box
at runtime.

Now, we begin building the GUI. As shown in Figure 13-10, we have split the screen vertically into three equal portions. On the left we show the source list box, and on the right we show the destination list box. In the center, we show two buttons: "add" and "remove." To achieve the desired position for the buttons, we create a panel and place it in the center of the screen. On the panel, we place two buttons, one below the other, as shown in the figure. First, we create a panel object by instantiating the **JPanel** class:

```java
JPanel panel = new JPanel();
```

A panel serves the purpose of a container in which the components can be placed. The same way we set the layout manager for our window for placing components on it, we create a layout manager for placing components on the panel:

```java
panel.setLayout(new GridLayout(4, 1, 20, 20));
```

We create an instance of the grid layout manager for this purpose. The imaginary grid consists of four rows and one column. We place two labels with no captions in the first and last rows to get some whitespace in the layout. In the two middle rows, we place the two buttons:

```java
panel.add(new JLabel());
panel.add(addButton);
panel.add(removeButton);
panel.add(new JLabel());
```

After adding the buttons to the panel, we then create a layout manager for the window using the following program statement:

```java
this.setLayout(new GridLayout(1, 3, 20, 20));
```

The layout used here is again a grid layout consisting of one row and three columns. We add the source list box to the first column, the panel to the second column, and the destination list box to the last column:

```java
add(source);
add(panel);
add(dest);
```

This completes the creation of the user interface. However, we need to complete one last thing—adding the event listener for our buttons, which we do using the following program statements:

```java
// Setting event handlers
addButton.addActionListener(this);
removeButton.addActionListener(this);
```

Now, let's discuss the event-handling code for our buttons. We implement the **actionPerformed** method as follows:

```java
public void actionPerformed(ActionEvent evt) {
```

We check the event source by calling the **getSource** method of the **ActionEvent** object:

```java
if (evt.getSource().equals(addButton)) {
```

If the user clicks the "add" button, the following processing is performed. We retrieve the current selection in the source list box by calling the **getSelectedValue** method of the **JList** class:

```
if (source.getSelectedValue() != null) {
```

The **getSelectedValue** method returns the current selection as an object. It returns **null** if the user has not selected any item from the list. We copy the selected value in a string variable and check whether it equals **null**:

```
String str = (String) source.getSelectedValue();
if (str != null) {
```

We add the retrieved element to the destination list's data model:

```
destModel.addElement(str);
```

We set the current index in the destination list box to its first item:

```
dest.setSelectedIndex(0);
```

We remove the transferred data item from the source list box by calling the **removeElement** method on the data model:

```
sourceModel.removeElement(str);
```

Finally, we set the selection in the source list to the first item:

```
source.setSelectedIndex(0);
```

If the user wants to move an item from the destination list box to the source list box, she has to select an item in the destination list and click the "remove" button. You provide the event handling for the "remove" button's **click** event as follows:

```
if (evt.getSource().equals(removeButton)) {
    if (dest.getSelectedValue() != null) {
        String str = (String) dest.getSelectedValue();
        if (str != null) {
            sourceModel.addElement(str);
            source.setSelectedIndex(0);
            destModel.removeElement(str);
            dest.setSelectedIndex(0);
        }
    }
}
```

This code is similar to the code for the "add" button's **click** event, except that the item from the destination list is transferred to the source list box.

In this section, you learned to use the **JList** control, which holds a list of items. You learned the use of **Adapter** classes, which provide null implementations to listener interface methods. You also learned to build complex layouts using a mixture of layout managers.

TIP

You will use several panels in creating a complex GUI. Each panel uses its own layout manager to get the desired placement of components. The panels themselves are placed in the parent container using one of the layout managers. You will learn this technique in the next chapter.

Summary

All graphical interface applications are event driven. The events may be generated internally by an application or they may be generated externally. For example, when you click a button or move the mouse, an external event occurs. An application may generate an event on its own for others to consume whenever a certain internal condition is satisfied. JDK 1.0 used the hierarchical event-processing model, where the event propagates up the container hierarchy until it gets consumed somewhere along the way. From JDK 1.1 onward, the event model changed to the delegation event model. In this model, we define event sources and listeners. An event *source* is an object that generates an event, and a *listener* is the one that waits for an event to occur and, when it does, consumes it. Any object can act like an event source, a listener and consumer, or both. A listener has to register with an event source for the type of event it is interested in. Whenever a source generates an event, it is dispatched to all the registered listeners. The event source maintains a list of registered listeners. Java classifies the events into different types, depending on the context. For example, you can have a set of events related to mouse clicks and mouse motion, a different set for window processing, another set for button or list box events, and so on.

Java provides the AWT and Swing classes to create GUI-based applications. The AWT components are considered heavyweight, whereas Swing components are considered lightweight because they are mostly written in Java itself. You create a GUI application by creating an application window. You place the various controls—buttons, labels, edit boxes, and so on—on the window using different layout managers. You implement the predefined interfaces to provide the event handlers in your classes. Java provides the adapter classes that provide the blank implementations for most of the event listener interfaces. This simplifies your coding because you only need to override the desired methods of the interface. The **ActionListener** interface has only one method; therefore, there is no need to define an adapter class for it. Many times, the event handlers are defined by creating inner anonymous classes.

In the next chapter, we cover in detail the various layout managers for building sophisticated GUIs.

CHAPTER
14

Creating Layouts

n the last chapter, you learned about building a graphical user interface (GUI). GUI applications use several components that are placed on the container using a layout manager. You briefly studied a couple layout managers in Chapter 13. This chapter will equip you with other layout managers for creating more advanced GUI screens. In particular, you will learn the following:

- Why you should use layout managers
- How layout managers work
- Using tools to create a layout
- Using BorderLayout, FlowLayout, CardLayout, GridLayout, GridBagLayout, and BoxLayout
- Creating a tabbed dialog box
- Using advanced layout managers such as GroupLayout and SpringLayout
- Turning off layout managers for absolute placements

Layout Managers

As discussed in the previous chapter, a layout manager takes the responsibility of placing the components at the appropriate positions on a container. In addition, the layout manager resizes and realigns these components when the user resizes the application window or whenever the container size varies according to the underlying platform. More than a decade ago, we had display monitors with different resolutions, such as CGA, EGA, and VGA. Developers had to port their applications to these different devices, which essentially meant developing a different GUI screen for each device. With the rise of layout managers, display device independence was achieved. Nowadays, with the introduction of mobile apps, this benefit is vanishing again because developers have to redesign the layouts of existing desktop applications for the small screen sizes of mobile phones and tablets. Learning about layout managers is still important because they offer true device independence when you're developing desktop applications.

So, what exactly is a layout manager? It is an object that controls the size and position of components in a container. The **LayoutManager** interface sets the standard for laying out containers. All layout managers implement this interface. Each type of container has some layout manager attached to it. As you saw in the previous chapter, for panel objects the default layout manager is **FlowLayout**. For window objects, the default layout manager is **BorderLayout**. If you do not use a layout manager, the components are placed using absolute coordinates. In such a case, when the parent container is resized, or when a user sets preferences such as font and locale, the relative positions of the components placed on the container do not adjust well and some overlaps in the component placements may occur.

Types of Layout Managers

In the early days, Java had only a few layout managers. Today, several layout mangers are available for your use. Each layout manager has its own purpose, and each one lays out components using its own predefined rules. As you have seen, the **FlowLayout** manager lays out components row-wise; when a row is filled, the next component added is placed in the next row. The components in a row may be added left to right, right to left, or centered with leading and trailing justification.

The **BoxLayout** manager is similar to the **FlowLayout** manager but provides additional functionality. BorderLayout can place a maximum of five visible components along the four borders and the center of the container. The **GridLayout** manager places the components in the cells of an imaginary grid, the size of which is decided by you. The **CardLayout** manager stacks components on top of each other like playing cards. This is very useful for creating tabbed dialog interfaces and wizards; however, due to the demand for creating tabbed dialog boxes, Java has introduced a class called **JTabbedPane** especially for this purpose. **GridBagLayout** is a very powerful layout manager that provides lots of flexibility in creating complex layouts but is complex to use. Although several layout managers are provided that have unique functionalities and purposes, developers typically use multiple layout managers on a single container to create sophisticated and complex layouts.

Building the GUI

To create the desired graphical user interface for your application, you first need to apply a layout manager to the application window. Next, you add the components to this window, which is essentially a container for them. These components are placed using the predefined rules in the layout manager. However, a component may provide size and alignment hints to the manager, which may or may not honor these requests. You can also control the space between these components. To support different locales in your application, you may wish to set the container's orientation. For example, Arabic is right-to-left, whereas English and most other languages are left-to-right.

Let's now look at the various steps in building a GUI. In the previous chapter, we applied the layout managers to the containers—a panel and a window. These have a default layout manager set. To apply a different layout manager, you would use code similar to

```
Container contentPane = frame.getContentPane();
contentPane.setLayout(new FlowLayout());
```

where **frame** is an object of type **JFrame** on which you want to arrange the components. To add a component, you use the code similar to this:

```
contentPane.add(aComponent);
```

In some situations, you may need to specify additional parameters in the **add** method. With some layout managers such as **GridBagLayout** and **SpringLayout**, you need to follow elaborate setup procedures before adding components. The Swing containers provide an API to add components to them. Before adding a component, you may specify its size preferences by calling the size hint methods: **setMinimumSize**, **setPreferredSize**, and **setMaximumSize**. Many layout managers do not honor these requests. However, **BoxLayout** and **SpringLayout** do. You may also provide alignment hints by calling the component's **setAlignmentX** and **setAlignmentY** methods, or by overriding its **getAlignmentX** and **getAlignmentY** methods.

TIP
Each component has a minimum, maximum, and preferred size.
A component class defines these sizes. A user can obtain these sizes
*by calling the respective **get** methods. To change the default values set*
by the component, you need to subclass it and override the respective
***set** methods. Layout managers do not necessarily honor these sizes.*

In some layout managers such as **GridLayout** and **BorderLayout**, you can specify the space between components. Some layout managers do this automatically. In some situations, you may also want to add some invisible components to get extra whitespace in your layout. The **BoxLayout** manager facilitates this. You may also create the apparent whitespace between components by adding empty borders to them, especially on panels and labels that do not have default borders.

To control the orientation of your layout, use the **setComponentOrientation** and **applyComponentOrientation** methods. The following code applies the right-to-left orientation to the content pane and its child components:

```
Container contentPane = this.getContentPane();
contentPane.applyComponentOrientation(ComponentOrientation.RIGHT_TO_LEFT);
```

Now that you have a general idea how to set up the layout manager and add components to a container using predefined constraints, let's move to the internal workings of a layout manager.

How Do Layout Managers Work?

The two primary tasks of a layout manager are to calculate the minimum/preferred/maximum sizes for a container and to lay out the container's child components. While laying the components, the manager looks at the designer-provided constraints, the container's properties, and the minimum/preferred/maximum sizes requested by the child components. A child component may itself be a container. In this situation, a child determines its own size based on the preceding factors and lays out components within itself. Thus, the system first determines the sizes of the containers at the bottom of its hierarchy. These sizes then percolate up the hierarchy, eventually determining the super-container's size. You need to call the **Window.pack** method to lay out the component hierarchy for the first time. Later on, you may use the **Container.validate** method to validate an invalid container. A container is considered valid if all its children are already laid out and valid. A child container may be considered invalid when it changes its size, alignment, or position. The **isValid** method can be used for testing validity. The **validate** method triggers the layout for the container and all its child containers down the component hierarchy. Eventually the container will be marked as valid.

When the component size changes—say, due to a font change or an explicit modification through the code—the component must be resized and repainted via calls to the **revalidate** and **repaint** methods. A revalidate request is passed up the container hierarchy until it encounters a top-level container or a container such as scroll pane that should not be affected by the current resizing. The container is then laid out again, resizing all affected components.

Let's now move on to the individual layout managers and study how each one works.

Using Layout Managers

In this section we cover how to use the layout managers we have discussed so far as well as the rationale behind using them. We will also look at a simple program example for each layout manager. So let's start with **BorderLayout**.

BorderLayout

A border layout fits components into five regions: North, South, East, West, and Center. Each region can contain no more than one component. If you place an additional component in a

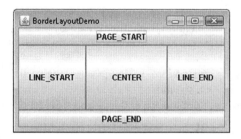

FIGURE 14-1. *Component placements in BorderLayout*

previously occupied region, the last added component will be shown on top and the previous component is completely hidden. Each region is identified with a constant: **NORTH**, **SOUTH**, **EAST**, **WEST**, and **CENTER**. While adding a component, you need to specify one of these constants. For a component placed in the center, specifying this constant is optional.

After the components have been placed, if you enlarge the window, the center area gets as much of the available space as possible. The components on the edges then fill up all the remaining space. Typically you won't use all the five regions. In general, developers use only the center area so that the component automatically resizes to the size of the window. Along with the center region, you may choose to use the South region to place status text for your application.

In the previous chapter, you used the **BorderLayout** manager. The component placements in this layout are shown in Figure 14-1.

When you used this layout manager in the previous chapter, the four regions were named after their directional orientation: North, South, East, and West. The remaining region was called Center. With JDK 1.4 onward, these regions are now called **PAGE_START**, **PAGE_END**, **LINE_START**, **LINE_END**, and **CENTER**, as shown in Figure 14-1.

NOTE
It is recommended that you use the new constants because they are now considered standard and also enable programs to adjust to different languages having different orientations.

Using NetBeans to Build the GUI

Because you have already hand-coded the placement of components using the **BorderLayout** manager in the previous chapter, we will now look at another way of creating GUIs using NetBeans. NetBeans enables you to create GUIs with ease without hand-coding the layout manager.

For this example we create a photo frame application that uses the **BorderLayout** manager for designing the interface. We create a frame and display a large size photograph at its center.

We provide four scroll buttons along the frame edges so that we can pan the displayed photo in four directions.

For our photo frame application, we either create a new project based on the Java Application template or add a **JFrame** form to an existing project. The menu for adding a new form is shown in Figure 14-2.

NetBeans displays the created form in design view. Right-click the form and select the Set Layout menu option. You will see the list of various layout managers. We will be covering the remaining layout managers from this list in this chapter. Select BorderLayout for the current application.

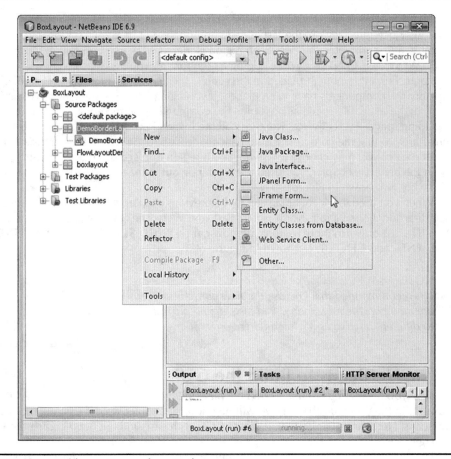

FIGURE 14-2. *Adding a JFrame form to the project*

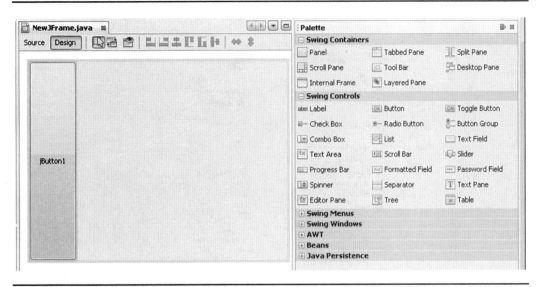

FIGURE 14-3. *Placing a Swing control from the palette*

NOTE
The default layout manager for a frame is **BorderLayout**. *Therefore, the preceding step is not necessary. It is included here to show you the procedure for setting a layout manager for any container.*

To set the caption for the application frame, select the Properties menu option. You will see the list of properties in the properties window. Set the title property to Photo Frame.

Now, drag a Button control from the palette of Swing controls onto the form, as shown in Figure 14-3.

As you move the dragged control onto the form, a dotted guideline will show you five different positions on the form where the button can be placed. Place the current button on the left edge. To change the default name, in the Inspector window click the button and edit its name (**leftButton** in this case). To set the button's properties, right-click it. A menu will pop up, as shown in Figure 14-4.

Select Properties. A properties dialog box will open. Set the text property to a less-than symbol (<). Next, select the Events tab. Click the down arrow in the **actionPerformed** method cell. Accept the suggested name for the method. An event handler with this name will now be added to your code.

Likewise, add three more buttons alongside the remaining three borders. Name them appropriately, set their captions, and create event handlers for them. Next, add a **JPanel** control to the center of the form. Add a **JLabel** control on top of it and set its icon property to **lake.jpg** or any other image file you wish to display (the lake.jpg file is available as a part of the download). Use a large size image so that you can pan it with the four button controls you have placed on the form. Set the text property of the label to a blank string. Your screen should look like the one shown in Figure 14-5 at this stage.

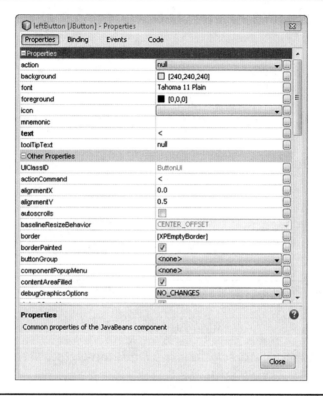

FIGURE 14-4. *Setting the properties of a component*

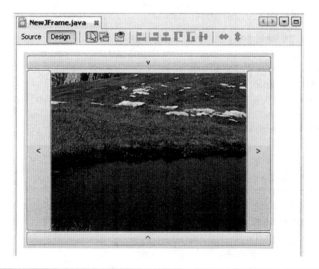

FIGURE 14-5. *Photo frame application in designer view*

Now it is time to add the code to your form. Select the Source tab and add the four event handlers and two static variables shown in bold in the full program given in Listing 14-1.

Listing 14-1   *Source Code for Photo Frame Application*

```java
public class PhotoFrame extends javax.swing.JFrame {

    static int xOffset = 0;
    static int yOffset = 0;

    /** Creates new form PhotoFrame */
    public PhotoFrame() {
        initComponents();
    }

    /** This method is called from within the constructor to
     * initialize the form.
     * WARNING: Do NOT modify this code. The content of this method is
     * always regenerated by the Form Editor.
     */
    @SuppressWarnings("unchecked")
    // <editor-fold defaultstate="collapsed" desc="Generated Code">
    private void initComponents() {
// Netbeans generated code not shown here
    }// </editor-fold>

    private void buttonRightActionPerformed(
            java.awt.event.ActionEvent evt) {
        // TODO add your handling code here:
        xOffset -= 10;
        jLabel1.setLocation(xOffset, yOffset);
    }

    private void buttonLeftActionPerformed(java.awt.event.ActionEvent evt) {
        // TODO add your handling code here:
        xOffset += 10;
        jLabel1.setLocation(xOffset, yOffset);
    }

    private void buttonTopActionPerformed(java.awt.event.ActionEvent evt) {
        // TODO add your handling code here:
        yOffset += 10;
        jLabel1.setLocation(xOffset, yOffset);
    }

    private void buttonBottomActionPerformed(
            java.awt.event.ActionEvent evt) {
        // TODO add your handling code here:
        yOffset -= 10;
        jLabel1.setLocation(xOffset, yOffset);
    }
```

```
        private void formComponentResized(java.awt.event.ComponentEvent evt) {
            // TODO add your handling code here:
            jLabel1.setLocation(xOffset, yOffset);
        }

        /**
         * @param args the command line arguments
         */
        public static void main(String args[]) {
            java.awt.EventQueue.invokeLater(new Runnable() {

                public void run() {
                    new PhotoFrame().setVisible(true);
                }
            });
        }
        // Variables declaration - do not modify
        private javax.swing.JButton buttonBottom;
        private javax.swing.JButton buttonLeft;
        private javax.swing.JButton buttonRight;
        private javax.swing.JButton buttonTop;
        private javax.swing.JLabel jLabel1;
        private javax.swing.JPanel jPanel1;
        // End of variables declaration
}
```

To pan the image, we use two static variables: **xOffset** and **yOffset**. The event handlers increment/decrement values of these variables. Calling the **setLocation** method on the label control moves the image on the screen appropriately to the new location.

To run this photo frame, right-click its source file name in the Projects window and select the Run File option. You will see the output shown in Figure 14-6. Click each of the four buttons to see how the image is panned.

Let's now examine the generated code that creates the application GUI. The **initComponents** method builds the GUI. In the beginning, it creates the instances of all the components we have placed on the form:

```
buttonTop = new javax.swing.JButton();
buttonRight = new javax.swing.JButton();
buttonBottom = new javax.swing.JButton();
buttonLeft = new javax.swing.JButton();
jPanel1 = new javax.swing.JPanel();
jLabel1 = new javax.swing.JLabel();
```

Next, it sets the action for closing the window:

```
setDefaultCloseOperation(javax.swing.WindowConstants.EXIT_ON_CLOSE);
```

Note that you will not need to implement the **WindowListener** interface as you did in Chapter 13 for closing the window.

FIGURE 14-6. *Screen shot of the photo frame application*

The code builder then adds the code for setting the caption and event handler for a button:

```
buttonTop.setText("v");
buttonTop.addActionListener(new java.awt.event.ActionListener() {

    public void actionPerformed(java.awt.event.ActionEvent evt) {
        buttonTopActionPerformed(evt);
    }
});
```

The button is then added to the requested location by first obtaining the container pane by calling the **getContentPane** method on the current object (which is a **JFrame** instance) and then calling its **add** method:

```
getContentPane().add(buttonTop, java.awt.BorderLayout.PAGE_START);
```

Likewise, the code generator sets up the three remaining buttons and adds them to the container. Next, the program sets the icon and the text for the label control:

```
jLabel1.setIcon
    (new javax.swing.ImageIcon(getClass().getResource("/lake.jpg")));
jLabel1.setText("jLabel1");
```

Finally, it adds the label to the panel and the panel itself to the center of the frame.

From this example, you can appreciate the ease with which the GUI can be constructed using tools such as NetBeans. However, developers always like to have control over what they do or at least prefer to have a thorough understanding of what's going on behind the scenes. Therefore, we discuss the rest of the layout managers by hand-coding them. Once you understand how they work, in practice, you can use the tools to build the GUI using any of these layout managers.

TIP

*In the **BorderLayout** manager, you can also control the gap between the components by calling its **setHgap** and **setVgap** methods.*

FlowLayout

This is a very simple layout manager and is the default for **JPanel** objects. The **FlowLayout** manager lays out the components in a directional flow, much like the lines of text in a paragraph. When one row is filled, the next component is placed on the next row. Although the default placement is left to right, you can change the orientation easily by setting the **componentOrientation** property of the container. Each component's preferred size is honored.

This layout is typically used to arrange buttons in a panel; for example, you would use this layout manager for creating a toolbar. The toolbar buttons are placed horizontally until no more buttons fit on the given line. A new row is automatically added for placing the remaining buttons. To control the alignment, the layout manger provides the **align** property. The five different permitted values for this property are **LEFT**, **RIGHT**, **CENTER**, **LEADING**, and **TRAILING**. The **LEFT** alignment left-justifies each row. The **RIGHT** alignment right-justifies each row. The **CENTER** alignment centers each line, as shown in Figure 14-7.

The **LEADING** alignment indicates that each row should be justified to the leading edge. For example, if the **ComponentOrientation** is set right-to-left, each row will be justified to the right. Similarly, the **TRAILING** alignment justifies to the trailing edge.

We will now look at how the **FlowLayout** manager places the components on its container and realigns them when the container size changes. To keep things simple, we will use only button controls as components. We place five buttons on a **JFrame** object and study their alignment upon window resizing. The code is given in Listing 14-2.

Listing 14-2   *Demonstration Program for FlowLayout*

```
import javax.swing.*;
import java.awt.*;

public class FlowLayoutDemoApp {

    public static void main(String[] args) {
        MyFrame frame = new MyFrame("FlowLayout Demo");
        frame.setSize(500, 300);
        frame.setVisible(true);
    }
}

class MyFrame extends JFrame {
```

FIGURE 14-7. *FlowLayout with center alignment*

```java
public MyFrame(String title) {
    super(title);
    setDefaultCloseOperation(JFrame.EXIT_ON_CLOSE);
    Container pane = getContentPane();
    pane.setLayout(new FlowLayout());
    pane.setComponentOrientation(ComponentOrientation.LEFT_TO_RIGHT);
    JButton button = new JButton("ONE");
    pane.add(button);
    button = new JButton("TWO");
    pane.add(button);
    button = new JButton("THREE");
    pane.add(button);
    button = new JButton("FOUR");
    pane.add(button);
    button = new JButton("FIVE");
    pane.add(button);
    }
}
```

As in the earlier example, we create a **MyFrame** class that inherits **JFrame** to demonstrate component placement. Calling the **setLayout** method on the container object sets the layout manager. The method receives an instance of **FlowLayout** as its argument:

```java
Container pane = getContentPane();
pane.setLayout(new FlowLayout());
```

We create a few Button instances and add them to the container. The placement orientation is set to left-to-right using the following statement:

```java
pane.setComponentOrientation(ComponentOrientation.LEFT_TO_RIGHT);
```

Because the default orientation is left-to-right, this statement is not necessary. However, you can experiment with a different orientation by changing the constant to **RIGHT_TO_LEFT**. When you run the application, you will see the output shown in Figure 14-8.

FIGURE 14-8. *Left-to-right component placement in FlowLayout*

FIGURE 14-9. *Right-to-left component placement in FlowLayout*

Now, if you change the orientation to **RIGHT_TO_LEFT** and run the program again, you will see the output shown in Figure 14-9.

The **FlowLayout** exhibits an interesting property. As mentioned earlier, it honors the component's preferred size. You must have noticed that the buttons displayed in our example have different widths—these are set by the size of the caption text. In other words, each button has a preferred size based on the size of its caption. Now, what happens if the container width is less than the total width of all the components placed on it? You can try this by resizing the window. A typical resized window is shown in Figure 14-10.

Note that after the first two components are placed, the layout manager is not able to fit button THREE on the same row; thus, it places it on the next row. Similarly, while placing FOUR, it has to use a new row due to lack of space on the second row.

Like the border layout discussed earlier, this layout manager also allows you to set the horizontal and vertical spacing between the components.

CardLayout

In this layout, the added components are stacked on top of each other just like a stack of playing cards. The layout manager provides methods to bring the next or the previous card to the top. You can also directly jump to the first, last, or any specified card in the stack. While adding a card to the stack, you can associate a string identifier with it so that it can be randomly accessed. One application of this is to create wizards that provide several tabs. Each tab has its own user interface, and the user can bring any desired card to the top by clicking the corresponding tab. You will learn how to create a wizard using the card layout manager with the help of the ready-to-use **JTabbedPane** class.

To explore how this layout manager functions, we construct a simple color panel application. The application contains several color panels stacked on top of each other. We provide two buttons to browse through this stack of "cards": The Next button brings the next card in the stack to the top, and the Previous button brings the bottom card on the top. Besides this, we also display a list of cards so that the user can jump directly to any one and bring it to the top.

The application user interface is shown in Figure 14-11.

FIGURE 14-10. *Component placements in FlowLayout after window resizing*

FIGURE 14-11. *Color panel application for demonstrating the CardLayout manager*

The full program is given in Listing 14-3.

Listing 14-3 *Demonstration Program for CardLayout*

```java
import javax.swing.*;
import java.awt.*;
import java.awt.event.*;
import javax.swing.event.*;

public class CardLayoutDemoApp {

    public static void main(String[] args) {
        ColorFrame frame = new ColorFrame("CardLayout Demo");
        frame.setSize(500, 300);
        frame.setVisible(true);
    }
}

class ColorFrame extends JFrame
        implements ActionListener, ListSelectionListener {

    private JButton cmdNext = new JButton("Next");
    private JButton cmdPrevious = new JButton("Previous");
    private JPanel displayPanel = new JPanel();
    private CardLayout cards = new CardLayout();
    private String[] colors = {"Red", "Orange", "Yellow",
        "Green", "Blue", "Indigo", "Violet"};
    private JList colorList = new JList(colors);
    private static int selectedColorIndex = 0;
```

```
    public ColorFrame(String title) {
        super(title);
        setDefaultCloseOperation(JFrame.EXIT_ON_CLOSE);
        cmdNext.addActionListener(this);
        cmdPrevious.addActionListener(this);
        colorList.addListSelectionListener(this);
        displayPanel.setLayout(cards);
        displayPanel.add(colors[0], new ColorPanel(Color.RED));
        displayPanel.add(colors[1], new ColorPanel(Color.ORANGE));
        displayPanel.add(colors[2], new ColorPanel(Color.YELLOW));
        displayPanel.add(colors[3], new ColorPanel(Color.GREEN));
        displayPanel.add(colors[4], new ColorPanel(Color.BLUE));
        displayPanel.add(colors[5], new ColorPanel(new Color(0x6600FF)));
        displayPanel.add(colors[6], new ColorPanel(new Color(0x8B00FF)));
        JPanel cmdPanel = new JPanel();
        cmdPanel.add(cmdPrevious);
        cmdPanel.add(cmdNext);
        Container pane = getContentPane();
        pane.add(colorList, BorderLayout.LINE_START);
        pane.add(displayPanel, BorderLayout.CENTER);
        pane.add(cmdPanel, BorderLayout.PAGE_END);
        colorList.setSelectedIndex(selectedColorIndex);
    }

    public void actionPerformed(ActionEvent evt) {
        cards.show(displayPanel, colors[selectedColorIndex]);
        if (evt.getSource() == cmdNext) {
            cards.next(displayPanel);
            selectedColorIndex++;
            if (selectedColorIndex > colors.length - 1) {
                selectedColorIndex = 0;
            }
            colorList.setSelectedIndex(selectedColorIndex);
        } else if (evt.getSource() == cmdPrevious) {
            cards.previous(displayPanel);
            selectedColorIndex--;
            if (selectedColorIndex < 0) {
                selectedColorIndex = colors.length - 1;
            }
            colorList.setSelectedIndex(selectedColorIndex);
        }
    }

    public void valueChanged(ListSelectionEvent lse) {
        selectedColorIndex = colorList.getSelectedIndex();
        cards.show(displayPanel, colors[selectedColorIndex]);
    }
}

class ColorPanel extends Panel {
```

```
    public ColorPanel(Color color) {
        setBackground(color);
        this.setLayout(new BorderLayout());
        add(new JLabel(
                "Value: " + String.format("%X", color.getRGB()),
                SwingConstants.CENTER),
                BorderLayout.CENTER);
    }
}
```

In this example, we construct a stack of color panels, with each panel having one of the colors of the rainbow. The **ColorPanel** class represents this panel. The class constructor accepts a color argument and sets the panel background to the specified color. It also displays the RGB value (along with its alpha value in the first two digits) on the panel.

The **ColorFrame** class constructs the user interface. As before, this is based on **JFrame**. The container creates a **displayPanel** that is displayed at its center using the default BorderLayout. On the left side, we add a **JList** control displaying the names of cards. At the bottom, we add a panel on which the Next and Previous buttons are placed using the default layout manager, which is a **FlowLayout**.

On the **displayPanel**, we set the layout manager to **CardLayout** and add a few color panels to it using the following statements:

```
displayPanel.setLayout(cards);
displayPanel.add(colors[0], new ColorPanel(Color.RED));
displayPanel.add(colors[1], new ColorPanel(Color.ORANGE));
...
```

The first parameter to the **add** method specifies the card name. We use this name to bring a desired card to the top. In the button actions, we simply call the **next** and **previous** methods of the **CardLayout** manager to bring to the top the next or previous card. The current card index is maintained in the class variable **selectedColorIndex**.

To process the selection in the **JList** control, we need to provide a listener to the list box events. This is done by implementing the **ListSelectionListener** interface. This requires the implementation of a sole **valueChanged** method of the interface:

```
public void valueChanged(ListSelectionEvent lse) {
```

In the method implementation, we first obtain the index of the user-selected item:

```
selectedColorIndex = colorList.getSelectedIndex();
```

We then bring the selected card to the top by using its name taken from the list model:

```
cards.show(displayPanel, colors[selectedColorIndex]);
```

Run the program. At the start, you will see a red panel. Select some other color from the list displayed on the left side. The panel color immediately shows the result of your selection. What actually happens is that the card at the selected color value is brought to the top. Now, try the Next and Previous buttons. The panel color changes and the corresponding color value is shown as a selected item in the list on the left. The RGB value of the current color is also displayed at the center of the panel.

TIP
The CardLayout *manager is very useful in creating a tabbed dialog box interface. However, Java provides a specially designed built-in class called* **JTabbedPane** *for creating a tabbed dialog box. You learn the use of this class toward the end of this chapter.*

GridLayout

If you wish to place the components in a table, you use the **GridLayout** manager. For example, suppose you want to create a mobile phone emulator in your application. You will need to create a keypad similar to the one on your mobile phone. The desired layout of this keypad is shown in Figure 14-12.

Before we look at how to construct this layout, let's quickly discuss this layout manager. In the **GridLayout** manager, you set the number of rows and columns for the table in the class constructor:

```
GridLayout(int rows, int cols)
GridLayout(int rows, int cols, int hgap, int vgap)
```

The second constructor specifies the horizontal and vertical gap between the cells. The layout manager adds the components row-wise. When one row is filled completely, the next component is added to the new row. The last row may contain empty cells if the number of components does not equal the total number of available cells. Each component always fills up the entire available cell area. Both the preferred and minimum sizes of a component are not honored. The horizontal and vertical gaps control the spacing between the cells and have no effect on the spacing between the cell and the container boundary. If you want zero spacing between the cells, use a constructor that takes only two arguments (that is, the number of rows and columns). Listing 14-4 shows how to construct a mobile phone keypad.

FIGURE 14-12. *A mobile phone keypad using GridLayout*

Listing 14-4   *Constructing a Mobile Phone Keypad Interface*

```java
import java.awt.GridLayout;
import javax.swing.*;

public class MobileKeypad extends JFrame {

    public MobileKeypad() {
        setTitle("Mobile Keypad");
        setDefaultCloseOperation(EXIT_ON_CLOSE);
        initGUI();
    }

    public static void main(String[] args) {
        MobileKeypad app = new MobileKeypad();
        app.setSize(220, 240);
        app.setVisible(true);
    }

    private void initGUI() {
        setLayout(new GridLayout(4, 3));
        add(new JButton("1"));
        add(new JButton("2"));
        add(new JButton("3"));
        add(new JButton("4"));
        add(new JButton("5"));
        add(new JButton("6"));
        add(new JButton("7"));
        add(new JButton("8"));
        add(new JButton("9"));
        add(new JButton("+"));
        add(new JButton("0"));
        add(new JButton("#"));
    }
}
```

As in the earlier cases, the user interface is created in the **initGUI** method. We simply set the layout manager to an instance of **GridLayout** with a size of four rows and three columns. After setting the manager, we add buttons to the container in the desired order to create the keypad.

GridBagLayout

This layout manager is very powerful, but at the same time it is also complex to use. Like the **GridLayout** manager, this layout manager places the components in grid cells. Unlike the **GridLayout** manager, the row heights and the column widths may not remain equal when the components are placed using this layout manager. The **GridBagLayout** manager honors the components' preferred sizes while determining the row heights and column widths. Also, a component may span multiple

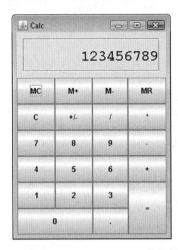

FIGURE 14-13. *Creating a calculator interface using GridBagLayout*

rows and columns. While adding a component, you set the constraints on its placement, as is done with the following code snippet:

```
JPanel pane = new JPanel(new GridBagLayout());
GridBagConstraints gridBagConstraints = new GridBagConstraints();
// set fields on gridBagConstraints
pane.add(theComponent, gridBagConstraints);
```

You create an instance of the **GridBagConstraints** class, set its desired fields, and pass it as a parameter to the **add** method.

To understand how this layout manager works, we will construct the calculator interface shown in Figure 14-13.

The GUI we are going to build contains several buttons and a label control that displays the output shown at the top of the window. Each button is placed in a certain grid cell. The grid itself consists of seven rows and four columns. The **equalto** button occupies the space of two rows and one column. The number 0 button occupies the space of one row and two columns. The top label for calculator output occupies the space of four columns and a row. Like in the case of **GridLayout**, you do not set the grid size while using this layout manager. Rather, the number of rows and columns is automatically computed when you add the components to the container with the specified constraints.

The full program for constructing the calculator GUI is given in Listing 14-5.

Listing 14-5 *Creating a Calculator Interface Using GridBagLayout*

```
import javax.swing.*;
import javax.swing.plaf.metal.MetalBorders;
import java.awt.*;

public class CalcInterface extends javax.swing.JFrame {
```

```java
    private JLabel jLabelOutput = new javax.swing.JLabel(
            "123456789", SwingConstants.RIGHT);
    private JButton jButtonMC = new javax.swing.JButton("MC");
    private JButton jButtonMPlus = new javax.swing.JButton("M+");
    private JButton jButtonMMinus = new javax.swing.JButton("M-");
    private JButton jButtonMR = new javax.swing.JButton("MR");
    private JButton jButtonC = new javax.swing.JButton("C");
    private JButton jButtonAddSub = new javax.swing.JButton("+/-");
    private JButton jButtondiv = new javax.swing.JButton("/");
    private JButton jButtonMul = new javax.swing.JButton("*");
    private JButton jButtonSeven = new javax.swing.JButton("7");
    private JButton jButtonEight = new javax.swing.JButton("8");
    private JButton jButtonNine = new javax.swing.JButton("9");
    private JButton jButtonSub = new javax.swing.JButton("-");
    private JButton jButtonFour = new javax.swing.JButton("4");
    private JButton jButtonFive = new javax.swing.JButton("5");
    private JButton jButtonSix = new javax.swing.JButton("6");
    private JButton jButtonAdd = new javax.swing.JButton("+");
    private JButton jButtonOne = new javax.swing.JButton("1");
    private JButton jButtonTwo = new javax.swing.JButton("2");
    private JButton jButtonThree = new javax.swing.JButton("3");
    private JButton jButtonZero = new javax.swing.JButton("0");
    private JButton jButtonDot = new javax.swing.JButton(".");
    private JButton jButtonEqual = new javax.swing.JButton("=");

    public CalcInterface() {
        super.setTitle("Calc");
        initGUI();
    }

    private void initGUI() {
        setDefaultCloseOperation(javax.swing.WindowConstants.EXIT_ON_CLOSE);
        GridBagConstraints constraints = new GridBagConstraints();
        constraints.ipady = 15;
        constraints.ipadx = 10;
        constraints.fill = java.awt.GridBagConstraints.BOTH;

        getContentPane().setLayout(new GridBagLayout());
        jLabelOutput.setFont(new Font("Monospaced", 1, 24));
        jLabelOutput.setBorder(new MetalBorders.TextFieldBorder());
        constraints.insets = new Insets(10, 10, 10, 10);

        constraints.gridwidth = GridBagConstraints.REMAINDER;
        getContentPane().add(jLabelOutput, constraints);
        constraints.insets = new Insets(0, 0, 0, 0);
        constraints.gridwidth = 1;
        constraints.gridx = 0;
        constraints.gridy = 1;
        getContentPane().add(jButtonMC, constraints);
        constraints.gridx = 1;
        constraints.gridy = 1;
```

```
getContentPane().add(jButtonMPlus, constraints);
constraints.gridx = 2;
constraints.gridy = 1;
getContentPane().add(jButtonMMinus, constraints);
constraints.gridx = 3;
constraints.gridy = 1;
getContentPane().add(jButtonMR, constraints);
constraints.gridx = 0;
constraints.gridy = 2;
getContentPane().add(jButtonC, constraints);
constraints.gridx = 1;
constraints.gridy = 2;
getContentPane().add(jButtonAddSub, constraints);
constraints.gridx = 2;
constraints.gridy = 2;
getContentPane().add(jButtondiv, constraints);
constraints.gridx = 3;
constraints.gridy = 2;
getContentPane().add(jButtonMul, constraints);
constraints.gridx = 0;
constraints.gridy = 3;
getContentPane().add(jButtonSeven, constraints);
constraints.gridx = 1;
constraints.gridy = 3;
getContentPane().add(jButtonEight, constraints);
constraints.gridx = 2;
constraints.gridy = 3;
getContentPane().add(jButtonNine, constraints);
constraints.gridx = 3;
constraints.gridy = 3;
getContentPane().add(jButtonSub, constraints);
constraints.gridx = 0;
constraints.gridy = 4;
getContentPane().add(jButtonFour, constraints);
constraints.gridx = 1;
constraints.gridy = 4;
getContentPane().add(jButtonFive, constraints);
constraints.gridx = 2;
constraints.gridy = 4;
getContentPane().add(jButtonSix, constraints);
constraints.gridx = 3;
constraints.gridy = 4;
getContentPane().add(jButtonAdd, constraints);
constraints.gridx = 0;
constraints.gridy = 5;
getContentPane().add(jButtonOne, constraints);
constraints.gridx = 1;
constraints.gridy = 5;
getContentPane().add(jButtonTwo, constraints);
constraints.gridx = 2;
```

```
        constraints.gridy = 5;
        getContentPane().add(jButtonThree, constraints);
        constraints.gridx = 0;
        constraints.gridy = 6;
        constraints.gridwidth = 2;
        getContentPane().add(jButtonZero, constraints);
        constraints.gridwidth = 1;
        constraints.gridx = 2;
        constraints.gridy = 6;
        getContentPane().add(jButtonDot, constraints);
        constraints.gridx = 3;
        constraints.gridy = 5;
        constraints.gridheight = 2;
        getContentPane().add(jButtonEqual, constraints);
        pack();
    }

    public static void main(String args[]) {
        new CalcInterface().setVisible(true);
    }
}
```

In the **initGUI** method, we first create a **constraints** object:

```
GridBagConstraints constraints = new GridBagConstraints();
```

We then set a few properties for this **constraints** object. These properties are common to all the components we are going to place on the container:

```
constraints.ipady = 15;
constraints.ipadx = 10;
constraints.fill = GridBagConstraints.BOTH;
```

The **ipady** and **ipadx** properties define the internal padding of the component, which is how much space to add to the minimum height or width of the component. Setting the **fill** property to the predefined **BOTH** constant indicates that the component should occupy all the available space in the given grid cell. The other possible values are **NONE**, **HORIZONTAL**, and **VERTICAL**. As the names suggest, the **HORIZONTAL** value makes the component stretch horizontally to fill the available width, the **VERTICAL** value makes the component stretch vertically, and **NONE** (the default) does not stretch the component at all.

NOTE
*Once any property on the **constraints** object is set, it is applicable to all the components that are placed thereafter using this **constraints** object. To avoid errors due to this, it is sometimes recommended that you create a new **constraints** object for every component you want to place. This would also mean additional coding on developer's part. The NetBeans GUI designer sets up an independent **constraints** object for each added object. This is probably because the code is generated automatically, so one need not worry about the effort in writing the additional code.*

Next, we set the layout manager for our container window:

```
getContentPane().setLayout(new GridBagLayout());
```

Now, we start adding the components to the container. The first component we are going to add is the label control. We set a few properties of the label:

```
jLabelOutput.setFont(new Font("Monospaced", 1, 24));
jLabelOutput.setBorder(new MetalBorders.TextFieldBorder());
```

These two statements set the font for the text in the label and set a border around the label boundary. We will now set a few additional constraints specific to this label:

```
constraints.insets = new Insets(10, 10, 10, 10);
```

Here, **insets** defines the external padding of the component, which is the minimum amount of space between the component and the edges of its display area. We set this for the label control so as to create big-sized output for the calculator. The next property we set is the **gridWidth**:

```
constraints.gridwidth = GridBagConstraints.REMAINDER;
```

The **gridWidth** property specifies the number of cells in a row for the component's display area. Because this is the first component being added and we want it to occupy the entire width of our grid, we set this property to **REMAINDER**, which specifies that this is the last component in the current row. Because we have already set the **fill** property to **BOTH**, this component will occupy the entire row. The other possible value that can be assigned to the **gridWidth** property is **RELATIVE**, which adds the next component to the same row immediately following the previously added component.

We now add the label to the container by calling the **add** method of the container:

```
getContentPane().add(jLabelOutput, gridBagConstraints);
```

Note that the second parameter specifies the **constraints** object we have set up so far. The layout manager applies the constraints specified in this **constraints** object while placing and aligning the label component. We will now start placing the various button controls. Because none of the buttons require additional whitespace in their display, we reset the insets to their default:

```
gridBagConstraints.insets = new Insets(0, 0, 0, 0);
```

We set **gridWidth** to 1 so that each component will occupy one column width. Note that, so far, the layout manager does not know the number of columns, which is decided only when we add all the remaining components. To add the first button, we first set its grid location by setting the **gridx** and **gridy** properties:

```
gridBagConstraints.gridx = 0;
gridBagConstraints.gridy = 1;
```

This indicates that the component to be added should be placed in Column 0, Row 1. Why does the row equal 1? Because our label occupies the first row. Note that the **gridx** property specifies the position along the x-axis, which is the column number. Likewise, the **gridy** property specifies the vertical positioning, which is the row number.

We now add the first button with the newly set **constraints** object:

```
getContentPane().add(jButtonMC, gridBagConstraints);
```

To add the remaining components, we simply need to specify the desired cell location for each component by changing the **gridx** and **gridy** properties; all other properties remain unchanged. Look at the code to see how a value for **gridx** and **gridy** is set before a new component is added. The maximum value for **gridx** is 3, indicating that we are not going to have more than four columns.

The trick comes in placing button 0, which occupies two columns' worth of space. We do this by using the following code fragment:

```
gridBagConstraints.gridx = 0;
gridBagConstraints.gridy = 6;
gridBagConstraints.gridwidth = 2;
getContentPane().add(jButtonZero, gridBagConstraints);
```

The button is placed in Column 0, Row 6 of the grid. We set its width to two columns by changing the **gridWidth** property.

Likewise, to place the **equalto** button, which is two rows high, we set the **gridHeight** property of the **constraints** object:

```
gridBagConstraints.gridheight = 2;
```

This completes our GUI. From this simple example, you can appreciate the flexibility available to you in this layout manager for building complex GUIs.

So far we have discussed the layout managers available in Java since its beginning. The next layout manager we discuss is **BoxLayout**, which was introduced in JDK 1.4.

BoxLayout

The **BoxLayout** manager is similar to the **FlowLayout** manager and provides additional functionality. This layout manager either stacks the components on top of each other or places them in a row, just like the flow layout. **BoxLayout** is good for creating forms-based applications. To illustrate this, we develop a forms-based application for creating a contacts database. The application focuses on creating the GUI and ignores the data storage functionality. The **ContactsDatabase** application has two panels—the one on the left captures the user name and contact number, and the one on the right displays all the contacts entered so far in the system as well as provides a facility to clear the entire database. The user interface of the application is shown in Figure 14-14.

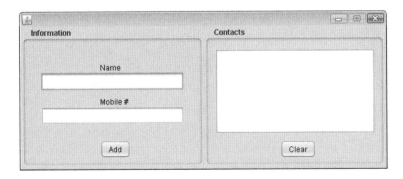

FIGURE 14-14.   *Creating a form-based user interface with BoxLayout*

Let's now study how the GUI is constructed. The entire source code for the **ContactsDatabase** application is given in Listing 14-6.

Listing 14-6 *Demonstration Program for BoxLayout*

```java
import java.awt.*;
import java.awt.event.*;
import java.util.logging.*;
import javax.swing.*;

public class ContactsDatabase extends JFrame implements ActionListener {

    private JPanel informationPanel;
    private JPanel listPanel;
    private JList contactList;
    private final JTextField jTextFieldName = new JTextField(20);
    private final JTextField jTextFieldMobile = new JTextField(20);
    private JButton jButtonAdd = new JButton("Add");
    private JButton jButtonClear = new JButton("Clear");

    public static void main(String[] args) {
        try {
            UIManager.setLookAndFeel(
                    "javax.swing.plaf.nimbus.NimbusLookAndFeel");
        } catch (ClassNotFoundException ex) {
            Logger.getLogger(
                    ContactsDatabase.class.getName()).log(Level.SEVERE,
                    null, ex);
        } catch (InstantiationException ex) {
            Logger.getLogger(
                    ContactsDatabase.class.getName()).log(Level.SEVERE,
                    null, ex);
        } catch (IllegalAccessException ex) {
            Logger.getLogger(
                    ContactsDatabase.class.getName()).log(Level.SEVERE,
                    null, ex);
        } catch (UnsupportedLookAndFeelException ex) {
            Logger.getLogger(
                    ContactsDatabase.class.getName()).log(Level.SEVERE,
                    null, ex);
        }
        ContactsDatabase mDIFrame = new ContactsDatabase();
    }

    public ContactsDatabase() {
        initGUI();
    }

    private void initGUI() {
```

```
        Box verticalBoxRight, verticalBoxLeft;

        setDefaultCloseOperation(JFrame.EXIT_ON_CLOSE);

        Container contentPane = getContentPane();
        contentPane.setLayout(new GridLayout(1, 2));
        verticalBoxLeft = Box.createVerticalBox();
        verticalBoxLeft.add(Box.createRigidArea(new Dimension(70, 20)));
        verticalBoxLeft.add(new JLabel("Name"));
        verticalBoxLeft.add(jTextFieldName);
        verticalBoxLeft.add(Box.createVerticalStrut(10));
        verticalBoxLeft.add(new JLabel("Mobile #"));
        verticalBoxLeft.add(jTextFieldMobile);
        verticalBoxLeft.add(Box.createVerticalStrut(25));
        verticalBoxLeft.add(jButtonAdd);
        jButtonAdd.addActionListener(this);
        informationPanel = new JPanel();
        informationPanel.add(verticalBoxLeft);
        informationPanel.setBorder(
                BorderFactory.createTitledBorder("Information"));
        contactList = new JList();
        contactList.setModel(new DefaultListModel());
        verticalBoxRight = Box.createVerticalBox();
        verticalBoxRight.add(new JScrollPane(contactList));
        verticalBoxRight.add(Box.createRigidArea(new Dimension(80, 10)));
        verticalBoxRight.add(jButtonClear);
        jButtonClear.addActionListener(this);
        listPanel = new JPanel();
        listPanel.setBorder(BorderFactory.createTitledBorder("Contacts"));
        listPanel.add(verticalBoxRight);
        contentPane.add(informationPanel);
        contentPane.add(listPanel);
        setSize(600, 250);
        setResizable(false);
        setVisible(true);
    }

    public void actionPerformed(ActionEvent e) {

        if (e.getSource() == jButtonAdd) {
            DefaultListModel contactsModel =
                    (DefaultListModel) contactList.getModel();
            contactsModel.addElement(jTextFieldName.getText()
                    + "   " + jTextFieldMobile.getText());
            jTextFieldName.setText("");
            jTextFieldMobile.setText("");
        } else {
            contactList.setModel(new DefaultListModel());
        }
    }
}
```

We'll first look at how the GUI is constructed. Then we'll discuss how to set the application's look and feel and use the logger for logging error messages, which is something that hasn't been covered so far in the book.

The **initGUI** method declares two variables of the **Box** type. A **Box** is a lightweight container that has its layout manager set to **BoxLayout**. By using this container, we won't need to create a separate container and its layout manager. Besides this, **Box** provides several class methods that are useful for containers that use **BoxLayout**. It also provides methods for creating several kinds of invisible components that affect layout. For fixed-size components, we use a glue component to control the components' positions. For a fixed amount of space between two components, we use a strut component, and for an invisible component that always takes up the same amount of space, you use a rigid area.

The program first sets the default action for the close icon so that the application window will close when the user clicks it:

```
setDefaultCloseOperation(JFrame.EXIT_ON_CLOSE);
```

Next, the program sets the **GridLayout** manager for the parent container:

```
Container contentPane = getContentPane();
contentPane.setLayout(new GridLayout(1, 2));
```

We set the grid of one row by two columns so that we can place the two panels horizontally, as shown in the figure. We then create a vertical box container by calling the **createVerticalBox** class method of the **Box** class:

```
verticalBoxLeft = Box.createVerticalBox();
```

This will be the left-side panel on which we place controls for capturing the user name and contact number. To set an equal amount of space in the layout of these components, we add a rigid area to the box:

```
verticalBoxLeft.add(Box.createRigidArea(new Dimension(70, 10)));
```

An x-dimension of 70 indicates that each component is placed 70 pixels from the left margin, and a y-dimension of 10 sets the vertical spacing from the top margin. We now add a label and a **TextField** control by calling the **add** method on the **Box** instance:

```
verticalBoxLeft.add(new JLabel("Name"));
verticalBoxLeft.add(jTextFieldName);
```

Now, we want to add some vertical space before the next component. We do this by creating a strut component:

```
verticalBoxLeft.add(Box.createVerticalStrut(10));
```

The vertical space equals 10 pixels in this example. Next, we add the label and a **TextField** for accepting the mobile number:

```
verticalBoxLeft.add(new JLabel("Mobile #"));
verticalBoxLeft.add(jTextFieldMobile);
```

Finally, we add a vertical space and a button to the container:

```
verticalBoxLeft.add(Box.createVerticalStrut(25));
verticalBoxLeft.add(jButtonAdd);
```

We now create a panel for the left side and add the previously created box container to it:

```
informationPanel = new JPanel();
informationPanel.add(verticalBoxLeft);
```

Note that we could add the box container directly to the parent container rather than creating another panel called **informationPanel**. The reason behind this is to set a titled border on this panel, which is done using the following statement:

```
informationPanel.setBorder(BorderFactory.createTitledBorder("Information"));
```

Likewise, we construct the right panel containing a list box and a Clear button. Both panels are then added to the parent container using its previously set grid layout:

```
contentPane.add(informationPanel);
contentPane.add(listPanel);
```

We create a fixed-size window for the application and do not allow the user to change its style with the following statements:

```
setSize(600, 250);
setResizable(false);
```

Now, let's discuss how to set the application's look and feel and how to use the logger for logging messages. The look and feel is set by calling the class method **setLookAndFeel** of the **UIManager** class:

```
UIManager.setLookAndFeel("javax.swing.plaf.nimbus.NimbusLookAndFeel");
```

The Nimbus look and feel was introduced in the Java SE 6 Update 10 release; it provides a cross-platform look and feel for your application. This is drawn with 2D vector graphics and can be rendered at any resolution, thus giving device independence to your application GUI. Calling this method requires you to capture several different kinds of exceptions, as seen in the code. The generated exceptions are stored in a log file using the logger provided in the **java.util.logging** package:

```
Logger.getLogger(
    ContactsDatabase.class.getName()).log(Level.SEVERE, null, ex);
```

The **log** method has several overloads. The one used here takes three parameters. The first parameter specifies the severity of the exception, the second parameter specifies a custom error string, which is set to null in this case, and the third parameter prints the string representation of the error that has occurred.

Finally, to complete the explanation of the entire application code, consider the event handler for the Add button. In this event handler, we obtain the model used by the list control and add the name and contact number to it:

```
DefaultListModel contactsModel = DefaultListModel) contactList.getModel();
contactsModel.addElement(jTextFieldName.getText()
        + "    " + jTextFieldMobile.getText());
```

As stated earlier, we could have used the instance of the BoxLayout manager to set the layout for our container. However, using a **Box** container is the preferred way of doing this for many users because it eases component placement and alignment via numerous built-in methods.

Here's something worth noting: In BoxLayout, the component's preferred height and width are ignored. So what happens when the application window is resized? If you reduce the width of the window beyond a certain level, the last added components do not show up on the window. This is because each component has a minimum size. The layout manager honors this size. Therefore, a component cannot be reduced to a size less than its minimum size. When the total container width is less than the sum of minimum widths of all the added components, the last added components disappear from the view.

Tabbed Dialog Box

Tabbed dialog boxes are widely used in many applications. You can use the CardLayout discussed earlier to create this kind of interface. However, Java provides a class called **JTabbedPane** to ease the construction of tabbed dialog boxes. The application we are going to create in this section contains two tabs. Each tab displays an independent form. The program in Listing 14-7 illustrates the use of this class.

Listing 14-7   *Demonstration Program for a Tabbed Dialog Box*

```java
import javax.swing.*;
import java.awt.*;

public class TabDemoApp {

    public static void main(String[] args) {
        TabFrame frame = new TabFrame("Tab Demo");
        frame.setSize(500, 200);
        frame.setVisible(true);
    }
}

class TabFrame extends JFrame {

    public TabFrame(String title) {
        super(title);
        setDefaultCloseOperation(EXIT_ON_CLOSE);
        initGUI();
    }

    public void initGUI() {
        JTabbedPane tabbedPane = new JTabbedPane();
        //Create the "cards".
        tabbedPane.addTab("Address", new AddressPanel());
        tabbedPane.addTab("Memo", new MemoPanel());
        getContentPane().add(tabbedPane, BorderLayout.CENTER);
    }
}
```

```
class MemoPanel extends JPanel {

    public MemoPanel() {
        setLayout(new BoxLayout(this, BoxLayout.PAGE_AXIS));
        add(new JLabel("Enter Memo"));
        add(new JTextField());
        add(new JButton("OK"));
    }
}

class AddressPanel extends JPanel {

    public AddressPanel() {
        setLayout(new BorderLayout(10, 0));
        JPanel leftPanel = new JPanel() {

            @Override
            public Dimension getPreferredSize() {
                Dimension size = super.getPreferredSize();
                size.width += 20;
                return size;
            }
        };
        leftPanel.setLayout(new GridLayout(4, 1, 10, 10));
        leftPanel.add(new JLabel("Name", JLabel.RIGHT));
        leftPanel.add(new JLabel("Address 1", JLabel.RIGHT));
        leftPanel.add(new JLabel("Address 2", JLabel.RIGHT));
        leftPanel.add(new JLabel("City", JLabel.RIGHT));
        add(leftPanel, BorderLayout.LINE_START);
        JPanel rightPanel = new JPanel();
        rightPanel.setLayout(new GridLayout(4, 1, 10, 10));
        rightPanel.add(new JTextField(20));
        rightPanel.add(new JTextField(10));
        rightPanel.add(new JTextField(15));
        rightPanel.add(new JTextField(5));
        add(rightPanel, BorderLayout.CENTER);
    }
}
```

As in the earlier cases, the GUI is built in the **initGUI** method. First, we create an instance of the **JTabbedPane** class:

```
JTabbedPane tabbedPane = new JTabbedPane();
```

Next, we add a card to this pane:

```
tabbedPane.addTab("Address", new AddressPanel());
```

Each tab in the dialog box has a card associated with it. This card is nothing but a panel object on which we will place a few components. The **addTab** method adds this panel to the tab panel. It also sets the name associated with the tab in its first parameter. The **AddressPanel** class extends **JPanel** and creates the GUI shown in Figure 14-15.

FIGURE 14-15. *Screen layout of Address panel*

We set the **BorderLayout** manager on this panel with a horizontal gap set to 10 pixels. We also set the preferred size by making its width 20 units more than the default preferred size. This creates some whitespace before the labels:

```
@Override
public Dimension getPreferredSize() {
    Dimension size = super.getPreferredSize();
    size.width += 20;
    return size;
}
```

Note the use of the **@Override** annotation, which was discussed in Chapter 11. To achieve the desired placement of components, we create two panels: **leftPanel** and **rightPanel**. We set the independent layout managers on these two panels and then add the components on them.

TIP
*To create complicated layouts, you usually split the container into smaller regions and place an independent container (a **panel** object) in each region. Each container uses its own layout manager for getting the desired placement of components.*

Next, we add one more tab called "Memo":

```
tabbedPane.addTab("Memo", new MemoPanel());
```

The **MemoPanel** class provides the GUI shown in Figure 14-16.

We use the **BoxLayout** manager here to construct the GUI. Instead of using the provided **Box** container, as in the earlier example, we'll now instantiate the **BoxLayout** class to demonstrate this second approach of using a box layout:

```
setLayout(new BoxLayout(this, BoxLayout.PAGE_AXIS));
```

The first parameter specifies the target container, and the second parameter specifies the axis along which to lay out components. The axis can be an x-axis or y-axis. It can also be a **LINE** or **PAGE** axis, where the direction is determined by the target container's **ComponentOrientation** property. Once the layout manager is created and attached to the container, we use the usual **add** method to add the components to the container.

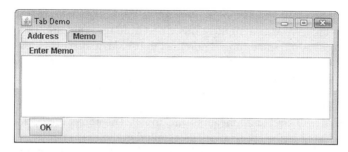

FIGURE 14-16. *Screen layout of the Memo panel*

Finally, we add the tab panel itself to the container:

```
getContentPane().add(tabbedPane, BorderLayout.CENTER);
```

Run the application and try clicking the two tabs to bring up the desired card. You may add any number of tabs to this tab panel. Each tab will have an associated card and an independent GUI.

Advanced Layout Managers

Besides the simple-to-use layout managers discussed so far, Java provides much more advanced and flexible layout managers—namely, the **GroupLayout** and **SpringLayout**. These layout managers are very complex to use and are mainly intended for builders of GUI tools. For example, NetBeans uses the **GroupLayout** manager to construct the user-painted GUI. It is recommended that you avoid using these layout managers if you are hand-coding a GUI. If you are curious to look at the code, simply create your GUI in NetBeans and examine the generated source code.

Besides these advanced layout managers, many third-party layout managers are available that you can use in your applications. If none of the provided layout managers meet your needs, you can create your own layout manager. For this, Java provides the **LayoutManager** interface. You need to create a class that implements this interface. This gives you total freedom and flexibility in designing your own layout manager.

In very rare situations, you may want to avoid using a layout manager and instead use absolute positioning to place the components. Note that, by default, some layout manager (**FlowLayout** or **BorderLayout**) is always in effect on a Java container. To turn off this layout manager, call the **setLayout** method with a **null** parameter. After this call, you need to specify the component's absolute location by calling its **setBounds** method.

Summary

This chapter discussed the many layout managers provided in Java. The layout managers place components on a container using some predefined rules. A layout manager makes it easier to adjust the GUI to different font sizes, to a container's changing size, and to different locales. Java provides several layout managers, each providing a certain kind of component placement. A **FlowLayout** lays the components row-wise. A **BorderLayout** places the components along the four borders of the container and its center. A **GridLayout** places the components in the cells of a grid with predefined dimensions. A **CardLayout** stacks the components on top of each other. A **BoxLayout** places the components along either the horizontal or vertical axis and is quite useful in creating form-based applications. The **GridBagLayout** allows for flexible placement of components, but at the same time is complex to use. Java also provides more advanced layout managers such as **GroupLayout** and **SpringLayout**, which are mainly intended for the use of GUI tool builders. Java also allows you to create your own layout manager classes. In addition, it allows you to turn off the default layout manager to facilitate placement at absolute coordinates.

Now that you have learned to build a GUI in a stand-alone application, in the next chapter you will learn a new kind of application—an applet. The applet life cycle is somewhat different from that of a stand-alone application, as detailed in the next chapter. You will learn to place the various GUI components on the applet and define their event handlers. More importantly, you will learn how to process user gestures such as mouse clicks, mouse motion, and keyboard input. So keep reading!

CHAPTER
15

Graphics and User
Gestures Processing

n Chapter 13, you learned about GUI building and event processing. In Chapter 14, you learned about creating sophisticated GUIs using layout managers. In those two chapters, the **JFrame** container was used to create a stand-alone Java application. In this chapter, you learn about another class of applications called *applets*. Applets have a somewhat different life cycle and runtime requirements than a stand-alone application. Applets require a web browser to run. Java does supply a command-line utility for testing applets; however, for an end user, using a browser is the preferred way of running an applet.

Along with applet programming, you learn lots of other techniques for detecting and processing user gestures in this chapter. You learn how to process mouse events and draw graphics on the screen. You create a popup menu for an application and learn to intercept keystrokes in a GUI application. Like in the earlier chapters, we use the Swing framework for developing applications in this chapter. Swing is a newer framework that supersedes the earlier AWT and offers many more advantages, although there is a lot of similarity in the use of Swing and AWT. Swing provides an equivalent for most of the components available in AWT. The names of these components are also identical, except for an uppercase **J** added in front of the name. All these new components have the same interface as their older counterparts, with a good number of additions to the interface in several cases. Sometimes, you may be able to convert your old AWT-based applications to newer Swing-based ones just by merely adding **J** in front of the component class names used in older applications.

Many developers these days use only Swing. Therefore, we will continue using it in this chapter, leaving AWT for those who have some special reason to stay with the older AWT APIs.

Here is what you will be learning in this chapter:

- Understanding the difference between an applet and a stand-alone application
- Creating applets
- Running applets
- Understanding the life-cycle methods of an applet
- Processing mouse click and motion events
- Creating popup menus
- Learning additional Swing and a few AWT components for which there are no Swing equivalents

What Is an Applet?

An *applet* is a Java program that can be embedded in a HTML page and opened in a browser. The HTML pages are located on a remote web server. When the client opens a HTML page in his browser, the HTML code gets downloaded to the client machine. Along with the HTML code, any Java applets embedded in the page also get downloaded to the client machine. The applet code then runs under the JVM installed on the client machine. Chapter 1 mentioned the misconception in the early days that the browser runs an applet. Although it is true that a browser is required to run an applet, the browser must be enabled with a JVM. If you turn off the JVM in a browser, it will not display an applet in its HTML page. An applet can be run without a browser, as you will see later in this chapter, by using the AppletViewer utility provided in JDK.

Also discussed in Chapter 1, if applet code is downloaded from a remote machine, it runs under several security restrictions, unless explicitly allowed greater freedom by the user. Contrary to this, a stand-alone application is available locally and is therefore not subjected to the same security restrictions. With the introduction of J2SE 1.2, applications are also subjected to security policies set by the user.

You will create applets whenever you want to make your applications available to your users from a remote machine. This means that the applications need not be preinstalled on the client machines. This is one of the greatest benefits in creating applets. The programs can now be deployed on remote servers, and the client can download and use the application on his machine whenever required. Because the client downloads the program every time he needs it, the client is assured to have the latest updates to it. This saves a lot of effort in distributing updates to your applications.

Creating applets is trivial. You simply declare a class that inherits from the **Applet** (AWT) or **JApplet** (Swing) class. It is said that developers like to get their hands dirty by quickly jumping in and coding. Therefore, we'll now get our hands dirty by creating an applet before discussing its life cycle.

Creating Your First Applet

As stated earlier, to create an applet you extend your class from **Applet** (of AWT package) or **JApplet** (of Swing package) and override its methods to provide the desired functionality. That's all that's required to create an applet. Once you create an applet class, you compile and embed it into an HTML page, which is opened in your browser for running the applet. You may embed multiple applets in an HTML page, which are positioned at the locations specified in the HTML code.

To add functionality to the applet, you override the appropriate methods of the applet class. One such method you will be overriding is the **paint** method. Whenever the applet needs repainting, the runtime calls its **paint** method. In your overridden **paint** method, you provide whatever drawing you wish to create on the applet's surface. The **paint** method for this purpose receives a device context (**Graphics**) object as its parameter. You use the various methods of the **Graphics** object to create some useful graphics. The code in Listing 15-1 shows how to create an applet and override its **paint** method to print a message on the applet's surface.

Listing 15-1   *First Java Applet*

```
import java.awt.*;
import javax.swing.JApplet;

public class FirstApplet extends JApplet {

    @Override
    public void paint(Graphics g) {
        g.drawString("Java programming is easy", 30, 30);
    }
}
```

The **JApplet** class is defined in the **javax.swing** package, so we need to import this in our source program. The **FirstApplet** class inherits **JApplet**, and we override the **paint** method. Whenever the applet needs repainting, the runtime calls this **paint** method. The **paint** method receives a **Graphics** object that allows the user to draw graphics on the applet's surface. In our case, the overridden **paint** method calls the **drawString** method of the **Graphics** object to display a string on the applet's surface. The string to be displayed is passed as the first parameter to the **drawString** method. The second and third parameters specify the x and y coordinates of a point where the string is to be displayed.

NOTE
*The **Graphics** class provides a lot more functionality than just drawing a string message. It provides the framework for all graphics operations within AWT and Swing. It plays two different but related roles. First, it is a graphics context that sets the background and foreground colors, the font, the drawing region, and the eventual destination (screen or image) of the graphics operations themselves. Second, the **Graphics** class provides methods for drawing simple geometric shapes, text, and images to the destination.*

Running the Applet

Place the code in Listing 15-1 in your favorite editor and store it under the filename FirstApplet.java. Compile the file to create a corresponding .class file. Next, you will need to write some HTML code to run this .class file in a browser window. The HTML code (FirstApplet.html) that does this is given in Listing 15-2.

Listing 15-2   *HTML Code for Running the Applet*

```
<HTML>
    <HEAD>
        <TITLE>First Applet</TITLE>
    </HEAD>
    <BODY>
        <H3><HR WIDTH="100%">First Applet<HR WIDTH="100%"></H3>
        <object  type="application/x-java-applet"
                height="200" width="300">
            <param name="code" value="FirstApplet"/>
            <param name="codebase" value="classes/"/>
        </object>
        <HR WIDTH="100%">
    </BODY>
</HTML>
```

In the HTML code, you set up the page title within the **TITLE** tag and set the page contents in the **BODY** tag. In the page body, we first print the heading "First Applet." To include the applet in the HTML body, we use the **object** tag:

```
<object  type="application/x-java-applet"
        height="200" width="300">
    <param name="code" value="FirstApplet"/>
    <param name="codebase" value="classes/"/>
</object>
```

The **type** parameter in the **object** tag specifies the type of application to run. The **width** and **height** parameters specify the size that the applet should occupy within the HTML page. The **code** parameter specifies the name of the .class file to run, and the **codebase** parameter specifies the path where the mentioned .class file can be found. This path is relative to the current folder from where the HTML code is opened.

NOTE
HTML tags are not case sensitive. To prove this point, we use a mix of upper- and lowercase tags in the preceding HTML code.

Once you have set up the HTML page and the .class file in the classes folder, simply open the page in your favorite browser. You will see the output shown in Figure 15-1.

Using AppletViewer

If you do not wish to use the browser every time you develop and test a new applet, you can use the AppletViewer utility provided as a part of the JDK. On the command prompt, type the following:

```
C:\360\ch15>appletviewer FirstApplet.html
```

The applet will now open and run within the AppletViewer application. The output is shown in Figure 15-2.

TIP
If you use NetBeans for developing your applets, right-click your applet source and click the Run File *option. NetBeans will start the AppletViewer and run your source applet within it.*

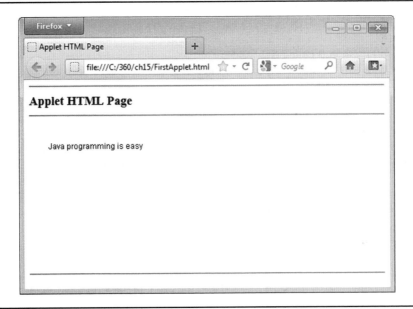

FIGURE 15-1. *Running the applet in a browser*

FIGURE 15-2.   *Running an applet in the AppletViewer application*

Understanding Applet Life-cycle Methods

When the applet runs, it provides several callback methods during its life cycle. You can override these methods to provide whatever functionality you want. The life-cycle methods are **init**, **start**, **paint**, **stop**, and **destroy**. You have already used the **paint** method in your first applet to draw some graphics on the applet.

The **init** method is typically used for creating resources required during the life of the applet. Usually, you build the GUI in the **init** method. The **start** method is called just before the applet starts executing. This happens when the applet is loaded the first time and whenever the user revisits the page that contains the applet.

NOTE
*The **init** method is called only once when the applet is loaded the first time, whereas the **start** method may be called several times during the applet's life cycle.*

The **stop** method is called just before the applet stops its execution. This happens whenever the user leaves the applet's page or quits the browser. Typically, the resources that are not required for the entire life cycle are allocated and deallocated in the **start** and **stop** methods, respectively. An example would be making a socket connection to the server.

CAUTION
Under the default security policy, an applet is not allowed to make a socket connection to any server other than the one from where it originated.

Because this socket connection is not required whenever the applet loses focus, you may make the connection in the **start** method and release it in the **stop** method. Another example would be playing an audio file; you can play the music while the applet is in focus and stop it whenever it goes in the background.

The **destroy** method is called before the applet is finally unloaded. You use this method to clean up the resources you may have allocated in the **init** method. Finally, the **paint** method is called several times during the applet's life cycle. It is first called by the runtime whenever it determines that the displayed contents must be refreshed onscreen. The **paint** method is then called whenever the programmer explicitly calls **repaint** or **update**.

To appreciate the practical applications of these methods, consider a video viewer applet. In developing such an applet, in the **init** method you might draw the viewer controls and start loading the video file. The **start** method would wait for the file to be fully loaded before playing it. The **stop** method would pause the video and not rewind it. Thus, the next invocation of the **start** method would continue the video from the last stopping point. The **destroy** method may remove the video from memory, implying that a call to **init** is required to start the video all over from the beginning.

Now that you have learned how to create an applet and understand its life-cycle methods, we will now create a very simple drawing tool (compared to the popular Paintbrush program) based on an applet. During the creation of this application, you will learn how to detect and process mouse clicks, mouse motion, and keyboard input. You will also create popup menus and use a few more Swing controls. Note that all the user-gesture-detection and -processing techniques described in this section can be applied to stand-alone Swing applications and are not restricted to use with applets.

Processing Mouse Events

A drawing tool typically uses a mouse as a pointing device for creating graphics. For drawing graphics on the application screen, your application must respond to user gestures such as mouse moves and mouse clicks. Whenever a user clicks a mouse button or moves the mouse, the mouse events occur. Java provides three listener classes for processing these mouse events. It differentiates between the mouse click and mouse motion events. The user moves the mouse around most of the time while using the computer. Thus, several mouse motion events are continuously generated as the mouse is moved. However, the user less frequently clicks the buttons on the mouse; thus, only a few mouse click events are generated during the program's use. Therefore, it makes sense to separate the mouse click and mouse motion event listener interfaces. Additionally, a listener interface is provided for receiving mouse wheel events. Let's first look at how to process mouse click events.

Mouse Clicks

To process mouse click events, Java provides the **MouseListener** interface. This interface provides five different methods corresponding to certain actions. When a mouse enters a component, a **mouseEntered** event is generated, and when it leaves the component, a **mouseExited** event is generated. Similarly, when a user presses the mouse button, a **mousePressed** event is generated, and when the button is released, a **mouseReleased** event is generated. Additionally, there is one more callback method, called **mouseClicked**. This is called whenever the user clicks (presses and releases) the mouse button.

To start building our drawing tool, we begin with processing mouse click events. Our application will simply print the coordinates where the mouse is clicked. The coordinates are printed at the click location. The full program is given in Listing 15-3.

Listing 15-3 *Processing Mouse Click Events*

```java
import java.awt.*;
import java.awt.event.*;
import javax.swing.JApplet;

public class GraphicsEditor extends JApplet {

    private Point pt = new Point(0, 0);

    @Override
    public void init() {
        addMouseListener(new MouseAdapter() {

            @Override
            public void mouseClicked(MouseEvent e) {
                pt = new Point(e.getX(), e.getY());
                repaint();
            }
        });
    }

    @Override
    public void paint(Graphics g) {
        if (pt.x > 0 && pt.x > 0) {
            String printString = String.format("(%d, %d)", pt.x, pt.y);
            g.drawString(printString, pt.x, pt.y);
        }
    }
}
```

In the **init** method, we set up the listener for the mouse events:

```java
addMouseListener(new MouseAdapter() {
```

Note that we use an anonymous class here to process mouse events. The other option would have been to implement the **mouseListener** interface. However, this would require providing the implementation for all five methods defined in the interface. Because we are interested in processing only a single mouse click event, the use of an adapter class is recommended. The adapter classes were discussed in Chapter 13. In the anonymous class, we override the **mouseClicked** method:

```java
public void mouseClicked(MouseEvent e) {
```

The method receives a parameter of type **MouseEvent** that contains the details of the mouse click event. From this parameter, we retrieve the x and y coordinates of the click point and assign those to the **pt** variable:

```java
pt = new Point(e.getX(), e.getY());
```

The program then calls the **repaint** method to post a paint request to the applet. This results in executing the applet's **paint** method.

CAUTION
*The **repaint** method may not result in an immediate invocation of the **paint** method. The applet screen is not refreshed on every click, and you will see the overlapped coordinates printed on each mouse click. When you resize the applet, the text will disappear from the screen.*

The **paint** method receives a parameter of type **Graphics**. This is a device context for printing graphics on the device:

```
public void paint(Graphics g) {
```

The **paint** method prepares a string containing the coordinates taken from the **pt** variable and prints it at the same location as **pt**:

```
String printString = String.format("(%d, %d)", pt.x, pt.y);
g.drawString(printString, pt.x, pt.y);
```

The **drawString** method of the **Graphics** class takes the string to be printed as the first parameter. The second and third parameters to the method specify the x and y coordinates, respectively, of the point where the string is to be displayed.

Now, when you run the applet and click the mouse anywhere on the applet surface, the program will read the coordinates where the mouse is clicked and print the same on the applet. Some typical output is shown in Figure 15-3.

Mouse Motion Events

Java provides an interface called **MouseMotionListener** to process mouse motion events. There are two types of motion events—one when the mouse is moved with the button pressed and the other without the button being pressed. Accordingly, the interface provides two methods: **mouseDragged** and **mouseMoved**. The **mouseDragged** method is called whenever the mouse button is pressed on a component and then dragged. The drag event is delivered to the component continuously until the time the mouse button is released. This may not happen within the component boundaries; however, the event continues to be delivered as long as the

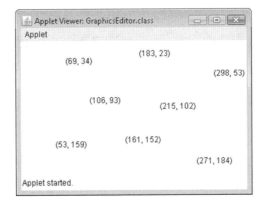

FIGURE 15-3. *Applet displays the coordinates of the clicked point*

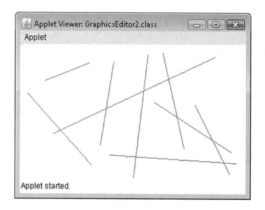

FIGURE 15-4. *Line-drawing applet*

button is not released. Because the drag-and-drop operation is platform dependent, this event may not be delivered during a native drag-and-drop operation. The **mouseMoved** method is invoked when the mouse cursor is moved over a component but no button has been pressed. We use this event in our application to draw lines.

Whenever the user clicks on the applet, the line drawing begins. To indicate this, we change the cursor from its default arrow shape to a crosshair. As the user moves the cursor, a line will be drawn from the starting point to the current cursor position, thus producing a rubber band effect. When the user clicks the mouse one more time, the drawing stops and a line is permanently drawn from the start position to the last position where the mouse was clicked. The user can continue drawing more lines by clicking the mouse one more time and dragging it to a new position. Some sample program output is shown in Figure 15-4.

The start and end coordinates of all the lines are stored in an **ArrayList**, which is a type of **Collection**. Collections are covered in Chapter 16. The applet displays all drawn line segments whenever it is repainted.

Listing 15-4 presents the code for our line-drawing applet.

Listing 15-4 *Line-Drawing Applet That Consumes Mouse Motion Events*

```
import java.awt.*;
import java.awt.event.*;
import java.util.*;
import javax.swing.JApplet;

public class GraphicsEditor2 extends JApplet {

    private Point ptFirst = new Point(0, 0);
    private Point ptSecond = new Point(0, 0);
    private Point ptOld = new Point(0, 0);
    private boolean isDrawing = false;
    private ArrayList<Line> lines = new ArrayList<>();
```

```java
@Override
public void init() {
    addMouseListener(new MouseAdapter() {

        @Override
        public void mouseClicked(MouseEvent e) {
            if (!isDrawing) {
                ptFirst = new Point(e.getX(), e.getY());
                ptSecond = new Point(e.getX(), e.getY());
                isDrawing = true;
                setCursor(new Cursor(Cursor.CROSSHAIR_CURSOR));
            } else {
                isDrawing = false;
                setCursor(new Cursor(Cursor.DEFAULT_CURSOR));
                lines.add(new Line(ptFirst, ptSecond));
            }
        }
    });

    addMouseMotionListener(new MouseMotionAdapter() {

        @Override
        public void mouseMoved(MouseEvent e) {
            if (isDrawing) {
                ptOld = ptSecond;
                ptSecond = new Point(e.getX(), e.getY());
                repaint();
            }
        }
    });
}

@Override
public void paint(Graphics g) {
    // erase earlier line
    g.setColor(Color.white);
    g.drawLine(ptFirst.x, ptFirst.y, ptOld.x, ptOld.y);

    // draw new line
    g.setColor(Color.red);
    g.drawLine(ptFirst.x, ptFirst.y, ptSecond.x, ptSecond.y);

    // draw all previous lines
    Iterator<Line> it = lines.iterator();
    while (it.hasNext()) {
        Line line = it.next();

        g.drawLine(line.getStartPoint().x, line.getStartPoint().y,
                line.getEndPoint().x, line.getEndPoint().y);
    }
}
}
```

```
class Line {

    private Point ptStart;
    private Point ptEnd;

    public Line(Point ptStart, Point ptEnd) {
        this.ptStart = ptStart;
        this.ptEnd = ptEnd;
    }

    public Point getEndPoint() {
        return ptEnd;
    }

    public Point getStartPoint() {
        return ptStart;
    }
}
```

The **GraphicsEditor2** class that inherits **JApplet** declares three **Point**-type variables:

```
private Point ptFirst = new Point(0, 0);
private Point ptSecond = new Point(0, 0);
private Point ptOld = new Point(0, 0);
```

The **ptFirst** variable stores the start point of a line segment, and the **ptSecond** variable stores its end point. The **ptOld** variable is used for storing the previous value of the end point. It also declares two more variables: **isDrawing** and **lines**. The **isDrawing** variable is of type **boolean** and is set to **true** whenever the user begins the line drawing by clicking the mouse button. This flag is reset when the user clicks the mouse button while in the drawing mode. The **lines** variable is of type **ArrayList**. You have already used this class in Chapter 12. You will learn more about this class in the next chapter. At this stage, just know that **ArrayList** is used for holding a list of objects. In our current case, the objects are of type **Line**. Each **Line** object stores the start and end points of each line segment. The definition of the **Line** class is very simple; it contains two **Point** variables, respective getter methods, and a class constructor.

In the **init** method, we set up the two listeners for processing both mouse click and motion events. We use the adapter classes for both the listeners to avoid some extra typing of methods we do not need. We use anonymous classes for both types of events. First, the mouse listener is implemented by instantiating the **MouseAdapter** class:

```
addMouseListener(new MouseAdapter() {
```

We override a single method of this class—**mouseClicked**:

```
public void mouseClicked(MouseEvent e) {
```

Within the method body, we check the drawing mode. If we're not currently drawing, we record the current mouse click position in both **ptFirst** and **ptSecond**:

```
if (!bDrawing) {
    ptFirst = new Point(e.getX(), e.getY());
    ptSecond = new Point(e.getX(), e.getY());
```

We then set the drawing mode to **true** and change the cursor to a crosshair:

```
isDrawing = true;
setCursor(new Cursor(Cursor.CROSSHAIR_CURSOR));
```

To change the cursor shape, we call the **setCursor** method of the **Component** class. The constructor takes a parameter that specifies the cursor shape. JDK provides several constants for predefined cursor shapes.

In the mouse click event, if the drawing mode is not active, we reset the **isDrawing** flag to **false**. We then change the cursor back to its original default shape:

```
setCursor(new Cursor(Cursor.DEFAULT_CURSOR));
```

Finally, we record the start and end point coordinates of the line segment in the **lines** collection:

```
lines.add(new Line(ptFirst, ptSecond));
```

TIP
*To store the two points, we could use a built-in **Rectangle** class rather than creating a **Line** class. The purpose behind creating a **Line** class is to add more properties, such as color, width, and so on, in later exercises.*

Next, we set up the listener for mouse motion events. Once again, we create an anonymous class by instantiating the required adapter class:

```
addMouseMotionListener(new MouseMotionAdapter() {
```

We then override the **mouseMoved** method:

```
public void mouseMoved(MouseEvent e) {
```

In the method body, we check whether the drawing mode is currently active; if it is, we record the coordinates of the current mouse position in the **ptSecond** variable and repaint the applet to show the line segment:

```
if (isDrawing) {
    ptOld = ptSecond;
    ptSecond = new Point(e.getX(), e.getY());
    repaint();
}
```

The last thing we need to do is override the applet's **paint** method for the actual drawing of the lines. In the **paint** method, we first set the drawing color to white by calling the **setColor** method of the **Graphics** object:

```
public void paint(Graphics g) {
    g.setColor(Color.white);
```

We draw the line by calling the **drawLine** method. The **drawLine** method receives four parameters. The first two parameters specify the x, y coordinates of the start point, and the last two parameters specify those of the end point:

```
g.drawLine(ptFirst.x, ptFirst.y, ptOld.x, ptOld.y);
```

This draws the line segment in white, which is the current background color. This will erase the earlier drawn line, if there is one, from the screen. We now draw another line segment in red:

```
// draw new line
g.setColor(Color.red);
g.drawLine(ptFirst.x, ptFirst.y, ptSecond.x, ptSecond.y);
```

Note that as we move the mouse on the screen, the value of **ptSecond** will keep changing. Drawing the line segment from the first point to the old second point in the background color effectively removes the earlier line from the screen. A new line segment is then drawn in red, producing a rubber-band effect as the cursor is moved around.

Additionally, in the **paint** method, we draw all the previously created line segments by iterating through the **lines** collection (this **Iterator** class is covered in more detail in the next chapter):

```
// draw all previous lines
Iterator<Line> it = lines.iterator();
while (it.hasNext()) {
    Line line = it.next();

    g.drawLine(line.getStartPoint().x, line.getStartPoint().y,
            line.getEndPoint().x, line.getEndPoint().y);
}
```

This completes our code discussion. Now, compile and run the program. Click the mouse anywhere on the applet. Release the mouse button and then move the mouse within the applet. As you move the mouse, you will see a line drawn in red from the first clicked point to the new mouse position. Click the mouse button one more time. A line is now drawn permanently, and the rubber-band effect is stopped. Click the mouse at another position on the applet to draw another line segment.

Creating Popup Menus

So far, you have learned just a few techniques of GUI programming. One of the important needs of a graphics application is a menu system. Menus are useful in general because they allow the user to navigate to different parts of the application easily, to make selections, to apply actions, and so on. Because an applet cannot have a conventional menu system, shown in the top bar of an application, it has to use popup menus. You learn how to create popup menus in this section. Although the technique discussed here is for an applet, it may very well be adapted to a stand-alone GUI application with a few minor changes. A popup menu appears on the screen whenever the user clicks the right mouse button. Therefore, you will also learn to process right-button clicks as the mouse event.

We will extend our graphics-drawing program of the previous section to allow the user to select the drawing color of the line segment. By right-clicking the applet, the user can select a color from a menu that pops up onscreen. This popup menu displays a few color choices to the user. The user

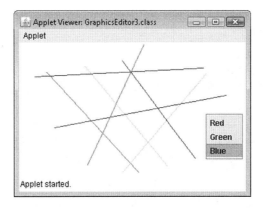

FIGURE 15-5.   *Popup menu on an applet*

selects a desired color by clicking the menu item. When he makes the selection, the popup menu disappears from the screen and the next line segment that's drawn will use the selected color.

The program output with the popup menu is shown in Figure 15-5.

The program that does all this is given in Listing 15-5.

Listing 15-5   *Selecting a Drawing Color Through a Popup Menu*

```java
import java.awt.*;
import java.awt.event.*;
import java.util.*;
import javax.swing.*;

public class GraphicsEditor3 extends JApplet
        implements ActionListener {

    private Point ptFirst = new Point(0, 0);
    private Point ptSecond = new Point(0, 0);
    private Point ptOld = new Point(0, 0);
    private boolean isDrawing = false;
    private ArrayList<Line> lines = new ArrayList<Line>();
    private JPopupMenu popMenu;
    private JMenuItem menuRed, menuGreen, menuBlue;
    private Color drawingColor = Color.red;
    private JApplet app;

    @Override
    public void init() {
        popMenu = new JPopupMenu("Colors");
        menuRed = new JMenuItem("Red");
        menuRed.addActionListener(this);
        menuGreen = new JMenuItem("Green");
```

```java
            menuGreen.addActionListener(this);
            menuBlue = new JMenuItem("Blue");
            menuBlue.addActionListener(this);
            popMenu.add(menuRed);
            popMenu.add(menuGreen);
            popMenu.add(menuBlue);
            addMouseListener(new MouseAdapter() {

                @Override
                public void mouseClicked(MouseEvent e) {
                    if (e.getModifiers() == InputEvent.BUTTON3_MASK) {
                        popMenu.show(e.getComponent(), e.getX(), e.getY());
                    } else if (e.getModifiers()
                            == InputEvent.BUTTON1_MASK) {

                        if (!isDrawing) {
                            ptFirst = new Point(e.getX(), e.getY());
                            ptSecond = new Point(e.getX(), e.getY());
                            isDrawing = true;
                            setCursor(new Cursor(Cursor.CROSSHAIR_CURSOR));
                        } else {
                            isDrawing = false;
                            setCursor(new Cursor(Cursor.DEFAULT_CURSOR));
                            lines.add(new Line(ptFirst, ptSecond, drawingColor));
                        }
                    }
                }
            });

            addMouseMotionListener(new MouseMotionAdapter() {

                @Override
                public void mouseMoved(MouseEvent e) {
                    if (isDrawing) {
                        ptOld = ptSecond;
                        ptSecond = new Point(e.getX(), e.getY());
                        repaint();
                    }
                }
            });
    }

    @Override
    public void paint(Graphics g) {
        // erase old line
        g.setColor(Color.white);
        g.drawLine(ptFirst.x, ptFirst.y, ptOld.x, ptOld.y);
        // draw new line
        g.setColor(drawingColor);
        g.drawLine(ptFirst.x, ptFirst.y, ptSecond.x, ptSecond.y);
```

```
            Iterator<Line> it = lines.iterator();
            while (it.hasNext()) {
                Line line = it.next();
                g.setColor(line.getLineColor());
                g.drawLine(line.getStartPoint().x, line.getStartPoint().y,
                        line.getEndPoint().x, line.getEndPoint().y);
            }
        }

        @Override
        public void actionPerformed(ActionEvent e) {
            if (e.getSource() == menuRed) {
                drawingColor = Color.red;
            } else if (e.getSource() == menuGreen) {
                drawingColor = Color.green;
            } else if (e.getSource() == menuBlue) {
                drawingColor = Color.blue;
            }
        }
    }

class Line {

    private Point ptStart;
    private Point ptEnd;
    private Color lineColor;

    public Line(Point ptStart, Point ptEnd) {
        this.ptStart = ptStart;
        this.ptEnd = ptEnd;
    }

    public Line(Point ptStart, Point ptEnd, Color lineColor) {
        this.ptStart = ptStart;
        this.ptEnd = ptEnd;
        this.lineColor = lineColor;
    }

    public Point getEndPoint() {
        return ptEnd;
    }

    public Point getStartPoint() {
        return ptStart;
    }

    public Color getLineColor() {
        return lineColor;
    }
}
```

As in earlier cases, the **GraphicsEditor3** class inherits **JApplet** and implements an action listener:

```
public class GraphicsEditor3 extends JApplet
    implements ActionListener {
```

An action listener is required for processing the menu-selection events. Whenever a user selects a menu item, an **ActionEvent** is generated.

NOTE
*There is no adapter class for the **ActionListener** interface because it has only a single method to implement.*

As before, we now declare a few class variables to store our **Point** objects, drawing mode, and line segments. To store the reference to the popup menu, we create a variable of type **JPopupMenu**, which is a built-in class in Swing:

```
private JPopupMenu popMenu;
```

Next, we declare three variables of type **JMenuItem**:

```
private JMenuItem menuRed, menuGreen, menuBlue;
```

We will be creating three menu items pertaining to three color choices for the line segment. We declare a **Color** variable and assign an initial value to it:

```
private Color drawingColor = Color.red;
```

In the **init** method, we instantiate the **JPopupMenu** class:

```
public void init() {
    popMenu = new JPopupMenu("Colors");
```

The class constructor receives a string argument, which is the name given to this menu. Note that you can create multiple menus in your application and select a different menu each time, depending on the application context. We use this name while referring to the desired menu. Next, we create a few menu items:

```
menuRed = new JMenuItem("Red");
menuRed.addActionListener(this);
menuGreen = new JMenuItem("Green");
menuGreen.addActionListener(this);
menuBlue = new JMenuItem("Blue");
menuBlue.addActionListener(this);
```

Each menu item has a string associated with it, which is displayed to the user. We also need to add an action listener to each menu item to process its action event whenever the user clicks the item. The action listener for all three menu items is set to the current applet instance, which provides the **actionPerformed** method. We add the three menu items to the popup menu by calling its **add** method:

```
popMenu.add(menuRed);
popMenu.add(menuGreen);
popMenu.add(menuBlue);
```

After creating the menu system, we set up the listener for processing the right mouse click events. Like in earlier examples, we use the anonymous adapter class:

```
addMouseListener(new MouseAdapter() {
```

In the **mouseClicked** event handler, we now check whether the user has clicked the right mouse button:

```
public void mouseClicked(MouseEvent e) {
    if (e.getModifiers() == InputEvent.BUTTON3_MASK) {
```

The **getModifiers** method helps us in determining which button is clicked. **BUTTON3_MASK** refers to the right button. If the right button is clicked, we display the popup menu to the user by calling its **show** method:

```
popMenu.show(e.getComponent(), e.getX(), e.getY());
```

The menu is displayed at the clicked location. When the user selects a certain menu item, an action event is generated. This results in calling the **actionPerformed** event handler:

```
public void actionPerformed(ActionEvent e) {
    if (e.getSource() == menuRed) {
        drawingColor = Color.red;
    }
```

In the event handler, we check the event source. Depending on the source, we set the **drawingColor** variable to an appropriate color.

The implementation of the **paint** method is the same as the earlier example, except that we set the drawing color to the user-selected value rather than a hard-coded color (red).

Customizing the Drawing Color

So far we have created a drawing tool that allows the user to draw lines on the screen and select the drawing color from one of three predefined options. Now, we will enhance our tool so that the user can set the drawing color to any color of his choice. Rather than providing a fixed set of color values, we allow the user to select RGB component values to set an arbitrary color. In the process, you will learn to use a few more Swing components. We use a scroll bar control to set the component color value in the range of 0 to 255. We also use a custom canvas on which the effect of the color selection will be displayed immediately. The **java.awt** package defines the **Canvas** class. Like a traditional canvas on which you paint, the instance of **Canvas** in Java is used for creating drawings. You typically draw primitives such as lines and circles on it to create a drawing. In this example, we use the canvas to display the user-selected color. We paint the entire canvas using this color. The user interface for the color selection dialog frame is shown in Figure 15-6.

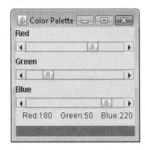

FIGURE 15-6. *User interface for customizing the drawing color*

The dialog frame displays three scroll bar controls to the user. The range of each scroll bar is 0 to 255. Each scroll bar corresponds to one of the three colors: red, green, or blue. When the user changes the scroll positions, the effective color is displayed on a custom canvas at the bottom of the screen. We also create another custom canvas that displays the currently set RGB values, which are shown just above the color custom canvas.

The complete code for the modified drawing editor is given in Listing 15-6.

Listing 15-6 *Scroll Bar and Canvas Demonstration*

```java
import java.awt.*;
import java.awt.event.*;
import java.util.*;
import javax.swing.*;

public class GraphicsEditor4 extends JApplet
        implements ActionListener {

    private Point ptFirst = new Point(0, 0);
    private Point ptSecond = new Point(0, 0);
    private Point ptOld = new Point(0, 0);
    private boolean isDrawing = false;
    private ArrayList<Line> lines = new ArrayList<Line>();
    private JPopupMenu popMenu;
    private JMenuItem menuRed, menuGreen, menuBlue, menuCustom;
    private Color drawingColor = Color.red;

    @Override
    public void init() {
        popMenu = new JPopupMenu("Colors");
        menuRed = new JMenuItem("Red");
        menuRed.addActionListener(this);
        menuGreen = new JMenuItem("Green");
        menuGreen.addActionListener(this);
        menuBlue = new JMenuItem("Blue");
        menuBlue.addActionListener(this);
```

```java
    menuCustom = new JMenuItem("Custom");
    menuCustom.addActionListener(this);
    popMenu.add(menuRed);
    popMenu.add(menuGreen);
    popMenu.add(menuBlue);
    popMenu.addSeparator();
    popMenu.add(menuCustom);

    addMouseListener(new MouseAdapter() {

        @Override
        public void mouseClicked(MouseEvent e) {
            if (e.getModifiers() == InputEvent.BUTTON3_MASK) {
                popMenu.show(e.getComponent(), e.getX(), e.getY());
            } else if (e.getModifiers()
                    == InputEvent.BUTTON1_MASK) {
                if (!isDrawing) {
                    ptFirst = new Point(e.getX(), e.getY());
                    ptSecond = new Point(e.getX(), e.getY());
                    isDrawing = true;
                    setCursor(new Cursor(Cursor.CROSSHAIR_CURSOR));
                } else {
                    isDrawing = false;
                    setCursor(new Cursor(Cursor.DEFAULT_CURSOR));
                    lines.add(new Line(ptFirst, ptSecond, drawingColor));
                }
            }
        }
    });

    addMouseMotionListener(new MouseMotionAdapter() {

        @Override
        public void mouseMoved(MouseEvent e) {
            if (isDrawing) {
                ptOld = ptSecond;
                ptSecond = new Point(e.getX(), e.getY());
                repaint();
            }
        }
    });
}

public void setClr(Color clr) {
    this.drawingColor = clr;
}

@Override
public void paint(Graphics g) {
    // erase old line
    g.setColor(Color.white);
```

```
        g.drawLine(ptFirst.x, ptFirst.y, ptOld.x, ptOld.y);
        // draw new line
        g.setColor(drawingColor);
        g.drawLine(ptFirst.x, ptFirst.y, ptSecond.x, ptSecond.y);

        Iterator<Line> it = lines.iterator();
        while (it.hasNext()) {
            Line line = it.next();
            g.setColor(line.getLineColor());
            g.drawLine(line.getStartPoint().x, line.getStartPoint().y,
                    line.getEndPoint().x, line.getEndPoint().y);
        }
    }

    @Override
    public void actionPerformed(ActionEvent e) {
        if (e.getSource() == menuRed) {
            drawingColor = Color.red;
        } else if (e.getSource() == menuGreen) {
            drawingColor = Color.green;
        } else if (e.getSource() == menuBlue) {
            drawingColor = Color.blue;
        } else if (e.getSource() == menuCustom) {
            (new ColorPalette("Color Palette",
                    this)).setVisible(true);
        }
    }
}

class Line {

    private Point ptStart;
    private Point ptEnd;
    private Color lineColor;

    public Line(Point ptStart, Point ptEnd) {
        this.ptStart = ptStart;
        this.ptEnd = ptEnd;
    }

    public Line(Point ptStart, Point ptEnd, Color clr) {
        this.ptStart = ptStart;
        this.ptEnd = ptEnd;
        this.lineColor = clr;
    }

    public Point getEndPoint() {
        return ptEnd;
    }
```

```java
    public Point getStartPoint() {
        return ptStart;
    }

    public Color getLineColor() {
        return lineColor;
    }
}

class ColorPalette extends JFrame implements AdjustmentListener {

    private GraphicsEditor4 applet;
    private JScrollBar redScroll =
            new JScrollBar(Scrollbar.HORIZONTAL, 0, 1, 0, 256);
    private JScrollBar greenScroll =
            new JScrollBar(Scrollbar.HORIZONTAL, 0, 1, 0, 256);
    private JScrollBar blueScroll =
            new JScrollBar(Scrollbar.HORIZONTAL, 0, 1, 0, 256);
    private ColorCanvas colorCanvas;
    private MessageCanvas messageCanvas;
    private int redValue, greenValue, blueValue;

    public int getBlueValue() {
        return blueValue;
    }

    public int getGreenValue() {
        return greenValue;
    }

    public int getRedValue() {
        return redValue;
    }

    public ColorPalette(String string, GraphicsEditor4 applet)
            throws HeadlessException {
        setTitle(string);
        this.applet = applet;
        initGUI();
    }

    private void initGUI() {
        setLayout(new GridLayout(8, 1, 5, 5));
        add(new JLabel("Red"));
        add(redScroll);
        add(new JLabel("Green"));
        add(greenScroll);
        add(new JLabel("Blue"));
        add(blueScroll);
        messageCanvas = new MessageCanvas(this);
        add(messageCanvas);
```

```
            colorCanvas = new ColorCanvas(this);
            add(colorCanvas);
            redScroll.addAdjustmentListener(this);
            blueScroll.addAdjustmentListener(this);
            greenScroll.addAdjustmentListener(this);
            setBounds(200, 200, 200, 200);
        }


        @Override
        public void adjustmentValueChanged(AdjustmentEvent e) {
            if (e.getAdjustable() == redScroll) {
                redValue = redScroll.getValue();
            }
            if (e.getAdjustable() == greenScroll) {
                greenValue = greenScroll.getValue();
            }
            if (e.getAdjustable() == blueScroll) {
                blueValue = blueScroll.getValue();
            }

            messageCanvas.repaint();
            colorCanvas.repaint();
            applet.setClr(new Color(redValue, greenValue, blueValue));
        }
    }

class MessageCanvas extends Canvas {

    private ColorPalette frame;
    private String strDisplay = "";

    MessageCanvas(ColorPalette frame) {
        this.frame = frame;
    }

    @Override
    public void paint(Graphics g) {
        strDisplay = "Red:" + String.valueOf(frame.getRedValue());
        strDisplay += " Green:" + String.valueOf(frame.getGreenValue());
        strDisplay += " Blue:" + String.valueOf(frame.getBlueValue());
        g.drawString(strDisplay, 10, 10);
    }
}

class ColorCanvas extends Canvas {

    private ColorPalette frame;

    ColorCanvas(ColorPalette applet) {
        this.frame = applet;
    }
```

```
    @Override
    public void paint(Graphics g) {
        Rectangle rect = getBounds();
        g.setColor(new Color(frame.getRedValue(),
                frame.getGreenValue(),
                frame.getBlueValue()));
        g.fillRect(0, 0, rect.width, rect.height);
    }
}
```

We add a new menu item to the existing popup menu by creating one more instance of **JMenuItem**, as shown here:

```
menuCustom = new JMenuItem("Custom");
menuCustom.addActionListener(this);
...
popMenu.addSeparator();
popMenu.add(menuCustom);
```

We process the click event on this custom menu with the following code:

```
} else if (e.getSource() == menuCustom) {
    (new ColorPalette("Color Palette", this)).setVisible(true);
}
```

Now let's look at the **ColorPalette** class that creates the dialog frame shown in Figure 15-6:

```
class ColorPalette extends JFrame implements AdjustmentListener {
```

The **ColorPalette** class implements the **AdjustmentListener** interface. This interface is required for processing the scroll bar events. Like the **ActionListener**, the **AdjustmentListener** interface has only one method to implement, so no adapter class is available for this interface.

Next, we declare a few class variables. First, we create a variable called **redScroll** of the **JScrollbar** type:

```
private JScrollBar redScroll =
            new JScrollBar(Scrollbar.HORIZONTAL, 0, 1, 0, 256);
```

The **redScroll** variable is initialized with an instance of **JScrollbar**. The class constructor takes five parameters. The first parameter indicates the scroll bar orientation, which is set to horizontal in this case. The other possible orientation is vertical. The second parameter indicates the initial value of the scroll bar. The value **0** here indicates that the scroll bubble will be at the leftmost position in the beginning. The third parameter indicates the visible amount of the scroll bar. Typically this represents the size of the bubble. The fourth and fifth parameters indicate the minimum and maximum values, respectively, of the scroll.

We create two more variables of the **JScrollbar** type, similar to **redScroll**, to represent the green and blue colors. After this, we declare two variables of custom class types:

```
private ColorCanvas colorCanvas;
private MessageCanvas messageCanvas;
```

ColorCanvas and **MessageCanvas** are custom classes used to display the selected color and the RGB values, respectively. Both these classes derive from a **Canvas** class and are discussed later. Finally, we declare three integer-type variables to store RGB values:

```
private int redValue, greenValue, blueValue;
```

In the **initGUI** method, we build the GUI. First, we set the layout manager, which is a grid layout having eight rows and one column:

```
setLayout(new GridLayout(8, 1, 5, 5));
```

We now add the appropriate labels and the previously created scroll bar controls in the first six rows of the grid:

```
add(new JLabel("Red"));
add(redScroll);
...
```

In the seventh row, we add an instance of **MessageCanvas**:

```
messageCanvas = new MessageCanvas(this);
add(messageCanvas);
```

In the eighth row, we add an instance of **ColorCanvas**:

```
colorCanvas = new ColorCanvas(this);
add(colorCanvas);
```

Finally, we set the event listener for each scroll bar control:

```
redScroll.addAdjustmentListener(this);
blueScroll.addAdjustmentListener(this);
greenScroll.addAdjustmentListener(this);
```

The applet class acts as an event listener for the scroll bar event. The event handler method receives a parameter of type **AdjustmentEvent**:

```
public void adjustmentValueChanged(AdjustmentEvent e) {
```

The **getAdjustable** method of the event object returns the control that generated this event. We first check this for the **redScroll** control. If this returns true, we read the current value of the control in the **nRed** variable:

```
if (e.getAdjustable() == redScroll) {
    redValue = redScroll.getValue();
}
```

Likewise, the program reads the current values of the remaining two scroll bar controls. Finally, the program repaints both canvases to reflect the current RGB values:

```
messageCanvas.repaint();
colorCanvas.repaint();
```

We will now discuss the custom canvas classes. Java provides a **Panel** class for placing components. Similarly, for drawing graphics, it provides a **Canvas** class. We create a custom class based on this **Canvas** class and provide the drawing functionality in its overridden **paint** method. Thus, our **MessageCanvas** class extends **Canvas**:

```
class MessageCanvas extends Canvas {
```

The class declares a variable of type **ColorPalette** that is our dialog frame class:

```
private ColorPalette frame;
```

When the frame instantiates the **MessageCanvas**, it passes its own reference (**this**) to the class constructor. The **MessageCanvas** class stores this in a local variable and then uses it later to access the members of the **ColorPalette** class:

```
MessageCanvas(ColorPalette frame) {
    this.frame = frame;
}
```

In the overridden **paint** method, we build the string by reading the current RGB values from the frame and then call the **drawString** method of the **Graphics** object to display it to the user:

```
public void paint(Graphics g) {
    strDisplay = "Red:" + String.valueOf(frame.getRedValue());
    strDisplay += "Green:" + String.valueOf(frame.getGreenValue());
    strDisplay += "Blue:" + String.valueOf(frame.getBlueValue());
    g.drawString(strDisplay, 10, 10);
}
```

The **ColorCanvas** class definition is similar to **MessageCanvas**, except for the implementation of its **paint** method. In the **paint** method, we fill the entire canvas area by obtaining its bounds, setting the fill color to the current RGB values taken from the frame, and calling the **fillRect** method of the **Graphics** object:

```
public void paint(Graphics g) {
    Rectangle rect = getBounds();
    g.setColor(new Color(frame.getRedValue(),
        frame.getGreenValue(),
        frame.getBlueValue()));
    g.fillRect(0, 0, rect.width, rect.height);
}
```

Now, compile and run the program. Click the right mouse button to view the popup menu. Select the Custom menu option. A dialog frame with three scroll bars appears. Change the scroll positions and observe the color change at the bottom of the frame. Now, click the applet and draw a line segment. The segment is drawn in the selected color. Try changing the color and draw more segments. Note that each line segment is drawn in the currently selected color.

Processing Keyboard Events

Finally, in this section, we discuss how to process keyboard events. For inputting text into your program, you will obviously prefer to use a **JTextField** control. However, if you want to type text directly on a drawing created in your application, you will need to process the keyboard events. To process the keyboard events, you need to implement the **KeyListener** interface. The **KeyListener** interface provides three callback methods. The **KeyPressed** method is invoked when the user presses a key. When the user releases a key, the **KeyReleased** method is called. When the user "types" a key (meaning presses and releases the key), the **KeyTyped** method is called.

In this section, you learn how to add a text caption at any desired point in your drawing. Rather than extending the code from Listing 15-6, which has already become quite bulky, I will demonstrate the technique by creating an independent application and leave the integration to you as an exercise. In our application, we will be able to input text at any location on the screen by clicking the mouse at that location. When the mouse is clicked, the cursor changes to text mode. As you type on the keyboard, the characters are displayed starting at the current location. To terminate the text entry, simply click the left button one more time. To input text at another location, follow the same procedure. The application remembers all previous text entries and displays them at their set locations.

Listing 15-7 shows the complete code for this application.

Listing 15-7 *Demonstrating Keyboard Processing*

```java
import java.awt.*;
import java.awt.event.*;
import java.util.*;
import javax.swing.JApplet;

public class KeyboardDemoApp extends JApplet {

    private Point pt = new Point(0, 0);
    private String strInput = "";
    private Boolean textMode = false;
    private ArrayList<Caption> captionList = new ArrayList<>();

    @Override
    public void init() {
        addMouseListener(new MouseAdapter() {

            @Override
            public void mouseClicked(MouseEvent e) {
                textMode = !textMode;
                if (textMode) {
                    requestFocus();
                    pt = new Point(e.getX(), e.getY());
                    setCursor(new Cursor(Cursor.TEXT_CURSOR));
                } else {
                    captionList.add(new Caption(pt, strInput));
                    setCursor(new Cursor(Cursor.DEFAULT_CURSOR));
                    strInput = "";
                }
            }
        });
```

```
        addKeyListener(new KeyAdapter() {

            @Override
            public void keyTyped(KeyEvent e) {
                strInput += e.getKeyChar();
                repaint();
            }
        });
    }

    @Override
    public void paint(Graphics g) {
        g.drawString(strInput, pt.x, pt.y);
        Iterator<Caption> it = captionList.iterator();
        while (it.hasNext()) {
            Caption caption = it.next();
            g.drawString(caption.getStrDisplay(),
                    caption.getPt().x,
                    caption.getPt().y);
        }
    }
}

class Caption {

    private Point pt;
    private String strDisplay = "";

    public Caption(Point pt, String strDisplay) {
        this.pt = pt;
        this.strDisplay = strDisplay;
    }

    public Point getPt() {
        return pt;
    }

    public String getStrDisplay() {
        return strDisplay;
    }
}
```

In the applet's **init** method, first we add a mouse listener by creating an instance of an anonymous class based on **MouseAdapter**:

```
addMouseListener(new MouseAdapter() {
```

In the overridden **mouseClicked** method, we toggle the state of the **textMode** variable:

```
textMode = !textMode;
```

When this variable is set to **true**, we are in the text input mode. In this mode, we record the coordinates of the clicked point and set the cursor to text mode:

```java
if (textMode) {
    requestFocus();
    pt = new Point(e.getX(), e.getY());
    setCursor(new Cursor(Cursor.TEXT_CURSOR));
```

On the second click, the **textMode** is set to **false**. This time, we record the input text and the point of display in the **Caption** object that is added to the **captionList** array:

```java
captionList.add(new Caption(pt, strInput));
```

The **Caption** class stores the caption text and the point at which this text is to be displayed. Next, we reset the cursor and nullify the string variable used for storing the input text:

```java
setCursor(new Cursor(Cursor.DEFAULT_CURSOR));
strInput = "";
```

Now comes the important point of this program—how to process keyboard input. Like in earlier programs, we use the adapter class to process keyboard events. In the **init** method, we add an instance of an anonymous **KeyAdapter** to the applet:

```java
addKeyListener(new KeyAdapter() {
```

The **KeyTyped** callback method receives the **KeyEvent** as its parameter:

```java
public void keyTyped(KeyEvent e) {
```

The **getKeyChar** method of the event object returns the Unicode corresponding to the key pressed by the user. We add this to the string variable and repaint the applet to display the string to the user:

```java
strInput += e.getKeyChar();
repaint();
```

In the applet initialization, we also call the **requestFocus** method to ensure that all keyboard inputs are sent to the applet when the applet is initially displayed to the user. Once an applet is running, the user may change the focus to some other application. When he returns to the applet, he will have to click the mouse on the applet surface to get the focus back on the applet. The keyboard input will then be sent to the applet.

The overridden **paint** method simply shows the constructed string at a specified fixed location by calling the **drawString** method of the **Graphics** class. It also iterates through the list of all previously entered captions and prints them on the screen:

```java
Iterator<Caption> it = captionList.iterator();
    while (it.hasNext()) {
        Caption caption = it.next();
        g.drawString(caption.getStrDisplay(),
            caption.getPt().x,
            caption.getPt().y);
    }
}
```

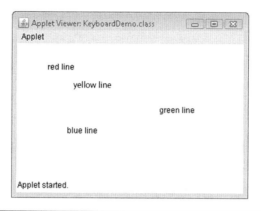

FIGURE 15-7. *Demonstrating keyboard input*

Some typical screen output is shown in Figure 15-7.

TIP
So far, you used an applet to draw some graphics on its surface.
However, an applet is a container and can therefore hold components
such as labels, text fields, list boxes, and so on. In other words, you
can build a complex GUI on the applet's surface. For building a GUI,
use the layout managers discussed in Chapter 14, create instances of
any desired components, and add them to the applet container.

Summary

In Java, you can create two types of client applications: stand-alone applications and applets. An applet is deployed on a remote server. A client downloads the applet code and runs it locally. Because applet code is always download from the server, applets have the latest updates, which eases maintenance tremendously. You create an applet by subclassing an **Applet** or **JApplet** class and overriding a few methods in it. During the life cycle of an applet, the **init**, **start**, **paint**, **stop**, and **destroy** methods are called. You override these methods to provide the desired application functionality in an applet. A GUI application may respond to mouse gestures. To process mouse clicks, Java provides the **MouseListener** interface, and to process mouse motion events, it provides the **MouseMotionListener** interface. An applet may require menus. You provide them via popup menus. Java provides a **Canvas** class that provides you with the surface for creating drawings. To process keyboard events, the **KeyListener** interface is provided.

In the next chapter, you will be learning one of the frequently used Java APIs—the **Collections** framework.

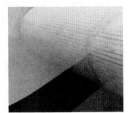

CHAPTER
16

Collections

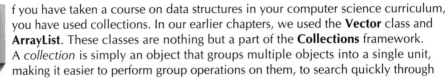 f you have taken a course on data structures in your computer science curriculum, you have used collections. In our earlier chapters, we used the **Vector** class and **ArrayList**. These classes are nothing but a part of the **Collections** framework. A *collection* is simply an object that groups multiple objects into a single unit, making it easier to perform group operations on them, to search quickly through thousands of sorted items, to insert and remove elements in the middle of an ordered sequence, and so on. Collections store and aggregate multiple data items so that they can be retrieved and manipulated with ease. In the earlier versions of Java (pre–J2SE 1.2) only the **Vector** and **Hashtable** classes were provided as part of Collections. The built-in **Array** class was used for creating arrays. Now, the Java platform provides a full-fledged Collections framework, which is a unified architecture for representing and manipulating various collections. You will learn to use the Collections framework in this chapter. In particular, you will learn the following:

- What the Collections framework is
- Interfaces defined in the Collections framework
- Various implementation classes of the framework
- Lists
- Sets
- Queues
- Maps
- Polymorphic algorithms

What Is the Java Collections Framework?

Many languages provide a collections framework, so it is very likely you have already used collections in other languages. For example, the Standard Template Library (STL) in C++ is a collections framework. Java introduced the Collections framework beginning in J2SE 1.2. Earlier to that it only had **Vector**, **Hashtable**, and built-in arrays. Each of these had different syntax and methods for accessing its members. Arrays use square brackets, **Vector** uses the **elementAt** method, and **Hashtable** uses **get** and **put** methods to access the members. Besides this, some of the methods in **Vector** are marked **final** and therefore cannot be inherited. Arrays have a fixed size, making it tricky to deal with those situations where the number of elements can dynamically vary at runtime.

What is desired is a standard interface for member access, a more powerful set of classes, and some built-in algorithms for sorting, searching, and so on. This is now achieved through the Collections framework. The Java Collections framework is not restricted to the aforementioned preexisting classes but rather contains much more—namely, interfaces, implementations, and algorithms.

The **Hashtable** and **Vector** classes have now been updated to implement the Collection interfaces. Many new collection implementations have been added, including **HashSet** and **TreeSet**, **ArrayList** and **LinkedList**, and **HashMap** and **TreeMap**. Each of these provides a unique advantage over the others. For example, **TreeSet** and **TreeMap** implicitly support ordering, making it lot easier to maintain a sorted list with no effort. Finding the smallest and largest element in a sorted list is very easy. You may sort the elements based on their natural sort order or provide your own comparator for sorting. Also, searching is made easier with the implementation of a binary search algorithm. The ordered insertion in collections usually results in a performance penalty, and in certain situations you may not need to order the collection elements. For example, in the previous chapter, we used **ArrayList** to maintain a list of graphics objects, where the ordering was not at all important. In some situations, you may want to maintain a key/value pair like the one in a word dictionary. For this, you would use **HashMap**. Thus, the Collections framework provides you with several types of collections to meet your current needs. Each type has a unique purpose, as you will learn as you read on.

Benefits of the Collections Framework

One of the biggest benefits that comes out of using the Collections framework is the set of standard interfaces it provides. Whether you are working on a **Set**, **List**, or **Map**, the interface remains the same. All the classes in the framework conform to a common API and thus become more regular and easily understood. The application type does not matter, and the user sees the same interface, whether he is developing a chat application, working on a SQL database, or creating a graphics editor like the one in Chapter 15. The standard interfaces make it easier to pass collection objects between methods as parameters or return values. Thus, a method can work on a wider variety of collections. All the collection classes have a common implementation that makes your code shorter and quicker to download. Also, any changes to this core implementation to enhance performance or add features are immediately available to your program code.

Earlier collections classes used **Enumeration** to traverse their elements. The Collections framework, on the other hand, introduced **Iterator**, which allows for element operations such as insertion and deletion. The **Iterator** is fail-fast, ensuring that you get an exception if the list you are iterating is modified by another user. Also, iterators such as **ListIterator** that operate on a list-based collection such as **Vector** allow bidirectional iteration and updating. As mentioned earlier, some of the collections allow you to maintain a sorted collection of objects, making it easy to find the first and the last based on a certain sort order and to perform quick searches.

The Collections framework also provides a static class called Collections that provides read-only and synchronized versions of existing collections. The read-only collections protect you from accidental changes to collection items, and synchronized versions are useful in developing multithreaded applications. You create a read-only set by calling the **unmodifiableSet** static method of the Collections class. You learn about the use of synchronized collection classes in thread programming later in the chapter.

What the Collections Framework Offers

The Java Collections framework consists of interfaces, implementations, and algorithms:

- **Interfaces**   Just like the Java interfaces you studied in the earlier chapters, these interfaces provide a uniform interface to the collections independent of the objects they represent. The various collection classes implement a common interface. The interface hierarchy is designed to account for the different types of data structures, such as lists, sets, queues, and maps.

- **Implementations**   These are concrete implementations for the various types of data structures, such as lists, sets, queues, and maps.

■ **Algorithms** These provide useful methods for performing common operations such as sorting and searching that are applied polymorphically to collections regardless of the object types they store.

In this chapter, you learn about all three of these aspects of the **Collections** framework.

The Collections Framework Interfaces

The interface hierarchy consists of two distinct trees. **List**, **Set**, and **Queue** fall under the **Iterable** tree. **Map** is somewhat different from these collections and therefore falls under a different tree all its own. Besides these, you have the **Iterator** interface that allows you to iterate through the elements of a collection. Finally, the **RandomAccess** interface is a marker to indicate that the implementing data structure class provides fast random access to its data. The interface hierarchy defined in the Collections framework is depicted in Figure 16-1.

List is an ordered collection that can contain duplicates. In a list, when you insert an element, you have control over where the element is inserted; therefore, you are able to retrieve an element by knowing its index. A **Vector** (which we used in previous chapters) falls under this category.

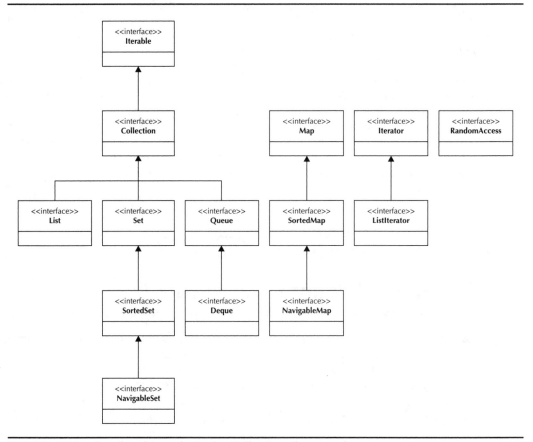

FIGURE 16-1. *Interface hierarchy in the Collections framework*

Set is a collection that cannot contain duplicate elements. More precisely, a set cannot contain a pair of elements, **e1** and **e2**, such that **e1.equals(e2)** is true. Also, it can contain at most one **null** element. This models the mathematical set abstraction. As an example, you could use a set to create a timetable of departing trains from a particular train station or to create a schedule of courses offered at the sophomore level. The **SortedSet** and **NavigableSet** interfaces extend the functionality defined by **Set**.

SortedSet is a set that provides a total ordering of its elements. It is used for naturally ordered sets and exposes the comparator object used for sorting. This interface provides methods to obtain subset views of the collection and the iterator that traverses the set in ascending element order. For ease of searching and traversal in such sorted sets, the **NavigableSet** interface was introduced in Java SE 6. Given a set of ordered numbers such as [..., 10, 15, 20, 35, 50, ...] you can easily determine the element greater than or less than 20 in a single method call of this interface. Methods such as **lower**, **higher**, **floor**, and **ceiling** are provided for this purpose. You can also use the **headSet** and **tailSet** methods to get a head or tail subset with respect to any element in the sorted set. **ConcurrentSkipListSet** and **TreeSet** are the two implementing classes for this interface.

Queue is a collection of multiple objects that you would like to insert into a collection before processing them. Just like in real life, we first form a queue of objects and then process them, maybe on a FIFO (first in, first out) basis. The interface provides methods for inserting, extracting, and inspecting elements; it is not necessary to extract elements in FIFO order. The interface provides a means of ordering elements as per their natural ordering or a supplied comparator.

Deque represents a double-ended queue, meaning that you are allowed to add and remove elements at both ends. The implementation can be used for LIFO (last in, first out) order, as in the case of a **Stack**, or FIFO order, as in the case of a **Queue**. The **Deque** provides methods to insert, remove, and examine the element. Each of these methods exists in two forms—one that throws an exception and the other that returns a **null** or **false** value, depending on the operation. For **Deque** implementations having capacity restrictions, the latter form is used. For example, the **offerFirst** method inserts the element specified in the method parameter at the front of the deque. If the insertion fails due to capacity restriction, a **false** value is returned. This is probably better than having an exception generated when you use the corresponding **addFirst** method.

BlockingDeque is a sub-interface of **Deque** that supports blocking operations during an insert or retrieval. Removing an element operation would block for the deque to become non-empty (if the deque is empty, the remove operation blocks until somebody inserts an element in it), and similarly inserting an element operation waits (blocks) for the space to become available in the deque. It supports four forms of methods:

- Methods that throw exceptions
- Methods that time out
- Methods that block (wait indefinitely)
- Methods that return a special value

Map provides a collection of key/value pairs. This is useful in creating dictionaries and such, where the objects are accessed using their keys. For example, a database of employee objects may be accessed using the employee IDs. Therefore, the ID in this case becomes the key, and the employee record becomes the value associated with the key. Just the way you have sorted and navigable sets, you have interfaces for creating sorted maps and navigating them using a tree-like structure. **SortedMap** provides a total ordering on its keys. The ordering is based on either the natural ordering of its keys or on a provided comparator. Along with the **NavigableSet** you saw earlier, Java SE 6 introduced the **NavigableMap** interface to provide similar navigational methods on a map that return the closest matches for given search targets. Methods such as **headMap** and **tailMap** are similar to **headSet** and **tailSet**, which you saw earlier for sets. In the case of **NavigableSet**, the methods typically returned a single value; in the case of **NavigableMap**, they return the key/value pair.

The **Iterator** interface provides methods for iterating through the elements of a collection. Finally, as mentioned earlier, **RandomAccess** is a marker interface that indicates that the implementing **List** class supports fast random access.

In summary, we say that the Collection interface is a group of objects. **Set** extends Collection but forbids duplicates. **List** extends Collection and also allows duplicates and introduces positional indexing. **Map** extends neither **Set** nor Collection. You can easily see from this discussion the amount of variety you have in creating different collections of objects, depending on your needs.

The Collections Framework Classes

The class diagram in Figure 16-2 shows the various classes you have for working with different kinds of collections. We will now discuss the four types of data structures individually—list, set, queue, and map—illustrated in this figure, along with code examples.

List

As stated earlier, the **List** data structure defines an ordered collection of elements. The user can precisely control the position where a new element is inserted in the list. To retrieve elements from the list, the user can use the index, which is the position in the list. Lists allow duplicates, meaning

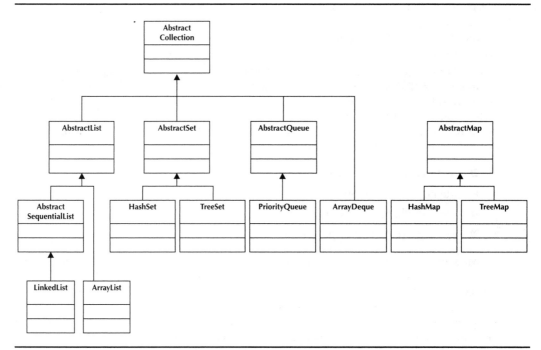

FIGURE 16-2. *Implementation classes in the Collections framework*

that a pair of elements, **e1** and **e2**, such that **e1.equals(e2)**, is allowed. Also, you can have multiple **null** elements, provided a **null** element is permitted in the first place (some implementations prohibit them). Note that sets do not allow such duplicates. A special iterator, called **ListIterator**, defined in this interface, besides its typical operations, allows element insertion and replacement as well as bidirectional access. The interface defines an **indexOf** method that takes an **Object** argument and, after searching the list, returns the index of the object, if found. The **get** method accepts an index as its argument and returns the element at the specified position. Such searches should be used with caution because many implementations perform costly linear searches. The interface also provides methods to efficiently insert and remove multiple elements at an arbitrary point in the list.

Java libraries define several implementations of this interface—a few examples are **ArrayList**, **LinkedList**, **Stack**, and **Vector**. We will now consider the use of the **List** interface through a code example based on the **LinkedList** implementation. The **LinkedList** class allows duplicate elements. A simple example of a list might be maintaining the names of players on a soccer team. The team can have two players with the same name (in some cases you might use a prefix such as Jr. to distinguish between the two). We will now write a program to create and manipulate a list of players. We will create two teams—one for men and the other for women. After adding five members to each team, we will print out the teams. We will then merge the two teams to create a mixed team. Later on, we will disqualify a few members and remove them from the mixed team. All this will certainly expose you to the various methods of the **List** interface. The program is given in Listing 16-1.

Listing 16-1   *Soccer Team Builder Based on the LinkedList Data Structure*

```java
import java.util.*;

public class SoccerTeam {

    public static void main(String[] args) {
        List<String> maleTeam = new LinkedList<>();
        maleTeam.add("John");
        maleTeam.add("Tom");
        maleTeam.add("Sam");
        maleTeam.add("Vijay");
        maleTeam.add("Anthony");
        System.out.println("Male Team: " + maleTeam);
        List<String> femaleTeam = new LinkedList<>();
        femaleTeam.add("Catherine");
        femaleTeam.add("Mary");
        femaleTeam.add("Shilpa");
        femaleTeam.add("Jane");
        femaleTeam.add("Anita");
        System.out.println("Female Team: " + femaleTeam);
        ListIterator<String> maleListIterator =
                maleTeam.listIterator();
        Iterator<String> femaleListIterator = femaleTeam.iterator();

        while (femaleListIterator.hasNext()) {
            if (maleListIterator.hasNext()) {
                maleListIterator.next();
```

```
        }
        maleListIterator.add(femaleListIterator.next());
    }
    System.out.println("Mixed Team: " + maleTeam);
    List<String> disqualify = new LinkedList<>();
    disqualify.add("Sam");
    disqualify.add("Tom");
    disqualify.add("Shilpa");
    maleTeam.removeAll(disqualify);
    System.out.println("Qualified Team: " + maleTeam);
}
}
```

In the **main** method, we first create the list with the following declaration:

```
List<String> maleTeam = new LinkedList<>();
```

Note that the collection classes now use generics. Therefore, we specify the type of object our list is going to hold in angular brackets. The **maleTeam** is the list that holds **String**-type elements. The instance of the **LinkedList** class is assigned to a **List**-type variable, which is a super-interface of the **LinkedList** class. After creating a list, we add a few items to it by calling the **List**'s **add** method:

```
maleTeam.add("John");
maleTeam.add("Tom");
...
```

To print the list of created members, we use our regular SOP (**System.out.println**) method:

```
System.out.println("Male Team: " + maleTeam);
```

Likewise, we create a list of female team members called **femaleTeam** and add a few members of the **String** type to it. We'll now merge the two teams. While merging the teams, we will mix the members of the two teams in an alternating fashion, adding the female players to the team of male players. Therefore, the mixed team will be stored in the **maleTeam** list. For this, we create two iterators:

```
ListIterator<String> maleListIterator = maleTeam.listIterator();
Iterator<String> femaleListIterator = femaleTeam.iterator();
```

Both iterator classes use generics; therefore, we need to provide the appropriate data type while creating them. The **ListIterator** class provides an **add** method that allows for the insertion of an object in the list. The **Iterator** class does not allow the insertion; it allows only the removal of an element. Thus, the **maleListIterator** is of type **ListIterator**, and the **femaleListIterator** is of type **Iterator**. After creating iterators, we define the following loop to copy the elements of the female team into the male team in alternating positions:

```
while (femaleListIterator.hasNext()) {
    if (maleListIterator.hasNext()) {
        maleListIterator.next();
    }
    maleListIterator.add(femaleListIterator.next());
}
```

The **hasNext** method returns **null** on encountering the end-of-list, and the **next** method returns the object from the list and advances the pointer in the list. After the **while** loop completes its execution, the mixed team is available in the **maleTeam** list, which we print to the terminal:

```
System.out.println("Mixed Team: " + maleTeam);
```

Now, to define a list of disqualified members, we create another list called **disqualify** and add the desired members to it:

```
List<String> disqualify = new LinkedList<>();
disqualify.add("Sam");
disqualify.add("Tom");
disqualify.add("Shilpa");
```

To remove the disqualified members from the mixed team, we use the **removeAll** method and pass the list of disqualified members to it as a parameter:

```
MaleTeam.removeAll(disqualify);
```

We then print the modified team for verification:

```
System.out.println("Qualified Team: " + maleTeam);
```

When you run the program, you will see the following output:

```
Male Team: [John, Tom, Sam, Vijay, Anthony]
Female Team: [Catherine, Mary, Shilpa, Jane, Anita]
Mixed Team: [John, Catherine, Tom, Mary, Sam, Shilpa, Vijay, Jane, Anthony, Anita]
Qualified Team: [John, Catherine, Mary, Vijay, Jane, Anthony, Anita]
```

From this simple example, you can see how easy it is to create and manipulate a list of objects using the **List** interface.

Optional Operations of the List Interface

The methods we used in Listing 16-1 were the mandatory implementations for an implementing class. The **List** interface also defines several methods that are optional in the sense that implementing classes need not use them, but must throw a runtime exception if they are not supported.

The interface defines four overloaded **add** methods and three overloaded **remove** methods that obviously take different sets of parameters. The **clear** method removes all the elements from the list. The **set** method takes two arguments—the index and the element—and replaces the element at the specified position in the list with the specified element. The **retainAll** method takes a Collection as an argument and retains only the elements in the list that are contained in the specified collection. We will now discuss a few implementations using some or all of these optional methods so that you get a feel for the various implementing classes of the **List** interface.

The **ArrayList** class used in the previous chapter is a resizable-array implementation of the **List** interface that implements all the aforementioned optional operations. One of the benefits of using this class is that the **size**, **isEmpty**, **get**, **set**, **iterator**, and **listIterator** operations run in constant time. The **add** operation runs in amortized constant time; adding n elements requires $O(n)$ time. The constant factor here is low compared to the corresponding **LinkedList** implementation. All other operations roughly run in linear time. Each instance of **ArrayList** has a capacity, which defines the size of the array used to store the elements in the list. This capacity grows dynamically as you add more elements to the list. Before adding a large number of elements, use the **ensureCapacity** operation to possibly reduce the amount of incremental allocation. This class is somewhat equivalent to the **java.util.Vector** class we used earlier, except that it is unsynchronized.

The **CopyOnWriteArrayList** defined in the **java.util.concurrent** package provides a thread-safe variant of **ArrayList**. In this class, all mutative operations, such as **add**, **set**, and so on, are implemented by creating a fresh copy of the underlying array, making it generally costly to use. Ordinarily, when you have more traversal operations than mutations, this implementation is preferred over synchronizing traversals yourself. This class permits **null**.

The **Vector** is another implementation of the **List** interface. It implements a "growable" array of objects. The size grows or shrinks as needed. Storage management can be optimized by using the **capacity** and **ensureCapacity** operations and the **capacityIncrement** field. The major benefit of using this class lies in the fact that the iterators returned by the **iterator** and **listIterator** methods are fail-fast. Concurrent external modifications to **Vector**'s structure result in the iterator throwing a **ConcurrentModificationException**. The iterator fails quickly and cleanly, saving you from encountering nondeterministic behavior in the future. Unlike the **LinkedList** and **ArrayList** from earlier, the **Vector** is synchronized.

The **Stack** is yet another implementation of the **List** interface. The **Stack** extends the **Vector**. Conventionally, it represents a LIFO stack of objects. When you create a **Stack** object, it contains no elements. The **Stack** class has existed since JDK 1.0. For a more complete and consistent set of LIFO operations, you should use the implementations of the **Deque** interface, discussed later in this chapter.

Having studied the various implementations of the **List** interface, we will now move ahead to study the **Set** data structure.

Set

The **Set** interface represents a collection that does not permit duplicate elements. The definition of duplicates in terms of the object identity remains the same as described previously. Due to this restriction, the interface places additional stipulations on its constructors and the **add**, **equals**, and **hashCode** methods. This interface models the mathematical set abstraction. **HashSet**, **LinkedHashSet**, **TreeSet**, **EnumSet**, and **CopyOnWriteArraySet** are some of the concrete implementations of this interface. We will discuss just two implementations: **HashSet** and **TreeSet**. Refer to javadocs for details about the other implementations.

HashSet

The **HashSet** implementation is backed by a hash table (a **HashMap** instance) and does not permit **null**. This class offers constant-time performance for basic operations such as **add**, **remove**, **contains**, and **size**, assuming the hash function disperses the elements properly among the buckets. The iteration time depends largely on the number of elements and the number of buckets in the backing **HashMap** instance; do not set the initial capacity too high and the load factor too low if iteration performance is important.

The implementation does not guarantee the iteration order. As a matter of fact, it does not even guarantee that the iteration order will remain constant over time.

This class is not synchronized. You can provide an external synchronization by wrapping the set as illustrated here:

```
Set s = Collections.synchronizedSet(new HashSet(5000, 0.75f));
```

The iterators are fail-fast, as described earlier for the **Vector**.

To illustrate the use of this class, let's look at a concrete example. Suppose we have been asked to write a program that accepts election voter names from the user. We will store these names in a set, with no duplicates allowed. In the case of a long list of names, the user might unknowingly enter the same name twice. This program should therefore ensure that the resultant set contains only distinct names and all duplicates are rejected without warning to the user. The program that does all this is given in Listing 16-2.

Listing 16-2 *Building a Set of Distinct Words Using the HashSet Class*

```java
import java.util.*;

public class DistinctWordSet {

    public static void main(String[] args) {
        int count = 0;
        Set<String> words = new HashSet<>();
        Scanner in = new Scanner(System.in);
        String str;
        while (!(str = in.nextLine()).equals("")) {
            count++;
            words.add(str);
        }
        System.out.println(". . .");
        System.out.println("Total number of words entered: " + count);
        System.out.println("Distinct words: " + words.size());
        System.out.println(". . .");
        Iterator<String> iterator = words.iterator();
        while (iterator.hasNext()) {
            System.out.println(iterator.next());
        }
    }
}
```

In the **main** method, we create an instance of **HashSet** that stores **String**-type objects:

```java
Set<String> words = new HashSet<>();
```

Next, we read the names from the user. We use the **Scanner** class (introduced in J2SE 5.0) to read input from the keyboard. The parameter to the class constructor is **System.in**, which is the default keyboard input:

```java
Scanner in = new Scanner(System.in);
```

We read multiple names from the user until he inputs a "blank" name:

```java
while (!(str = in.nextLine()).equals("")) {
```

The **nextLine** method of the **Scanner** class returns a **String**. As long as this string does not equal a blank string, we keep on asking for a new name from the user. We add the input string to the **Set** we created earlier:

```java
words.add(str);
```

In case of a duplicate entry, the **add** method simply refuses to add it to the set. After the **while** loop terminates, the set contains only the distinct words. We print both the total number of input words and the number of distinct words to the terminal:

```
System.out.println("Total number of words entered: " + count);
System.out.println("Distinct words: " + words.size());
```

We also print the contents of the created set to the terminal for verification by creating and using an iterator:

```
Iterator<String> iterator = words.iterator();
while (iterator.hasNext()) {
    System.out.println(iterator.next());
}
```

Sample output from the program is shown here:

```
John
Jack
Sam
Anthony
Jack
Bill

. . .
Total words: 6
Distinct words: 5
. . .
Bill
Jack
Anthony
Sam
John
```

Note that the user has entered a total of six names, out of which five are unique. The name Jack has been entered twice. The final list contains only one occurrence of Jack.

TreeSet

TreeSet uses a tree for storage. Objects are stored in sorted, ascending order. The elements are ordered using their natural ordering or by a comparator provided at the set creation time. Therefore, when you iterate over the set elements, the order of elements is constant. By passing the comparator object to the constructor, you can set a different ordering than the natural ordering of the elements. You create a comparator object by instantiating a built-in **Comparator** class. You will need to define your own comparison in its **compare** method. The operations, such as **add**, **remove**, and **contains**, are guaranteed to perform in log(n) time, making this a better choice over **ArrayList** for fast retrievals from large amounts of sorted information. Like **HashSet**, this class, too, is not synchronized.

To illustrate this class, let's look at a concrete example. Suppose we have to create a team of players. We will store this list of players in a **TreeSet**. For each player, we store his name and age.

We will create a **Player** class for storing this information. We will define the default ordering based on the players' age. Later on, we will create another sorted list based on the existing list that sorts the elements of the list by player name. You will understand how easy it is to sort the team on different fields when you use this class. The program is given in Listing 16-3.

Listing 16-3   *Building a Sortable Team Based on TreeSet*

```java
import java.util.*;

public class SortableTeam {

    public static void main(String[] args) {
        SortedSet<Player> ageSortedTeam = new TreeSet<>();
        ageSortedTeam.add(new Player("John", 21));
        ageSortedTeam.add(new Player("Sam", 20));
        ageSortedTeam.add(new Player("Anthony", 18));
        ageSortedTeam.add(new Player("Bill", 19));
        ageSortedTeam.add(new Player("Jack", 22));
        System.out.println("Team - by age");
        printSet(ageSortedTeam);
        System.out.println("------------------");
        SortedSet<Player> nameSortedTeam =
                new TreeSet<>(new Comparator<Player>() {

            public int compare(Player a, Player b) {
                return a.getName().compareTo(b.getName());
            }
        });
        nameSortedTeam.addAll(ageSortedTeam);
        System.out.println("Team - alphabetical");
        printSet(nameSortedTeam);
        System.out.println("------------------");
    }

    static void printSet(Set set) {
        Iterator iterator = set.iterator();
        while (iterator.hasNext()) {
            Player player = (Player) iterator.next();
            System.out.println(player.getName() + " - Age:"
                    + player.getAge());
        }
    }

    private static class Player implements Comparable<Player> {

        private String name;
        private int age;
```

```
        public Player(String name, int age) {
            this.name = name;
            this.age = age;
        }

        public int getAge() {
            return age;
        }

        public String getName() {
            return this.name;
        }

        public int compareTo(Player other) {
            return age - other.age;
        }
    }
}
```

Let's first look at the **Player** class. We will store the instances of this class in the team we create in the main application:

```
private static class Player implements Comparable<Player> {
```

The class is declared **private** and defined as an inner class to the **SortableTeam** class. Because we will not use the **Player** class outside this sample application, we declare it **private** so as to shield its definition from other classes in the application.

The **Player** class implements the **Comparable** interface that operates on the **Player** data type. As part of the **Comparable** interface implementation, we need to implement the **compareTo** method:

```
public int compareTo(Player other) {
    return age - other.age;
}
```

The **compareTo** method returns the difference between the age of the current object and the age of the received object. This defines the default ordering while inserting the objects of the **Player** type in the tree. Besides this **compareTo** method, the class defines the conventional constructor that takes two parameters and initializes the object's state. We also create two getter methods to retrieve the **age** and **name** fields. Now, let's look at the main application.

In the **main** method, we create an instance of **TreeSet** that operates on a **Player** data type:

```
SortedSet<Player> ageSortedTeam = new TreeSet<>();
```

We add a few elements to the **ageSortedTeam**:

```
ageSortedTeam.add(new Player("John", 21));
ageSortedTeam.add(new Player("Sam", 20));
    ...
```

Note that when the elements are inserted, they will be ordered based on the comparator provided in the class definition; they will be arranged in the ascending order of each player's age. To verify this, we print the set by calling the **printSet** method, which is discussed later:

```
printSet(ageSortedTeam);
```

Now, we create another list that is sorted alphabetically by player name. To do this, we create another instance of the **TreeSet** class:

```
SortedSet<Player> nameSortedTeam =
            new TreeSet<Player>(new Comparator<Player>() {
```

To the constructor, we pass an instance of **Comparator** (remember the use of anonymous classes from previous chapters). The **compare** method receives two parameters of the **Player** type:

```
public int compare(Player a, Player b) {
```

We obtain the players' names from the two received objects by calling the getter method. The **compareTo** method compares two strings and returns their alphabetical ordering:

```
return a.getName().compareTo(b.getName());
```

After we have constructed the ordered set with a new ordering method defined, we need to add elements to it. We do this by calling the **addAll** method:

```
nameSortedTeam.addAll(ageSortedTeam);
```

The **addAll** method takes a parameter, which is an existing set of players. All the elements of the **ageSortedTeam** will now be added to the new set; however, during insertion, the new ordering mechanism is used. We verify this ordering by printing the list to the terminal:

```
System.out.println("Team - alphabetical");
printSet(nameSortedTeam);
```

Finally, we discuss the implementation of the **printSet** method. This is a **static** method of the class that accepts a **Set**-type parameter:

```
static void printSet(Set set) {
```

In the method body, we first create an iterator:

```
Iterator iterator = set.iterator();
```

We iterate through all the elements of the set by calling the **hasNext** method:

```
while (iterator.hasNext()) {
```

The **next** method retrieves the object from the set. We typecast this to the **Player** type:

```
Player player = (Player) iterator.next();
```

We get the name and the age attributes of the **Player** object and print them to the terminal:

```
System.out.println(player.getName() + " - Age:" + player.getAge());
```

When we run the program, we see the following output:

```
Team - by age
Anthony - Age:18
Bill - Age:19
Sam - Age:20
John - Age:21
Jack - Age:22
------------------
Team - alphabetical
Anthony - Age:18
Bill - Age:19
Jack - Age:22
John - Age:21
Sam - Age:20
------------------
```

Note that the first list is arranged by the players' age, whereas the second one is arranged alphabetically by the players' name.

TIP
*Here are some pointers for deciding between using **Set** and **List**.*
*A **TreeSet** consumes a little bit more memory than an **ArrayList**. This*
*is because a **TreeSet** uses a tree data structure to store its information,*
where each node in the tree is an object that keeps pointers to its
parent, the left branch, the right branch, the element, and more.
*In comparison, an **ArrayList** is a simple array with the elements.*
*Also, inserting an element in a **TreeSet** is faster than the insertion in*
***ArrayList**. This is because when you insert an element in an arbitrary*
*position in an **ArrayList**, on average half the list will have to be shifted*
by one position. This takes O(n) time, which means inserting into a list
containing 1,000,000 elements will take 1,000 times as long as the
time taken to insert into a list of 1,000 elements. On the other hand,
*a **TreeSet** needs to traverse the depth of the tree, which takes O(log(n))*
time. Therefore, if the set contains 1,000,000 elements, it takes only
twice as long as when the set contains 1,000 elements.

We'll now move on to the next type of data structure—a queue.

Queue

A *queue* is a collection that is designed for holding elements prior to processing. Queues typically order elements in FIFO order, although this is not always true. The **PriorityQueue** implementation, described next, orders elements based on their natural ordering or according to the supplied comparator. Besides basic operations, **Queue** provides additional methods for insertion, extraction, and inspection. To insert an element, you use the **offer** method instead of the typical **add** method.

To remove an element, you use **poll** instead of the typical **remove**, and to inspect you use **peek** instead of the regular **element** method. The **offer**, **poll**, and **peek** methods return a special value instead of throwing an exception in case of failure. The **Queue** interface does not define blocking methods; however, the **BlockingQueue** interface that extends the **Queue** interface blocks on an element to appear or for the space to become available. The **Queue** implementation generally does not allow **null** insertion; the exception is the **LinkedList** implementation. You should generally avoid the insertion of **null** because it is also used as a special return value by the **poll** method.

Java libraries provide several implementations of the **Queue** interface—a few examples are **PriorityQueue**, **PriorityBlockingQueue**, **LinkedList**, and **ArrayDeque**. Refer to the javadocs for a detailed study of the different implementations. In this section, we discuss just one implementation: **PriorityQueue**.

The **PriorityQueue** class represents an unbounded priority queue based on a priority heap. The elements are ordered according to their natural ordering or by a comparator provided at the queue construction time. A sorted order is always permanently imposed on the elements it contains. The highest-priority element is at the head of the queue, and the lowest is at its tail. Removing the highest-priority element and adding a new element operation are both efficient. Searching for an element that is not at the head of the queue is usually inefficient.

You would typically use priority queues in situations where you want to add elements in any order but retrieve them in sorted order, and where you do not necessarily retrieve the elements all at once. A typical application of this is building a Huffman compression tree, where you need to sort something gradually, occasionally peeking at the topmost element, altering it, and placing it back into the tree. Other typical applications might be performing a heapsort and creating a job scheduler.

An example where a priority queue might be useful is in the allocation of the CPU to waiting threads. Generally, several processes running on the system create threads that are posted in a queue for execution. The threads have different priorities. The operating system executes all threads with the highest priority first, followed by the threads at the next priority level, and so on. We will now write a program that does this allocation of CPU time. In this example, the thread priorities range from 0 to 9, with 0 being the highest priority and 9 being the lowest.

CAUTION
Generally, for thread priorities, 0 is the lowest priority and 9 (or whatever is the highest level) is considered the highest priority. We use the reverse order in this example because this is the natural ordering for integers. To change to descending ordering, you need to provide your comparator, which is discussed in later examples in this chapter.

We assume that the processes will create threads and put them in a queue for execution. The size of this queue is 100. Therefore, at any moment, we may have up to 100 threads for allocation. We will rearrange all these threads based on their priorities in a priority queue. We will then simply allocate the CPU cycles by picking the element at the top of the queue, one after another. For all threads having the same priority level, we do not further distinguish between them on the basis of their time of creation. Therefore, it's possible for a thread created later than another thread (both with the same priority) to get the CPU earlier than the other one.

The program that does this allocation is given in Listing 16-4.

Listing 16-4   *Building a Thread Scheduler Using the PriorityQueue Class*

```java
import java.util.*;

public class ThreadScheduler {

    public static void main(String[] args) {
        List<Integer> list = new ArrayList<>();
        for (int i = 0; i < 100; i++) {
            list.add((int) (Math.random() * 10));
        }
        PriorityQueue<Integer> threadQueue = new PriorityQueue<>();
        threadQueue.addAll(list);
        System.out.println("Waiting threads...");
        for (Integer thread : threadQueue) {
            System.out.print(thread + ",");
        }
        System.out.println("\nDeploying threads...");
        while (!threadQueue.isEmpty()) {
            System.out.print(threadQueue.remove() + ",");
        }
    }
}
```

In the **main** function, we first declare an array to store the waiting threads:

```java
List<Integer> list = new ArrayList<>();
```

We create 100 threads with a random priority in the range of 0 to 9 assigned to each one:

```java
for (int i = 0; i < 100; i++) {
    list.add((int) (Math.random() * 10));
}
```

Next, we create a **PriorityQueue** class instance that operates on the **Integer** data type:

```java
PriorityQueue<Integer> threadQueue = new PriorityQueue<>();
```

We fill this queue with the elements of our thread list by calling the **addAll** method:

```java
threadQueue.addAll(arrayList);
```

We now print the list of all waiting threads:

```java
System.out.println("Waiting threads...");
for (Integer thread : threadQueue) {
    System.out.print(thread + ",");
}
```

To allocate the CPU, we remove the thread from the top of the queue and print its priority level to the user terminal:

```
System.out.println("\nDeploying threads...");
while (!threadQueue.isEmpty()) {
    System.out.print(threadQueue.remove() + ",");
}
```

When we run the program, we see output similar to the following:

```
Waiting threads...


0,0,0,0,0,1,3,2,1,0,0,1,4,3,4,2,2,1,2,1,2,1,0,2,3,6,6,5,7,7,6,6,3,4,4,2,4,2,
2,4,2,3,3,2,5,4,3,6,3,5,6,7,7,7,8,9,8,9,9,9,8,9,8,9,8,6,3,8,6,5,7,7,4,8,7,5,
3,3,7,9,8,5,3,7,4,7,8,9,2,8,7,9,8,9,7,9,7,6,3,6,


Deploying threads...


0,0,0,0,0,0,0,0,1,1,1,1,1,1,2,2,2,2,2,2,2,2,2,2,2,2,3,3,3,3,3,3,3,3,3,3,3,3,
3,4,4,4,4,4,4,4,4,4,5,5,5,5,5,6,6,6,6,6,6,6,6,6,6,7,7,7,7,7,7,7,7,7,7,7,7,
7,7,8,8,8,8,8,8,8,8,8,8,9,9,9,9,9,9,9,9,9,9,
```

Note that the threads are deployed strictly according to their priorities, and until the threads with higher priorities finish, threads at lower priorities starve.

Map

A **Map** represents an object that maps keys to values. It cannot contain duplicate keys; each key can map to at most one value. This is typically used in building word dictionary applications. Java libraries define several implementations of the **Map** interface. We just discuss one implementation in this section: **HashMap**. As usual, refer to javadocs for information on the other implementations. The **HashMap** permits the use of **null** values and keys. The **HashMap** does not make any guarantee that the retrieval order will remain constant over time. It provides constant-time performance for basic operations such as **get** and **put**, assuming that the hash function disperses the elements properly among the buckets. To have the **HashMap** work efficiently, we use its two parameters—initial capacity and load factor. The load factor controls when the capacity should be increased. Note that **HashMap** stores only object references; if you want to store primitive data types, use wrapper classes. This class is not synchronized. For synchronized access, use **java.util.Hashtable** instead. You will learn the pros and cons of using synchronized access in Chapter 17.

We will now discuss the use of the **HashMap** class through a concrete example. Suppose we are building a word list typically used by students taking the Graduate Record Examination (GRE), where for each word we want to store its type, synonym, and antonym. The list should be searchable by a keyword. After the search, the aforementioned three attributes of the word should be displayed. This user of the program should be able to modify any of the entries as well as print the entire word list on demand. The program in Listing 16-5 does all this.

Listing 16-5 *Building a GRE Word List Using HashMap*

```java
import java.util.*;

public class GREWordList {

    static Map<String, Word> wordList = new HashMap<>();

    public static void main(String[] args) {
        wordList.put("Abate", new Word("verb", "subside",
                "alienate,increase,extend,amplify,continue,enlarge"));
        wordList.put("Abeyance", new Word("noun",
                "suspended action", "continuance"));
        wordList.put("Abscond", new Word("verb",
                "depart secretly and hide",
                "appear,emerge, show,stay,remain"));
        wordList.put("Abstemious", new Word("adj",
                "sparing in eating and drinking",
                "intemperate,glutonous"));
        wordList.put("Admonish", new Word("verb", "warn, reprove",
                "acclaim,commend,praise,compliment,countenance"));
        printList();
        // Look up a value
        System.out.println("\nValue for abscond " + wordList.get("Abscond"));
        // Modify an entry
        wordList.put("Abate", new Word("verb", "subside,moderate",
                "alienate,increase,extend,amplify,continue,enlarge"));
        // Remove entry
        wordList.remove("Abstemious");
        System.out.print("\nAfter modifications:");
        printList();
    }

    static private void printList() {
        System.out.println("\nAll Entries:");
        for (Map.Entry<String, Word> entry : wordList.entrySet()) {
            String key = entry.getKey();
            Word value = entry.getValue();
            System.out.println("key=" + key + ", value=" + value);
        }
    }

    private static class Word {

        private String type;
        private String synonym;
        private String antonym;

        public String getAntonym() {
            return antonym;
        }
```

```
        public String getSynonym() {
            return synonym;
        }

        public String getType() {
            return type;
        }

        public Word(String type, String synonym, String antonym) {
            this.type = type;
            this.synonym = synonym;
            this.antonym = antonym;
        }

        @Override
        public String toString() {
            return "[" + type + "; " + synonym + "; " + antonym + "]";
        }
    }
}
```

In the declaration, we first create an instance of the **HashMap** class:

```
static Map<String, Word> wordList = new HashMap<>();
```

The **HashMap** class uses two generic parameters. We set the first parameter to the type **String** and the second parameter to the type **Word**, which is a user-defined class (discussed later). In the **main** method, we add a few entries to the map, as follows:

```
wordList.put("Abate", new Word("verb", "subside",
                "alienate,increase,extend,amplify,continue,enlarge"));
...
```

The first parameter to the **put** method is the key, and the second parameter is its value, which in this case is an instance of the **Word** class. Note that the **Word** constructor requires three parameters—the first parameter specifies the type of word, the second parameter specifies synonyms, and the third parameter specifies antonyms. After building the list, we print the entire list by calling the **printList** method (discussed later). To look up an entry in the list, we call the **get** method:

```
// Look up a value
System.out.println("\nValue for abscond " + wordList.get("Abscond"));
```

The key to search for becomes the parameter to the **get** method. On return, it gives the value stored in the map. This value is printed by using the overridden **toString** method of the **Word** class.

To modify an entry, we simply call the **put** method with the desired key and the new value. This will replace the value for the existing key:

```
// Modify an entry
wordList.put("Abate", new Word("verb", "subside,moderate",
                "alienate,increase,extend,amplify,continue,enlarge"));
```

To remove an entry from the list, we call the **remove** method with the desired key as its parameter:

```
// Remove entry
wordList.remove("Abstemious");
```

The implementation of the **printList** method is very straightforward. We use the **for-each** loop to iterate the list. For each entry, we use the getter methods to retrieve the key and its value and then print them to the terminal using SOP:

```
for (Map.Entry<String, Word> entry : wordList.entrySet()) {
    String key = entry.getKey();
    Word value = entry.getValue();
    System.out.println("key=" + key + ", value=" + value);
}
```

The **Word** class declaration is very straightforward. It contains three class variables, with the corresponding getter methods and a constructor to initialize these variables at the time of construction. The overridden **toString** method provides the formatted output of the three fields.

Algorithms

The Collections class in the framework provides implementations of several useful algorithms. These are polymorphic and therefore can be applied to any type of collection. This class provides many popular algorithms, such as binary search, sort, shuffle, max, min, frequency, and so on. These algorithms are defined as static methods of the Collections class.

We'll cover the use of some of these algorithms with the help of a program. We will first create a set of 100 random numbers as sample data for our program. We will sort these numbers based on their natural ordering by calling the built-in sort algorithm. We will then apply a binary search algorithm to locate a particular test number. We will also find the largest and the smallest number in the set. Then, we will determine the frequency of occurrence of a certain test number by using the provided frequency algorithm. We will then proceed to find the number of distinct elements by creating a sorted **HashSet**. We shuffle this newly created set and sort it in ascending order to determine top 10 picks. Isn't this exciting? The program given in Listing 16-6 teaches you all these techniques.

Listing 16-6   *Demonstrating the Power of Built-in Collection Algorithms*

```
import java.util.*;

public class CollectionAlgorithms {

    public static void main(String[] args) {
        List<Integer> list = new ArrayList<>();
        for (int i = 0; i < 100; i++) {
            list.add((int) (Math.random() * 100));
        }
        Collections.sort(list);
        System.out.println("Sorted Array: " + list);
```

```
        int testNumber = 10;
        int index = Collections.binarySearch(list, testNumber);
        if (index >= 0) {
            System.out.println("Number " + testNumber
                    + " found at index: " + index);
        } else {
            System.out.println("Number " + testNumber + " not found");
        }
        System.out.println("Max number: " + Collections.max(list));
        System.out.println("Min number: " + Collections.min(list));
        System.out.println("Frequency of " + testNumber + ": "
                + Collections.frequency(list, testNumber));
        Set<Integer> sortedList = new HashSet<>();
        sortedList.addAll(list);
        System.out.println("Number of distinct elements: " + sortedList.size());
        list.clear();
        list.addAll(sortedList);
        Collections.shuffle(list);
        List<Integer> topTenList = list.subList(0, 10);
        Collections.sort(topTenList);
        System.out.println("Top 10: " + topTenList);
    }
}
```

To demonstrate the use of algorithms, we first create an array of integers:

```
List<Integer> list = new ArrayList<>();
```

We fill this array with 100 random numbers in the range 0 to 99:

```
for (int i = 0; i < 100; i++) {
    list.add((int) (Math.random() * 100));
}
```

We then sort the contents of this array by calling the **sort** method of the Collections class:

```
Collections.sort(list);
```

The **sort** method stores back the result in the same array. We print this array to verify the sorting:

```
System.out.println("Sorted Array: " + list);
```

Next, we perform a binary search on this sorted array to locate a desired number:

```
int index = Collections.binarySearch(list, testNumber);
```

The **binarySearch** method takes two arguments: The first argument specifies the list on which a search is to be performed, and the second argument specifies the search element. On completion, it returns the index at which the specified number is found. If the search element is not found, it returns a negative number.

To determine the largest number in the array, we use the **max** method:

```
System.out.println("Max number: " + Collections.max(list));
```

Likewise, to determine the smallest number, we use the **min** method. Both methods take the list to be searched as the argument.

To determine the frequency of occurrence of a certain number in the list, we use the **frequency** method:

```
Collections.frequency(list, testNumber));
```

The first parameter to the **frequency** method is the list to be searched, and the second argument is the search element.

Next, we create a set of distinct elements from our set. For this, we use the **HashSet** class:

```
Set<Integer> sortedList = new HashSet<>();
```

We add all the elements of our list into this new set by calling the **addAll** method:

```
sortedList.addAll(list);
```

The **addAll** method adds only the distinct elements to the set. We determine and print the size of this set by calling its **size** method:

```
sortedList.size());
```

Next, we shuffle the elements of this set and list the top 10 numbers from the shuffled set as the winners. For this, we use the **shuffle** method. Because the **shuffle** works only on the **List** interface, we need to copy the elements of our set into a list. We first clear the existing contents of the list by calling its **clear** method and then add all the elements of the set into it:

```
list.clear();
list.addAll(sortedList);
```

The **shuffle** method now shuffles the contents of the modified list:

```
Collections.shuffle(list);
```

To pick the top 10 numbers from this new list, we call the **subList** method. The first parameter specifies the start index and the second parameter specifies the end index for the sublist:

```
List<Integer> topTenList = list.subList(0, 10);
```

We now sort this new set and print it to the user console as a set of top 10:

```
Collections.sort(topTenList);
System.out.println("Top 10: " + topTenList);
```

When we run the program, typical output would be as follows:

```
Sorted Array: [0, 1, 2, 2, 3, 4, 5, 5, 6, 9, 11, 11, 12, 12, 13, 14, 14, 16,
16, 17, 17, 17, 18, 19, 19, 22, 24, 25, 25, 27, 29, 29, 30, 30, 31, 33, 36,
40, 40, 41, 41, 42, 43, 44, 45, 48, 48, 50, 50, 51, 52, 52, 53, 55, 55, 55,
56, 57, 57, 58, 58, 59, 60, 62, 63, 64, 65, 65, 66, 66, 67, 67, 68, 68, 68,
68, 69, 71, 72, 74, 75, 76, 77, 79, 80, 80, 82, 84, 85, 87, 88, 89, 90, 91,
93, 94, 94, 97, 98, 99]
Number 10 not found
Max number: 99
Min number: 0
Frequency of 10: 0
Number of distinct elements: 71
Top 10: [1, 4, 17, 41, 52, 62, 64, 72, 75, 84]
```

This simple example demonstrates the power of just a few algorithms. The Collections class provides several more of them. You are encouraged to go through the documentation to learn more about these algorithms.

TIP
The Collections framework also makes it easy to write your own custom algorithms that can operate on a generic collection.

Summary

In this chapter, you studied Java's Collections framework. The framework defines interfaces, implementation classes, and algorithms that operate polymorphically on various collection classes. The interfaces provide a unified look to the various collection implementations. The classes provide the implementations of several popular data structures. You studied the use of lists, sets, queues, and maps. The Collections class in the framework provides implementations of several useful algorithms as the **static** methods of the class. These algorithms work polymorphically on the collection classes and therefore can be applied to them easily without considering the data type they operate upon. The Collections framework also makes it viable for you to develop custom algorithms that operate polymorphically on various collection classes.

The next three chapters cover another very important feature of Java language programming— threads. As you might have guessed, thread programming is a vast subject.

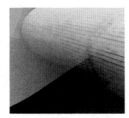

CHAPTER
17

Threads

or many of you, the concept of threads might not be a new one. Many popular languages support threading, either inherently or through the use of external libraries. In spite of this, it is possible that you might not have used threads at all—most of the time, when you write a program, creating threads is not a general requirement. What's more, writing multithreaded code is hard and debugging such code makes it worse. So do we really need to care about learning threads? Yes, we do. The programs you studied so far in the book have been trivial, focusing on a certain Java language feature. In real-life applications, it is hard to find a Java program that does not use threading. In fact, Java developers considered threading to be so important that the threading libraries were introduced from the beginning in JDK 1.0.

Let's discuss why we should use threading. Multithreaded code can provide a huge speed boost, especially when it runs on modern computers containing multiple CPUs and cores. Consider a simple application that sums up an enormous list of numbers. Splitting the summing process in two halves (or, even better, multiple parts) and assigning each half to an independent person would obviously speed up the entire computation. When each person finishes his totaling, the ultimate sum may be computed by adding the partial results. And that is what we do in a parallel program. A task that can be split into parts is divided and executed on multiple CPUs, and those parts are run in parallel, thus increasing the program throughput substantially. Summing a large set of numbers is just one example where the parallelism of an algorithm can be exploited; in many other situations in real life such parallelism can be observed. Consider the case of a stock exchange, where multiple trades occur simultaneously on the exchange in real time. All such trades are executed using the same algorithm. Without threads, it would be impossible to meet the demands traders place on these exchanges. We discuss many applications in the securities domain (and other domains) in this and the next two chapters to demonstrate the power of threading.

NOTE
Not all applications benefit from multiple threads, and some cannot be multithreaded.

Even if your machine does not contain a multiple-core CPU, there are reasons for using threads in your applications. Consider a simple file-copy program. While copying a file, the user will want the ability to cancel the copying process at any time. This can be implemented by creating a separate thread that continually monitors user input sources, such as the keyboard and mouse, and that can cause an interruption in the copy process whenever a user request to do so is detected. These two threads may not truly run in parallel if only one core is available in the machine. In such cases, the operating system pretends to run multiple threads at the same time by time-slicing the CPU—that is, constantly switching between the two threads. This gives the illusion to the user of doing two things at the same time.

These days, multicore machines have become so common that it is hard to find a single-core machine in today's market. Parallel programming has become important in exploiting the power of these machines. Java SE 8 and 9 help you parallelize your program code with many new language/API additions.

Thread programming is a complex topic. Fortunately, Java provides many simple constructs to create and use threads. In fact, many features of the threading system are built into the core language itself. As stated earlier, threading support has been available since JDK 1.0. The J2SE 5.0 introduced a concurrency framework that makes it easier to create concurrent programs that support parallelism and share data among multiple threads. Java SE 7 made further enhancements by supporting fine-grained parallelism in algorithms. In this and the next two chapters, you learn many techniques for creating threaded applications and exploiting the full potential of modern multicore machines. So let's begin by discussing what a thread is and then a few basics of thread programming in this chapter.

In particular, you will learn the following in this chapter:

- What a thread is
- The types of threads
- Thread priorities
- Thread scheduling
- Creating threads
- The static methods of **Thread** class
- Essential operations on threads
- Thread synchronizations
- Object locks
- The deadlocks

Processes and Threads

Before we delve into programming, let's first go over what a thread is. You have heard about processes in operating systems. So what is a process? When an application is loaded in memory and made ready to run, we say that a process is created.

A multitasking operating system creates several processes and runs them on multiple CPUs or the cores of a single CPU. In the rare situation that you have a single-core CPU in your box, the OS will switch the CPU between these processes, giving you the illusion of concurrently running processes. Processes are usually large and can be further split into smaller units of execution. For example, a spreadsheet application may allow the user to interact with it while it performs calculations in the background. A word processing application might perform a background spell check while the user edits the document. To implement these kinds of features, the developer splits the process into two units—one that is responsible for calculations and the other for handling user interactions. Such units of execution are called *threads*. The application developer may create multiple threads by partitioning the application into a number of logical units and creating a thread for each. In some situations, this can dramatically improve application performance and user responsiveness, thus providing a rich experience to its users.

The life cycle of all the threads created in your application is managed by the operating system. The operating system periodically allocates the available cores to waiting threads so that each one gets a chance to execute its code. Such allocation may be on a simple round-robin basis or may use a more sophisticated algorithm. The same way the operating system assigns the CPU to a thread, it also has the privilege of taking away the CPU from a running thread. Scheduling threads while ensuring that no thread is starved for CPU time forever itself becomes a highly complex algorithm to implement; fortunately, we do not have to bother with this—the operating system developers have taken care of it for us.

A thread undergoes several stages during its entire life cycle, as detailed next.

Thread States

The operating system (OS) maintains a queue of "ready-to-run" threads. A newly created thread is added at the bottom of this queue. The OS picks up a thread from the top of the queue and allocates the CPU to it within a fixed slice of time. After this time slice is over, the thread is returned to the bottom of the queue and the next waiting thread at the top of the queue is allocated to the CPU. This process continues forever, and each thread gets its own turn periodically. The different states of a thread are depicted in Figure 17-1.

Eventually, a thread may finish its job. Such a thread will be put into the *dead* state. A thread that's dead cannot be restarted and should be garbage-collected. What happens when you try to restart a dead thread is explained later in this chapter.

A thread may voluntarily block itself. This happens when a thread is waiting for some I/O operation to occur, or it could simply be generous enough to yield control to another waiting thread. A thread may go to sleep for a specified amount of time and enter a Blocked state. A blocked thread will wake up after a specified amount of time and/or when the external operation on which it has been waiting is completed. The OS wakes up these sleeping threads. A thread that is woken up will not be allocated the CPU immediately. Instead, it will be returned to the bottom of the Ready to Run queue and will eventually be allocated to the CPU.

As stated previously, a thread might need to wait for some external event to occur. For example, a thread might need to wait for some other thread to complete its job before proceeding with its own program code. The OS maintains a queue of threads waiting on other objects. When the object the thread is waiting on is ready, it signals the waiting thread. The waiting thread will then be brought into the queue of ready-to-run threads, where eventually it will receive the CPU cycles. Note that more than one thread could be waiting on the same object. In this case, a notification is sent to all such waiting threads.

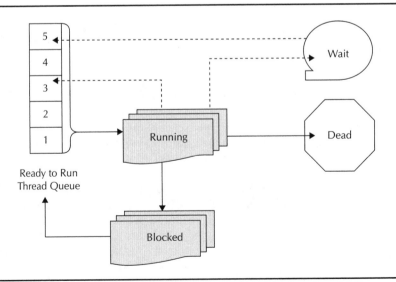

FIGURE 17-1. *Thread states*

Having seen how an OS implements threading, let's look at how the JVM implements it. To understand the different implementations of the JVM on different platforms, first you need to know what a thread priority is and how threads are scheduled for execution.

Thread Priorities

With several threads running on a system, you may want to prioritize their execution. You do so by assigning a priority level to each thread. In Java, the thread priority levels range from 1 to 10. The priority 0 is reserved for the virtual machine. Java also provides a few predefined constants for setting the thread priority. **MAX_PRIORITY** designates the top priority of 10, **MIN_PRIORITY** designates the minimum priority of 1, and **NORM_PRIORITY** specifies the normal priority of 5. A thread with a higher priority gets the CPU first. The OS maintains a separate queue for all threads belonging to each priority level (refer to Figure 17-2).

Because threads with the higher priority level get the CPU first, this implies that a thread with a lower priority will starve for CPU cycles forever if the higher-priority threads never finish. However, this is not exactly true. The OS periodically raises the priority of these "starving" threads until they reach the currently executing thread priority level. At this level, each thread will eventually get its time slice. After the time slice is over, the thread will be returned to the queue of its original priority.

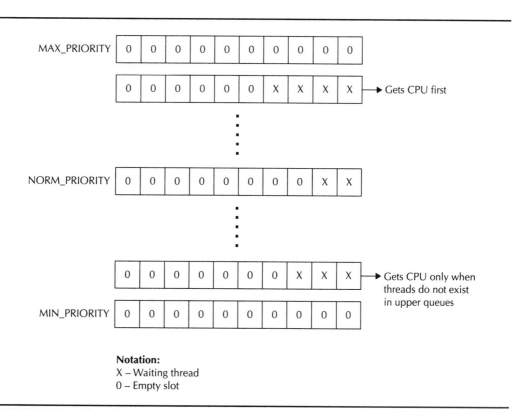

FIGURE 17-2.   *Thread priority queues*

CAUTION
The thread scheduling described here is generic. A JVM vendor may implement a different scheduling policy than the one described here, most likely to take advantage of the underlying platform's implementation, as you will see in the section that follows.

Next, we briefly look at preemptive and nonpreemptive scheduling.

Thread Scheduling

The two strategies for scheduling threads on the CPU are preemptive and nonpreemptive scheduling. In case of preemptive scheduling, a thread with a higher priority (the moment it is created or acquires a higher priority) will preempt the running thread and acquire the CPU for execution. A preemptive scheduling scheme may also use time slicing, whereby threads at the same priority level will be allocated the CPU for a maximum of a certain fixed time interval. Windows NT is an example of a preemptive OS.

In case of nonpreemptive scheduling, a running thread continues using CPU cycles even if a thread with a higher priority exists. Thus, a running thread may be required to relinquish the CPU voluntarily so that other threads get a chance to execute. In this scheme, a badly written program can lock up your OS (a system hang-up). Nonpreemptive scheduling may also be time-sliced, where the user may decide the amount of time for the slice. For example, Windows 3.1 is a nonpreemptive OS, where the user can switch from one application to another by making the desired application active. Thus, the user decides the length of time for which the CPU is allocated to a running application. The active application continues using the CPU until the user makes it inactive by switching to another application.

A JVM may derive its functionality of thread scheduling from the underlying OS. Therefore, you should be careful when coding threads in Java because the application behavior may change depending on the underlying platform.

JVM Threading Implementations

Each JVM has its own implementation of the threading model, depending on its vendor and the platform for which it is written. While implementing a threading model, it may exploit the features provided by the underlying platform or it may have its own model that is not based on the model implemented by the underlying platform. We will now look at some of the JVM implementations on several popular platforms. Java is a platform-independent language, so studying the different implementations of JVMs is mainly unimportant to a developer. However, in a few cases, understanding these variations in implementation details do matter, as you will see shortly.

Green Threads

The most common threading model is the simple *green thread* model. In this model, each thread is an abstraction within the virtual machine; the OS does not know anything about the threads that exist in the JVM. Thus, from the OS perspective, the JVM is a single process and a single thread. It means that whenever a JVM creates a thread, it must hold all information related to the thread within the thread object itself. Such information includes the thread's stack, a program counter to track the currently executing instruction, and other bookkeeping data. The VM also becomes responsible for context switching and the entire life cycle (discussed previously). As far as the OS is concerned, it is executing a single thread of execution of JVM code and whatever code switching is happening inside the JVM is unknown to it. These types of threads are also called *user-level threads* because they exist only within the user level of the OS. In the early days of Java, this green thread model was fairly common.

NOTE
Most operating systems are logically divided into two parts: user level and system level. The OS kernel runs at the system level, and the user applications run at the user level. To use the OS services, the program transits from the user level to the system level. After the service is provided, the OS switches from system to user level, restricting privileges to a running program.

Windows Implementation

The native threading model in 32-bit Windows uses a one-to-one mapping between Java threads and operating system threads. Because Windows provides only seven priority levels, there is some overlap when Java's 11 distinct priority levels are mapped to the Windows levels. These mappings vary among the different implementations of the JVM on the same Windows platform. Therefore, your program may exhibit slightly different behavior on JVMs provided by different vendors. The scheduling of Java threads is now subject to the underlying scheduling of OS threads.

The actual Windows thread scheduler is more complex than the simple priority-based scheduler described earlier. It uses a complex priority calculation, taking into consideration how recently a thread has run. The actual priority is the difference between the assigned priority and a value that indicates the elapsed time since the last run. This value is continually adjusted so that the thread will acquire a CPU eventually at some point in time. A thread that has not run for a very long time gets a temporary priority boost, thus preventing threads from absolute starvation and at the same time giving preference to a higher-priority thread over a lower-priority one. Likewise, threads that have a keyboard or mouse focus are given a priority boost. This complex mechanism of actual priority computation results in an unpredictable order of thread execution, but at the same time ensures that threads do not starve.

Solaris Implementation

The older Solaris 7 had system-level lightweight processes (known as LWPs) in addition to user-level threads. Java threads were considered equivalent to user-level threads and there was an M-to-N mapping between these user-level threads and LWPs. Developers were allowed to influence the priorities of these user-level threads and not those of LWPs. In Solaris 9, there is a one-to-one mapping quite similar to Windows; however, the implementation as compared to the Windows implementation is quite different. Solaris 8 supported both models and allowed the user to make a selection. The CPU-intensive Java programs perform better with the one-to-one mapping model and therefore you may find that certain Java applications run faster on Solaris 9 than Solaris 7. Like Windows, Solaris uses a complex priority calculation, ensuring that all threads get an adequate amount of CPU time without starving for a long period of time. In Solaris, there are 60 different runnable priorities and 128 application-level priorities. In Java versions up to J2SE 1.4 (inclusive), priorities were mapped to the full range of 0 to 127. The default priority was therefore in the middle of this range, whereas the default priority for a C/C++ program was 127. Therefore, when a CPU-intensive C program was run along with a CPU-intensive Java program, the Java program was always at a disadvantage. In J2SE 5.0, this was taken care of and now all Java threads with a priority of **NORM_PRIORITY** or higher are mapped to the 127 level.

Linux Implementation

Prior to J2SE 1.3, the virtual machines on the Linux platform mostly used the green thread model, with only a few using the native threads. The Linux kernel back then did not support a large number of concurrent threads. J2SE 1.3 added support for native threads; however, the kernel still did not provide optimal support for threaded applications. The new kernels use the Native POSIX Thread Library. This library provides a one-to-one mapping between Java and kernel threads as well as complex priority calculations similar to other operating systems. J2SE 1.4.2 is the first version to support this new kernel.

One last term we should discuss before digging into code is the *daemon thread*.

Daemon Versus Non-Daemon Threads

There are two types of threads in Java:

- Daemon threads
- Non-daemon (user) threads

A daemon thread terminates automatically as soon as the parent thread that created this thread terminates. A non-daemon thread, however, continues to live even when the parent dies. As long as there is at least one thread alive, we say that the process is alive. When all non-daemon threads along with the remaining daemon threads of an application die, we say that the process is dead. Every Java application has at least one non-daemon thread, which is the main thread. When the program quits this thread or the user closes the application, the main thread dies. However, the process can continue to live if it has already spawned other non-daemon threads. You will learn how to create both types of threads in the sections that follow.

Creating Threads

Java implements thread functionality by using the following classes/interfaces:

- The interface **Runnable**
- The class **Thread**
- The class **ThreadGroup**

To create threads in your Java program, you need to implement the **Runnable** interface in your Java class. As a part of the interface implementation, you provide the implementation of the **run** method. In the **run** method, you program the desired functionality for your thread:

```
class WorkerThread implements Runnable {

    public void run() {
        ...
    }
}
```

After creating this thread class, you need to create its instance of the **Thread** class and pass an object of the preceding class as a parameter to the **Thread** class constructor. This is done as follows:

```
Thread t = new Thread (new WorkerThread());
```

The created thread executes the **run** method defined in the **WorkerThread** class. When the **run** method completes its execution, the thread becomes dead and cannot be rescheduled for another run.

Alternatively, you can create a thread by subclassing the **Thread** class:

```
class WorkerThread extends Thread {

    public void run() {
        ...
    }
}
```

In this case, you are overriding the **run** method to implement your own desired functionality. Once your thread class is created, some other thread will need to instantiate it and invoke its **start** method. The following code snippet illustrates how to achieve this:

```
Thread t = new WorkerThread();
t.start();
```

When you start the thread, this does not mean it gets the CPU immediately. Rather, it is put in the Ready to Run queue, discussed earlier, where eventually it will receive a CPU time slice for execution.

TIP
*Implementing **Runnable** is considered an object-oriented approach and is recommended over the technique of subclassing the **Thread** class. Also, if your class is already extending some other class, you will not be allowed to extend from **Thread** class simultaneously.*

The **ThreadGroup** class allows you to group all logically related threads into a single group, whereby you will be able to apply simultaneous changes to all such threads belonging to a single group. For example, you can raise the priorities of all threads belonging to a certain group to the maximum priority by calling the **setMaxPriority** method on the group object. You can mark all threads within a group as "daemon" or "non-daemon" by calling its **setDaemon** method. A group of threads responsible for printing documents can be sent a simultaneous notification for aborting printing. By default, all threads you create belong to the same group. However, it is possible to create additional groups of your own and add newly created threads to them. A thread group may contain other thread groups. Thus, you can build a tree hierarchy for your threads.

TIP
J2SE 5.0 introduced better features for operating on a collection of threads, making the use of a thread group somewhat redundant.

Creating Your First Threaded Application

The application we develop in this section draws two superimposed sine waves on the application screen. These waves are animated and keep moving to the right as the time progresses. The application interface is shown in Figure 17-3.

FIGURE 17-3. *Output of a threaded sine wave animator*

To create the animation, we create two threads: One thread draws a vertical line whose end coordinates are the points on a sine wave, and the other thread periodically calls the **repaint** method on the first thread to redraw the line. Before redrawing the line, however, it makes sure the line is shifted in the x-direction by a fixed amount. This gives the effect of a moving sine wave from left to right. To make things more dramatic, the equations for computing the top and bottom y-coordinates of the line are kept different by using different sine wave frequencies in the two calculations. You may want to run the application first for a better understanding of how it works. The entire program code is given in Listing 17-1, followed by its explanation.

Listing 17-1   *A Threaded Sine Wave Animator*

```java
import java.awt.*;
import javax.swing.JFrame;

public class SineWaveAnimator extends JFrame implements Runnable {

    private int frame = 0;

    public SineWaveAnimator() {
        setTitle("Sine Wave Animator");
        setDefaultCloseOperation(EXIT_ON_CLOSE);
        setSize(500, 200);
        setVisible(true);
    }

    public static void main(String[] args) {
        SineWaveAnimator app = new SineWaveAnimator();
        Thread animator = new Thread(app);
        animator.setDaemon(true);
        animator.start();
    }

    public void run() {
        while (true) {
            repaint();
```

```
        try {
            Thread.sleep(100);
        } catch (InterruptedException e) {
        }
        frame++;
    }
}

@Override
public void paint(Graphics g) {
    Rectangle d = getBounds();
    g.clearRect(0, 0, d.width, d.height);
    int h = d.height / 2;
    for (int x = 0; x < d.width; x++) {
        int y1 = (int) ((1.0 + Math.sin((x - frame) * 0.09)) * h);
        int y2 = (int) ((1.0 + Math.sin((x + frame) * 0.01)) * h);
        g.drawLine(x, y1, x, y2);
    }
}
}
```

The **SineWaveAnimator** is our main class and extends its functionality from **JFrame**. It also implements the **Runnable** interface. Thus, it will need to implement the **run** method:

```
public class SineWaveAnimator extends JFrame implements Runnable {
```

The instance of this class will be submitted to the **Thread** class constructor; the object of **Thread** class will execute the **run** method of this class. Before discussing the implementation of the **run** method, let's look at the code in the **main** method. In the **main** method, we create a new thread by calling the **Thread** class constructor, as follows:

```
Thread animator = new Thread(app);
```

The constructor receives the instance of our main application class as a parameter. We mark this thread as a daemon thread so that it gets cleaned up whenever its parent thread dies:

```
animator.setDaemon(true);
```

To start the thread, we call its **start** method:

```
animator.start();
```

The **start** method puts the created thread in the Ready to Run queue discussed earlier. Thus, at this stage, we have two application threads—one is the **main** thread that was started as a part of the application startup, and the second is the **animator** thread we created in the **main** method. Now, let's look at the implementation of the **run** method.

The **run** method simply keeps on calling the **repaint** method in an infinite loop:

```
while (true) {
    repaint();
```

So that the second thread has an opportunity to run, it puts itself to sleep for a specified amount of time in the same **while** loop:

```
try {
    Thread.sleep(100);
} catch (InterruptedException e) {
}
frame++;
```

The **sleep** method takes a parameter that specifies the number of milliseconds for which the thread should sleep. During this sleep time, the thread is put into the blocked state. After the sleep time is over, the JVM will awaken the thread and put it in the Ready to Run queue. Thus, the thread will not get the CPU for a guaranteed minimum period of 100 milliseconds in our case. Note that usually it takes longer than 100 milliseconds to get the CPU due to other threads waiting in the queue. Whenever it gets the CPU, the thread continues with its rest of the work (which is incrementing the frame number) in our infinite **for** loop and again goes to sleep when it encounters another call to the **sleep** method.

Note that the **Thread.sleep** method is enclosed in a **try-catch** block. This is a checked exception that must be caught or re-thrown. A sleeping thread may be interrupted from its sleep and awakened by another thread. Thus, a thread may receive a CPU time slice earlier than its sleeping period of 10 milliseconds provided some other thread interrupts it. You learn about this interrupt processing and exception handling during interruptions in the sections that follow.

In the exception handler, we do nothing and proceed with another iteration of the **while** loop. Before starting another iteration, we increment the **frame** counter, which moves the x-position of the sine wave during its painting.

Finally, in the **paint** method, which gets called whenever we call the frame's **repaint** method, we draw a vertical line. We first obtain the dimensions of the drawing area by calling the **getBounds** method on the container:

```
Rectangle d = getBounds();
```

We clear this area on every **repaint** operation to erase the previously drawn line by calling the **clearRect** method of the **Graphics** context:

```
g.clearRect(0, 0, d.width, d.height);
```

We now draw a series of vertical lines throughout the width of the container by using a **for** loop:

```
for (int x = 0; x < d.width; x++) {
```

The top coordinate of the desired line is computed using the following statement, which uses the sine function:

```
int y1 = (int) ((1.0 + Math.sin((x - frame) * 0.09)) * h);
```

Likewise, the bottom coordinate is computed using the following statement:

```
int y2 = (int) ((1.0 + Math.sin((x + frame) * 0.01)) * h);
```

The constants 0.09 and 0.01 in these equations decide the sine wave frequencies. Finally, the vertical line is drawn between the two computed coordinates via a call to the **drawLine** method of the **Graphics** class:

```
g.drawLine(x, y1, x, y2);
```

Note that we keep the same x-value for the two end coordinates so as to draw a vertical line.

When you run the program, two threads will be running. One thread draws the vertical lines throughout the container width, and the second thread periodically keeps on shifting the position of these lines to the right, thus giving an illusion of a moving sine wave.

Creating Non-Daemon Threads

The program we just discussed terminates properly, cleaning all the spawned threads. This is because the **animator** thread we created in the program was a daemon thread and therefore was terminated when the **main** thread died as a result of closing the application.

TIP
*When code running in some thread creates a new **Thread** object, the new thread becomes a* daemon *thread if and only if the creating thread is a daemon. Also, the initial priority of the created thread equals the priority of the creating thread.*

To help you better understand the implications of creating non-daemon threads in your programs, we will discuss another threaded application. We will write a thread class that generates and displays a list of prime numbers to the user console. The application thread will create an instance of this thread class and set it to run along with itself. We will study the two cases of when this worker thread is marked "daemon" and "non-daemon," respectively. Look at the code in Listing 17-2.

Listing 17-2 *Prime Number Generator in a Non-Daemon Thread*

```
public class PrimeNumberGenerator {

    public static void main(String[] args) {
        Thread primeNumberGenerator = new Thread(new WorkerThread());
        primeNumberGenerator.setDaemon(true);
        primeNumberGenerator.start();
        try {
            Thread.sleep(10);
        } catch (InterruptedException e) {
        }
    }
}

class WorkerThread implements Runnable {

    public void run() {
        long i = 1;
        while (true) {
```

```
            long j;
            for (j = 2; j < i; j++) {
                long n = i % j;
                if (n == 0) {
                    break;
                }
            }
            if (i == j) {
                System.out.print("   " + i);
            }
            i++;
        }
    }
}
```

We create a class called **WorkerThread** that implements **Runnable**. In the **run** method, we generate prime numbers and print each generated number to the user console. (Note that we won't go into the details of the algorithm for prime number generation here.) In the **main** method of the application class, we create a **Thread** instance by passing the **WorkerThread** object in its constructor:

```
Thread primeNumberGenerator = new Thread(new WorkerThread());
```

We mark this instance as "daemon."

CAUTION
*The thread instance must be marked "daemon" or "non-daemon" before it is started; otherwise, it acquires its default state depending on the state of its creator. A thread created on a user thread becomes non-daemon by default. Therefore, in the preceding code, we have explicitly called **setDaemon** to mark the created thread as daemon.*

Next, we schedule the created thread to run by calling its **start** method. We then put the current thread to sleep for 10 milliseconds, giving the worker thread an opportunity to run.

Run the application and observe its output. You will see a list of prime numbers on the console. Every time you run the application, the last generated number varies, indicating that the worker thread is getting a different amount of CPU time on each run. Now modify the parameter to the **setDaemon** method by setting it to **false**. Run the application and you will find that the random-number-generation process never stops indicating that the worker thread continues to run even though the main thread has died after a while. Thus, a non-daemon thread continues to run even when its creator is dead. To terminate the application, you need to kill the process by pressing CTRL-C (on Windows) or the appropriate key combination according to your operating system.

CAUTION
In a nonpreemptive OS (which is difficult to find these days because most are now preemptive), there may be a difference in the execution of the preceding code depending on how the native thread or threads that make up the Java process are affected by the competing priorities of other processes on the OS.

Now that you understand how to create threaded programs, let's look at a few details of **Thread** class, such as its constructors and the various static methods it provides.

Thread Class Constructors

As mentioned earlier, there are two ways to create a thread in your application. One is to implement the **Runnable** interface, and the other is to extend your class from the **Thread** class. This is possible because the **Thread** class itself implements the **Runnable** interface, and that is why you could create a class extending a **Thread** class to create threads. The **Thread** class is defined as follows:

```
public class Thread extends Object implements Runnable
```

Thus, to create a thread, you would extend your class from a **Thread** class and override its default **run** method implementation. Another way of creating threads, as you know, is to implement a **Runnable** interface in your class. You then pass an instance of this **Runnable** object to the **Thread** class constructor. You have already used this technique in the previous examples.

Besides the constructor that takes a **Runnable** instance as a parameter, the **Thread** class defines several more constructors that accept the two more types of parameters and their combinations. The two other types of parameters are the **String** that specifies the name for the created thread and the **ThreadGroup** that specifies the group to which the created thread will be added. A thread may be referred to later in the code by its assigned name after it is created. As mentioned earlier, you will use the **ThreadGroup** to group the threads for performing certain common operations on them collectively.

Static Methods of Thread

The **Thread** class defines several static methods. As you are aware, the static methods can be invoked without creating an instance of the class. We will discuss a few frequently used static methods.

The **activeCount** method returns the number of active threads in the current thread's thread group. For example, if you add the following statement in the **main** method of your **PrimeNumberGenerator** class, discussed earlier, you will get the number of active threads in the current thread group along with its name printed to the console:

```
System.out.printf("Number of active threads in the %s group equals %d%n",
    primeNumberGenerator.getThreadGroup().getName(), Thread.activeCount());
```

The preceding statement generates the following output on the console:

```
Number of active threads in the main group equals 2
```

Note that the **getThreadGroup** method is not a class method and therefore requires an instance to operate upon.

TIP
*You can obtain a reference to the instance of the currently running thread by calling the **Thread.currentThread** method.*

The **getName** method returns the name of the **ThreadGroup** on which it is invoked.

The **yield** method yields the control of execution to another waiting thread at the same priority. The **sleep** method voluntarily puts the current thread to sleep for the specified amount of time. The time may be specified as a number of milliseconds or a number of milliseconds plus a number of nanoseconds.

The **enumerate** method returns the details on each thread belonging to the current thread group and its subgroups. Add the following code fragment to the **main** method of the **PrimeNumberGenerator** class:

```
Thread[] threads = new Thread[Thread.activeCount()];
Thread.enumerate(threads);
for (Thread t : threads) {
    System.out.printf("%s\tpriority:%d%n", t.getName(), t.getPriority());
}
```

Run the program and you will get the following output:

```
main          priority:5
Thread-1          priority:5
```

The two threads in the **main** thread group are named **main** and **Thread-1**; both have a priority level of 5, which is the normal priority.

Finally, the **currentThread** static method returns a reference to the currently executing thread object. Other static methods are defined in the **Thread** class, which you should look up in the documentation. We discuss some of the remaining ones, when required, in the remainder of this chapter. Next, we focus on some of the essential and common operations on a thread.

Some Essential Operations on Thread

Once a thread object is created, you can carry out many different operations on it, as listed here:

- Setting the Daemon/Non-daemon property
- Starting/stopping a thread
- Suspending/resuming a thread
- Yielding to other threads
- Changing priorities
- Waiting on other objects
- Interrupting threads
- Joining to another thread

We will now discuss each of these operations in the following sections.

Setting the Daemon Property

A thread object may be marked as "daemon" or "non-daemon" by calling its **setDaemon** method. We used this operation in some of our earlier code.

Starting the Thread

Calling its **start** method starts a thread object and schedules the thread for execution. The created thread will execute the **run** method of the **Runnable** object. It is illegal to call a **start** method more than once. If you do so on a thread that is still executing its code defined in the **run** method, the JVM will throw an **IllegalThreadStateException**. When the **run** method runs to completion, we say that the thread is dead. You should not call the **start** method on a dead thread. If you do so, no exception is thrown to you. The JVM detects that the thread is dead and does not call its **run** method. Interestingly, calling the **isAlive** method after invoking the **start** method on a dead thread returns **true**. However, be assured that the **run** method will never be executed again. If your **Thread** class defines methods in addition to its mandatory **run** method, you will be able to invoke these methods on a thread object that is dead. This means that the object of a dead thread is not removed from the system and is available to you as any other object.

Stop, Suspend, and Resume Operations

The stop, suspend, and resume operations mentioned in the preceding task list have been deprecated since J2SE 1.2. You should refrain from calling the **stop**, **suspend**, and **resume** methods because they are prone to causing deadlocks (discussed later). Just so you know what these methods are, a thread may be stopped by calling the **stop** method, a thread may be suspended by calling the **suspend** method, and a suspended thread may be resumed by another running thread by calling the **resume** method.

Yielding Control

A thread may voluntarily yield control to another waiting thread by calling the **yield** method. Usually a thread awaiting a certain result created by another thread with the same priority will yield its control. Let's look at a situation of where you would use **yield**. The java. NIO2 allows you to lock a file. Consider a case where multiple threads may be accessing a single file—some readers and other writers. Both readers and writers will lock the file while accessing it to ensure data integrity and consistency. Both readers and writers may be running at the same priority level. Now, a reader who is holding the lock on the file may periodically yield its control to another contending thread that is waiting to write some new content to the file. This way, the writer threads are ensured to always get a better opportunity to write the latest news to the file.

TIP
*The **yield** is a hint to the VM that a thread can take a break but is not done. Unfortunately, Java cannot guarantee deterministically the scheduling of its threads, so **yield** is a hint rather than a stronger requirement. Moreover, the designers did not actually specify whether this hint allows threads of a lower priority to gain some CPU time, or just the ones at the same priority (although the latter is how most implementations have interpreted it). In any event, this is a method that is not frequently called; it can be used by more advanced developers when "tuning" an application to see if they can squeeze out better throughput.*

When you call **yield**, another waiting thread with the same priority as the running thread gets the CPU. If no waiting thread has the same priority, the control returns to the currently running thread. Logically, what happens here is that the thread that executes **yield** remains in the runnable state, except that it is moved to the bottom of its priority queue. The JVM may now pick up a new thread for execution from this queue, assuming that no higher priority threads exist at this point of time. There is no guarantee which thread will be selected for execution. The scheduler may pick the thread that has yielded control, even though other threads are available at the same priority.

Yielding control is just being nice to other threads at the same priority level. It's a thread's way of saying, "I've had enough CPU time and want to let others have an opportunity to run; I will run the rest of my code at a later time. If no other threads can be run, give the CPU back to me and I will continue with the rest of my code." This is different from executing the **sleep** method, where the thread says, "I do not want to run for *n* milliseconds. Even if no other thread wants to run, don't make me run."

Setting the Priority

You may change the priority of a thread by calling its **setPriority** method. We discussed thread priorities in depth earlier in this chapter.

Waiting on Other Objects

A thread may wait for some object to signal that the object on which it is waiting is now ready to use by calling the *obj*.**wait()** method from the running thread, where *obj* refers to the object the current thread wants to wait on. You will learn the use of this method later in this chapter when we discuss thread synchronization.

Interrupting Threads

You need to learn three important methods to understand interrupts: **interrupt**, **isInterrupted**, and **interrupted**. A running thread may be interrupted in its work by some other thread or itself. When a thread is interrupted, it does not mean that the thread will stop whatever it is doing. It's like patting your friend on his shoulder—he might ignore your interruption and continue with whatever he was doing. However, he will remember your patting and might listen to you at a later time. Something similar happens in the case of threads. A thread has an internal flag that is set to **true** whenever it is interrupted. The **interrupted** method returns the status of this flag. This is a static method and therefore does not require an object reference. Also, a call to this method clears the flag. Therefore, if you call this method twice, the second call will always return **false**, assuming that the thread has not been interrupted one more time between your two calls to the **interrupted** method.

When a thread is first created, it has not been interrupted so far; therefore, calling the **interrupted** method on it will return **false**. To interrupt the thread, you call the **interrupt** method on it. Thus, if the reference to your thread is **animator**, you would use the syntax **animator.interrupt()** to interrupt it. This sets the interrupt flag in the **animator** thread. The thread would continue its work except in special cases when it is sleeping or waiting for an object, which are explained further. A call to the **interrupted** method within the thread's body would now return **true**. What happens in those situations where the thread is in sleep mode (that is, after the thread has executed the **Thread.sleep()** method) or is waiting on an object (that is, when it has executed the **wait** method, which is discussed later in this chapter)? In these situations, because the thread is in a blocked state, it cannot respond to an interrupt. To overcome this situation, the designers of Java have made it mandatory to wrap the **sleep** and **wait** commands in a **try/catch** block and you have to catch the **InterruptedException**. That is why most developers do not provide any code in the **InterruptedException** block; in other words, it is okay not to handle this exception in most of the situations (see the Tip at the very end of this section for more information). You can just add a comment in this block to explain to the reader what happens when this exception is raised. For a very detailed explanation on dealing with **InterruptedException**, refer to http://www.ibm.com/developerworks/java/library/j-jtp05236/index.html.

If the thread is not sleeping or waiting, you may use the **interrupted** method to check whether it has been interrupted. The following code fragment shows how to do this:

```
public void run() {
    while (true) {
        // do your stuff here
        if (Thread.interrupted()) {
            // deal with the interrupt
        }
        // do more stuff
    }
}
```

Finally, we come to the remaining method, **isInterrupted**. This method is similar to the **interrupted** method in the sense that it returns the status of the interrupt flag. However, this method is nonstatic and therefore requires an object reference for invocation. Also, a call to this method does not clear the flag.

We will now demonstrate the use of these methods through a program example. We will modify our earlier prime number generation program for this purpose. The main thread after starting the thread that continually generates the prime numbers will wait for keyboard input. When the user hits the ENTER key, we interrupt the number generator thread, which on its own will decide the logical point for stopping and will terminate itself at an appropriate time. We also create another lazy worker thread in the same application that does not do any work other than sleep. We will send an interrupt to this thread, which is sleeping, and observe how the thread is awakened.

NOTE
Running this code from a command prompt will display the generated prime numbers on the console as the generator thread waits to be interrupted, which occurs when the user hits the ENTER key. NetBeans unfortunately does not update its console until the thread is interrupted, at which time it dumps all previously generated prime numbers to the console.

Look at the program in Listing 17-3 for the implementation of these features.

Listing 17-3 *Understanding Interrupt Processing in Threads*

```
import java.io.*;

public class ControlledPrimeNumberGenerator {

    public static void main(String[] args) {
        Thread primeNumberGenerator = new Thread(new WorkerThread());
        primeNumberGenerator.start();
        InputStreamReader in = new InputStreamReader(System.in);
        try {
            while (in.read() != '\n') {
            }
```

```
            } catch (IOException ex) {
                ex.printStackTrace();
            }
            primeNumberGenerator.interrupt();

// uncomment the following lines to introduce a delay
// before checking the interrupt status
//          try {
//              Thread.sleep(100);
//          } catch (InterruptedException ex) {
//          }

            if (primeNumberGenerator.isInterrupted()) {
                System.out.println("\nNumber generation has "
                        + "already been interrupted");
            } else {
                System.out.println("Number generator "
                        + "is not currently running");
            }
            Thread lazyWorker = new Thread(new LazyWorker());
            lazyWorker.start();
            System.out.println("\nRunning lazy worker");
            try {
                Thread.sleep(100);
            } catch (InterruptedException ex) {
            }
            lazyWorker.interrupt();
        }
}

class WorkerThread implements Runnable {

    public void run() {
        long i = 1;
        while (true) {
            long j;
            for (j = 2; j < i; j++) {
                long n = i % j;
                if (n == 0) {
                    break;
                }
            }
            if (i == j) {
                System.out.print("   " + i);
            }
            i++;

            if (Thread.interrupted()) {
                System.out.println("\nStopping prime "
                        + "number generator");
```

```
                return;
            }
        }
    }
}

class LazyWorker implements Runnable {

    public void run() {
        try {
            Thread.sleep(100000);
        } catch (InterruptedException ex) {
            System.out.println("Lazy worker: " + ex.toString());
        }
    }
}
```

In the **main** method, we create a thread that runs the **WorkerThread** for generating prime numbers:

```
Thread primeNumberGenerator = new Thread(new WorkerThread());
```

We start this thread as usual by calling its **start** method:

```
primeNumberGenerator.start();
```

Next, we wait for the user to press the ENTER key on the keyboard:

```
while (in.read() != '\n') {
}
```

After the user input is received, we interrupt the number generator thread:

```
primeNumberGenerator.interrupt();
```

This sets the interrupt flag in the designated thread. Note that it will not stop the **primeNumberGenerator** thread, which may choose to ignore this interruption completely.

Next, we check the status of the interrupt flag in the **primeNumberGenerator** thread, which mostly remains **true** at this time, assuming that the **primeNumberGenerator** thread has not got a chance to process the request and reset its interrupt flag so far:

```
if (primeNumberGenerator.isInterrupted()) {
    System.out.println("\nNumber generation has "
                + "already been interrupted");
} else {
    System.out.println("Number generator " + "is not currently running");
}
```

If you make the main thread sleep for a certain amount of time (uncomment the commented lines in the program to do so) before calling the preceding code, the **primeNumberGenerator** thread will have probably processed the request and reset its internal flag. In this situation, you see the message printed in the preceding **else** clause. To honor and process the interrupt request, the **WorkerThread**, in its infinite **while** loop, checks the status in each iteration by calling the **Thread.interrupted** method:

```
if (Thread.interrupted()) {
    System.out.println("\nStopping prime " + "number generator");
    return;
}
```

If the thread has been interrupted, we print a message to the user and return to the caller, effectively terminating the thread's **run** method.

Finally, let's look at the lazy worker thread. In the **run** method of **LazyWorker**, we simply cause the thread to sleep for a very long time:

```
try {
    Thread.sleep(100000);
} catch (InterruptedException ex) {
    System.out.println("Lazy worker: " + ex.toString());
}
```

Whenever the thread is awakened from its sleep, we print the message to confirm the reason for the interruption.

The **main** method simply creates an instance of **LazyWorker** and starts it. The main thread puts itself to sleep for some time before sending an interrupt to **LazyWorker** thread. Sample output is shown here:

```
31531   31541   31543   31547   31567   31573   31583   31601   31607   31627   31643
31649   31657   31663   31667   31687   31699   31721   31723   31727

Number generation has already been interrupted

Running lazy worker
   31729
Stopping prime number generator
Lazy worker: java.lang.InterruptedException: sleep interrupted
```

Note that the output shows the number 31729 generated even after the thread was interrupted. This is because the number generator thread has not got its CPU slot before the main thread prints the "has already been interrupted" message to the terminal.

If you introduce the **Thread.sleep** statement, the interrupt, and **isInterrupted** calls, you will get output similar to what's shown here:

```
43541   43543   43573   43577   43579   43591   43597   43607   43609   43613   43627
   43633
Stopping prime number generator
Number generator is not currently running

Running lazy worker
Lazy worker: java.lang.InterruptedException: sleep interrupted
```

Now, the program prints the message stating that the number generator has already honored our interrupt request. Finally, observe the request processed by the lazy worker thread. The message shows that the thread was interrupted in its sleep.

TIP

*A blocking method, when it catches the **InterruptedException**, clears the interrupt status flag. If you want to preserve the evidence that the interruption occurred so that code higher up on the call stack can learn about it, call the **interrupt** method to set the flag once again, as shown in the code fragment here:*

```
catch (InterruptedException e) {
    // Restore the interrupted status
    Thread.currentThread().interrupt();
}
```

Joining

A thread may **join** with another thread; in such a case, the thread that wants to join with another thread will have to wait for the other thread to complete its job (that is, run to completion) before it continues. If the other thread never completes its job, the joining thread will have to wait indefinitely. To overcome this situation, a thread may join for a specified period of time. In this case, the thread will acquire control after the other thread has run to completion or the specified time period is over, whichever occurs first.

Thread Synchronization

From our discussions so far, it is obvious that CPU allocation for thread execution is totally asynchronous and therefore the thread execution order cannot be assumed. When these threads access a common resource, keeping its state consistent becomes a great challenge in thread programming. If a thread has partially modified a resource when it loses the CPU, no other thread should be given access to this resource unless and until the first thread acquires the CPU again and completes its modification of the resource, leaving it in a consistent state at all times. Consider the stock exchange scenario, where several buyers may be trying to grab a stock's sale order placed at a very attractive price. The inventory that is the sale quantity for this order now becomes a common resource that many buyers compete over to acquire. The access to this resource must be carefully guarded and synchronized. In a banking scenario, the simultaneous withdrawals by many concurrent users may leave the bank's cash repository in an inconsistent state, which certainly the bank won't want to have happen. A web-based bulletin board may be written to concurrently by many users—one user giving sports updates, another user discussing political news, and other users just gossiping. Without controlled access to this bulletin board, the articles can get mixed up at times.

In many situations in real life, you need to guard a common resource for which many compete. The problem is solvable and is typically done using resource-locking techniques. Many low-level constructs are available for providing synchronized access to a common resource. If you have taken a course on operating systems, you have encountered terms such as *semaphores, monitors,* and *critical sections.* Java initially abstracted most of these from developers by introducing a single

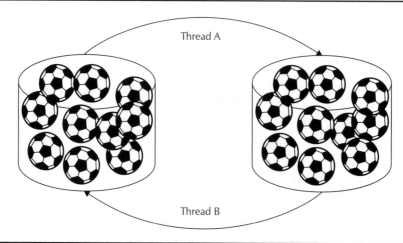

FIGURE 17-4. *Threads transfer balls from one bucket to another*

keyword, **synchronized**, in its initial version. Beginning in J2SE 5.0, access to these low-level constructs was provided. You will learn these other constructs in the next chapter. In this chapter, we focus on the **synchronized** keyword to better understand the thread synchronization.

To explain the synchronization issues and understand their solutions, we start with a concrete example.

Bucket Transfers

Let's suppose we have two buckets of balls and two threads, as illustrated in Figure 17-4. One thread transfers a few balls from the left bucket into the right one, while the other thread does the reverse operation. When a thread performs a transfer, it removes a few balls from one bucket and puts them in the other bucket. Both these operations should be atomic (done as a single unit) to keep the total system consistent. The total system consists of both the buckets and their contents. At any time after the transfer is completed, the total number of balls in the two buckets together must always remain constant. This can be achieved only if access to both buckets is guarded during each transfer. Therefore, a thread should acquire exclusive access to both the buckets until the transfer is complete, and only then can a consistent system state be guaranteed.

We will now discuss the program code that implements the bucket transfers so you can see what happens when we do not have guarded access to the buckets. The full source for the bucket transfers is given in Listing 17-4.

Listing 17-4   *Bucket Ball Game Demonstrating Thread Synchronization*

```
public class BucketBallGame {

    private int bucket[] = {10000, 10000};
    private static boolean RIGHT_TO_LEFT;
```

```java
    public static void main(String[] args) {
        new BucketBallGame().doTransfers();
    }

    private void doTransfers() {
        for (int i = 0; i < 10; i++) {
            new Thread(new TransferThread(!RIGHT_TO_LEFT)).start();
            new Thread(new TransferThread(RIGHT_TO_LEFT)).start();
        }
    }

    public void transfer(boolean direction, int numToTransfer) {
        if (direction == RIGHT_TO_LEFT) {
            bucket[0] += numToTransfer;
            bucket[1] -= numToTransfer;
        } else {
            bucket[0] -= numToTransfer;
            bucket[1] += numToTransfer;
        }
        System.out.println("Total: " + (bucket[0] + bucket[1]));
    }

    private class TransferThread implements Runnable {

        private boolean direction;

        public TransferThread(boolean direction) {
            this.direction = direction;
        }

        @Override
        public void run() {
            for (int i = 0; i < 100; i++) {
                transfer(direction, (int) (Math.random() * 2000));
                try {
                    Thread.sleep((int) (Math.random() * 100));
                } catch (InterruptedException ex) {
                }
            }
        }
    }
}
```

We first create two buckets by declaring an integer array of size 2:

```java
private int bucket[] = {10000, 10000};
```

We also define a constant for determining the transfer direction:

```java
private static boolean RIGHT_TO_LEFT;
```

In the **main** method, we create an application instance and call its **doTransfers** method:

```
new BucketBallGame().doTransfers();
```

In the **doTransfers** method, we create 10 instances of our **TransferThread** class that transfer balls from left to right and 10 more instances that transfer from right to left:

```
for (int i = 0; i < 10; i++) {
    new Thread(new TransferThread(!RIGHT_TO_LEFT)).start();
    new Thread(new TransferThread(RIGHT_TO_LEFT)).start();
}
```

TransferThread is our thread, which is a private inner class and discussed later.

Subtracting the desired number from the first bucket and adding the same to the second bucket performs the transfer of balls:

```
bucket[0] += numToTransfer;
bucket[1] -= numToTransfer;
```

After the transfer is over, we print the total number of balls from the two buckets:

```
System.out.println("Total: " + (bucket[0] + bucket[1]));
```

Finally, we look at the transfer thread class implementation:

```
private class TransferThread implements Runnable {
```

The class constructor receives a parameter, which we copy into a class variable for further use. In the **run** method, we perform 100 transfers:

```
public void run() {
    for (int i = 0; i < 100; i++) {
```

For each transfer, we create a random number in the range of 0 to 1999:

```
transfer(direction, (int) (Math.random() * 2000));
```

We then cause the thread to sleep for a random time, in the range of 0 to 100 milliseconds:

```
Thread.sleep((int) (Math.random() * 100));
```

Now, run the application and observe the output. Initially, the output shows a total of 20,000, which is correct because the number of balls in each bucket is 10,000. For a first few iterations, this total remains 20,000; however, after a while this total changes to a figure other than 20,000. Typical partial output is shown here:

```
Total: 20000
Total: 20000
Total: 20386
Total: 20386
Total: 20386
```

How is it that the total does not remain constant at 20,000? Have we lost some balls? In some runs, you will find the total is more than 20,000. Are new balls created then? No. The answer to the original question is that we do not perform the ball removal and insertion operations as an atomic unit—that is, as a unit that is not broken up. When one thread removes the balls from the bucket, before it puts them into the second bucket, another thread gets the CPU. This new thread modifies the bucket states without the knowledge of what the first thread has done. This leaves the total system in an inconsistent state. To solve this problem, we must perform the ball removal and insertion operations atomically. In other words, even if the running thread loses the CPU in between the two operations, no other thread should be given access to the buckets unless and until the first thread resumes and completes its previously uncompleted operation. To achieve this, Java provides a simple keyword called **synchronized**. Let's make a small change in our program to implement this synchronization. Simply put the **synchronized** keyword between the **public** and **void** literals in the **transfer** function declaration, as shown here:

```
public synchronized void transfer(boolean direction, int numToTransfer) {
```

Now run the program and observe the output. You will find that the output now remains constant to 20,000. This is because each time only one thread at a time can perform a transfer.

Producer/Consumer Problem

The scenario described in the previous section is a very trivial situation used for demonstrating synchronized access to a common resource. In real-life situations, you would require synchronization between many contending threads. Java provides a special wait/notify mechanism to achieve this—and that is what we will be discussing in this section. To teach wait/notify implementation, it is common to use a pedagogical producer/consumer problem, which is what we'll do here.

We will first look at the classical producer/consumer problem in thread programming (see Figure 17-5) and then show its implementation in a Java program.

Consider a situation where we have an empty bucket. A producer produces a pack of balls and puts it in the bucket. As soon as the pack is placed, the consumer (who is waiting for the pack) immediately picks it up. The producer now creates another pack and puts it in the bucket. As soon as this pack of balls is in the bucket, the waiting consumer is notified and again immediately picks

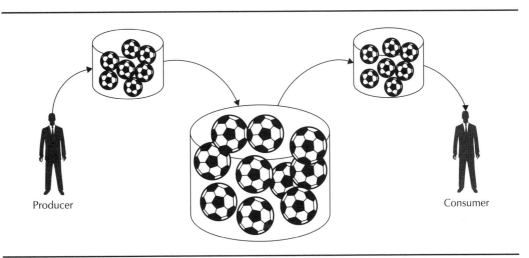

FIGURE 17-5. *Producer/consumer scenario*

up the pack from the bucket. This process continues in tandem, where the producer keeps on producing packs of balls and the consumer keeps on consuming those packs as soon as they are available in the bucket. Note that the producer and consumer work independent of each other. Therefore, the consumer must be notified whenever the producer adds a pack to the bucket. Java provides the wait/notify construct to implement this functionality. The use of this functionality is illustrated in Listing 17-5.

Listing 17-5 *A Producer/Consumer Scenario in Thread Programming*

```java
public class ProducerConsumerGame {

    public static void main(String args[]) {
        Bucket bucket = new Bucket();
        new Thread(new Producer(bucket)).start();
        new Thread(new Consumer(bucket)).start();
    }
}

final class Consumer implements Runnable {

    private Bucket bucket;

    public Consumer(Bucket bucket) {
        this.bucket = bucket;
    }

    public void run() {
        for (int i = 0; i < 10; i++) {
            bucket.get();
        }
    }
}

final class Producer implements Runnable {

    private Bucket bucket;

    public Producer(Bucket bucket) {
        this.bucket = bucket;
    }

    public void run() {

        for (int i = 0; i < 10; i++) {
            bucket.put((int) (Math.random() * 100));
        }
    }
}

class Bucket {
```

```
    private int packOfBalls;
    private boolean available = false;

    public synchronized int get() {
        if (available == false) {
            try {
                wait();
            } catch (InterruptedException e) {
            }
        }
        System.out.println("Consumer Got: " + packOfBalls);
        available = false;
        notify();
        return packOfBalls;
    }

    public synchronized void put(int packOfBalls) {
        if (available) {
            try {
                wait();
            } catch (InterruptedException e) {
            }
        }
        this.packOfBalls = packOfBalls;
        available = true;
        System.out.println("Producer Put: " + packOfBalls);
        notify();
    }
}
```

In the **main** method, we first create a bucket:

```
Bucket bucket = new Bucket();
```

We discuss the **Bucket** class later. In the **main** method, we create and start two threads:

```
new Thread(new Producer(bucket)).start();
new Thread(new Consumer(bucket)).start();
```

The **Producer** thread produces the balls and puts them in the bucket after they are produced. The **Consumer** thread waits for the balls to become available in the bucket and then removes them from the bucket when they do become available.

The **Consumer** class implements **Runnable** and receives the **Bucket** object as an argument to its constructor. In the **run** method, the consumer fetches the pack of balls from the bucket 10 times.

```
for (int i = 0; i < 10; i++) {
    bucket.get();
}
```

To fetch the pack, it calls the **get** method of the **Bucket** class.

Like the **Consumer** class, **Producer** is a thread class that receives a reference to the **Bucket** object at the time of its construction. In the **run** method, it puts 10 packs in the bucket. The pack size is set to a random number in the range 0 to 99:

```
for (int i = 0; i < 10; i++) {
    bucket.put((int) (Math.random() * 100));
}
```

Let's now discuss the most important class—**Bucket**. The **Bucket** class declares two class variables:

```
private int packOfBalls;
private boolean available = false;
```

Here, **packOfBalls** indicates the number of balls added to the bucket at any point in time, and **available** is a **boolean** flag that is set to **true** whenever a pack is added to the bucket and is reset after the pack is removed from the bucket. The **get** method is used for retrieving the pack from the bucket:

```
public synchronized int get() {
```

The **get** method is synchronized because the method implementation uses the **wait** method, which can be used only within a synchronized method or block. In the **get** method, we test the condition of the **available** flag. If the flag is reset, we simply wait on the current object for the condition to become **true**:

```
if (available == false) {
    try {
        wait();
    } catch (InterruptedException e) {
    }
}
```

The JVM will awaken this thread whenever some other thread sets the **available** condition. When this happens, we reset the flag, notify the consumer, and return the value of **packOfBalls** to the caller:

```
available = false;
notify();
return packOfBalls;
```

The producer ensures that the **packOfBalls** value is set before waking the waiting consumer thread. This is done in the **put** method. The **put** method of the **Bucket** class is also **synchronized** because it uses the **notify** method in its implementation:

```
public synchronized void put(int packOfBalls) {
```

The **put** method first checks whether it is allowed to put the balls in the bucket by checking the bucket's **available** status. If the bucket is not available, the method waits for it to become available:

```
if (available) {
    try {
        wait();
    } catch (InterruptedException e) {
    }
}
```

It then copies the received parameter in the class variable, **packOfBalls**, and sets the **available** flag to **true**:

```
packOfBalls = numberOfBalls;
available = true;
```

It then calls the **notify** method to inform the consumer that the balls are now available in the bucket for its consumption:

```
notify();
```

Therefore, whenever the producer calls the **put** method on the **Bucket**, a notification is sent to the waiting consumer. The consumer uses the **get** method to wait and retrieve the pack of balls whenever it is available. The process will continue in tandem forever. Sample, partial output is shown here:

```
Producer put: 64
Consumer got: 64
Producer put: 92
Consumer got: 92
Producer put: 60
Consumer got: 60
```

This producer/consumer problem is observed in many real-life situations. Consider a chat room application where many users concurrently read/write their messages in a single room. If the getter/setter methods are not synchronized, messages will get jumbled up. A similar thing happens for a bulletin board that is read and written concurrently by many users. An auction site might receive many bids and offers for a single item in a very short period of time. Therefore, access to the board that displays the last bid/offer must be synchronized. If a single bank account is accessible by a group of users, the deposits and withdrawals must be synchronized. A typical database application where several records are read, written, and modified in a single table must provide synchronized access to the table to avoid data corruption. These situations illustrate the need for the proper synchronization of common resources in real-life applications.

Object Locks

When you use the **synchronized** keyword, it actually obtains a lock on the current object. In Java, every object has an associated lock. You have so far seen the use of the **synchronized** keyword on the method declarations. This, however, can be used on any block of code. For example, you may provide an atomicity of operations on a block of code by enclosing it in a synchronized block, as shown here:

```
synchronized (this) {
    // program statements;
}
```

This synchronized statement obtains a lock on the current object specified by the **this** keyword and executes all the program statements enclosed in the curly braces as an atomic operation. Instead of **this**, which is just a reference to the current object, you may use any other object reference. The program will obtain a lock on this specified object.

CAUTION
Be aware that this will lock the whole object while execution of the block is occurring on the "winning" thread. Therefore, any other thread will have to wait to call any other method on that object.

When to Synchronize

Synchronization is essential for avoiding data corruption and race conditions that can lead to a program crash, incorrect results, or unpredictable behavior. Even worse, these conditions are likely to occur rarely and sporadically. Thus, an application may pass all its test conditions in a development environment, yet fail sporadically in a production environment. Such problems are hard to detect and reproduce. This, however, does not imply that you should synchronize each and every method. In fact, doing so can lead you into a deadlock if the calls to synchronized methods are not properly ordered, as explained in the next section. Inappropriate or excessive synchronization also leads to an application's poor performance. A synchronized call to an **empty** method may be 20 times slower than the corresponding unsynchronized call. To understand why, let's discuss what **synchronized** really means.

The **synchronized** semantics guarantees that only one thread has access to the protected section at any given time. Consider a case where you have two threads running on two different processors, both having access to a common variable. This variable obviously resides in the common main memory of your machine. Both processors may cache this variable. Thus, in the absence of synchronization, the two threads may see a different value to a common variable read from the processors' respective caches. When synchronizing on a monitor, the Java Memory Model (JMM) requires this cache to be immediately invalidated after the lock is acquired and then flushed before it is released. Flushing the cache frequently can be expensive. This explains the performance penalty in using synchronization.

NOTE
Other platforms typically implement the critical section facilities with an atomic "test and set bit" machine instruction, thus making them perform better than the Java platform in similar situations.

It is important to understand that even when a program contains only a single thread running on a single processor, a synchronized method call will take longer to execute than an unsynchronized method call. If the synchronization requires contending for the lock, the performance penalty is substantially greater. This is because before a lock is obtained, several thread switches and system calls may be happening in the system.

Therefore, the bottom line is this: A multithreaded program requires a good balance between synchronizing enough to protect your shared data from corruption and yet not so much as to risk a deadlock or cause poor performance. Using a **volatile** keyword can result in a more efficient way to synchronize as explained in the sidebar.

Using volatile for Thread Synchronization

Marking the variable with the **volatile** keyword ensures that the same value is seen by all threads at any given point in time—the threads are not allowed to keep local copies of a **volatile** variable. Consider the following code fragment:

```
private int sharedVariable;

synchronized public int getSharedVariable() {
    return sharedVariable;
}

synchronized public void setSharedVariable(int sharedVariable) {
    this.sharedVariable = sharedVariable;
}
```

Here, the access to the **sharedVariable** is guarded by setting the accessor/mutator methods as **synchronized**. A better way to do this is with the following code:

```
volatile private int synchronizedSharedVariable;

public int getSynchronizedSharedVariable() {
    return synchronizedSharedVariable;
}

public void setSynchronizedSharedVariable(int synchronizedSharedVariable) {
    this.synchronizedSharedVariable = synchronizedSharedVariable;
}
```

Now, we have marked the variable as **volatile** instead of making the access methods **synchronized**. This is more efficient because **volatile** only synchronizes the value of just one variable between the thread and main memory, whereas synchronizing a method requires it to provide synchronization for all its variables between the thread and main memory besides locking and releasing a monitor.

The Deadlock

One of the major problems in thread programming is the occurrence of deadlocks in programs that are not carefully designed. When two or more threads compete to obtain a lock on a shared resource and none of them can proceed until the other releases the lock it holds, a deadlock occurs and none of the competing threads can continue. This is like when two people are standing at a door, both holding it open for the other to pass through. Such a situation should obviously be avoided. Figure 17-6 shows an example of a deadlock.

In this figure, the two threads perform synchronized access to their code. Consider the situation where Thread 1 obtains a lock on Object A and then loses the CPU. Now Thread 2, which gains the CPU, obtains a lock on Object B and executes a few code lines before losing the CPU. Thread 1, which now has the CPU, proceeds with its code to obtain a lock on Object B. However, because

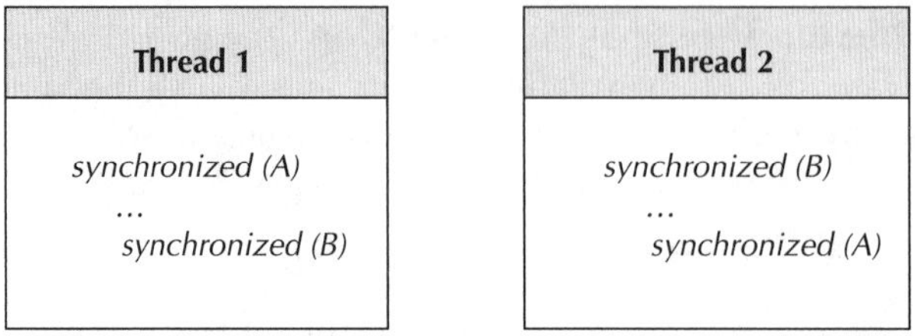

FIGURE 17-6. *A deadlock situation*

Object B has been locked by Thread 2, it cannot proceed and has to wait until the lock on Object B is released by Thread 2. Now, Thread 2 gains the CPU one more time and proceeds with its own code, in which it tries to obtain a lock on Object A. Because Object A has previously been locked by Thread 1, Thread 2 cannot continue unless the lock on Object A is released by Thread 1. You can see that each thread must wait on the other to release its lock and therefore neither can proceed. This situation is called *deadlock*.

Solutions to Deadlock

Deadlocks have no simple solution. They can be avoided only by careful coding. However, three techniques can be used to help you in detecting and preventing deadlocks in your code:

- Lock ordering
- Lock timeout
- Deadlock detection

Lock Ordering

In our earlier example, deadlock can be avoided by maintaining the order in which the locks are obtained and released by two threads. If locks on multiple objects are obtained and released in the same order by both threads, a deadlock cannot occur. Thus, if both threads in our example obtain the locks in the order Object A first, followed by Object B, a deadlock will not occur. The general rule here is that in case of multiple locks, if all locks are always taken in the same order by any thread, deadlocks cannot occur. However, knowing about all the locks needed ahead of taking any of them may not always be the case.

Lock Timeout

Putting a timeout on lock attempts helps in preventing a deadlock situation. Let's look at how this happens. If a thread does not succeed in obtaining all the necessary locks within the given timeout period, it will back up, freeing all locks taken so far. It then waits for a random amount of time before making another attempt to obtain the locks. The random amount of waiting time gives a fair opportunity for others to obtain locks. The problem with this technique is that the **synchronized** keyword has no facility to specify this timeout. To use a timeout facility, use the **java.util.concurrent.locks.Lock** interface introduced in J2SE 5.0 for thread synchronization.

The **ReentrantLock** class in the same package implements this interface. The use of this class is illustrated in the following code snippet:

```
Lock lock = new ReentrantLock();
lock.lock();
// critical section
lock.unlock();
```

You may use the **tryLock (long timeout, TimeUnit timeUnit)** method to specify the timeout for attempts to acquire a lock.

To demonstrate how to use this **Lock** implementation, we modify the **BucketBallGame** class discussed previously. To maintain the integrity of the entire system, earlier we used the **synchronized** keyword on the **transfer** method. The same effect can be achieved by using locks, as shown in the modified class in Listing 17-6.

Listing 17-6   *Modified Bucket Ball Game Using Locks*

```java
import java.util.concurrent.locks.ReentrantLock;

public class ModifiedBucketBallGame {

    private int bucket[] = {10000, 10000};
    private static boolean RIGHT_TO_LEFT;
    ReentrantLock lock = new ReentrantLock();

    public static void main(String[] args) {
        new ModifiedBucketBallGame().doTransfers();
    }

    private void doTransfers() {
        for (int i = 0; i < 10; i++) {
            new Thread(new TransferThread(!RIGHT_TO_LEFT)).start();
            new Thread(new TransferThread(RIGHT_TO_LEFT)).start();
        }
    }

    public void transfer(boolean direction, int numToTransfer) {
        lock.lock();
        if (direction == RIGHT_TO_LEFT) {
            bucket[0] += numToTransfer;
            bucket[1] -= numToTransfer;
        } else {
            bucket[0] -= numToTransfer;
            bucket[1] += numToTransfer;
        }
        System.out.println("Total: " + (bucket[0] + bucket[1]));
        lock.unlock();
    }

    private class TransferThread implements Runnable {
```

```
        private boolean direction;

        public TransferThread(boolean direction) {
            this.direction = direction;
        }

        @Override
        public void run() {
            for (int i = 0; i < 100; i++) {
                transfer(direction, (int) (Math.random() * 2000));
                try {
                    Thread.sleep((int) (Math.random() * 100));
                } catch (InterruptedException ex) {
                }
            }
        }
    }
}
```

The changes made to the original class definition are shown in bold typeface. We create the **Lock** instance as an instance variable:

```
ReentrantLock lock = new ReentrantLock();
```

Once a lock object is available, we can enclose the critical section code anywhere in the program by calling the **lock** method at the beginning of the critical section and the **unlock** method at the end. Look at the placement of the **lock.lock** and **lock.unlock** statements in the listing. The code enclosed between these two calls would be executed as an atomic operation, and the system's integrity is never compromised.

Deadlock Detection

If both these remedies of lock ordering and timeout are not feasible, we can resort to deadlock detection, which is definitely a more difficult solution of deadlock prevention. In this solution, we record every request and acquire a lock by all threads. Generally, this is stored in a map or graph for ease of traversal. When a request for a lock is denied, the thread traverses this lock graph to check for deadlocks. Consider the lock graph shown in Figure 17-7.

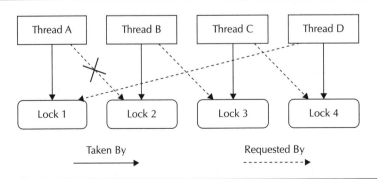

FIGURE 17-7. *Graph used in deadlock detection*

Here, Thread A is holding Lock 1 and has requested Lock 2. The request fails. Therefore, Thread A tries to find out why the request failed. It realizes from the graph that Lock 2, which it has requested, is currently being held by Thread B. Now it moves further in the graph to detect that Thread B is waiting for Lock 3. Continuing on, it finds out that Thread C is holding Lock 3, which is requested by Thread B. Going further, it detects that Thread C is waiting on Lock 4, which is currently held by Thread D. One more step and it finds out that Thread D is waiting for Lock 1, which is held by Thread A itself. Now, Thread A knows that a deadlock has occurred and its request for Lock 2 will not be fulfilled until the deadlock is resolved. So how do we resolve it?

A possible approach would be to release all locks and withdraw all pending requests, and then wait a random amount of time before every thread tries acquiring the desired locks. There is no guarantee that this second attempt of acquiring locks all over again would succeed, and we may be required to repeat the entire process several times, especially if the number of threads involved is large. A possible remedy to this could be to do a priority-based backup, where only certain threads that have been assigned lower priorities are made to back up, while other threads continue holding their locks. The priority for the backup itself may be randomly assigned whenever a deadlock is detected.

From these discussions, we can make one conclusion for sure: Avoiding deadlocks is not always easy, but careful coding can mitigate the situation.

Summary

Thread programming is considered one of the most important aspects of learning a new language, and at the same time it is the most complex aspect to learn. In this chapter, you learned how to create and use threads in your Java applications. A thread is a single unit of execution within an operating system process. A process may contain multiple threads. The OS schedules these threads on the CPU based on a predetermined scheduling policy. We discussed the preemptive and nonpreemptive scheduling policies. Each thread is assigned a certain priority. In the case of preemptive scheduling, a thread with a higher priority preempts the running thread, whereas in the case of nonpreemptive scheduling, a running thread continues using the CPU even when a thread with a higher priority is waiting. The JVM may derive its thread-scheduling functionality from the underlying platform. We discussed the variations in JVM implementations on various popular platforms. Threads are assigned a priority level. Java defines these levels in the range 1 to 10. A separate queue for scheduling threads on the CPU is maintained for threads at each priority level.

To create threads in Java, you have two mechanisms. One is to implement the **Runnable** interface, and the other one is to subclass the **Thread** class. Implementing the **Runnable** interface is the recommended way. The **Thread** class provides several static methods to perform various thread-related operations. You studied several of these methods in this chapter.

When multiple threads access a common resource, resource contention may occur. To avoid this, you need to use locking mechanisms. Java provides an easy way of locking resources with the use of the **synchronized** keyword. You learned the synchronization techniques with the help of two code examples. In the next chapter, you learn about the concurrency framework introduced in J2SE 5.0.

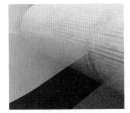

CHAPTER
18

Blocking Queues
and Synchronizers

A s you saw in the previous chapter, the Java language has had support for threads and concurrency from day one. You have seen the use of synchronization primitives such as **synchronized** and **volatile**, and the use of the **Thread** class. These concurrency primitives addressed the needs of the then-available hardware technology (in 1995), where all commercially available machines offered only a single-core CPU for processing. The threads in those days provided asynchrony, rather than concurrency, which was adequate for the demands of that time. Now, by default, all machines come with a multicore processor; your machine may even have multiple processors. So these days, software developers need to write applications that leverage parallelism to fully exploit the available hardware.

The question is, what kinds of applications can leverage this parallelism? In many situations, the parallelism helps in improving application performance. Consider the use-case of an automated price quote system. Such a web application requires access to three databases—the pricing database, which provides the item's base price; the customer database, which provides the discount structure for a customer; and the shipping database, which provides the basic shipping costs for various modes of shipping. The computations and results provided by these three database accesses are independent of each other; in the end, the three results are aggregated to generate a final price quote, as depicted in Figure 18-1.

Let's look at a few more use-cases where implementing parallelism can help. A game with multiple animations can benefit from forking each animation to run on an independent processor. An image-processing application, where each pixel in an image needs some sort of manipulation,

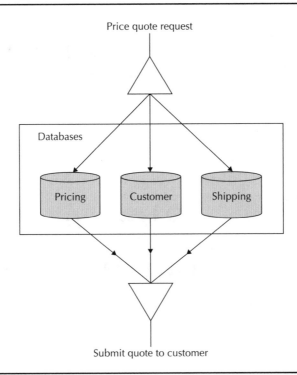

FIGURE 18-1. *Using parallelism in an automated price quote system*

such as reversing its color, will benefit from splitting the number of pixels into smaller groups and assigning each group to an independent core for processing. A game can be more exciting when multiple events take place concurrently. A healthcare application may run various tests concurrently to determine a patient's diagnosis. An application that evaluates portfolios needs to communicate with various markets concurrently. There is no end to this list; you will be able to find several areas where parallelism can help improve application performance and generate a richer user experience.

From our discussions, do not jump to the conclusion that every application must use the concurrency framework that you are going to learn about in this and the next chapter. Typical sequential operations cannot be split into parallel programs and would continue running in a single thread. The kinds of applications we've looked at so far in this book, which are inherently small, do not require parallelism. Many GUI applications also do not require explicit thread programming from the developer's perspective.

In general, you would use the concurrency framework for a variety of performance-scaling needs as well as for splitting heavy linear tasks into smaller tasks that can be executed concurrently. Generally, CPU-intensive applications will be ideal candidates for exploiting parallelism.

You have seen the use of the **interrupt**, **join**, **sleep**, **notify**, and **wait** methods to implement concurrency in our programs. The use of these methods was a bit tedious. J2SE 5.0 came up with a higher-level framework to provide easier, simpler, and less-error-prone handling of threads. This is called a concurrency framework, and it enables you to write applications that it can apply multiple threads to. In turn, the VM maps those multiple threads onto the available multiple hardware threads. On the other hand, if you write a single-threaded application (say, a **for** loop that iterates through millions of records), the VM can only use one execution thread to do the work. And this can only map to one hardware thread, even if 127 other hardware threads are idle. Higher-level concurrency APIs can help you rewrite this into a multithreaded application. A lot of art and science is involved in how different VM implementations map Java threads to hardware threads on different systems. The important thing to note is that modern VMs on multiple-core/multiple-processor architectures do make a mapping that is of great benefit to multithreaded applications. So let's start with the various synchronization constructs introduced in J2SE 5.0.

In particular, you will learn the following constructs in this chapter:

- Blocking queues
- Countdown latches
- Semaphores
- Barriers
- Phasers
- Exchangers

Blocking Queues

Many synchronization problems can be formulated with the help of blocking queues. A *blocking queue* is a queue that blocks when a thread tries to dequeue from an empty queue or tries to enqueue an item into a full queue. A thread trying to remove an item from an empty queue blocks until some other thread puts an item into that queue. Similarly, a thread trying to insert an item into a queue that is full will block until some other thread removes an item from that queue. The blocking may be implemented by using either the polling or the wait-notify mechanism discussed in the last chapter. In the case of polling, a reader thread calls the **get** method on the queue periodically until a message becomes available in the queue. In case of the wait-notify mechanism, the reader thread simply waits on the queue object that notifies it whenever an item is available for reading.

In real life, you come across many situations where these blocking queues can be used. Consider buying a ticket at the railway booth. When you approach the counter, you find line of people (that is, a queue). You stand at the end of the queue and wait for your turn to come. The person at the counter takes requests from the beginning of the queue—one request at a time. Serving a request requires a few synchronization operations that take place at the counter. Once one person is served, the next person in the line gets an opportunity. When more customers arrive at the station, the queue grows dynamically. The size of a queue may be restricted due to space limitations at some railway stations. The ticket officer who deals with only one customer at a time becomes a point of key synchronization in this entire scenario. Both the consumer (the traveler) and the producer (the ticket issuer) are relieved of the duty of taking care of synchronized access to the shared resources (travel tickets). Without the implementation of a disciplined queue in this scenario, all travelers would jump to get their hands on whatever tickets are available at the counter, and chaos would ensue.

Another real-life scenario where blocking queues come to the rescue is in the implementation of a chat server. In a typical chat application, multiple users communicate with each other concurrently. The application has many reader and writer threads. The reader threads take incoming messages and put them on the main message queue. The writer threads take messages off the queue, one at a time, and send them to the appropriate chat clients. The use of a queue effectively decouples the reading and writing processes. At any given time, if the queue is full, the reader thread that has a message to post will have to wait for a slot to be available in the queue. Similarly, if the queue is empty, all writer threads will have to wait until a message becomes available in the queue. Thus, even if the speeds (connection and data transfer speeds) at which the readers and writers operate vary greatly, the integrity of the data (messages) is never compromised.

Blocking queues are also useful in many other scenarios, such as a bulletin board service, a stock-trading system, and more. You will see many practical applications of blocking queues and their uses as you read further.

Characteristics of Blocking Queues

The typical characteristics of a blocking queue may be summarized as follows:

- Blocking queues provide methods to add items to them. Calls to these methods are blocking calls, where the inserter of an item in the queue has to wait until space becomes available in the queue.

- The queues provide methods to remove items from them. Once again, these are blocking calls, and takers are made to wait for an item to be put into an empty queue.

- The **add** and **remove** methods may optionally provide a timeout on their wait operations and may be interruptible.

- Generally, the **put** and **take** operations are implemented in separate threads, thus providing good isolation between the two types of operations. Also, they generally achieve this without blocking the entire queue, thus improving the concurrency of these operations significantly.

- You cannot insert **null** elements in a blocking queue.

- A blocking queue may be bound by capacity.

■ The implementations are thread-safe. However, bulk operations such as **addAll** may not be necessarily performed atomically and may sometimes fail after a few elements have been added.

■ A blocking queue does not intrinsically support a "close" or "shutdown" operation to indicate that no more items can be added.

From these characteristics, one can easily deduce that the primary application of a blocking queue would lie in the producer-consumer scenario described in the previous chapter. These queues can safely be used with multiple producers and multiple consumers.

The BlockingQueue Interface

J2SE 5.0 introduced this blocking queue construct as a part of the concurrency framework. The **BlockingQueue** interface facilitates queue construction and provides several methods for operating on a queue. Once a queue is constructed, you can use the **add** or **remove** method to add or remove an element from the queue, as the names suggest. These methods throw some exceptions in the case of a failure. A queue generally has a restricted size. If such a queue gets full, an **add** operation on it fails. Similarly, a **remove** operation on an empty queue fails. Besides these very obvious **add/remove** methods, the **BlockingQueue** interface provides **put** and **take** methods, which block if the operation does not succeed. The **put** method blocks until an empty slot is available in the queue, and the **take** method waits until an element is added to an empty queue. The **BlockingQueue** also provides special methods called **offer** and **poll**. These methods do not block; on the contrary, they return a special value to the caller so that the caller can decide whether to wait or to proceed further with its work. Both these methods also provide a timeout version, where they wait for the operation to succeed for a specified amount of time.

Implementations of the BlockingQueue Interface

J2SE 5.0 provides several implementations of the **BlockingQueue** interface. This section describes these various implementations.

ArrayBlockingQueue

The **ArrayBlockingQueue** class implements a bounded blocking queue backed by an array. This implements FIFO (first-in, first-out) ordering. New elements are inserted at the tail end, and retrieval takes place from the head of the queue. The tail end of the queue is the element that's on the queue for the shortest amount of time, and the head element is the one on the queue for the longest amount of time. This queue is of the fixed size, where the size is decided at the time of its construction. The array capacity cannot be increased at a later time. An overloaded constructor also allows you to specify the fairness policy for ordering waiting threads. If this policy is set to true, all blocked operations for insertion or removal will be processed in FIFO order. By default, this is set to false, indicating that the ordering may not be fair to the waiting threads. Although this can cause starvation and predictability problems, it produces better throughput.

NOTE
In a situation where many threads compete for a shared resource, a greedy thread may acquire it and make it unavailable to those waiting for it for long periods of time. This situation is called starvation, *where the waiting threads starve for the resource to become available.*

Another variation of the constructor takes a **Collection** parameter, through which you can supply the initial data items to the queue.

LinkedBlockingQueue

The **LinkedBlockingQueue** extends the concept of the array-blocking queue by making the maximum capacity optional. You may still specify the capacity to prohibit excessive expansion. If you do not specify the capacity, the default is the max integer value. Not having a limit on the capacity can be advantageous because the producers do not have to wait if the consumers are behind schedule in picking up the items. Like the array-based queue, an overloaded constructor can accept the initial feed from a collection. This queue generally has higher throughput than an array-based queue, but at the same time has less-predictable performance. Most operations on this queue run in constant time, except for the remove operations, which run in linear time.

PriorityBlockingQueue

A **PriorityBlockingQueue** is an unbounded queue, where you can decide on the priority ordering of the elements, the same as **PriorityQueue** from Chapter 16. Priority can be decided by the natural ordering of elements or by a comparator supplied by you. According to a priority queue's ordering, an attempt to insert noncomparable objects results in a **ClassCastException**. If the system resources are exhausted, an add operation may fail even though it is an unbounded queue. If the elements have equal priorities, their ordering is not guaranteed. To enforce ordering in such situations, you need to provide your own classes or comparators on secondary keys.

DelayedQueue

A **DelayedQueue** is a specialized priority queue where the ordering is based on the delay time of each element—the time remaining before an element can be removed from the queue. The **DelayedQueue** requires the objects to remain resident on the queue for a specified amount of time before they are retrieved. The implementation allows element retrieval only when its delay has expired. The element having the furthest (longest) delay is considered to be at the head of the queue and is the first one available for retrieval. If the delay for none of the elements has expired (in other words, all elements have a positive delay time), then the **poll** operation will return **null** because nothing can be retrieved. A **peek** operation on such a queue will still allow you to see the first unexpired element. The **size** method returns a total count of both expired and unexpired elements.

SynchronousQueue

The **SynchronousQueue** implementation defines a blocking queue in which an insert operation must wait for a corresponding remove operation, and vice versa. This is typically used in handoff designs, where an object running in one thread must sync up with an object running in another thread. A common application of this would be in a work-sharing system, where enough consumers are available to ensure that producers do not have to wait to hand over their tasks. Also, the converse is true in the same sense that enough producers are available to ensure consumers do not have to wait. In fact, a synchronous queue does not have any internal capacity—not even the capacity to hold a single object. Therefore, a **peek** operation would always return **null** because nothing is available on the queue. The only time an object is available on the queue is when you are trying to remove it. If you know Ada, you probably know its rendezvous channels; a synchronous queue is quite similar to these. This class supports an optional fairness policy that, when set to true, grants threads access in FIFO order. A synchronous queue is an obvious choice when you need a task-handoff design where one thread needs to sync with another one.

TransferQueue

Java SE 7 introduced a new interface called **TransferQueue** that extends the **BlockingQueue**. Like a synchronous queue, here a producer may wait for consumers to receive elements. For this, the **transfer** method was added to this new interface. The existing **put** method of the **BlockingQueue** enqueues elements without waiting for receipt. The **transfer** method is a blocking call; the **tryTransfer** version of the **transfer** method is a nonblocking call with an optional timeout. The interface provides **getWaitingConsumerCount**, which returns an estimate of the number of consumers waiting to receive elements via **take** or a timed **poll** method. The **hasWaitingConsumer** method tests whether at least one consumer is waiting to receive an element. A **TransferQueue** may be capacity bounded like other blocking queues. The **LinkedTransferQueue** provides a concrete implementation of this interface.

We will now look at the use of blocking queues with the help of an example.

Stock-trading System

Consider the operation of a stock market, where millions of trades take place during the hours of operation. Furthermore, consider all the traders placing buy and sell orders on IBM or Microsoft stock. We will create a blocking queue to allow these traders to add sell orders to this queue as well as to pick up the pending orders. At any given time, if the queue is full, a trader will have to wait for a slot to become empty. Similarly, a buyer will have to wait until a sell order is available in the queue. To simplify the situation, let's say that a buyer must always purchase the full quantity of stock available for sale and that no partial or over-purchases can be made. This is illustrated in Figure 18-2.

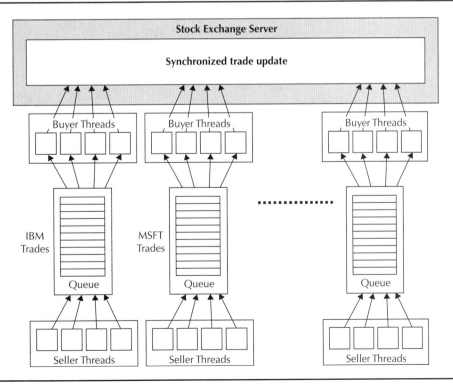

FIGURE 18-2.   *Using blocking queues in a stock-trading system*

The multiple sellers put their sell orders in the queue. The queue is obviously created and maintained by the stock exchange server. When a buyer comes in, he picks up an order from the top of the queue and buys whatever quantity is available in the current sell order. This requires synchronized access to the database and other resources on the server. The updates to these resources are made by the underlying code on the server. Neither buyers nor sellers are responsible for implementing any synchronization mechanism in their code. This is an example of a blocking queue. The stock exchange server will create and operate such queues for each traded scrip on the exchange.

The implementation of this scenario is given in Listing 18-1.

Listing 18-1 *Stock Exchange Trade Server Based on Blocking Queues*

```java
import java.io.IOException;
import java.util.concurrent.*;

public class StockExchange {

    public static void main(String[] args) {
        System.out.printf("Hit Enter to terminate%n%n");
        BlockingQueue<Integer> orderQueue =
                new LinkedBlockingQueue<Integer>();
        Seller seller = new Seller(orderQueue);
        Thread[] sellerThread = new Thread[100];
        for (int i = 0; i < 100; i++) {
            sellerThread[i] = new Thread(seller);
            sellerThread[i].start();
        }
        Buyer buyer = new Buyer(orderQueue);
        Thread[] buyerThread = new Thread[100];
        for (int i = 0; i < 100; i++) {
            buyerThread[i] = new Thread(buyer);
            buyerThread[i].start();
        }
        try {
            while (System.in.read() != '\n');
        } catch (IOException ex) {
        }
        System.out.println("Terminating");
        for (Thread t : sellerThread) {
            t.interrupt();
        }
        for (Thread t : buyerThread) {
            t.interrupt();
        }
    }
}

class Seller implements Runnable {

    private BlockingQueue orderQueue;
```

```
        private boolean shutdownRequest = false;
        private static int id;

        public Seller(BlockingQueue orderQueue) {
            this.orderQueue = orderQueue;
        }

        public void run() {
            while (shutdownRequest == false) {
                Integer quantity = (int) (Math.random() * 100);
                try {
                    orderQueue.put(quantity);
                    System.out.println("Sell order by "
                            + Thread.currentThread().getName()
                            + ": " + quantity);
                } catch (InterruptedException iex) {
                    shutdownRequest = true;
                }
            }
        }
    }

    class Buyer implements Runnable {

        private BlockingQueue orderQueue;
        private boolean shutdownRequest = false;

        public Buyer(BlockingQueue orderQueue) {
            this.orderQueue = orderQueue;
        }

        public void run() {
            while (shutdownRequest == false) {
                try {
                    Integer quantity = (Integer) orderQueue.take();
                    System.out.println("Buy order by "
                            + Thread.currentThread().getName()
                            + ": " + quantity);
                } catch (InterruptedException iex) {
                    shutdownRequest = true;
                }
            }
        }
    }
```

In the **main** function, we create an instance of **LinkedBlockingQueue**:

```
BlockingQueue<Integer> orderQueue = new LinkedBlockingQueue<Integer>();
```

Because the **LinkedBlockingQueue** has unlimited capacity, traders are able to place any number of orders in the queue. If we had used an **ArrayBlockingQueue** instead, we would have been restricted to a limited number of trades on each scrip.

Next, we create an instance of **Seller** that is a **Runnable** class (the implementation is discussed later):

```
Seller seller = new Seller(orderQueue);
```

We create 100 instances of our traders who put their sell orders in the queue. Each sell order will have a random quantity. We thus create an array of 100 threads and schedule them for execution:

```
Thread[] sellerThread = new Thread[100];
for (int i = 0; i < 100; i++) {
    sellerThread[i] = new Thread(seller);
    sellerThread[i].start();
}
```

Likewise, we create 100 buyers who pick up the pending sell orders:

```
Buyer buyer = new Buyer(orderQueue);
Thread[] buyerThread = new Thread[100];
for (int i = 0; i < 100; i++) {
    buyerThread[i] = new Thread(buyer);
    buyerThread[i].start();
}
```

Once the producer and consumer threads are created, they keep running forever, placing orders on and retrieving orders from the queue and blocking themselves periodically, depending on the load at the given time. We need some means of terminating the application. Thus, the **main** thread now waits for the user to hit the ENTER key on the keyboard:

```
while (System.in.read() != '\n');
```

When this happens, the **main** function interrupts all the running producer and consumer threads, requesting that they abort and quit:

```
System.out.println("Terminating");
for (Thread t : sellerThread) {
    t.interrupt();
}
for (Thread t : buyerThread) {
    t.interrupt();
}
```

Now, let's look at the implementation of **Seller**, which implements the **Runnable** interface and provides a constructor that takes our **OrderQueue** as its parameter. The **run** method sets up an infinite loop:

```
public void run() {
    while (shutdownRequest == false) {
```

In each iteration, we generate a random number for the trade quantity value:

```
Integer quantity = (int) (Math.random() * 100);
```

The order is placed in the queue via a call to its **put** method. Note that this is a blocking call, so the thread will have to wait for an empty slot in the queue, just in case the queue has a limited capacity specified at the time of its creation.

```
orderQueue.put(quantity);
```

For the user's benefit, we print the sell order details, along with the details of the thread that has placed this order, to the user console:

```
System.out.println("Sell order by "
        + Thread.currentThread().getName() + ": " + quantity);
```

The **run** method will run indefinitely, placing orders periodically in the queue. This thread can be interrupted by another thread via a call to its **interrupt** method. This is what the **main** thread does whenever it wants to stop the trading. The **interrupt** method generates the **InterruptedException**. The exception handler simply sets the **shutdownRequest** flag to **true**, which causes the infinite loop in the **run** method to terminate:

```
} catch (InterruptedException iex) {
    shutdownRequest = true;
```

Finally, let's look at the implementation of **Buyer**, which is mostly similar to **Seller**, except for its **run** method, which we'll study now. The **run** method picks up a pending trade from the top of the queue by calling its **take** method:

```
Integer quantity = (Integer) OrderQueue.take();
```

Note that the method will block if no orders are available in the queue. Once again, we print the order and thread details for the user's knowledge:

```
System.out.println("Buy order by "
        + Thread.currentThread().getName() + ": " + quantity);
```

Note that now we need synchronized access to the server resources to perform atomic updates on the server. This now becomes the responsibility of the server implementation, and the seller and buyer threads do not have to worry about synchronization issues.

Some typical program output is shown here:

```
Buy order by Thread-136: 46
Buy order by Thread-135: 26
Sell order by Thread-82: 75
Buy order by Thread-133: 96
Sell order by Thread-83: 54
Buy order by Thread-132: 22
Sell order by Thread-84: 29
Sell order by Thread-85: 79
Sell order by Thread-86: 76
Buy order by Thread-131: 35
Sell order by Thread-87: 89
```

The program terminates when the user hits the ENTER key on the keyboard.

If we had not used the blocking queues in this program, there would be contention in accessing the trades placed on an unsynchronized queue. Everybody would try grabbing an order selling a stock below the current market price. Multiple traders would pick up the same order, and chaos and fights among traders would break out. Because the blocking queue ensures synchronized access to the queue, the integrity of trades is never compromised.

We used the **LinkedBlockingQueue** in the preceding example; however, we could have used a priority-based queue so that the trades are automatically arranged based on their bids and offers. An order with the highest bid and the lowest offer always tops the queue. To use the priority-based queue, we would need to provide an appropriate comparator.

In the next section, we discuss the use of the newly introduced **LinkedTransferQueue** class (in Java SE 7).

The LinkedTransferQueue Example

We already discussed this class and some of its methods earlier in the chapter, so in this section we jump directly into its application. We will develop a "lucky number" generator that produces a number using randomization and hands it over to a waiting customer. We create 10 customer (consumer) threads. The consumer threads are created with a time gap of two seconds. If a consumer is available, the lucky number generator thread (which is our producer) will produce a number and hand it over to the consumer. Once a consumer receives its lucky number, it quits. Thus, each consumer will get exactly one number. The lucky number generator, along with 10 consumers, is given in Listing 18-2.

Listing 18-2   *A Lucky Number Generator Based on TransferQueue*

```java
import java.util.Random;
import java.util.concurrent.*;

public class LuckyNumberGenerator {

    public static void main(String... args) {
        TransferQueue<String> queue = new LinkedTransferQueue();
        Thread producer = new Thread(new Producer(queue));
        producer.setDaemon(true);
        producer.start();
        for (int i = 0; i < 10; i++) {
            Thread consumer = new Thread(new Consumer(queue));
            consumer.setDaemon(true);
            consumer.start();
            try {
                Thread.sleep(2000);
            } catch (InterruptedException ex) {
            }
        }
    }
}

class Producer implements Runnable {
```

```
        private final TransferQueue<String> queue;

        Producer(TransferQueue<String> queue) {
            this.queue = queue;
        }

        private String produce() {
            return " your lucky number " + (new Random().nextInt(100));
        }

        public void run() {
            try {
                while (true) {
                    if (queue.hasWaitingConsumer()) {
                        queue.transfer(produce());
                    }
                    TimeUnit.SECONDS.sleep(1);
                }
            } catch (InterruptedException ex) {
            }
        }
    }

    class Consumer implements Runnable {

        private final TransferQueue<String> queue;

        Consumer(TransferQueue<String> queue) {
            this.queue = queue;
        }

        public void run() {
            try {
                System.out.println(" Consumer "
                        + Thread.currentThread().getName() + queue.take());
            } catch (InterruptedException ex) {
            }
        }
    }
```

In the **main** method, we create an instance of **TransferQueue** that stores **String** objects:

```
TransferQueue<String> queue = new LinkedTransferQueue();
```

The method then creates a single producer thread and starts it:

```
Thread producer = new Thread(new Producer(queue));
```

The producer thread takes the queue we just created as its parameter. After creating the producer thread, the program creates 10 consumer threads with a gap of two seconds in between every 2 threads:

```
Thread consumer = new Thread(new Consumer(queue));
```

The **Producer** that implements **Runnable** stores the **TransferQueue** object received in its constructor in a private field. The **run** method creates an infinite program loop, and we check whether a consumer is waiting for a lucky number; if so, we create a lucky number and transfer it to the waiting consumer:

```
if (queue.hasWaitingConsumer()) {
    queue.transfer(produce());
}
```

The producer thread then sleeps for one second before checking for another waiting consumer.

The **Consumer** class also implements **Runnable**, and in its **run** method it receives the lucky number by calling the **take** method on the **TransferQueue** object:

```
System.out.println(" Consumer "
            + Thread.currentThread().getName() + queue.take());
```

Once a lucky number is obtained, the consumer thread terminates. Some typical program output is shown here:

```
Consumer Thread-1 your lucky number 26
Consumer Thread-2 your lucky number 53
Consumer Thread-3 your lucky number 22
Consumer Thread-4 your lucky number 58
Consumer Thread-5 your lucky number 25
Consumer Thread-6 your lucky number 76
Consumer Thread-7 your lucky number 73
Consumer Thread-8 your lucky number 67
Consumer Thread-9 your lucky number 17
Consumer Thread-10 your lucky number 41
```

Synchronizers

J2SE 5.0 added several synchronization constructs to the language as a part of the **java.util.concurrent** package. It includes classes that offer semaphores, barriers, latches, and exchangers. We will now study the use of these classes for synchronization.

Semaphores

Semaphores are useful when you want *n* number of entities to access a shared resource in a synchronized way. A typical application of semaphores is observed in server applications where multiple threads compete for resources that are in some way limited in number. For example, a website with a lot of concurrency may receive several requests at any given time for certain data stored in an internal database on the server. Because the database connections are expensive in terms of time to create and resources held, you might create only a limited number of connections and keep them in a pool. When a web request arrives to access the data, the server application hands over one of the connections to it, provided one is available in the pool at that instance of time. If not, the web request is made to wait until some connection is returned to the pool by one of the existing users. In some situations, the server application may also decide to increase the pool size if the demand is high. The semaphores help you in achieving this functionality, as you will see shortly.

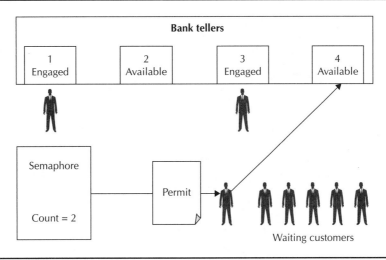

FIGURE 18-3. *A banking scenario that implements semaphores*

Semaphores allow *n* number of entities to access *m* number of resources in a synchronized way. Contrast this with the use of the **synchronized** keyword, which allows access only by a single entity. To explain this better, let's look at a practical situation (see Figure 18-3).

A bank has multiple tellers to serve its customers. Consider this a semaphore count. When a customer walks into the bank, he acquires a permit to engage the teller. After the agent is engaged, the semaphore count is reduced by one. When all the available agents are engaged, the count becomes zero. Now, when a new customer arrives, he cannot obtain a permit and therefore has to wait until an agent becomes available. When the customer finishes his business, he releases his permit, resulting in an increase in semaphore count. The new customer can now get a permit. Thus, multiple customers can now get synchronized access to the bank resources.

The **Semaphore** class implements the semaphores in Java. When you instantiate this class, you specify the number of permits. To acquire a permit, you use the **acquire** method. You may acquire more than one permit by specifying it as a parameter to the **acquire** method. This is a blocking call that blocks itself until a permit is available, or until the waiting thread is interrupted. If you do not want the thread to block on a permit, use the **tryAcquire** method. It returns **false** if the required number of permits is not available. The method takes an optional parameter that specifies the amount of time for which the thread will wait for the permit to become available.

The implementation of our bank teller example is given in Listing 18-3.

Listing 18-3 *Bank Teller Implementation Based on Semaphores*

```
import java.util.concurrent.*;

public class Bank {

    private final static int COUNT = 100;
    private final static Semaphore semaphore =
            new Semaphore(2, true);
```

```java
public static void main(String[] args) {
    for (int i = 0; i < COUNT; i++) {
        final int count = i;
        new Thread() {

            @Override
            public void run() {
                try {
                    if (semaphore.tryAcquire(10,
                            TimeUnit.MILLISECONDS)) {
                        try {
                            Teller.getService(count);
                        } finally {
                            semaphore.release();
                        }
                    }
                } catch (InterruptedException ex) {
                }
            }
        }.start();
    }
}
}

class Teller {

    static public void getService(int i) {
        try {
            System.out.println("serving: " + i);
            Thread.sleep((long) (Math.random() * 10));
        } catch (InterruptedException ex) {
        }
    }
}
```

The **Bank** class declares two **static** variables. The **COUNT** variable controls the number of customers who will visit the bank. The **semaphore** variable holds a reference to the created **Semaphore**:

```java
private static final int COUNT = 100;
private final static Semaphore semaphore = new Semaphore(2, true);
```

The first parameter to the **Semaphore** constructor specifies the number of permits. In this case, we have set it to 2, indicating that the bank has only two agents. The second parameter specifies the fairness setting. When set to **true**, it indicates the FIFO behavior—first come, first served. Because overhead is involved in maintaining a queue of customers, this fairness setting need not always be efficient. As discussed earlier, the default setting is **false**, where a customer arriving later may obtain the permit earlier.

In the **main** method, we set up a loop to process requests from all 100 customers:

```
for (int i = 0; i < COUNT; i++) {
```

For each customer, we create an anonymous thread:

```
new Thread() {
```

In the overridden **run** method, the thread tries to acquire a permit by calling the **tryAcquire** method of the **Semaphore** class:

```
public void run() {
    try {
        if (semaphore.tryAcquire(10, TimeUnit.MILLISECONDS))
```

The first parameter specifies the amount of time to wait, and the second parameter specifies the unit of time. The **TimeUnit** class defines several constants that allow you to specify the unit of time, even in terms of the number of days. In our case, the thread waits for 10 milliseconds to acquire a permit. If a permit is not obtained within this amount of time, the thread simply gives up and continues with its work. This means that the customer no longer waits in the bank and just walks away. If the permit is obtained, the thread requests the service by calling the **getService** method on the **Teller** class, which is discussed later:

```
Teller.getService(count);
```

The **getService** method takes a parameter that identifies the current iteration count and thus the executing thread. After the thread is done with the banker, it releases the permit by calling the **release** method on the **semaphore** object:

```
} finally {
    semaphore.release();
}
```

Note that we have created an instance of an anonymous **Thread** class. To start this, we call the **start** method on the created instance.

Now, let's look at the **Teller** class. The **Teller** class defines one **static** method called **getService**:

```
static public void getService(int i) {
```

In the method, we print the **id** for the currently executing thread:

```
try {
    System.out.println("serving: " + i);
```

We make the thread sleep for a random amount of time:

```
Thread.sleep((long) (Math.random() * 10));
```

The sleep time varies, anywhere from 0 to 10 milliseconds. This is done to simulate the condition that each customer will take a variable amount of time with the agent. Due to this, when you run the program multiple times, you will find that the number of customers served on each run differs from the previous runs.

The output from two sample runs is shown here:

Run 1:

```
serving: 1
serving: 7
serving: 9
serving: 93
serving: 94
```

Run 2:

```
serving: 0
serving: 7
serving: 5
```

In the second run, obviously the customers were too impatient with the speed of the tellers and quickly left the bank. Now, try changing the customer wait time from 10 milliseconds to a higher value. You will now find that a greater number of customers is now served. This is because the customers are now willing to spend more time in the bank waiting for an agent to become available. You can also experiment by changing the number of permits to allocate more agents.

Barriers

A barrier is like a common crossover point, where everybody waits to join up with the others in the team before crossing over. This is illustrated in Figure 18-4.

All members of the team decide to meet at one end of the bridge before crossing over. Once a member arrives, he has to wait for others to reach the same junction. When everyone hits the barrier, the program can continue with the next task. Once a barrier (that is, a meeting point) is decided, any other team can use the same barrier to synchronize their actions.

Java provides the barrier implementation in the **CyclicBarrier** class. Using this class, a set of threads is made to wait for each other to reach a common barrier point. This is typically used in programs where a fixed-sized party of threads must occasionally wait for each other before they

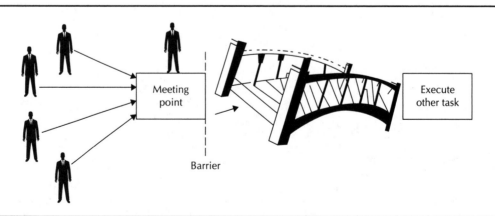

FIGURE 18-4. *Illustrating a barrier type of synchronization construct*

can all proceed further. For example, in horse racing, all horses must reach the starting gate before the race starts. This barrier is considered *cyclic* because it can be reused after all waiting threads are released.

The **CyclicBarrier** class constructor takes a parameter that decides the number of members in the team. Each member of the team, after completing its work, arrives at the barrier and waits by calling its **await** method. When all the members arrive at the barrier, the barrier is broken and the program can proceed. Another variation of the constructor takes an additional parameter that refers to a **Runnable** class, which is executed after the barrier breaks.

To illustrate the use of this class, we will write a program that computes **ln (1–x)**, where **ln** is the natural logarithm. The definition is given here:

$$\ln\,(1\text{-}x)\ =\ -\ (x\ +\ x^2/2\ +\ x^3/3\ +\ x^4/4\ +\ \ldots)\ \text{where}\ |x|\ <\ 1$$

We will create a thread that computes a single term of this series. Thus, to compute 10 terms, we will create 10 threads. Each thread puts the result in a common array and waits at a barrier for the others to finish. When everybody finishes, a waiting thread computes the array sum and displays the result to the user. The implementation is given in Listing 18-4.

Listing 18-4   *Natural Logarithm Calculator Demonstrating a Cyclic Barrier*

```
import java.util.concurrent.*;

public class NaturalLogCalc {

    private static final int numberOfTerms = 10;
    private static double[] termArray = new double[numberOfTerms];
    private static final float x = 0.2f;

    public static void main(String[] args) {
        CyclicBarrier barrier = new CyclicBarrier(numberOfTerms, new Runnable() {

            @Override
            public void run() {
                System.out.println("Computing series sum");
                double sum = 0;
                for (double term : termArray) {
                    sum += term;
                }
                System.out.println("ln (1-" + x + ") equals " + -sum);
            }
        });
        for (int i = 0; i < numberOfTerms; i++) {
            new Thread(new TermCalc(barrier, i)).start();
        }
        System.out.println("Waiting...");
    }

    private static class TermCalc implements Runnable {
```

```
        private int termIndex;
        private CyclicBarrier barrier;

        public TermCalc(CyclicBarrier barrier, int termIndex) {
            this.barrier = barrier;
            this.termIndex = termIndex;
        }

        @Override
        public void run() {
            double result = Math.pow(x, termIndex + 1) / (termIndex + 1);
            termArray[termIndex] = result;
            System.out.println("Term " + (termIndex + 1) + ": " + result);
            try {
                barrier.await();
            } catch (InterruptedException ex) {
                ex.printStackTrace();
            } catch (BrokenBarrierException ex) {
                ex.printStackTrace();
            }
        }
    }
}
```

The **NaturalLogCalc** class declares a few **static** variables:

```
private static final int numberOfTerms = 10;
private static double[] termArray = new double[numberOfTerms];
private static final float x = 0.2f;
```

The **numberOfTerms** decides the number of terms in the series to compute. The **termArray** provides an array to store the result of each computation. The static variable **x** sets the value for **x** in the expression **ln (1–x)**. The **main** method creates an instance of the **CyclicBarrier** class:

```
CyclicBarrier barrier = new CyclicBarrier(numberOfTerms, new Runnable() {

    public void run() {
        System.out.println("Computing series sum");
        double sum = 0;
        for (double term : termArray) {
            sum += term;
        }
        System.out.println("ln (1-" + x + ") equals " + -sum);
    }
});
```

The first parameter to the constructor decides the number of parties. This is set to the number of terms we want to compute. This naturally equals the number of threads we will create for computing terms. The second parameter to the constructor is an instance of the **Runnable** class that will be executed after the barrier is broken. We use an anonymous class here. In the overridden **run** method, the program computes the sum of all elements of the **termArray** and prints the result to the user.

The **main** program now proceeds to create the threads for computing individual terms:

```
for (int i = 0; i < numberOfTerms; i++) {
    new Thread(new TermCalc(barrier, i)).start();
}
```

The **TermCalc** is a **Runnable** class. Let's look at its implementation:

```
private static class TermCalc implements Runnable {
```

The class is declared **private** because it will be used only within the enclosing class. It is also declared **static** so that it is accessible within the static **main** method. In the **run** method, we compute the term value and store it in the **termArray** at an appropriate index:

```
public void run() {
    double result = Math.pow(x, termIndex + 1) / (termIndex + 1);
    termArray[termIndex] = result;
```

After the computation is done, the thread waits at the barrier:

```
barrier.await();
```

After everybody arrives at the barrier, the thread comes out of its **await** method call and proceeds to completion. At this stage, the **termArray** is fully filled and the main program can proceed to compute the sum of all the terms. When you run the program, you will see output similar to the following:

```
Waiting...
Term 1: 0.20000000298023224
Term 3: 0.002666666785875958
Term 7: 1.8285716193063003E-6
Term 10: 1.0240001525879009E-8
Term 8: 3.2000003814697465E-7
Term 6: 1.0666667620341019E-5
Term 4: 4.0000002384185847E-4
Term 2: 0.020000000596046452
Term 5: 6.400000476837173E-5
Term 9: 5.688889651828388E-8
Computing series sum
ln (1-0.2) equals -0.22314355275894068
```

Note that every time you run the program, you will see a different order of execution for the threads. Try changing the value of **x** and the number of terms to compute and observe the execution results.

Countdown Latches

This is yet another synchronization tool provided beginning in J2SE 5.0. In some ways, a countdown latch is like a generalized barrier from the previous section. It provides methods that allow threads to wait for a condition; the only difference is that in the case of a barrier, the threads wait on other threads, whereas in the case of a latch, threads wait for a certain count to reach zero. You specify this count in the constructor. When this count reaches zero, all waiting threads are released.

After the count reaches zero, the latch is not reset and the condition that is now set to **true** remains **true** forever. Note that in the beginning, the latch condition starts out with a **false** status. We will now look at the concept of a countdown latch in the context of the stock-trading server discussed previously.

In our earlier stock-trading example, which was discussed in the context of blocking queues, we created several buyer and seller threads. Ideally, all these trades should have equal privilege when the first order is placed on the exchange. However, because our program creates threads in a definite chronological order, it is likely that the threads created first will find an opportunity to execute before the other threads created later. To avoid this situation, we can make all the threads wait with their orders until we give them the go-ahead signal. This is the purpose of the countdown latch, which is why Java provides the **CountDownLatch** class. We specify the count in its constructor. The **countDown** method decrements the count by one. Each thread, whenever it is ready, is made to wait for this count to become zero by calling the **await** method. Thus, we create all the threads, making each thread wait in its **run** method. After we have created all the threads, we bring the count down to zero. Now, the threads will proceed with their execution. Which thread gets the CPU first is now solely decided by the thread scheduler.

Likewise, when the stock exchange closes its operations at the end of the trading day, it may need to confirm that all running threads have completed fully before proceeding with further cleanup. This can be achieved by setting the count to 200 (note that we have created a combined total of 200 threads of producers and consumers). We will ask each thread to decrement the count by calling the **countDown** method at the end of its **run** method. We make the **main** thread wait until this count becomes zero. Thus, the **main** thread cannot proceed until all threads signal their successful completion of the **run** method. Once this happens, the **main** thread will continue with any further cleanup operations.

The modified program that implements these countdown latches is given in Listing 18-5.

Listing 18-5 *Enhanced Stock Exchange Using a Countdown Latch*

```java
import java.io.IOException;
import java.util.concurrent.*;

public class EnhancedStockExchange {

    public static void main(String[] args) {
        BlockingQueue<Integer> orderQueue =
                new LinkedBlockingQueue<Integer>();
        CountDownLatch startSignal = new CountDownLatch(1);
        CountDownLatch stopSignal = new CountDownLatch(200);
        Seller seller = new Seller(orderQueue, startSignal, stopSignal);
        Thread[] sellerThread = new Thread[100];
        for (int i = 0; i < 100; i++) {
            sellerThread[i] = new Thread(seller);
            sellerThread[i].start();
        }
        Buyer buyer = new Buyer(orderQueue, startSignal, stopSignal);
        Thread[] buyerThread = new Thread[100];
        for (int i = 0; i < 100; i++) {
            buyerThread[i] = new Thread(buyer);
```

```
            buyerThread[i].start();
        }
        System.out.println("Go");
        startSignal.countDown();
        try {
            while (System.in.read() != '\n');
        } catch (IOException ex) {
        }
        System.out.println("Terminating");
        for (Thread t : sellerThread) {
            t.interrupt();
        }
        for (Thread t : buyerThread) {
            t.interrupt();
        }
        try {
            stopSignal.await();
        } catch (InterruptedException ex) {
        }
        System.out.println("Closing down");
    }
}

class Seller implements Runnable {

    private BlockingQueue orderQueue;
    private boolean shutdownRequest = false;
    private static int id;
    private CountDownLatch startLatch, stopLatch;

    public Seller(BlockingQueue orderQueue,
            CountDownLatch startLatch, CountDownLatch stopLatch) {
        this.orderQueue = orderQueue;
        this.startLatch = startLatch;
        this.stopLatch = stopLatch;
    }

    public void run() {
        try {
            startLatch.await();
        } catch (InterruptedException ex) {
        }
        while (shutdownRequest == false) {
            Integer quantity = (int) (Math.random() * 100);
            try {
                orderQueue.put(quantity);
                System.out.println("Sell order producer # "
                    + Thread.currentThread().getName()
                    + ": " + quantity);
            } catch (InterruptedException iex) {
```

```
                shutdownRequest = true;
            }
        }
        stopLatch.countDown();
    }
}

class Buyer implements Runnable {

    private BlockingQueue orderQueue;
    private boolean shutdownRequest = false;
    private CountDownLatch startLatch, stopLatch;

    public Buyer(BlockingQueue orderQueue,
            CountDownLatch startLatch, CountDownLatch stopLatch) {
        this.orderQueue = orderQueue;
        this.startLatch = startLatch;
        this.stopLatch = stopLatch;
    }

    public void run() {
        try {
            startLatch.await();
        } catch (InterruptedException ex) {
        }
        while (shutdownRequest == false) {
            try {
                Integer quantity = (Integer) orderQueue.take();
                System.out.println("Buy order consumer # "
                    + Thread.currentThread().getName()
                        + ": " + quantity);
            } catch (InterruptedException iex) {
                shutdownRequest = true;
            }
        }
        stopLatch.countDown();
    }
}
```

In the **main** method, we create two latches as follows:

```
CountDownLatch startSignal = new CountDownLatch(1);
CountDownLatch stopSignal = new CountDownLatch(200);
```

Note that the count for the start signal is set to 1 and that for the stop signal is set to 200. Thus, one single countdown operation on the start signal will release all its waiting threads for execution. The stop signal count has to go from 200 to 0 before the waiting main thread can proceed. Each of our individual buyer and seller threads will decrement the count by one. We send the references to these latches in the **Buyer** and **Seller** constructors:

```
Seller seller = new Seller(orderQueue, startSignal, stopSignal);
```

At the beginning of the **run** method of both **Buyer** and **Seller**, we add the following code:

```
try {
    startLatch.await();
} catch (InterruptedException ex) {
}
```

Thus, after the thread is created, it is made to wait on the **startLatch** for a go-ahead signal. In the **main** method, after we have created all the threads, we execute the following statement:

```
startSignal.countDown();
```

The **countDown** method brings the start latch count to zero. Now, all created threads can begin their execution. All these ready-to-run threads will acquire the CPU based on the scheduling policy of the underlying platform. The point is that each trader gets an equal priority to make the first trade.

At the end of the **run** method of both the **Buyer** and **Seller** classes, we add the following statement:

```
stopLatch.countDown();
```

This decrements the stop count by one. In the **main** method, we wait on this count to become zero by executing the **await** method:

```
try {
    stopSignal.await();
} catch (InterruptedException ex) {
}
System.out.println("Closing down");
```

The program proceeds only when the **stopSignal** count goes to zero. By this time, every trader has had a chance to complete its pending trade. The **main** thread can now proceed with rest of the cleanup.

Phaser

Java SE 7 introduced a new reusable synchronization barrier called **Phaser** that is similar in functionality to **CyclicBarrier** and **CountDownLatch**; however, this class provides for more flexible usage. The barriers you've studied so far worked on a fixed number of parties. A phaser works with a variable number of barriers, in the sense that you can register a new party at any time and an already registered party can deregister itself upon arrival at the barrier. So the number of parties registered to synchronize on a phaser may vary over time. Like a **CyclicBarrier**, a phaser can be reused. This means that after a party has arrived at a phaser, it may register itself one more time and await another arrival. Thus, a phaser will have many generations. Once all the parties registered for a particular phase arrive at the phaser, the phase number is advanced. The phase number starts with zero and, after reaching **Integer.MAX_VALUE**, wraps around to zero again. On a phase change, an optional action may be performed by overriding its **onAdvance** method. This method can also be used to terminate the phaser; once the phaser is terminated, all synchronization methods immediately return and attempts to register new parties fail.

Another important feature of a phaser is that it may be tiered. This allows you to arrange phasers in tree structures to reduce contention. A smaller group obviously has fewer parties contending for synchronization. Arranging a large number of parties into smaller groups would thus reduce contention. Even though it increases the total throughput, building a phaser requires more overhead. Finally, one more important feature of a phaser is its monitoring. An independent object can monitor the current state of a phaser. This monitor can query the phaser for the number of parties registered and the number of parties that have arrived and have not arrived at a particular phase number.

Now, let's look at the use of the **Phaser** class with a practical example. Suppose we want to write a horse-racing simulation game. We could consider the starting gate of the race to be the barrier; when all the horses arrive at the starting gate, the race may begin. The time that each horse needs to reach the starting gate may vary considerably and therefore synchronization at the barrier is required. Once the race begins, each horse will deregister from the phaser, and the same phaser (starting gate) may be reused for another race, scheduled at a later time. The complete simulation program is presented in Listing 18-6.

Listing 18-6 *A Horse-racing Simulation Program Using Phaser*

```java
import java.util.*;
import java.util.concurrent.Phaser;
import java.util.concurrent.atomic.AtomicInteger;

public class HorseRace {

    private final int NUMBER_OF_HORSES = 12;
    private final static int INIT_PARTIES = 1;
    private final static Phaser manager = new Phaser(INIT_PARTIES);

    public static void main(String[] args) {
        Thread raceMonitor = new Thread(new RaceMonitor());
        raceMonitor.setDaemon(true);
        raceMonitor.start();
        new HorseRace().manageRace();
    }

    public void manageRace() {
        ArrayList<Horse> horseArray = new ArrayList<Horse>();
        for (int i = 0; i < NUMBER_OF_HORSES; i++) {
            horseArray.add(new Horse());
        }
        runRace(horseArray);
    }

    private void runRace(Iterable<Horse> team) {
        log("Assign all horses, then start race");
        for (final Horse horse : team) {
            final String dev = horse.toString();
            log("assign " + dev + " to the race");
            manager.register();
            new Thread() {

                @Override
                public void run() {
                    try {
```

```
                      Thread.sleep((new Random()).nextInt(1000));
                  } catch (InterruptedException ex) {
                  }
                  log(dev + ", please await all horses");
                  manager.arriveAndAwaitAdvance();
                  horse.run();
              }
          }.start();
      }
      try {
          Thread.sleep(1000);
      } catch (InterruptedException ex) {
      }
      log("All arrived at starting gate, start race");
      manager.arriveAndDeregister();
  }

  private static void log(String msg) {
      System.out.println(msg);
  }

  private static class Horse implements Runnable {

      private final static AtomicInteger idSource = new AtomicInteger();
      private final int id = idSource.incrementAndGet();

      @Override
      public void run() {
          log(toString() + ": running");
      }

      @Override
      public String toString() {
          return "horse #" + id;
      }
  }

  private static class RaceMonitor implements Runnable {

      @Override
      public void run() {
          while (true) {
              System.out.println("Number of horses ready to run: "
                      + HorseRace.manager.getArrivedParties());
              try {
                  Thread.sleep(1);
              } catch (InterruptedException ex) {
              }
          }
      }
  }
}
```

We define the maximum horse count as 12, which is the typical average for big horse races. We create a phaser by passing the initial count for the number of parties as 1:

```
private final static int INIT_PARTIES = 1;
private final static Phaser manager = new Phaser(INIT_PARTIES);
```

As more horses (parties) register on this phaser, the number of parties awaiting the synchronization barrier will increase.

In the **main** method, we declare a thread variable called **raceMonitor** for holding a reference to a thread object that independently monitors the number of horses that have arrived at the starting gate. We create a monitoring thread that monitors the number of horses that have arrived at the starting gate at a particular instance of time:

```
Thread raceMonitor = new Thread(new RaceMonitor());
raceMonitor.setDaemon(true);
raceMonitor.start();
```

After this, we create an application instance and call its **manageRace** method:

```
new HorseRace().manageRace();
```

In the **manageRace** method, we create an array for holding the **Horse** objects and initialize it with the instances of **Horse**s. We start the race by calling the **runRace** method, which takes this horse array as an argument.

In the **runRace** method, each **Horse** in the team is registered with the phaser via a call to its **register** method:

```
manager.register();
```

After this registration, we wait for a variable amount of time before calling the **arriveAndAwaitAdvance** method. The current thread then arrives at the phaser and waits for others to arrive.

After all horses arrive at the starting gate, the main thread sleeps for one second and then we call the **arriveAndDeregister** method to release each horse from the starting gate. Now, the actual race begins. We can use the phaser again to start another race by reregistering a set of horses.

The implementation of the **Horse** class is very straightforward. In the **run** and **toString** methods, we simply print a message to the user. The most important thing in this class is the generation of the unique ID for each horse. To create a unique ID, we would have used the synchronization techniques we covered so far to increment the field **ID**. The class **AtomicInteger** provides this facility with improved efficiency and without the use of synchronization constructs. We create a static variable by instantiating the **AtomicInteger** class:

```
private final static AtomicInteger idSource = new AtomicInteger();
```

The **incrementAndGet** method atomically increments the value of this variable by one:

```
private final int id = idSource.incrementAndGet();
```

Note that creating multiple instances of the **Horse** class causes them to contend for this variable.

The **RaceMonitor** thread class calls the **getArrivedParties** method on the **manager** (phaser instance) to periodically print the number of horses that have arrived at the starting gate.

Typical partial output on a sample run is given here:

```
Number of horses ready to run: 0
Assign all horses, then start race
assign horse #1 to the race
assign horse #2 to the race
assign horse #3 to the race
Number of horses ready to run: 0
assign horse #4 to the race
assign horse #5 to the race
...
horse #3, please await all horses
horse #7, please await all horses
Number of horses ready to run: 5
horse #12, please await all horses
All arrived at starting gate, start race
Number of horses ready to run: 12
horse #5: running
horse #12: running
horse #9: running
horse #6: running
```

The output shows the various states of the application. In the beginning, we assign 12 horses to the race. As horses arrive at the starting gate, they wait for all the others to arrive. Once all the horses arrive, we start the race. In the output, you will see several periodic monitoring messages that tell you how many horses have reached the starting gate at a particular instance of time.

Exchangers

An exchanger allows two threads to exchange objects at a rendezvous point; this is generally useful in pipeline designs. An exchanger is often used when a producer and consumer want to exchange a resource. Remember the producer-consumer problem from the previous chapter? We used wait-notify in its implementation; the same could now be achieved using exchangers. The difference is that in the producer-consumer scenario, the producer produces objects, puts them in a shared channel, and notifies the consumer. The consumer then picks up the produced objects from the shared channel. In the case of an exchanger, each thread presents some object upon entry into the **exchange** method and receives an object presented by the other thread upon its return from the **exchange** method. Typically this is used in writing communications software where there are two threads—one that collects some data in a communication buffer and the other that empties the buffer and processes the data. The first thread waits until its buffer is completely filled. At this time, it will exchange its full buffer with an empty buffer provided by the consumer thread. The process will continue in a loop, where in each iteration the producer waits for its buffer to be completely filled and then exchanges it for an empty buffer from the consumer.

The producer puts the items to exchange in its buffer. When the buffer gets full, the producer waits for the consumer with an empty buffer where the contents can be transferred. Similarly, the consumer consumes the items from its buffer. When the buffer is empty, the consumer waits for the producer. When waits occur, the two buffers are exchanged and then both parties can continue. For this to work satisfactorily, you must be sure that the producer is going to produce items on an ongoing basis; otherwise, the items already added to the buffer will sit there waiting for the buffer to get full.

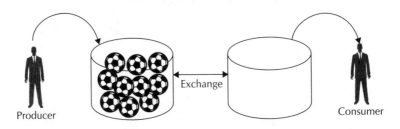

FIGURE 18-5. *Exchanger in action*

Java implements this functionality with the help of the **Exchanger** class. The class constructor does not take any parameters, except for the type of object to exchange:

```
Class Exchanger<V>
```

The **exchange** method performs the actual exchange:

```
public V exchange(V x) throws InterruptedException
```

Another variation of the **exchange** method allows you to define a timeout during which the thread remains dormant. Let's now look at an example of using this class (see Figure 18-5).

The producer produces items and hands them over to the consumer on an on-going basis. Both are given baskets. Initially, both baskets are empty. The producer produces the items and puts them in his basket. The consumer keeps waiting for the items to be ready. When the producer's basket gets full, the two baskets are exchanged. This will be done with the help of the **Exchanger** class. The exchange does not require the use of any of the synchronization mechanisms discussed in the previous chapter. The **Exchanger** class takes care of all the needed synchronization while accessing the two baskets in two threads. Now, the producer has an empty basket and the consumer has a full basket. The producer will produce more items and fill his empty basket, while the consumer will consume the items from his full basket. Eventually, the producer's basket will become full and the consumer's basket will become empty. Another exchange will take place at this time, and the process repeats itself. We will now write a program to implement this operation (see Listing 18-7). Note that the program does not contain any explicit synchronization constructs.

Listing 18-7 *Producer/Consumer Implementation Using Exchanger*

```
import java.util.*;
import java.util.concurrent.Exchanger;

public class ProductExchanger {

    public static Exchanger<List<Integer>> exchanger =
            new Exchanger<List<Integer>>();

    public static void main(String[] args) {
        Thread producer = new Thread(new Producer());
```

```
        Thread consumer = new Thread(new Consumer());
        producer.start();
        consumer.start();
        try {
            while (System.in.read() != '\n') {
            }
        } catch (Exception ex) {
            ex.printStackTrace();
        }
        producer.interrupt();
        consumer.interrupt();
    }
}

class Producer implements Runnable {

    private static List<Integer> buffer = new ArrayList<Integer>();
    private boolean okToRun = true;
    private final int BUFFSIZE = 10;

    public void run() {
        int j = 0;
        while (okToRun) {
            if (buffer.isEmpty()) {
                try {
                    for (int i = 0; i < BUFFSIZE; i++) {
                        buffer.add((int) (Math.random() * 100));
                    }
                    Thread.sleep((int) (Math.random() * 1000));
                    System.out.print("Producer Buffer: ");
                    for (int i : buffer) {
                        System.out.print(i + ", ");
                    }
                    System.out.println();
                    System.out.println("Exchanging ...");
                    buffer = ProductExchanger.exchanger.exchange(buffer);
                } catch (InterruptedException ex) {
                    okToRun = false;
                }
            }
        }
    }
}

class Consumer implements Runnable {

    private static List<Integer> buffer = new ArrayList<Integer>();
    private boolean okToRun = true;
```

```
    public void run() {
        while (okToRun) {
            try {
                if (buffer.isEmpty()) {
                    buffer =
                        ProductExchanger.exchanger.exchange(buffer);
                    System.out.print("Consumer Buffer: ");
                    for (int i : buffer) {
                        System.out.print(i + ", ");
                    }
                    System.out.println("\n");
                    Thread.sleep((int) (Math.random() * 1000));
                    buffer.clear();
                }
            } catch (InterruptedException ex) {
                okToRun = false;
            }
        }
    }
}
```

The **ProductExchanger** class first creates an instance of **Exchanger**:

```
public static Exchanger<List<Integer>> exchanger =
    new Exchanger<List<Integer>>();
```

The exchanger operates on a list of integers as specified in the type parameter of its constructor. This is declared **public** and **static** so that it can be accessed by the producer and consumer thread classes without creating the class instance. The **main** method simply creates the two threads and starts them:

```
Thread producer = new Thread(new Producer());
Thread consumer = new Thread(new Consumer());
producer.start();
consumer.start();
```

To terminate the program, the **main** thread waits indefinitely for the user to hit the ENTER key:

```
while (System.in.read() != '\n') {
}
```

When this happens, both producer and consumer threads are interrupted in their work:

```
producer.interrupt();
consumer.interrupt();
```

Note that this is the nice way of stopping a running thread. You make a request to the running thread by interrupting it and then let the running thread decide when to stop. It would usually do so after finishing whatever it is currently doing and comes to the logical end of a running process.

Now, let's look at the producer class:

```
class Producer implements Runnable {
```

First, we create an empty buffer for the producer to hold our **Integer** items:

```
private static List<Integer> buffer = new ArrayList<Integer>();
```

In the **run** method, we set up an infinite loop. The **okToRun** flag is set to **true** by default. It will be reset when the thread is interrupted. When this occurs, the loop will break.

```
while (okToRun) {
```

We now check whether the buffer is empty. If it is, we add a few random numbers to it until the buffer is filled completely:

```
if (buffer.isEmpty()) {
    try {
        for (int i = 0; i < BUFFSIZE; i++) {
            buffer.add((int) (Math.random() * 100));
        }
```

We then put the thread to sleep for a random amount of time to simulate the condition that producing and filling items take some finite amount of time:

```
Thread.sleep((int) (Math.random() * 1000));
```

The program now prints the buffer's contents for the user's knowledge:

```
System.out.print("Producer Buffer: ");
for (int i : buffer) {
    System.out.print(i + ", ");
}
```

At this stage, the producer thread requests an exchange with the exchanger. To do this, it calls the **exchange** method on the **exchanger** object defined in the **main** program:

```
buffer = ProductExchanger.exchanger.exchange(buffer);
```

The **exchange** method takes the **buffer** to exchange as its parameter. After the exchange is performed, the returned value will be the exchanged buffer, which in our case is going to be an empty buffer. A call to the **exchange** method makes the calling thread wait for another thread to arrive at this exchange point. When the other thread arrives, it transfers its object to it, receiving the object given by the second thread in return. Note that a waiting thread may be interrupted, and if that happens, it will no longer continue to wait on the other thread. If the current thread has its interrupted status set upon entry into the **exchange** method, an **InterruptedException** is thrown and the thread's interrupted status is cleared. When a thread calls an **exchange** method, if at that time another thread is already waiting at the exchange point, it is awakened and scheduled to run. The waiting thread receives the object passed in by the current thread and the current thread returns immediately. If no other thread is waiting at the exchange when a thread calls the **exchange** method, it is made to wait at the exchange point. It continues doing so until the point when some other thread enters the exchange or interrupts the current thread.

Finally, in the exception handler we simply reset the **okToRun** flag so that the infinite loop will terminate on its next iteration:

```
} catch (InterruptedException ex) {
    okToRun = false;
}
```

Now, let's look at the **Consumer** class. As with the **Producer** class, we create an empty buffer for the use of the consumer:

```
class Consumer implements Runnable {
    private static List<Integer> buffer = new ArrayList<Integer>();
```

In the **run** method, we set up an infinite loop that is terminated only when the thread is interrupted:

```
while (okToRun) {
```

We test whether the buffer is empty; if it is, we initiate an exchange. Note that the actual exchange does not take place until both parties are ready for an exchange. If the producer thread fills its buffer before the consumer thread is able to empty its buffer, the producer thread is made to wait at the exchange point. Similarly, if the consumer buffer clears its buffer before the producer is able to fill its buffer completely, the consumer is made to wait at the exchange point. When both buffers are ready for an exchange (that is, when the producer buffer is full and the consumer buffer is empty), the exchange takes place:

```
if (buffer.isEmpty()) {
    buffer = ProductExchanger.exchanger.exchange(buffer);
```

After the exchange, we print the buffer contents to verify that the consumer has actually received the items:

```
System.out.print("Consumer Buffer: ");
for (int i : buffer) {
    System.out.print(i + ", ");
}
```

To simulate the condition that the consumer will take a finite amount of time to consume all the contents of the basket, we cause the thread to sleep for a variable amount of time before emptying the buffer:

```
Thread.sleep((int) (Math.random() * 1000));
buffer.clear();
```

Typical program output is shown here:

```
Producer Buffer: 19, 19, 35, 25, 53, 55, 15, 41, 50, 14,
Exchanging ...
Consumer Buffer: 19, 19, 35, 25, 53, 55, 15, 41, 50, 14,

Producer Buffer: 65, 39, 21, 53, 95, 80, 90, 70, 25, 32,
Exchanging ...
Consumer Buffer: 65, 39, 21, 53, 95, 80, 90, 70, 25, 32,
```

```
Producer Buffer: 7, 26, 60, 24, 4, 54, 74, 22, 71, 52,
Exchanging ...
Consumer Buffer: 7, 26, 60, 24, 4, 54, 74, 22, 71, 52,

Producer Buffer: 20, 34, 50, 14, 91, 75, 39, 7, 98, 63,
Exchanging ...
Consumer Buffer: 20, 34, 50, 14, 91, 75, 39, 7, 98, 63,

Producer Buffer: 49, 49, 78, 72, 1, 40, 43, 79, 7, 35,
Exchanging ...
Consumer Buffer: 49, 49, 78, 72, 1, 40, 43, 79, 7, 35,
```

Note that after each exchange, the contents of the consumer buffer are identical to the contents of the producer buffer. Thus, the buffers were exchanged as expected without the use of any explicit synchronization constructs.

Summary

In this chapter, you studied many synchronization constructs provided in Java beginning in J2SE 5.0. The use of these constructs relieves developers from employing any explicit synchronization in their programs. Many synchronization needs can be modeled and solved using blocking queues. Java provides several classes to implement blocking queue functionality, where you can create both bounded and dynamically growing queues. You can prioritize the objects in the queue for obtaining the service, and you can also decide on a delayed service for each object.

Besides blocking queues, J2SE 5.0 defines semaphores, countdown latches, barriers, and exchangers. Semaphores allow the sharing of *n* shared resources among competing threads. The countdown latch makes threads wait until the running threads bring a count value down to zero. A barrier is a common point where the running threads meet after completing their individual work. After each thread arrives at the barrier, a new task can be initiated. Until then, the new task is made to wait. The exchanger allows an easy exchange between the individual buffers of the producer and the consumer. The producer fills the buffer to its completion, and the consumer consumes the items from its buffer until it becomes empty. When both the conditions are met (that is, the producer buffer is full and the consumer buffer is empty), the exchanger performs an exchange of the two buffers.

This chapter covered many synchronization constructs. The need for concurrency-enabled programs is even bigger than the synchronization mechanisms discussed in this chapter. You will understand these needs and how Java addresses them, including its latest Fork/Join framework, in the next chapter.

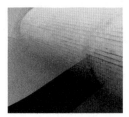

CHAPTER
19

Callables, Futures,
Executors, and Fork/Join

he last two chapters covered various aspects of thread programming. Thread programming is a vast subject. So far we have discussed how to create threads, the various thread-synchronization issues, how deadlocks occur, and the different mechanisms introduced in J2SE 5.0 to deal with thread synchronization. The Concurrency framework defines several more classes that reflect the additional aspects of thread programming we have not covered so far. The last chapter covered the different types of blocking queues and several constructs for synchronization. This chapter now focuses on the more advanced features of thread programming, including the latest additions in Java SE 7.

If you are a developer of highly scalable large-scale applications, you will need the features covered in this chapter. This chapter will definitely help if you want to develop highly scalable, CPU-intensive, real-time applications with lots of concurrency deployed on server farms for scalability and performance. You will learn how to create a thread pool, how to submit tasks to a thread pool so that they run concurrently, how to obtain the results of concurrent tasks, how to monitor their processing, and so on. You will learn how to parallelize a large task by dividing it into subtasks and executing them concurrently. This includes a good coverage of the newly introduced (Java SE 7) Fork/Join framework.

Specifically, here is what you'll learn in this chapter:

- What callables and futures are
- Understanding the **Callable** interface
- Understanding the **Future** interface
- Using **FutureTask** class
- Understanding executors
- Creating and using thread pools
- Scheduling tasks for future execution
- Repeating a task with some periodicity
- Retrieving the result of a first completed task
- Understanding the Fork/Join framework
- Understanding thread-safe collections

Callables and Futures

So far you have seen that to create a thread, you need to either implement the **Runnable** interface or extend your class from the **Thread** class. This is simple enough; however, the created thread has a serious limitation—its **run** method cannot return a value to its creator. Therefore, many programmers have resorted to such inelegant techniques as writing to a file to return the results. Another problem with **Runnable** is that it cannot throw any checked exceptions, so you must handle all exceptions that occur during the code execution in the **run** method itself. Fortunately, J2SE 5.0 addressed this programmer need and provided what is called a **Callable** and a **Future**. So what are they? Whereas **Thread** is a class that simply models an execution of a task with no expected result, a **Callable** is a construct that models execution of a task that produces a result. A **Future** takes this one step further and models the execution of a task that allows for interrogation of its progress and retrieval of its result.

Prior to J2SE 5.0, if you wanted a thread to return a value to its creator, you would probably write code similar to this:

```
Thread worker = new Thread(new WorkerThread());
worker.start();
worker.join();
String value = getSavedValue();
```

Although nothing is inherently wrong with this code, J2SE 5.0 provides a different and better approach to this problem. You can now use the **Callable** interface for this purpose. A **Future** helps in monitoring the **Callable** and retrieves its result. So let's look at the **Callable** and **Future** interfaces.

The Callable Interface

A **Callable** interface is similar to a **Runnable** interface with a single-parameterized method called **call**:

```
public interface Callable<V> {
    V call() throws Exception;
}
```

The **call** method can return any type, as specified by the generic parameter. Note that unlike the **run** method in **Runnable**, the **call** method throws a checked exception. To implement **Callable** with no return value, use **Callable<Void>**.

You cannot directly submit a **Callable** into a **Thread** for its execution. You need to use **ExecutorService** to execute the **Callable** object. You do so by calling its **submit** method:

```
<T> Future<T> submit(Callable<T> task)
```

The **submit** method returns a **Future** object.

The Future Interface

When a caller submits a task to an executor, it returns a **Future** object to the caller. The interface is declared as

```
interface Future <V>
```

where **V** represents the result type returned by the **Future**'s **get** method. The caller can use this **Future** object to gain control over the requested task. The **get** method returns the result to the caller. This method waits if the computation is not yet over. The overloaded **get** method accepts a timeout as its parameter and waits, if necessary, for, at most, the given time for the computation to complete and then retrieves its result, if available. The **isDone** method checks whether the task is completed and returns **true** if so. The **cancel** method attempts to cancel the execution of the task, and the **isCancelled** method returns **true** if the task was cancelled before it completed normally.

FutureTask is a wrapper class that implements both the **Future** and **Runnable** interfaces and provides a convenient way to convert a **Callable** into both a **Future** and a **Runnable**.

How Callable and Future Work

To understand how to use **Callable** and **Future** in your applications, look at the diagram in Figure 19-1.

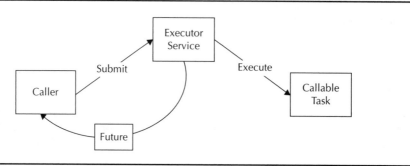

FIGURE 19-1.   *Callable and Future at work*

The block on the right side shows a callable task. This is a Java class that implements the **Callable** interface. The **Callable** interface contains a sole **call** method that a class developer must implement. The **call** method usually contains the service implementation. To invoke this service, you must instantiate the callable task class and run its **call** method. Because you want this to be done asynchronously, you need some mechanism to invoke the **call** method. The **Callable** interface is not like the **Runnable** interface, which can be submitted to the constructor of a **Thread** class for execution. Java provides another class called **ExecutorService** to run a callable task. The caller first creates or obtains an instance of **ExecutorService** and submits a callable task for execution. The framework then returns a future object to the caller. This future object can be used to check the status of a callable and to retrieve the result from the callable.

We will now look at how to use these interfaces to invoke an asynchronous operation that, upon completion, returns a result to the caller.

Using Callables in Parallelizing Large Tasks

In this scenario, we have a cement-manufacturing company that maintains its sales data in a spreadsheet, where the column represents the number of cement bags sold in a particular month and the row represents the ID of the company to which the bags are sold. If there are N number of customers, we will have an $N \times 12$ matrix, where 12 is the number of months in a year (see Figure 19-2).

Now, we will develop a program that computes the annual sales turnover for the company. For this, we need the total number of bags sold throughout the year to all customers. For a large customer base, this totaling could take a substantial amount of time. Therefore, we will perform the yearly total for each customer in a separate thread. Assuming that we are running the application on a multicore/multi-CPU machine, these yearly computations will be done in parallel, thus increasing the total throughput of the program.

We create a thread that computes the sum of all elements in a given row. Thus, we can create multiple threads and ask each one to compute the row sum for an independent row. Because each of the row calculations is wholly independent from the others, we can do these computations in parallel. Note that an algorithm cannot be arbitrarily split into parts. We need to look carefully where work can be split into units and each unit executed independently of the others.

When all threads finish their job, we take the total of all the individual sums, and this will be the desired result.

	Jan	Feb	Mar	Apr	...	
Client ID: 100	11	24	54	31	29	Sum1
						+
Client ID: 101	72	32	21	76	22	Sum2
						+
Client ID: 102	56	33	39	32	41	Sum3
						+
Client ID: 103	81	21	16	19	42	Sum4
						+
...	12	54	19	33	43	...
						+
...	32	46	72	23	22	...
						Total

FIGURE 19-2. *Multiple threads totaling each row of a matrix*

CAUTION
*If you sum the total matrix in the following example by creating a double **for** loop, it would most likely take less time to execute compared to the thread pool approach used in this example. This is because creating and managing the thread pool itself takes a substantial amount of processing time. The use of a thread pool and executor service would be justified when the matrix size becomes sufficiently large and the algorithm complexity for each thread increases substantially.*

The implementation of this annual sales turnover calculator is given in Listing 19-1.

Listing 19-1 *Annual Sales Turnover Calculator*

```
import java.text.DateFormatSymbols;
import java.util.*;
import java.util.concurrent.*;

public class AnnualSalesCalc {

    private static int NUMBER_OF_CUSTOMERS = 100;
    private static int NUMBER_OF_MONTHS = 12;
    private static int salesMatrix[][];

    private static class Summer implements Callable {
```

```java
        private int companyID;

        public Summer(int companyID) {
            this.companyID = companyID;
        }

        public Integer call() {
            int sum = 0;
            for (int col = 0; col < NUMBER_OF_MONTHS; col++) {
                sum += salesMatrix[companyID][col];
            }
            System.out.printf(
                    "Totaling for client 1%02d completed%n", companyID);

            return sum;
        }
    }

    public static void main(String args[]) throws Exception {

        generateMatrix();
        printMatrix();

        ExecutorService executor = Executors.newFixedThreadPool(10);
        Set<Future<Integer>> set = new HashSet<Future<Integer>>();
        for (int row = 0; row < NUMBER_OF_CUSTOMERS; row++) {
            Callable<Integer> callable = new Summer(row);
            Future<Integer> future = executor.submit(callable);
            set.add(future);
        }
        int sum = 0;
        for (Future<Integer> future : set) {
            sum += future.get();
        }
        System.out.printf("%nThe annual turnover (bags): %s%n%n", sum);
        executor.shutdown();
    }

    private static void generateMatrix() {
        salesMatrix = new int[NUMBER_OF_CUSTOMERS][NUMBER_OF_MONTHS];

        for (int i = 0; i < NUMBER_OF_CUSTOMERS; i++) {
            for (int j = 0; j < NUMBER_OF_MONTHS; j++) {
                salesMatrix[i][j] = (int) (Math.random() * 100);
            }
        }
    }

    private static void printMatrix() {
        System.out.print("\t\t");
```

```
        String[] monthDisplayNames =
                (new DateFormatSymbols()).getShortMonths();
        for (String strName : monthDisplayNames) {
            System.out.printf("%8s", strName);
        }
        System.out.printf("%n%n");
        for (int i = 0; i < NUMBER_OF_CUSTOMERS; i++) {
            System.out.printf("Client ID: 1%02d", i);
            for (int j = 0; j < NUMBER_OF_MONTHS; j++) {
                System.out.printf("%8d", salesMatrix[i][j]);
            }
            System.out.println();
        }
        System.out.printf("%n%n");
    }
}
```

The **AnnualSalesCalc** class declares two integer constants—**NUMBER_OF_CUSTOMERS** decides the number of rows for our matrix, and **NUMBER_OF_MONTHS** decides the number of columns. The **salesMatrix** field represents a two-dimensional array of integers that is not yet created. We will create the matrix in the **main** method. Next, we declare a class that computes the row sum:

```
private static class Summer implements Callable {
```

The **Summer** class is declared as an inner class to **AnnualSalesCalc** and is **private** and **static**. Because this class is not used elsewhere, it is declared **private**. It is declared **static** because it is called in the static **main** method. The class also implements the **Callable** interface. The constructor accepts an integer value that is the customer ID and stores it in a class variable for further use.

As a part of the interface, we need to provide an implementation of the **call** method. In our case, we declare the **call** method to return an **Integer** data type:

```
public Integer call() {
```

The **call** method returns a generic type that can be mapped to any real data type. In our example, this is mapped to the **Integer** data type. The method now computes the sum of all elements within the specified row of the matrix by using a **for** loop:

```
int sum = 0;
for (int col = 0; col < NUMBER_OF_MONTHS; col++) {
    sum += salesMatrix[customerID][col];
}
```

After the summation is complete, the program prints a message to the user indicating that the task by the current callable object is done and returns the computed result to the caller whenever it is asked for:

```
System.out.printf("Totaling for client 1%02d completed%n", customerID);
return sum;
```

Now, let's look at the **main** method that uses this callable task. In the **main** method, we first call **generateMatrix** to generate a matrix and **printMatrix** to print the generated matrix to the console. The implementation of both these methods is discussed later.

As discussed in the previous section, we need an executor service to invoke the **Callable** object. The **Executors** class provides this service:

```
ExecutorService executor = Executors.newFixedThreadPool(10);
```

The **newFixedThreadPool** is a static method of the **Executors** class that accepts an integer parameter. The value of this parameter determines the number of threads created by this method. The method creates a fixed pool of threads that can be used for running different tasks. The method returns an instance of the **ExecutorService** class.

TIP

Creating and destroying threads is usually time consuming. Also, a thread that runs to its completion cannot be reused and must be garbage-collected. Creating a pool of threads helps in overcoming these difficulties. When you create a thread pool, the threads from the pool will be reused to perform a certain task many times. Thread pools are discussed in more detail later in this chapter.

Next, we declare a **Set** (refer to Chapter 16 for more on sets) for storing the **Future** objects that can be used for monitoring the submitted tasks. A **Future** object takes a generic parameter. In our example, we set this to the **Integer** data type. Thus, our **Future** object will return an **Integer** object to the caller:

```
Set<Future<Integer>> set = new HashSet<Future<Integer>>();
```

Now, for each row of the matrix, we instantiate the **Summer** class, which is a **Callable** object:

```
for (int row = 0; row < NUMBER_OF_CUSTOMERS; row++) {
    Callable<Integer> callable = new Summer(row);
```

The **Summer** class implements the **Callable** interface and is discussed later. As seen in the preceding statement, the **Callable** interface accepts a generic parameter of type **Integer** that is the return data type used by its **call** method. To run this callable object, we call the **submit** method on the **executor** object we created earlier:

```
Future<Integer> future = executor.submit(callable);
```

The **submit** method submits the **callable** object to one of the threads from its pool. The method returns a **Future** object to the caller. The caller can use the **get** method on this **Future** object to obtain the computation results. We add the returned **Future** object to our set so that ultimately we can take the sum of all the elements of this set to compute the grand total:

```
set.add(future);
```

After submitting all the tasks, the **main** function computes the grand total by using the following **for each** loop:

```
int sum = 0;
for (Future<Integer> future : set) {
    sum += future.get();
}
```

Note that the program calls the **get** method on each **future** object stored in the set. The **get** method returns the computation result whenever it is ready. The results may come in totally unordered. Therefore, this is analogous to the barriers in the previous chapter. When results from all **future** objects are obtained, the **for** loop terminates. After the grand total is computed, we print it to the console:

```
System.out.printf("%nThe annual turnover (bags): %s%n%n", sum);
```

Finally, we shut down the executor service so as to free all its allocated resources:

```
executor.shutdown();
```

Let's now look at the implementation of the **generateMatrix** method:

```
private static void generateMatrix() {
```

This method creates our **salesMatrix** array of integers:

```
salesMatrix = new int[NUMBER_OF_CUSTOMERS][NUMBER_OF_MONTHS];
```

The entire array is initialized by assigning a random number in the range of 0 to 99 for each element. We use randomization here so that the program output differs on every run:

```
for (int i = 0; i < NUMBER_OF_CUSTOMERS; i++) {
    for (int j = 0; j < NUMBER_OF_MONTHS; j++) {
        salesMatrix[i][j] = (int) (Math.random() * 100);
```

The **printMatrix** method simply iterates through all array elements and prints its values to the user console. Some typical program output is shown here:

```
               Jan  Feb  Mar  Apr  May  Jun  Jul  Aug  Sep  Oct  Nov  Dec

Client ID: 100  37   16   81   51   68   31   50    0   18   86    7   16
Client ID: 101  31   36   14    4   67   26   26   74   51   41   49   54
Client ID: 102  18   37   93   43   15   44   17    9   69   13   56    4
Client ID: 103  58   78   17   73   19   34   54   11   22   34   74   83
...
Totaling for client 195 completed
Totaling for client 196 completed
Totaling for client 197 completed
Totaling for client 198 completed
Totaling for client 199 completed

The annual turnover (bags): 59601
```

Note the ordering of the row computations. Each time you run the application, you may get a different order, depending on how much time each thread takes to complete its task and how the threads are scheduled for execution. You can experiment by increasing the matrix dimension and studying the program output. If you increase the matrix dimension to a large value, comment out the **printMatrix** statement to avoid cluttering the output on your console.

The FutureTask Class

The **FutureTask** class implements both **Runnable** and **Future** interfaces. Therefore, it provides asynchronous computation due to its **Runnable** interface and provides the facility to cancel the task through the future object returned to the caller. This class can be used to wrap a **Callable** or **Runnable** object. For example, in the program code discussed in Listing 19-1, you can comment out the line that contains the **executor.submit** call and add the next two lines shown here:

```
// Future<Integer> future = executor.submit(callable);
FutureTask<Integer> future = new FutureTask<Integer>(callable);
future.run();
```

The **run** method invokes the task and sets its result to the **future** object.

Alternatively, you may submit the instance of a **FutureTask** to an **Executor** for execution, as follows:

```
executor.submit(future);
```

Because the **FutureTask** class also implements the **Future** interface, an instance of it can be used to cancel the task, check its status, and so on. We will now look at how to cancel a job using the **Future** object.

Creating Cancellable Tasks

In this demonstration, you learn how to create a task that can be cancelled before it runs to completion. As mentioned earlier, to cancel a task, we use the **Future** object returned to us by an executor. For task creation and execution, we will use the **FutureTask** class discussed in the previous section.

In this demonstration, we continue with our stock exchange case study and develop a simulator that can process millions of trade requests concurrently. We will pump in thousands of trade requests into our simulator. The simulator contains a large pool of threads that executes these requests. We will also write an evil thread, which randomly picks up a few orders and tries to cancel them. If the order has already been executed, the cancellation request will fail. If a thread is not allocated to process a pending order before the cancellation request arrives, the order will be cancelled. If the trade order execution is in progress and the thread can be interrupted, a cancel request arriving during the processing will terminate the rest of the processing, effectively cancelling the order. We will be able to verify these situations in the test results. Our "evil" thread, in practical terms, represents customers sending cancellation requests to the stock exchange after placing their orders. The program that simulates this stocks order processor is given in Listing 19-2.

Listing 19-2   *A Stocks Order Processor Demonstrating Cancellable Tasks*

```
import java.util.*;
import java.util.concurrent.*;

public class StocksOrderProcessor {

    static final int MAX_NUMBER_OF_ORDERS = 10000;
    static private ExecutorService executor =
            Executors.newFixedThreadPool(100);
    static private List<Future> ordersToProcess = new ArrayList();

    private static class OrderExecutor implements Callable {

        int id = 0;
        int count = 0;

        public OrderExecutor(int id) {
            this.id = id;
        }

        public Object call() throws Exception {
            try {
                while (count < 50) {
                    count++;
                    Thread.sleep(new Random(
                        System.currentTimeMillis() % 100).nextInt(10));
                }
                System.out.println("Successfully executed order: " + id);
            } catch (Exception ex) {
                throw (ex);
            }
            return id;
        }
    }

    public static void main(String[] args) {
        System.out.printf("Submitting %d trades%n", MAX_NUMBER_OF_ORDERS);
        for (int i = 0; i < MAX_NUMBER_OF_ORDERS; i++) {
            SubmitOrder(i);
        }
        new Thread(new EvilThread(ordersToProcess)).start();
        System.out.println("Cancelling a few orders at random");
        try {
            executor.awaitTermination(30, TimeUnit.SECONDS);
        } catch (InterruptedException ex) {
            ex.printStackTrace();
        }
        System.out.println("Checking status before shutdown");
        int count = 0;
```

```
            for (Future f : ordersToProcess) {
                if (f.isCancelled()) {
                    count++;
                }
            }
            System.out.printf("%d trades cancelled%n", count);
            executor.shutdownNow();
        }

    private static void SubmitOrder(int id) {
        Callable<Integer> callable = new OrderExecutor(id);
        ordersToProcess.add(executor.submit(callable));
    }
}

class EvilThread implements Runnable {

    private List<Future> ordersToProcess;

    public EvilThread(List<Future> futures) {
        this.ordersToProcess = futures;
    }

    public void run() {
        Random myNextKill = new Random(System.currentTimeMillis()
                % 100);
        for (int i = 0; i < 100; i++) {
            int index =
                myNextKill.nextInt(StocksOrderProcessor.MAX_NUMBER_OF_ORDERS);
            boolean cancel = ordersToProcess.get(index).cancel(true);
            if (cancel) {
                System.out.println("Cancel Order Succeeded: " + index);
            } else {
                System.out.println("Cancel Order Failed: " + index);
            }
            try {
                Thread.sleep(myNextKill.nextInt(100));
            } catch (InterruptedException ex) {
                ex.printStackTrace();
            }
        }
    }
}
```

The **StocksOrderProcessor** class creates a fixed pool of 100 threads to execute the orders using the following declaration:

```
static private ExecutorService executor =
        Executors.newFixedThreadPool(100);
```

It also creates an **ArrayList** to hold the references to the orders to be executed:

```
static private List<Future> ordersToProcess = new ArrayList();
```

We declare an inner private class called **OrderExecutor** that performs the business logic for executing the order. The class **OrderExecutor** implements **Callable** so that an executor can invoke it asynchronously:

```
private static class OrderExecutor implements Callable {
```

In the class constructor, we pass an integer **id** to track the order number:

```
public OrderExecutor(int id) {
    this.id = id;
}
```

In the **call** method, we simply count up to 50. Before each count, we place the thread to sleep for a variable amount of time:

```
try {
    while (count < 50) {
        count++;
        Thread.sleep(new Random(System.currentTimeMillis() % 100).nextInt(10));
    }
```

By causing the thread to sleep for a variable amount of time, we simulate the fact that each order processed takes a different amount of time to execute. At the end of the **call** method, we return the **id** so that we can later verify which orders ran to completion.

In the **main** method, we submit a huge number of orders to the order processor:

```
for (int i = 0; i < MAX_NUMBER_OF_ORDERS; i++) {
    SubmitOrder(i);
}
```

The **SubmitOrder** method creates a **Callable** instance that will be run at some later time. Each **Callable** instance is tracked with a unique ID:

```
Callable<Integer> callable = new OrderExecutor(id);
```

Each created task is submitted for processing by calling the **submit** method of the **ExecutorService** class. We store the future object returned by the **submit** method in our array list of pending orders:

```
ordersToProcess.add(executor.submit(callable));
```

After submitting a large number of trade requests, the **main** method creates an evil thread that attempts to cancel a few orders at random:

```
new Thread(new EvilThread(ordersToProcess)).start();
```

The **EvilThread**, whenever it gets its time slot, creates a few cancellation requests and executes them on the future objects stored in our pending orders list. We discuss the construction of **EvilThread** shortly.

At this stage, some of our orders might have already been processed. The simulator will continue processing the rest. If the order has been cancelled before the executor allocates a thread, it will never run. To allow sufficient time to complete all the pending orders, we request the executor to hang on for 30 seconds. This, in practical situations, would be the time for which the stock exchange is open for trading.

```
executor.awaitTermination(30, TimeUnit.SECONDS);
```

Depending on the speed and capabilities (number of cores/CPUs) of your machine, you may need to adjust this wait time to ensure that the main thread does not prematurely terminate before all pending trade requests get a chance to execute on the simulator.

NOTE
The executor can wait precisely until all its assigned tasks run to completion. We discuss this in the next section.

After the preceding timeout, we get a summary of how many orders were successfully cancelled. This is done with a simple **for** loop, shown here:

```
int count = 0;
for (Future f : ordersToProcess) {
    if (f.isCancelled()) {
        count++;
    }
}
```

For each **Future** object in our collection of orders, we call its **isCancelled** method. This method returns **true** if the execution of the corresponding **Future** object was successfully cancelled.

At the end of the **main** method, we shut down the executor to free all its allocated resources:

```
executor.shutdownNow();
```

Now, let's look at the design of the **EvilThread** class. In the class constructor, we send our list of pending orders so that the thread may send cancellation requests to a few of the **Future** objects in this list:

```
public EvilThread(List<Future> futures) {
    this.ordersToProcess = futures;
}
```

In the **run** method, we create 100 cancellation requests. The **Future** object for cancellation is selected at random:

```
int index = myNextKill.nextInt(StocksOrderProcessor.MAX_NUMBER_OF_ORDERS);
boolean cancel = ordersToProcess.get(index).cancel(true);
```

Calling the **cancel** method on the future object sends the cancellation request. We set the parameter to the **cancel** method to **true**, indicating that if the job is already in progress, it may be interrupted in its work. The **cancel** method returns a **boolean** result that indicates the success or failure of the cancellation request. In between every two requests, we place the thread to sleep for a random amount of time:

```
Thread.sleep(myNextKill.nextInt(100));
```

Partial output of the sample run is presented here:

```
Successfully executed order: 2730
Successfully executed order: 2620
Successfully executed order: 2631
Cancel Order Succeeded: 4405
Successfully executed order: 2595
Successfully executed order: 2586
...
Successfully executed order: 2594
Successfully executed order: 2660
Cancel Order Failed: 958
Successfully executed order: 2652
Successfully executed order: 2693
Successfully executed order: 2680
...
Checking status before shutdown
86 trades cancelled
```

In the output, you can see that the cancellation of order 4405 succeeds because this order has not yet been run. At this time, orders in the range of 2600–2700 are being processed. You can also observe that the cancellation request for order 958 failed because the order was already executed, which you can verify by looking at the earlier log. At the end we see the summary of cancelled orders. Note that out of 100 requests, 86 were successfully cancelled. This number will change on every run and will also depend on your machine configuration.

Executors

You have already seen the use of executors in your previous programs. The **Executors** class allows you to create a pool of threads and returns an **ExecutorService** object to you. The executor provides a standard means of decoupling task submission from task execution. Besides the basic thread life-cycle support, it provides functions for statistics gathering, application management, and monitoring. This is based on a producer-consumer design pattern that scales well for large concurrent applications.

Using this service object, you can execute an instance of a **Runnable** or **Callable** class. You simply need to submit this instance to the service object. The service picks up a thread from the pool and hands your runnable object to it for execution. When the thread completes its execution, it is not destroyed. Rather, it is returned to the pool for executing another task in the future. This saves the overhead of creating and destroying threads.

The **Executors** class has a number of static methods for creating thread pools. You have already seen the use of the **newFixedThreadPool** method. The **newFixedThreadPool** method creates a thread pool of a fixed size. The threads will be assigned from this pool to the requesting task. If a thread remains idle, it is not destroyed and is kept in the pool for an indefinite amount of time. The **Executors** class also provides a method that creates a pool where the idle threads are automatically destroyed after 60 seconds. This is called **newCachedThreadPool**. Because the threads are automatically destroyed after a fixed period of time, they are also automatically created whenever required. Therefore, you may find the **newCachedThreadPool** to be more efficient in terms of memory footprint in situations where your demand for threads varies drastically over a period of time. The **Executors** class also defines a method called **newSingleThreadExecutor**. As the name suggests, this creates only a single thread of execution. However, after one task is over, the thread is not destroyed and can be reassigned to another task. In the case of multiple simultaneous requests, a queue will be maintained of all the pending requests and the thread will execute these jobs sequentially.

The **Executors** class also provides another interesting method. This is called **newScheduledThreadPool** and may be considered a replacement to **java.util.Timer**. The method creates a fixed thread pool for scheduled execution. It returns a **ScheduledExecutorService** object that provides several methods for the scheduled execution of tasks. We will now discuss the various methods of this class.

Creating a Thread Pool for Scheduled Executions

Sometimes, you may want to create a thread that begins its execution after a specified time delay. For example, you can set an alarm to ring after a specified amount of time elapses. In some situations, you may want to run the thread repeatedly at a fixed rate or with a fixed delay between subsequent executions. A typical application of this is a virus scanner. Such a utility starts automatically every day at the scheduled time. Thus, it repeats itself every 24 hours. You would use an executor service implemented in the **ScheduledExecutorService** class that runs the virus scanner once every 24 hours. If you have multiple disks to scan or even a single disk with a large capacity, you may prefer splitting this scan task into multiple units, where each unit scans a particular disk or a part of a large disk.

Another application where this service is useful is a news aggregator. The aggregator collects the latest news from various web-based sources and queues them on the client machine for view. The news retrieval from the various sources may be done concurrently and will take a variable amount of time, depending on the connectivity to the concerned source. The synchronization of news items between the client and the various sources will be done periodically. If the frequency at which this synchronization is performed is high, an overlap will occur between the new synchronization task and the currently running task that has not yet finished retrieving all the news. In such situations, it is better to run the tasks at a fixed delay between subsequent executions. The **ScheduledExecutorService** class allows you to do this.

The ScheduledExecutorService Class

The **ScheduledExecutorService** class provides a method called **schedule** for future execution of a task. It provides two overloads to this method:

```
<V>ScheduledFuture<V> schedule(Callable<V> callable, long delay, TimeUnit unit)
ScheduledFuture<?> schedule(Runnable command, long delay, TimeUnit unit)
```

The method takes three parameters: the **Callable** or **Runnable** class instance, the delay time, and the time unit. The method schedules the task specified by **Callable** or **Runnable** to run after the given time delay. The unit for time measure is specified by the third parameter of the method. The method returns a future object to the caller.

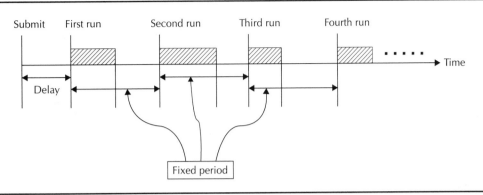

FIGURE 19-3. *Executing a task at a fixed rate*

Besides this simple delayed execution, the class provides a method called **scheduleAtFixedRate** that allows you to specify the rate at which the specified task is repeatedly executed. The first run occurs after the given delay. The subsequent executions of the task start at delay + period, delay + (2 × period), and so on. This kind of scheduling may be used for the virus scanner discussed earlier and is illustrated in Figure 19-3.

The **scheduleWithFixedDelay** method executes the specified task for the first time after the given delay. After this, the task is executed repeatedly with a fixed delay between the completion of a run and the start of the next run. This kind of scheduling may be used in the news aggregator applications discussed earlier. This is illustrated in Figure 19-4.

Let's now look at the use of this class with a program example.

Demonstrating Scheduled Task Execution

The program presented in this section demonstrates how to schedule a task that repeats at a fixed rate. The application is a virus scanner with a fixed-rate repeat. When the scan starts, the application pops up a window on the screen that shows the scan status. The scanning stops after all the files on

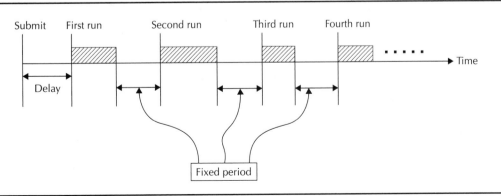

FIGURE 19-4. *Executing a task with a fixed delay*

the disk are traversed. Each scan may take a variable amount of time, which is simulated by the scan thread sleeping for a variable amount of time. After the scan, the status window is closed and then reopens when a new scan begins at the next scheduled time. The periodically repeating virus-scanning program is given in Listing 19-3.

Listing 19-3   *A Periodically Repeating Virus Scanner*

```
import java.awt.*;
import java.text.DateFormat;
import java.util.*;
import static java.util.concurrent.TimeUnit.*;
import java.util.concurrent.*;
import javax.swing.*;

class VirusScanner {

    private static JFrame appFrame;
    private static JLabel statusString;
    private int scanNumber = 0;
    private static final ScheduledExecutorService scheduler =

                    Executors.newScheduledThreadPool(5);
    private GregorianCalendar calendar = new GregorianCalendar();
    private static VirusScanner app = new VirusScanner();

    public void scanDisk() {
        final Runnable scanner = new Runnable() {

            public void run() {
                {
                    try {
                        appFrame.setVisible(true);
                        scanNumber++;
                        Calendar cal = Calendar.getInstance();
                        DateFormat df = DateFormat.getDateTimeInstance(
                           DateFormat.FULL, DateFormat.MEDIUM);
                           statusString.setText(" Scan   " + scanNumber
                           + " started at " + df.format(cal.getTime()));
                        Thread.sleep(1000 + new
                        Random().nextInt(10000));
                        appFrame.setVisible(false);
                    } catch (InterruptedException ex) {
                        ex.printStackTrace();
                    }
                }
            }
        };

        final ScheduledFuture<?> scanManager =
                scheduler.scheduleAtFixedRate(scanner, 1, 15, SECONDS);
```

```
    scheduler.schedule(new Runnable() {

        public void run() {
            scanManager.cancel(true);
            scheduler.shutdown();
            appFrame.dispose();
        }
    }, 60, SECONDS);
}

public static void main(String args[]) {
    appFrame = new JFrame();
    Dimension dimension =
                Toolkit.getDefaultToolkit().getScreenSize();
    appFrame.setSize(400, 70);
    appFrame.setLocation(
            dimension.width / 2 - appFrame.getWidth() / 2,
            dimension.height / 2 - appFrame.getWidth() / 2);
    statusString = new JLabel();
    appFrame.add(statusString);
    appFrame.setVisible(false);
    app.scanDisk();
}
}
```

The **VirusScanner** creates a thread pool by calling the **newScheduledThreadPool** method on the **Executors** class:

```
private static final ScheduledExecutorService scheduler =
                Executors.newScheduledThreadPool(5);
```

For multiple concurrent scans, we use the threads from this pool. **scanDisk** is the method that does all the hard work. First, we create a thread class:

```
final Runnable scanner = new Runnable() {
```

In the **run** method, we show the elsewhere-created status window to the user:

```
appFrame.setVisible(true);
```

We display the scan number and the time at which the scan started in the status window. We now cause the current thread to sleep for a variable amount of time:

```
Thread.sleep(1000 + new Random().nextInt(10000));
```

The constant addition factor of 1000 ensures that the window will remain open for a minimum of one second. In an actual program, you would have the virus-scanning code in place of this **sleep** statement. We put the thread to sleep here to give the illusion that the scanning is in progress for a certain amount of time. When the thread is awakened from its sleep, we hide the status window, giving the feeling to the user that the current scan cycle is over.

To run this scanner periodically at a fixed rate, we used the previously created scheduler:

```
final ScheduledFuture<?> scanManager =
                    scheduler.scheduleAtFixedRate(scanner, 1, 15, SECONDS);
```

This scanner task runs every 15 seconds after an initial delay of 1 second. The scheduler returns a future object that we will use to cancel the scanning after a certain period of time. To allow this cancellation, we create another anonymous thread:

```
scheduler.schedule(new Runnable() {

    public void run() {
        scanManager.cancel(true);
        scheduler.shutdown();
        appFrame.dispose();
    }
}, 60, SECONDS);
```

NOTE
*All timings in this program are given in seconds so that you can see
the effect of the simulation. In a real application, you would perform
the virus scan once a day or every couple of hours.*

In the **run** method of this thread, we cancel the scanner task, shut down the scheduler, and dispose of the status window. This thread runs only once after a time delay of 60 seconds. Therefore, our simulation will run periodically for a total of one minute. Every 15 seconds the virus scan status window pops up on the screen and will stay there for a variable amount of time, with a minimum of 1 second.

Finally, in the **main** method, we simply create the status window, set its location, and call the **scanDisk** method. Note that the main thread terminates immediately after this, and the threads created in the **scanDisk** method continue to leave throughout the next minute.

Obtaining the Results of the First Completed Execution

So far you have seen how to submit tasks to an executor for immediate, delayed, and periodic runs. You also know that an executor may provide and maintain multiple threads so that your jobs can be executed concurrently. When you submit multiple jobs to an executor, there may be situations where you want to process the result of whatever job is completed rather than waiting on each task to complete individually. The **get** method of the executor we have used so far waits for the job completion. In case of multiple task submissions, you would create a loop for obtaining the results of each computation, which may look like this:

```
for (Future<T> result : results)
    result.get();
```

Thus, the results are obtained sequentially. If a particular task takes too long to reach completion, the current **get** call will block onto it. Even if other tasks have finished earlier, you will not be able to obtain their results. To overcome this problem, the **ExecutorCompletionService** class comes to your rescue. It monitors the tasks submitted to an executor. You wait for the results to come out, one after another, by calling the **take** method. It returns the **Future** object representing the next completed task, waiting if none are completed. This class is useful in many practical situations where you want to proceed as soon as some tasks complete. For example, you may submit multiple requests to an automated price quote system, where each request takes a variable amount of execution time depending on several factors in its computations. As soon as a result is available for any of the submitted tasks, you want to present the quote to the waiting customer rather than making him wait for all other tasks to compute their individual quotes. We will now consider the use of this service via a concrete example.

Demonstrating the ExecutorCompletionService Class

When you submit multiple tasks to an executor, these tasks run concurrently and finish in a variable amount of time. In many situations, you would be interested in knowing when a task reaches its completion. For this, Java defines a class called **ExecutorCompletionService** that helps you in monitoring a task's completion. Upon completion, tasks are placed on a queue that can be accessed using the **take** method of the **ExecutorCompletionService** class. This is a lightweight class that can be used without incurring much of the overhead for processing a group of tasks.

As an example, consider a task that computes **m** raised to **n** (m^n), where **m** is a real number and **n** is an integer in the range 0 to 1000. We will use simple multiplication to compute the result. The time taken to compute the result will largely depend on the number of multiplication operations we need to perform, which is basically the value of **n**. We will create multiple tasks and submit them to the **Executor**, as we did in earlier examples. We then create an instance of **ExecutorCompletionService** by passing the previously created executor as a parameter to its constructor. The service will keep on monitoring the completed tasks. As the results come out, we print them to the terminal. The full program is given in Listing 19-4.

Listing 19-4   *Retrieving the First Available Result from Multiple Tasks*

```java
import java.util.ArrayList;
import java.util.concurrent.*;
import java.util.concurrent.locks.*;

public class MultipleServices {

    public static class Exp implements Callable {

        private double m;
        private int n;

        public Exp(double m, int n) {
            this.m = m;
            this.n = n;
        }

        public Double call() {
            double result = 1;
            for (int i = 0; i < n; i++) {
                result *= m;
```

```
                    try {
                        Thread.sleep(10);
                    } catch (InterruptedException ex) {
                        ex.printStackTrace();
                    }
                }
                System.out.printf("%nComputed %.02f raised to %d%n", m, n);
                return result;
            }
        }

        public static void main(String[] args) {
            ExecutorService executor = Executors.newFixedThreadPool(10);
            ArrayList<Callable<Double>> tasks = new ArrayList<Callable<Double>>();

            for (int i = 0; i < 10; i++) {
                double m = Math.random() * 10;
                int n = (int) (Math.random() * 1000);
                System.out.printf("Created task for computing: "
                        + "%.02f raised to %d\n", m, n);
                tasks.add(new Exp(m, n));
            }

            ExecutorCompletionService service =
                    new ExecutorCompletionService(executor);
            for (Callable<Double> task : tasks) {
                service.submit(task);
            }
            Lock lock = new ReentrantLock();
            for (int i = 0; i < tasks.size(); i++) {
                try {
                    lock.lock();
                    Double d = (Double) service.take().get();
                    System.out.printf("Result: %E%n", d);
                    lock.unlock();
                } catch (InterruptedException ex) {
                    ex.printStackTrace();
                } catch (ExecutionException ex) {
                    System.out.println("Error detected during task execution");
                }
            }
            executor.shutdown();
        }
    }
```

We first create a callable task:

```
public static class Exp implements Callable {
```

The class constructor accepts the values of **m** and **n** as parameters and stores them in the instance fields. The **call** method repeatedly performs the multiplication operation to compute the value of m^n:

```
public Double call() {
    double result = 1;
    for (int i = 0; i < n; i++) {
        result *= m;
```

After each iteration, we cause the thread to sleep for a few milliseconds to introduce a deliberate delay in the computation:

```
Thread.sleep(10);
```

After the **for** loop terminates, we print a message to the user and return the result of computation to the caller:

```
System.out.printf("%nComputed %.02f raised to %d%n", m, n);
return result;
```

In the **main** method, we create a fixed thread pool by using the **ExecutorService**:

```
ExecutorService executor = Executors.newFixedThreadPool(10);
```

We declare an array of **Callable** tasks. We create multiple tasks and add those to the array for deferred execution:

```
ArrayList<Callable<Double>> tasks = new ArrayList<Callable<Double>>();
```

To create the tasks, we set up a **for** loop. For each task, we generate random values for **m** and **n** so that execution takes a different amount of time for each task. Each created task is added to the **tasks** array:

```
for (int i = 0; i < 10; i++) {
    double m = Math.random() * 10;
    int n = (int)(Math.random() * 1000);
    tasks.add(new Exp(m, n));
}
```

Next, we create an instance of **ExecutorCompletionService** by passing the previously created **executor** as a parameter to its constructor. The service will now monitor the completion of jobs submitted to the executor service:

```
ExecutorCompletionService service = new ExecutorCompletionService(executor);
```

To submit the tasks to the executor, we call its **submit** method:

```
for (Callable<Double> task : tasks) {
    service.submit(task);
}
```

To check whether any of the tasks has completed its work, we set up a **for** loop and call the **take** method on the **service** object:

```
Lock lock = new ReentrantLock();
for (int i = 0; i < tasks.size(); i++) {
    try {
        lock.lock();
        Double d = (Double) service.take().get();
        System.out.printf("Result: %E%n", d);
        lock.unlock();
    } catch (InterruptedException ex) {
```

Note that the **take** method waits for the first result to become available. The loop that iterates 10 times retrieves the results of the 10 submitted tasks, one after another, as they become available. When the result becomes available, we retrieve its value by calling the **get** method on the returned future object. We print the returned value to the user console.

```
System.out.printf("Result: %E\n", d);
```

Note that we execute the **get** method and the print statement in a synchronized block so that the task's purpose and its output always appear together on the console.

At the end, we shut down the service:

```
executor.shutdown();
```

This ensures that all existing tasks get an opportunity to run to completion and that no new tasks will now be accepted. Calling the **shutdown** method does not mean that all previously submitted tasks will be cancelled at once. On the contrary, it just initiates an orderly shutdown so that all previously submitted tasks get an opportunity to run to completion. However, calling **shutdown** ensures that no new tasks will now be accepted. Additionally, Java defines a few more policies for shutdown. If **ExecuteExistingDelayedTasksAfterShutdownPolicy** is set to **false**, existing delayed tasks whose delays have not yet elapsed are cancelled. If **ContinueExistingPeriodicTasksAfterShutdownPolicy** is set to **true**, future executions of existing periodic tasks will be cancelled.

Typical partial output is shown here:

```
Created task for computing: 1.68 raised to 151
Created task for computing: 4.03 raised to 894
Created task for computing: 4.13 raised to 666
Created task for computing: 4.66 raised to 671
Created task for computing: 0.50 raised to 944
Computed 1.68 raised to 151
Result: 7.000069E+33
Computed 1.13 raised to 245
Result: 3.925909E+12
Computed 6.29 raised to 278
Result: 1.264098E+222
Computed 5.15 raised to 360
Result: 1.416120E+256
```

Compare the order in which the tasks are submitted with the order in which the results are retrieved and printed. Clearly, the tasks that complete earlier print their results to the console before the other tasks that are still in progress.

This kind of application, where a single task of computing exponentials on a large set of numbers can be split into smaller independent tasks, becomes an ideal candidate for concurrent programming. Given the multicore machines available on the market today, each subtask would run on an independent core and the program throughput would increase appreciably. So always look out for situations where a large linear task can be divided into smaller independent tasks and, wherever permissible, use the executor service to run these tasks in parallel. The executor completion service allows you to monitor the completion of these tasks and gives you the output of the task that completes first. The order in which the tasks complete need not match the order in which they are submitted.

Fork/Join Framework

The applications in this and the previous two chapters no doubt exploited the parallelism provided by the modern-day computers; however, we still need finer-grained parallelism. For example, consider the computation of Fibonacci numbers using a recursive algorithm. In the Fibonacci solution, the following takes place:

$$\text{fibonacci}(n - 1) + \text{fibonacci}(n - 2)$$

We can assign each of these two tasks to a new thread, and when they complete we add up the two results. In fact, the computation of each factor can be further divided into two parts; the process can continue until the computation becomes a simple linear problem. These kinds of algorithms are called *divide and conquer,* where a big problem is divided into smaller ones and the results are combined to conquer the solution. These kinds of algorithms are easy to parallelize, and this is the fine-grained parallelism we are looking for. Java SE 7 introduced a new framework called the Fork/Join framework to simplify the implementation of this type of divide-and-conquer algorithm. This framework, developed by Doug Lea, is based on his original paper from June 2000 (refer to http://gee.cs.oswego.edu/dl/papers/fj.pdf). Figure 19-5 shows the structure of a Fork/Join algorithm.

A large task is divided into several parts that are queued for later computation. A queued task may divide itself into further smaller parts. A thread picks up the task from the queue and executes it. When all threads complete, the partial results are combined to generate a final result. "Fork" refers to the division of tasks, and "Join" refers to the merging of the results. Each worker thread

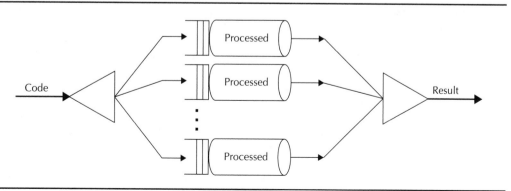

FIGURE 19-5. *Processing of a Fork/Join algorithm*

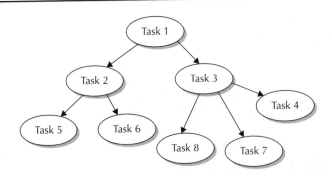

FIGURE 19-6. *A recursive divide-and-conquer algorithm*

maintains a double-ended queue of tasks. Tasks are executed in youngest-first order. When a worker thread has no more tasks to execute, it attempts to steal a task from another worker's deque tail. If it fails to steal and has no other work to do, it backs off. The advantage of this stealing is reduced contention because stealers steal from the opposite end of the deque than workers. Also, the stolen tasks are the larger units of work that lead to further recursive division. Note that the recursive divide-and-conquer algorithms generate larger tasks early. This divide-and-conquer model is depicted in Figure 19-6.

A big task such as Task 1 is divided into two or more subtasks. Each subtask is further divided into new subtasks, until a subtask becomes simple enough to solve. The subtasks are solved recursively.

To understand the Fork/Join framework, you need to understand two classes—**ForkJoinPool** and **ForkJoinTask**—which we will now discuss.

The ForkJoinPool Class

The class **ForkJoinPool** is an **ExecutorService** for running **ForkJoinTask**s. This class differs from other kinds of **ExecutorService**s by employing the work stealing described earlier. During its construction, you may specify the pool size as a parameter to the constructor. If you use a no-argument constructor, by default, it creates a pool of size that equals the number of available processors. Although you specify an initial pool size, the pool adjusts its size dynamically in an attempt to maintain enough active threads at any given point in time. The **ForkJoinPool** provides methods for the management and monitoring operations on submitted tasks. Another important difference compared to other **ExecutorService**s is that this pool need not be explicitly **shutdown** upon program exit because all its threads are in daemon mode.

There are three different ways of submitting a task to the **ForkJoinPool**. In the case of a desired asynchronous execution, you call its **execute** method with **ForkJoinTask** as a parameter. In the task itself, you need to call its **fork** method to split the work between multiple threads. If you want to await on obtaining the result, you call the **invoke** method on the pool. Inside the **ForkJoinTask** you then call its **invoke** method. The **invoke** method commences performing this task and returns its result after the task is completed, or it throws an unchecked exception or **Error** if the underlying computation fails. Lastly, you can submit the task to the pool by calling its **submit** method, which returns a **Future** object that you can use for checking status and obtaining the result on its completion.

TIP
*Use a single **ForkJoinPool** for all parallel-tasks execution in a program; otherwise, its use will not justify the overhead involved in its construction and bookkeeping of a large number of threads.*

The ForkJoinTask Class

This is an abstract class for creating tasks that run within a **ForkJoinPool**, described previously. The **RecursiveAction** and **RecursiveTask** are the only two direct, known subclasses of **ForkJoinTask**. When submitted to a **ForkJoinPool**, it begins its execution. As its name indicates, **ForkJoinTask** employs two operations—fork and join. Once started, it usually starts other subtasks. The join operation awaits the task's completion and extracts its results when the task completes. The **ForkJoinTask** implements **Future** and is, therefore, a lightweight form of **Future**. The implementation of the **get** method of the **Future** interface can be used for waiting on the computation to be completed and then retrieving its result. You may use the **invoke** method for performing the task; it returns the result after the task completes. The **invokeAll** method can accept a collection of tasks as its argument—the method forks all tasks in the specified collection and returns after each task completes or if an exception is encountered.

The **ForkJoinTask** class provides several methods for checking the execution status of a task. The **isDone** method returns **true** if a task completes in any way. The **isCompletedNormally** method returns **true** if a task completes without cancellation or encountering an exception, and **isCancelled** returns **true** if the task was cancelled. Lastly, **isCompletedAbnormally** returns **true** if the task was either cancelled or encountered an exception.

You would not generally subclass the **ForkJoinTask** class directly; rather, you would create a class based on **RecursiveTask** or **RecursiveAction**, which are the abstract subclasses of the **ForkJoinTask** class. The **RecursiveTask** class is used when a task returns a result, and the **RecursiveAction** is used when it does not return a result. In both cases, you would need to implement the **compute** method in your subclass that performs the main computation desired by the task.

You should perform only relatively small amounts of computations (typically 100 to 10,000 computational steps) in a **ForkJoinTask**. In the case of larger tasks, the benefits of parallelism diminish quickly. For smaller tasks, memory and task maintenance turns out to be expensive. You should usually split a large task into smaller subtasks, typically via recursive decomposition. All these things may sound too complicated to you; however, the use of this framework in practical situations is very easy, as you will see soon.

We will now look at a concrete implementation that shows how to use the Fork/Join framework for implementing divide-and-conquer algorithms. Instead of using the conventional algorithm for generating Fibonacci numbers, we will take on a slightly more complex problem to illustrate the use of this framework.

Sorting an Enormous Array of Floats

Suppose we have a very large chunk (say, a million records) of floating-point numbers. We are required to write a program to sort these numbers in ascending order. The well-known sorting techniques running on a single thread would take an unduly long time to create a sorted array. This kind of problem perfectly fits the divide-and-conquer paradigm. We will split the entire input array into smaller arrays and sort each one independently. We will keep on merging the sorted arrays into a larger array to create the final sorted array.

The complete sort program is presented in Listing 19-5.

Listing 19-5 *Parallel Merge Sort Based on the Fork/Join Framework*

```java
import java.util.concurrent.*;

public class ParallelMergeSort {

    private static ForkJoinPool threadPool;
    private static final int THRESHOLD = 16;

    private static void sort(Comparable[] objectArray) {
        Comparable[] destArray = new Comparable[objectArray.length];
        threadPool.invoke(new SortTask(objectArray,
                destArray, 0, objectArray.length - 1));
    }

    static class SortTask extends RecursiveAction {

        private Comparable[] sourceArray;
        private Comparable[] destArray;
        private int lowerIndex, upperIndex;

        public SortTask(Comparable[] sourceArray,
                Comparable[] destArray,
                int lowerIndex,
                int upperIndex) {
            this.sourceArray = sourceArray;
            this.lowerIndex = lowerIndex;
            this.upperIndex = upperIndex;
            this.destArray = destArray;
        }

        @Override
        protected void compute() {
            if (upperIndex - lowerIndex < THRESHOLD) {
                insertionSort(sourceArray, lowerIndex, upperIndex);
                return;
            }

            int midIndex = (lowerIndex + upperIndex) >>> 1;
            invokeAll(new SortTask(sourceArray, destArray, lowerIndex, midIndex),
                new SortTask(sourceArray, destArray, midIndex + 1, upperIndex));
            merge(sourceArray, destArray, lowerIndex, midIndex, upperIndex);
        }
    }

    private static void merge(Comparable[] sourceArray,
            Comparable[] destArray, int lowerIndex,
```

```
                 int midIndex, int upperIndex) {
        if (sourceArray[midIndex].compareTo(
                sourceArray[midIndex + 1]) <= 0) {
            return;
        }

        System.arraycopy(sourceArray, lowerIndex,
                destArray, lowerIndex, midIndex - lowerIndex + 1);

        int i = lowerIndex;
        int j = midIndex + 1;
        int k = lowerIndex;

        while (k < j && j <= upperIndex) {
            if (destArray[i].compareTo(sourceArray[j]) <= 0) {
                sourceArray[k++] = destArray[i++];
            } else {
                sourceArray[k++] = sourceArray[j++];
            }
        }
        System.arraycopy(destArray, i, sourceArray, k, j - k);
    }

    private static void insertionSort(Comparable[] objectArray,
            int lowerIndex, int upperIndex) {
        for (int i = lowerIndex + 1; i <= upperIndex; i++) {
            int j = i;
            Comparable tempObject = objectArray[j];
            while (j > lowerIndex
                    && tempObject.compareTo(objectArray[j - 1]) < 0) {
                objectArray[j] = objectArray[j - 1];
                --j;
            }
            objectArray[j] = tempObject;
        }
    }

    public static Double[] createRandomData(int length) {
        Double[] data = new Double[length];
        for (int i = 0; i < data.length; i++) {
            data[i] = length * Math.random();
        }
        return data;
    }

    public static void main(String[] args) {
        int processors = Runtime.getRuntime().availableProcessors();
        System.out.println("No of processors: " + processors);

        threadPool = new ForkJoinPool(processors);
        Double[] data = createRandomData(1000);
```

```
        System.out.println("Original unsorted data:");
        for (Double d : data) {
            System.out.printf("%3.2f  ", (double) d);
        }
        sort(data);
        System.out.println("\n\nSorted Array:");
        for (Double d : data) {
            System.out.printf("%3.2f  ", d);
        }
    }
}
```

In the **main** method, we first obtain the number of available processors on the machine where the code is currently running:

```
int processors = Runtime.getRuntime().availableProcessors();
```

We will create a thread pool of this size, which is the optimal number for running on the available hardware. If you create a pool of a higher size, contention for the available CPUs will occur. We create the thread pool by instantiating **ForkJoinPool** and passing the pool size as a parameter to its constructor:

```
threadPool = new ForkJoinPool(processors);
```

After creating the thread pool in the **main** method, we construct an array of some random data:

```
Double[] data = createRandomData(1000);
```

The implementation of **createRandomData** is very straightforward—it uses the **Random** class to generate data points in the range of 0 to 1,000 and initializes each element of the array with this randomly generated data. The number of data points created equals the argument to the function, which in this case is **1000**. Making this figure large will prove the efficiency of our parallel-sort algorithm, but we have kept this at a reasonable level for testing purposes. The **main** method then prints this random data for our knowledge. We call the **sort** method to sort the generated data and once again print it to the console so the user can verify the sorting.

Let's now look at the implementation of the **sort** method. The **sort** method accepts the object array, the elements of which are to be sorted in ascending order:

```
private static void sort(Comparable[] objectArray) {
```

We declare a temporary destination array of equal size to store the result of sorting:

```
Comparable[] destArray = new Comparable[objectArray.length];
```

We then create a **SortTask** and submit it to our thread pool by calling its **invoke** method:

```
threadPool.invoke(new SortTask(objectArray,
                destArray, 0, objectArray.length - 1));
```

The **SortTask** takes four parameters: the array to be sorted and the destination array for the sorted objects as well as the start index and the end index in the source array, between which the elements are to be sorted. The **SortTask** is the heart of our program. It derives its functionality from the **RecursiveAction** class. Note that because our sorting algorithm does not directly return a result to its caller, we create our task based on **RecursiveAction**. Had our algorithm returned a value, as in the case of Fibonacci number calculation, we would have derived our class from **RecursiveTask**. As part of creating a concrete implementation for the **SortTask** class, we need to override the abstract method **compute**. In the **compute** method, we check the number of elements to be sorted—if it is less than the predefined **THRESHOLD (16)**, we call the **insertionSort** method to sort its elements:

```
if (upperIndex - lowerIndex < THRESHOLD) {
    insertionSort(sourceArray, lowerIndex, upperIndex);
    return;
}
```

Otherwise, we create two subtasks and call them recursively. Each subtask receives its source data array as half of the original array. The first subtask is created by constructing a **SortTask** instance as follows:

```
new SortTask(sourceArray, destArray, lowerIndex, midIndex)
```

The second subtask is created by the following code:

```
new SortTask(sourceArray, destArray, midIndex + 1, upperIndex)
```

The **midIndex** in these two constructors defines the midpoint of the original array. The two tasks are submitted to the pool by calling

```
invokeAll (task1, task2)
```

where **task1** and **task2** are the previously created two tasks.

Note that this process of splitting a task into subtasks continues recursively until each subtask becomes small enough (when the number of elements in the array is less than **THRESHOLD**). All the split subtasks are submitted to the pool recursively, and when they complete, the **compute** method calls **merge**:

```
merge(sourceArray, destArray, lowerIndex, midIndex, upperIndex);
```

Understanding the **merge** and **insertionSort** methods is left as an exercise for the reader (they should not be too difficult to understand).

Now, try running the program. You may experiment with different array sizes and also add code to determine the execution time to fully appreciate the efficiency of divide-and-conquer algorithms. Partial output of the program is shown here:

```
No of processors: 4

598.44   261.95   496.39   496.92   476.67   320.68   618.45   263.29   649.88
417.24   925.36   317.36   899.89   564.64   405.76   230.71   849.37   232.94
242.52   407.35   354.44   384.48   856.25   223.49    61.96   132.42   232.37
222.20   677.12   754.12   392.38   561.74   327.93   498.97   757.74   796.42
597.76   931.88   886.19    42.08   325.37   449.34   635.51   646.15   144.01
 94.04   228.72   642.97   946.81   877.13   957.41   530.22    25.55   494.06
366.14   250.76   532.89   590.16   711.51   706.68   165.47   596.75   282.87
668.37   556.00
```

. . .

```
 0.43    1.22    3.97    5.39    5.52    6.52    7.51    7.55    9.71   10.29
11.77   12.15   13.10   15.26   16.68   19.06   20.71   21.96   22.25   23.07
23.23   25.01   25.10   25.55   25.88   26.62   28.82   29.03   29.08   29.28
35.80   38.77   40.47   41.55   41.82   42.08   50.57   51.18   52.09   54.49
55.08   55.16   55.83   56.03   56.57   56.73   56.77   61.72   61.83   61.96
62.28   63.58   67.49   69.79   70.12   70.98   71.54   71.66   72.54   76.14
80.60   83.45   84.11   85.58   86.20   91.09   92.13   92.45   94.04   96.69
97.42   97.59   98.15  100.05  100.50  101.34
```

Before concluding this chapter, let's look at the thread-safe collections, which were first introduced in J2SE 5.0.

Thread-safe Collections

The collections we discussed in Chapter 16 are not thread-safe. Therefore, if multiple threads access a collection, data corruption may occur unless the developer provides his own synchronizations. The new collection classes introduced in J2SE 5.0 have created wrappers on the existing classes, providing concurrency to those classes.

The **Vector** and **Hashtable** classes provided in the initial release of Java were thread-safe. However, as of J2SE 1.2, these were deprecated and declared obsolete. They were replaced by the **ArrayList** and **HashMap** classes, which are not thread-safe. To introduce thread safety, Java provided synchronization wrappers. Thus, you could create a thread-safe **List** or **Map** using the following declarations:

```
List<E> synchArrayList = Collections.synchronizedList(new ArrayList<E>());
Map<K, V> synchHashMap = Collections.synchronizedMap(new HashMap<K, V>());
```

Although this solved the concurrency issues at that time, it is now recommended that you use the newly created collection classes. With the introduction of concurrency utilities in J2SE 5.0, Java provided concurrent implementations for maps, sorted sets, and queues. The blocking queue we used earlier is thread-safe. The two new classes, **ConcurrentHashMap** and **ConcurrentSkipListMap**, provide the map implementations. The **ConcurrentSkipListSet** implements a set, and **ConcurrentLinkedQueue** provides the queue implementation, as their names suggest. They employ sophisticated algorithms to minimize contention and to provide concurrency in data access.

Because they support concurrency, they return *weakly consistent iterators,* which may or may not reflect all modifications made to the underlying data structure after it was constructed. However, they are not guaranteed to return a value twice and also do not throw a **ConcurrentModificationException**, as in the case of collection classes in the **java.util** package. For the insertion and removal of associations in a map, the new classes provide methods called **putIfAbsent** and **remove** for this purpose. The **putIfAbsent** method ensures that only one thread adds an item to the cache. The **remove** method atomically removes the key and value, if present, in the map. Finally, the **replace** method atomically replaces a value associated with the specified key.

One of the major additions to this **java.util.concurrent** package in Java SE 7 is the introduction of the **ConcurrentLinkedDeque** class. This is an unbounded concurrent deque (double-ended queue) based on linked nodes. You would use this class when many threads in your program want to share a collection, where the concurrent insertion, removal, and access operations are guaranteed to execute safely across multiple threads.

Collections can be used in many practical scenarios. For example, in the stock exchange server scenario, the trades may be maintained in some type of collection; in an online chat application, the different threads of communication may be maintained in some form of collection. A data logger application may collect data from many concurrent channels and put it in some form of collection. In all such practical situations, using these thread-safe collections can save you a lot of headaches in managing the concurrency of these shared objects.

In conclusion, if you need concurrency in collections, it is better to use the newly introduced classes in the **java.util.concurrent** package. If you do not need concurrency in your programs, continue using the older classes in the **java.util** package.

The ThreadLocalRandom Class

We'll discuss one more addition to Java SE 7 in the Concurrency framework before closing this chapter: the **ThreadLocalRandom** class. This class defines a random number generator isolated to the current thread. You will use this class when multiple tasks in your program use random numbers in parallel in thread pools. Rather than sharing an object of a **Random** class, as we have been doing in all our programs so far, you would use **ThreadLocalRandom**, which results in less overhead and contention in concurrent programs. Typically, to generate a random number using this class, you use the syntax **ThreadLocalRandom.current().nextLong(*n*)**, where *n* is the upper bound for the generated number and the lower bound is zero. Of course, you get variations on the **next** method that generate integers and double numbers. The overloads on these allow you to set both lower and upper bounds. So consider using this class in your concurrent programs if you need random numbers in your threads.

Summary

The **Runnable** interface allows you to create a task that can be run asynchronously by submitting it to a thread. When such asynchronous execution runs to its completion, it neither implicitly notifies its creator nor returns the results to it. The caller and future concepts introduced in J2SE 5.0 help overcome this situation. A caller is created by implementing a **Callable** interface. It has a sole method named **call**. This method is executed asynchronously, just the way the **run** method executes in the **Runnable** interface. The caller who wants to execute this asynchronous method must create an instance of a **Callable** object and submit it to an **Executor** for execution. The executor returns a **Future** object to the caller for monitoring, controlling, and obtaining the results of the method execution. Such execution may take place immediately after its submission or may be delayed for the specified time. The task may also be repeatedly executed at a fixed rate or with a fixed delay between subsequent runs. The **Executors** class provides these facilities. You learned the use of the **ExecutorService** class for managing the life cycle and to track the progress of asynchronously submitted tasks. The **ScheduledExecutorService** class helps in scheduling commands after a given delay, or to execute them periodically. This chapter also introduced you to the newly added Fork/ Join framework, which explores fine-grained parallelism in your algorithms.

The chapter concluded with a brief discussion of the thread-safe collections introduced in J2SE 5.0. Most of the methods of these thread-safe collection classes are the same as their earlier counterparts. The chapter discussed a few new methods of these collection classes. In the next chapter, you learn another important feature—network programming.

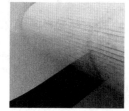

CHAPTER
20

Network Programming

o far you have learned many aspects of Java programming. The last three chapters covered the important topic of thread programming. In this chapter, you will learn another important feature in Java—network programming. As a matter of fact, network programs are so common that you might be wondering why we did not cover them earlier in the book. Network programs most of the time are multiuser applications. These are essentially client/server applications, where a single server application serves many clients. The server application, because it uses the same application logic for serving different clients, requires the use of threads for efficient processing. Therefore, it would have made little sense discussing network programming without first covering threads.

Network programming plays a vital role in today's distributed computing era. Whatever applications you use these days generally require a collaboration with applications running on other machines—whether local or remote. This requires applications to support network programming. There are many examples of network applications in real life. The Yahoo! or Google chat application you use everyday is a network application. An online stock-trading application is a network application. Checking your bank balances online involves yet another network application. Browsing oracle.com in your web browser involves a network application. In fact, any web-based application requires network programming, and that's what you will be learning in this chapter.

Java, right from its beginning, provided excellent support for network programming. JDK 1.0 provided a rich set of libraries for creating networked applications; in fact, at one stage, Java was "advertised" as a network programming language.

You will be learning the following in this chapter:

- Network programming concepts
- Creating a socket connection to a remote server
- Reading the home page of any website
- Using the **URL** class to download any webpage
- Spying for incoming cookies from websites
- Writing a server application
- Serving multiple clients simultaneously
- Writing a practical file storage server application
- Understanding the use of the **InetAddress** class
- Writing a multicast server and client

Networking

To understand how different computers connected on a network communicate with each other, let's consider the telephone network within the premises of a fictional office. In the office, a telephone receptionist is appointed. The receptionist waits on incoming calls. When the phone rings, she responds to the call and connects the caller to the requested person. The two parties—the caller and the requested person in the organization—communicate with each other without the receptionist overhearing the conversation. The receptionist now waits for another call. When a new call comes in, once again she responds to the call and connects the new caller to someone in the organization. The process continues until all the incoming lines available in the office are busy. Anyone calling the office number will now get a busy signal. This entire process is illustrated in Figure 20-1.

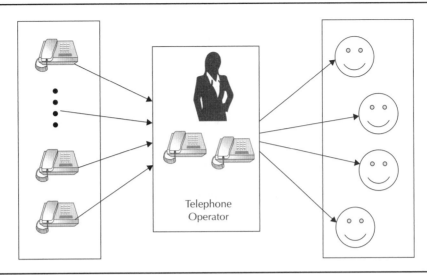

FIGURE 20-1. *Our office telephone network*

A similar process occurs when multiple computers connected in a physical network want to communicate with each other over a centralized server. We will first consider the case of two computers communicating with each other, and later on expand the idea to multiple computers. The case of *point-to-point* communication is illustrated in Figure 20-2.

For two machines to communicate with each other based on the network programming model, one of the machines must be in listening mode, as in the case of the telephone operator in the office scenario. The machine shown on the right side in Figure 20-2 is a listener to the incoming calls. Every machine connected to a network has a certain unique IP (Internet Protocol) address. The server sets up a port on which it is continually listening for incoming requests. An IP and port are similar to an office telephone number. Your office telephone has a fixed number that you let your clients know. The clients dial this number to connect to your office. Similarly, any machine that wants to connect to the server (the machine on the right in Figure 20-2) uses the known IP and the port number while making the connection. How does the client connect to the server? We say that the client makes a socket connection to the server by creating a **Socket** object from the classes

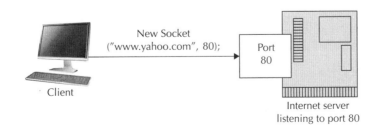

FIGURE 20-2. *Two machines communicating with each other in a network programming model*

provided in the Java library. So what is a socket? A *socket* is a software endpoint that establishes bidirectional communication between a server and a client. A socket associates the server program with a specific IP and port number. A client anywhere in the physical network holding a reference to this socket communicates with the server program using this socket. The client obtains this socket object with the following statement:

```
Socket s = new Socket("www.yahoo.com", 80);
```

The **Socket** constructor takes two arguments: The first argument is the URL (Uniform Resource Locator) string, and the second argument is a port number. The URL represents the IP address of the server. Each server connected to the Internet has a unique address provided by an organization called InterNIC, which provides worldwide Internet domain name registration services. The port number is any number in the range 0 to 0xFFFF that you designate to your server application. Note that a certain range of numbers has been reserved universally for certain kinds of applications. When you create server applications, you will have to be sure not to use the reserved port numbers. The port number 80 is one such reserved number on which an HTTP (Hypertext Transfer Protocol) server is set up. Several other constructors are defined in the **Socket** class; some of these use the **InetAddress** class we will be discussing later in the book. You are encouraged to look up the API documentation to learn the other constructors.

When a **Socket** object is successfully created, the two machines will communicate with each other with the help of an established socket, which is general terminology used in the network programming model to indicate an endpoint of a communication link between the two processes. Java and some other languages use the name "Socket" to refer to a socket connection.

After a socket connection is established, we use the streams to send data back and forth between the two processes. A socket holds two streams—one for data input and the other for data output. This is shown in Figure 20-3.

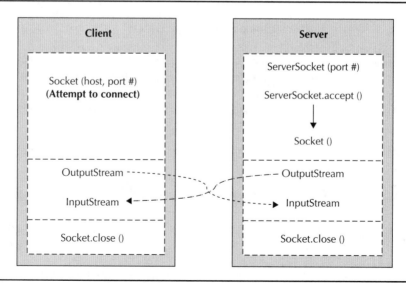

FIGURE 20-3. *Using streams on a TCP/IP socket connection*

The server creates a server socket and keeps listening on it for incoming requests. A client makes a socket connection to the server. The server may accept or reject the client request. If a request is accepted, the client and server are connected using a common socket. The client opens input and output streams on the created socket. To send data to the server, it writes to the output stream. To read data coming from the server, it reads the input stream. When the communication is over, generally the client will close the socket, breaking the link between the two machines. Let's look at this concept further via a concrete program example.

Simple Home Page Reader

When you surf on the Net, your browser makes connections to HTTP servers located worldwide and retrieves the contents of the pages hosted by those sites. For example, when you type a typical URL (such as http://www.oracle.com) into your browser, a socket connection is made to the remote server hosted by Oracle, an HTTP request gets its contents, its home page (index.html) is fetched, and finally the page contents are displayed in the browser's client area. The browser interprets the HTML tags in the page contents and renders formatted output in its display area. We will now develop an application that does exactly this for a browser, but at a very crude level. In particular, our application will not have an HTML interpreter and will simply display the page contents in plain-text format on the console.

First, the application makes a socket connection to a well-known IP and port number. Once a socket connection is established, it opens the input and output streams on it. Then it sends a **GET** request through the output stream to the server. The server may respond to the request by sending the contents of its home page to our application. The client simply waits for the server to respond, and whenever the contents arrive, it reads and prints them to the console line by line.

The home page reader application is shown in Listing 20-1.

Listing 20-1 *A Web Home Page Reader Application Using Sockets*

```
import java.net.*;
import java.io.*;
import java.util.Scanner;

public class HomePageReader {

    public static void main(String[] args) {
        try {
            Socket socketObject = new Socket("www.yahoo.com", 80);
            try {
                OutputStream outStream = socketObject.getOutputStream();
                String str = "GET / HTTP/1.0\n\n";
                outStream.write(str.getBytes());
                InputStream inStream = socketObject.getInputStream();
                Scanner reader = new Scanner(inStream);
                while (reader.hasNextLine()) {
                    String line = reader.nextLine();
                    System.out.println(line);
                }
            } finally {
```

```
            socketObject.close();
        }
    } catch (Exception e) {
        e.printStackTrace();
    }
   }
 }
}
```

Java defines its network classes in the **java.net** package. Therefore, we first import this package into our application:

```
import java.net.*;
```

In the **main** function, we make a socket connection by constructing an object of the **Socket** class:

```
Socket socketObject = new Socket("www.yahoo.com", 80);
```

The first argument to the constructor is the IP address of a known domain—in this case, it is Yahoo!. You could also replace this IP address with the string **"87.248.122.122"**, which is the physical IP assigned to yahoo.com and is subject to change at any time in future. All the web browsers listen to the standard port number 80 for serving contents based on HTTP. Therefore, we specify a port number of 80 in the preceding statement.

NOTE
If you are running this code in your office environment, a proxy server may be installed for HTTP connections. In this case, you need to use another constructor that specifies the type of proxy to be used.

```
Socket socketObject = new Socket(new Proxy(Proxy.Type.Socks,
                        new InetSocketAddress("socks.abcom.com", 1080)));
socketObject.connect (new InsetSocketAddress(www.yahoo.com, 80));
```

If this attempt to connect fails, the program generates an exception. We catch this exception and print the stack trace to understand the type of error that occurred. If the connection succeeds, the program obtains the output stream associated with the connected socket.

```
OutputStream outStream = socketObject.getOutputStream();
```

Next, we construct an HTTP **GET** request:

```
String str = "GET / HTTP/1.0\n\n";
```

GET is the most common HTTP method. It says, "Get me this resource." The resource itself is specified as the next token in the string. The slash (/) in the preceding statement indicates the desired resource, which means "Get me the contents of the default home page file from the path '/' at the specified host address." The home page may be index.html or default.html or any other file, as decided by the server. The protocol used for communication is HTTP version 1.0, as specified by the next token in the preceding string. We now send this string to the server through the output stream object we obtained earlier:

```
outStream.write(str.getBytes());
```

Now, we need to read the response from the server. For this, we obtain the input stream object from the socket connection:

```
InputStream inStream = socketObject.getInputStream();
```

We create a **Scanner** object and repeatedly read the contents provided by the server until no more lines are found:

```
Scanner reader = new Scanner(inStream);
while (reader.hasNextLine()) {
    String line = reader.nextLine();
    System.out.println(line);
}
```

At the end, the program closes the socket connection:

```
} finally {
    socketObject.close();
}
```

NOTE
It is important that your application closes the socket connection after its use. The open sockets are not garbage-collected and need to be explicitly closed for freeing the resources.

When you run the program, you will get the following output:

```
HTTP/1.0 200 OK
Date: Thu, 09 Jun 2011 07:56:48 GMT
P3P: policyref="http://info.yahoo.com/w3c/p3p.xml", CP="CAO DSP COR CUR ADM
DEV TAI PSA PSD IVAi IVDi CONi TELo OTPi OUR DELi SAMi OTRi UNRi PUBi IND
PHY ONL UNI PUR FIN COM NAV INT DEM CNT STA POL HEA PRE LOC GOV"
Cache-Control: private
Set-Cookie: IU=deleted; expires=Wed, 09-Jun-2010 07:56:47 GMT; path=/; domain=.yahoo.com
Set-Cookie: PH=deleted; expires=Wed, 09-Jun-2010 07:56:47 GMT; path=/; domain=.yahoo.com
...
Content-Type: text/html;charset=utf-8
Age: 2
Server: YTS/1.20.0

<!DOCTYPE html>
<html lang="en-US" class="y-fp-bg y-fp-pg-grad  bkt701" style="">
<!-- m2 template  -->
<head>
    <meta http-equiv="Content-Type" content="text/html; charset=utf-8">

    <title>Yahoo!</title>
    <meta http-equiv="X-UA-Compatible" content="chrome=1">
```

The complete output is not shown here. Obviously, the output on your machine will differ, depending on the current home page hosted at the time. Note the **html** tag toward the end of the shown output. Your browser interprets this HTML code and renders a formatted output in its client area. Because our client application does not understand these HTML tags, it simply gives the output in text format.

The home page reader application discussed here is a pretty low-level application that uses sockets directly. Java provides a higher abstraction to retrieve a webpage hosted on any server in the world. You will now learn about two new classes—**URL** and **URLConnection**—for doing this.

The URL Class

The **URL** class makes accessing web resources as easy as accessing a local file on your machine. URL stands for Uniform Resource Locator. The syntax for a URL is specified as follows:

```
scheme://domain:port/path?query_string#fragment_id
```

A sample URL string looks like this:

```
http://www.oracle.com/us/technologies/java/index.html
```

The "http" part of the URL represents the scheme, popularly known as the protocol. The "www.oracle.com" part is the domain. The port, when not specified, takes a default value of 80. The substring "/us/technologies/java/index.html" specifies the path. This particular URL string does not contain the query_string subpart.

The Java **URL** class is an abstraction of the URL identifier. It provides functions for opening a connection to a specific URL, reading/writing data from/to this URL, and reading/writing header information as well as performing several other operations on the URL. You will be using the same I/O classes from the **java.io** package to read from and write to a URL that you used on files and socket connections.

The **URL** class provides several overloaded constructors. In its simplest form, it takes a single string parameter that specifies the URL, as just illustrated. The other versions accept protocol, host, port, and other types of parameters. You are encouraged to look up the javadocs for further details. The **openConnection** method opens a connection to the remote object. It provides several **get** methods to retrieve the parts of the URL string. You use the **getInputStream** and **getOutputStream** methods to obtain the input and output streams, respectively, for reading from and writing to a remote URL.

The URLConnection Class

Opening a connection on the **URL** instance returns an object of type **URLConnection**. This is an abstract class that represents a communication link between the application and a URL. **HttpURLConnection** and **JarURLConnection** provide the concrete implementations of this class. Once a connection is established, you call the **setDoInput** method to set the inward communication from the server to the application, which is the default. Similarly, to write to the server, you set the connection to the output mode by calling the **setDoOutput** method; the default value for the **doOutput** flag is **false**.

Let's now consider an example that shows the use of **URLConnection** class. We will develop a simple webpage browser in the next section that uses the **URL** and **URLConnection** classes. Unlike the home page reader discussed earlier, this application is able to read from a remote web object using several available protocols.

Webpage Reader

The webpage reader application first constructs a URL object based on the specified URL string. Then it opens a connection on this URL and reads the contents in the specified remote object. The application code is given in Listing 20-2.

Listing 20-2 *A URL-based Webpage Reader*

```java
import java.io.InputStream;
import java.net.*;
import java.util.Scanner;

public class WebPageReader {

    public static void main(String[] args) {
        try {
            String strURL =
                    "http://www.oracle.com/us/technologies/java/index.html";
            URL url = new URL(strURL);
            URLConnection connection = url.openConnection();
            InputStream inStream = connection.getInputStream();
            Scanner reader = new Scanner(inStream);
            while (reader.hasNextLine()) {
                String line = reader.nextLine();
                System.out.println(line);
            }
            reader.close();
        } catch (Exception e) {
            e.printStackTrace();
        }
    }
}
```

The **main** method declares a URL string **strURL**, as follows:

```java
String strURL = "http://www.oracle.com/us/technologies/java/index.html";
```

This URL string can be anything you want. If the string points to an invalid URL, the program will catch an exception at runtime. You may also use other protocols such as **ftp** to retrieve the contents of the remote object using FTP (File Transfer Protocol).

The following statement constructs a URL object:

```java
URL url = new URL(strURL);
```

A connection to this URL is made by calling the **openConnection** method on it that returns an object of type **URLConnection**:

```java
URLConnection connection = url.openConnection();
```

To read the data from the remote object, we obtain the input stream from the connection object:

```java
InputStream inStream = connection.getInputStream();
```

Now, we can use our usual **InputStream** methods to read the contents from the remote machine and print them to the console. At the end, we close the input stream by calling its **close** method. Invoking the **close** method on the **InputStream** or **OutputStream** of a **URLConnection** after a request may free network resources associated with this instance, unless particular protocol specifications specify different behavior for it.

So far we've looked at the client side of network programming. Before moving on to server programming, I will like to discuss one more important class—**java.net.HttpCookie**.

The HttpCookie Class

A website uses a cookie to send state information to a user's browser, and a browser uses the cookie to return the state information to the original site. Websites use cookies for client session management, personalization, and tracking a user's web-browsing habits. If you look at the output of the program given in Listing 20-1, presented earlier, you will notice the presence of **Set-Cookie** fields in it. The general syntax of an HTTP response is shown here:

```
HTTP/1.1 200 OK
Content-type: text/html
Set-Cookie: user=sanjay
Set-Cookie: password=10101; Expires=Wed, 19 Jun 2021 12:00:00 GMT
...
(content of page)
```

The web server sends these lines of **Set-Cookie** when it wants the browser to store cookies. The **Set-Cookie** is a directive to the browser to store the cookie and send it back in future requests to the server. If the browser does not support cookies or if cookies are disabled, obviously this directive is ignored. The browser, in its new request, sends the cookies back to the server using the following general syntax:

```
GET /technetwork/java/index.html HTTP/1.1
Host: www.oracle.com
Cookie: user=sanjay; password=10101
Accept: */*
```

The server now knows that the new request is related to the previous one. The server may answer the request by sending the requested page, possibly adding other cookies.

The **HttpCookie** class represents these cookies in Java. It provides several methods to parse the cookie contents. Methods include **getDomain**, **getName**, **getValue**, **hasExpired**, and so on. You will be using some of these methods in the **CookieSpy** program we are going to discuss shortly. To retrieve the cookies from the HTTP response, the class provides a static parse method that returns a list of **HttpCookie** objects constructed from the **Set-Cookie** and **Set-Cookie2** header strings. Like the getter methods, the class provides several setter methods that a server uses after creating a cookie object.

To handle cookies, the **java.net** package provides two more classes (**CookieManager** and **CookieHandler**) and two interfaces (**CookiePolicy** and **CookieStore**). The **CookieManager** provides a concrete implementation of **CookieHandler** that provides methods for getting/putting cookies besides other functions. The **CookiePolicy** implementation decides the policy for accepting/ rejecting cookies. Lastly, as its name indicates, the **CookieStore** represents storage for cookies. You will be using these interfaces and classes in the **CookieSpy** program.

Spying for Cookies

Generally, websites don't tell you when they send cookies to your machine. Although cookies cannot carry viruses and cannot install malware on your computer, they can be used to track your browsing activities (which is considered an invasion of privacy by law in some countries). Also, hackers can steal them to gain access to your web account and other sensitive information the cookies may contain. Therefore, we will develop a spy program that lists out the cookies sent to your machine by any website you usually browse. The code for the **CookieSpy** program is given in Listing 20-3.

Listing 20-3   *A Spy Utility for Web Cookies*

```java
import java.io.IOException;
import java.net.*;
import java.text.SimpleDateFormat;
import java.util.List;

public class CookieSpy {

    private final static String TIME_FORMAT_NOW = "HH:mm:ss";
    private final static SimpleDateFormat sdf =
            new SimpleDateFormat(TIME_FORMAT_NOW);

    public static void main(String[] args) {
        try {
            String urlString = "http://www.yahoo.com";

            CookieManager manager = new CookieManager();
            manager.setCookiePolicy(new CustomCookiePolicy());
            CookieHandlet.setDefault(manager);

            URL url = new URL(urlString);
            URLConnection connection = url.openConnection();
            Object obj = connection.getContent();
            List<HttpCookie> cookies = manager.getCookieStore().getCookies();
            for (HttpCookie cookie : cookies) {
                System.out.println("Name: " + cookie.getName());
                System.out.println("Domain: " + cookie.getDomain());
                long age = cookie.getMaxAge();
                if (age == -1) {
                    System.out.println( "This cookie will expire when "
                            + "browser closes");
                } else {
                    System.out.printf( "This cookie will expire in %s "
                            + "seconds%n", sdf.format(age));
                }
                System.out.println("Secured: "
                        + ((Boolean) cookie.getSecure()).toString());
                System.out.println("Value: " + cookie.getValue());
                System.out.println();
            }
        }
```

```
            } catch (MalformedURLException e) {
                System.out.println("Invalid URL");
            } catch (IOException e) {
                System.out.println("Error in I/O operation");
            }
        }
    }
}

class CustomCookiePolicy implements CookiePolicy {

    public boolean shouldAccept(URI uri, HttpCookie cookie) {
//          return uri.getHost().equals("yahoo.com");
        return true;
    }
}
```

The **main** method first creates an instance of the **CookieManager** class:

```
CookieManager manager = new CookieManager();
```

Besides the no-argument constructor used here, the **CookieManager** class provides another constructor that takes two parameters—a **CookieStore** and a **CookiePolicy**. You would use this constructor if you want the manager to use your customized store and policy for accepting/rejecting cookies. If you just want to use customized policies and not a customized store, the **CookieManager** provides a method called **setCookiePolicy** to set your own policies and continue using its default store. In our case, we set our customized policy:

```
manager.setCookiePolicy(new CustomCookiePolicy());
```

We then set this manager as the default in the **CookieHandler**:

```
CookieHandler.setDefault(manager);
```

CookieHandler is at the core of all cookie management. It uses the manager set in the preceding statement to use the customized store and policies, if provided. When you get a response to your web request, this handler will intercept the response and store the cookies, if any, in its store. To send a web request and get a response, we use the following code:

```
URL url = new URL(urlString);
URLConnection connection = url.openConnection();
Object obj = connection.getContent();
```

We now obtain the list of received cookies by calling the **getCookies** method of the **CookieStore**:

```
List<HttpCookie> cookies = manager.getCookieStore().getCookies();
```

For each cookie in the list, we print its various members:

```
for (HttpCookie cookie : cookies) {
    System.out.println("Name: " + cookie.getName());
        ...
}
```

Now, let's look at the **CustomCookiePolicy** class that implements **CookiePolicy**. The interface provides one sole method, called **shouldAccept**, that we implement as follows:

```
public boolean shouldAccept(URI uri, HttpCookie cookie) {
    return true;
}
```

The method simply returns **true**, suggesting that regardless of the values of the two parameters it receives, it would accept any cookie. Now, suppose you want to accept the cookies conditionally; for example, you may decide not to accept any cookies coming from yahoo.com. You would do so by replacing the preceding **return** statement with the following:

```
return uri.getHost().equals("yahoo.com");
```

Now, try running this code on the specified Yahoo! site. You will see output similar to the partial output shown here:

```
Name: fpc
Domain: www.yahoo.com
This cookie will expire in 14:15:35 seconds
Secured: false
Value: d=uaopc3ToR..MGhrtVbW1DjiAHEDyLTGUEf5vFfdiCC7FuBeb8LMu5F3UeMm8JVNlFQC
1qCLoe0znpglXs3uofuX2K.K6CbZgF5Nj6Hwgpw7ObWN.Ajw4KorrSpr2uXwbVrOImaiy63kmORX
5_uqAfZ5gy1rurYE3edYAQQpADepRpDSXEKDch8kue7Zjdrl171ByPn8-&v=2

Name: B
Domain: .yahoo.com
This cookie will expire in 23:03:20 seconds
Secured: false
Value: 04h4rp96vgq4i&b=3&s=9p

Name: fpc_s
Domain: in.yahoo.com
...
```

Try setting the policy so as to reject cookies from yahoo.com, as explained earlier. This time, you will not get any cookies listed on your terminal. Try the program with different sites such as google.com to see what cookies it sends to your machine.

One last thing to cover before we close this section: the implementation of a custom cookie store. The default cookie store provided in Java's implementation should suffice in most cases. You would want to implement your own store should you wish to keep cookies in your own persistent storage. To create your own store, you create a custom store class that implements **CookieStore**:

```
class CustomCookieStore implements CookieStore {
```

As a part of the interface implementation, you need to provide definitions for the **add**, **remove**, and **removeAll** methods as well as the **get**, **getCookies**, and **getURIs** methods. You may create a store in an internal **HashMap** or persistent storage on your disk. The **CookieManager** will automatically call your **add** method to save cookies for every incoming HTTP response, and it will call the **get** method to retrieve cookies for every outgoing HTTP request. Remember, it is your responsibility to remove any cookie instances that have expired.

Having seen how to write the client applications that communicate with a remote server, we will now cover how to write an HTTP server application.

Echo Server Application

In the previous section, you learned how to write a client application. In this section, you will learn how to write a server application. The server application requires you to use the **ServerSocket** class. This class implements server sockets. A *server socket* is a socket (endpoint of communication— remember the definition of *socket* given previously) that waits for requests to come in over the network. Based on the request, it performs some operation and optionally returns a result to the requester.

In this section, we develop an echo server application. The echo server sets up a server socket listening on a certain port for incoming client requests. A client makes a connection to the server using this port number and writes some data to our echo server. The echo server will read the data and send it back to the client "as is." The full program is given in Listing 20-4.

Listing 20-4 *A Server That Echoes Back the Client Message*

```java
import java.net.*;
import java.io.*;

public class EchoServer {

    private static ServerSocket server = null;

    public static void main(String[] args) {
        byte buffer[] = new byte[512];
        new Thread(new Monitor()).start();

        try {
            server = new ServerSocket(10000);
            System.out.println("Server Started");
            System.out.println("Hit Enter to stop the server");

            while (true) {
                Socket socketObject = server.accept();
                InputStream reader = socketObject.getInputStream();
                reader.read(buffer);
                OutputStream writer = socketObject.getOutputStream();
                writer.write(buffer);
                socketObject.close();
            }
        } catch (SocketException e) {
            System.out.println("Server is down");
        } catch (IOException ex) {
            ex.printStackTrace();
```

```
            }
        }

    private static void shutdownServer() {
        try {
            server.close();
        } catch (IOException ex) {
        }
        System.exit(0);
    }

    private static class Monitor implements Runnable {

        public void run() {
            try {
                while (System.in.read() != '\n') {
                }
            } catch (IOException ex) {
            }
            shutdownServer();
        }
    }
}
```

We declare a class field of type **ServerSocket**:

```
private static ServerSocket server = null;
```

In the **main** function, we declare a buffer for storing the data that comes from the input stream:

```
byte buffer[] = new byte[512];
```

We create a **Monitor** thread and submit it for execution:

```
new Thread(new Monitor()).start();
```

The **Monitor** thread waits for the user to hit the ENTER key and then closes the server. The **Monitor** class is discussed later.

We create a server socket by instantiating the **ServerSocket** class:

```
server = new ServerSocket(10000);
```

The class constructor takes one argument that specifies the port number on which the server would be listening. In our example, the server listens to incoming requests on port 10000. Note that you cannot arbitrarily pick up any number for assignment to a port. There are many ports that are already reserved. A few well-known reserved ports include port 80 (HTTP), port 21 (FTP), port 25 (SMTP), port 23 (Telnet), and port 53 (DNS). The port numbers range from 0 to 65535 and are divided into three ranges: the well-known ports (0 through 1023), the registered ports (1024 through 49151), and the dynamic and/or private ports (49152 through 65535). For a complete list of ports, refer to the IANA registry (www.iana.org/assignments/port-numbers). A value of 0 in the port numbers registry indicates that no port has been allocated. Passing 0 as an argument to the **ServerSocket** constructor results in the automatic allocation of a port.

After the server socket is created, we need to make it wait for the input requests. This is done by calling its **accept** method:

```
Socket socketObject = server.accept();
```

The **accept** method is a blocking call and will wait indefinitely until a client request is received. When it breaks from this blocking call, it returns an object of the **Socket** type. This is your socket connection to the client who is currently connected to you. Just the way the client opens input and output streams on the connected socket, similarly the server program obtains the input and output streams on the connected socket. The following statement obtains the input stream from the socket:

```
InputStream reader = socketObject.getInputStream();
```

The program now reads the data from the input stream by calling the **read** method of the **InputStream** class:

```
reader.read(buffer);
```

We now obtain the output stream on the socket and write the buffer contents to it:

```
OutputStream writer = socketObject.getOutputStream();
writer.write(buffer);
```

Finally, we close the socket by calling its **close** method:

```
socketObject.close();
```

The program now does another iteration of the **while** loop, where it will block again for another request from a client. Because this is an infinite loop, we need some means of shutting down the server. This is exactly the purpose behind creating the **Monitor** thread.

The **Monitor** class implements **Runnable**, and its **run** method simply blocks itself for keyboard input from the user:

```
while (System.in.read() != '\n') {
}
```

The loop ignores all input except the ENTER key. At this event, it calls the **shutdownServer** method of the application. In the **shutdownServer** method, we close the server socket and quit the application by calling the **System.exit** method:

```
server.close();
```

Closing the socket also results in closing an associated channel, if any. After the server socket is closed, any thread currently blocked in **accept** throws a **SocketException**. We catch this exception and print the "Server down" message to the user. Note that if there is no thread that is currently blocked in the **accept** method, this message will not be printed to the console. Later on in this chapter, you will be developing a multiuser server application that creates multiple threads, each thread holding its own socket connection. In this situation, the chances of a **SocketException** occurring are greater, and you will likely see the "Server down" message on the console.

With any other type of exception, we print a stack trace. Note that the **SocketException** is a subclass of **IOException**:

```
} catch (SocketException e) {
    System.out.println ("Server is down");
} catch (IOException ex) {
    ex.printStackTrace();
}
```

Now, let's look at what kinds of exceptions can occur in this code. Creating an instance of **ServerSocket** can generate three types of exceptions: An **IOException** is generated if an I/O error occurs while opening the socket, a **SecurityException** occurs if a security manager exists and its method does not allow this operation, and an **IllegalArgumentException** occurs if the **port** parameter is outside the specified range of valid port values. A call to the **accept** method may generate four different types of exceptions: **IOException**, **SecurityException**, **SocketTimeoutException**, and **IllegalBlockingModeException**. The first two types of errors occur under the conditions explained earlier. The **SocketTimeoutException** error occurs if a timeout was previously set and has now been reached. The **IllegalBlockingModeException** occurs if this socket has an associated channel that is in nonblocking mode and there is no connection ready to be accepted. The **close** method throws an **IOException** if an I/O error occurs while closing the socket. As mentioned earlier, closing the server socket will make the thread blocked in the socket's **accept** method throw a **SocketException**.

Testing the Echo Server Application

To test the echo server application, compile and run the code in a command window. You will see the message "Server Started" on the console. The server keeps waiting for clients to connect. We will use the client HomePageReader.java, developed in the previous section. Simply modify the URL and the port number in the socket connection statement as follows:

```
Socket socketObject = new Socket("localhost", 10000);
```

The URL is now set to **localhost**, which specifies the IP for your local machine. The port is set to 10000, which is where our echo server is listening to incoming requests.

Recompile the client program and run it from a different command window. The client program will print the following message in its command window:

```
GET / HTTP/1.0
↵

↵
```

Note that it prints your **GET** request along with the two newline characters embedded in the request. Thus, the server echoes back the client message "as is." You may try changing the request string and observe the program output. Now, shut down the server by terminating the server application and try running the client application. You will see an error message printed to the console informing you that the connection to the server is refused.

Serving Multiple Clients

The echo server developed previously is capable of serving only a single client at a time. While it is serving one client, if another client tries to connect to the server, the new client will get the "connection refused" error. A client may try repeatedly to make a socket connection for a predefined timeout period.

TIP

*To specify a timeout for making a socket connection, use the following code snippet. The second parameter to the **connect** method specifies the time in milliseconds. The first parameter to the **connect** method is an instance of the **InetSocketAddress** class that specifies the URL and the port number to which you wish to connect.*

```
Socket socketObject = new Socket();
socketObject.connect(new InetSocketAddress("localhost", 10000), 100);
```

If the server response time is much smaller than the frequency at which the client requests arrive at the server, the "connection refused" error may not occur frequently and would be acceptable to the clients. If the client receives this error; at the most, it will have to retry connecting to the server, with a good possibility that the next time the connection will succeed. However, if the server takes a long time to process the client request and to send a response to the client, this "connection refused" error may not be acceptable to many waiting clients. We will now modify our server application so that it can provide better service to the simultaneous multiple clients. The idea is depicted in Figure 20-4.

As in the previous case, our server application listens to the incoming requests on a designated port. Multiple clients will connect to the server using this port number. Whenever a client requests a connection, the server spawns a thread and passes the connected socket to the created thread. The client and this thread will now communicate with each other using the connected socket. For every client that requests a connection to the server, the server application creates a new thread and assigns it to the requesting client. Thus, we can now have multiple clients connecting to the server at the same time, and these clients are served by independent threads assigned by the

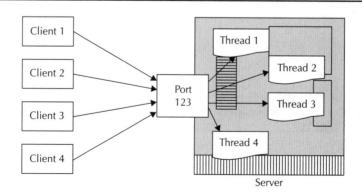

FIGURE 20-4. *Serving multiple clients by creating threads on the server*

server. When large numbers of clients attempt to connect to the server, the server may eventually run out of resources, and in such a case the connection to the new client would be refused. This situation will not occur that frequently, as in the earlier case. We will now modify our echo server application to implement this concept.

Serving Simultaneous Clients

To serve multiple clients, the modified server application will need to create a thread for each received client request. We will pass the connected client socket to this thread so that the client and the corresponding thread can communicate directly with each other. The server will now be free to receive the next client request. The modified **EchoServer** application is given in Listing 20-5.

Listing 20-5   *A Threaded Server Application That Services Multiple Clients*

```java
import java.net.*;
import java.io.*;
import java.util.concurrent.*;

public class EchoMultiServer {

    private static ServerSocket server = null;
    private static ExecutorService threadPool;

    public static void main(String[] args) {
        try {
            threadPool = Executors.newCachedThreadPool();
            threadPool.submit(new Monitor());
            server = new ServerSocket(10000);
            System.out.println("Server listening on port 10000 ...");
            System.out.println("Hit Enter to stop the server");
            while (true) {
                Socket socketObject = server.accept();
                System.out.println("Thread created");
                threadPool.submit(new EchoThread(socketObject));
            }
        } catch (SocketException e) {
            System.out.println("Server is down");
        } catch (IOException ex) {
            ex.printStackTrace();
        }
    }

    private static void shutdownServer() {
        try {
            server.close();
        } catch (IOException ex) {
        }
        threadPool.shutdown();
        System.exit(0);
    }
}
```

```
        private static class Monitor implements Runnable {

            @Override
            public void run() {
                try {
                    while (System.in.read() != '\n') {
                    }
                } catch (IOException ex) {
                }
                shutdownServer();
            }
        }
    }


class EchoThread implements Runnable {

    private Socket socketObject = null;
    private byte buffer[] = new byte[512];

    public EchoThread(Socket socketObject) {
        this.socketObject = socketObject;
    }

    @Override
    public void run() {
        try {
            try {
                InputStream reader = socketObject.getInputStream();
                reader.read(buffer);
                OutputStream writer = socketObject.getOutputStream();
                writer.write(buffer);
            } finally {
                socketObject.close();
            }
        } catch (Exception e) {
            e.printStackTrace();
        }
    }
}
```

In the **main** method, we create a cached thread pool for executing our worker threads and a single instance of the **Monitor** thread:

```
threadPool = Executors.newCachedThreadPool();
```

We create a **Monitor** thread and submit it for execution:

```
threadPool.submit(new Monitor());
```

The **Monitor** thread waits for the user to hit the ENTER key and then closes the server. The **Monitor** class was discussed earlier with the **EchoServer** class.

We also create an instance of **ServerSocket** listening to port 10000:

```
server = new ServerSocket(10000);
```

We then set up an infinite loop for accepting client requests:

```
while (true) {
    Socket socketObject = server.accept();
```

The **accept** method call is a blocking call that waits for client requests to arrive. After a client request arrives, the **accept** method returns a **Socket** object. We now create a thread and pass this socket object in the thread's constructor and submit the created thread to the thread pool for execution:

```
threadPool.submit(new EchoThread(socketObject));
```

The program loops back to the **accept** method, where it waits for another client to connect. The **EchoThread** class implements the **Runnable** interface:

```
class EchoThread implements Runnable {
```

The class constructor receives a **Socket** object as a parameter and copies it to a local variable for later use. In the **run** method, we obtain the input stream on the socket object and read the data into the buffer from the input stream:

```
InputStream reader = socketObject.getInputStream();
reader.read(buffer);
```

We write this data back to the output stream on the same socket. Thus, whatever data we receive from the client is echoed back to the client:

```
OutputStream writer = socketObject.getOutputStream();
writer.write(buffer);
```

Finally, we close the socket by calling its **close** method.

```
socketObject.close();
```

Note that the **EchoThread** simply sends back the received string to the client. If this thread were to do something more, such as accessing a server resource, you would be required to implement the various synchronization techniques you learned in the previous chapters to ensure resource integrity.

Running the EchoMultiServer Application

To run the **EchoMultiServer** application, you first compile the application using the **javac** compiler. After the program compiles successfully, you run it on the command prompt as follows:

```
C:\360\ch20>java EchoMultiServer
```

When the server starts, it prints an appropriate message to the user console and waits for the clients to connect.

Testing the EchoMultiServer Application

To test the **EchoMultiServer** application, we will modify our earlier **HomepageReader** application. The modified program creates 100 clients, each making an independent socket connection to the multiserver. You will observe that the server serves all these clients concurrently. The modified client application is shown in Listing 20-6.

Listing 20-6 *A Client Application for Testing the Multiserver*

```java
import java.io.*;
import java.net.*;
import java.util.Scanner;

public class EchoMultiClient {

    private static int counter;

    public static void main(String[] args) {
        for (int i = 0; i < 100; i++) {
            counter++;
            new Thread(new Client(counter)).start();
        }
    }

    private static class Client implements Runnable {

        private int counter;

        public Client(int counter) {
            this.counter = counter;
        }

        public void run() {
            try {
                Socket socketObject = new Socket();
                socketObject.connect(
                    new InetSocketAddress("localhost", 10000), 1000);

                try {
                    OutputStream oStream = socketObject.getOutputStream();
                    String str = "Hello from Client " + counter;
                    oStream.write(str.getBytes());
                    InputStream inStream = socketObject.getInputStream();
                    Scanner in = new Scanner(inStream);
                    while (in.hasNextLine()) {
                        String line = in.nextLine();
                        System.out.println(line);
                    }
                    Thread.sleep(10);
                } finally {
                    socketObject.close();
```

```
                   }
               } catch (Exception e) {
                   e.printStackTrace();
               }
           }
       }
   }
```

In the **main** method, we simply create a loop to instantiate 100 client threads:

```
for (int i = 0; i < 100; i++) {
    counter++;
    new Thread(new Client(counter)).start();
}
```

The **client** is a **Runnable** class that accepts the **counter** as a parameter to its constructor. The **counter** is a static class field that numbers the created threads:

```
private static class client implements Runnable {
```

The **client** is declared **private** and **static**, the same as our previous declarations. The run method creates a **Socket** and binds it to the **localhost** at port 10000. We also set a timeout of 1,000 milliseconds just to ensure that the client tries for a successful socket connection for a reasonable amount of time:

```
public void run() {
try {
    Socket socketObject = new Socket();
    socketObject.connect(
            new InetSocketAddress("localhost", 10000), 1000);
```

The rest of the client code is similar to the socket client application discussed in Listing 20-1. It basically writes a message to the server and prints the "server returned" message to the console. When you run the application, you will see the following typical output:

```
Hello from Client 8
Hello from Client 9
Hello from Client 15
Hello from Client 12
Hello from Client 4
Hello from Client 11
Hello from Client 17
...
```

Also, observe the server console. You will notice that several threads are created. Each created thread prints an informative message to the console. The server output is shown here:

```
Thread Created
Thread Created
Thread Created
...
```

Try changing the timeout in the socket connection statement. If this time is set to a low value, you may see a few timeout exceptions on the console. If you do not get any timeouts, it means the server is running really fast to serve all these clients promptly. You might now introduce a deliberate time lag between the two **accept** calls in the server's infinite **while** loop by placing the thread to sleep for some time.

Writing a File Storage Server Application

Now that you have learned the basics of network programming, we will discuss how to develop a more practical application. We will be developing a file storage server where you can upload a file of your choice. For this, the server will need to create a server socket and listen to the incoming requests. A client makes a connection to the server and sends a file to the server for storage. The server receives the file contents over the established socket connection to the client, and it stores the file by appending a unique string to its filename. The client can later on request the file back from the server. In this case, the file stored on the server will be downloaded to the client machine.

We will discuss the construction of both the server and client applications. First, let's look at the server implementation.

A Cloud Storage Server

The file storage server sets up a server socket and waits for the client requests. A client request consists of a command followed by a filename and its contents. The command is an integer value of 0 or 1, where 0 indicates the request for storage and 1 indicates a request for retrieval. The server accepts only text-based files for storage. The complete program is given in Listing 20-7.

Listing 20-7 *A File Storage Server Application*

```java
import java.io.*;
import java.net.*;
import java.util.logging.*;

public class CloudStorageServer {

    private static ServerSocket server;

    public static void main(String[] args) {
        Socket requestSocket = null;
        new Thread(new Monitor()).start();

        try {
            server = new ServerSocket(10000);
            System.out.println("Server started:");
            System.out.println("Hit Enter to stop server");
            try {
                while (true) {
                    requestSocket = server.accept();
                    new Thread(
                            new RequestProcessor(requestSocket)).start();
                }
            } finally {
                requestSocket.close();
            }
```

```java
        } catch (Exception ex) {
            Logger.getLogger(
                    CloudStorageServer.class.getName()).log(Level.SEVERE,
                    null, ex);
        }
    }

    private static void shutdownServer() {
        try {
            server.close();
        } catch (IOException ex) {
        }
        System.exit(0);
    }

    private static class Monitor implements Runnable {

        public void run() {
            try {
                while (System.in.read() != '\n') {
                }
            } catch (IOException ex) {
            }
            shutdownServer();
        }
    }

    private static class RequestProcessor implements Runnable {

        private Socket requestSocket;

        public RequestProcessor(Socket requestSocket) {
            this.requestSocket = requestSocket;
        }

        @Override
        public void run() {
            try {
                DataInputStream reader =
                        new DataInputStream(requestSocket.getInputStream());
                DataOutputStream writer = new DataOutputStream(
                        requestSocket.getOutputStream());
                int cmd = reader.readInt();
                String fileName = reader.readUTF();
                String message;
                if (cmd == 0) {
                    message = "Put ";
                } else {
                    message = "Get ";
                }
                message += fileName + " requested";
                System.out.println(message);
```

```java
                    if (cmd == 0) {
                        uploadFile(reader, fileName);
                    } else if (cmd == 1) {
                        downloadFile(writer, fileName);
                    }
                } catch (IOException ex) {
                    Logger.getLogger(
                            CloudStorageServer.class.getName()).log(Level.SEVERE,
                            null, ex);
                }
            }

            private void uploadFile(DataInputStream in, String fname) {
                try {
                    BufferedWriter writer = new BufferedWriter(
                            new FileWriter("server-" + fname));
                    String str;
                    while (!(str = in.readUTF()).equals("-1")) {
                        writer.write(str);
                        writer.newLine();
                    }
                    in.close();
                    writer.close();
                    System.out.println("'" + fname
                            + "' saved under name '" + "server-" + fname + "'");
                } catch (IOException ex) {
                    Logger.getLogger(
                            CloudStorageServer.class.getName()).log(Level.SEVERE,
                            null, ex);
                }
            }

            private void downloadFile(DataOutputStream out, String fname) {
                try {
                    BufferedReader reader = new BufferedReader(
                            new FileReader("server-" + fname));
                    String str = reader.readLine();
                    while (str != null) {
                        out.writeUTF(str);
                        str = reader.readLine();
                    }
                    out.writeUTF("-1");
                    reader.close();
                    out.close();
                } catch (IOException ex) {
                    Logger.getLogger(
                            CloudStorageServer.class.getName()).log(Level.SEVERE,
                            null, ex);
                }
            }
        }
    }
}
```

The **main** function creates a server socket listening to port 10000:

```
server = new ServerSocket(10000);
```

It sets up an infinite loop that awaits client requests. When a request is received, it creates a thread for processing the request and passes the socket object to it during its construction:

```
while (true) {
    requestSocket = server.accept();
    new Thread(
        new RequestProcessor(requestSocket)).start();
}
```

Now, let's look at the thread implementation that processes the request:

```
private static class RequestProcessor implements Runnable {
```

The **RequestProcessor** is a **static private** inner class. The class constructor receives a **Socket** object as a parameter and stores it in its instance field.

The **run** method creates **DataInputStream** and **DataOutputStream** objects on the socket connection:

```
DataInputStream reader = new DataInputStream(requestSocket.getInputStream());
DataOutputStream writer = new DataOutputStream(requestSocket.getOutputStream());
```

The **readInt** method of the **DataInputStream** class reads the command from the client application:

```
int cmd = reader.readInt();
```

The **readUTF** method reads the name of the file that the client is going to upload:

```
String fileName = reader.readUTF();
```

We call the **uploadFile** or **downloadFile** method, depending on the user's command.

In the **uploadFile** method, we create a file in the server's current working directory with the prefix "server-" added to the filename and then create a **BufferedWriter** on it:

```
BufferedWriter writer = new BufferedWriter(new FileWriter("server-" + fname));
```

The program now continuously reads from the input stream and writes to the output file created in the server's current working directory until the string "-1" is received, which marks the end-of-file condition:

```
while (!(str = in.readUTF()).equals("-1")) {
    writer.write(str);
    writer.newLine();
}
```

At the end, we attempt to close both the input and output streams:

```
in.close();
writer.close();
```

In the **downloadFile** method, we create a reader on the previously stored file:

```
BufferedReader reader = new BufferedReader(new FileReader("server-" + fname));
```

We now read the file line by line and send its contents to the output stream using a **while** loop:

```
String str = reader.readLine();
while (str != null) {
    out.writeUTF(str);
    str = reader.readLine();
}
```

We mark the end-of-data condition by writing "-1" to the output stream. Finally, we attempt to close both files. Note that in the case of an error, the server simply logs the error, which the server administrator can look up at a later time; no error is reported to the client.

Having discussed the server code, we will now discuss the client implementation.

A Cloud Store Client

The cloud store client developed in this section can both upload and download a file from the remote sever. This is a command-line application that accepts two parameters: The first parameter specifies the **get/put** command, and the second specifies the filename. The program establishes a socket connection to the remote server and uses it for uploading/downloading the specified file. The client program is given in Listing 20-8.

Listing 20-8   *A File Upload/Download Program*

```
import java.io.*;
import java.net.*;

public class CloudStore {

    public static void main(String[] args) {
        Socket requestSocket = null;

        if (args.length < 2) {
            System.out.println("Usage: java CloudStore get/put filename");
            System.exit(0);
        }

        int cmd = 0;
        switch (args[0]) {
            case "get":
                cmd = 1;
                break;
            case "put":
                cmd = 0;
                break;
        }
```

```
        String fileName = args[1];
        try {
            try {
                requestSocket = new Socket();
                requestSocket.connect(
                        new InetSocketAddress("localhost", 10000));
                DataOutputStream writer = new DataOutputStream(
                        requestSocket.getOutputStream());
                writer.writeInt(cmd);
                writer.writeUTF(fileName);
                if (cmd == 0) { //put
                    BufferedReader reader = new BufferedReader(
                            new FileReader(fileName));
                    String str = null;
                    while ((str = reader.readLine()) != null) {
                        writer.writeUTF(str);
                    }
                    writer.writeUTF("-1");
                    System.out.println(filename + " uploaded successfully");
                    reader.close();
                    writer.close();
                } else { //get
                    DataInputStream reader = new DataInputStream(
                            (requestSocket.getInputStream()));
                    BufferedWriter fileWriter = new BufferedWriter(
                            new FileWriter(fileName));
                    String str = null;
                    while (!(str = reader.readUTF()).equalsIgnoreCase("-1")) {
                        fileWriter.write(str);
                        fileWriter.newLine();
                        System.out.println(str);
                    }
                    reader.close();
                    fileWriter.close();
                }
            } finally {
                requestSocket.close();
            }
        } catch (Exception e) {
            e.printStackTrace();
        }
    }
}
```

In the **main** method, the client establishes a socket connection. (I used the same machine for running the server, so the server is specified as **localhost**.) If you use a remote server, specify the appropriate URL for the server or its IP address.

```
requestSocket = new Socket();
requestSocket.connect(new InetSocketAddress("localhost", 10000));
```

The client application now opens **DataOutputStream** on the output stream of the established socket:

```
DataOutputStream writer = new DataOutputStream(requestSocket.getOutputStream());
```

The **writeInt** method writes the command, and the **writeUTF** method writes the filename to the socket stream:

```
writer.writeInt(cmd);
writer.writeUTF(fileName);
```

To read the contents of the file specified on the command line, we use the **BufferedReader** class:

```
BufferedReader reader = new BufferedReader(new FileReader(fileName));
```

The program reads the file contents, line after line, by calling the **readLine** method of the stream reader class and writes the read contents to the output stream by calling its **writeUTF** method:

```
while ((str = reader.readLine()) != null) {
    writer.writeUTF(str);
}
```

At the end, we write the string "-1" to the output stream to indicate the end of contents:

```
writer.writeUTF("-1");
```

CAUTION
The use of "-1" as the EOF marker might not be appropriate because your text file might contain this string, resulting in a partial reading of the file at the client's end. When you use low-level sockets for communication, you need to be careful in designing the proper protocol and handshaking between the two machines.

For downloading the previously stored file, we open a **DataInputStream** on the socket connection:

```
DataInputStream reader = new DataInputStream((requestSocket.getInputStream()));
```

We also create a file for writing the downloaded contents:

```
BufferedWriter fileWriter = new BufferedWriter(new FileWriter(fileName));
```

We keep on reading from the input stream until we receive the terminating string specified by -1:

```
while (!(str = reader.readUTF()).equalsIgnoreCase("-1")) {
```

For each line read, we write its contents followed by a newline character to the local file:

```
fileWriter.write(str);
fileWriter.newLine();
```

We also print the read line to the user's console for a quick look at the downloaded file:

```
System.out.println(str);
```

Testing the File Upload/Download Utility

Compile the server application, open a command window, and then start the server using the following command:

```
C:\360\ch20>java CloudStorageServer
```

You will see the following message on your console:

```
Server started:
Hit Enter to stop server
```

The server is now waiting for the client requests. Open another command window and run the client using the following command:

```
C:\360\ch20>java CloudStore put notes.txt
```

The program will upload the notes.txt file to the server. The file must be available in the local folder from where the application is run. After the file is uploaded, the application prints a message to the user:

```
notes.txt uploaded successfully
```

Note that this message is not a guarantee that the server received the file contents without errors and saved it on its local storage. The server does not return any error conditions to the client. To check whether there were any errors in this operation, you will need to check the server console. You will see the following message on the server console if the file was successfully saved:

```
put notes.txt requested
'notes.txt' saved under name 'server-notes.txt'
```

You can verify the physical presence of this file on the server in the working directory where you started the server application and check its contents. To download the previously uploaded file, use the following command:

```
C:\360\ch20 java CloudStore get notes.txt
```

The contents of the previously uploaded notes.txt file will be downloaded from the server and stored in the local file with the same name in the working directory where you started the client application.

NOTE
To focus on socket programming, we have kept the server and client applications simple by avoiding the handshaking in communications, especially for error reporting. To develop an application similar to this for uploading/downloading files to a remote machine, you would probably use a web container and servlets/JSPs (Java Server Pages). A web container would use sockets for communication like the one described in this application.

The InetAddress Class

The **InetAddress** class is a utility class that represents an IP address, which is either a 32-bit or 128-bit unsigned number used by Internet Protocol (IP). The protocols such as Transmission Control Protocol (TCP), User Datagram Protocol (UDP), and Stream Control Transport Protocol (SCTP) are built on top of IP. The instance of this class consists of an IP address and possibly its corresponding host name. The class converts numeric addresses to host names, and vice versa. The other networking classes that you have studied previously, such as **Socket** and **ServerSocket**, use this class for identifying hosts.

The class does not have any public constructors, which means you cannot create any arbitrary addresses. All created addresses must be checked with DNS (Domain Name System). To create an **InetAddress** object, you must use one of the available factory methods. The **getLocalHost** factory method returns the **InetAddress** object that represents the local host. The **getByName** method accepts the host name as its parameter and returns the corresponding **InetAddress** object. Both methods throw an **UnknownHostException** if they are unable to resolve the host name. The **getAllByName** factory method returns an array of **InetAddress** objects that represent all the addresses the given name resolves to—note that DNS mappings allow you to associate a single name with a set of machines (IP addresses). This method may throw an **UnknownException** like the other two methods if it cannot resolve the name to at least one address.

The class provides various getter methods that return the host name, address, and so on. The **isMulticastAddress** method checks whether the **InetAddress** is an IP multicast address. **Inet4Address** and **Inet6Address** are the two direct, known subclasses of this class. As the name indicates, **Inet4Address** represents an IP version 4 address and **Inet6Address** represents an IP version 6 address. For so many years, we have been using IPv4 addresses that consist of four parts—each being a byte of data. The IPv6 address consists of eight 16-bit pieces and will soon be in use as the Internet keeps growing.

We have used a variation of the class **InetSocketAddress** in our earlier examples while connecting to a remote server. The simple example given in Listing 20-9 illustrates the use of this class.

Listing 20-9 *DNS Resolution Application*

```java
import java.net.*;

public class DNSLookup {

    public static void main(String[] args) {
        InetAddress[] inetHost = null;
        try {
            System.out.println("List of Google servers");
            inetHost = InetAddress.getAllByName("www.google.com");
            for (InetAddress address : inetHost) {
                System.out.println(address);
            }
            System.out.println("\nList of CNN servers");
            inetHost = InetAddress.getAllByName("cnn.com");
            for (InetAddress address : inetHost) {
                System.out.println(address);
            }
            System.out.println("\nLocal machine");
```

```
            System.out.println(InetAddress.getLocalHost().toString());
        } catch (UnknownHostException ex) {
            ex.printStackTrace();
        }
    }
}
```

In the **main** method, we call the **getAllByName** static method of the **InetAddress** class. The method takes a host as the parameter and returns an array of the associated IP addresses. First, we list out all servers hosted by Google and then by CNN. At the end, we list out the IP address of our local machine. When you run this application, you will see output similar to the following (note that by the time you run this code, Google/CNN might have changed/added a few servers):

```
List of Google servers
www.google.com/74.125.236.48
www.google.com/74.125.236.49
www.google.com/74.125.236.50
www.google.com/74.125.236.51
www.google.com/74.125.236.52

List of CNN servers
cnn.com/157.166.224.26
cnn.com/157.166.226.26
cnn.com/157.166.255.19
cnn.com/157.166.224.25
cnn.com/157.166.255.18
cnn.com/157.166.226.25

Local machine
Poornachandra-Sarangs-iMac.local/10.0.1.2
```

From this output, you can see that Google has hosted their website on five different IPs, whereas CNN hosts their website on six known servers. The output shows that the local machine has only one IP associated with it (which, of course, goes without saying).

Broadcasting Messages

So far what you have seen in this chapter is the development of client/server applications, where one or more clients connect to a known server and communicate with it. This communication takes place over TCP, which provides reliable, ordered delivery of a stream of bytes from a program running on one computer to another program running on another computer. In some situations, you might need to make a general broadcast of a message on a network, without caring about the guaranteed and orderly delivery of data. Consider the case of a news network that continually transmits news on its channel regardless of whether anyone is watching. A client that connects to the channel receives the news currently being broadcast. All previous broadcasts are not delivered to the client. A client might not even be interested in the past broadcasts.

We will now develop such an application in Java using a **DatagramSocket**, which is Java's mechanism for network communication via UDP instead of TCP. This class represents a socket that is used for sending and receiving datagram packets. It can be used for sending multiple packets on a network. When multiple packets are sent from one machine to another, each one may take a different route and therefore the packets at the receiving end may not arrive in the same order as the sending order. In situations where datagrams are used, this is acceptable. For example, consider a server that broadcasts news on a channel; the order in which the news items are received by the client rarely matters. In some cases, the packets could be lost in the transit and the client might not receive them. Consider a server that broadcasts atomic clock time ticks on the network. Let us say that the server broadcasts a message every second. If a few of these messages are lost, the client does not care because it is usually interested in the current time and not all the older beeps that the server has broadcasted.

We will now discuss the construction of such a broadcasting server. We cover the server application first, followed by a client that receives the current broadcasts from the server.

Writing a Stock Quotes Server

Our server application will broadcast the latest trade executed on the stock exchange. Such broadcasts take place periodically as trades are executed. The server application is given in Listing 20-10.

Listing 20-10   *Exchange Server Broadcasting Trades*

```java
import java.io.*;
import java.net.*;
import java.text.SimpleDateFormat;
import java.util.Calendar;

public class StockTradesServer {

    public static void main(String[] args) {
        try {
            Thread tradesGenerator = new Thread(
                    new StockTradesGenerator());
            tradesGenerator.setDaemon(true);
            tradesGenerator.start();
            System.out.println(
                    "Stock trades broadcast server started");
            System.out.println("Hit Enter to stop server");
            while (System.in.read() != '\n') {
            }
        } catch (IOException ex) {
            System.out.println("Error starting server");
        }
    }

    private static class StockTradesGenerator implements Runnable {

        private DatagramSocket broadcastSocket = null;
        private String[] stockSymbols = {"IBM", "SNE", "XRX", "MHP", "NOK"};
        private static final String TIME_FORMAT_NOW = "HH:mm:ss";

        public StockTradesGenerator() {
            try {
```

```java
            broadcastSocket = new DatagramSocket(4445);
        } catch (SocketException ex) {
            System.out.println("Error making socket connection");
        }
    }

    public void run() {
        byte[] buffer = new byte[80];

        try {
            while (true) {
                int index = (int) (Math.random() * 5);
                float trade = generateRandomTrade(index);
                String lastTrade = String.format("%s %.2f @%s",
                        stockSymbols[index], trade, now());
                buffer = lastTrade.getBytes();

                try {
                    InetAddress groupBrodcastAddresses =
                            InetAddress.getByName("230.0.0.1");
                    DatagramPacket packet = new DatagramPacket(buffer,
                            buffer.length, groupBrodcastAddresses, 4446);
                    broadcastSocket.send(packet);
                    Thread.sleep((long) (Math.random() * 2000));
                } catch (Exception ex) {
                    System.out.println("Error in communication");
                }
            }
        } finally {
            broadcastSocket.close();
        }
    }

    private float generateRandomTrade(int index) {
        float trade = (float) Math.random();

        switch (index) {
            case 0:
                trade += 118;
                break;
            case 1:
                trade += 29;
                break;
            case 2:
                trade += 8;
                break;
            case 3:
                trade += 26;
                break;
            case 4:
                trade += 14;
                break;
```

```
            }
            return trade;
        }

        private String now() {
            Calendar cal = Calendar.getInstance();
            SimpleDateFormat sdf = new SimpleDateFormat(TIME_FORMAT_NOW);
            return sdf.format(cal.getTime());
        }
    }
}
```

The **main** method of the application creates and runs an instance of **StockTradesGenerator** that generates random trades periodically for a predefined list of stocks:

```
Thread tradesGenerator = new Thread(new StockTradesGenerator());
tradesGenerator.setDaemon(true);
tradesGenerator.start();
```

The main application thread terminates when the user hits the ENTER key.

In the **StockTradesGenerator** thread class, we declare a **DatagramSocket** variable and a few strings that represent some of the stock symbols:

```
private DatagramSocket broadcastSocket = null;
private String[] stockSymbols = {"IBM", "SNE", "XRX", "MHP", "NOK"};
```

The class constructor creates an instance of **DatagramSocket** that binds to port 4445:

```
broadcastSocket = new DatagramSocket(4445);
```

In the **run** method, we set up an infinite loop for broadcasting the trade as and when it executes on the exchange. To simulate a real-life-like situation, we pick up the stock symbol from the **stockSymbols** array at random. We also generate the trade price at random and add it to a fixed value for each stock symbol:

```
int index = (int) (Math.random() * 5);
float trade = generateRandomTrade(index);
```

We now format the last trade (the generated price and the current time) in a string and get its contents in a byte buffer:

```
String lastTrade = String.format("%s %.2f @%s", stockSymbols[index], trade, now());
buffer = lastTrade.getBytes();
```

The method **now** gets the current system time and formats it using a predefined formatter. The program then sets up an IP address for broadcast:

```
InetAddress groupBrodcastAddresses = InetAddress.getByName("230.0.0.1");
```

A datagram packet is constructed by instantiating the **DatagramPacket** class:

```
DatagramPacket packet = new DatagramPacket(buffer, buffer.length,
                        groupBrodcastAddresses, 4446);
```

The first parameter to the constructor defines the packet contents, the second parameter decides the contents' length, the third parameter specifies the IP, and the fourth parameter specifies the port number. The packet is broadcast on the network by calling the **send** method of the socket:

```
broadcastSocket.send(packet);
```

We sleep for some time before sending the next packet:

```
Thread.sleep((long) (Math.random() * 2000));
```

Because this is a server application, we maintain a log of exceptions for the administrator to examine at a later time. So let's look at what kind of exceptions this server application may generate at runtime. Constructing a **DatagramSocket** may generate a **SocketException** or a **SecurityException**. A **SocketException** is generated if the socket could not be opened or could not bind to the specified local port. The **SecurityException** is generated if a security manager exists and its **checkListen** method does not allow this operation. The **DatagramPacket** constructor we have used in our application does not throw any exceptions. The class declares a few more overloaded constructors. The constructors that take a **SocketAddress** as one of the parameters may throw an **IllegalArgumentException** and a **SocketException**. The constructor we have used here takes **InetAddress** as one of the parameters. The **getByName** method of the **InetAddress** class may throw an **UnknownHostException** if no IP address for the specified host can be found. A **SecurityException** may be thrown for the usual reasons that the security manager exists and its **checkConnect** method does not allow the current operation. Finally, the **send** operation of **DatagramSocket** may generate various exceptions. Obviously, it would throw an **IOException** if an I/O error occurs during sending. A **SecurityException** occurs for the usual reasons that the security manager exists and the **checkMulticast** or **checkConnect** method does not allow the send operation. The method may throw a **PortUnreachableException** if the socket is connected to a currently unreachable destination port—throwing of this exception is not guaranteed. If the socket has an associated channel, which is in nonblocking mode, the method will throw an **IllegalBlockingModeException**. Lastly, if the socket is connected and the connected address and packet address differ, an **IllegalArgumentException** would be thrown. Note that when any of these exceptions occur, we log them on the server and do not attempt to inform the client, which is really not required because this type of communication (datagram) is not really guaranteed.

When you run the application, the server keeps broadcasting the trade packets continuously. Let's now look at a client application that connects to the server and displays the contents of the received packets on its console.

Writing the Stock Trader Client

The stock trader client connects to the multicast stock trades server described in the previous section and prints trade information to the user console whenever such information is received from the server. The full source for the client is given in Listing 20-11.

NOTE
*We intentionally declare the **main** method of the following client application as throwing an **IOException** so as to keep the exception-handling code away from the main application logic and not clutter it up. As said in Chapter 8, a good practice is to handle errors close to where they occur.*

Listing 20-11 *Client Program That Receives Trades from a Stock Exchange Server Application*

```java
import java.io.*;
import java.net.*;

public class StocksTrader {

    public static void main(String[] args) throws IOException {

        MulticastSocket socket = new MulticastSocket(4446);
        InetAddress address = InetAddress.getByName("230.0.0.1");
        socket.joinGroup(address);

        for (int i = 0; i < 10; i++) {
            byte[] buffer = new byte[256];
            DatagramPacket packet = new DatagramPacket(buffer, buffer.length);
            socket.receive(packet);
            String received = new String(packet.getData(), 0, packet.getLength());
            System.out.println("Last Trade: " + received);
        }
        socket.leaveGroup(address);
        socket.close();

    }
}
```

The **main** method creates an instance of **MulticastSocket** that binds to port 4446:

```java
MulticastSocket socket = new MulticastSocket(4446);
```

The program builds an **InetAddress** corresponding to the broadcast address set up in the server:

```java
InetAddress address = InetAddress.getByName("230.0.0.1");
```

We call the **joinGroup** method on the socket to bind it to the multicast group:

```java
socket.joinGroup(address);
```

We then read the last 10 trades broadcast by the server. For this, we create a **DatagramPacket** and pass it as a parameter to the **receive** method of the socket instance:

```java
DatagramPacket packet = new DatagramPacket(buffer, buffer.length);
socket.receive(packet);
```

Note that **receive** is a blocking call and therefore waits for the server broadcast. After receiving the packet, we retrieve its contents in a string:

```java
String received = new String(packet.getData(), 0, packet.getLength());
```

The **getData** method retrieves the packet contents, and the **getLength** method returns the length of its contents. The program then prints these contents to the console:

```java
System.out.println("Last Trade: " + received);
```

After reading the last 10 trades, we disconnect the socket from the multicast group and close it:

```
socket.leaveGroup(address);
socket.close();
```

Let's now look at the various exceptions this program may generate. The **MulticastSocket** constructor may generate an **IOException** if an I/O error occurs while creating the socket. It may also throw a **SecurityException** if the **checkListen** method of the existing security manager does not allow this operation. The **joinGroup** method may generate an **IOException** if an error occurs while joining or the specified address is not a multicast address. It throws a **SecurityException** if the **checkMulticast** method of the existing security manager does not allow the join operation. The **leaveGroup** method may generate an **IOException** and **SecurityException** for reasons similar to a join operation. The **receive** operation on the socket may generate various kinds of exceptions. An **IOException** is thrown if an I/O error occurs. A **SocketTimeoutException** occurs if a timeout was previously set and it has expired. The **PortUnreachableException** is thrown if the socket is currently connected to an unreachable destination, and lastly the **IllegalBlockingModeException** is thrown when the associated channel of the socket is in nonblocking mode. On the occurrence of any of these errors, we simply print a stack trace to the user console for detailed information on the type of error that occurred. Typically, for network applications, the stack trace helps in better understanding and diagnosing, if required, the type of error rather than using a customized error message.

Running the Server and Client

To run the server, on a new command window type the following command:

```
C:\360\ch20>java StockTradesServer
```

Leave the server running in this window and open another window for starting the client. Type the following command to run the client:

```
C:\360\ch20>java StocksTrader
```

You will see the following messages printed on the console.

```
Last Trade: NOK 14.56 @10:01:58
Last Trade: XRX 8.32 @10:01:59
Last Trade: SNE 29.62 @10:01:59
Last Trade: NOK 14.08 @10:02:01
Last Trade: IBM 118.78 @10:02:02
Last Trade: MHP 26.33 @10:02:03
Last Trade: SNE 29.32 @10:02:05
Last Trade: IBM 118.51 @10:02:05
Last Trade: SNE 29.66 @10:02:06
Last Trade: IBM 118.97 @10:02:08
```

Note that the output on your machine will differ from the preceding output and will differ on every run due to the randomization used to generate trades.

Support for SCTP

So far you have seen the use of two network protocols—TCP and UDP. Another option is SCTP. It provides the reliable, ordered delivery of data like TCP but operates in the message-oriented fashion like UDP. It is session oriented, and an association between the two endpoints must be established before any data can be transmitted. The connection between two endpoints is referred to as an association between those endpoints. It has direct support for multihoming. This means that an endpoint may be represented by more than one address. This is illustrated in Figure 20-5.

Each address may be used for sending and receiving data, thus providing network redundancy. Endpoints exchange a list of addresses during association setup. One address is designated as a primary address; the peer communicates to this default address.

The I/O operations operate on messages, and message boundaries are preserved. Each association may support multiple independent logical streams. This is illustrated in Figure 20-6.

The data packet now includes stream identifiers in addition to the usual sequence numbers. SCTP monitors the association paths using a built-in heartbeat. If a path failure is detected, it sends traffic over the alternate path. The application need not even know that a failover recovery occurred. Failover can also be used to maintain network application connectivity. Thus, SCTP provides a powerful mechanism for supporting high availability and increased reliability.

Along with SCTP, there is also a need for other protocols such as the Session Initiation Protocol (SIP), which is used for negotiating and defining a communication session's parameters. To explain the purpose and enrollment process, you use the Session Description Protocol (SDP), which defines a format for session characterization and media definition. SDP can be used with a number of transport protocols, such as Session Announcement Protocol (SAP), SIP, HTTP, and others.

The Java API now defines a new package, **com.sun.nio.sctp**, to support SCTP. The API and implementation are publicly accessible, so you can write your network applications based on SCTP. However, SCTP is not a part of the Java SE platform at this time.

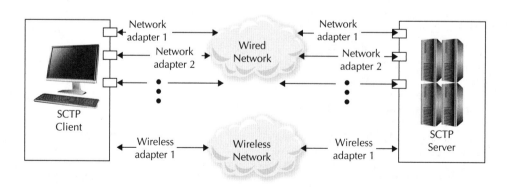

FIGURE 20-5. *Multihoming in an SCTP connection*

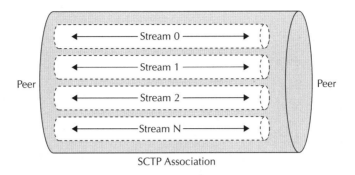

FIGURE 20-6. *SCTP association containing multiple streams*

Summary

In this chapter, you studied another important set of classes from the Java libraries for networking. Java right from its beginning provided good support for creating network applications. The **java.net** package provides a set of classes for this purpose. The **Socket** class represents a client socket, and a **ServerSocket** class is used for creating a server application. The communication over the socket is abstracted using stream classes. You open an input stream for reading from a socket and an output stream to send data out on a socket. To serve multiple clients, you would create a thread on the server for each accepted request. You pass the connected socket object to this thread. The client and the thread on the server communicate with each other using this socket.

In this chapter, you learned to write home page and webpage reader applications based on the **URL** and **URLConnection** classes. You also developed a cookie spy application that checks on the incoming cookies sent by websites. You developed an echo server that responds to requests coming from many concurrent clients.

The network applications include programs such as chat, file server, and news broadcast. You learned to create a simple file storage server that allows clients to upload files on the server. You also learned the use of the **InetAddress** class that represents an IP address.

The communication in a network application need not always be point-to-point. In certain situations such as a news broadcast, the server will broadcast messages on a channel on a continuous basis. A client connects to the server and receives the currently broadcasted messages. Java supports this functionality through the use of the **DatagramSocket** and **DatagramPacket** classes. In addition to TCP and UDP, Java libraries now support SCTP.

In the next chapter, you learn a few more classes from the Java libraries.

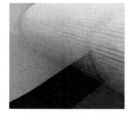

CHAPTER
21

Utility Classes

ach of our previous chapters was dedicated to a specific topic. This chapter, however, is different from earlier chapters. Java provides several utility classes for various purposes. This chapter covers some of these utility classes. Covering the entire set of these classes is beyond the scope of a single book, so I have picked only the most commonly used classes and discuss only their important methods. In particular, we cover the **String** class, the date and time classes, and the Reflection and Introspection mechanism. Under these three headings, here is what you will be learning in this chapter:

- The **String** class
  - The various techniques of string manipulations
  - Comparing string objects
  - Creating formatted output
- Date and time classes
  - The **Calendar** class
  - The **GregorianCalendar** class
  - Developing a local time converter application
- The Introspection and Reflection mechanism of Java
  - Understanding the **Class** class
  - Using the **Method** class for dynamic invocation
  - Creating a class browser application for dynamic discovery and execution of an unknown class

The String Class

We have used the **String** class in earlier chapters to represent an array of characters. At that time, we did not use the powerful functionality provided in this class for manipulating strings. We will now cover several of these methods in this chapter. Such methods include concatenating strings, extracting a substring from a given string, and replacing a sequence of characters with another sequence. We discuss just a few important methods of this class to demonstrate its usefulness in practical situations.

A Few Important Methods

The **String** class provides a method called **substring** that is used for extracting a part of a given string. Both start and end indices may be specified while calling this method, as follows:

```
public String substring(int beginIndex)
public String substring(int beginIndex, int endIndex)
```

The **beginIndex** argument specifies the index in the string where the extraction begins, and the **endIndex** argument specifies the ending index up to which the extraction is performed. The first method, which takes only one argument, extracts until the end of the string.

You can check the presence of a substring within a given string by calling the **contains** method. The **contains** method returns **true** if the specified character sequence is found in a given string:

```
public boolean contains(CharSequence s)
```

You can replace any character in the string with another character by using the **replace** method. The **replace** method replaces all occurrences of a given character with the specified new character.

```
public String replace(char oldChar, char newChar)
```

A few more variations of the **replace** method are available:

```
public String replace(CharSequence target, CharSequence replacement)
public String replaceAll(String regex, String replacement)
public String replaceFirst(String regex, String replacement)
```

As the first method indicates, it replaces all occurrences of a given character sequence with the new character sequence. The **replaceAll** method replaces the substring that matches the given regular expression with the **replacement** string.

TIP
*A regular expression is a string of characters that describes a pattern used to find matches in other character sequences. The **java.util.regex** package supports regular expression processing. You are encouraged to go through the tutorial provided on the Oracle site (http://docs.oracle.com/javase/tutorial/essential/regex/) to learn more about regular expressions.*

The **replaceFirst** method replaces the first occurrence of a substring that matches the regular expression specified in the first parameter by the **replacement** string.

In your programming career, you have certainly encountered a situation where you are required to process a CSV (comma-separated values) file. The **split** method of the **String** class helps you process such a file. The **split** method separates out the tokens in a given string on the specified delimiter. There are two variations of the **split** method:

```
public String[] split(String regex)
public String[] split(String regex, int limit)
```

The only difference between the two methods is the limit set in the second method that restricts the number of tokens separated. Both methods return tokens in a string array.

Finally, the **format** method of the **String** class allows you to format a given string using **printf**-style formatters.

We will now use a concrete example to demonstrate the use of these methods.

TIP
*Look up the **String** class in javadocs to learn about several more useful methods you can use in daily practice.*

Practical Demonstration of String Methods

The best way to understand the usefulness of the **String** class methods is to try them out in a practical situation. To demonstrate these methods, we will manipulate the following string:

```
"IBM,09/09/2009,87,100,80,95,1567823"
```

This string represents the end-of-day (EOD) quotes for IBM listed on a stock exchange. Typically, stock exchanges supply the EOD data in this format for all stocks trades during the day. An application developer needs to parse this string to extract the various fields and use them in his code. Such comma-delimited strings are very common. A program such as Microsoft Excel (or any other spreadsheet application) is able to export and import data from CSV files. In this section, you learn how to parse such a string into its individual tokens using the various methods available in the **String** class.

In the given string, the various fields are separated with a comma delimiter. In practice, you may use any other character as a delimiter, but the comma is the most popular character used as a delimiter. The first field in the preceding string represents the stock symbol; the second field specifies the trade date (which is not really required if this line represents an EOD quote). The next four fields indicate opening, high, low, and closing prices, respectively, on the specified trade date. The last field specifies the total trade volume for the day. We will now apply various methods of the **String** class on this input string to understand their purpose. The program in Listing 21-1 demonstrates the use of several methods of the **String** class.

Listing 21-1   *Stocks EOD Parser Based on String Methods*

```java
public class StocksEODParser {

    private static String trade = "IBM,09/09/2009,87,100,80,95,1567823";

    public static void main(String[] args) {

        // retrieving a substring
        String dateField = trade.substring(4, 14);
        System.out.println("Substring field date equals " + dateField);

        // locating a character sequence
        if (trade.contains("09/09/2009")) {
            System.out.println("This is a trade on 09/09/2009");
        }

        // replacing a character
        String str = trade.replace(',', ':');
        System.out.println("After replacing delimiter: " + str);

        // replacing a character sequence
        str = trade.replace("100", "101");
        System.out.println("After replacing trade price 100: " + str);

        System.out.println("Splitting string into its fields");
        String[] fields = trade.split(",");
```

```
    for (String strFields : fields) {
        System.out.println("\t" + strFields);
    }

    float hilowDifference =
            Float.parseFloat(fields[3]) - Float.parseFloat(fields[4]);
    str = String.valueOf(hilowDifference);
    System.out.println("Difference in Hi to Low price: $" + str);
    System.out.println(String.format(
            "Formatted HiLow Difference: $%.02f", hilowDifference));
    }
}
```

First of all, in the **main** method, we use the **substring** method to extract the date field from our IBM trade string:

```
String dateField = trade.substring(4, 14);
```

The **substring** method extracts the character sequence starting at index 4 and ending at index 14. This sequence represents the date field, which is then printed to the user console. Refer to the program output at the end of this section while studying the effect of these methods.

The **contains** method checks whether our input string contains a substring specified in its parameter. In our case, we check whether the trade string contains the substring 09/09/2009. This should return **true**.

```
if (trade.contains("09/09/2009"))
```

Next, we replace the field delimiter (comma) with a colon character by calling the **replace** method and then assign it to a new variable, **str**:

```
String str = trade.replace(',', ':');
```

We change the closing price of the stock from 100 to 101 by using the following statement:

```
str = trade.replace("100", "101");
```

The **replace** method in this statement replaces a given character sequence with a new sequence.

We separate out the tokens in the input string by calling the **split** method and then print their values to the console in a **for-each** loop:

```
String[] fields = trade.split(",");
for (String strFields : fields) {
    System.out.println("\t" + strFields);
}
```

Next, we compute the difference between the high and low prices. To do this, we need to convert the field values into their corresponding **float** types. This is done by using the **parseFloat** method of the **Float** class:

```
float hilowDifference = Float.parseFloat(fields[3])
                        - Float.parseFloat(fields[4]);
```

Note that **fields[3]** represents the high price and **fields[4]** represents the low price. To convert the difference to a **String** type, we use the **valueOf** method of the **String** class:

```
str = String.valueOf(hilowDifference);
System.out.println("Difference in Hi to Low price: $" + str);
```

TIP
*To print the value of a float, you could simply append it to another string ("" + **hilowDifference**) and output the resultant string.*

We use the static **format** method to format a given float number to add a trailing zero:

```
System.out.println(String.format(
                "Formatted HiLow Difference: $%.02f", hilowDifference));
```

When you run the program, you will get the following output:

```
Substring field date equals 09/09/2009
This is a trade on 09/09/2009
After replacing delimiter: IBM:09/09/2009:87:100:80:95:1567823
After replacing trade price 100: IBM,09/09/2009,87,101,80,95,1567823
Splitting string into its fields
        IBM
        09/09/2009
        87
        100
        80
        95
        1567823
Difference in Hi to Low price: $20.0
Formatted HiLow Difference: $20.00
```

Comparing Strings

It is interesting to know what happens when you compare two strings for equality. Generally, to compare two objects, you would use the comparison operator (==). In this case, we look at what happens when you use a comparator operator for comparing two strings. Consider the program given in Listing 21-2.

Listing 21-2 *Program to Compare Two String Objects*

```java
public class StringComparator {

    public static void main(String[] args) {
        String str1 = "This is a test string";
        String str2 = new String(str1);
        String str3 = "This is a test string";

        System.out.println("str1.equals(str2) returns " + str1.equals(str2));
        System.out.println("str1==str2 returns " + (str1 == str2));
```

```
            System.out.println("str1.equals(str3) returns " + str1.equals(str3));
            System.out.println("str1==str3 returns " + (str1 == str3));
    }
}
```

The program output is shown here:

```
str1.equals(str2) returns true
str1==str2 returns false
str1.equals(str3) returns true
str1==str3 returns true
```

Now let's analyze the output. The first comparison statement uses the **equals** method to compare **str1** to **str2**. In the case of a **String** class, the **equals** method compares the contents of the two operands. Because **str1** and **str2** both contain the same character sequence, this comparison returns **true**. The next comparison uses the equality operator. Because **str1** and **str2** are two distinct objects, the comparison returns **false**, although the object contents are identical. Note that **str2** is an object created by calling the **String** class constructor. The third comparison, again, uses the **equals** method. As you would expect, this returns **true** because the contents of both **str1** and **str3** are identical. Now, what about the last comparison statement? Should this not return **false**? The two variables **str1** and **str3** are distinct and are individually initialized. Although this is the case, the compiler creates only one object for the variables **str1** and **str3** because both objects contain the same character sequence.

CAUTION
*If you wish to compare the contents of two string objects, always use the **equals** method. Do not use the equality operator for comparison.*

Creating Formatted Output

J2SE 5.0 introduced **printf**-style formatting in Java. This is done through the introduction of the **Formatter** class in the **java.util** package. The **format** method of this class allows you to specify the formatting for your output string. The following code snippet demonstrates how to use the formatter:

```
StringBuilder stringBuilder = new StringBuilder();
Formatter formatter = new Formatter(stringBuilder);
formatter.format("Max float value: %10e\n", Float.MAX_VALUE);
System.out.println(stringBuilder);
```

This results in printing the following output message to the console:

```
Max float value: 3.402823e+38
```

NOTE
*The **StringBuilder** class was introduced in J2SE 5.0 and represents a mutable sequence of characters. The use of this class for creating mutable strings is recommended over the earlier **StringBuffer** class due to its performance.*

The format specifier **%10e** used in the preceding string is identical to the specifiers used in the **printf** statement in the C language. Therefore, you can use familiar specifiers such as **%d**, **%f**, and **%6.02f** while formatting your output string. However, this specifier offers more facilities than its counterpart in C. The general form is as follows:

```
% [ argument_index$ ] [ flags ] [ width ] [ .precision ] conversion
```

The first optional parameter indicates the index in the argument list. Therefore, you will be able to use arguments in any order in your formatted string. The optional **flags** is a set of characters that modify the output format. This set depends on the applied conversion. The **width** specifies the minimum number of characters to be written as output. The **precision** restricts the number of nonzero characters. The **conversion** describes the type of object being formatted. Common types are **f** for float, **t** for time, **o** for octal, and so on. We discuss this format specifier form further via a programming example later in this section.

Rather than using the **Formatter** class, you can use the newly added **printf** method in the **java.io.PrintStream**, **java.io.PrintWriter**, and **java.lang.String** classes. The overloaded **printf** method in these classes also allows you to specify the locale used while formatting the output. We will now look at how to use this formatting feature through a program example. The program in Listing 21-3 produces some formatted output.

Listing 21-3   *Demonstrating the New Formatter Class*

```java
import java.util.*;

public class StringFormatter {

    public static void main(String[] args) {
        float rate = 12.5f;
        int quantity = 100;
        float total = 1250;

        System.out.printf("Rate: %1$.2f Quantity:%2$d Total:%3$.2f\n",
                        rate, quantity, total);
        System.out.printf("Total: %3$.2f Quantity:%2$d Rate:%1$.2f\n\n",
                        rate, quantity, total);

        float f = (float) 123456789.98;
        System.out.printf("US - Price: %,.2f\n", f);
        System.out.printf(Locale.FRANCE, "France - Price: %,.2f\n", f);
        System.out.printf(Locale.GERMANY, "German - Price: %,.2f\n", f);
        System.out.printf(Locale.CHINA, "China - Price: %,.2f\n\n", f);

        Calendar calendar = Calendar.getInstance();
        System.out.printf("The current local time is %tr on "
                + "%<tA, %<tB %<te, %<tY.%n", calendar);
        System.out.printf(Locale.FRANCE, "The current local time is %tr on "
                + "%<tA, %<tB %<te, %<tY.%n", calendar);
        System.out.printf(Locale.GERMANY, "The current local time is %tr on "
                + "%<tA, %<tB %<te, %<tY.%n", calendar);
```

```
System.out.printf(Locale.CHINA, "The current local time is %tr on "
        + "%<tA, %<tB %<te, %<tY.%n", calendar);
    }
}
```

Before we examine the code, let's look at the program output:

```
Rate: 12.50 Quantity:100 Total:1250.00
Total: 1250.00 Quantity:100 Rate:12.50

US - Price: 123,456,792.00
France - Price: 123 456 792,00
German - Price: 123.456.792,00
China - Price: 123,456,792.00

The current local time is 03:28:58 PM on Monday, June 13, 2011.
The current local time is 03:28:58 PM on lundi, juin 13, 2011.
The current local time is 03:28:58 PM on Montag, Juni 13, 2011.
The current local time is 03:28:58 下午 on 星期一, 六月 13, 2011.
```

Now, study the first two formatting statements. Each uses three arguments. The arguments in the string to be formatted are specified as numbers (1, 2, and 3). The first statement uses the arguments in the specified ascending order. The second statement uses the third argument in the first placeholder and the first argument in the last placeholder. Observe how the output changes when we change the index order of the arguments.

Next, we print a floating-point number in different locales. The default is U.S. and is therefore not mentioned in the first **printf** statement. The subsequent **printf** statements state the desired locale in the first argument. Study the output to see how the number formatting changes depending on the set locale.

Finally, we print the current time and date in different locales. The statement **Calendar.getInstance()** returns a **Calendar** object that represents the current system time. The **Calendar** class is discussed in the next section. Look at the format string used for formatting the time and date fields:

```
%tr on %<tA, %<tB %<te, %<tY.%n
```

The **t** in the preceding string indicates the type as time. The conversion character **r** indicates that the time is formatted using the 12-hour clock format **hh:mm:ss am/pm**. The character **A** indicates the use of the locale-specific full name of the day of the week. The **B** indicates the locale-specific full month name. The **e** indicates the day of the month, formatted as two digits (that is, 1–31). The **Y** indicates the year formatted as at least four digits, with leading zeros as necessary.

TIP
For a complete list of conversion characters, which is very exhaustive, refer to the JDK documentation.

Observe how the date and time fields vary depending on the locale used.

In the next section, we discuss another important class that provides the time and date functionality in Java.

The Calendar Class

Java provides a rich set of functionality for time and date manipulations. The most important class in this category is **GregorianCalendar**, which is defined in the **java.util** package:

```
public class GregorianCalendar extends Calendar
```

This class supports both Julian and Gregorian calendar systems. It provides several constructors and useful methods for time representation and arithmetic. A few important methods of this class are discussed in this section.

The GregorianCalendar Methods

The various constructors for this class are listed here:

```
public GregorianCalendar();
public GregorianCalendar(TimeZone zone)
public GregorianCalendar(Locale aLocale)
public GregorianCalendar(TimeZone zone, Locale aLocale)
public GregorianCalendar(int year, int month, int dayOfMonth)
public GregorianCalendar(int year, int month, int dayOfMonth,
                         int hourOfDay, int minute, int second)
```

The no-argument class constructor constructs a **Calendar** object using the current time in the default time zone with the default locale. The other variations allow you to specify the time zone and/or locale at the time of construction. The last two methods allow you to specify the various date and time parameters so that a calendar instance can be created for any date other than the current instance of time.

The **add** method of this class takes two parameters: The first parameter specifies the field of the **Calendar** class to which the amount of time specified by the second parameter is added:

```
public void add(int field, int amount)
```

To understand this method, look at the following code snippet:

```
Calendar calendar = Calendar.getInstance();
System.out.printf("The current local time is %tr on "
                + "%<tA, %<tB %<te, %<tY.%n", calendar);
calendar.add(Calendar.MONTH, -5);
System.out.printf("The time 5 months ago is %tr on "
                + "%<tA, %<tB %<te, %<tY.%n", calendar);
```

Running this code generates the following output:

```
The current local time is 04:25:00 PM on Monday, June 13, 2011.
The time 5 months ago is 04:25:00 PM on Thursday, January 13, 2011.
```

The code creates a **Calendar** instance with the current system time, default time zone, and locale. We now subtract five months from this time by specifying the field **Calendar.MONTH** in the **add** method. The new time shows the month as January versus the original month in the current instance of June, so this is correct. When such additions are performed, the **add** method applies the rules of the calendar on which it is operating. The preceding output also reflects that the day on January 13 is Thursday, whereas the day in the original time is Monday. Thus, the **add** method has performed the correct date and time computations.

Several methods in the **Calendar** class allow for date comparison. For example, the **after** and **before** methods allow a direct comparison with another time object to determine whether the time specified by the current object occurs after or before the other time:

```
public boolean after(Object when)
public boolean before(Object when)
```

The **compareTo** method provides a comparison between two time objects:

```
public int compareTo(Calendar anotherCalendar)
```

There are **get** and **set** methods for getting and setting the time zone of the current object. Because the best way to learn the use of this class is through a practical example, we will now discuss the construction of an application called Local Time Converter to illustrate the power of **Calendar**.

The Local Time Converter Application

The Local Time Converter application tells you what the time is anywhere in the world, corresponding to the current time at your location. The application displays a huge list of locations, which is predefined in the Java libraries. Converting the time from one zone to another is a very simple task, thanks to excellent facilities provided in the **Calendar** class. Let's look at the application code given in Listing 21-4.

Listing 21-4 *Local Time Converter*

```
import java.awt.*;
import java.awt.event.*;
import java.text.SimpleDateFormat;
import java.util.*;
import java.util.List;
import javax.swing.*;

public class LocalTimeConverter extends JFrame {

    private final String TIME_FORMAT_NOW = "HH:mm 'on' dd MMM yyyy";
    private final SimpleDateFormat sdf = new SimpleDateFormat(TIME_FORMAT_NOW);

    public static void main(String[] args) {
        LocalTimeConverter app = new LocalTimeConverter();
        app.setTitle("Local Time Converter");
        app.setDefaultCloseOperation(JFrame.EXIT_ON_CLOSE);
        app.init();
        app.setBounds(100, 100, 700, 500);
        app.setVisible(true);
    }

    private void init() {
        final JPopupMenu popup = new JPopupMenu();
```

```java
final JMenuItem menuItem = new JMenuItem();
popup.add(menuItem);

menuItem.setBackground(Color.yellow);
menuItem.setForeground(Color.blue);

final JLabel localTime = new JLabel(getTimeNowAsString(), JLabel.CENTER);
localTime.setHorizontalTextPosition(JLabel.CENTER);
localTime.setFont(new Font("Tahoma", Font.PLAIN, 24));
localTime.setForeground(new Color(0, 0, 255));
add(localTime, BorderLayout.PAGE_START);

List<String> zoneList = new ArrayList<String>();
zoneList.addAll(Arrays.asList(TimeZone.getAvailableIDs()));
Collections.sort(zoneList);

final JList listOfZones = new JList(zoneList.toArray());
listOfZones.setSelectionMode(
        ListSelectionModel.SINGLE_INTERVAL_SELECTION);
listOfZones.setLayoutOrientation(JList.HORIZONTAL_WRAP);
listOfZones.setVisibleRowCount(-1);
listOfZones.addMouseListener(new MouseAdapter() {

    private Calendar calendar;
    private String selectedZone;

    @Override
    public void mouseClicked(MouseEvent e) {
        localTime.setText(getTimeNowAsString());
        int index = listOfZones.locationToIndex(e.getPoint());
        if (index > -1 && !(listOfZones.isSelectionEmpty())) {

            selectedZone = (String) listOfZones.getSelectedValue();
            computeTimeAtSelectedZone();

            // display time for remote zone in the popup
            String timezoneName = TimeZone.getTimeZone(selectedZone).
                    getDisplayName();
            menuItem.setText("Local time @ " + selectedZone + " "
                    + sdf.format(calendar.getTime()) + " "
                    + timezoneName);

            popup.show(e.getComponent(),
                    e.getX(), e.getY() + 10);
        }
    }

    private void computeTimeAtSelectedZone() {
        // reset calendar to local timezone
        calendar = new GregorianCalendar();
        long currentTime = calendar.getTimeInMillis();
```

```
                // get time offset of local timezone wrt GMT
                int localOffset = calendar.getTimeZone().
                        getOffset(Calendar.ZONE_OFFSET);

                // get time offset of remote timezone wrt GMT
                calendar.setTimeZone(TimeZone.getTimeZone(selectedZone));
                int remoteOffset = calendar.getTimeZone().
                        getOffset(Calendar.ZONE_OFFSET);

                // difference in two timezones
                int totalOffset = -remoteOffset + localOffset;

                // add offset to current local time
                currentTime -= totalOffset;

                // set time in remote zone
                calendar.setTimeInMillis(currentTime);
            }
        });

        JScrollPane listScroller = new JScrollPane(listOfZones);
        add(listScroller, BorderLayout.CENTER);
    }

    private String getTimeNowAsString() {
        Calendar calendar = new GregorianCalendar();
        String strLocalTime = "Local Time-"
                + sdf.format(calendar.getTime()) + " "
                + calendar.getTimeZone().getDisplayName();
        return strLocalTime;
    }
}
```

The Local Time Converter is a Swing-based application. The application class
LocalTimeConverter derives from **JFrame**. We first define a few constants:

```
final String TIME_FORMAT_NOW = "HH:mm 'on' dd MMM yyyy";
final SimpleDateFormat sdf = new SimpleDateFormat(TIME_FORMAT_NOW);
```

In the **main** method, we create an application instance and make the application frame visible
to the user. The application's **init** method provides its full functionality. In **init**, we create a **popup**
and a **menuItem**:

```
final JPopupMenu popup = new JPopupMenu();
final JMenuItem menuItem = new JMenuItem();
```

These identifiers are declared **final** because they will be used within a mouse-event-listener
inner class. Remember the inner class cannot access variables defined outside its scope unless
they are declared **final**. When the user clicks the desired zone in the application-displayed list,
we will pop up this menu showing the time in the selected zone.

Next, we create a **JLabel** and add it to the top of our display container:

```
final JLabel localTime = new JLabel(now(), JLabel.CENTER);
```

We will display the local time in this label. We then collect the list of time zones. The **TimeZone.getAvailableIDs** method returns an array of all predefined time zones in its library:

```
List<String> zoneList = new ArrayList<String>();
zoneList.addAll(Arrays.asList(TimeZone.getAvailableIDs()));
Collections.sort(zoneList);
```

We add this sorted list of zone names to a **JList** control:

```
final JList listOfZones = new JList(zoneList.toArray());
```

Now comes the important part. We add a mouse listener to the **JList** control:

```
listOfZones.addMouseListener(new MouseAdapter() {
```

We declared an anonymous inner class because this class may not be usable elsewhere. We override the **mouseClicked** event handler. Every time the user clicks the mouse on an item in the zones list, we first obtain and display the current time:

```
localTime.setText(now());
```

The **now** method, which is defined in the outer class, uses the **format** method of the **SimpleDateFormat** class to format the date and time.

We obtain the index in the list at the clicked point by using the **locationToIndex** method:

```
int index = listOfZones.locationToIndex(e.getPoint());
```

The time at the selected zone corresponding to the current time in local zone is computed in the **ComputeTimeAtSelectedZone** method, which is discussed later on. This method sets the **calendar** object to the remote zone, which we use for displaying the time in the popup menu. This is done in the following code:

```
String timezoneName = TimeZone.getTimeZone(selectedZone).getDisplayName();
menuItem.setText("Local time @ " + selectedZone + " "
                 + sdf.format(calendar.getTime()) + " " + timezoneName);
popup.show(e.getComponent(), e.getX(), e.getY() + 10);
```

Now, let's look at the time conversion, which as stated earlier, is done in the **ComputeTimeAtSelectedZone** method. The trick for converting the time is to take the difference in time between the two time zones by using the built-in classes and then add this difference to the current local time to obtain the time at the new zone. For doing this, we use the built-in **Calendar** and **Timezone** classes to perform the time arithmetic and get a user-readable time-formatted string.

We first create an instance of **GregorianCalendar** and obtain the current time in long format:

```
calendar = new GregorianCalendar();
long currentTime = calendar.getTimeInMillis();
```

We then obtain the time offset of the local time zone with respect to GMT:

```
int localOffset = calendar.getTimeZone().getOffset(Calendar.ZONE_OFFSET);
```

To get the time offset of the second zone, we need to set our calendar to the new zone:

```
calendar.setTimeZone(TimeZone.getTimeZone(selectedZone));
```

The **getTimeZone** method returns a **TimeZone** for the time zone string specified in its parameter. We obtain the time offset at the newly set calendar with the following statement:

```
int remoteOffset = calendar.getTimeZone().getOffset(Calendar.ZONE_OFFSET);
```

We compute the time difference in the two time zones and add it to the current time of the local zone:

```
int totalOffset = -remoteOffset + localOffset;
currentTime -= totalOffset;
```

We then set the calendar instance to this new time:

```
calendar.setTimeInMillis(currentTime);
```

The date and time corresponding to this calendar are now printed in the popup menu, as described previously. The program output is shown in Figure 21-1.

Try clicking different time zones and observe the corresponding local time in the selected zone.

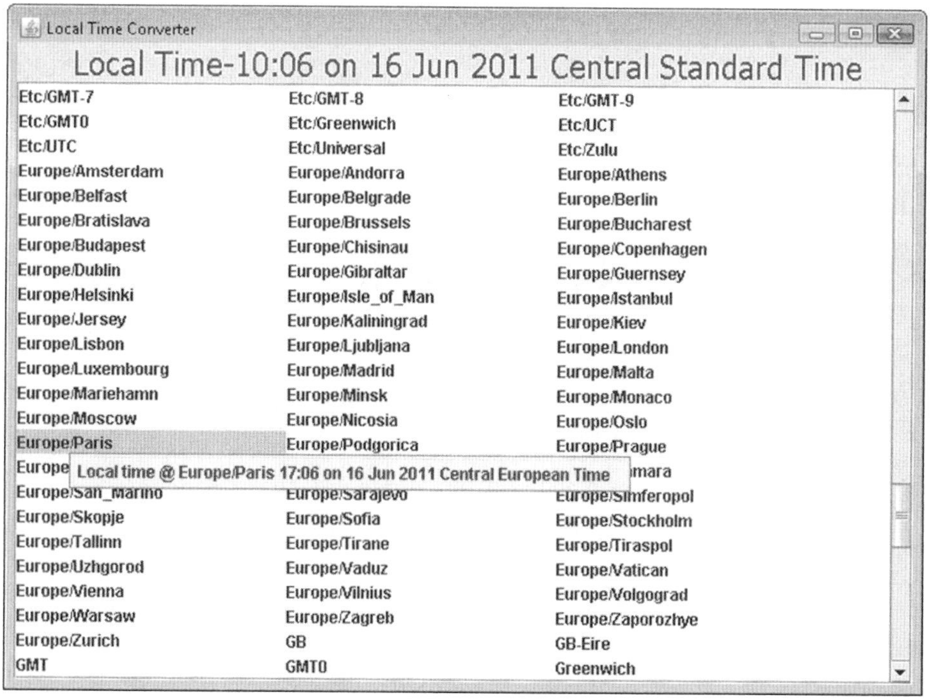

FIGURE 21-1. *Local time converter program output*

CAUTION
If you are still using versions older than Java SE 7, the preceding time computations may not reflect DST (Daylight Savings Time) at the local and remote time zones. Refer to www.oracle.com/technetwork/java/ javase/timezones-137583.html#intro for Java's implementation of time zones and DST.

Introspection and Reflection

Chapter 1 mentioned the *dynamic* feature of the Java language, which was a buzzword in the list of initial features of Java. This dynamic nature of Java is implemented in the introspection and reflection mechanism. Reflection allows a program to examine the internals of any class or object at runtime. Introspection builds on this facility. Using introspection, running code can ask an object for its class, ask a class for its methods and constructors, find out the parameters and the return type each method takes, load an unknown class, create objects and arrays of the discovered class, and invoke methods on the newly created objects. This is the dynamic nature of Java, where all these things are done at runtime without the compiler's knowledge of the class that is loaded at runtime. To give you a quick look at what introspection and reflection can do, consider the code in Listing 21-5.

Listing 21-5   *Dynamic Method Invoker*

```java
public class DynamicInvoker {

    public static void main(String[] args) {
        DynamicInvoker app = new DynamicInvoker();
        app.printGreeting("Jonny", 5);
        System.out.println("\nDynamic invocation of printGreeting method");
        try {
            app.getClass().getMethod("printGreeting", new Class[]{
                    Class.forName("java.lang.String"), Integer.TYPE}).
                invoke(app, new Object[]{"Sanjay", new Integer(3)});
        } catch (Exception ex) {
            ex.printStackTrace();
        }
    }

    public void printGreeting(String name, int numberOfTimes) {
        for (int i = 0; i < numberOfTimes; i++) {
            System.out.println("Hello " + name);
        }
    }
}
```

The **DynamicInvoker** is a very simple application that creates its instance in the **main** method and invokes its **printGreeting** method, which prints a greeting to the person specified in its first parameter, the number of times specified by the second parameter. This example shows the invocation of the same method by obfuscating its call. This is done in the following program statement:

```
app.getClass().getMethod("printGreeting", new Class[]{
        Class.forName("java.lang.String"), Integer.TYPE}).
    invoke(app, new Object[]{"Sanjay", new Integer(3)});
```

This produces output similar to the earlier call to the **printGreeting** method on the **app** object, except for a name change and the number of times the message is printed.

So, one benefit of this dynamic invocation is the obfuscation and verbosity of the method calls in your code. Of course, this also comes with a disadvantage of runtime checking versus the compile-time checking of a method call. Some people may still consider this as an advantage. Are there any better reasons for using introspection and reflection?

Introspection has a wide variety of applications. You may use it for writing plug-ins—the application discovers the methods of a plug-in at runtime and invokes them. JUnit uses introspection to identify the test methods that begin with the word "test" and invokes them in order. In a Web Services implementation, a client can discover the service's interface from a UDDI registry and obtain the service via dynamic coding. You could even develop your own javadocs-type application by introspecting the classes at runtime.

This feature has been available in the language since its inception, and the Reflection API became a part of core Java with the release 1.1 of the JDK. In JDK 1.1, new methods were added to the **java.lang.Class** class and the new package **java.lang.reflect** was introduced.

We will now use this feature by constructing an interesting application that discovers any unknown class at runtime, instantiates it, and invokes methods on it. Before we discuss the construction of this application, we will look at a very important class, called **Class**, on which this entire introspection and reflection mechanism is based.

The Class Class

Java defines a class called **Class**. Because this is a **final** class, you cannot extend it in your programs.

```
public final class Class<T> extends Object
        implements Serializable, GenericDeclaration, Type, AnnotatedElement
```

Whenever the Java runtime loads a class in memory, it creates an instance of this class **Class** to represent a loaded class or an interface. You can obtain a reference to this object by calling the **getClass** method of the **Object** class from which all the classes in Java are derived. You can also use the **forName** method of the class **Class** to load an unknown class and obtain a reference to its **Class** object. The **Class** class provides several methods to introspect the class that it represents. For example, you can obtain the class name, its modifiers, constructors, methods, attributes, and so on. Not only that, but you will be able to create another object of the class that it represents and also an array of objects. Thus, this provides the dynamic nature of Java we have been talking about so far.

The **getName** method of this class returns the fully qualified name of the class that this **Class** object represents. The **getModifiers** method returns the Java language modifiers for the represented class or interface:

```
public int getModifiers()
```

These modifiers are encoded in an integer and must be decoded using the methods of the class **Modifier**. As you know, the modifiers are **public**, **protected**, **private**, **abstract**, and so on.

The **Modifier** class defines **static** fields to represent these various modifiers and provides accessor methods on them. For example, the **isAbstract** method tests for the presence of the **abstract** modifier, the **isFinal** method tests whether it is **final**, and so on.

The **getMethods** method returns an array of **Method** objects reflecting all the public methods of the represented object, including all those inherited from a superclass and superinterface:

```
public Method[] getMethods() throws SecurityException
```

Likewise, the **getConstructors** method returns an array of all public constructors:

```
public Constructor<?>[] getConstructors() throws SecurityException
```

Both methods may throw a **SecurityException**. Let's look at the conditions under which this exception is thrown. First, for this exception to be thrown, the security manager must be present. Second, the invocation of the **checkMemberAccess(this, Member.PUBLIC)** method on it denies access to methods/constructors within this class. The permission denial in this case indicates that this method/constructor does not have public access and therefore cannot be invoked with dynamic discovery. There is one more situation under which the **SecurityException** is thrown: if the caller's class loader is not located in the class hierarchy of the class loader of the current class and invoking the **checkPackageAccess** method on the security manager denies access to the package of this class. In other words, if the loaded class belongs to a package other than the current class, the current class may not have the package permissions to the loaded class, so in that case a **SecurityException** will be thrown.

Several other important methods are available that reveal more information about the class that the **Class** class represents. However, two important methods need to be mentioned here for the class browser application we are going to develop next.

The **forName** method accepts the class name as its argument and returns a **Class** object that represents the specified class:

```
public static Class<?> forName(String className) throws ClassNotFoundException
```

Thus, this method is very useful in injecting a compile-time unknown Java class into the runtime environment for dynamic instantiation. The method will throw the **ClassNotFoundException** if the class cannot be located.

To instantiate the loaded class, you call the **newInstance** method:

```
public T newInstance() throws InstantiationException, IllegalAccessException
```

The **newInstance** method creates an object that this class **Class** represents. You will get the **IllegalAccessException** if the class or its no-argument constructor is not accessible. You get the **InstantiationException** exception under the following situations:

- The **Class** represents one of the following:
  - An abstract class
  - An interface
  - An array class
  - A primitive type
  - Void

- The class has no nullary constructor (that is, a no-argument constructor—either a default constructor provided by the compiler or one defined by the programmer).
- The instantiation fails due to some other reason.

Besides this, you may also get a **SecurityException** under exactly the identical conditions described for the **getMethods** and **getConstructors** methods.

Using the **forName** method allows you to use objects of a type not known at development time. You will find several useful applications of this feature. The best-known use is to load the new or latest JDBC drivers dynamically in your code. What's more, using this feature, you can add new features to your application, maybe having several installations worldwide, by providing this dynamic discovery feature in the initial release of your application. For example, a preinstalled word processing program may use the newly created thesaurus or the new spell-check library.

NOTE
JDBC stands for Java Database Connectivity and is a Java application-programming interface that allows Java programmers to access a database management system from Java code.

Once an object of the dynamically discovered class is created, you can invoke the discovered methods on it to use the object for your purposes. For this, you need to use the **Method** class, discussed next.

The Method Class

The **Method** class is important to us for the dynamic invocation of a method at runtime:

```
public final class Method extends AccessibleObject
        implements GenericDeclaration, Member
```

Like the class **Class**, this is a **final** class that we cannot extend. It provides several getter methods to extract all the details of the represented method. We will just discuss a few important methods of this class relevant in the current context.

The **getParameterTypes** method returns an array of **Class** objects representing the formal parameter types this method takes:

```
public Class<?>[] getParameterTypes()
```

From the size of the array, we can determine the number of parameters required for invoking the method. The type of each parameter is obtained from the **Class** object that an array element holds.

The method return type is obtained by calling the **getReturnType** method on the **Method** object:

```
public Class<?> getReturnType()
```

This method returns a **Class** object from which the type of return value can be ascertained.

Finally, the most important method to us for executing the method at runtime is the **invoke** method:

```
public Object invoke(Object obj, Object... args)
                throws IllegalAccessException,
                    IllegalArgumentException,
                    InvocationTargetException
```

The **invoke** method invokes the underlying method represented by this **Method** object. The first parameter, **obj**, specifies the object on which the method is invoked. The **args** parameter specifies the arguments used for the method call. The return value, if any, is returned as an **Object** type after the method completes successfully.

Now that we have covered the basics of introspection and reflection, we will discuss the construction of a class browser application that demonstrates how to use these classes in practical terms.

The Class Browser Application

The class browser application is a GUI Swing-based application. To understand the application functionality, let's first look at its interface, shown in Figure 21-2. At the top of the application window, you enter the name of the class you want to introspect. Clicking the Accept button introspects the specified class and displays its public constructors and methods. This also creates an instance of the class using its no-argument constructor. The screenshot also shows what

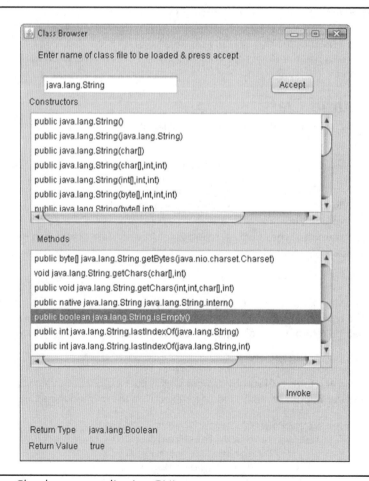

FIGURE 21-2. *Class browser application GUI*

happens when you invoke a method on this created object. To invoke a method, you select it from the list presented and click the Invoke button. The method return value and its type are shown at the bottom of the screen.

Introspecting the **String** class does not show its instantiation visually. Therefore, to give you a visual demonstration of the dynamic instantiation of the introspected class, we will create a test class that is GUI based. We will first discuss the construction of this test application and then proceed to the explanation of the class browser.

The Introspection Test Application

The test application creates a frame window with the message "Hello" displayed at its center. It declares a few public methods that allow another object to change the display color, font, and the text of the message displayed at its center. Our class browser will discover these methods and invoke them by passing the appropriate number of parameters to each. You will be able to see the effect of invocation of these methods visually. The introspection test application code is given in Listing 21-6.

Listing 21-6   *The Introspection Test Application for the Class Browser*

```java
import java.awt.*;
import java.awt.event.*;
import javax.swing.*;

public class IntrospectionTestApplication extends JFrame {

    private String displayString = "Hello";
    private Font textFont = new Font("Arial", Font.PLAIN, 20);
    private Color textColor = new Color(255, 0, 0);
    private JLabel labelDisplay;

    IntrospectionTestApplication() {
        super("Introspection Test");
        setBounds(200, 200, 200, 200);
        setResizable(false);

        labelDisplay = new JLabel("Hello", JLabel.CENTER);
        add(labelDisplay, BorderLayout.CENTER);

        addWindowListener(new WindowAdapter() {

            @Override
            public void windowClosing(WindowEvent evt) {
                dispose();
            }
        });
        setVisible(true);
    }

    public static void main(String args[]) {
        new IntrospectionTestApplication();
    }
```

```
    public void setDefaultString() {
        displayString = "Hello";
        labelDisplay.setText(displayString);
    }

    public void setDisplayColor(short red, short blue, short green) {
        textColor = new Color(red, blue, green);
        labelDisplay.setForeground(textColor);
    }

    public void setDisplayString(String str) {
        displayString = str;
        labelDisplay.setText(displayString);
    }

    public void setFontSize(int size) {
        textFont = new Font("Arial", Font.PLAIN, size);
        labelDisplay.setFont(textFont);
    }
}
```

The **IntrospectionTestApplication** extends its functionality from **JFrame**. The class declares a few variables for setting the display message, the font, and the color used for display. The class constructor sets the window caption and its default size. We create an anonymous adapter to hide the window when its close button is clicked, and finally we display the window to the user. The **main** method simply instantiates the application class.

The class declares several public methods for the purpose of testing our class browser application. The four setter methods take a different number of parameters and perform the task suggested by their name. What is important to us is understanding how the class browser detects how many parameters a method requires, the type of each parameter, and how these parameters are constructed with real values and then passed to the dynamic invocation. You will understand all this when we discuss the class browser, next.

The Class Browser

The full source of the class browser application is given in Listing 21-7.

Listing 21-7   *Program Demonstrating Introspection and Reflection*

```
import java.awt.*;
import java.awt.event.*;
import java.lang.reflect.*;
import javax.swing.*;

public class ClassBrowser extends JFrame implements ActionListener {

    private JButton buttonAccept = new JButton("Accept");
    private JButton buttonInvoke = new JButton("Invoke");
    private JLabel returnType = new JLabel();
    private JLabel returnValue = new JLabel();
    private DefaultListModel constructors = new DefaultListModel();
```

```java
    private DefaultListModel methods = new DefaultListModel();
    private JList listConstructors = new JList(constructors);
    private JList listMethods = new JList(methods);
    private JScrollPane jScrollPane1 = new JScrollPane();
    private JScrollPane jScrollPane2 = new JScrollPane();
    private JTextField textClassName =
            new JTextField("IntrospectionTestApplication");
    private String strClassName;
    private Class theClass;
    private Object obj;
    private String argumentValue;

    public ClassBrowser() {
        initComponents();
    }

    public void setArgumentValue(String argumentValue) {
        this.argumentValue = argumentValue;
    }

    private void initComponents() {
        setTitle("Class Browser");

        setDefaultCloseOperation(JFrame.EXIT_ON_CLOSE);
        setResizable(false);
        getContentPane().setLayout(new java.awt.GridBagLayout());
        GridBagConstraints gridBagConstraints = new java.awt.GridBagConstraints();
        gridBagConstraints.gridx = 0;
        gridBagConstraints.gridy = 0;
        gridBagConstraints.gridwidth = 7;
        gridBagConstraints.insets = new java.awt.Insets(11, 23, 0, 0);
        getContentPane().add(new JLabel(
                "Enter name of class file to be loaded & press accept"),
                gridBagConstraints);
        gridBagConstraints = new java.awt.GridBagConstraints();
        gridBagConstraints.gridx = 7;
        gridBagConstraints.gridy = 1;
        gridBagConstraints.gridwidth = 9;
        gridBagConstraints.gridheight = 2;
        gridBagConstraints.insets = new java.awt.Insets(18, 18, 0, 20);
        buttonAccept.addActionListener(this);
        getContentPane().add(buttonAccept, gridBagConstraints);
        jScrollPane1.setViewportView(listConstructors);
        gridBagConstraints = new java.awt.GridBagConstraints();
        gridBagConstraints.gridx = 0;
        gridBagConstraints.gridy = 4;
        gridBagConstraints.gridwidth = 16;
        gridBagConstraints.fill = java.awt.GridBagConstraints.BOTH;
        gridBagConstraints.ipadx = 257;
        gridBagConstraints.ipady = 71;
        gridBagConstraints.weightx = 1.0;
        gridBagConstraints.weighty = 1.0;
```

```
        gridBagConstraints.insets = new java.awt.Insets(6, 10, 0, 20);
        getContentPane().add(jScrollPane1, gridBagConstraints);
        jScrollPane2.setViewportView(listMethods);
        gridBagConstraints = new java.awt.GridBagConstraints();
        gridBagConstraints.gridx = 0;
        gridBagConstraints.gridy = 6;
        gridBagConstraints.gridwidth = 16;
        gridBagConstraints.fill = java.awt.GridBagConstraints.BOTH;
        gridBagConstraints.ipadx = 257;
        gridBagConstraints.ipady = 81;
        gridBagConstraints.weightx = 1.0;
        gridBagConstraints.weighty = 1.0;
        gridBagConstraints.insets = new java.awt.Insets(6, 10, 0, 20);
        getContentPane().add(jScrollPane2, gridBagConstraints);
        gridBagConstraints = new java.awt.GridBagConstraints();
        gridBagConstraints.gridx = 8;
        gridBagConstraints.gridy = 7;
        gridBagConstraints.gridwidth = 8;
        gridBagConstraints.insets = new java.awt.Insets(18, 17, 0, 0);
        buttonInvoke.addActionListener(this);
        getContentPane().add(buttonInvoke, gridBagConstraints);
        gridBagConstraints = new java.awt.GridBagConstraints();
        gridBagConstraints.gridx = 0;
        gridBagConstraints.gridy = 5;
        gridBagConstraints.insets = new java.awt.Insets(11, 10, 0, 0);
        getContentPane().add(new JLabel("Methods"), gridBagConstraints);
        gridBagConstraints = new java.awt.GridBagConstraints();
        gridBagConstraints.gridx = 0;
        gridBagConstraints.gridy = 3;
        gridBagConstraints.insets = new java.awt.Insets(1, 10, 0, 0);
        getContentPane().add(new JLabel("Constructors"), gridBagConstraints);
        gridBagConstraints = new java.awt.GridBagConstraints();
        gridBagConstraints.gridx = 0;
        gridBagConstraints.gridy = 1;
        gridBagConstraints.gridwidth = 6;
        gridBagConstraints.ipadx = 183;
        gridBagConstraints.insets = new java.awt.Insets(19, 10, 0, 0);
        getContentPane().add(textClassName, gridBagConstraints);
        gridBagConstraints = new java.awt.GridBagConstraints();
        gridBagConstraints.gridx = 0;
        gridBagConstraints.gridy = 8;
        gridBagConstraints.gridwidth = 2;
        gridBagConstraints.insets = new java.awt.Insets(29, 10, 0, 0);
        getContentPane().add(new JLabel("Return Type"), gridBagConstraints);
        gridBagConstraints = new java.awt.GridBagConstraints();
        gridBagConstraints.gridx = 0;
        gridBagConstraints.gridy = 9;
        gridBagConstraints.gridwidth = 3;
        gridBagConstraints.insets = new java.awt.Insets(6, 10, 11, 0);
        getContentPane().add(new JLabel("Return Value"), gridBagConstraints);
        gridBagConstraints = new java.awt.GridBagConstraints();
        gridBagConstraints.gridx = 3;
```

```
            gridBagConstraints.gridy = 8;
            gridBagConstraints.gridwidth = 2;
            gridBagConstraints.ipadx = 48;
            gridBagConstraints.insets = new java.awt.Insets(29, 16, 0, 0);
            getContentPane().add(returnType, gridBagConstraints);
            gridBagConstraints = new java.awt.GridBagConstraints();
            gridBagConstraints.gridx = 3;
            gridBagConstraints.gridy = 9;
            gridBagConstraints.insets = new java.awt.Insets(6, 18, 11, 0);
            getContentPane().add(returnValue, gridBagConstraints);
            pack();
        }

    public static void main(String args[]) {
        try {
//          UIManager.setLookAndFeel("javax.swing.plaf.nimbus.NimbusLookAndFeel");
            ClassBrowser app = new ClassBrowser();
            app.setBounds(220, 30, 470, 600);
            app.setVisible(true);
        } catch (Exception ex) {
            ex.printStackTrace();
        }
    }

    @Override
    public void actionPerformed(ActionEvent aevt) {
        Object source = aevt.getSource();
        if (source == buttonAccept) {
            strClassName = textClassName.getText();

            if (strClassName.equals("")) {
                return;
            }
            constructors.clear();
            methods.clear();
            returnValue.setText("");
            returnType.setText("");

            try {
                theClass = Class.forName(strClassName);
            } catch (Throwable exp) {
                constructors.addElement(
                        "You have entered the class name incorrectly");
                constructors.addElement("Please input a new class name");
                textClassName.requestFocus();
                return;
            }
            try {
                obj = theClass.newInstance();
            } catch (Exception e) {
                constructors.addElement(e.toString());
            }
```

```
            displayMethods();
        } else if (source == buttonInvoke) {
            invokeSelectedMethod();
        }
    }

    private void displayMethods() {
        Method methodList[] = theClass.getDeclaredMethods();
        Constructor constructorList[] = theClass.getDeclaredConstructors();

        for (int count = 0; count < constructorList.length; count++) {
            constructors.addElement(constructorList[count].toString());
        }
        for (int count = 0; count < methodList.length; count++) {
            methods.addElement(methodList[count].toString());
        }
        listMethods.requestFocus();
    }

    private void invokeSelectedMethod() {

        returnType.setText("");
        returnValue.setText("");
        int index = listMethods.getSelectedIndex();
        Method classMethods[] = theClass.getDeclaredMethods();
        Class inputParameters[] = classMethods[index].getParameterTypes();
        Object[] params = new Object[inputParameters.length];
        for (int i = 0; i < inputParameters.length; i++) {
            (new InputFrame(this, inputParameters[i].getName(),
                    true)).setVisible(true);
            if (inputParameters[i].isAssignableFrom(
                    java.lang.Short.TYPE)) {
                params[i] = new Short(argumentValue);
            } else if (inputParameters[i].isAssignableFrom(
                    java.lang.Boolean.TYPE)) {
                params[i] = Boolean.valueOf(argumentValue);
            } else if (inputParameters[i].isAssignableFrom(
                    java.lang.Character.TYPE)) {
                params[i] = new Character(argumentValue.charAt(0));
            } else if (inputParameters[i].isAssignableFrom(
                    java.lang.Byte.TYPE)) {
                params[i] = new Byte(argumentValue);
            } else if (inputParameters[i].isAssignableFrom(
                    java.lang.Integer.TYPE)) {
                params[i] = new Integer(argumentValue);
            } else if (inputParameters[i].isAssignableFrom(
                    java.lang.Long.TYPE)) {
                params[i] = new Long(argumentValue);
            } else if (inputParameters[i].isAssignableFrom(
                    java.lang.Float.TYPE)) {
```

```
                params[i] = new Float(argumentValue);
            } else if (inputParameters[i].isAssignableFrom(
                    java.lang.Double.TYPE)) {
                params[i] = new Double(argumentValue);
            } else {
                params[i] = argumentValue;
            }
        }
        try {
            Object returnObject = classMethods[index].invoke(obj, params);
            returnValue.setText(returnObject.toString());
            returnType.setText(returnObject.getClass().getName());
        } catch (java.lang.IllegalAccessException iae) {
            System.out.println("Invalid operation");
        } catch (Exception e) {
            returnValue.setText(e.toString());
        }
    }
}


class InputFrame extends JDialog implements ActionListener {

    private ClassBrowser app;
    private JTextField inputText = new JTextField(15);
    private JButton buttonOK = new JButton("OK");

    InputFrame(ClassBrowser app, String name, boolean model) {
        super(app, model);
        setTitle(name);
        this.app = app;
        init();
    }

    private void init() {
        setBounds(50, 50, 200, 100);
        setLayout(new FlowLayout());
        add(inputText);
        add(buttonOK);
        buttonOK.addActionListener(this);
    }

    @Override
    public void actionPerformed(ActionEvent evt) {
        if (evt.getSource() == buttonOK) {
            app.setArgumentValue(inputText.getText());
            dispose();
        }
    }
}
```

The **ClassBrowser** class that extends a **JFrame** constructs its GUI in the **initComponents** method. Here, we use NetBeans to create the layout and then copy the IDE-generated code (which was trimmed to save space). Therefore, you may find this initialization to be a little longer than the GUI applications we have discussed so far in the book. This is one of the reasons to hand-code the GUI rather than using an IDE—to save on the number of lines of code.

The **main** method sets the application's look and feel, creates an application instance, sets the window size, and then makes it visible. We have also reduced the number of exceptions the **setLookAndFeel** method requires us to catch to the more-generic **Exception** type.

Most of the action that interests us occurs in the **actionPerformed** method, which is called when either the Accept or Invoke button is clicked.

When the user clicks the Accept button, we read the class name entered by the user:

```
if (source == buttonAccept) {
    strClassName = textClassName.getText();
```

After checking that the entered name is not null, we clear the two list boxes:

```
constructors.clear();
methods.clear();
```

Now we try to load the class by calling the **forName** method of the class **Class**. The method receives the class name as its parameter:

```
theClass = Class.forName(strClassName);
```

If the class is loaded successfully, we instantiate it by calling the **newInstance** method on the **Class** object:

```
obj = theClass.newInstance();
```

Now, to display the list of constructors and methods, we call **displayMethods** (which is discussed later):

```
displayMethods();
```

If the user has clicked the Invoke button, we call the **invokeSelectedMethod** (which also is discussed later):

```
else if (source == buttonInvoke) {
    invokeSelectedMethod();
}
```

Now, let's look at the implementation of the **displayMethods**. Here, we first obtain the list of methods by calling the **getDeclaredMethods** on the **Class** object:

```
Method methodList[] = theClass.getDeclaredMethods();
```

The list of methods is returned as an array of **Method** objects. Likewise, we get the list of all the constructors by calling the **getDeclaredConstructors** method:

```
Constructor constructorList[] = theClass.getDeclaredConstructors();
```

The list of constructors is returned in an array of **Constructor**s. We add the list of constructors and methods in their respective list boxes.

Now, let's look at what happens when a method is dynamically invoked. The dynamic invocation takes place in the **invokeSelectedMethod**. First, we get the index of the selected method in the list box:

```
int index = listMethods.getSelectedIndex();
```

To obtain the list of input parameters on the selected method, we call the **getParameterTypes** method on the **Method** object:

```
Class inputParameters[] = classMethods[index].getParameterTypes();
```

The method returns an array of **Class** objects. To read the method parameters from the user, we first construct an **Object** array to store the input parameter values:

```
Object[] params = new Object[inputParameters.length];
```

The size of the array is set to the length of the **inputParameters** array. For each input parameter, we construct a frame and ask the user to input the parameter value:

```
for (int i = 0; i < inputParameters.length; i++) {
    (new InputFrame(this, inputParameters[i].getName(),
            true)).setVisible(true);
```

To construct a frame for inputting the parameter value, we instantiate the **InputFrame** class, discussed later. The second parameter to the **InputFrame** constructor is set to the parameter type, which will be displayed as the frame title.

We now set up a big **if-elseif** ladder to validate the input type with all known data types while copying the parameter value into the **params** array:

```
if (inputParameters[i].isAssignableFrom(java.lang.Short.TYPE)) {
    params[i] = new Short(argumentValue);
} else if (inputParameters[i].isAssignableFrom (java.lang.Boolean.TYPE)) {
    params[i] = Boolean.valueOf(argumentValue);
} else if (inputParameters[i].isAssignableFrom (java.lang.Character.TYPE)) {
...
```

Once all the parameters are read, we invoke the method by calling **invoke** on the **Method** object:

```
Object returnObject = classMethods[index].invoke(obj, params);
```

The first parameter to the **invoke** method specifies the object on which the method is invoked, and the second parameter specifies the list of parameters that the method takes. This call causes the method to execute on the specified object.

Finally, let's look at the **InputFrame** class, which is dialog box based:

```
class InputFrame extends JDialog implements ActionListener {
```

The **init** method constructs the GUI and sets up the action listener for the button. In the action event handler, we simply read and assign the user input and eventually dispose of the dialog box.

Try running the application. In the class name field, enter **IntrospectionTestApplication** and click the Accept button. The test application window appears with a default "Hello" message displayed at its center. You will also notice the list of constructors and methods being displayed in the main application window. Now, select the **setDisplayString** method and click the Invoke button. An instance of our **InputFrame** class pops up. Enter some string in the displayed dialog box and click the OK button. The text in the test application window immediately changes to the newly entered value. Likewise, you can try invoking the **setFontSize** and **setDisplayColor** methods. The first method accepts only one parameter that specifies the font size. The second method accepts three parameters. Therefore, when you invoke it, you will find the **InputFrame** instance popping up three times on your screen. Each time you will input a desired number in the range of 0 to 255, corresponding to the component value in RGB. Finally, you can try invoking one more method—**setDefaultString**. This method does not take any parameters and changes the displayed string in the test application to its default value.

Now, test the application with other predefined classes in the Java libraries. For example, try the **java.lang.String** class. When you click the Accept button, the class will call its no-argument constructor and create a **String** object that is empty. Select the **length()** method in the list and invoke it. At the bottom of the screen, you will see the return type as **java.lang.Integer** and the return value of **0**. Try another method, such as **isEmpty**. The return type will now be **java.lang .Boolean** and the value is **true**. Now, try the **charAt(int)** method. The **InputFrame** appears, asking you to enter an **int**-type parameter. Enter some value and click OK. You will see the exception **java.lang.reflect.InvocationTargetException** printed in the output. You may now try other methods to understand how the dynamic invocation really works.

CAUTION
*The class browser application constructs an instance of the specified class using its no-argument constructor, provided one is available. As an exercise, modify the preceding code so that the user can select the type of constructor while instantiating the class. You will need to detect the number and types of parameters that the constructor requires and accept those inputs from the user using **InputFrame**.*

Disadvantages

You have so far seen the power and flexibility provided by the introspection and reflection mechanism. However, all this power does not come without a cost. The introspection and reflection method calls have substantial performance overhead. The reflection makes the code much more complex and harder to understand as compared to direct method calls. The type-safety in the code is also compromised to some extent. Therefore, use this mechanism with care and only when it is absolutely needed.

What's Next?

What you learned in this book is just the tip of the iceberg when it comes to Java programming. Java offers a whole lot more. What you have gained to this point will give you a head start in learning those new APIs. So let's look at what else is available.

Figure 21-3 illustrates the various packages available in Java SE 7.

User Interface Toolkits	AWT			Swing		Java 2D	
	Accessibility	Drag n Drop	Input Methods	Image I/O	Print Service	Sound	
Integration Libraries	IDL	JDBC	JNDI	RMI	RMI-IIOP	Scripting	
Other Base Libraries	Beans	Int'l Support	Input/Output	JMX	JNI	Math	
	Networking	Override Mechanism	Security	Serialization	Extension Mechanism	XML JAXP	
lang and util Base Libraries	lang and util	Collections	Concurrency Utilities	JAR	Logging	Management	
	Preferences API	Ref Objects	Reflection	Regular Expressions	Versioning	Zip	Instrumentation

Java SE API

FIGURE 21-3. *List of Java SE APIs (courtesy of Oracle Corporation)*

In this book, you studied AWT and Swing to develop GUI-based applications. If you want to do advanced 2D graphics and imaging, use the set of classes provided in Java 2D. To make your applications accessible to persons with disabilities, use the Java Accessibility API. This provides support for assistive technologies such as screen readers, speech-recognition systems, and refreshable Braille displays. Java provides excellent support for internationalizing your Java applications that can be adapted to various languages and regions without engineering changes.

To integrate your Java application with legacy and other applications, Java provides several integration libraries. The JDBC libraries allow you to access many different kinds of database engines. RMI allows you to create distributed Java technology–based applications that use JRMP (Java Remote Method Protocol). RMI-IIOP allows your existing Java client applications access to CORBA (Common Object Request Broker Architecture) servers that use the widely accepted IIOP (Internet InterORB Protocol).

Beginning in Java SE 6, a new framework is available that permits Java applications to host script engines and access them through your Java code, just the way you use JDBC drivers to access databases. Many web-based applications use scripting languages such as JavaScript and can now benefit from all the advantages provided by the Java platform. The XML JAXP libraries provide good support for processing XML (Extensible Markup Language), which has been widely accepted as the language of data exchange in standalone, distributed, and mobile platforms.

The list is endless. Keep studying—and welcome to the world of Java programming.

Summary

In this chapter you studied several utility classes provided in the Java libraries. The **String** class provides several methods for manipulating strings. You used the **substring** method to extract a sequence of characters from a given string. The **contains** method allows you to check the presence of a substring in a given string. You used the **replace** method to replace a character or a character sequence with another one in the specified string object. The **format** method allows you to create a formatted output in a string. To compare two strings, use the **equals** method. This will cause the comparison of the string contents. Do not use the equality operator to compare two strings for equality. The newly added **Formatter** class allows you to include C-style formatting in your Java applications.

Java provides time and date representation through a **Calendar** class. The **GregorianCalendar** is a concrete implementation of **Calendar** that provides several methods for representation of time and date. You used this class in a practical application that finds the time at several worldwide locations, corresponding to the current time instance at your location.

The introspection and reflection mechanism is a powerful feature of the Java language that provides its dynamic nature. The **java.lang** package provides a class called **Class** that represents a class loaded in memory. You use an instance of this class to get the details of the loaded class. Such details are very exhaustive and include the class modifiers, the public methods, the public constructors, and more. The **forName** method of this class allows you to inject any compile-time unknown class in the runtime system. Once a class is available at runtime, you can create objects of its type by calling the **newInstance** method on it. The **getDeclaredMethods** method returns the list of public methods in an array of **Method** objects. The **invoke** method of the **Method** class permits the dynamic invocation of a method.

The chapter concluded with a list of other APIs available in Java SE 7 that you should learn as you continue your studies.

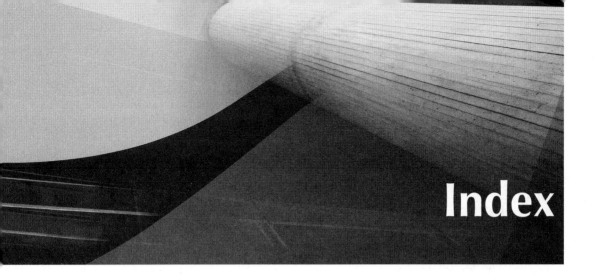

Index

D

O

Q

R

Y

GET YOUR FREE SUBSCRIPTION
TO *ORACLE MAGAZINE*

Oracle Magazine is essential gear for today's information technology professionals. Stay informed and increase your productivity with every issue of *Oracle Magazine*. Inside each free bimonthly issue you'll get:

- Up-to-date information on Oracle Database, Oracle Application Server, Web development, enterprise grid computing, database technology, and business trends
- Third-party news and announcements
- Technical articles on Oracle and partner products, technologies, and operating environments
- Development and administration tips
- Real-world customer stories

If there are other Oracle users at your location who would like to receive their own subscription to *Oracle Magazine*, please photocopy this form and pass it along.

Three easy ways to subscribe:

① **Web**
Visit our Web site at **oracle.com/oraclemagazine**
You'll find a subscription form there, plus much more

② **Fax**
Complete the questionnaire on the back of this card
and fax the questionnaire side only to **+1.847.763.9638**

③ **Mail**
Complete the questionnaire on the back of this card
and mail it to **P.O. Box 1263, Skokie, IL 60076-8263**

ORACLE®

Want your own FREE subscription?

To receive a free subscription to *Oracle Magazine*, you must fill out the entire card, sign it, and date it (incomplete cards cannot be processed or acknowledged). You can also fax your application to +1.847.763.9638. **Or subscribe at our Web site at oracle.com/oraclemagazine**

○ **Yes, please send me a FREE subscription** *Oracle Magazine*.　　○ No.

○ From time to time, Oracle Publishing allows our partners exclusive access to our e-mail addresses for special promotions and announcements. To be included in this program, please check this circle. If you do not wish to be included, you will only receive notices about your subscription via e-mail.

○ Oracle Publishing allows sharing of our postal mailing list with selected third parties. If you prefer your mailing address not to be included in this program, please check this circle.

If at any time you would like to be removed from either mailing list, please contact Customer Service at +1.847.763.9635 or send an e-mail to oracle@halldata.com. If you opt in to the sharing of information, Oracle may also provide you with e-mail related to Oracle products, services, and events. If you want to completely unsubscribe from any e-mail communication from Oracle, please send an e-mail to: unsubscribe@oracle-mail.com with the following in the subject line: REMOVE [your e-mail address]. For complete information on Oracle Publishing's privacy practices, please visit oracle.com/html/privacy/html

X _____
signature (required)　　　　　　　　　　　date

name　　　　　　　　　　　　　　　title

company　　　　　　　　　　　　　e-mail address

street/p.o. box

city/state/zip or postal code　　　　　telephone

country　　　　　　　　　　　　　fax

Would you like to receive your free subscription in digital format instead of print if it becomes available? ○ Yes ○ No

---

YOU MUST ANSWER ALL 10 QUESTIONS BELOW.

① WHAT IS THE PRIMARY BUSINESS ACTIVITY OF YOUR FIRM AT THIS LOCATION? (check one only)

- ☐ 01 Aerospace and Defense Manufacturing
- ☐ 02 Application Service Provider
- ☐ 03 Automotive Manufacturing
- ☐ 04 Chemicals
- ☐ 05 Media and Entertainment
- ☐ 06 Construction/Engineering
- ☐ 07 Consumer Sector/Consumer Packaged Goods
- ☐ 08 Education
- ☐ 09 Financial Services/Insurance
- ☐ 10 Health Care
- ☐ 11 High Technology Manufacturing, OEM
- ☐ 12 Industrial Manufacturing
- ☐ 13 Independent Software Vendor
- ☐ 14 Life Sciences (biotech, pharmaceuticals)
- ☐ 15 Natural Resources
- ☐ 16 Oil and Gas
- ☐ 17 Professional Services
- ☐ 18 Public Sector (government)
- ☐ 19 Research
- ☐ 20 Retail/Wholesale/Distribution
- ☐ 21 Systems Integrator, VAR/VAD
- ☐ 22 Telecommunications
- ☐ 23 Travel and Transportation
- ☐ 24 Utilities (electric, gas, sanitation, water)
- ☐ 98 Other Business and Services _____

② WHICH OF THE FOLLOWING BEST DESCRIBES YOUR PRIMARY JOB FUNCTION? (check one only)

CORPORATE MANAGEMENT/STAFF
- ☐ 01 Executive Management (President, Chair, CEO, CFO, Owner, Partner, Principal)
- ☐ 02 Finance/Administrative Management (VP/Director/ Manager/Controller, Purchasing, Administration)
- ☐ 03 Sales/Marketing Management (VP/Director/Manager)
- ☐ 04 Computer Systems/Operations Management (CIO/VP/Director/Manager MIS/IS/IT, Ops)

IS/IT STAFF
- ☐ 05 Application Development/Programming Management
- ☐ 06 Application Development/Programming Staff
- ☐ 07 Consulting
- ☐ 08 DBA/Systems Administrator
- ☐ 09 Education/Training
- ☐ 10 Technical Support Director/Manager
- ☐ 11 Other Technical Management/Staff
- ☐ 98 Other

③ WHAT IS YOUR CURRENT PRIMARY OPERATING PLATFORM (check all that apply)

- ☐ 01 Digital Equipment Corp UNIX/VAX/VMS
- ☐ 02 HP UNIX
- ☐ 03 IBM AIX
- ☐ 04 IBM UNIX
- ☐ 05 Linux (Red Hat)
- ☐ 06 Linux (SUSE)
- ☐ 07 Linux (Oracle Enterprise)
- ☐ 08 Linux (other)
- ☐ 09 Macintosh
- ☐ 10 MVS
- ☐ 11 Netware
- ☐ 12 Network Computing
- ☐ 13 SCO UNIX
- ☐ 14 Sun Solaris/SunOS
- ☐ 15 Windows
- ☐ 16 Other UNIX
- ☐ 98 Other
- ☐ 99 None of the Above

④ DO YOU EVALUATE, SPECIFY, RECOMMEND, OR AUTHORIZE THE PURCHASE OF ANY OF THE FOLLOWING? (check all that apply)

- ☐ 01 Hardware
- ☐ 02 Business Applications (ERP, CRM, etc.)
- ☐ 03 Application Development Tools
- ☐ 04 Database Products
- ☐ 05 Internet or Intranet Products
- ☐ 06 Other Software
- ☐ 07 Middleware Products
- ☐ 99 None of the Above

⑤ IN YOUR JOB, DO YOU USE OR PLAN TO PURCHASE ANY OF THE FOLLOWING PRODUCTS? (check all that apply)

SOFTWARE
- ☐ 01 CAD/CAE/CAM
- ☐ 02 Collaboration Software
- ☐ 03 Communications
- ☐ 04 Database Management
- ☐ 05 File Management
- ☐ 06 Finance
- ☐ 07 Java
- ☐ 08 Multimedia Authoring
- ☐ 09 Networking
- ☐ 10 Programming
- ☐ 11 Project Management
- ☐ 12 Scientific and Engineering
- ☐ 13 Systems Management
- ☐ 14 Workflow

HARDWARE
- ☐ 15 Macintosh
- ☐ 16 Mainframe
- ☐ 17 Massively Parallel Processing

- ☐ 18 Minicomputer
- ☐ 19 Intel x86(32)
- ☐ 20 Intel x86(64)
- ☐ 21 Network Computer
- ☐ 22 Symmetric Multiprocessing
- ☐ 23 Workstation Services

SERVICES
- ☐ 24 Consulting
- ☐ 25 Education/Training
- ☐ 26 Maintenance
- ☐ 27 Online Database
- ☐ 28 Support
- ☐ 29 Technology-Based Training
- ☐ 30 Other
- ☐ 99 None of the Above

⑥ WHAT IS YOUR COMPANY'S SIZE? (check one only)

- ☐ 01 More than 25,000 Employees
- ☐ 02 10,001 to 25,000 Employees
- ☐ 03 5,001 to 10,000 Employees
- ☐ 04 1,001 to 5,000 Employees
- ☐ 05 101 to 1,000 Employees
- ☐ 06 Fewer than 100 Employees

⑦ DURING THE NEXT 12 MONTHS, HOW MUCH DO YOU ANTICIPATE YOUR ORGANIZATION WILL SPEND ON COMPUTER HARDWARE, SOFTWARE, PERIPHERALS, AND SERVICES FOR YOUR LOCATION? (check one only)

- ☐ 01 Less than $10,000
- ☐ 02 $10,000 to $49,999
- ☐ 03 $50,000 to $99,999
- ☐ 04 $100,000 to $499,999
- ☐ 05 $500,000 to $999,999
- ☐ 06 $1,000,000 and Over

⑧ WHAT IS YOUR COMPANY'S YEARLY SALES REVENUE? (check one only)

- ☐ 01 $500, 000, 000 and above
- ☐ 02 $100, 000, 000 to $500, 000, 000
- ☐ 03 $50, 000, 000 to $100, 000, 000
- ☐ 04 $5, 000, 000 to $50, 000, 000
- ☐ 05 $1, 000, 000 to $5, 000, 000

⑨ WHAT LANGUAGES AND FRAMEWORKS DO YOU USE? (check all that apply)

- ☐ 01 Ajax
- ☐ 02 C
- ☐ 03 C++
- ☐ 04 C#
- ☐ 05 Hibernate
- ☐ 06 J++/J#
- ☐ 07 Java
- ☐ 08 JSP
- ☐ 09 .NET
- ☐ 10 Perl
- ☐ 11 PHP
- ☐ 12 PL/SQL
- ☐ 13 Python
- ☐ 14 Ruby/Rails
- ☐ 15 Spring
- ☐ 16 Struts
- ☐ 17 SQL
- ☐ 18 Visual Basic
- ☐ 98 Other

⑩ WHAT ORACLE PRODUCTS ARE IN USE AT YOUR SITE? (check all that apply)

ORACLE DATABASE
- ☐ 01 Oracle Database 11*g*
- ☐ 02 Oracle Database 10*g*
- ☐ 03 Oracle9*i* Database
- ☐ 04 Oracle Embedded Database (Oracle Lite, Times Ten, Berkeley DB)
- ☐ 05 Other Oracle Database Release

ORACLE FUSION MIDDLEWARE
- ☐ 06 Oracle Application Server
- ☐ 07 Oracle Portal
- ☐ 08 Oracle Enterprise Manager
- ☐ 09 Oracle BPEL Process Manager
- ☐ 10 Oracle Identity Management
- ☐ 11 Oracle SOA Suite
- ☐ 12 Oracle Data Hubs

ORACLE DEVELOPMENT TOOLS
- ☐ 13 Oracle JDeveloper
- ☐ 14 Oracle Forms
- ☐ 15 Oracle Reports
- ☐ 16 Oracle Designer
- ☐ 17 Oracle Discoverer
- ☐ 18 Oracle BI Beans
- ☐ 19 Oracle Warehouse Builder
- ☐ 20 Oracle WebCenter
- ☐ 21 Oracle Application Express

ORACLE APPLICATIONS
- ☐ 22 Oracle E-Business Suite
- ☐ 23 PeopleSoft Enterprise
- ☐ 24 JD Edwards EnterpriseOne
- ☐ 25 JD Edwards World
- ☐ 26 Oracle Fusion
- ☐ 27 Hyperion
- ☐ 28 Siebel CRM

ORACLE SERVICES
- ☐ 28 Oracle E-Business Suite On Demand
- ☐ 29 Oracle Technology On Demand
- ☐ 30 Siebel CRM On Demand
- ☐ 31 Oracle Consulting
- ☐ 32 Oracle Education
- ☐ 33 Oracle Support
- ☐ 98 Other
- ☐ 99 None of the Above